RENEWALS 458-4574

DATE DUE

Down a Path of Wonder
ROBERT CRAFT

Part One: Music
Schoenberg, Stravinsky, Webern

Part Two: Literature
Mallarmé, Joyce, Eliot, Auden

Part Three:
Travel Diaries 2001–2004
Cambodia, Italian Vignettes, Seville

This book is dedicated to all those, near and far, who inspired me to write it, especially to Michael Tanner, Oxford; Carragh Thompson, Patmos; Jonathan Brown, Zimbabwe; Allen Shawn, Stanley Baron, Richard Frisch, and Carol and Fred Sherry, Manhattan.

Published by Naxos Books, an imprint of Naxos Rights International Ltd
© Robert Craft 2006
www.naxosbooks.com

Printed in the UK by Biddles Ltd, Norfolk
Design and layout: Hannah Davies, Fruition – Creative Concepts
All photographs of Stravinsky are the property of the author.
Front cover: Schoenberg in Vienna, c. 1910; Stravinsky in Paris, May 1913;
          Robert Craft, by Alexander Craft

10-digit ISBN: 1-84379-217-6
13-digit ISBN: 978-1-84379-217-8

Acknowledgements

I wish to thank the editors of the *Times Literary Supplement*, the *New York Review of Books* and *The Musical Quarterly* for permission to reprint revised versions of essays that originally appeared in their pages. I also want to express my appreciation for the constant inspiration and support of my wife Alva and my sister Phyllis Crawford. A special gratitude is reserved for my editorial assistant and dear friend Olivia Pittet for her painstaking deciphering of my manuscripts, and her numerous suggested improvements in them. I also thank all those at Naxos Books, above all Genevieve Helsby and Nicolas Soames, who brought about the publication of the book, editor Richard Wigmore and designer Hannah Davies.

Table of Contents

Part Two: Literature 289

Part Three: Travel Diaries 2001–2004 501

Index 545

Preface

The title *Down a Path of Wonder* comes from a *New York Times* article by Allan Kozinn introducing a Schoenberg festival in Merkin Hall, New York. The 'path of wonder' is the step-by-step discovery of Schoenberg's music.

—————•—————

The Table of Contents seems to be only remotely related to the two composers who are the principal subjects of the book. But as the reader moves from chapter to chapter, connections will become evident. My life with Stravinsky naturally drew me into his social and artistic spheres, principally with George Balanchine, Aldous Huxley, T.S. Eliot, Evelyn Waugh, W.H. Auden, Christopher Isherwood and Isaiah Berlin. Stravinsky had met James Joyce in Paris in 1922 and in the 1930s kept himself informed about him through their mutual friend Paul Léon. Of course the composer did not know Mallarmé, but he was the most revered figure in Stravinsky's French circle, which was dominated by his close friend Paul Valéry. The story about Mallarmé and Whistler, however, is purely a result of my own research.

I did not know Anton Webern, but he became a part of my life and was a major influence on Stravinsky, who had met him in Vienna in 1926. Webern would become, posthumously, Stavinsky's closest link with Schoenberg. The articles on other musicians are based on personal experiences. Otto Klemperer was a friend of both of the subject composers. I became acquainted with him through Stravinsky in 1950, and with his daughter, Lotte, at the time of her mother's death in Munich in 1956. Virgil Thomson remained on amiable terms with Stravinsky throughout his thirty American years, and was also the only significant critic to champion Schoenberg's 1942 Piano Concerto. The brief chapter on the New York Philharmonic broadcasts has been included because it contains the unique reference to the *spiccato* ('off-the-string') style that Stravinsky employed in all his performances of nineteenth-century music, Tchaikovsky's as well as his own.

Farther afield, one of my motives for visiting Cambodia was to study thirteenth-century Angkorian bas-relief sculptures of musical instruments, such as the khong vong, the sralai and the roneat ek, as well as the Khmer harmonic language formed by a heptatonic tuning system. Music also lured me to Andalusia, where Columbus's son had famously collected manuscripts of Renaissance polyphony.

R.C.
1 April 2006

Part One: Music
Schoenberg, Stravinsky, Webern

Chapter 1

Remembering Schoenberg

On 5 July 1950, after a cordial exchange of letters,[1] I called on
Arnold Schoenberg in his Brentwood Park (West Los Angeles) home
in connection with a New York concert in which I would conduct
his Septet-Suite and *Pierrot lunaire.* Approaching his house, I was
startled by the sight of stained-glass windows on the south side,
more so when I learned that they were in his studio. The idea of
A Survivor from Warsaw being composed in a Southern Baptist
country church, which is where the *vitraille* seemed to belong, was
incongruous. When Schoenberg entered the room, small, thin, frail
and clinging to his wife's right arm, I was struck by the softness and
high pitch of his voice. We shook hands, sat in adjoining chairs, and
listened to a scratchy amateur recording of the first performance of
the Septet Suite, which he conducted in Paris on 15 December 1927.
The playing was of virtuoso quality, given the date, but he criticised
it with every page-turn in the score, and complained throughout
that his tempi were too slow. At the end, nevertheless, he seemed
to be inwardly smiling, pleased with the music and for the moment
forgetting about its neglect.

Afterwards he conceded that the piano part is 'the most difficult
of my writings for the instrument', but recalled that the piece had
been rehearsed innumerable times. For my part, I realised that I

---

[1]   My handwritten (pencil) letter is in the Schoenberg Institute in Vienna.

would have to devote much more study to it. He mentioned the need of more attention to dynamics, articulation and nuances of tempo, and added that this was one of his favourite creations.

I said that I wanted to record his Four Orchestral Songs, Opus 22, and ventured to observe that the large size of the orchestra was an obstacle. He answered that orchestras of this dimension were common in Central Europe at the time the songs were composed (during World War I). When I said that I could organise the small ensembles required for the second and third songs, he replied that the full effect of the changing colours and volumes would be lost without all four, besides which they were interconnected by thematic and other relationships. As the songs were unknown in the US, he was curious as to how I had learned them. I had to admit that I had never heard them but had spent many hours with the six-staff study-score trying to imagine them.

The intensity of the man, and the power of his concentration while listening to the music, charged the atmosphere to an almost unbearable degree. But he was gentle and kindly, and, I thought, grateful for a young person's interest in and obvious dedication to his music. I revered him above anyone in the world – yes, even above Stravinsky, for by this time Stravinsky was 'family' to me, and it was impossible to live with him thinking all the time about his historical stature. I reflected on the similarities of the two men, the mental energy and focus, pride and vulnerability, isolation and alienation, and the absurdity of their common exile in movieland.

As I prepared to leave, Schoenberg inscribed my score of *Pierrot lunaire*: 'To Mr. Robert Craft, cordially Arnold Schoenberg. Expecting a good performance, July 5, 1950.' As he did so, I regretted that I had not brought Stravinsky's programme for the Berlin performance, on 8 December 1912, to which his ticket stub, 'Saal links, Reihe 5 Platz 5', was attached, and, from the same scrapbook, the clipping from a London *Daily Mail* interview with him a few weeks later: 'The Viennese are barbarians. They chased Schoenberg away to Berlin. Now Schoenberg is one of the greatest creative spirits of our day.' Surely this would have meant something to the older composer. Moreover, even though Schoenberg did not know that Stravinsky had completed

The Rite of Spring only two weeks before their Berlin meeting, in November 1912, or even know what it was, he may have perceived that, of any musician alive, Stravinsky, perhaps even before Webern and Berg, had the most developed ear with which to recognise 'the great creative spirit' in *Pierrot lunaire.*

To this day I regret that I did not attempt to arrange a meeting between the two titans. No doubt I realised that Stravinsky was not ready for it, since he was almost totally unacquainted with Schoenberg's music. All that he had heard of it was the Chamber Symphony, which Ernest Ansermet conducted on a broadcast with Stravinsky's Octet on 8 January 1928, and the *Accompaniment to a Cinematographic Scene,* actually the first performance of the piece – Schoenberg was ill and not present – by Klemperer in Berlin on 6 November 1930. Stravinsky had heard Schoenberg's arrangements of two Bach Chorale Preludes, also conducted by Klemperer in Berlin, and heard them again later, on a programme with *Le Sacre du printemps,* at the Salle Gaveau in Paris on 15 December 1931, conducted by Igor Markevitch. Stravinsky had also heard a rehearsal of Schoenberg's Septet-Suite in Venice in 1937; of *Verklärte Nacht,* in its ballet form as *Pillar of Fire,* in 1943 in San Francisco; and the Prelude to *Genesis,* at a recording session in Hollywood in 1944, during which he and Schoenberg sat at opposite sides of the room and did not meet. How different the situation would have been in 1952. Then Stravinsky would have gone to him, addressed him as 'Meister' – Stravinsky's letter to him of 27 May 1919 addresses him as 'Honoured Master'– reminisced with him about Berlin in 1912, and thanked him for presenting the premieres of the original instrumental versions of *Pribaoutki, Berceuses du chat* and the string quartet and piano four-hand pieces in Schoenberg's Vienna Society for Private Musical Performances.

In truth, the thought that a meeting could have been arranged between the two men, who had lived only a few miles apart for eleven years but never communicated, disturbs me more now than ever because of a letter discovered after Vera Stravinsky's death in 1982. Writing on Monday 13 April 1953 to her husband in Caracas, where he was conducting concerts, she says, in part:

> On Sunday there was a concert by the New Music Quartet: Schoenberg, Webern, and Berg. Bob asked Mrs Schoenberg if she would like to come to our house and go to the concert together. She accepted with pleasure and arrived with her beautiful daughter. I gave them some Scotch. The first thing she said was: 'This should have happened twenty years ago. It was not Schoenberg's or Stravinsky's fault, but that of people in between.' She is very nice, very direct, but very nervous. She talks a great deal and drinks copiously. She gives the impression of someone who has been hurt all her life...

I was very pleased to learn that the Schoenbergs had also been thinking about the question. That same day, Mrs Schoenberg wrote to Mrs Stravinsky: 'Thank you for taking the initiative and for the wonderful evening. I and Nuria enjoyed your company. Hope to see you again in my house. With herzlichsten Grüssen.'

Schoenberg's biographer, H.H. Stuckenschmidt, describes Stravinsky during a visit to him in April 1949 'warmly' asking about 'the great old man', and it was known then that Schoenberg had criticised René Leibowitz's and Theodor Adorno's attacks on Stravinsky. But one doubts that Schoenberg ever wanted a visit from 'Der Kleine Modernsky', his sobriquet for his counterpart in the 1920s. The violinist Samuel Dushkin, who was playing in concerts with Stravinsky in Los Angeles in 1935 and 1937, told me that he had unsuccessfully tried to arrange a meeting during both tours. It did not help that Dushkin's accompanist, Erich Itor Kahn, a twelve-tone composer and disciple of Schoenberg, was on intimate terms with Stravinsky. Also in 1937, Otto Klemperer escorted Schoenberg to hear Stravinsky conduct *The Firebird* in Los Angeles with the local orchestra, but could not persuade Schoenberg to go backstage. All that is known of his reaction to the concert is the remark 'I could not bow that way', a reference to the hand-on-heart, waist-deep, Russian-style acknowledgement.

In San Francisco on 26 January 1943, the Stravinskys attended a Ballet Theater performance of Schoenberg's *Pillar of Fire*, conducted by him. They were greatly impressed by the music and the ballet, but did not pay any compliments afterwards to the composer or the choreographer, Anthony Tudor, a longtime friend of theirs. The Stravinskys were staying in Oakland with the Milhauds, who escorted them to the performance. Darius, on good personal, if not musical, terms with Schoenberg, had seen him a day or two earlier, and would surely have urged Stravinsky to greet him. True, Stravinsky had to rehearse *Petrushka* early the next morning and conduct it in the evening. Nevertheless, here was an opportunity. One also wonders about the role of Sol Hurok, who had engaged both composers and visited both when he was in Los Angeles the week before. (He lunched with the Stravinskys on the 17th.) The role of Pierre Monteux is also curious, since his relationships with both men were cordial, and since he had lunched with the Stravinskys in San Francisco on the 28th. Monteux would have had to attend Schoenberg's premiere. It is also possible that the Schoenbergs and the Stravinskys were on the same night train to Los Angeles on the 28th.

An entry in Vera Stravinsky's diary for 1 August 1943 says that 'Igor unsuccessfully tries to find out whether or not Alma Mahler-Werfel had also invited Schoenberg' for dinner the next night. This seems to indicate that Stravinsky wished to avoid direct contact with his 'rival' even socially. On 7 July 1948, a large gathering of Hollywood notables, including Schoenberg, Stravinsky and Thomas Mann, attended a dinner for Frau Alma at the Beverley Hills Hotel, but the two composers managed not to meet. Mme Stravinsky's diary informs us that the dinner was 'terribly boring'.

In the autumn of 1949 Stravinsky was in the Los Angeles audience that heard Schoenberg deliver an ironic acceptance speech to the Austrian Consul-General who had conferred the 'Freedom of the City of Vienna' on him. In New York at the time to conduct Berg's Chamber Concerto, I returned to hear Stravinsky describe the occasion sympathetically: Schoenberg, whose eyesight seemed weak, read from a clutch of papers, each containing only a few words written in large letters. I knew then that Stravinsky would happily have paid his respects, but I did not find an opportune occasion to ask him.

Stravinsky was in New York in the spring of 1950, working with Auden on the auction scene in *The Rake's Progress* and posing for

Marino Marini's two bronze heads. On 10 April he accompanied me
to a studio at WOR to resolve the question of what to do with my
too-slow recording of the last part of *Renard*, soon to be released by
Ross Russell's Dial Records.[2] I mention this only because Russell was
in correspondence at the same time (August 1949 – May 1951) with
Schoenberg, ten of whose compositions were issued by Dial, and in
April 1950 Ernst Krenek seems to have told Schoenberg that Dial
had recorded *Renard*.

My concert in New York on 21 October 1950 went remarkably
well. The pianist, Eduard Steuermann, had played in the premieres
of both works and in many subsequent performances of *Pierrot
lunaire*. The other *Pierrot* instrumentalists had also played it before.
Ross Russell, in the audience, told his diary that he had heard an
'Entire 12-tone concert including a stirring three-dimensional
performance of *Pierrot lunaire* with Erika Wagner-Stiedry and
Steuermann'. Back in California I received a letter of thanks from
Schoenberg, dated 4 November: 'News of your performances are
very enjoyable', and 'cordial greetings'.

Schoenberg wrote to me on a reprint that I had sent to him of his
1928 Canon for the Concertgebouw:

> I possess one copy of this canon... There are four different
> tonalities and the task of the cello part is to make them
> understandable. But it must be checked, whether the cello part
> is not only to be used when all the four voices are together.
> Probably I have examined it at the time, but I don't recall it. In
> case the sound is disturbing with the fifth voice, the cello so

---

2   Russell's diary for 12 April 1950 describes this:
     Met Stravinsky with Robert Craft at WOR, where we listened to playbacks
     of *Renard* with I.S. proposing one troublesome change... according to Craft
     [he is] a disciplined voluptuary. [My stupid phrase] He loves to eat, drink,
     attend interesting parties. He is a true genital type, relaxed, secure, curious,
     observant, with perhaps important anal secondary characteristics (keeps all
     correspondence, programs, etc., etc.) Believes his music is always absolutely
     correct and logical, will brook no change. Physically he is curious. Short...
     stooped, with the strong, flat, thick hands of a farmer. Long arms, short
     legs. Long head with small crown. Big nose, thick voluptuous lips, marvelous
     manner of an old time aristocrat. Simple, direct, solicitous, dignified (he is a
     count by birth).

near to the bass voice, I recommend to double the cello in the lower octave by the double-bass.

In the event, Stravinsky transcribed Schoenberg's condensed score of four clefs on one line into a five-stave full-score, which I duly performed and recorded at a tempo to make the harmony 'understandable'. The cellist Emmet Sargent tuned the C string of his cello down to A, as Schoenberg requires, and octave doubling was not needed.

When I visited Schoenberg on 6 July 1951, he was too ill to come downstairs. I heard his voice from upstairs, nevertheless, and we talked through his wife before listening 'together', the composer at the top of the stairs, I at the bottom, to an acetate recording of his Violin Concerto played by Tibor Varga.[3] Later that thrilling afternoon, Schoenberg, with great kindness and generosity, inscribed my scores of *Erwartung* and *Die glückliche Hand.*

In 1950 the conductor Hermann Scherchen had founded a music publishing company, Ars Viva, in Gravesano (Zurich), and wrote to Schoenberg for permission to publish the 'Golden Calf' scene from *Moses und Aron* in a private edition. On 26 November the composer answered a request from the Maggio Fiorentino, initiated by Scherchen, to perform the opera, suggesting that only the second act be presented. Then, on 29 June 1951, Schoenberg wrote to Scherchen that the second act is 'really the only act which I want to be performed' and contracted with him to publish and perform the 'Golden Calf' excerpt. This was played on 2 July 1951 at a special concert in Darmstadt, conducted by Scherchen. A tape, expedited to the composer the next day, reached him a few days before his death. I heard it in his house on 7 July.

Six days later, Schoenberg was dead.[4] His wife told me later that

---

3   Died in 2003, aged eighty-two.
4   On 16 July I wrote to my sister, Phyllis: 'Great Schoenberg is dead. It was a terrible shock to me, partly because I saw him a few days before, but mostly because I have been thinking about him more and more, and because his music is taking me over. How glad I am that I had played some of it these last years and had you send that telegram for his birthday last September. Cabbalistic all his life, he worried about 13 and died as he predicted on the 13th. I will make my November concert a memorial program.' (The Stravinskys had originally planned to return to New York after the Venetian performances of *The Rake's Progress* in September, but delayed it by three months.)

the first telegram received was from Stravinsky, and that it was greatly appreciated. Stravinsky wanted to, but finally did not attend the funeral, fearing, in view of local myths about antipodes and rivalries, that his presence might be misconstrued.

In 1952 I conducted four memorial programmes of Schoenberg's music at the Los Angeles concert series 'Evenings on the Roof'. After that and throughout 1953 I was a frequent guest in the Schoenberg home, where I rehearsed the Serenade. While I was dining there on 11 October 1953, Mrs Schoenberg gave me a sheet of paper covered with writing, as well as music notations – one of them the opening theme of *Die Meistersinger* – in Schoenberg's hand. She had found it while emptying a drawer of his papers and kindly said that I should think of it as a gift 'in all senses'. What I read was: 'Do not discourage people, friends, they will "break" the Schbg clique. Encourage Craft. Also Mitropoulos.' I was overwhelmed.

Schoenberg perfectly understood that his possessive old guard – friends, disciples, pupils – resented the intrusion of young upstarts from the shallows of American culture. Many years later, Otto Klemperer's daughter, Lotte, wrote to me from her home in Zurich that Schoenberg had written much the same message to Erika Wagner-Stiedry in a letter dated 2 January 1951, now in the Stiedry Archives in the Swiss city: 'My young friend Mr Craft is slowly working himself into my music by performing my music a lot and finally he will succeed. I should like to see all of my friends encourage such people as Craft.'

On 12 September 1954, Stravinsky wrote to Gertrud Schoenberg:

> Mrs Schoenberg, this day of 13 September must be kept high in
> every musician's mind, and I am deeply regretful not to be able
> to attend your noble musical gathering to commemorate the
> great Arnold Schoenberg. Most sincerely, Igor Stravinsky.

But the two saw each other many times after that. She attended a concert at UCLA, conducted by Lukas Foss, which juxtaposed *A*

Survivor from Warsaw and Symphony of Psalms, and another concert of 5 June 1966, in which I conducted *Die glückliche Hand.* She dined at the Stravinskys for the last time on 2 November 1965, and presented him with a facsimile of the *Jakobsleiter* manuscript.

Stravinsky began to study Schoenberg's music in 1952, but tended to hide his acquisitions of it. Instead of writing directly to Schoenberg's publishers, he asked his own publisher, Boosey & Hawkes, to procure the orchestra and piano scores of the Piano Concerto. A note from John Roberts in Toronto, postmarked 9 May 1962, informs Stravinsky that Schoenberg's *Genesis* Prelude was photographed as requested before the score was returned to its publisher – Stravinsky having attended my recording session of the piece with the CBC Radio Orchestra but not wanting his interest in it to be known. Stravinsky's archives contain letters to his publishers in London asking them to obtain tapes of works by Schoenberg from German radio stations and the BBC. On 23 September 1963, Stravinsky wrote to Boosey & Hawkes with instructions for the printing of his *Abraham and Isaac.*

> The vocal score should be sent to Israel and the adding of the Hebrew letters and the spelling of the English phonetics should be done according to the State rules, or uses in the University of Jerusalem. This, incidentally, is how Schoenberg's *De Profundis* was published, Hebrew on top, Latin underneath, English on the flyleaf.

It remains to be said that Stravinsky made possible my Columbia Records Schoenberg series of the 1950s and 1960s by consenting to record his own music for Columbia only on condition that Columbia record Schoenberg's with me, and by giving time from his own recording sessions to the Schoenberg project. In June 1957 part of the finale of Schoenberg's Variations, Op. 31 was taped on time allotted for Stravinsky's recording of *Agon.* Further, Stravinsky personally induced two violinists to learn Schoenberg's Concerto, going to Israel Baker's home in the Hollywood hills more than once to convince him of the importance of the piece, and during a concert tour in Israel (actually during a boat ride on the Dead Sea) Stravinsky urged Zvi

Zeitlin to learn it. But Stravinsky's greatest tribute was the adaptation of Schoenbergian principles in his own music. Ultimately, Stravinsky may prove to have been one of Schoenberg's greatest benefactors.

Not until the year 2000, however, did the musical establishment begin to understand that the Stravinsky-Schoenberg opposition was artificial, and that *Agon*, *In Memoriam: Dylan Thomas*, the *Requiem Canticles* and all the other Stravinsky masterpieces do not sound in any way Schoenbergian. They sound Stravinskian. What the two composers shared was the belief that the present must come out of the past. In the words of Michael Oliver, the 'irreconcilables of the twentieth century were not Stravinsky and Schoenberg but Stravinsky and Boulez. [The latter's] doctrine of amnesia, of writing music that continually denies the past in its search for the future, is in direct conflict with Stravinsky.'

Chapter 2

Down a Path of Wonder

'Schoenberg *particularly* moves, excites, and amazes young listeners,' the composer Allen Shawn says, 'particularly those who seek, first and foremost, contact with a great imagination. Students recognise that Schoenberg's language is strong, complex, honest, and also deeply traditional.'[1] He might have added that, as a rule, more new musical ideas are presented at the same time in Schoenberg's music than in that of any of his contemporaries, and that much of what happens is more interesting.

Shawn devotes separate chapters to the larger and historically crucial works, *Gurrelieder, Erwartung, Die glückliche Hand, Pierrot lunaire, Moses und Aron*; but we begin with Richard Dehmel's poem, *Verklärte Nacht*, which inspired the composer's earliest significant opus. In this instance, Shawn quotes him on his creative processes. Following Schopenhauer, Schoenberg believed that intuition is the first and most essential attribute for every artist. He wrote that at the beginning of *Verklärte Nacht* he had had 'an overall plan of surrounding the tonic D with the tonalities a half-step above and below it, E flat and C sharp, ending the first part with the one above, beginning the second part with D major, then moving a half-step below, and finally modulating back to D'.

With characteristic wit, Schoenberg ascribed the development of

---

1   *Arnold Schoenberg's Journey*, by Allen Shawn, New York, 2002.

the piece from this pre-concept to 'the diligent effort of my brain working "behind my back", without seeking my approval'. A decade later, crossing the Rubicon into atonality in *The Book of the Hanging Gardens*, he observed, with equal acumen: 'I am following an inner compulsion that is stronger than education, and obeying a law that is natural to me, and therefore stronger than my artistic training'.

Late in life, after losing sympathy with Dehmel's *fin-de-siècle* aesthetics, Schoenberg nevertheless wrote record-album notes for the music, identifying the emotions of the characters in the poem to corresponding musical themes that also conjure the moonlit atmosphere. But as Shawn knows, Schoenberg was always a programmatic composer, and even some of his most 'abstract' music conceals a scenario. Thus the String Trio dramatises a harrowing medical experience: the composer's heart had stopped beating but was revived by the injection of a needle directly into it. So, too, the plotless Piano Concerto follows a programme, in this case simply of subjective moods.

Nowadays *Gurrelieder,* Schoenberg's largest-scale masterpiece (1900–1911) and his only immediately successful one, is still downgraded as 'Wagnerian'. Shawn's rebuttal is exact: the 'more "Wagnerian" passages... [are] less earthbound than Wagner, more limpid... more contrapuntal and more architectural'. This is well said, and could have been elaborated with reference to the tenderness in Waldemar's arias 'So tanzen die Engel' and 'Du wunderliche Tove', and to the ethereality of Tove's 'Nun sag' ich dir', recapitulated, wonderfully transformed, in the English horn lament introducing the Wood Dove's elegy for her. The debt to Wagner's harmonic language and use of leitmotifs is acknowledged, as is the centrality of 'love-death', 'Denn wir geh'n zu Grab ersterbend im seligen Kuss!', ecstasies different in kind from Wagner's. In the last part, Waldemar, in a forest echoing with apparitions of Tove's voice, her eyes, and her laughter, reminds us of Phèdre's reverie of Hippolytus: 'deep in the woods your image follows me'.

Gurrelieder seems to me, as it does to Shawn, more opera than oratorio. Readily imagining it being staged, by the end of the Prelude, in which plump orchestral raindrops turn to mizzle – Wagner discovering Debussy – one expects a curtain to open. The music is always scenic and nature-evocative: the water, the woods, the 'Mitternacht Zeit', the fluttering and cooing that frames the Wood Dove aria, the prancing of Waldemar's horse, the sepulchral sonority of blended bassoons and bass clarinets before the funeral chorus of Waldemar's men. Shawn is right: the raptures of Waldemar and Tove are other-worldly. Waldemar's blasphemous rage against a god who would 'take away a beggar's only lamb' can end only in the king's own death. In an opera, this would require new characters – The Peasant, The Fool, The Speaker, this last with the most innovatory music of all, anticipating the *Sprechstimme* of *Pierrot lunaire*, and thereby partly rescuing the whole from the 'time-warp' *Gemütlichkeit* which, as Shawn says, it has suffered.

One large question remains: how could Schoenberg have kept the gargantuan composition on ice for ten years, orchestrating it when he could find time, and simultaneously composing those other radically different masterpieces, *Pelleas und Melisande,* the Chamber Symphony, the George songs, the Five Pieces for Orchestra, *Erwartung* and *Die glückliche Hand?*

———•———

A letter from Schoenberg to a conductor planning to perform *Gurrelieder* exposes more of the composer's wit:

> ... the singers' microphones [in Stokowski's RCA recording] are so loud that they cover the orchestra. You don't hear the orchestra for almost the whole performance... All the soloists are rather poor. The worst is the singer of Klaus Narr, who does not sing but speaks, and if he sings, he usually sings a melody of his own. The other, who is almost as bad, is the speaker, who makes the opposite mistake: he sings all the time, and he sings his own melodies, [which] of course, [are] not shaped so that they fit the harmony. I did not want to have melodies. I was able to write melodies myself when I wanted them.

No doubt such remarks sound more sarcastic than originally intended, as in the following from Schoenberg's letter to Mahler of 29 December 1909, after hearing a performance of his Seventh Symphony:

> Ferdinand Löwe, the conductor, was obviously trying very hard to carry out the score directions exactly... I often had the feeling that one thing or another ought to have been done differently [but] there is no reason why he... should be expected to understand the work, considering how many years he has been conducting without ever having understood anything.

Shawn supplies the essentials of Schoenberg's biography, interspersed with analyses of his character. The great composer was born in Vienna on 13 September 1874, the son of a shoemaker who died when the child was sixteen, leaving him to support his mother and younger sister and brother. The other great tragedy of Schoenberg's life came in July 1908, when his young friend, the artist Richard Gerstl, who was giving lessons in painting to him, eloped with his thirty-one-year-old wife. Gerstl, in a fit of remorse, committed suicide. Schoenberg responded by drafting a will, one of the most revealing documents ever written by a great composer:

> I have cried, behaved like someone in despair – had thoughts of suicide... have plunged from one madness to another... in a word I am totally broken... I deny the fact that my wife betrayed me... She did not betray me, for my imagination had already pictured everything that she has done. My capacity for premonition had always seen through her lies and suspected her crimes long before she herself had thought to commit them – the fact that she betrayed me is thus of no importance to me... She lied – I believed her. Wrong! She did not lie to me. For my wife does not lie. The soul of my wife is so at one with my soul that I know everything about her. Therefore she did not lie; but she was not my wife, that's how it is... It was the man she took me for that my wife lied to and betrayed. He was her creation; she could do what she wanted with him.

Coincidental or otherwise, Schoenberg's music became atonal during this crisis, but had long been moving in that direction.

To a great extent, Schoenberg's character was formed by the rejection and open hostility with which his music was initially received, and thereafter neglected. He fought back but naturally became embittered in the process. Shawn chronicles some of the early skirmishes with critics and audiences, primarily to account for the composer's apparent show of contempt for other musicians, and his demands of fealty from friends and advocates. As for the latter, the correspondence reveals that he distrusted some of even his closest supporters, and tyrannised certain pupils, most notably Alban Berg, whom he tended to treat as a factotum. In America, near the end, he began to suspect that a 'clique' from his former cenacle was discouraging younger performers of his music. His friend Oscar Levant noted that 'Schoenberg is quick to defend himself even when not attacked', and that conversations with the composer consisted mainly of 'exchanging his ideas with him'.

Writing to Schoenberg on 12 July 1909, Richard Strauss says: 'It interests me very much to see everything you write'. Schoenberg responded by sending the scores of four of his Five Pieces for Orchestra with a letter asking Strauss to perform them in one of his concerts. The reader should be reminded that however low Schoenberg's opinion of Strauss's operas after *Salome, Elektra* and, surprisingly, *Intermezzo*, he always regarded these three works highly, and that Strauss used Schoenberg's *Harmonielehre* in the musical education of his grandson. Not surprisingly, the four pieces were over Strauss's head, as a letter makes clear, in which he declines to perform 'such daring experiments in content and sound'. Privately, Strauss doubted that Schoenberg himself could actually 'hear' what he was writing, and though we now know that he could, the affirmation has taken a long time.

Schoenberg played the cello as a young man, but did not master it or any instrument, being obliged to give the necessary practice time to supporting his widowed mother, wife, and children by orchestrating operettas and operas for publishers and preparing piano reductions of the same; one of the latter was *The Barber of Seville*. Steeped in music, he spent such time as he could find studying and composing it. One astonishing consequence of this is that in the music world in which he developed, and in which most composers worked at the piano, Schoenberg, who wrote the most innovative, technically demanding and altogether superior music for the instrument – *Pierrot lunaire*, the Suites Opus 25 and 29, and the Concerto – could not play it. In 1949, after composing the *a cappella* chorus *Dreimal tausend Jahre* (Three Destructions of the Temple), he required the help of a pupil to play two of the four simple lines, unable to manage all four of them himself.

Schoenberg knew the sound characteristics, the qualities and possibilities of every instrument more profoundly than any other composer of his time, and expanded the orchestral palette beyond any other, with new combinations of instruments, new means of articulation and new explorations of extreme registers. As he once wrote to Mahler, 'Middle of the road experiences do not happen to me'. His reworking of the Monn Cello Concerto, ridiculed a generation ago as unplayable, is now taught in conservatories; and his Violin Concerto, demanding more of the player than any other music ever conceived for the instrument, is only now, seventy years later, being discovered. While composing it, Schoenberg purchased a violin, in order to test the fingerings himself for each of his successive quadruple stops and successive harmonics. Needless to say, the piece is much more than a trial of the technical equipment of the player. The Concerto was Schoenberg's own favourite of all his orchestral compositions.

Only the fifth of the Five Pieces for Orchestra is entirely atonal and hence without pedal points, ostinati and octave doublings. Schoenberg changed his mind concerning this last, writing to René Leibowitz on 1 October 1945:

> You will find in all the works between 1906 and 1921 occasional doubling in octaves, [but] the fear that it might produce similarity to tonal treatment proved to be an exaggeration,

because very soon it became evident that it had – as a mere
device of instrumentation – no influence upon the purpose of
construction.

What the last phrase means is simply that he had been careful not to
grant pitch priority to any one of the twelve notes in the chromatic
scale, but finally understood that this would not happen. Indeed, the
octaves at climaxes in *Erwartung* (1909) are a *dramatic* resource.
They powerfully underline the protagonist's words in the passage
revealing that she murdered her lover out of jealousy, having
imagined a 'sorceress and a harlot with her lily-white arms around
you'. The protagonist had seen the bare-armed woman on the balcony
of a house at the edge of the forest in which she is seeking her lover.
By doubling the vocal part here in four octaves, played *fortissimo* in
the orchestra and *molto ritardando*, the melody and its words are
pre-eminent.

Erwartung and Die glückliche Hand are two of the most intricate,
puzzling, dense and exquisite scores in all music. Shawn's chapters
on them are perspicacious. True, he does not resolve the longstanding
dispute between those who credit Schoenberg with directing the
conception and even the actual writing of Marie Pappenheim's
Erwartung libretto, and those who attribute it to Freud's and Breuer's
Studies on Hysteria, through Pappenheim's cousin Bertha, who had
been Breuer's patient. But the idea of Schoenberg following anyone's
directions is inconceivable, and he famously refused to see Freud
himself.

Shawn's talents as a teacher are brilliantly evident in the *Erwartung*
essay. He suggests a way 'for the listener unable to read music to
learn to love these beautifully wrought bits of song, these desperate
outcries... Follow it a minute at a time, text in hand, hearing it not as
a generalised type of music but as a specific narrative in sound. As
dreamlike as *Erwartung* is, its structure and the way it establishes
a sense of musical place is remarkable.' Further, he identifies the
Erwartung protagonist's moments of contact with external reality,
the first being the kiss she bestows on the corpse of her dead lover.
Shawn remarks that 'We find ourselves listening to this piece, and

after only a very few notes we are simply in it. Like the protagonist, we often feel lost, but we also periodically find ourselves in very distinct places.'

Shawn's assertion that Schoenberg 'obliterated any obvious supports of the structure', however, could be contested on one count: the four scenes are demarcated by, respectively, two bangs on the timpani, an orchestral ostinato without the singer, and a few moments of absolute quiet. Shawn's humour surfaces in a comparison of the singer's 'obsessive returns to the first oboe note in the first bar (C sharp) as if to a sore tooth', and he has found the *mot juste* for the final bar of the music and of the dream-world of the drama: it 'evaporates'.

Erwartung is better known than *Die glückliche Hand*, concerning which Shawn's observations are original and important. He remarks that the orchestral interlude at the beginning of Scene Three starts like a fugue with a Beethovenian rhythm, 'a daring allusion to a past style'. But he does not mention the oddity that the unharmonised 'fugue' subject is assigned to unison bass instruments, a passage like no other in all Schoenberg. The orchestral interlude leading to Scene Four is equally novel in rhythm and orchestration. The bumpy, jagged rhythm, corresponding to the rocky landscape of the scenario, is some of the most exciting music Schoenberg ever wrote, and the instrumentation, featuring brass, especially low-register horns, is completely new.

Shawn proposes that the small mixed chorus, part sung, part whispered, at the beginning and end of the piece, can be 'viewed as a kind of precursor to *Moses und Aron*'. Though *Die glückliche Hand* is not a religious work, Shawn hears echoes of Hasidic chant in it:

> The leader of the prayer used to exclaim each verse with mystic fervor. The congregation repeated it... but with minor changes and in a faster tempo, [shifting] key centers frequently, unconsciously creating an atmosphere of unbridled, almost primeval, religious fervor. Of these observations, the most immediately recognizable is the comparison of the tenor solo emerging from the chorus groups at bar 17 with the voice of a

cantor. Although Schoenberg did not have a religious upbringing, his mother came from an Orthodox family of cantors. The Jewish music Schoenberg would have heard growing up was word-based, and prayers were chanted at home in a rhythmical but unmetered manner. While Schoenberg comes from the tradition of Bach, Beethoven, Wagner, Brahms, and Mahler, there may also be, at least unconsciously, the tradition of the music associated with Judaism.

Die glückliche Hand is perhaps the 'furthest-out' of Schoenberg's creations. The formal framework is perfectly symmetrical, the first and last scenes beginning with the same music, an ostinato pattern, concluding with a small off-stage wind band playing raucous street music in a different meter from the orchestra's, with which, however, it is co-ordinated. Whereas the orchestra is huge, the chorus is a group of twelve solo singers whose contrapuntal parts are doubled to produce curious shiftings of emphasis. The allegory of the plot is difficult to interpret, though clearly the protagonist, a tortured, Cellini-like artist, creator of beautiful objects, is Schoenberg himself, failing, as usual, to possess the woman who enchants him. He is identified simply as 'Mann', as the protagonist of *Erwartung* was simply 'Frau', and the masculinity of the opus contrasts consistently with the femininity of the earlier work. The baritone (Schoenberg) sings only a few notes, a declaration of love in a never-before-or-since high vocal range. But *Die glückliche Hand* should be staged, since the scheme of coloured lighting, notated in a system of Schoenberg's invention, is closely co-ordinated with the music. A live performance video is necessary if we are to know the work on all its levels.

Pierrot lunaire should also be thought of as a theatre piece. Its tone, Shawn believes, 'lies between comedy and tragedy'. Yes, but the emotions are parodistic, not real, and the genius in the music as a whole is that each of the twenty-one miniature pieces succeeds in creating a distinct mood. Shawn's musical analysis will be useful even to those who are not score readers. He does not call attention to the returns of tonality, except to note the frequent employment of implied triadic constructions in the successions of thirds in the harmony. Complete triads distinguish 'Eine blasse Wäscherin', a piece I think of as tonal in its entirety, partly because of its tonal harmonies at the beginning, at bars nine and ten in the flute, and in the repetition on the same pitches in the flute figure in the last three bars, where, additionally, the violin emphasises tonic G and dominant D. But perfect triads occur again near the end of the final number, and of numbers 5, 7, 15, 17, 19, 20, as well as in the instrumental quartet interlude. Numerous melodic fragments throughout the masterpiece now strike us as tonal (*viz.* the cello melody in the Serenade, along with the five-bar piano ostinato accompaniment).

———◆———

The aptly titled 'Moses and Arnold' chapter contains an absorbing discussion of 'the multidimensionality of the word for God in the Hebrew language', as well as of the use of *Sprechstimme* for Moses, who in the Bible is 'slow of speech and slow of tongue'. In the Midrashic tradition, stammering was Moses' affliction. Rashi, in the eleventh century, used the word *balbus*, which, in contemporary French, would make Moses *balbutiant.* Pharaoh's attendants supposedly placed two bowls before the infant Moses, one containing jewels, the other glowing coals. If the infant is a true worshipper of Amon-Ra, he will reach for the coals, if a potential Hebrew usurper, he will go for the jewels. When the child's hand moves toward the jewels, an angel of God moves it to the coals, and the burning coal he brings to his mouth leaves him orally impaired. In Exodus VI Moses refers to his 'uncircumcised' lips, meaning an incompletely opened aperture. In Exodus IV Moses says 'I am slow of speech and of a slow tongue'. Exodus VII says that his brother Aaron is his spokesman.

Moses' part at the beginning of the score, the Burning Bush scene, is marked *möglichst langsam* (as slow as possible), and in an introductory note Schoenberg indicates that the reason for the fermatas in the orchestra parts is to give the singer freedom to take more time. After this initial passage, the tempo is established by the music. Moses is allowed, but not required, to sing bars 208-14 in the First Act.

———•———

Shawn rates the Piano Concerto above the one for violin. But it is the latter that haunts and exalts me, while the Piano Concerto merely delights me and raises my spirits. The Violin Concerto, Shawn concludes, is 'more a picture of a great piece than a great piece'. The distinction is over my head. The Piano Concerto is lighter in mood, considerably shorter, and much more frequently performed. The ending of its *Rondo giocoso* movement, moreover, reminds me, rhythmically and melodically, of Prokofiev, and the continuous octave doublings bother me; I have not adjusted to Schoenberg's retraction of his own interdiction against them.

One final work that deserves to be better known is that shortest of Schoenberg's masterpieces, *A Survivor from Warsaw*, a music drama in six to seven minutes. Shawn's observations about it are astute:

> Schoenberg paints a dramatic scene of the utmost immediacy and directness... It is universal and alive and contains nothing of a 'Memorial' character... One is instantly brought into the reality of the horrifying situation as a participant, not as an observer.

The recognition of Schoenberg's stature as the musical colossus of his time is taking longer than that of any of the great composers. This book is intended to help the process by bringing new understanding to the man and his music.

Chapter 3

Schoenberg, Einstein and Zionism

In engrossing detail, E. Randal Schoenberg, the composer's grandson, has recorded the different paths by which Schoenberg and Einstein decided that their dedication to Jewish political affairs would take second place only to their musical and scientific work.[1] But while Einstein's role is part of contemporary history, Schoenberg's involvement has been unknown. Told from his side, this new version subjects Einstein's changing political positions to bitter criticism, notably in a polemic, 'Einstein's Mistaken Politics', published here for the first time.

In 1914 the political views of the two men could hardly have been further apart. Antimilitarist, virtually alone among German scientists in opposing the Great War, Einstein signed a 'Manifesto to Europeans' advocating 'internationalism, pacifism and socialism'. Schoenberg, pro-war and serving for part of it in the Imperial Austrian army, claimed to be a monarchist as late as 1950. He soon discovered that the war 'was being waged not only against foreign enemies, but at least as heavily against inner ones. And to the latter belonged... the Jews' (letter to Dr Stephen Wise, New York, 2 May 1934). So, too, in 1929 Einstein recalled that 'when I came to Germany [from Zurich] fifteen years ago, I discovered for the first time that I was a Jew. I owe this discovery more to gentiles than to Jews.'

---

1   *The Journal of the Arnold Schoenberg Institute*, Los Angeles, 1987.

By 1921 Einstein's experience of anti-Semitism had attracted him to the Zionist movement. Early in the year he predicted that he would 'be forced to leave Germany within ten years'. In late March, in company with Chaim Weizmann, he departed on a two-month tour in America, where 'I first discovered the Jewish people', and where he was to become Zionism's most famous advocate. But Einstein's subsequent political career, beginning with his flight to Holland after Hitler's 1923 Beer Hall *putsch*, is as well known as Schoenberg's has been obscure.

At the beginning of 1925, Schoenberg, a long-sufferer from anti-Semitism, wrote to Einstein requesting a meeting to discuss Zionism. The letter, which was not answered, began with a protracted account of Schoenberg's 'position in German artistic life', including the complaint that a Berlin musicologist listed him not in order of importance but alphabetically. 'Though I am considered, at least abroad, to be the leading German composer,' Schoenberg wrote, the Germans were ready to relinquish predominance in music if they could avoid linking him to it, and 'in their hatred of me, the Jews and the Swastika bearers are of one mind'. He goes on to digress on an unexplained connection between the musical art of the Netherlands in the early Renaissance and the Talmud and cabbala until, in the next-to-last paragraph, Zionism is mentioned only in order to say that he 'deviates' from its 'propaganda'. Einstein, who must have thought his correspondent deranged, did not answer. Greatly offended by the snub, Schoenberg wrote to a friend: 'I had to swallow a very terrestrial treatment from this astronomer who sees far too distantly but overlooks what is close at hand'.

Whereas Einstein rejected all forms of aggression and nationalism – for him, Jewish internationality was its nationality – Schoenberg approached 'the Jewish problem' militantly: 'The re-establishment of a Jewish state can come about only in the manner that has characterised similar events throughout history: not through words but through the success of arms.' Schoenberg feared that in the Diaspora the Jews had lost their 'fighting spirit', the spirit of the Maccabees. Meanwhile, Einstein had warned against 'the establishment of a Jewish state without the agreement of the Arabs'.

Again in 1930 Schoenberg wrote to Einstein seeking his support for a testimonial honouring the architect Adolf Loos, and without referring to the 'Jewish problem'. This time Einstein responded, but, on grounds that he was insufficiently acquainted with Loos's work and felt too distant from it to make a judgement, did not comply. Schoenberg drafted an irate answer, but wrote instead to Loos's wife: 'Loos has in his field at least the same importance as I do in mine. And you know perhaps that I pride myself in having shown mankind the way for musical creativity for at least the next hundred years.'

In 1931–2, both Schoenberg and Einstein avoided Berlin as much as possible, and in the latter year Einstein left Germany permanently. By this time his every word on the political situation was receiving world publicity and, of course, total distortion in the German press. The imprudence of his criticisms of Germany greatly disturbed Schoenberg – 'he must surely... have learned that they have given occasion for far-reaching revenge against innocent people' – or 'hostages at risk', as Stefan Zweig called them in a letter to Romain Rolland, refusing to join a protest – and the anti-German boycott of 1932 horrified the composer. The Zionists admit that they cannot help the German Jews, he wrote, but 'Mr Einstein is endangering the lives of the Jews who have had to remain. Does he not consider what consequences the boycott decision can have for the Jews in Germany?'

In mid-summer 1933, Schoenberg confided in a letter to Anton Webern that 'Zionist affairs are more important for me than my art... I have decided... to work in the future solely for the national state of Jewry'. The resolve was carried out, without any sacrifice of his art, until the creation of the State of Israel. But while Schoenberg thought that Jewish unity could be achieved only through 'devotion to a single, abstract idea', the idea of the one God, Einstein felt no ties at all with the faith of his fathers. Years before, he wrote to a friend that when his wife and children had turned Catholic, 'It's all the same to me'.

One of Schoenberg's main tenets was that anti-Semitism should not be opposed. His grandson emphasises that 'the fight against anti-Semitism rather than for Judaism' was always the main disagreement between Schoenberg and other Zionists. 'To oppose anti-Semitism is nonsense', one of the composer's notes reads,

> and the only Jews who could want to do this seriously are those who want to stabilise the conditions of Diaspora into infinity... Anti-Semitism is the natural and necessary answer for the claim 'chosen people'. To fight anti-Semitism is... like fighting envy. Mr Einstein does not have the courage to see anti-Semitism as a given reality, to put up with it... something which it was not possible to eliminate in the whole history of mankind.

In 1920 Einstein had expressed a version of the same opinion: 'It may be thanks to anti-Semitism that we are able to preserve our existence as a race.' But by the early 1930s he had understood the necessity of fighting Germany – an about-face from the pacifism that had momentarily undermined his credibility. Schoenberg seized on this: 'Mr Einstein is a kind of Janus face... He is against war in general, except for one against Germany.' When Schoenberg eventually understood that the survival of civilisation was at stake, he supported Einstein's call for preparation against German rearmament.

On 7 October 1933, Einstein sailed for the United States to take up the position that he would hold for the rest of his life at Princeton's Institute for Advanced Study, and it was at Princeton, when Einstein and his wife attended Schoenberg's 'Twelve-Tone Lecture' on 6 March 1934, that the two men finally met. Three weeks later, on 1 April, they were photographed together after a Carnegie Hall concert to raise money for the Settlement of German-Jewish Children in Palestine and the New York Zionist Region, a concert honouring Einstein as well, a 'Tribute of Music to Science'.

One more exchange of letters took place, with results similar to the appeal on behalf of Loos. In August 1938, Schoenberg sent a rambling letter seeking a recommendation for a professorship in astrology (from *Einstein!*) for Schoenberg's friend, the violinist, physician and professional astrologer Oskar Adler. Einstein answered briefly that he had read Adler's book and considered it 'so well written that it presents a real danger for immature intellects'. He suggested that

Schoenberg and his friends should 'try to find means of support for him as a musician', yet offered to write on Adler's behalf 'if in so doing I don't have to indirectly support astrology'. The composer's grandson does not tell us what happened.

The essay's most arresting remark is one of Einstein's, dated 1936: 'The intellectual decline brought on by a shallow materialism is a far greater menace to the survival of Jewry than numerous external foes who threaten its existence with violence.'

Chapter 4

Schoenberg and Kandinsky

About a third of the forty-five or so letters from Kandinsky to
Schoenberg[1] were written by Kandinsky's pupil and partner
Gabriele Münter. The seventeen Schoenberg letters are apparently
all that survive, though Kandinsky's replies indicate that more
were received. The book is filled out with related writings by
both men; with photographs, including colour reproductions of
Schoenberg's paintings, as well as Kandinsky's; and with essays
by the editor and translator, some of which compound verbal and
interpretative problems in the letters. But the best of the exchanges
are indispensable for anyone concerned with painting and music in
the years immediately preceding World War I.

Schoenberg's Second String Quartet and Three Pieces for Piano,
Op. 11, in a Munich concert in January 1911, aroused an artistic
'empathy' in Kandinsky that compelled him to communicate with the
composer. Schoenberg did not concur with the notions set forth in
Kandinsky's initial letter, that in both painting and music 'today's
dissonances are tomorrow's consonances', and that '*construction* is
what has been so woefully lacking in the painting of recent times'.
The composer replied that since 1909 he has been seeking, if not
amorphousness, 'complete freedom from all forms', and he quotes the

---

1   *Arnold Schoenberg–Wassily Kandinsky: Letters, Pictures and Documents.* Edited by Jelena
Hahl-Koch, translated by John C. Crawford, London, 1984.

now classic definition from his *Harmonielehre*: 'Dissonances are only different from consonances in degree; they are nothing more than remote consonances.' He also challenges 'construction' as 'a word of yours with which I do not agree'. No reason is given for the objection, but Schoenberg must have had beliefs similar to Chesterton's 'A thing constructed can only be loved after it is constructed, while a thing created is loved before it exists'. Essence precedes existence.

By the end of the year, Schoenberg denies the usefulness of theory:

> I do not agree when you write... that you would have preferred to present an exact theory... We search on and on (as you yourself say) with our feelings. Let us endeavour *never* to lose these feelings to a theory. [14 December 1911]

A month earlier Schoenberg had told Kandinsky: 'In a few days I will have begun a series of 8-10 lectures on "Aesthetics and the Theory of Composition"... as you can well imagine, the object is to overturn both.' (11 November 1911)

On 'points of contact' between the arts, Schoenberg accepted Kandinsky's observations concerning 'colour in comparison to musical timbre', but, probably deciding that his correspondent would not be able to grasp the implications of atonality, the composer avoided the subject and turned to generalities. On style, for instance, Schoenberg wrote:

> Although I have certainly developed very much... I have not *improved*, but my style has simply got better, so that I can penetrate more profoundly into what I had already had to say earlier and am nevertheless capable of saying it more concisely and more fully.

His elaborations on this distinction regrettably weaken it by introducing the false opposition of 'not what I say but how I say it', as if a poem could be 'said' in some other way (prose).

Kandinsky invited Schoenberg to contribute music, graphic work, and critical articles to *Der blaue Reiter*, and the two artists were soon exchanging photographs of their paintings. Compliments followed, Schoenberg expressing his appreciation of the work of Emil Nolde and pleasure in the 'salutary simplicity' of Münter's paintings, in which 'goodness and love are hidden'. Kandinsky contributed an article on Schoenberg's pictures for the 1912 *Festschrift* about the composer, who acknowledged it with a stunning remark: 'You are such a full man that the least vibration always causes you to overflow.'[2]

Kandinsky resumed the correspondence after World War I, saying that he had been living in Russia for seven years, totally isolated from the West. Schoenberg answered that during the same period he led a hand-to-mouth existence in Vienna, with religion as his 'one and only support'. The name 'Schoenberg', he added, may now be less well known because of his music than because of the feats of his football-playing son Georg. By this time Schoenberg is complaining about his disciples: 'These atonalists! Damn it all, I did my composing without any "ism" in mind.'

In 1923 Kandinsky invited Schoenberg to become a director of a reorganised Bauhaus music school. The response could hardly have been more jolting: Schoenberg would like to teach, but cannot accept, having learned the lesson that 'I am a Jew'. He charges Kandinsky with anti-Semitism, of having been aware 'of what really happened' during Schoenberg's summer stay in Mattsee, where the Germans had made him feel unwelcome, an experience that deprived him of 'the peace of mind to work at all'. Alban Berg wrote to his wife that anti-Semitic restrictions imposed by the town council had forced Schoenberg to leave Mattsee. Though the underlying provocation seems not to have been the Mattsee incident, and though Schoenberg was mistaken about Kandinsky's role in the persecution of Jews

---

2   The imagery in Schoenberg's letters of the same period to Ferruccio Busoni is on the same high level of imagination. In Busoni's 'concert arrangement' of the second of Schoenberg's piano pieces, Op. 11, he changed the original and began with an octave effect that Schoenberg's version subtly anticipates. Schoenberg reacted by observing to him that 'A hero who will shoot himself in the third act must be portrayed in the first act in such a way that an intuitive person can have a presentiment of his fate'. Referring to the same arrangement, Schoenberg says that where the entry of a chord is for him 'as if someone had pressed away a tear', in Busoni's version, 'the person blows his nose as well'.

in Russia, Kandinsky's answer is not satisfactory.[3] Neither he nor Schoenberg can have anything to do with 'lumping together', even though 'particular characteristics, negative and positive', are found in individuals and in nations. Among his friends, Kandinsky counts more Jews than Russians or Germans. (This old story served as the basis of the misconceived 1984 exhibition in Bayreuth, 'Wagner and the Jews'.) A 'Jewish problem' exists, Kandinsky goes on, and he regrets not having had the benefit of Schoenberg's views about it, since it must be examined by human beings 'who are free'.

Schoenberg's reply is psychologically revealing and profoundly moving:

> When I walk along the street, and each person looks at me to see whether I'm a Jew or a Christian, I can't very well tell each of them that I'm the one that Kandinsky and some others make an exception of, although of course that man Hitler [this was written in 1923] is not of their opinion.

Happily the two men became trusted friends again later in the 1920s. In 1936, when they resumed their correspondence, both of them were refugees, Schoenberg in Los Angeles, Kandinsky in Paris.

———◆———

In the growing literature on Schoenberg's own painting, a review essay (24 October 2003)[4] by *The New York Times*'s Roberta Smith is one of the most helpful to date. She was introducing the Schoenberg, Kandinsky, and Blue Rider Exhibition at the Jewish Museum on Fifth Avenue, New York. The thirty-six paintings by Schoenberg substantially outnumber the others – only thirteen by Kandinsky and

---

3   This writer heard the story in greater detail from Kandinsky's widow, Nina, in Venice in August 1956, and again in New York at the home of the Guggenheim Museum Director, Thomas Messer, in the 1960s.

4   Among the correspondence provoked by reviews of this exhibition, the *Times Literary Supplement* for 2 April 2004 printed a letter from Gerald N. Izenberg (Department of History, Washington University, St Louis, Missouri) that includes the sentence: 'Having examined the unpublished correspondence between Kandinsky and Gabriele Münter, his partner in the years before the First World War, I can attest to direct expressions of anti-Semitism on Kandinsky's part.'

twelve by the *Blaue Reiter* group. Moreover, they include, for the first time in America, the *Impression III (Concert)* that inspired Kandinsky to write to Schoenberg in the first place, in January 1911. Ms Smith describes the picture as 'unusually raw' for Kandinsky, by which, at this stage in the painter's journey into abstraction, she means the recognisable piano and the attentive audience. Ms Smith writes:

> Schoenberg was a... genuine, if somewhat capricious, hit-and-miss painter. His efforts... center on self-portraits and are variously outsiderish, abstract and conventionally representational... Schoenberg's paintings move in and out of Kandinsky and Company's push for modernism... moving ahead then dallying behind.

Ms Smith's comparison of the artists' historical situation is perceptive:

> Kandinsky's roiling paintings, radical in their time, may have lost much of their ability to shock, assuming a secure place in both the history of art and public consciousness. But Schoenberg's tumultuous music... remains relatively unassimilated, emblematically modern. It demands your complete attention and is not about to fade into any easy-listening background.

She also recognises that 'strikingly advanced' as many of Schoenberg's paintings are, they are more accessible than his music. But the push for Modernism lets us down: 'It is interesting to remember that Kandinsky's favorite paintings by Schoenberg were the more conventional, full-faced portraits... You wonder if Kandinsky ever suspected that Schoenberg's maverick paintings might be every bit as daring as his own.'

Chapter 5

A Survivor from Warsaw

A Survivor from Warsaw is a fully formed music drama of only six
to seven minutes' duration. The economy of statement and formal
compression are extreme, even for Schoenberg. No idea is repeated
in the same way. The effectiveness of the work depends on dramatic
contrasts: speaking (narration) versus singing (the chorus); English
(past-tense recollections in the Narration) versus German (present-
tense reality in the impersonation of the Sergeant); the association
of bugle calls and military drum rhythms with the Germans, and of
irregular rhythms in the strings with their limping and ragged Jewish
victims; the fragmentation of the first part of the piece versus the
unity and continuity of the choral ending (Auden: 'Group singing
in unison reduces the sense of diversity and strengthens the sense
of unity'); the limitation to small groups of instruments in the first
part in contrast to the full orchestra in the last; the fluctuating tempi
and metres in the first part versus the constant metre and scarcely
inflected tempo in the last.

The horror and hypertension of the scene is established in the
first few seconds by distorted and dissonant bugle calls accompanied
by violins and basses playing comminatory tremolandos at extreme
ranges, and by a piercing snare-drum roll. The picture is filled out
and intensified by nerve-shattering instrumental effects: sudden,
rhythmically disjunct outbursts of trills in the upper woodwinds
and trombone; flutter-tonguing in muted trumpets; rapidly repeated

notes in bassoons, oboe, and high xylophone; high, needlelike stabs of violin harmonics; tapping on the strings with the wood of the bow *(col legno battuto)*, and the use of *sul ponticello, saltando* and loud detonations in low basses and high winds. Perhaps the most effective orchestral scene change is in the accompaniment by percussion alone of the Sergeant's first command, and in the characterisation of his emptiness and puppet-like rigidity by the repetition of his motive in the hollow sonority of the xylophone.

The return of the bugle calls after the word 'sleep' is a structural device as well as a cruel irony. So, too, is the soft pre-echoing in muted horn near the beginning of the first six notes of *Sh'ma Yisroël*, the Hebrew prayer (Deuteronomy 6) recited at the immanence of a death, and, for protection, attached in mezuzahs to the doorposts of homes. People went to the gas chambers reciting, or singing, the *Sh'ma Yisroël.* (As musical precedent, Massenet's *Hérodiade* includes a setting of the prayer.)

The *Survivor* is as remarkable for its orchestral volumes as for its timbres. The two most dramatic moments in the narrative are those where the narration leaves description for action: the first quotation, in German, of the Sergeant, and the singing, in Hebrew, of the *Sh'ma Yisroël.* Both of these events are dependent upon orchestral scene-changing, which Schoenberg effects by radical changes in volume. As aforesaid, the Sergeant is accompanied by percussion alone, the *Sh'ma Yisroël* by the full orchestra, which has been saved for this moment and used heretofore only in groups and solo-instrument combinations. At this point, too, the musico-dramatic style, fragmented until now, gives way to unity and continuity.

The musico-dramatic technique employs several devices of preparation, as well as of identification. For only two examples, the melody of the Hebrew hymn of triumph is anticipated near the beginning by a muted horn sounding its first six notes softly and in the background. Further, the music accompanying the narrator's final speech, 'like a stampede of wild horses', is anticipated near the beginning by the music to the words, 'the grandiose moment when they all started to sing'. In both of these examples the later passage connects in retrospect with the earlier as a formative link.

On the analogy of marble not outlasting immortal rhymes, *A Survivor from Warsaw* is a living monument to the victims of the Holocaust, hence more powerful than a museum. It should have been heard at the end of *Schindler's List*, not only because of its incommensurable superiority to the commercial film score, but because of the feeling of triumph conveyed by Schoenberg's music at the end. The entrance of the chorus is one of the most moving moments in twentieth-century music.

The twos-against-threes of the 'stampede of wild horses' is a capital invention, and so is the simple trick of changing the narrator's speed: as the victims count, the words 'one' and 'two' are evenly paced, but the words 'three' and 'four' are twice as fast, an effect of genius.

Where does the *Survivor* lie in the Schoenberg pantheon? At a higher eminence, I think, than anyone has accorded it. It is protest music, a new genre in music. The ending is the most moving he ever wrote – compare it with the *MGM* ending of his *Genesis* Prelude, where, without words to inspire him, he forgets his own Three Satires, Op. 28, on composers who end in C major after wandering about in a no-man's-land of tonalities. As for relating the *Survivor* to Schoenberg's music as a whole, one thinks first of that other dramatic narrative, the too wordy *Ode to Napoleon.* But the listener is also reminded of *Moses und Aron* in the dramatic use of contrasting singing and speech, and of the String Trio in the exploitation of accented string harmonics.

A Survivor from Warsaw was composed in 1947. The initial performance, on 4 November 1948, was by the Albuquerque Civic Symphony, Kurt Frederick conducting.

Chapter 6

'The Emperor of China'

Everything I have written has a certain inner likeness to myself.
Schoenberg, to Alban Berg

Fewer than half of the 800 items in this far from completely collected Berg–Schoenberg correspondence have been included in this English-language volume of *The Berg–Schoenberg Correspondence*,[1] but the selection seems trustworthy, and, for better or worse, most readers will not be left feeling starved for more. Nor are they likely to object very strongly to the cuts and substituted summaries in several items from Berg, whose letters outnumber Schoenberg's more than three to one and in total are approximately six times longer. Berg's side of the correspondence is a trove of historically important information, but he is so lacking in candour, after learning what will and will not go down, that the reader can hardly wait for Schoenberg's replies. Schoenberg, of course, the same man to everybody, never diplomatic, never political, has the more original mind.

Berg's thralldom to Schoenberg and the contrast of their antithetical personalities – Schoenberg: small, quick, dynamic; Berg: tall, ponderous, effete, hyper-Romantic – provide the main interest. The two rarely discuss music at the level of discovery and innovation

---

1   *The Berg-Schoenberg Correspondence.* Selected letters. Translated by Juliane Brand and Christopher Hailey, London, 1987.

in composing. On the evidence of this book, Schoenberg, introrse in his creativity, did not confide in Berg on such matters, nor even mention the existence of *Pierrot lunaire* to him until a few days before its premiere. For exchanges about music, apart from questions pertaining to the publication of Schoenberg's works and comments on concerts and their preparation, we can look forward to Schoenberg's and Berg's letters to Webern, with whom, the editors inform us, both composers were 'much readier to share... artistic motivation'.

The first communications, during the summer of 1911, are from Berg. At the age of twenty-six, he had just completed six years of study (1904–10) with Schoenberg but could not break the teacher–pupil dependency, and had made no mark as a composer on his own. Schoenberg, at thirty-seven, had written epoch-making music (not yet performed), already had a European reputation, and, a year later, with *Pierrot lunaire*, would be recognised as the most influential composer of the age. As a musical radical without precedent, an intellectual cult figure – his pupils became his disciples – he was more harshly attacked than any other composer in music history. In consequence, he became rebarbative, prickly, spiteful, not least to his most successful pupil, Alban Berg. After more than a decade of abortive attempts to be heard in Vienna without an audience scandal, Schoenberg organised a society for private performances that excluded critics and non-member audiences.

Schoenberg's letters are epigrammatic ('the modern-minded cling to the abstruse and enjoy it only if it remains unclear to them'); ironical ('the people seemed to despise me as much as if they knew my music'); tactless (he acknowledges Berg's gift of a book with 'I never... would have considered acquiring [it] for myself... The ones I want are missing'); and bullying ('I am extremely annoyed, for I realise how irresponsibly you treated the matter... Now I know I cannot depend on you'). Yet Schoenberg remained Berg's polestar through thick and thin.

Schoenberg's humour balances his testiness: 'Enter rehearsal numbers as follows – a number every 10th bar;... at the 20th bar – 2; at the 30th bar – 3;... at the 82,756,930th bar – 8,275,693.' Schoenberg the teacher dominates the book, and its most memorable lines are his laws, musical and moral. Do not 'skirmish with journalists; it intensifies hate but lessens contempt'. Urging Berg to 'get involved in practical music making', Schoenberg gives matchless advice on how to conduct a rehearsal: 'Talk as little as possible. Never try to be witty...' At least one remark belongs in Bartlett's: 'Of course he seems to have quite "a mind of his own" and that is probably where he is weakest.'

Berg, in contrast, is effusive and expletive-prone (countless sentences begin with 'Oh'); like Queen Victoria, he underscores compulsively. He is hyperbolic ('How right you are in this, as in everything', 'My debt to you... has long since exceeded infinity'), obsequious and self-abasing ('I must *thank you* for your *censure*'); religiose (on a photo of Mahler's birthplace: 'Doesn't this resemble the shelter in which Christ was born?'); and lachrymose ('Of the inner joy I felt when I read your words, I cannot speak – for that there are only tears').

Berg's epistolary style provokes what he refers to as Schoenberg's 'affectionate admonitions', though the affection is hard to find:

> Dear Berg... Please number your questions so I can find them more easily when I answer you. [There are] so many excuses, parenthetical asides, 'developments', 'extensions' and stylisations that it takes a long time to figure out what you are driving at... your formalities... Break that habit!

And later: 'One sentence on each point, *clear and concise...* Surely by now you have learned from my letters.' Schoenberg even complains about the length of Berg's address, whereupon self-addressed envelopes are sent. But Berg's style does not change, even though he drafts his letters.

When the correspondence begins, Berg is in Vienna, Schoenberg at Starnbergersee, where he has fled because a neighbour in his Vienna apartment house has alleged that the composer's nine-year-old daughter was corrupting his five- and eleven-year-old sons. In the beginning, and as it will be thereafter, most of the letters centre on a real or imagined slight. The initial misunderstanding, for which

Berg sends treacly apologies, is the possibility that he has 'overrated' Schoenberg, something Schoenberg 'fears'. This leads to a new career for Berg as Schoenberg's factotum. He is soon mediating with an attorney in the affair with the neighbour: arranging to sublet Schoenberg's apartment, dispose of the contents, find a mover, oversee the shipment of furniture to Berlin; making panhandling calls on well-known music and art patrons in a campaign to raise money for Schoenberg's support. Schoenberg also puts Berg to work correcting the proofs and compiling the indexes for his book on harmony, although, as the author writes, 'It probably won't appear any time this century'. Needless to say, these onerous and time-consuming tasks are unremunerated, except for the 'honour' and 'privilege'.

The reader should bear in mind from the outset that Berg was unaware of the revolutionary creations of Schoenberg's most richly productive year, 1908–09, and the breakthrough to atonality that is still the central event of twentieth-century music, and the only music he knew of the composer he literally worshipped ('dear idolised Herr Schoenberg', 'your holy person'). Berg was never able to keep pace with Schoenberg, and as late as 1928 remarked on his wish to become 'as familiar with your later works as I believe I am with the first half'.

The correspondence concerns Berg's labours in connection with his transcription of Schoenberg's mammoth *Gurrelieder* for piano, as well as correcting its proofs, checking the orchestra parts for mistakes, and writing the concert guide. Predictably, Schoenberg rejects Berg's first and second efforts with the piano reduction as 'too difficult', and raises for him the awful prospect of having to do it over yet again: 'You'll make a simpler one next time.' But Berg's corrected proofs are also returned to him, because of the 'incredibly many errors... I think you frequently misread transposing instruments and various other things'. Even Schoenberg's compliment on the subsequent vetting includes a remark about remaining errors. When the piece is finally scheduled for performance and Schoenberg wants to have the orchestra parts compared to the score, Berg, back up for once and showing an instinct for self-preservation, estimates that this would take 'at least five hours a day for five weeks'.

As Berg starts on the *Gurrelieder* guide, Schoenberg warns

him against 'poetry' and 'flowery adjectives'. When it is finished, Schoenberg tells him to apply an editorial bistoury and 'cut 15-30 pages', which amounts to half of it! 'Don't let me influence your decision,' he adds, as if Berg's reactions were unforeseeable: 'The least criticism from you... robs me of almost *all* hope.' Years later, Schoenberg returned to the subject of Berg's guides:

> [if you do any more] you shouldn't design them so they are practically unintelligible without the score... In... the *Gurrelieder* guide... there is a bit too much "scientific" text with
> $$x^2 X y^3 + ab. 2[3q5 \pm (f X 1^2 ---/ + X I^{\text{bpa}}?!---4fffsf]: 26^a A.$$

The pattern of humble offerings from Berg and crushing responses from Schoenberg does not change until the premiere of *Wozzeck* (1925), after which Berg is accorded, but cannot fully accept, equal footing. Early in the correspondence Schoenberg admits that 'the minute I see something, I immediately feel an urge to contradict'. One letter from him begins: 'Dear Berg, I am sorry to have to tell you that you are wrong, although you used almost two pages trying to prove you were right'. When Berg talks about the 'fun' he is having with his 'radio set', Schoenberg says that 'turning it off remains the greatest pleasure'. When Berg sends some windy observations about kite-flying, Schoenberg pounces on him with 'Your conclusion about the flight of kites is wrong,' followed by the correct explanation in a few sentences, one of them containing the thought that 'only the immaterial possesses stability', on which Berg battens.

After Berg claims a 'tempo-machine' as his brainchild, Schoenberg says that he described 'exactly the same device' to a friend two years earlier. In response to Berg's gift of a book about the Jesuits, Schoenberg tells him that it 'only confirms a number of things I had already thought myself'. Yet Schoenberg is no less annoyed when Berg's letters do not come: 'Why haven't I heard from you? Have you lost all interest in me?' In the second year of the First World War, Schoenberg remarks that it might be 'easier to bring about world peace than clear the air between us'. But the belligerence is always on his side.

Was Schoenberg paranoid? According to his widow, as the

present writer can testify from correspondence as well as numerous conversations with her, Schoenberg believed that he was jinxed, that an encroaching malignant force foredoomed him and his work to misadventure. His references in these letters to a 'persecution complex' and to his periods of 'self-delusion' are probably not of much significance, since he is constantly analysing himself (as well as Berg, whose asthma he dismisses as 'autosuggestion'). But such statements as 'I must always be prepared for the nightly ambush of conspirators' and 'I detect a hint of defection in the slightest negligence' certainly sound like danger signals, as does his 'accusation' that Berg was 'cultivating' his friendship 'only with an eye to posterity'.

Yet the correspondence is more surprising in testimony of the opposite kind, in the many proofs that, so far from being a 'misfit', Schoenberg was an eminently sane, well-integrated and socially responsible citizen, fully able to 'function' and to 'cope'. At the beginning of the First World War, this 'decadent' and 'neurasthenic', as he was abused throughout the Establishment world, became a feisty patriot, rallying to the Austrian cause and criticising pacifists such as Karl Kraus. He prods Berg, much less sanguine about the draft, into buying war bonds ('an amount commensurate with your circumstances'), and reminds him that 'more than ever it is important to be a man... In a few months you may have to wield a bayonet.'

Berg, too, is forever analysing himself, in music as well as letters, identifying with Wozzeck at some level, portraying his temperament in the Chamber Concerto, impersonating himself in *Lulu* in the character Alwa, in the asthmatic breathing of Schigolch, and, on his deathbed, in Lulu herself ('Lulu c'est moi', following Flaubert on Emma Bovary). Berg knew Freud personally, and was an advocate of psychoanalysis, in which he signally failed to interest Schoenberg. He wrote to Schoenberg that Webern's account of psychoanalytic therapy, after three months as a patient of Alfred Adler, 'seems very plausible and reasonable'. But Schoenberg did not react. Nor does he comment on Otto Weininger's crackpot theories about the sexes as repeated by Berg – 'How can a woman's illogic stand up to a man's logic?' – or on Berg's references to such manifestations of the *psychopathia sexualis* as his sister's lesbianism ('a most unpleasant family matter'), Adolf Loos's pederastic activities, or Berg's repeated speculations about the deepest origins of illness being mental (Groddeck). Schoenberg's ceaselessly inventing mind does not have time for non-probative hypotheses of this kind, and he does not feel the need of help with his psyche.

What does rouse Schoenberg is Berg's conviction – which may have come from, and at any rate was confirmed by, Wilhelm Fliess's *Vom Leben und Tod* – that the number 23 had always played a crucial role in his life: 'Dear Berg... Everyone has a number like that... You must see that you become less dependent on these lucky and unlucky numbers by doing your best to *ignore* them!' – this from twelve-tone music's triskaidekaphobe, who, sharing the superstition that governs the numbering of floors in modern American high-rise buildings, wrote '12A' in his later manuscripts above the bar before 14.

In December 1912, Berg mailed the score of his *Altenberg Lieder* to Schoenberg for possible inclusion in a concert. When Berg proposed to simplify Schoenberg's task by sending a piano reduction, Schoenberg took offence – 'I am quite able to read the orchestral score' – and went on to criticise the music for betraying a 'too obvious desire to use new means'. He nevertheless liked 'a number of passages' and, at 'first glance', of course, thought the songs 'beautifully orchestrated'. True to form, Berg thanked him for his 'kind words acknowledging that the score can make a pretentious impression', and proceeded with a complicated explanation that Schoenberg probably did not read. Ultimately Schoenberg programmed the two songs that were not Berg's first choices, and omitted the final, haunting one, whose performance the young composer most wanted, but which would not have been heard anyway, since the music and the Peter Altenberg texts provoked protests that led to a brawl in the audience and brought the concert to an end.

Far more striking and original than Schoenberg's own orchestral songs to that date (Six Songs, Op. 8), the *Altenberg Lieder* mark a huge leap in Berg's development, the emergence of the theatrical, lyrical and structural gifts that would attain full expression in *Wozzeck*. All five of them, but especially the last, display a distinctive melodic character. Surely an intuition of this influenced Schoenberg's choice.

What becomes clear from the letters and other sources is that Schoenberg did not believe in Berg's promise as a composer, that he regarded Webern as the more highly endowed pupil and recommended his, but not Berg's, music to publishers. A year and a half beyond the *Altenberg Lieder*, and with the score of two of Berg's new orchestra pieces as further tokens of his genius, Schoenberg could still disappoint him with: 'I can't say anything about your work just yet'. Writing to Berg in 1929, Theodor Adorno reminds him that he, Berg, had confessed to being greatly upset after the 1913 *Altenberg* performance ended in a scandal and Schoenberg dissociated himself from him. But this discovery could also be interpreted as an instance of Berg's duplicity, since no hint of anything of the kind can be found in his letters to Schoenberg at the time.

Schoenberg's reaction to the *Altenberg Lieder* recurred on a larger scale with the stunning success of *Wozzeck* in Berlin in December 1925, an event that would soon be seen as the peripeteia in Berg's fortunes, as well as in his relationship with Schoenberg. Two years earlier, after finishing the opera, Berg had disparaged it in comparison with *Erwartung*, 'that concentration without its equal in music' – which is true – as '3 acts of verbosity and loquaciousness' – which is false and gratuitous.

Seeing *Wozzeck* a month after the premiere, and with no preparatory study of the score, Schoenberg sent Berg a brief note, resorting to the hackneyed device of criticising the performance first: 'The orchestra stumbles... the singers exaggerate... [the] sets [are] irritating.' Then he vouchsafes an opinion of the work: 'Some things I don't find good,' he writes, singling out the topographical feature of Berg's vaulting style: 'Every scene builds to a great orchestral FFF.' Here the reader must remember that when the opera was first performed, Schoenberg was writing chamber music in a neoclassical style, far from Berg's passionate ebullitions. But on the whole 'it is very impressive and there is no doubt that I *can* be proud of such a student'.

Berg's craven reply is exasperating: 'That you really didn't need to feel ashamed of me as a student makes me very happy.' Virtually overnight *Wozzeck* had catapulted him to a pre-eminent position among the handful of great living composers, and to a popularity that

Schoenberg would never know. In the last year of Berg's life Schoenberg acknowledged: 'You... alone in our cause, managed to win general recognition'. The infrequent letters of the decade from *Wozzeck* to Berg's death reflect on both sides Berg's change of status, as well as his ability to balance the two claims of artistic success and loyalty to Schoenberg. But the servility remains, an undiscardable habit.

Unlike Schoenberg, who concentrated almost exclusively on himself as a source of creativity in music, painting and literature, Berg had an ear and a mind for other voices. We are not surprised to learn from the letters that the composer who recognised the greatness of Georg Büchner also sent Kafka's *Country Doctor* collection, Dostoyevsky's *Idiot* and Broch's *Sleepwalkers* to Schoenberg. Yet Berg could not bring himself to countervail his literary-critical perceptions to those of his teacher. In one mid-1920s letter he quotes some less-than-immortal lines from a poem by Schoenberg and, to the reader's mortification, calls them 'surely among the most sublime in the German language'.

The editors needlessly warn that Berg's musical judgements are 'too often coloured by his eagerness to please Schoenberg' and that they betray a 'snobbishness that belongs to the less appetising legacies of the Schoenberg circle'. A fanaticism, rather. In fact, what Berg really thought about the music of his contemporaries is impossible to discover. Not that we distrust his verdict on an opera by Szymanowski as 'very boring and superfluous'. But such comparatively favourable judgements as those on Charpentier's *Julien* ('very fine music') and Prokofiev's *Love for Three Oranges* ('very engaging, flowing music', albeit in the salon class) were too obviously put forward for the reason that the composers were beneath competition. This much is shown by the total silence about Stravinsky. Culture clashes notwithstanding, Berg, an inveterate theatre-goer, might have been expected to notice Nijinsky's *Petrushka*, if not the music, in Diaghilev's January 1913 Vienna season. But, then, *The Rite of Spring*, performed throughout Berg's world in the 1920s, is not mentioned, and in reporting to Schoenberg on a Vienna performance of his *Pelleas*, Berg fails to mention that *Les Noces* was on the same programme.

One other omission is still more conspicuous. We wonder, not for long, why Berg's bulletins about the fates of operas by the likes of

Schillings and Lenau do not include *Der Rosenkavalier*, which was triumphing just down the street. Richard Strauss had helped Schoenberg at one time, then criticised him, thus becoming an unmentionable – which explains why the reader ignorant of other literature on the subject would have no way of knowing of Strauss's immense consequence in German and Viennese musical life in the quarter of a century covered by these letters. Apart from a calculated remark about revising downward an opinion of *Elektra,* and a description of Strauss's 'latest operas' as an 'uninterrupted stream of mush', his name scarcely appears. (A footnote states that Schoenberg and Berg heard the first version of *Ariadne* together in Berlin.) As shown in this correspondence, Berg's monotheism compelled him to stoop, as he kneeled, to conceal his true feelings about *Salome*, to which *Wozzeck* owes a very audible debt.

The correspondence is herewith published in English first, before any German edition. The editors attribute their coup to 'the intense interest of American scholars in the period and in the composers', and to the persistence of the 'quest'. In their case this has meant searching through the files of newspapers and periodicals, comparing other correspondence, tracing obscure acquaintances, and much more.

When, if ever, will we see the Schoenberg–Webern and Webern–Berg correspondence? According to the editors, 'postwar publication on the so-called Second Viennese School was... more reliant upon fond recollection... than historical scholarship'. Part of this criticism can be levelled at Joan Allen Smith's book of interviews[2] with survivors (and their next of kin) of Schoenberg's Vienna circle, all of whom refer to him with a reverence appropriate to the canonisation process. But the other part does not apply. Smith's scholarship is sound, and her book adds substantially to existing character studies of Schoenberg, as for example those published in *The Journal of the Arnold Schoenberg Institute*, as well as of Berg and Webern (*ibid*), 'the two sentinels watching outside Schoenberg's house [to make sure] that nobody [comes] near it'.

Ms Smith tells us that her presentation of oral history is based

2   *Schoenberg and His Circle. A Viennese Portrait*, London (Macmillan), 1980.

on a technique of juxtaposition employed by Karl Kraus and Walter Benjamin. Perhaps. But this particular side-by-side testimony of different witnesses to events of more than half a century ago yields many remarkable similarities and no significant disagreements. The reservations about the book that the reader may have are that the twenty-five interviewees – pupils, performing musicians and friends (including Oskar Kokoschka) – were induced to speak American ('Mahler wasn't a soft guy') rather than their native tongues. The false starts, anacoluthons and verbal fumbles are all faithfully retained (the *ipsissima verba*), and the exegetical and background matter with which their recollections are introduced and interlarded is helpful only for those seeking a first acquaintance with Schoenberg's world.

One of the most valuable chapters contains the complete programmes, December 1918 – December 1921, of Schoenberg's Society for Private Musical Performances in Vienna, in which Schoenberg and Webern participated as conductors and, on one occasion, Ravel as piano accompanist for his Mallarmé songs. This most important concert series of the modernist period turned limited resources to advantage by replacing large orchestra works with specially prepared chamber-music arrangements, and two-, four- and six-hand piano reductions, some of which, by masters including Webern, are of permanent value. From Smith's listings, which identify the *Vortragsmeister*, or coach, for each piece, we learn that Schoenberg himself rehearsed the major Debussy scores, Scriabin's *Poème de l'extase* and the Mahler symphonies. The predominance of Reger in numbers of performances (almost sixty) begs some questions, and might have generated one or two from Smith, since Reger's music was so little known in the United States, and Schoenberg named him in the line of descent from Wagner: 'Mahler, Reger, Strauss, and Debussy to the harmony of today'.

Berg's function in the Society at one time is recalled by Felix Greissle, Schoenberg's son-in-law:

> ... to see whether there were enough chairs in the hall, and that they were at a certain distance... I remember Schoenberg coming... 'The chairs are completely cockeyed. This is

ridiculous. What did you do here?' Berg, without saying a word, took a tape measure out of his pocket and measured and said, 'You said you wanted so and so many centimetres; it's really all right; it's half a centimetre more.'

Nothing in the book conveys the living Schoenberg so much as two other anecdotes. The first is an account by Greissle of his attempt to move in with Schoenberg in Berlin in 1923:

> After his first wife died, and when he felt very lonely, my wife and I offered to live with him, which we did, for a couple of months; it was very, very difficult. We used to have fights almost every day about really minor matters, and so one day, it was impossible to live further with him. We packed and moved out into our apartment... That same day, at night ... somebody threw pebbles at my window. I opened the window and down there was Schoenberg. He said very meekly, 'May I come up?' So I said, 'Oh, please do come up by all means.' And he came up, he apologised, and he said, 'I'm sorry. You are of course absolutely right, you cannot live with me, that's impossible.'

The narrator of the other story is Marcel Dick, violia player of the Kolisch Quartet:

> There was a graphologist in Vienna... Webern and Steuermann... took an envelope that had an address on it in Schoenberg's handwriting... The... expert described completely what kind of person he was in amazing detail and accuracy... When he ended his presentation, he said, '... this man thinks he's the emperor of China'... In California, ... Schoenberg celebrating his seventieth birthday [in 1944] and... noticing that a group of his old friends were whispering around in a corner and laughing, said... 'What are you laughing at?'... Finally, one of them took courage and... told him the story of... the graphologist and that he said that the man thinks he's the emperor of China. 'What, what? Well, didn't you tell him that I am?'

Chapter 7
Schoenberg and Dika

In 1936, a piece of music by 'eleven-year-old Dika Newlin' (actually born on 22 November 1923) attracted the attention of the film-music composer Vladimir Bakaleinikoff, who had just returned from Hollywood to Michigan after attending one of Arnold Schoenberg's classes. As a friend of the girl's parents, Bakaleinikoff persuaded them to send her to study with Schoenberg, saying that he was the world's foremost teacher of composition, and that any sacrifice would be worth the goal. This came to pass three years later. The diaries Dika kept between the ages of fifteen and eighteen about her lessons with the master contain the only intimate views of Schoenberg so far published, as well as the first detailed account of his teaching in his American period. For these reasons, *Schoenberg Remembered*[1] will be read by generations to come.

On one level, the book is a chronicle of classroom events and of the author's progress as a student. But the main interest is in the battle between the pupil's and the teacher's egos. Something of Schoenberg's is known from other sources, but never so intimately observed as by Ms Newlin. In Schoenberg's sessions in musical analysis she quickly emerges as a kind of challenger. The kiddy-composer stands in her corner opposite Schoenberg and provides what may be the unique three-dimensional portrait of the great man in his American period.

---

1   *Schoenberg Remembered: Diaries and Recollections, 1938-1976*, New York, 1980.

In some ways the contestants were well matched. First of all, their self-esteem seems about equal: 'All the local lights present were making much of him, and of me, too...' the bobbysox Dika writes. Second, neither teacher nor pupil has even the semblance of a superego in the usual interpretation of the term; Schoenberg, of course, requires none, thanks to his high endowment of intuitive powers. Then, too, both combatants are peculiarly able to arouse guilt feelings. 'Probably I should not go to him,' Dika writes, after a spat, 'but will do so this time to give him a chance to redeem himself.' And, 'I had prepared for [the oral exam] by making myself up to look interestingly ill.' The aspiring composer worships the renowned master, but has a mind of her own, and speaks it in her diaries on almost everything Schoenberg says or does, both in areas of agreement – 'Schoenberg and I shared this taste,' the sixteen-year-old writes on one occasion – and disagreement – 'He thinks Verdi is a great composer. I do not concur'.

Although Ms Newlin might see the matter differently, Schoenberg emerged the winner; at the end of her third year, he did not invite her to return, this despite her triumph in being awarded a University Fellowship ('I was the indubitable first out of 142 applicants'). On the night of the performance of her string quartet, 6 June 1941, she had 'thought of staying away, to give Uncle Arnold a well-deserved punch, but [I] let my better nature get ahead of me'. This cherubic side directed her to sit 'in the back of the auditorium by myself, and [wear] a hat with a veil, so he got scared for fear that I'd left town without bidding him a fond farewell!... He refrained from insulting anybody all evening...'

Apart from the two principals in the ego department, the only others of any consequence in the cast are Schoenberg's family, his dog, and Leonard Stein (d. 2004), later the composer's assistant, who, though not indexed, appears *passim*, frequently as the focal point of one disaster or another:

> Stein broke a record today by bringing one measure of orchestration. Uncle Arnold had to spend nearly the whole hour explaining what was wrong with it. He wrote 12 p's over it and crossed out all the notes...

Since six *pppppp*'s would mean quiet to the limit of audibility, twelve would mean not to be heard at all.

The author's classmates provide little more than a backdrop. A similar situation had apparently existed in East Lansing, where young Dika was secretly given high school entrance exams after only three years of grade school, her 'diminutive presence' having angered her classmates' parents, who 'feared that I might give their children an "inferiority complex"'! (She adds, characteristically, 'It wasn't the last time I would be perceived as a threat...') At UCLA she was soon doing more work than the other members of Schoenberg's classes ('I had to present my variations... I brought the number up to seven; no one else had more than three'). Receiving his highest marks, 'I was invited to become a private pupil'. Whatever the effects of her brilliance and domineering personality on her faceless fellow students, *they* are mentioned only because of their poor showings: 'Y. was slow on the uptake,' and as for Miss E.,

> I might have commented that Schoenberg wouldn't get music out of *her* manuscripts, but confined myself to saying that, so far as I remembered, we had not handed in our variations on that day. At that, I think she would like to have killed me!

On one occasion Schoenberg berated Ms Newlin for the sloppiness of her writing:

> 'No more, Miss Newlin, no more. There's no use, I cannot help you. I cannot read one word of these hieroglyphics... I absolutely refuse to look at your music so long as it is like this. You *must* write a clear manuscript. Why you not write like Miss Temple, hm?'

Miss Temple, in Newlin's words, was 'a neat but untalented student'. A few days later, in another class, Newlin remarks that 'Schoenberg did not look at our work today. A cursory look at Miss Temple's current masterpiece got him shuttled off to a discussion of chorale harmonization...'

At times, the advanced composition students' classroom could be mistaken for a kindergarten. Here is a scene from the 'Structural Functions' class:

> When he asked me to describe the codettas and retransition [in the first section of the first Razumovsky Quartet], I did so in this way: 'The retransition begins in measure 98.' That didn't seem to satisfy him; he asked several others for the answer, but didn't seem to be satisfied with theirs, either. Finally, he asked,... 'Why... do you not see that the codettas end in measure 97 and not in measure 98?' 'But that's what Miss Newlin said!' shouted Abraham... 'But you did not say this!... You said that the codettas end in measure 98!' 'I did not!... I said the retransition began in 98!...' 'Mr Stein, ... did I misunderstand her? Did she say this? Now, don't become embarrassed; tell me frankly if she said it, for I might have misunderstood her!' 'Well,' muttered Stein, 'all I heard was 98.' (He has to keep his job, you know!) 'Mr Abraham,... did she say it? Swear to tell the truth, the whole truth, and nothing but the truth!... Say yes or no!' 'YES!' (chorus of assent from the whole class). 'And I still say she did not say it!' [from Schoenberg]

At this point, the reader should be informed that Dika Newlin eventually became a devoted advocate of Schoenberg's music and artistic principles. At twenty-three, she would publish a classic study of Schoenberg and his two Austrian predecessors, Bruckner and Mahler, the first in English to exhibit a profound knowledge of their interconnections and of the subject as a whole. Shortly after that, in 1947, she translated René Leibowitz's *Schoenberg et son école*,[2] one of the most influential books in American musical life in the early 1950s. Late in life, she became a punk rocker, and, in succession, a horror-movie star, marketed by her collaborator, the film-maker Michael Moore. She also founded a nightclub band called Apocowlypso.

---

2   *Schoenberg and His School*, New York, 1949.

The most troublesome aspect of *Schoenberg Remembered* is in the question of genre. Nearly all of the book is in diary form, yet much of it reads like a memoir. Newlin's foreword asserts that apart from using pseudonyms and initials to protect people's identities (such as 'St.' for Schoenberg's assistant!) and normal English spelling for the composer's pronunciation, 'the diaries are as I originally wrote them'. At the end of the volume, however, she refers to her work of 'editing... for the reader of the present day'. But these editorial additions and changes are so voluminous that they require demarcation by italics, brackets, footnotes, typeface or other means. For instance, after only nine entries, she writes of Schoenberg's 'character (Which I never did admire, by the way. I always thought him mean...)'. This, transparently, is the conclusion of a later date, and not, as the entry begins, an observation of 'this afternoon'. So, too, in the phrase already quoted referring to fellow student Miss E., 'so far as I remembered', why is the verb in the past tense, when the action is in the present, and would the author be likely to forget what she had said only a few hours before? Moreover, 'by the way' and 'you know' are not diarists' expressions. And who is the addressee in such questions as 'Did you ever hear of such a mix-up in your life?'

It must also be said that the language of the diaries is confusing. The fifteen-year-old can write a sentence such as 'After any prolonged period of highly concentrated and alembicated happiness, a corresponding period of depression should occur...' yet refer to Schoenberg as 'Nuncie', 'Schoenie', 'Arnelie', 'a scream', 'goofy', 'loopy', and call his home 'the dear old loony-bin'. She often makes Schoenberg sound Japanese. 'Ah so,' he says, and 'This all the same', 'This fine', as if he rarely used verbs. Furthermore, in 1940, such expressions as 'I trow' and the 'latest wrinkle' are anachronistic, from past and future time zones. Some of the writing is downright awful, as when she says that libraries were 'handy hideouts for peaceful proofreading, far from frenetic felinity', and 'Uncle Arnold was infernally diabolical'. How can an intellectual and multilingual woman be so unthinking? Is it a case of Eliot's distinction, with reference to Thomas Carlyle, between intellect and intelligence?

Withal, nearly every page contains illustrations of Schoenberg's reputation as a great teacher. He says of a colleague, 'All he must do is teach what he knows; this easy; what I do, I teach the student what *he* must know; and this hard.' Newlin observes that, for Schoenberg,

> ... a rule is like a law of nature, and admits of absolutely no exceptions. Hence, he gives us but few rules... but much advice. This latter is not meant to be followed slavishly, but rather to develop our ear so that we can use our own judgment... He sees no sense in teaching us to write... in the... 'Palestrina style'.

In truth, this is the quiddity of Schoenberg's approach. For him, to teach a pupil how to duplicate the music of an unrepeatable past made no sense. His goal was to make his students self-reliant and to instill in them an understanding of music from the inside – i.e., to think creatively rather than academically, in, for example, a 'scholarly', but sterile, analysis of sonata form. Newlin paraphrases him on the subject of too-rapid emotional change in the traditional use of the major key for the subordinate theme in a minor-key piece; in the post-Beethoven era Schoenberg illustrated this weakness of 'turning too quickly from clouds to sunshine' in a reference to Brahms's C minor Quartet. (But surely the key, by itself, does not necessarily establish the mood. Schubert, for instance, can be as sad in the major mode as in the minor.)

Newlin tells us, as well, that Schoenberg distinguished 'modern' thematic counterpoint from an earlier kind based on motives. He mentioned that contrapuntal art in his own music consists in combining two or more themes in as many ways as possible, whereas in the older counterpoint all of the voices are strictly derived from the given motive.

One item will surprise musicians. Schoenberg, Newlin says, 'doesn't believe in teaching harmony and composition concurrently', harmony being so complex a subject that to learn it while composing would require too much time. But what, then, is the student composer's harmonic language? Schoenberg, self-taught in this regard, evidently believed that others should follow his example. But after three-quarters of a century, the harmonic dimension in his own so-called twelve-tone music remains its greatest obstacle for the general audience.

The book is as illuminating about the quirks of Schoenberg's mind outside music as in it, and about the idiosyncrasies of his personality and character. Unfortunately, the author directs us to what she considers to be his most acute remarks and most eccentric behaviour without any explanation. Thus she introduces as a 'terribly funny incident' the composer's attempt to mend a loose-seated chair, ending in an accident of a splinter in his finger: 'He screamed and yelled bloody murder, made the most terrifying faces, and pulled... until the blood came.' But what is funny about this? She also cites as 'typically Schoenbergian naïveté' the composer's 'exclamation' one day, 'in a voice replete with childish joy and wonderment', 'Oh look, it rains! Is it not wonderful?' But what one wonders is why the observation is peculiarly Schoenbergian and naïve. One incident, presented as revealing of Schoenberg's self-centredness, the story of his runaway dog, Roddie, provides a convincing insight into his character. Not considering that all dogs have natural urges, and, at one time or another, take off on their own, Schoenberg was ready to punish the pet by giving it away: 'He won't have a dog that is so disloyal.'

The author seems not to have comprehended one of Schoenberg's most famous witticisms. According to her, 'he admitted having made... errors in the *Gurrelieder,* where he wrote low B's for the cello and viola' (actually one low B in the third division of cellos at figure 100). But the story is that when someone observed to him that he had written a non-existent note in the final *tutti* to that work, he riposted: 'Leave it out, we won't hear it anyway'.

Readers can decide for themselves if 'cruel' is a justified adjective to describe many of Schoenberg's remarks to his students. Yet it must be remembered that Schoenberg, at the summit of his art, was obliged, in one class, to teach as many as thirty-six pupils, of whom only two or three, if any, could have been qualified to receive the instruction he was able to offer. A related consideration that the author overlooks is that the harsh abuse suffered by the composer all his life did not thicken his epidermis, and that in a sense he was only giving back what he had received. At times, his treatment of the 'harassed' and 'docile' Leonard Stein does seem truculent, as when Mr Stein 'appears with no work and gives the excuse that he has been moving'. (Schoenberg's response is, 'I think you've been moving all year'.) Miss Newlin vengefully records a remark to her that 'the judges know so little that they will surely give the prize to someone like you, or to someone who knows even less, if this is possible'.

Schoenberg Remembered is nevertheless a valuable contribution to the history of a now buried and forgotten Los Angeles. The present reviewer, who knew all of the places and most of the people mentioned in it, read the book with some nostalgia. Here are Peter Yates's Evenings on the Roof and the rehearsal orchestra of film-studio musicians, which was conducted by both Stravinsky and Schoenberg (and, for that matter, by this reviewer, who remembers Alma Mahler and Bruno Walter together attending his rehearsal of *Petrushka* and Haydn's Symphony No. 31) in a high school auditorium. And here on page after page are Klemperer, Krenek and other fascinating musicians, though none more so than the subject of the book, of whom it may be said, as he himself said of J.S. Bach, he had an 'infinite knowledge of the biology of tone'.

To complete the record, it must be mentioned that in 1945 Schoenberg singled out Dika Newlin 'among the younger and lesser-known' composers in whom he had 'found talent and originality'.

Chapter 8

Notes on the Chamber Symphony, *The Book of the Hanging Gardens*, Five Pieces for Orchestra, *Erwartung*, Four Orchestral Songs, Serenade, Violin Concerto

Chamber Symphony (1906)

Introducing Schoenberg's pre-atonal works, programme annotators often begin by attempting to explain the piece's anticipation of atonality, while at the same time tracing its antecedents in *Tristan* and *Parsifal*. But the single-movement Symphony requires total concentration on itself alone, and no part of the listener's mind, if he or she is to digest it fully, can be spared for musings about where the composer once was and where he is going. It is the densest, most compact and rapidly moving music up to its time (1906).

Schoenberg himself outlined the form in terms of rehearsal numbers in the score:

I   Sonata-allegro (Beginning to No. 38)

II   Scherzo (Nos 38-60)

III Development (Nos 60-77)

IV   Adagio (Nos 77-90)

V   Recapitulation and Finale (Nos 90-100)

The overt Wagnerisms in the *Adagio* may seem surprising at this stage in Schoenberg's evolution, but the never-mentioned, though blindingly obvious, Beethoven ancestry is more germane. The propulsive power and the tug and pull of impending tonal-harmonic resolutions bring to mind the work of no other composer. So does the cohesiveness of different movements within a single one, as in the recapitulation of the Scherzo in the finale of Beethoven's C minor Symphony. The repeated hammer blows near the end of Schoenberg's exposition, in the passage for the horn upbeats to *tutti* chords, also recall the repeated *forte* chords in the first movement of the 'Eroica'.

Utterly new in Schoenberg are the sudden rhythmic interchanges in the Scherzo, the transferring of the time-value of the beat to a note of greater (or lesser) value, and the constantly changing tempi. No sooner is a steady pulsation established than the word *steigernd* (quickening, intensifying) appears, the mood begins to shift, and the music is soon charging ahead and off the emotional fever chart.

In later years Schoenberg claimed that the Symphony was 'a first attempt to create a chamber orchestra'. He might have added 'and the last', since no one has subsequently composed anything comparable to it. A criticism sometimes levelled against the piece is that an ensemble of ten winds and five strings is inherently unbalanced. Schoenberg knew this, of course, but his fifteen instruments never play 'one on one'. In full ensemble episodes they are carefully doubled, which was the composer's chief means of obtaining balanced volumes, as well as differentiations of colour.

Instruments of different timbres play in unison in Bach cantatas. Similarly, in one triple *forte* unison passage near the beginning of the Symphony the upper woodwinds combine on a single line, producing a new, wonderfully plangent sonority. Among the novel doublings, those of the flute and small clarinet in their lowest registers with the bassoon in a medium high one, and of a violin playing a fast triplet accompaniment figure *pizzicato* together with the piccolo playing it legato, must be mentioned. But it should also be said that some of Schoenberg's instrumental demands have become possible only with a new generation of virtuoso players, a bassoonist who can double-tongue groups of six notes at a metronomic 160 to the beat, a double bassist whose treble harmonics are full tones at exact pitch instead of out-of-tune pipsqueaks, a violinist who executes wide intervals perfectly in tune in the top register – and with players who know the whole as well as their parts. Only then does a coherent performance of the piece become a possibility.

The Book of the Hanging Gardens, Op. 15
Fifteen Poems from Stefan George's *Das Buch der hängenden Gärten*

Schoenberg had set poems by Stefan George before *The Hanging Gardens* (1908), most notably the *Litanei* (Litany) and *Entrückung* (Rapture), the third and fourth movements of his Second String Quartet, which add a high soprano voice to the instruments. Composer and poet seem to have had no personal connection. One reason could be that as charismatic leaders of cults, they too much resembled each other.

In 1889, in Paris, George began to attend Mallarmé's 'Tuesday afternoons', where he soon attracted the most intelligent young literati in the German-speaking world, among them Hugo von Hofmannsthal. George, a homosexual, tried to disguise his inclinations by referring to lovers in gender-neutral terms ('you', 'my child'). The texts of *The Hanging Gardens* are love poems, the only ones George ever addressed to a woman (in this case the wife of Richard Dehmel, author of the poem that inspired Schoenberg's *Verklärte Nacht*). But we are told nothing about the relationship between her and the man, except that they are destined to separate. We are also unable to visualise the scene, which includes white marble Baroque fountains, storks, ponds, a desert, Northern garden flowers and tropical palms. Furthermore, there is no consistent narrative and there are no 'events'.

At the very beginning of the song-cycle we are struck by the syncopations of the single-line accompaniment. The vocal line is one of the most memorable of the entire group; a climax builds quickly and a piano coda, which echoes the introduction, follows soon after. The second song is confined to the lowest octave of the voice. Its dotted rhythmic style and piano doubling of pitches and rhythm recalls Schumann. The fourth song is distinguished by its changing metres and frequent doubling of piano and voice. In the fifth song, in which twelve out of only eighteen bars employ bass octaves, the beauty of the quiet, tender melodic line, repeated in a perfect canon between voice and piano in bars ten and twelve, is remarkable. The sixth song is also notable for piano and vocal doubling, but in the seventh song the piano part is entirely in the treble clef, much of it confined to three-part harmony, the first part to two-part harmony, and the middle section to single-note piano accompaniment.

Perhaps the most passionate in the entire cycle, Song VIII ('If I today do not come nigh thee'), which features the augmented triad, is the only one in rapid tempo. Beginning with Song IX, the piano part becomes increasingly predominant. Introductions become longer, and in the final song the piano plays thirty-one bars alone and accompanies the voice in only nineteen bars. The melody in Song X is repeated, always with changes of harmony, more times than in any other Schoenberg opus in this period, and at the beginning the voice repeats the piano exactly, and the piano part is closer to the vocal part than in any other song. A striking moment is the affirmation of the D major tonality on the downbeat of the second last bar, and the conclusion in the same key, shifting to a Neapolitan sixth chord.

In Song XI, the shape of the opening bars of the accompaniment reminds us of the beginning of the first of the Five Pieces for Orchestra, particularly in the recapitulation at the end of the piece. Again, in Song XII, the piano and vocal parts double at the centre of the piece, and again the piano part is reduced to a single line towards the end. In Song XIII, the tessitura is remarkably low, as well as small in compass. The emphasised triplet rhythm is another feature. Schoenberg's biographer Hans Stuckenschmidt identifies this song as 'the first composition in which all connections with traditional conceptions of key and consonances are left behind', and further suggests that 'Schoenberg's peculiar superstitious relation to the number 13' began here.

Song XIV, the shortest and least dense of the fifteen, has been called 'hectic, nervous, almost stormy', but this description must refer to one or the other of two earlier, unpublished versions. The scholarly analysis of this quiet, gentle and very short little piece, published in the *Journal of the Arnold Schoenberg Institute*, November 1984, sheds no light either on the relationships of the other versions or on the song itself. In this song perhaps Schoenberg's and George's nature mysticism come closest. A special effect will be noted by the use of the pedal. As aforesaid, Song XV, the longest in the opus and with the longest introduction and coda, features the piano as much as the voice. Pure triadic harmonies are prominent in bars eight and thirty-one. The song engages a greater range of dynamics, from *pianissimo* to *molto forte*, than any of the others, and the coda is more notable for a succession of octaves in the left hand of the piano part than any other work by Schoenberg.

The first performance of *The Hanging Gardens* took place in the Ehrbar Hall, Berlin, on 14 January 1910, sung by Martha Winternitz-Dorda. Schoenberg's messianic programme note for the occasion reads, in part:

> With the George songs I have for the first time succeeded in approaching an ideal of expression and form which has been in my mind for years. Until now, I lacked the strength and confidence to make it a reality. But now that I have set out along this path once and for all, I am conscious of having broken through every restriction of a bygone aesthetic; and though the goal towards which I am striving appears to me a certain one, I am, nonetheless, already feeling the resistance I shall have to overcome: I feel that even the least of temperaments will rise in revolt, and suspect that even those who have so far believed in me will not want to acknowledge the necessary nature of this development. So it seemed a good thing to point out, by performing the *Gurrelieder* – which years ago were friendless, but today have friends enough – that I am being forced in this direction not because my invention or technique is inadequate, nor because I am uninformed about all the other things the prevailing aesthetics demand, but that I am obeying an inner

compulsion, which is stronger than my upbringing: that I am obeying the formative process which, being natural to me, is stronger than my artistic education.

Schoenberg's pupil Egon Wellesz quotes him to the effect that the initial words of the text meant nothing to him while composing, and that he claimed to have understood the poetic context only days after finishing the music:

> There to my great astonishment I discovered that I was never more faithful to the poet than when, led as it were, by the first direct contact with the opening sounds, I felt instinctively all that must necessarily follow from these initial sounds. Then it became clear to me that it is with a work of art as with every perfect organism... It is so homogeneous in its constitution that it discloses in every detail its truest and inmost being. Thus I came to a full understanding... of Stefan George's poems from their sound alone... the external agreement between music and text - declamation, tempo, and tonal intensity - has little to do with inner meaning.

Five Pieces for Orchestra

The Five Pieces for Orchestra and *Erwartung*, written immediately afterwards, embody Schoenberg's artistic credo:

> Art belongs to the unconscious. One must express oneself directly. Not one's taste, or one's upbringing, or one's intelligence, knowledge, or skill. Not all these acquired characteristics, but that which is inborn, instinctive.

Composed in 1909, the Five Pieces for Orchestra, untitled originally, were performed for the first time by Sir Henry Wood and the Queen's Hall Orchestra on 3 September 1912, in the Royal Albert Hall, London. Schoenberg's diary for 27 January 1912 tells us that the publisher wants titles for the orchestral pieces, for publisher's reasons. Maybe I'll give in, since I've found titles that are at least possible. On the whole, unsympathetic to the idea. For the wonderful thing about music is that one can say everything in it, so that he who knows understands everything; and yet one hasn't given away one's secrets, the things one doesn't admit even to oneself. But titles give you away. Besides, whatever has to be said has been said by the music. Why, then, words as well? If words were necessary, they would be there in the first place. But music says more than words. Now, the titles which I may provide give nothing away, because some of them are very obscure and others highly technical. To wit:

I. Premonitions (everyone has those)

II. The Past (everyone has that, too)

III. Chord-Colours (technical)

IV. Peripetia (general enough, I think)

V. The Obbligato (perhaps better the 'fully-developed' or the 'endless') Recitative

There should be a note that these titles were added for technical reasons of publication and not to give a 'poetic' content.

'Premonitions'

The basic melodic-intervallic, harmonic and rhythmic materials are exposed in the first three bars. The three-note motive of the upper line (cellos), with its repetition in sequence (cellos and oboe), describes an augmented triad on the longer, emphasised notes F, A, C sharp, the pedal harmony that underlies the music from bar twenty-three to the end. The last three notes of the piece become a principal motive in the 'Obbligato Recitative', and hence help to interconnect the Five Pieces. Still another motive, in faster note values, becomes a bridge from the start-and-stop introduction to the continuous main section of the piece. The three-note motive returns prominently near the end of 'Premonitions'. A steady tempo is established in the next passage, which exposes the principal motive at the climax of the piece.

No one has written about 'Premonitions' with as much insight as

Larry Kart, book editor of the *Chicago Tribune*:

> The discontinuous continuity of 'Premonitions' is the most
> extreme case in all Schoenberg. Even *Erwartung* is not
> comparable in this regard; though there is a near continuous
> avalanche of new material in that work, it is linked to a
> character, a drama, and a text, no matter how disordered all
> three may be. Nor does the emotional-musical texture of any
> Berg work seem as genuinely extreme as that of 'Premonitions',
> while the eruptive-disruptive aspects of 'Premonitions' have a
> quite different relationship to Schoenberg. It is as though this
> music that threatens to rend the fabric of music itself were
> being greeted by its maker with both delight (at the onset of an
> unparalleled fecundity of invention) and terror.

'The Past'

The second piece, in contrasting slow tempi to the first, exposes the
fundamental materials at the beginning and makes extensive use
of ostinati. True to the title, the first melody is 'old-fashioned' in
sentiment, as well as in its surprisingly literal returns. The transfixingly
beautiful final cadence begins with an upward D minor arpeggio in
the celesta that connects with the piccolo, which then repeats the
first melodic interval of the piece above three final notes in the
clarinets, recognised by every musical ear, consciously or otherwise
– Brentano's distinction between sensory and noetic perception – as
the first three notes of 'Premonitions' in reverse order.

'Chord-Colours'

> Schoenberg, *Harmonielehre*, 1911: 'I cannot unreservedly agree
> with the distinction between colour and pitch. I find that a note
> is perceived by its colour, one of whose dimensions is pitch.
> Colour, then, is the great realm, pitch one of its provinces...
> If the ear could discriminate between differences of colour, it
> might be feasible to invent melodies that are built of colours

(*Klangfarbenmelodien*). But who dares to develop such theories?'

Rhythmic and motivic activity, dynamic and harmonic change, increase and quicken, until boiling point, two-thirds of the way through, then abruptly deconvect and return to the near stasis of the beginning. 'Colours' is a *crescendo–diminuendo* of movement, as distinguished from the melodic–harmonic returns in 'The Past', and the alternation of instrumental colours is the means by which the 'changing chord' is kept in motion. The five-note chord is stationary at the beginning. A repeated, gradually changing chord[1] overlaps and blends with itself in different orchestral combinations, thereby creating an antiphonal effect of canonic movement, at the distance of two beats in the upper parts and of one beat in the bass, the note C played by viola *sola* on the strong beats and by bass on the weak. Schoenberg's performance directions serve notice that 'Colours' is 'without motives to be brought out', or thematic development. All the same, the melodic structure shapes the piece. In the first section, this reduces to A natural, B flat and A flat, repeated several times. In the second section (bars 12–19), the pitch range, edging upward, is marked by harmonic relocation and a new application of the changing-colours principle: a different instrument, or combination of instruments, plays each different note of a chord, spreading the chord out, so to speak, and sustaining it. The third section (bars 20–30) joins more events in more movement, and at the zenith, with the beat subdivided into units of three and four, the flux of overlapping and dovetailing colour particles challenges the analytical powers of even the keenest ear. The 'leaping-fish'[2] motive, introduced in the second section, is heard eight times from there to the end, its six upward-directed forms at the same pitches, and its

---

1 'The color of a sustained chord keeps changing,' Schoenberg's pupil Erwin Stein wrote in *The Elements of Musical Form*. But the pitches change, too, and the colour does not 'keep' changing at the outset but is limited to two regularly alternating and overlapping combinations.

2 In 1949 Schoenberg renamed the piece 'Morning by a Lake', but he had always called it that privately (E. Wellesz: *Arnold Schoenberg*, London (Dent), 1925), and had even identified a 'leaping-fish' motive.

two downward-directed ones at their same pitches, an indication of Schoenberg's need at this stage to establish tonal identities.

'Peripetia'

Peripetia, a sudden change of fortune, a sudden change of direction.
Rudolf Kassner

As in 'Premonitions', the thematic materials are set forth in the first part of the piece, but their development here is successive rather than superimposed. The prominence of the augmented triad is another link with 'Premonitions': the trumpet 'smear' that follows the chord in bar two and returns at the end of the piece consists of seven parallel augmented triads.

The ever-changing tempo, as the title allows, and the rubato character are in extreme contrast to the quasi-motionless 'Colours' and the even-keeled, one-tempo 'Obbligato Recitative' that follows. The highlights of 'Peripetia' are the rich thematic intrigue of as many as six voices toward the middle (bars 283–99), and the ending. The latter begins with three canonic pairs twirled in motion like a juggling act over three other polyphonic parts, followed by the swarming of the whole orchestra to a tremendous crash, which includes a whistling noise produced by drawing a cello bow along the rim of a cymbal (following the principle of rubbing the rim of a drinking glass with humected finger). The crash is followed by a gurgle in the clarinets, the *coup de grâce*, and a dust-settling tremolo in the lower strings.

'The Obbligato Recitative'

Unlike the other pieces, number five makes no use of ostinato and sustained chords, changes of tempo and metre. The rhythmic vocabulary, moreover, all but excludes triplets and is largely restricted to dotted and even-note figures: one of the latter, a rest at the beginning of a bar followed by five even notes, occurs seventeen times. 'The Obbligato Recitative' can be described as a composition in three- to six-voice atonal polyphony in which a leading line, indicated by Schoenberg, moves rapidly high and low through the orchestra, always speaking in a different voice. The form is dramatic and does not reflect any classical plan of exposition, development, recapitulation: two incomplete climaxes are followed by a third, fulfilled and extended, and a quiet ending in which the same chord is relayed through three overlapping combinations of instruments.

The first motive reappears, transposed, in the cellos, violas and then flute. The musicologist Carl Dahlhaus remarked on the 'rigorous avoidance of melodic restatement', but restatements occur as early as bar four, which repeats, untransposed, most of the principal-voice clarinet part of bar two. Another high-profile instance of repetition is the falling minor-third in the same clarinet phrase: it reappears in the violas, octave-doubled by oboes, soon after, as well as in the section ending immediately before the start of the first aborted climax, then in the top line at the breaking point of the next climax, and again in the final one. In fact, the coherence of the piece depends upon these motives, on the continuity of the leading melodic voice as it passes through one combination of instruments to another, and on the contrast between close chromatic movement and wide intervals.

The instrumental voicing of the harmony is unprecedented. For one example, in the second phrase of the ultimate climax, the lowest line is played by trombones, tuba, bass clarinet and bassoons, while the basses and cellos play middle voices. These chords, the densest in modern full-orchestra harmony, are perfectly balanced, perfectly transparent.

Erwartung
Monodrama in One Act for Soprano and Orchestra

The text is the interior monologue of a Woman who has probably killed the lover with whom, nevertheless, she is anticipating a rendezvous. The action, which may have been dreamed, takes place between twilight and dawn, and near, as well as in, a forest. It consists of her search for him, the discovery of his still-bleeding corpse, and finally the realisation that 'light will dawn for all others, but I am all alone in my darkness'. Here the words 'Tausend Menschen' are set to the same music Schoenberg composed for them in his song 'Am Wegrand', Op. 6 No. 6 (1905). At the end of the first of the four scenes, the Woman overcomes her fears and enters the forest on a path. At the beginning of the equally short second scene, she feels lost at first, then remembers that her lover had been in the same place, the first clue to her culpability in his murder. The second clue comes when she imagines hearing someone, seeing something move, and mistaking a tree stump for a dead body. The third clue, in the even shorter third scene, surfaces while she contemplates the moon, imagines something black dancing, and fleetingly wonders if it is her lover's body. The musical tension increases from quiet agitation to a peak of orchestral volume, during which she calls for her lover's help. The scene changes during an ostinato, one of the most prominent of many in the opus, in which the Woman exits. The speed of the ostinato figure increases and then decreases, suggesting the chugging of a train as it approaches and recedes.

At the beginning of the fourth and final scene, the Woman emerges onto a road, from which perspective a house with a balcony is visible in the moonlit background. The music is quiet and virtually motionless, a chord sustained by seven instruments, the vocal part imitating the Woman's weary trudging. As she remarks of the 'empty, bloodless moon and cloudless sky', a motive in octaves, bassoon and contra-bassoon, a hauntingly hollow sound, introduces an ostinato: tone-painting of exquisite subtlety, formed by alternating five-note chords played in harmonics by combinations of solo strings, and by a muted violin and celesta alternately playing a quintuplet figure.

Back in the forest the Woman suddenly sees a bench and a man's body lying on the ground next to it, glazed eyes staring lifelessly, blood dripping from a heart wound. She touches the corpse's face, hair, mouth, and, placing one of its cold hands on her breast, recognises the body as her lover's. In the stream-of-consciousness text from here to the end we learn that the lover had promised to meet her here tonight, but that his attentions have been falling off in recent months, that he has not visited her in the last three days, but may have been seeing another woman, whose 'white arms' the Woman imagines having seen extended toward him from the balcony of the background house. Again and again she speaks of the depths of her love for him, begging him to 'Wake up, wake up. I love you so,' but these expressions of tenderness and passion are mixed with reproaches. Why have 'they' killed him? she asks, though it is now clear that her magnetic return to the scene of the crime convicts her of the murder. The octave-doubling in the orchestra of her phrase 'die Frau mit den weissen Armen' makes it stand out more than any other passage in the piece.

Dawn breaks at the end, and the nightmare, as Schoenberg himself called it, concludes in a single, miraculous bar of music. After the Woman's last words, 'Oh, are you there?' shrieked out over the full orchestra playing her minor-third leitmotif, the music dissolves in a quiet 'whoosh'. High strings and flutter-tonguing woodwinds play ascending chromatic scales, while muted lower strings, playing *sul ponticello tremolando*, execute downward chromatic scales. But the leading orchestral line is that of the contrabasses, which enter on the second half of the bar and play a descending whole-tone scale *pizzicato*. The speed increases by rhythmic subdivision, doublets, triplets, sextuplets, double sextuplets, and a forty-eight-note, four-octave upward glissando in the celesta, throughout the bar, while the pulse remains steady. The progressively higher and lower lines extend the pitch spectrum so that the highest and lowest notes are heard at the very end, broadening the music spatially. The change of colour with each subdivision of the beat is complex beyond aural analysis.

The most innovative features of *Erwartung* are the continual variation of orchestral textures, and the constantly changing tempi. Not only are the instrumental combinations new, but the instruments themselves are required to produce new sounds. Thus the harpist inserts tissue paper between the strings at one point, and at another one of the percussionists scrapes the rim of a cymbal with the bow of a string bass. Apart from evoking the sounds of night-time nature, and creating atmosphere, the orchestra 'expresses' the Woman's anxieties, morbid fears, yearnings, desperation, hatred of her 'hostile' rival with 'white arms', and always trance-like mental state.

In a work of only 427 bars, the metronome markings shift 111 times, and between them are instructions for more than eighty additional tempo controls: *fermati, ritenuti, accelerandi, etwas drängend, etwas beschleunigen, etwas zurückhaltend.* Rarely does the beat remain constant for more than a few bars, and at times different metronomic numbers are assigned to several individual bars in succession. Near the beginning of the fourth scene, a fast figure moving from woodwinds to strings to brass must be played faster than the general beat of the orchestra (i.e. out of tempo), and at another place in the same scene the basses are required to play *pizzicato*, each player at his own fastest-possible individual speed (i.e. *not* together). Obviously no recorded, and probably no unrecorded, performance has as yet realised most of these tempo nuances.

Postscriptum: The viola solo at bars 252–3 is not found in any set of the orchestra parts, a proofreader's error going back to 1924.

Four Orchestral Songs

In a 1932 broadcast talk from Frankfurt introducing a performance of the Four Orchestral Songs, Op. 22, Schoenberg averred that 'my feeling for form, modelled on the great masters, and my musical logic... must guarantee that what I write is formally and logically correct, even if I do not realise it... [but whereas the third and fourth songs] do not dispense with logic, I cannot prove it'. He went on to say that he hears relationships in the work that he is unable to discern through the eye, and that 'Only in this way is it possible to perceive the similarity between the first bar of the orchestral introduction [to No. 3] and the first bar of the vocal part'. Then, addressing the question of shapes and proportions, he conceded that 'compositions for texts are inclined to allow the poem to determine their form, at least outwardly', in a correspondence of 'declamation, tempo, and dynamics'.

It seems characteristic of Schoenberg that his most original and lapidary orchestration is found in a vocal work, one, moreover, in which he had composed the singer's part in the first and fourth songs before beginning to sketch the orchestral accompaniment. Further, in that balance of tradition and innovation which is the foundation of Schoenberg's musical philosophy, the traditional element in the Four

Songs is in the setting of the texts. He generally follows Brahms in duplicating the accent patterns of the verses in the music, even though, as he says, the 'logic' in Brahms's songs, as distinguished from the inexplicable logic in his own, 'can be demonstrated through purely melodic analysis'. Also on the traditional side are the ostinatos and pedal-point harmonies, a feature of the first song, 'Seraphita', as well as the third and fourth songs, in the case of No. 4 with a distribution of accents spread through four lines of violins and violas, an original idea that he did not exploit in any other work.

The innovatory side is best exemplified in the instrumentation. Consider the spatial relationships. At the end of the first song, 'Seraphita', the twenty-four violins sustain a long note in a high register, while *pizzicato* cellos and xylophone play a repeated note, and the basses intone a descending line to their lowest range. The distance between highest and lowest levels has never been greater. The final, four-note cadence, under the sustained high violin note, begins with a parallel downward half-step in ten parts followed by the simultaneous drop of an octave in four parts, yet the effect is the same as that of a classical close.

Schoenberg singled out the 'preponderantly soloistic' style of the orchestration. In the brief second song, the ensemble is reduced from sixty to only sixteen instruments, each one a 'solo part' until the broadening, climactic middle section that underscores the word 'Eitelkeit', where both the lower treble and lower bass lines are doubled. But the sizes of the ensembles in each of the four songs are remarkably different, and only that of 'Vorgefühle', the last of them, employs a standard symphony orchestra. 'Seraphita' enlists the most novel aggregation: clarinets are the only woodwinds, and six of the same kind (mid-range) begin the piece with a unison cantilena, in which the articulation and volumes change with every note of the long-line legato melody, in correspondence with the mainly minor-second and minor-third ambitus of the intervallic construction. The sonority is plaintive, doleful, and never heard before or since. The instruments fan out to six parts in the middle of the piece, but return to their unisons later.

Clarinets are the featured instruments through the opus, playing in extraordinary combinations in all the songs. Five of the sixteen instruments in the second song are clarinets representing three different ranges. In the third song, three bass clarinets, joined by a contrabass, add new, richly dark colours to the orchestral palette. The fourth song requires three normal and one bass clarinet, but the clarinet colour remains dominant. Before this wonderful creation, the art of instrumentation had been concerned chiefly with contrasts and mixtures, not with exploring the deployment of several of the same instruments on the same part, nor with the exploitation of combinations of a single family.

All four songs are framed by orchestral introductions and codas, amounting, in 'Seraphita', to a third of the playing time of the whole. The melodic intervals and rhythms of vocal figures are sometimes stated in the orchestra first, and, in the case of 'Seraphita', not once but twice before the first vocal entrance.

In contrast to the thoughts (anacoluthons) of the protagonist of *Erwartung*, the texts of the Four Songs, three of them poems by Rilke, inspired long-line melodic phrases. The musical images evoked by the texts are remarkably traditional in kind. The crashing cymbal, the loud bursts of the brass, and the jagged *forte* passages in the violins in 'Seraphita' are not different in genre from the storm music of Wagner, and the setting of Rilke's beautiful line, 'auf deiner Meere Einsamsein' ('the vastness of your oceans lone'), with its slow rise in pitch with the word 'Meere', and fall in a great arc on the word 'Einsamsein' to the deepest vocal register, reminds us of passages in *Tristan* and *Parsifal*. A triplet figure in the three bass clarinets, echoed later in the voice, evokes the motion of the sea, recalling a principal motive in Debussy's *La Mer*. The next line, 'let me accompany your rivers', inspires more musical imagery in the overlapping phrases of smoothly flowing semiquavers. The last words of the poem, 'and tread, to some blind ancient cleaving', are perfectly fitted to an evenly treading ostinato figure in flutes and cellos.

In his 1932 analysis of the Songs, Schoenberg acknowledged that the 'poetry assisted my feelings, insights, occurrences, impressions'. Let it be said that the musical emotion, in the dark days during World War I, intensely personal in its feelings of resignation and agitation, is conveyed by the orchestra at the beginning of *Vorgefühle*, 'I sense the winds which come and must endure them', and the sense of abandonment at the end of the same song, in which the composer must have believed that the poem was addressed directly to him:

> ... I can already sense the storm, and surge like the sea.
>
> And spread myself out and into myself downfall
>
> and hurtle away and am all alone
>
> In the great storm.

Serenade

Among the Serenade's most immediately striking characteristics are its exuberant mood, melodiousness, borrowings of Classical form-models, and the unprecedented repetition (for Schoenberg) of entire segments: forty-six bars of the middle section of the first movement return as the last movement, half of the Minuet is repeated, and a third of the Dance Scene. Uniquely in Schoenberg's music, the first movement is without tempo modification from beginning to end.

'Viennese strumming', Leoš Janáček wrote after hearing the piece in Venice in September 1925, referring to the mandolin-guitar foundation of the sonority. The *pizzicati* and bouncing on the strings of the wood of the violin, viola and cello bows, and the flutter-tonguing of the clarinets, extend and complement the articulation of the strummed and plucked instruments. At the beginning of the repeated section of the first movement, these effects of bariolage are the focus of the music.

The Minuet, a quiet, mellow piece, is more song than dance, while the Trio, which begins with a viola/guitar ostinato, is more dance than song. The Variations, the most delectable movement of the seven, consists of a comparatively long theme in the clarinet, and six brief variations, each with the same number of bars as the theme. The Coda, with its dialogues between the clarinets, then between guitar and mandolin, and its gradual slackening of pace to the end, is one of Schoenberg's most beautiful, intricately carved jewels.

The Petrarch 'Sonnet' (No. 217 in Schoenberg's score, but No. 256

in the standard Italian editions) is the Serenade's centrepiece, at once the most highly organised movement of the seven, and the most chaotic-sounding. At the start, the violin plays the first two notes of a twelve-tone series as a melodic fragment. Each note is followed by a mandolin/guitar chord containing the remaining ten pitches of the chromatic scale. The twelve pitches are then exposed in melodic order in the vocal part, and repeated in the same order twelve times (the twelfth is incomplete), but with differences in octave registers and in the position of the series *vis-à-vis* the musical phrases. The first of the twelve notes becomes, successively, the second, third, fourth and fifth note in the next four phrases, for the reason that Petrarch's eleven-syllable line leaves a leftover note of the series each time. Since the original first note becomes the last note before the final, longest and most hectic of the three instrumental interludes that separate the poem's four stanzas, and notes two to twelve follow after a considerable break, Schoenberg obviously did not intend the series to be heard integrally. The instrumental accompaniment provides musical images for textural references, evoking a lion's roar with fearsome glissandos and tremolos in the strings and clarinets, and, at the word 'death', introducing a pulsation wonderfully alien to the metre of the rest of the piece.

The melodies of the Dance Scene, the most popular movement, are also its most immediately memorable. The full *Ländler* melody (clarinet) and its counter-melody are repeated several times untransposed, rare instances of same-pitch repetition in Schoenberg's 'atonal period'. Worth iterating, too, is the interruption of the four-metre ostinato in the mandolin and, later, violin, relieving the three-in-one rhythm.

The violin sings the 'Song Without Words' first, followed by cello then bass clarinet. The guitar accompaniment, major thirds doubled by viola and cello at the end of the first phrase, recalls 'O Alter Duft', the nostalgic ending of *Pierrot lunaire.* The final March repeats the first movement, with alterations, including the return of the *Ländler* as a counter-melody, and, shortly before the end, a brief, slow inset combining the principal melodies of the two preceding movements.

Violin Concerto

Schoenberg completed the first movement on 9 February 1934, a year and a half before Alban Berg began his Concerto for the same instrument. The piece is dedicated to 'Meinen lieben Freund und Kampfgenossen Dr. Anton von Webern' ('My dear friend and fellow warrior'). The Concerto was the composer's favourite among his orchestral works.

Of the three movements – 'Poco Allegro', 'Andante Grazioso' and 'Allegro' – the second is dated 27 August 1936, the third, less than a month later, 23 September 1936. Louis Krasner, the Concerto's first 'conqueror', as Schoenberg called him, commissioned the work and gave its premiere in Philadelphia on 6 December 1940, with Leopold Stokowski conducting the Philadelphia Orchestra. Schoenberg's brother-in-law, the left-handed violinist Rudolf Kolisch, recommended Krasner to Schoenberg through Otto Klemperer.

On 11 February 1938, Schoenberg wrote to Krasner:

> Kolisch has spoken very favourably to me about you and recommended strongly that I turn over to you the first performance of my Violin Concerto. Nevertheless, I believe it would be necessary for you first to have a look at the music. The difficulties of this work are different ones and greater than those of the Berg Concerto. Also you do not know whether this kind of music suits you. Unfortunately, I cannot myself send you the score, since I have only one copy. But perhaps... it might be possible for you to look up my son-in-law, Felix Greissle, Mödling bei Wien, Jakob Thomastrasse 6, telephone 751/VI. He is just now working on a piano reduction of this work and could perhaps make a photostat copy of it...

Krasner commented on this astutely in a reminiscence:

> ... Schoenberg's pointed reference to the differences both in the kinds and the degrees of difficulties encountered in the

two works is in itself significant. Quite rightly, he raises the question of his concerto's suitability, that is, whether it 'lies well', for me. The implication is that suitability in Berg does not necessarily mean suitability in Schoenberg. In any case, it is clear that the Schoenberg Concerto, from its very genesis, is a totally different work from the Berg. Schoenberg proudly conceived his concerto in grand style and with a flair for the violin. It is knowingly designed and reflects his eagerness to explore new challenges for the instrument. Its technical innovations are thoroughly and ingeniously researched and thoughtfully developed.

Krasner goes on:

> After I played the concerto for Schoenberg [the occasion is not dated], he triumphantly exclaimed to me, 'You see, I knew it could be played because actually I was able to manage every note of it on the violin with my own hands.' One was reminded of the 'unplayable' and 'unviolinistic' reports that were circulated about the Brahms Concerto [admired by Schoenberg]... Those criticisms were easily overcome, but in the case of the Schoenberg Concerto, the charges have been more intense and longer lasting.

Krasner reports that the first two performances in Philadelphia – the work was repeated the next day – 'had to overcome an excessive number of problems, antagonisms, and tensions. There must have been considerable giggling and disturbance because after the first movement Stokowski turned to the Friday afternoon audience and stressed the historic significance of the premiere.' Schoenberg wrote to Krasner on 17 December: '...You must know yourself that you have achieved something which must be called "a historical fact", whether my music will survive or not.'

The third performance, on 30 November 1945, took place in Minneapolis and was conducted by Dimitri Mitropoulos, who had memorised the score in two weeks. Thereby hangs a tale. It seems that Krasner did not bring his violin score to the first rehearsal because he also had memorised it. When Mitropoulos began to call bar numbers, however, Krasner had no means of finding them, but fortunately Mitropoulos had also memorised the numbers, and could sing the solo violin part for him at each one.

On 2 December 1945, Schoenberg wrote to Krasner asking for an account of the reception of the piece:

> Especially the following points are of great interest to me:
> 1. Is everything clear in my tempo marks?
> 2. How is the orchestra dynamically? Does the violin always easily dominate, or are there dark spots, where it is difficult or even impossible to be heard?
> 3. Do all the *Hauptstimmen*, H⁻, distinctly come to the fore?
> 4. Can you name sections which according to your impressions, or [those of] friends of yours, have been
>   a) distinctly disliked by the audience or by music lovers; or
>   b) agreeable to the same or others?
>
> Do not resent these questions: you and Mr Mitropoulos are the only two persons at present who can answer them. It would be nice if you would also [ask] Mr Mitropoulos about these problems.

Schoenberg's sketches for the Concerto contain two annotations that refer to his obsession with the baleful influence on his life of the number 13 (his birthdate). First, he describes his discovery, during an interruption in the composition, that '169 = 13 x 13'. (Bar 169 marks a sudden change of character and tempo.) Second, he writes: 'Nobody will believe me – but when I numbered bar 222 in the score, I thought to myself, "Up to now I haven't made any mistakes in the bar-numbering this time." And then I thought at once, "But it couldn't last." And a minute later I discovered that I left out the number in bar 223 – which is on *page 13*, where I interrupted my work.' (The metre of bar 223, 9/4, is unusual.)

The Violin Concerto reintroduces morsels of tonality for the first time in Schoenberg's work since the last of the 1930 unaccompanied male choruses. Some instances of this are startling. In bars 197–204, first movement, the solo violin plays five bars of a triplet figure of minor thirds followed by three bars of the same octave-changing figure of major thirds. The spacing of the thin and transparent orchestral accompaniment allows the violin harmony to dominate or separate out. Then, near the beginning of the second movement (bars 276–82), the repeated A to C figure in the violin establishes a sense of A minor, as the repeated F to A flat triplet figure in the cellos does of F minor in bars 305–11. The predominance of D minor in the conclusion of the third movement is the strongest of all. With one exception, the last fourteen bars begin with D, the 'tonality' of the first theme of the movement, and of its recapitulation.

'Do you think one is any better off for knowing this [pitch construction]?' Schoenberg wrote to Kolisch about the series of another of his twelve-tone compositions.

> I can't quite see it that way. My firm belief is that for a composer who does not yet quite know his way about with the use of series it may give some idea of how to set about it – a purely technical indication of the possibility of getting something out of the series. But this isn't where the aesthetic qualities reveal themselves, or, if so, only incidentally.

This last statement is unchallengeable. Is an understanding of the pitch structure essential to a full appreciation of it? For this, the reader should consult Milton Babbitt's brilliant analysis of the Concerto. He is particularly enlightening on Schoenberg's presentation of simultaneous sets, as when the solo violin plays one form and the bassoon another. After enlightening us that the composer restricts his sets to four during the first fifty-eight bars of the piece, then changes the tonal area from bar fifty-nine, Babbitt affirms that this is analogous to a change of tonal centre in a tonal-system composition.

Pitch-functions apart, the Violin Concerto should be approached as essentially a work of melodic development and variation. Its phrase-lengths and shapes, tempo contrasts, rhythmic figurations, repetition, metric variation (2/2, 3/4, 2/2), melodic structure, even, to some extent, the treatment of the orchestra, are extensions of the language of Brahms.

The constantly changing orchestral textures require a high degree of concentration, though the character of the music is always clearly delineated. The *alla marcia* last movement, which begins with the work's longest orchestral *tutti*, has the greatest drive and continuity, despite the long cadenza, and the ending is Schoenberg's most majestic. The violin cadenzas differ from those of the past in their far wider exploitation of the technical possibilities of the instrument, but their placement at the ends of the first and third movements, and their use of primary thematic material, are traditional. The same can be said of the recapitulations of opening themes at the ends of movements, and at the beginning of the last movement cadenza. Traditional, too, is the orchestral *tutti* that follows the final cadenza, and its thematic repetition: nine of its fourteen bars reiterate the movement's opening motive, and at the same two pitches.

The instrumentation is typical of Schoenberg, for instance in the doublings of oboes, clarinets and bassoons as one voice in a canon at the octave with the violins in a *tutti* in the second movement. But the demands on solo wind instruments are less extreme than in other Schoenberg orchestral works. The melodic content of the Concerto is remarkably simple, appealing and memorable.

Chapter 9

Anton Webern

My involvement with the music of Anton Webern began in 1947 at a Juilliard rehearsal of the Concerto for nine instruments conducted by René Leibowitz. Less than a decade later, I would complete a four-LP Webern album that enabled music lovers to become acquainted with his all but unknown creations. The performances were woefully inadequate, but they helped others to achieve better ones, and the album stimulated a worldwide awareness of the composer. I discovered this shortly thereafter, during a fuelling stop on Wake Island, when a Swiss passenger from another flight, recognising Stravinsky walking with me, introduced himself to me with 'I want to thank you for your Webern recordings'.

In Vienna, in 1956, I visited Webern's daughter, Amalie Mattel, as well as friends of the composer, including the soprano Ilona Steingruber, who, only ten days before, had sung Webern's last two cantatas with me at the Domaine Musical in Paris. Her husband, Friedrich Wildgans, son of the poet and author of the first Webern biography, invited me to dinner and to examine the sketches for his unfinished last composition. On the following day I met the editor at Universal Edition who had been providing the photocopies of Webern manuscripts from which I had extracted the vocal and instrumental parts for my recordings. In Munich, Karl Amadeus Hartmann, Webern's pupil (1942) and sturdy supporter of his music in the postwar concert series Musica Viva, had described to me the composer's home life at Maria Enzersdorf, the Vienna suburb, in a tiny upstairs apartment, and remembered him passionately analysing Schoenberg's *Erwartung*.

Back in California I would learn much more about Webern from Ernst Krenek. There, too, I encouraged Hans Moldenhauer in his research for a Webern biography, responding to his continuing inquiries and helping to find a publisher for what became an 800-page tome.

————◆————

By the mid-1950s a Webern movement seemed to dominate the music world, albeit based on a misunderstanding concerning the traditional–classicist origins of this *avant-la-lettre* modernist. Anton von Webern was born in Vienna on 3 December 1883, to a family ennobled in 1731 by the Habsburg Emperor Charles VI. Although the child's home environment was not musical, he was given piano lessons from the age of five. His parents did not oppose his choice of career, but they considered their son's pieces 'too nervous' and 'all over before they start'. Like his contemporary, Stravinsky, Webern married his first cousin and fathered four children, the first of whom appeared abruptly six weeks after the wedding. The new grandparents were so displeased by this that, despite continuing financial support, they did not invite the young family to visit at Christmas.

Webern seems to have been the first major twentieth-century composer educated in Renaissance polyphonic music. He received a doctorate from the University of Vienna for his transcriptions of the second book of Heinrich Isaac's *Constantinus Choralis* and Johannes Bressart's *Sacris solemnis*, learning mensural notation and the construction of the isorhythmic motet from the latter. Webern's essay on the Isaac transcription proclaims the Netherlandish-style of the sacred works of Josquin, Pierre de la Rue and Isaac as the apogee of musical art, and further contends that 'in comparison with Ockeghem and Obrecht, there reigns in Isaac's work a much greater liveliness and independence of the individual parts'. Webern must have been stunned by *Pierrot lunaire*, the polyphonic masterwork of the twentieth century, but why did he not confide this to his diary or sketchbook?

The axial event in Webern's life, his decision in the autumn of 1904 to study with Schoenberg, is also, and inexplicably, not mentioned in the diary. The affinity that developed between teacher and pupil can in some measure be attributed, apart from their hyper-intense creative personalities, to their similar provincial backgrounds, materially straitened circumstances, and small, less than physically prepossessing, appearance. When Schoenberg's wife eloped with the young painter Richard Gerstl in 1908, it was Webern who convinced the tortured, confused woman to return, as well as Schoenberg to receive, if not to forgive, her. This would have been an inconceivable intrusion if Webern had not been Schoenberg's closest intimate.

The most shattering experience of Webern's own life heretofore was the sudden, premature death of his mother in 1906. This is generally accepted as the underlying cause of his later 'nervous breakdown', but the hostile critical and public reaction to his Five Pieces for String Quartet and Six Pieces for Orchestra, both written in her memory, undoubtedly assisted. A year after the premiere of *Pierrot*, when Webern began to show signs of emotional instability, Schoenberg advised him to consult a psychoanalyst, and for three months in the autumn of 1913 Webern was a patient of Freud's former associate, Alfred Adler, whose reputation had been established by his success in the treatment of inferiority complex. The only communications concerning Webern's progress are said to be in his still unpublished letters to Schoenberg, whose newest masterpieces had evidently inspired the younger man but also overwhelmed him to the extent of destroying his self-confidence.

Webern could be described as a nature mystic, in his own words, a 'metaphysical theosophist', as well as a Catholic, albeit one who believed that Beethoven's birthday should be celebrated on a par with Christmas. The reserved and introspective young composer was also an autochthonous Austrian nationalist warped by an 'unshakable faith in the German spirit which indeed has created, almost exclusively, the culture of mankind'. A rustic, whose early music employs cowbells, guitar and mandolin, his preferred avocations were mountaineering and the study of Alpine plants and flowers. He spoke a Tyrolean dialect, but, except for Church Latin, Italian musical terminology and the etymology of philosophical words in classical Greek, knew no foreign tongue.

Webern's mystic-horticultural inclinations help to explain his close friendship, beginning in 1926, with the like-minded poet and painter Hildegard Jone, a married neighbour in nearby Mödling, whose verses inspired his future vocal works. She was apparently too 'spiritual' and 'pure' to have been his paramour, but however that may have been, the qualitative decline from the composer's previous selections of poetry by Goethe, Rilke, Trakl, Stefan George and Avenarius (Richard Wagner's nephew) to Jone's naïve pantheistic texts is puzzling. Another of her attractions for Webern would have been her direct descent from Beethoven's friend the Countess Deym.

Webern gave as much time to arranging the works of others as to the creation of his own. His career as composer is chiefly remarkable for postponements of premieres, the ridicule of audiences, and the vilification of critics biased in principle against his Schoenbergian-infused music. As a conductor, Webern vacillated in his choices of employment, and abruptly resigned from most of the jobs he accepted. By the age of forty, nevertheless, he had become an esteemed conductor, highly regarded for both his musical depth and technical exactitude. His punctiliousness is seen in an excerpt from a 1938 letter to Hermann Scherchen apropos his forthcoming BBC performance of the Bach-Webern six-part *Fuga-Ricercata* from *The Musical Offering*:

> The rubato you ask me about is intended to indicate that I think of these bars of the Fuga subject as played with movement – every time, even with all the later additional counterpoints, *accel.*, *rit.*, finally merging into the *poco allargando* of the last notes of the subject. For I feel this part of the subject, this chromatic progression (g–b), to be essentially different from the first five notes, which I think of as being very steady, almost stiff (i.e., in strict tempo, since the tempo is set by this phrase), and which in my view finds an equivalent in character in the last five notes. More precisely, I intend the 'rubato' to be like this: from g via f sharp to f faster, then holding back a little on the e flat (accent by the harp), and again rubato on the trombone progression (including the tied e flat of the horn where the trombone has a crochet rest in bar 6)...

> One more important point for the performance of my arrangement: nothing must be allowed to take second place. Not even the softest notes of the muted trumpet can be allowed to be lost. Everything is of primary importance. Is it not worthwhile to awaken this music asleep in the seclusion of Bach's own abstract presentation, and thus unknown or unapproachable by most people?

As a young man Webern held posts as *répétiteur* and assistant conductor at the Vienna Opera and at opera houses in Danzig, Prague and Stettin, but because he balked at having to prepare repertory he found contemptible none of these appointments lasted very long. Beginning in the early 1920s, after Schoenberg's Vienna Society for Private Performances had disbanded,[1] Webern persisted for longer periods in respected conducting positions in Vienna. He directed the Singverein, 1923–33 and the Workers' Symphony Concerts, 1922–33, as well as the Ravag (Austrian Radio), until dismissed in 1934 after conducting an all-Mendelssohn programme, the ostracising of the great composer already having begun. Webern's repertory ranged from Bach to Glazunov, but focused on Beethoven and Mahler, presenting more of the latter's music than any other conductor, at a time when it was rarely played. The attraction of opposites here is ironic, since some of Mahler's pieces were the longest ever written, while Webern's are famously and incomparably the shortest. 'If a programme is too long,' Schoenberg quipped, 'add a piece by Webern.' And whereas a Mahler symphony may seem like an omnium gatherum, every Webern opus is exclusive unto itself, never digressing from its own confined character and inner logic. The shock of Webern, and it is still there, is in its intensity of concentration. Next to Schoenberg, Mahler was

---

1   This organisation gave weekly concerts from 1919 to 1921, and occupied Webern chiefly in preparing piano transcriptions and chamber-group reductions of large orchestra works. Some of Schoenberg's rules for this non-pareil elitist enterprise should be mentioned. The performers had to be 'young and less well-known artists, to avoid the display of irrelevant virtuosity and individuality; nothing should be performed from memory; rehearsals must be unlimited; and the audience was forbidden to show signs of approval or disapproval' (neither obsibilations nor applause). Only card-carrying members and visiting foreign musicians could be admitted.

the most important influence in the young composer's life, and he learned the art of conducting exclusively by observing Mahler.

In 1932 Webern conducted the first concert of American music, Ives included, in Vienna. He also led a male chorus in Mödling, but resigned when it refused to accept a Jewish vocal soloist. After this, he wrote to Schoenberg, in Boston, of 'feeling the most vehement aversion against my own race because of the anti-Semitism of so many of its members'.

Even at today's distance Webern's blindness to the impending catastrophe of the National Socialist Party seems incomprehensible. It had quickly condemned his music as 'degenerate', banned its publication and performance, and, later, as a disciple of Schoenberg, forbidden him to conduct and to teach, thereby depriving him of his only sources of income. Yet he seems not to have contemplated emigration, no doubt realising that with his large, three-generation family, lack of money and of prospects of support elsewhere, any move would have been impossible. Contrast his situation in 1933 with Schoenberg's, a world-renowned composer with a contract to teach in Boston, only two dependents, and many American friends, all factors facilitating his move to the United Sates. Webern's vain belief in the supremacy of German culture was ultimately responsible for his own violent, premature death.

An adamantine streak in Webern's personality emerges during the many crises in his career, and was always evident in his music. The temporary break with his idol, Schoenberg, and the move away from him in Mödling, so soon after moving there only to be near him, exposes the obduracy. So does his abandonment of the directorship of the Workers' Concerts, after years of successful and enthusiastically received performances, simply because a trombone player criticised his rehearsal procedures. Webern's abrupt but permanent departure, refusing even to listen to the entreaties of the other players, seems irrational. Before the *Anschluss* (1938) he had been dismissed from a teaching position at the Vienna Israelite Institution for the Blind. After that he became increasingly reclusive. Not surprisingly, *Walden* and Emerson's *Solitude*, first read in 1911, were two of his favourite books. Thereafter, Webern's livelihood came from secret private teaching; sporadic conducting engagements in London (the BBC), Zurich, Barcelona, Winterthur, Vienna; and from such journeyman's jobs as arranging, proofreading and evaluating (mostly rejecting) new music submitted for publication:

> [X's] Four Songs are entirely amateurish, miserable, cheap! Indescribable. [Y's] *Albumblätter* is impossible! [Z's] Violin Concerto: I cannot recommend it. Inventions clearly based on Grieg... How poor it all is. Constant irrelevant modulations... Since we are being driven about all the time there is no idea of form.

On 7 June 1944, as the Russian Army gradually advanced westward, two of Webern's daughters and their children fled to the town of Mittersill in the Pinzgau Mountains, where one of their families owned a house. On 24 July, Webern and his wife joined them there, but on their return to Vienna on 18 August he found an order to report for 'labour allocation'. Conscripted into service as an air-raid warden, he was uniformed and assigned to living quarters. He wrote to Hildegard Jone: 'I am not allowed to live at home anymore, snatched utterly from my work. My duties are roughly those of a mason, carrying sand and so on. Endless grind from 6 am.'

On 14 February 1945, Webern's son Peter, an army recruit, was killed in the bombing of a train in Yugoslavia. On 31 March, a few days before the Russian occupation of Vienna, the destitute, starving sixty-one-year-old composer and his wife set out on foot for Mittersill, trains no longer being available to civilians, or not running at all. Mercifully, on reaching the railroad terminal at Neulengbach, they were able to purchase tickets for the remainder of the journey. Their daughter Amalie met them and brought them to her home, where Webern, suffering from dysentery and malnutrition, had to share a small house with sixteen other people.

The local choirmaster, Cesar Bresgen, who had met Webern before, left a recollection of him at this time, 'repeatedly busy at a shabby little table with a pencil and compass occupied with geometrical figures or lines and signs'. Bresgen describes seeing him on a mountain path shortly before his death and hearing him talk about 'flowers, fungi, ferns, mosses, lichens'.

In an early letter to Alban Berg, Webern wrote:

> ... it is not the beautiful flowers in the usual Romantic sense that move me. My object is the deep, bottomless, inexhaustible meaning in all. I got to know a tiny plant, a little like a lily of the valley, homely, humble, hardly noticeable, but for me it contains all tenderness, emotion, depth, purity... I want to progress in the purely physical knowledge of all these phenomena. That is why I always carry my Botany lexicon with me.

During the summer of 1945, the US Army dispatched soldiers to Mittersill to curtail black-marketing activities and illegal currency exchanges between the residents and its own personnel. A curfew and blackout had been imposed on the neighbourhood where Webern's son-in-law, Bruno Mattel, a suspect in this trafficking, resided. On 15 September Webern shared a meal at the Mattel home. Afterwards he stepped outside to smoke a cigar, American contraband obviously, and provided by Mattel. Not understanding a 'hands-up' order by an American soldier posted outside the building, Webern struck a match. The guard shot him three times in the chest and abdomen. Contradictory versions of this unwitnessed savagery have appeared, but the three bullet holes were visible on a wall of the house for many years. The marksman, alleging that he had been assaulted with an iron bar, which Webern would have been too weak to lift, let alone wield, was acquitted. The music of the Requiem mass held in Mittersill's small Baroque church was Gregorian. Five people followed the coffin to the cemetery.

The biography of Webern's creative mind is more difficult to comprehend than that of the man, who was simply another artist brutally treated at the hands of life. But the analyses of the music are often of little help to the listener. One of the most important discoveries in Webern's sketchbooks is that this supposedly most abstract of all composers was actually responding to his natural world impressionistically – or expressionistically – but in terms of his own mode, which, of course, was light years from Strauss's Alpine Symphony. In fact Webern had outlined an extra-musical programme for his Quartet, Op. 22 before composing a note:

> 1st movement: Quiet (Annabichl, mountains), perhaps Variations
>
> 2nd movement: Slow; Introduction to 3. (Schwabegg) (Soloists only)
>
> 3rd movement: Rondo (Dachstein, snow and ice, crystal clear air, cosy, warm, sphere of the high pastures) – coolness of the first spring (Anninger, first flora, primroses, anemones [hepatica], pulsatilla).
>
> IInd Secondary theme (Soldanella, flowers of the highest region)
>
> Theme (IIIrd time) The children on ice and snow.
>
> Repetition of 1st secondary theme. (Sphere of the alpine roses)
>
> IInd secondary theme, light, sky. IV.
>
> Coda: Outlook into the highest region.

Ernst Krenek, who grew up in the same landscape as Webern and knew him as well as anyone like him could be 'known', defended him against accusations of 'cold cerebralism and of reducing music to meaningless calculations' simply by remarking that 'his music evokes the image of the tense stillness of the highest mountain peaks'.

In conversation, Krenek extended the topographical image, associating the extremely wide intervals characteristic of the composer with the jagged contours of the Styrian Koralpe, which had been visible to Webern from his family home; his father was buried at Annabichl, his mother at Schwabegg. The Quartet's second movement is a paradigmatic game, and the suggestion that it might be a game of 'children on ice and snow' is intriguing, even though the specification refers to a third movement ultimately not included in the piece.

Most of Schoenberg's music, for comparison, is overtly

programmatic, and in conventional ways, but Webern's exploitation of the 'twelve-tone system' is manifoldly different from that of its progenitor's, as the latter quickly understood. Curiously, Krenek seems surprised that the twelve-tone technique of Webern's Trio attaches complete forms of the series end to end, but since it was his first entirely twelve-tone work, this seems only natural. His next composition, the *Symphonie*, uses more than one series simultaneously and aims in a completely new aesthetic direction, the compounding of Beethovenian sonata form with the polyphonic purity of the sixteenth-century Netherlanders. Hereafter, Webern pursued a goal of simplification, call it reductionism, the Concerto, Op. 24 becoming virtually diagrammatic. Schoenberg contemporaneously explored ever greater involutions, during which his aesthetic seems to revert to Brahms, never more so than in the 1936 Violin Concerto dedicated to 'Anton von Webern'.

Most performances of Webern's music tend to follow only minimally the composer's directions *vis-à-vis* tempi, dynamics, phrasing, articulation and expressive character. Of these elements, tempo is the most important, yet no recording of, for example, the *Symphonie* presents the music anywhere near the speed of Webern's metronomic indications, with the result that the masterpiece, journalistically well described by Virgil Thomson as 'spun steel', sounds as limp as the melting watch by Dali looks.

The first movement of the *Symphonie* is distinguished by its spaciousness, sense of continuity, regularity of metre and pulsation, and ethereal sound. From the start, the listener is aware of underlying structures – horizontal and vertical symmetries, mirrors, palindromes and, more specifically, the Venn diagram for four terms – but one's musical pleasure is only subliminally related to such formal concepts. The second movement, in contrast, consists of eight discrete variations and a coda, all clearly distinguished by changes of instrumentation and tempo. Halfway through are two curious interlude-like bars, strikingly reminiscent of Debussy. Both melodically and harmonically, the music here (repeated minor thirds) is manifestly tonal. Webern had programmed a piece by Debussy on 17 April 1928, only shortly before composing this part of the *Symphonie*, which may or may not have influenced him. What can be conjectured is Webern's realisation that the return to triadic harmony in 'Eine blasse Wäscherin' (*Pierrot lunaire*) legitimated his flirtation with tonality.

The study of Webern's songs with instruments ought properly to start with the Latin canons for Maundy Thursday and Good Friday, if only because of their brevity and accessibility as closed forms, simple linearity, and limitation to either one or two instruments. His next song cycle, *Three Traditional Rhymes*, is immeasurably more difficult to absorb because of the great increase in rhythmic complexity and the density of the three-part instrumental accompaniment. The *Rhymes* contradict the assertion that Webern's vocal music is 'absolute', as opposed to 'programmatic'. In fact, the songs 'express' the emotions and reflect the meanings of the texts through extensions of traditional formulae, as well as through new ones. In the opening lyric, pulsation, metre and tempo are regular throughout, in correspondence with the simplicity of the verse, though the triplet rhythm (violin/clarinet) is new. In the second song, the *forte* dynamics, the clashing of rhythmic patterns and the repeated grumbling rhythm in the viola vividly evoke the scourging and crown-of-thorns of the text. The third song, the death agony on the cross, is also 'expressionistic'. The singer's unaccompanied shriek on C sharp *in alt* on the word 'Rette', the apex of the piece, is dramatic realism. The rhythmically vaporous instrumental ending may be the most subtle Webern ever wrote.

The next and last of the instrumental song cycles, like the first of the *Rhymes*, begins with a pastoral love lyric, 'Schätzerl klein'.[2] The exuberant mood of the second song is suggested by the strumming guitar at the beginning, and the continuing sequence of joyous high

---

2   The original manuscript of this brief (thirteen-bar) piece, in the collection of Robert Blackley, Twelfth Street, Manhattan, shows a great many differences with the printed version, eleven of them in dynamics, twenty-three in note accents, nine in *crescendi* and *diminuendi*, four in slur or phrase marks, three in verbal directions. The metronome is 48 in the manuscript v. 54 in the printed score, and bar eight in the manuscript ties the clarinet to a quaver, versus a semiquaver in the printed score. Additionally, there are eleven further details in the manuscript not found in the printed score, and eight in the printed score not found in the manuscript. Moreover, the manuscript of the piece has a title, *Volkslied*. Webern was the most fastidious, some might say finicky, of composers.

and low vocal leaps, breathtaking for all concerned. The 'carnation' must refer to the incarnation that follows consummation, since the flower blossoms at home. The language, in dialogue form – in the order Virgin, Christ and *Vater* – suggests a parallel to Lower Austrian roadside shrine carvings and painted iconic images of the Holy Family. The third song, a Latin hymn, begins softly with a duet for the accompanying instruments intoning single melodic lines, but the music that follows is a song of religious exaltation.

The String Trio marks Webern's largest step in the perfect fusion of his materials. If the songs with instruments are static and can be compared to intricately carved 'jewels', each expressing an emotion inspired by a poem or a prayer, the Trio, in contrast, is all ongoing movement, development and variation, in accordance with purely musical ideas. It is also Webern's first entirely twelve-tone composition. The dissolution of regular-beat pulsation and of the traditional components of thematic structure in the first movement may perplex the listener. From the beginning, and without following a score, one hears four violin notes. After the second, the cello contributes two more notes, at which point the ear tries to relate the six notes rhythmically. This suspension of pulsation, a major incident in the history of music, extends into the middle of the next bar, where the cello plays the same note twice, *pizzicato*. The listener suspects that the cello is introducing an incipient motive, and in fact the repeated-note idea gradually becomes more prominent and forms the basis of a lively exposition. Only one structural device in the sonata-allegro second movement need be mentioned: the recurring brief passages of rhythmic unisons in otherwise complex counter-rhythmic contexts. The idea occurs for the first time near the end of the introduction, where the three instruments play accelerating, space-splintering hemi-demi-semiquavers in the same co-ordinated rhythmic units. This happens several times, but with notes of differing time values.

Webern wrote to Schoenberg that the tempo and dynamic markings in the Trio had cost him a great effort, and that he needed 'time to understand what I have written', a revealing remark: the calculations in the composing process ultimately depend upon the indefinable 'force that through the green fuse drives the flower'. Webern's diary tells us that the Vienna premiere 'went very well, even if only a few listeners understood something of it'. A Berlin performance prompted a congratulatory letter from Schoenberg, but one in Stettin was boisterously rejected, and the next one, at an International Society for Contemporary Music concert in Count Chigi-Saracini's palace in Siena, provoked audience ructions. Someone shouted an appeal to Mussolini to close down the festival. Webern, who was not present, described the fracas – as told to him by Berg – in a letter to Schoenberg: 'During the first bars of the second movement the restlessness became so great that Kolisch [the violinist] decided to call a halt.'

As with the Trio and the *Symphonie*, the Quartet for tenor saxophone, violin, clarinet and piano raised the question of whether to give the piece a third movement, two-movement compositions being a cornerstone of Webern's aesthetic philosophy at the time. On 9 September 1930, he wrote to Berg: 'I almost find the work complete because of the perfect opposition provided by the great contrast inherent in the two finished movements.' After seeing the score, Berg responded: 'This Quartet is a miracle... there is nothing in the entire world of music production that attains even approximately such a degree of originality' (19 August 1932). Schoenberg also wrote to thank Webern for the 'fabulous piece', and now, more than seventy years later, the Quartet is being recognised as one of the happiest of Webern's creations. The composer revealed what few would have suspected: that the Scherzo in Beethoven's Sonata, Op. 14 No. 2 was a model for the second, *giocoso* movement, which includes composers' insider jokes such as the re-use of the metronomic unit of the slow movement for the fast one, and a final *Presto* for only one note.

———◆———

I conclude with a plea to the next generation of musicians to fulfil the composer's instructions regarding tempi, dynamics, phrasing, articulation and expressive character. Recordings of Webern's music that are virtually innocent of these considerations continue to appear. In one luxuriously boxed set, more attention has been expended on the photographs of the conductor and the promotional prose than on the quality of the performance. For example, in the last and greatest of the instrumental songs, *Ave, Regina coelorum*, Op. 18 No. 3, the *ritardando* in bar fifteen is ignored, hence the singer's high D shriek in bar sixteen arrives in bar fifteen, more than a beat too soon. A bit later the *molto ritardando* in bar nineteen, a carefully measured deceleration leading to the instrumental coda, is overlooked, with the result that the formal idea of the piece, the matching of the tempi of the prelude and postlude, is lost. In the same album, the string Trio receives a hard-driven, slapdash performance by one of the most prestigious ensembles on the musical scene. The result is a massacre. Not only dynamics but also changes of tempo are absent. At bar twenty-six in the second movement, for example, the players charge through a metronomic red light apparently unaware that the music for a while thereafter is slower and utterly different in character.

The producer of the album disregards Webern's own choices of the pieces he wished to form the canon of his works, namely those with opus numbers. He clearly did not want his fledgling efforts (the dull Piano Quintet and *Sommerwind*) included, or the unpublished cello sonata, the two tiny 1920s piano pieces, and the twenty-three early songs with piano, all of them filler that dissipates the 'hard gemlike flame' of this least diffuse of composers. Webern would have been appalled as well by the mechanical groupings of his works according to instrumentation – the string pieces, early and late, side by side, and the monotonous placement of songs one after the other.

Chapter 10

Vive Kl'Empereur

The Later Years

Biographies of conductors tend to bog down in rotas of rehearsals, performances, cancellations, recording sessions, and in discussions of repertory, managerial business and the pros and cons in press notices. The first volume of Peter Heyworth's *Otto Klemperer*[1] provides this information, along with a balanced survey of his achievements as a musician and his erratic behavior. Volume Two, incomplete at the time of the author's death, was finished by another writer and published after a hiatus of thirteen years. The emphasis of the sequel is on the running chronicle of the conductor's personal idiosyncrasies, and the eventual triumph of his will. The Klemperer story is the most bizarre in the annals of music's great *maestri*.

Like all of his known paternal ancestors, Nathan Klemperer, the conductor's father, was born in the Prague ghetto. His wife, Otto's mother, descended from a Sephardic family, was brought up in Hamburg, like her only son. Otto seems to have inherited his talent and intelligence from her, as well as his manic-depressive illness. At age thirty-four, Otto, deeply religious by nature, converted to Catholicism, not opportunistically, as his idol Mahler had had to do

---

1   Peter Heyworth, *Otto Klemperer: His Life and Times, Volume I, 1885–1933*, Cambridge, 1983; *Volume II, 1933–1973*, Cambridge, 1996.

under Austrian law, but out of 'intellectual conviction, and belief in God and the efficacy of prayer'. He remained a communicant, a more fervent one in manic phases, when he would go to Mass daily. Near the end of his life he returned to Judaism, partly as a gesture of solidarity with Israel, partly as a result of revelations concerning Papal quiescence during the Holocaust.

The earliest manifestation of the cyclothymic malady that blighted Klemperer's life occurred in his twentieth year (1905), while he was a music student in Berlin. In Hamburg, in 1912, where he was a conductor at the Stadttheater, he eloped during a wild manic phase with the soprano Elisabeth Schumann, a married woman. Returning to the city after a five-day spree with her, he was challenged to a duel by her husband, but declined the invitation: 'Let him shoot ducks.' The cuckold avenged himself at the end of Klemperer's next performance of *Lohengrin*, approaching the conductor from behind while he was still standing on his podium, shouting at him to turn around, striking him twice on the left side of his face with a riding crop, and knocking him into the orchestra pit. This public scandal was the first of a great many that would feed the press and plague Klemperer's career. He fell out of love as abruptly as he had fallen into it. The singer returned to her husband and bore him a son.

In the first volume of the biography Heyworth maintains that a manic-depressive disorder is endogenous, caused by chemical changes in the body, rather than a 'neurosis'. Updating this, Volume Two refers to it as a psychosis, while allowing that circumstances could and did affect the intensity of Klemperer's mood swings. Since 'the impairment of contact with reality' is one of the definitions of the term, its application to the conductor is clearly warranted. Item: as late as the beginning of 1933 Klemperer believed that racial persecution in the Third Reich could be averted by baptising the country's Jews. He actually proposed that a 'Jewish palatinate guard be formed to protect Hitler'.

In April 1933 Klemperer left Berlin for Zurich, which would become his home after World War II, and, in 1973, place of interment. In May 1933, in Florence, he met the philosopher Dietrich von Hildebrand, who perceived that the conductor 'hated the Nazis above all because they had dismissed him', and not because of their 'terrible doctrine'.

He was not an ideologue, obviously, and his 'artistic allegiances took precedence over political issues'. A month or two later he had progressed to the point of acknowledging 'the readiness of the world outside Germany to accommodate the barbarians in Berlin', and in 1940 he hailed the fall of Paris as a 'miracle', looking forward to the capitulation of Britain as the beginning of an era of peace. Only after the war did he recognise the catastrophe of Hitler. On his return to America after a 1946 European concert tour, he told an interviewer: 'I never met anyone who said he was a Nazi... The Germans are sorry they lost the war – period!...' All the same, in Baden-Baden, a year later, when asked whether he would prefer an oboist who had been a National Socialist to a less good one with irreproachable political credentials, he replied, 'The Nazi, of course'. With characteristic inconsistency he avoided his pre-war friend, the politically ambivalent Wilhelm Furtwängler, but received the ardent Nazi Herbert von Karajan cordially.

Klemperer fulfilled engagements in Budapest and Vienna in the late spring of 1933, conducting Béla Bartók's Second Piano Concerto in both cities. During rehearsals, the composer 'sat in the auditorium with a metronome in front of him'. In Vienna, where Bartók performed the solo part, Klemperer was impressed by 'The beauty of his tone, the energy and lightness of his playing'. When it became known that Klemperer wished to establish himself in Vienna, he was given spacious rooms on the ground floor of the former imperial palace of Schönbrunn. But he wished to explore possibilities in America, and after protracted negotiations signed a contract to conduct the forthcoming season of the Los Angeles Philharmonic.

Professionally and personally, Klemperer's American years (1933–47) were the unhappiest in his life. He was forced to play music he did not like, such as the early Sibelius symphonies and that of César Franck, and hinterland American orchestras did not meet his standards or play to his taste. He found the Buffalo orchestra 'miserably mediocre', and in 1937, after conducting the Chicago, wrote to his wife that it 'doesn't *sound* well. Sour violins! It reminds me vividly (and with shudders) of certain German orchestras... It is particularly difficult for me to work with such orchestras. There aren't – it must be said – enough Jews... They have the *warmth* of tone that is indispensable for music.'

Arriving alone in Los Angeles in October 1933, he took an immediate dislike to the enormous, sprawling village and soon began to loathe it. His letters grouse about the 'lack of intellectuality', 'the vast distances', the absence of a 'real city... with architecture', the 'bad service and unspeakable food' in his hotel. His position as Music Director required that he attend 'lunches, at which there is an appalling amount of talk and as good as nothing happens'. What irritated him most was the obligation to participate in the Easter Sunrise Service in Hollywood Bowl and Forest Lawn. A report on one of these smarmy observances as it transpired in 1936 appeared in the *Los Angeles Times*:

> High on a treetop, above a sleeping city, burned a huge cross. Silently, reverently, in the darkness before dawn, 30,000 persons found their way to the Tower of Legends in Forest Lawn Memorial Park... the Philharmonic trumpeters sounded a single long note into the East. And just as the last star faded, the gigantic congregation bowed their heads.

Klemperer conducted the preludes to *Parsifal* and *Die Meistersinger*, then partook of an Easter egg breakfast with the orchestra board.

Thanks to rifts and feuds, German *émigré* society in Los Angeles was 'far from a happy family party'. What 'united the Diaspora' was a 'dislike of American bread and American children and a contempt for Anglo-Saxon cultural standards'. One wonders how Arnold Schoenberg endured these and other aggravations, but the narrative of Klemperer's stormy relationship with him during the first part of the period exposes the strain. A glimpse of their association in Berlin during the four or five preceding years is necessary for an understanding of the relationship in California. When Klemperer conducted Schoenberg's *Die glückliche Hand* at the Kroll Opera, the staging drove the composer wild with fury, and Klemperer foolishly let it be known that he did not have a high opinion of the piece itself. When Schoenberg finally wrote to him, the language reveals the atrabilious side of the composer's never equable temperament: 'the shock of the Berlin productions of my stage works, the atrocities that were committed by scepticism, lack of talent, ignorance and frivolity'. Uncomfortable with English at first, and feeling isolated 'among a population they found alien and philistine', the two men were brought together by their common backgrounds and interests. Unfortunately the conductor's neglect of Schoenberg's music in the late-Romantic idiom as well as of his twelve-tone music – he could 'perceive its logic but was not convinced of its expressive power' – precluded any very close connection between them.

During his first Los Angeles season, Klemperer invited Schoenberg to a banquet. The composer responded with a note:

> I was yesterday obliged to decline an invitation in your honour. You know I have no reason to show you more respect than you have shown me. But that is not my motive in this case... I find it outrageous that these people, who for twenty years have suppressed my music in this area, should now want to use me as a stage-prop, just because I happen to be here.

In April 1936, when Klemperer did not answer an invitation from Schoenberg to visit him, the composer wrote to him, rancorously:

> I find it inappropriate that the extent of our meetings should be determined by you... Anyone should consider it a pleasure as well as an honour if I enjoy seeing him often... My sense of order tells me that every civilised person owes me tribute for my cultural achievements.

Three weeks later, however, Schoenberg accepted Klemperer as a private pupil. The conductor recalled that these lessons were 'among the greatest experiences of my life as a musician'. He also remembered that 'Schoenberg looked through what I had written, corrected it in a very wise manner, and we analysed Bach motets... the greatest thing Schoenberg taught us is that there is no real difference between consonance and dissonance.'

Schoenberg's recollection was that Klemperer's 'incompetence became known to me... when I had to realise that he was unable to harmonise a chorale'. In April 1940 the composer wrote to another conductor explaining that he had reproached Klemperer because in six years in Los Angeles he had not performed any work of his,

> with the exception of the String Suite for *school* orchestra (which, though it was written by no less a person than Schoenberg, does not represent the sense of my historical task)... after the usual excuses: box office, board of directors, lack of rehearsal... he was driven into a corner... and forced to admit that my music has become 'alien' to him...

———●———

Klemperer's highs and lows were more violent and extreme during his American period than they had been in Europe, but other, no less alarming disorders became evident as well. In 1935 he began to complain of imbalance and deafness in his right ear. He started to lurch, sway, and even grope as he walked, and once, rising to speak at a fund-raising dinner for Hollywood Bowl, he toppled across the table, upsetting a water pitcher. Four years later, after consulting with his cousin, a physician in Boston, he entered the Lahey Clinic, celebrated for its school of neurosurgery. An acute neuroma, a tumour on the nerve that controls hearing and balance, was discovered. The surgery that removed it left the right side of his body partly paralysed, the facial muscles to the extent that the side of the mouth twisted downward and the eyelid could not close. A further but unsuccessful operation to ameliorate these impediments resulted in partial atrophy of the tongue, causing him to speak indistinctly. His recuperation was retarded by meningitis that required five daily lumbar punctures without anaesthetic. Even so, the worst consequence of the operation was that it exacerbated the manic phase that had already begun and extended it into the most prolonged of his life.

In Heyworth's account, 1940 was the most terrible year, with the exception of a successful concert series that Klemperer managed to conduct in Mexico in the spring. By this time he had abandoned his wife and was living in New York with a newfound, but married, mistress. Back in California in the summer, he resided in clinics at Arrowhead and Santa Barbara, chaperoned by his sixteen-year-old daughter, Lotte, who, when his lady friend from the East joined him, fled through a window and returned to her mother in Los Angeles. Klemperer's next move was to a hotel in Pasadena from which he was soon asked to leave because he had entered the swimming pool fully dressed. When he appeared at his Los Angeles home with his mistress in tow, his cruelly humiliated wife evacuated it, threatening divorce. He replied to her in writing that he would not consider divorce since *he* had 'not the least grounds for one'. He and his concubine returned to New York, but only a month later he was again in Los Angeles. The novelist Vicki Baum, wife of Richard Lert, conductor of the Pasadena Symphony Orchestra, wrote to a friend:

> Something seems to have damaged [Klemperer's] self-control. He tears around like a maniac, getting into conflicts with the police all the time. He is a Hoffmanesque figure with a black patch on one eye, his roaring voice, his paralyzed walk, and his tragic pursuit of every female that crosses his way.

Heyworth describes him in New York at the beginning of 1941:

> ... his clothes were covered with stains and cigarette burns. He... had difficulty directing food into his mouth... with his huge height, booming voice, eye patch and changes of mood that were liable to switch from hilarity to rage within a few seconds, he could be a terrifying figure.

Still in New York in the autumn, Klemperer conducted a concert series at the New School for Social Research. At rehearsals he placed what looked like a revolver but was actually a water pistol on his conductor's desk. In an automobile accident in Arizona in the same year, he drew the pistol on the arriving police and was jailed. In the last weeks of 1940 and the first two of 1941, he nevertheless conducted five acclaimed concerts with the WPA Symphony Orchestra in Carnegie

Hall, proving that his musical faculties were intact. The sixth concert had to be conducted by a substitute, for the reason that Klemperer, failing to subdue his Lotharian instincts, had pushed his way into the apartment of his soprano soloist. She managed to thwart him, but in the next morning's rehearsal he 'shouted so persistently at her that the manager ordered [him] to leave the hall'.

The conductor's New York doctors convinced him to enter a New Jersey sanitarium, but he was quickly expelled from it for singing too loudly. He proceeded to a similar establishment in Rye, New York, without realising that it was a mental home. The physician in charge telegraphed Klemperer's wife in California, asking her to sign committal papers, but by this time he had absconded. An eight-state police alarm described him as 'dangerous and insane', words that Klemperer read 'with much amusement' in a *New York Times* headline the next day. Not surprisingly, the Los Angeles Philharmonic Orchestra, of which he was still director, did not re-engage him for the next half-season. Surprisingly, his wife took him back.

If the low point of Klemperer's artistic fortunes was the March 1943 bus tour with a pick-up orchestra, to Albany, Binghamton, Sandusky, East Liverpool and Danville (Virginia), the personal pits seem to have been the period in 1944, 'the most intensely manic in his life' in a sanitarium in Evanston, Illinois, where he 'became so excited that his arms and legs had to be strapped to his bed'. After a month of this he was given insulin shock therapy. In another rambunctiously manic state, bar-hopping in Los Angeles in the middle of the night, he was beaten, robbed and left bloodied in the middle of the street until found by police in the morning.

In contrast, the main afflictions suffered in the 1950s and 1960s were physical accidents. Arriving in Montreal for a concert in 1951, he missed his step leaving the airport, fell heavily and fractured the neck of his left femur. After a five-hour operation, he was confined to a hospital for a month and unable to conduct for six more. In Germany, in February 1954, a critic described the start of a Klemperer concert: 'The side door opens… A physically broken man supported on a stick makes his way to the conductor's desk and, held by nearby musicians, lets himself fall into a chair.' That same year, Heyworth reminds us,

Klemperer, aged sixty-nine, was 'about to enter into one of the most fruitful periods of his career'. This refers, above all, to the twelve years of his directorship of the Philharmonia Orchestra, London,[2] and the concerts and rich legacy of recordings with the orchestra.

In 1955 he underwent an emergency appendectomy, and, six weeks later, a procedure to remove a prostate tumor. In September 1958, as he fell asleep while smoking a pipe, his bedclothes began to smoulder; hoping to prevent a fire, he ignited one by pouring a bottle of highly flammable spirits of camphor over the bed. He suffered second- and third-degree burns on fifteen percent of his body and life-threatening days of kidney failure due to the loss of body fluids. A skin-grafting operation followed and another one in March 1959. In the summer of 1966, in St Moritz for a holiday, he slipped on a short flight of stairs, fell, fractured his left hip, and, because of the risk of operating on a man in his eighties at that mountain altitude, had to be taken to Zurich in an ambulance – a seven-hour trip. The litany of his ailments before and after includes cystitis, pericarditis, bronchitis, bursitis, cataracts and pneumonia. Towards the end, too, he was prone to falling asleep while conducting recordings, and in one instance the Philharmonia finished a record without waking him. Klemperer, clearly, was indestructible.

The conductor's zany behaviour was of course not confined to the United States. Some of it seems like deliberate crudeness, as when Oskar Kokoschka came to see him about a project to design sets for *The Magic Flute* and was greeted with 'I would have preferred Picasso'; or boorishness, as when, during a dinner party at Bernard Berenson's in Florence, he asked for a glass of water and proceeded to rinse his dentures in it; or raw tactlessness, as when, on first meeting Wieland Wagner, the composer's grandson, he opened the conversation by asking 'What was it like sitting on the Führer's knee?' When Paul Hindemith called for questions at the end of his 1947 Salzburg lecture, Klemperer raised his hand and loudly asked, 'Where is the lavatory?' Other incidents are inexplicable. At his hotel in Engadine, 'he played tennis by himself, hitting the ball over the

---

2   From 1964–77 the New Philharmonia.

net and then walking to the other side of the court to return it'. Still other happenings can be interpreted as intended to be funny or cute, as when he appeared in Iron-Curtain Budapest conducting with the trousers of his dress clothes stuffed into high rubber boots, and when he arrived at a formal dance in St Moritz attired in a Tyrolean hat, lederhosen, socks and suspenders, which failed to amuse but succeeded in embarrassing everyone present.

Televised orchestral concerts offer close-up footage of conductors as their musicians see them, beating time, cueing, manipulating dynamic levels, emoting. Klemperer, in his later years, performed these functions at the absolute minimum, partly because he was physically unable to register sentiments histrionically. Yet he communicated his musical meanings merely through the expressive use of his eyes, and drew performances from players and singers surpassing what they had thought of as the limits of their abilities. Regrettably, none of the many musicians quoted to this effect in Heyworth's book ventures an explanation of how this was achieved.

Klemperer's stature as conductor can only be attributed to his ability to establish a magnetic field between himself and his musicians, and to communicate or impose his concept of the music on them. In the best of his performances, supremely in his 1964 recording of *The Magic Flute*, every phrase is alive and meaningful, every note infused with feeling. True, Klemperer's tempi diverged widely. He set speed records, fast as well as slow, his 'Eroica' clocking in at forty-eight minutes in 1959 and at fifty-eight in 1970. Questions of technique are irrelevant. He understood that nothing can be instilled into a student that is not already there, and did not believe that conducting is a teachable art: 'What one can teach about conducting is so minimal that I could explain it to you in a minute.' Among the current oversupply of technically proficient conductors no one succeeds in generating a therm of Klemperer's quality of emotion. Competent observers have remarked that 'his gestures were often imprecise', and that in the later years he 'barely gestured at all'. In the early years a Hamburg reviewer wrote that 'the exaltation with which he used his baton in a Bach concerto makes one fear that when he eventually conducts *Tristan* those within reach will be in danger of their lives...'

Otto Klemperer would not have fulfilled his genius without the love and ministrations of his wife, Johanna, and daughter, Lotte, whose letters and personal interviews are Heyworth's principal source. When Klemperer, in Budapest, was insisting that Johanna, in Los Angeles, join him there, she answered, touchingly, through Lotte:

> You rightly ask, where are the intellectual pleasures? Those lie within oneself and are independent of *where* one lives, my little one. People, in case one is dependent on them... are the same everywhere... I'm not interested in concerts, as neither Toscanini nor Klemperer is to be heard here. What I do miss, my dear one, is you.

Lotte, for the last thirty-three years of her father's life, was his impresario, nurse, confidante, guiding light and guardian angel.

Chapter 11

Sunday Afternoon Live

Sedgwick Clark, producer of *New York Philharmonic: The Historic Broadcasts, 1923-1987*, tells us that the album's twelve hours of recorded music were chosen by him after listening to 'hundreds of hours of live music-making'.[1] But since he provides no information about the winnowing process or the other choices that had been under consideration, critical comment on these subjects is limited to guesswork. Ultimately the discussion of repertory is lowered, or perhaps raised, to the level of *de gustibus.*

Clark reveals that he and Kurt Masur, music director of the New York Philharmonic (1991-2002), decided to restrict the contents of the records to broadcasts, Masur being 'keen on preserving the spontaneity of live performances'. But so far from guaranteeing spontaneity, a high proportion of live performances are moribund, and not a few are altogether brain-dead. What they do promise are distractions resulting from bronchial disorders, the crepitations of programme page-turning, the shifting of positions in seats, and other extraneous noises, as exemplified in varying degrees in all ten of the album's CDs. Studio recordings, on the other hand, have been known to convey both the naturalness and the unprompted instinctiveness that define spontaneity. Clark would

---

1   *New York Philharmonic: The Historic Broadcasts, 1923-1987.* Ten compact discs of digitally remastered recordings. New York Philharmonic Special Editions.

probably maintain that all of this is beside the point, which is that live broadcasts, thanks in part to coughs, nasal expurgations, etc., impart a sense of being there.

Another Masur precondition was that 'only conductors no longer active on the podium' – i.e., not alive – 'would be considered'. The reason for this mandate is withheld, perhaps because Masur himself, of the only three maestros to whom it could apply, did not wish to participate. One wonders if Rafael Kubelík, who died in August 1996, was still among the quick when his still unsurpassed performance of Bartók's *Bluebeard's Castle* was nominated for inclusion, since this, the longest piece in the album, alone filling one of the twelve hours, is not likely to have been a last-minute choice.

The selection of conductors and soloists may have taken precedence over the selection of repertory, as musical politics often does over music. Of the twenty-one conductors represented, Bruno Walter receives the lion's share of performing time. He and Toscanini have entire discs to themselves, and Walter has a substantial part of a second one as well. The absence of Wilhelm Furtwängler is thus all the more glaring, since he and Toscanini were the chief contenders for the position of music director of the orchestra in the late 1920s, and no one would rank him below Willem van Hoogstraten, Josef Krips, Erich Leinsdorf and John Barbirolli, who do appear. Controversy about Furtwängler's wartime career in Germany can hardly have been an issue in this decision, since the ardent Nazi collaborator Willem Mengelberg is included, and the conductor Karl Böhm, an out-and-out Nazi, is referred to glowingly in the album booklet's history of the orchestra, while Furtwängler, who had a major role in its musical development, is not mentioned.

The account of the early years neglects to explain why Walter Damrosch's New York Symphony Society and not the Philharmonic was chosen for Carnegie Hall's baptismal concert, which was partly conducted by Tchaikovsky. Nor is anything said about the Philharmonic's connection, a little later in the 1890s, with Antonín Dvořák, who was teaching in a New York conservatory. The then director of the orchestra, Anton Seidl, a friend of the Czech composer, reawakened his interest in Wagner. (A Philharmonic performance in

1894 of the second Victor Herbert Cello Concerto inspired Dvořák to write his own enduringly popular one.)

The Philharmonic's beginnings are dim. It presented only three concerts in its inaugural season, 1842, and by 1875-6, thirty-three years later, the number had increased by only three more. Still another thirty-three years elapsed before the total rose to eighteen. Not until Gustav Mahler became principal conductor, in 1909, did they expand to fifty-four, and he died after his second season.

Josef Stransky succeeded him, then Mengelberg, in whose nine-year reign the principal guest conductors were Stravinsky, Toscanini, Furtwängler, Klemperer and Erich Kleiber. In 1928, Toscanini was appointed sole conductor, and the period until he retired in 1937 is acknowledged as the orchestra's golden age. The unenviable position of successor fell to the young, little-known John Barbirolli, whose incumbency, as should have been foreseen, provoked controversy and discontent. The well-regarded Artur Rodzinsky took over during the war years, with George Szell and Bruno Walter as the most prominent guest conductors. In 1947 Walter was named 'musical adviser'. Two seasons later Leopold Stokowski and Dimitri Mitropoulos were designated 'joint-resident' conductors, an unsatisfactory arrangement that led to Stokowski's resignation after a few weeks.

Mitropoulos's nine subsequent years with the orchestra are widely remembered as troubling. The former Greek Orthodox ordinand, the most phenomenally gifted performing musician of his time, was too gentle and forbearing in his relations with the players. Discipline declined, and, with it, artistic standards. His programmes – Mahler symphonies, concert performances of Strauss's *Elektra* and Berg's *Wozzeck*, Schoenberg's Five Pieces for Orchestra, Violin Concerto, Orchestral Variations, *Erwartung*, *A Survivor from Warsaw* – were too progressive for Philharmonic subscribers. Virgil Thomson's cruel description of his contortions on the podium – 'He whipped [the orchestra] up as if it were a cake, kneaded it like bread, shuffled and riffled an imaginary deck of cards, wound up a clock, shook a recalcitrant umbrella, rubbed something on a washboard and wrung it out' – helped to undermine his position and support.

Mitropoulos's phenomenal memory apparently unnerved the

players. The booklet quotes John Shaeffer, a member of the orchestra's bass section: 'Mitropoulos did the whole season without using a score, rehearsals as well as concerts...' (Schoenberg would have disapproved of this: '... In my Society for Private Performances in Vienna I did not allow playing from memory. I said: "Our musical notation is a puzzle picture which one cannot look at often enough in order to find the right solution."') But Mitropoulos was reading photographically memorised scores, not simply following melodic and dynamic contours as others do who conduct 'by heart'. To demonstrate how a passage should sound, or expose wrong notes, he would go to a piano and, as in his rehearsals of Schoenberg's Serenade for a concert at the Museum of Modern Art, play music of the greatest harmonic complexity for which no piano arrangement existed. Mitropoulos is represented in the Historic Broadcasts only in the ungrateful role of accompanist to Francis Poulenc in his *Concert champêtre*, and to David Oistrakh in Shostakovich's First Violin Concerto, pieces that can have had little interest for the conductor. In 1958, two years before Mitropoulos's premature death, he resigned in favour of his competitive friend Leonard Bernstein, who survived in the glamorous but gory arena for eleven years.

Among the album's many outstanding performances, the most treasured by the present writer is the Brahms Violin Concerto rendered by Jascha Heifetz and Arturo Toscanini in 1935. In the more than six decades since the broadcast, and in spite of all the interim improvements in recording technology, the allure of the young Heifetz's tone has not been surpassed. As interpreted by him and Toscanini, the music takes possession of the listener's imagination and will not let go. No matter that in two or three places in the first movement the violinist takes off in his own, slightly faster tempo: the nuances of speed contribute to the excitement. Toscanini is left only a fraction of a second behind. The orchestra's descending string-triplet octaves just before the end are ragged, the only blemish of the kind in the presentation. In the interests of intonation, Heifetz occasionally substitutes harmonics, an old trick of his, a gross solecism in his commercial recording of Mozart's A major Concerto, but smoothly blended and scarcely noticeable here. Landing very slightly flat on a high note, Heifetz instantly adjusts the pitch in a way that makes the tiny miscalculation sound like an attractive planned effect.

Coughing is rarer here than elsewhere in the set, but other incidental noises include what sounds like a muffled revolver shot during the cadenza (the suicide of an aspiring violinist?), and two notes from what could be the timpanist 'tuning up' during the second bar of the second movement.

Brahms's Second Symphony receives a first-rate performance by Fritz Reiner, its second movement at the perfect tempo, thanks to his decision to follow Brahms's bowings: the cellos play the first phrase of their opening theme on a single bow, which reduces the possibility of dragging. The first and third movements are almost as good, but the fourth is rushed, as if the conductor had to answer a call of nature. Brahms, represented by two of his strongest pieces, as Mozart and Beethoven are not, is thus the album's winning composer. In the restaurant of the Hotel Berkeley, Paris, one day in the autumn of 1957, Françoise Sagan, attractive, intelligent, chic, came to Stravinsky's table and introduced herself to him. He responded by answering the title question of her book: 'Enchanté, Madame. Oui, j'aime Brahms.' He explained to her that, like Brahms, he wanted more than anything to be worthy of the past.

The repertory of the collection will baffle musicians. Haydn is absent, though his symphonies and masses were Bernstein's forte, and Beethoven is represented by only one masterpiece, the C minor Piano Concerto (No. 3). Schubert, Schumann, Weber, Berlioz, Liszt, Dvořák are missing, and, surprisingly, so is Mahler,[2] though in his place is a stunning account of Bruckner's Ninth by Otto Klemperer, albeit patchily hidden under frying-bacon surface noise. Mozart is represented only by early pieces, including the Three-Piano Concerto, in the composer's two-piano arrangement, but from which, delectable as it is, little or nothing stays with the listener. The A major Symphony No. 29 is here, but in a punchy, string-heavy and poorly articulated performance. Since Italian music is entirely absent, one supposes that

---

2   In 1998 the Philharmonic issued a boxed set of twelve CDs containing New York Philharmonic broadcast performances of all Mahler's symphonies and two of his song cycles.

a token Verdi or Rossini overture under Toscanini's magic wand was not available. *La Mer*, conducted by his tragically short-lived protégé Guido Cantelli, is more Italian than Gallic.

Some presences are likewise inexplicable. Sir Henry Wood's bombastic arrangement of Bach's D minor Toccata and Fugue is out of place, as, for a different reason, are the arias from *Fledermaus*. The two 'fragments' – shellac 'shards' – from Mengelberg's 1924 performance of Strauss's *Death and Transfiguration* are merely frustrating. But these feelings are offset by Toscanini's electrifying account of Salome's Dance of the Seven Veils. They were included, no doubt, to extend by a decade the time frame, 1923–87, claimed in the album's title. Nothing at all is offered from the period between 1924 and 1934. Poulenc's *Concert champêtre* and Fauré's dreary Requiem are questionable choices, though the latter was apparently intended as homage to Nadia Boulanger, the composer's pupil, who conducts it. One could do without William Walton's Capriccio, Strauss's bloated family-portrait tone-poem *Symphonia domestica* (magisterially conducted by Bruno Walter, though it was a Mitropoulos warhorse), and Sibelius's *En Saga* (Toscanini), which repeats its themes and relentless rhythm too many times. This writer remains ambivalent about the first Chopin Concerto, a non-piece orchestrally speaking, but how otherwise would we hear Artur Rubinstein play the krakowiak?

No milestone twentieth-century music is included. Something by Schoenberg had to be, and the *Ode to Napoleon* is an astute compromise, sidestepping the historically important pieces yet conveying the intensity and temperament of the composer's late works. The music itself, for those who think they don't like Schoenberg, is partly obscured by the drawled recitation of Byron's repetitive poem. One of the surprises of the set is Leonard Bernstein, no advocate of the Schoenberg school, conducting Berg and Webern very well, though the high level of audience noise during Webern's very short Symphony makes it difficult to hear.

How was the virtual absence of Stravinsky justified? Certainly the four-minute *Fireworks*, half Rimsky-Korsakov, half Paul Dukas, does not adequately represent a composer who transformed the language of music. The likely reason for the absence of the Symphony in Three

Movements, commissioned by the Philharmonic, is that the solo cello in the middle movement mistakenly plays in the bass rather than the tenor clef in the broadcast (and commercial recording). But why was the 7 April 1940 broadcast of *The Rite of Spring* excluded? This musical earthquake would have provided measurements of the orchestra's ability at a time when the piece was seldom heard. Perhaps the broadcast performance does not bear comparison with the studio recording, made a few days earlier, which does great credit to the Philharmonic. Unlike the *Rite*, Strauss's *Domestica* attests to no more than the orchestra's powers of endurance.

The same time that might have been allocated to the *Rite* is occupied by Stravinsky's recording of Tchaikovsky's Second Symphony from the same 1940 broadcast. The fleet-footed execution employs the neatest string – or, rather, off-the-string – staccato articulation on any of the ten discs. But the charming, elegant music is minor, and other broadcast recordings of Stravinsky's interpretation are available. His performance of Rimsky-Korsakov's *Sadko* tone poem, recorded by the orchestra on 17 January 1937, would have represented the Russian Nationalist School, otherwise excluded.

Charles Munch's debonair, sprightly *L'Après-midi d'un faune* is a happy resuscitation, a welcome change from the heavy-breathing, carnal interpretation popular nowadays, which overemphasises the *molto crescendo* in the D flat major section, traditionally co-ordinated with Nijinsky's 'ejaculation'. But Munch inadvertently picks up speed while switching away from subdivided beats in bar seventeen.

Bartók's *Bluebeard* is the lone representative of pre-World War I musical modernism. One lauds the choice partly because it is a risky one, a theatre piece, lugubrious in mood, dependent to a degree on visual tie-ins of lighting and colour symbolisms, an opera sung in untranslatable octosyllabic Magyar (an English text is provided). Confined to the slow-moving dialogue between Bluebeard and Judith, his last wife, the work is static, yet attains dramatic intensity as Mrs Bluebeard's inquisitiveness gradually turns into jealousy.

The music, consisting largely of a succession of ostinati, lacks movement. Yet the score is a gallery of orchestral attractions, and the contrast between Bluebeard singing or speaking in simple rhythms and modalities, and Judith's lighter, triple-time music, is *géniale*. The orchestra is always paramount, nevertheless, and the instrumental timbres and their combinations are original and masterful; a performance in piano reduction is unimaginable. No other composer has employed the organ in an orchestra with such skill and to such majestic effect. The dissonances are no less remarkable. The minor-second is to *Bluebeard* what the major-second is to *Petrushka*, completed in the same year (1911). Clark rightly observes that the plunge from Debussy's *Faune* into *Bluebeard*, which follows in the album, is not so precipitous. But *Pelléas et Mélisande*, not the *Faune*, is Bartók's model, especially in the chant-like vocal style. The Bluebeard in this recording has the required range of *Pelléas*'s Arkel at the beginning, and later of Golaud.

The album's two most recent specimens of twentieth-century music are Shostakovich's First Violin Concerto (1954) and John Corigliano's Clarinet Concerto (1977). Whereas Sedgwick Clark's experience of the former was 'searing', this present writer was unable to derive any calefaction from it. The steady-paced, largely on-the-beat music is monotonous, whether in the turgid passacaglia or the lickety-split scherzo and two-four finale, and the alternation of fast and slow is routine and stale. The opus is devoid of engaging musical ideas, its brand of key-signature tonality is without harmonic interest, and the whole is academic to the extent that the cadenza sounds like a conservatory exercise. Here the coughing fits are enlivening.

The choice of the Clarinet Concerto must have been a difficult one, given the dimensions of the American composers' lobby. The music touches bases with prevalent styles and gives the percussionists and sound engineers their heads. But never mind. It attains Corigliano's goal: 'I wish to be understood. I think it is the job of the composer to reach out to his audiences with every means at his disposal. Communication should be a primary goal.'

What the album establishes is that the eclipse of the coast-to-coast Sunday matinée broadcasts by the New York Philharmonic in the 1930s, 1940s and 1950s marks a huge step in the dumbing down of America.

Chapter 12

'Virge'

Lunch with Virgil Thomson... one of the few people... who have
something to say on the subject of music and say it with great
feeling and style and freshness, and, indeed, written, truth.

Isaiah Berlin, 12 June 1945

Virgil Thomson: Composer on the Aisle[1] provides important
amplifications and sortings-out of fact and fiction in Thomson's own
and other versions of his life. His own remains the best-written life
of an American musician,[2] but Anthony Tommasini's ranks not far
below it in that regard and has the advantages of being more complete
and truthful. His fluent, easy-going style, free of fustian, thickets,
ponderosities, is indebted to Thomson's. Much of the material is familiar
– the Missouri Baptist background, the discovery of intellectual and
musical precocity, the Harvard years, life in *l'entre deux guerres* Paris
– but a surprising amount is new and revelatory. The book subtracts
several cubits from Thomson's stature as a person.

Thanks to 'exclusive full access' to Virgil Thomson's papers at
Yale, and to some that he withheld, including intimate letters and
a receipt from a Brooklyn bail bondsman, the book is 'the first full-
scale account of Thomson's experiences as a composer, influential

---

1   By Anthony Tommasini, New York, 1997.
2   *Virgil Thomson* by Virgil Thomson, New York, 1960.

critic, and gay man'. Thomson himself was silent concerning the last of these categories, and the fact of it, though too obvious to be closetable, has not heretofore been brought into the open with a frankness that includes an index of sexual partners, which, though shorter than Leporello's, seems to have been on the way to catching up. Increasingly, 'Virgil attracted a coterie of young gay male friends', Tommasini tells us, adding that 'star-struck students, including quite a few handsome gay men, sat at his feet...' Not the least valuable aspect of the new biography is its contribution to sexual sociology and the understanding of changing mores during Thomson's long life (1896–1989).

The story of his brief incarceration after a 1942 police raid on a male bordello operated by one Gustave Beekman near the Brooklyn Navy Yard is upsetting to read and must have been frightening to experience. How long and how frequently he had patronised the establishment is apparently not known, but the *New York Herald Tribune*, in the person of Geoffrey Parsons, Thomson's employer as well as the paper's chief editorial writer and 'overseer of all things cultural', managed to arrange for his release and to keep a lid on his involvement in the scandal. The truth circulated privately at the *Tribune* and a bit beyond, but with the exception of a remark in the *Daily Mirror* by Walter Winchell to the effect that one of the big fish in the police net was an unnamed musician who has 'many gunning for him' reached neither the tabloids nor the extortionists.

The success of the cover-up was due in part to Beekman's identification of a more prominent client, the senior senator from Massachusetts, David Walsh, and a press campaign to expose him that deflected attention from the mystery musician. Alben Barkley, the Senate majority leader and future vice-president, and J. Edgar Hoover, 'who, we now know, understood what it meant to be homosexual', quickly quashed the charges against the senator; but Beekman, with no powerful friends, spent twenty years in Sing Sing Prison, the savage penalty of the period, on a single charge of sodomy.

Thomson was unnerved again some years later when Jerome D. Bohm, one of his assistants at the *Tribune,* served a prison term for pederasty, after a teenage boy, 'questioned... about some abrasions around his anus' during a routine examination by his doctor, gave a lurid account of 'goings-on' in Bohm's weekend Connecticut household. Perhaps understandably, if cravenly, Thomson turned down Bohm's plea to appear as a character witness at his trial, as well as, two years later, his petition for reinstatement in his job at the *Tribune*.

As expected, the best of the book is in the chapter on Thomson's heyday as chief music critic of the *Tribune* (1940–54). A mutual friend wrote to Gertrude Stein to tell her the news: 'Dear Baby Woojums [Alice B. Toklas was Mama Woojums]... Virgil is the music critic of the *N.Y. Herald-Tribune* and has made a sensation.' In fact, his wit, debonair tone and anti-establishment point of view were soon revolutionising the music world. He took on the entrenched powers of the day, among them Olin Downes, the stodgy music critic of the rival 'voice of the majority' *New York Times*, the Columbia Concerts, the largest artists' agency in the country, the Metropolitan Opera, and even the reigning maestro, Arturo Toscanini, who, Thomson wrote, reduced the mighty second movement of Beethoven's Seventh Symphony to a 'barcarole'.

Here are some excerpts from Thomson's debut review (11 October 1940):

> The Philharmonic-Symphony Society of New York opened its ninety-ninth season last evening in Carnegie Hall. There was little that could be called festive about the occasion. The menu was routine, the playing ditto...
>
> Beethoven's overture to 'Egmont' is a classic hors d'oeuvre. Nobody's digestion was ever spoiled by it and no latecomer has ever lost much by missing it. It was preceded, as is the custom nowadays, by our National Anthem, gulped down standing, like a cocktail... [The somberness of last night's version] is due, I think, to an attempt to express authority through mere weighty blowing and sawing in the middle and lower ranges of the various orchestral instruments, rather than by the more classical method of placing every instrument in its most brilliant and grateful register in order to achieve the maximum of carrying power and of richness...

> ... Twenty years residence on the European continent has
> largely spared me Sibelius. Last night's Second Symphony was
> my first in quite some years. I found it vulgar, self-indulgent
> and provincial beyond all description. I realize that there are
> sincere Sibelius lovers in the world, though I must say I've
> never met one among educated professional musicians...
>
> ... The concert, as a whole... was anything but a memorable
> experience. The music itself was soggy, the playing dull and
> brutal. As a friend remarked... 'I understand now why the
> Philharmonic is not part of New York's intellectual life.'

Geoffrey Parsons' memo to Thomson on his review keeps pace with
the celerity of his protégé's mental movements, and it is a pity that
we are not told more about this perceptive editor who, realising that
Thomson could be a boon to the paper, had foresightedly chosen him
in the first place:

> The Sibelius paragraph was the one considerable blunder. You...
> committed the one cardinal sin of criticism, that of appearing
> to condescend. When you cited the opinion of 'musically
> educated' people, you made every illiterate and amateur who
> disagreed with you simply snort... 'What the hell, the experts
> have always been wrong... Provincial is Sibelius? Well, then,
> that's what I like.'... A cult is a cult and must be approached
> patiently and calmly – the way you would a nervous horse...

Parsons does not challenge, as he should have, the greater blunder
that to miss *Egmont* is no great loss, or say that Downes, as New
York's most prominent music critic and an ardent Sibelius champion,
is too overtly Thomson's target. But to judge from his deletion in the
galleys of an offensive remark about the 'undistinguished audience',
one supposes that he saw through Thomson's opportunistic intent
to shock, and at the same time realised that not since G.B. Shaw had
anyone written about music with such directness, wit and daring.

The next day Thomson reviewed the Boston Symphony Orchestra's
opening concert of the season in its home city. He expressed

reservations about Koussevitzky's performance of Beethoven's Fifth, and about the programme: 'The first two movements of [Vaughan Williams's] *A London Symphony* are long and episodic, disjointed...' This time Parsons was delighted: 'Peaches and cream from every point of view... You struck exactly the right note... of wise, modest, generous, urbane, constructive comment.' Of the Beethoven, Thomson had observed that:

> At the back of every conductor's mind is a desire to make his orchestra produce a louder noise than anyone else's orchestra can produce, a really majestic noise, a Niagara Falls of sound... You can tell when it is coming by the way he goes into a brief convulsion at that point. The convulsion is useful to the conductor because it prevents his hearing what the orchestra really sounds like while his fit is on...

Performances of Thomson's own music increased in tandem with the growth of his influence as a critic, then decreased abruptly when he left the newspaper. This surprised no one except Thomson himself, we are told, which indicates that the shrewd observer of *The Musical Scene*, as this now-classic survey of musical criticism is titled, failed to see that the impresarios, conductors and performers who had programmed his music feared his power as a critic but had low opinions of his composing talent. In fact the literature about his music is undistinguished. His advocates rely on nebulous, impressionistic descriptions, in the main. Tommasini himself, who plainly loves it – the 'serenely beautiful' Stabat Mater, the 'poignant grandeur' of the *Oraison funèbre* – does not discuss it in a musically enlightening way. To characterise the Piano Sonata No. 2 as a 'beguiling mix of resignation and whimsy' conveys a sensitiveness to moods, perhaps, but nothing about musical substance. Similarly, to be told that the 'Handelian andante' of the Violin Sonata 'grows shockingly intense' is unhelpful. (Intense in what ways, and why shockingly?) And when a technical matter is touched upon, the results undermine the reader's confidence.

A *New York Times* review of Tommasini's book states that Thomson is 'not a great composer... but he certainly is the composer of two great operas'. One or the other statement is of course invalidated by the syllogistic squeeze, but, in any case, what makes the operas 'great' is not divulged. The first of them, *Four Saints in Three Acts*, has no plot, no real characters in any recognisable sense, and no emotion, unless the pre-curtain discussion to Act Four of whether there should be a fourth act is considered suspenseful. Two Teresas of Avila and Ignatius of Loyola, the principal saints, repeat children's rhymes, random remarks, word games, and ask questions. One of the latter, 'Can women have wishes?' hints at Gertrude Stein's feminism, and, by hindsight, the subject of her second Thomson libretto, *The Mother of Us All* (Susan B. Anthony), a cavalcade of nineteenth-century Americana. The diatonic and harmonically rudimentary music of *Four Saints*, whether *faux-naïf* or the real kind, is a patchwork of waltzes, marches, hymns, quotations ('My Country 'Tis of Thee', 'God Save the King'), connected, or disconnected, by singsong recitative and chant.

Tommasini exposes some of the less attractive aspects of Thomson's personality as they became manifest during the long struggle (from 1927) to bring *Four Saints* to the stage. Charming with prospective backers, and uncharacteristically restrained in his tussle with Baby Woojums over money – 'We want to sell the damn thing,' she wrote, 'and we got to have the reclame... believe me it is not for anything 'xcept selling...' – Thomson was 'surly and short-tempered with everyone else'. Tommasini does not shirk such epithets as bitchy, bossy, bullying, imperious, but stronger ones – contumelious, monstrously egotistical – are needed for Thomson's treatment of Beatrice Wayne Godfrey, the St Teresa in the first production. A revival of the opera had been organised in honour of Thomson's ninetieth birthday, and members of his entourage had thoughtfully arranged for the wheelchair-confined eighty-two-year-old to attend. When he got wind of this plan, Thomson flew into paroxysms of rage, refused to have the 'old fat black lady' there, and sent one of his minions to inform her. She later told Tommasini that 'he didn't want to share the attention with me... That's Virgil. He is so afraid somebody will take something from him.'

Thomson's interest in the 'homosexual subculture of Harlem', where 'men could find men to have sex with', led to his decision to cast *Four Saints* 'entirely with Negro singers'. This inspiration appalled Baby Woojums – 'I do not care for the idea of showing the negro bodies' – but one of his letters intended to change her mind exposes his, and the period's, condescension and plantationism: 'Negroes objectify themselves very easily, and I think the explanation is all part of the "threshold of consciousness" idea – they live on the surface of their consciousness.' No doubt such views echo inherited and regional ones, Thomson's ancestors having taken sixty of their slaves with them in the move from Virginia to Missouri in the 1830s. They had intended to settle in Illinois but kept going when they learned that slavery would soon become illegal there.

The behaviour of Thomson and his collaborators, John Houseman, the director, and Frederick Ashton, the choreographer, in speaking French in front of the all-black cast when not wanting to be understood, is unconscionable. Ashton, moreover, 'campy and flamboyant', had himself photographed with three naked young male dancers in a pose intended to mean, as Tommasini interprets it, 'How I love and care for these beautiful, simple black boys'. Thomson later recalled that by the time the show closed on Broadway, the choreographer had 'slept with two or three of them. They were pretty as hell, you know.'

The book's account of Thomson's third, last, and least successful opera, *Lord Byron*, gives the impression that the failure must be attributed in part to the composer's natural peevishness and his attempt to control every detail of the production. Tommasini describes a rehearsal during which 'Byron' and three *beaux idéals* fellow poets were trying out their tight-fitting nineteenth-century breeches: Thomson 'bounded toward the stage, pointed at their crotches, and shouted: "Everybody hang to the left, hang to the left"... [The men] attempted to arrange their bulges in some semblance of conformity.' But *Byron* does have characters, intelligible situations and traditional operatic forms – arias, duets, choruses and ensembles. The music is said to reflect English, Irish and Scottish ballads, but to some listeners they sound more like Missouri parlour pieces. The opera fails because its dramatic purpose is unclear, and because the music strives for, but never achieves, passion. The quoted excerpts, changing with the geography, include 'Auld Lang Syne' and 'London Bridge is falling down'.

Composer on the Aisle relates for the first time the origins of the fifty-year friction between Thomson and Roger Sessions, a 'personal enemy' who debunked the notion of an American school, 'advocated rigorous international standards' and represented 'the modernism of complexity', as Thomson himself did the 'modernism of simplicity'; John Clare's line comes to mind: 'Give me no high-flown fangled things.' By mid-century, the validity of the 'dissonance-saturated international style' was no longer contested, Tommasini writes, but 'the public wasn't exactly buying it either'. Misreading the portents, Thomson predicted that 'Our century's second half... will certainly witness the fusion of all the major modern devices into a new classical style...' In reality, the faceless international kind prevailed until the time of Philip Glass's *Einstein on the Beach* (1976).

The personal animus between Thomson and Sessions was fuelled by the latter's devastating review, in *Modern Music*, of Thomson's *Sonate d'église* at its premiere in Paris in May 1926, and by Thomson's discovery that Sessions had pressured the composer-critic Theodore Chanler into reviewing *Four Saints* negatively. A letter from Chanler to Thomson's biographer, Kathleen Hoover, explains that Sessions 'was five years my senior, and I was very much under the spell of his remarkable mind...' The hostility on Sessions's side is attributable to a 1947 Thomson review trashing his compositions as 'learned, laborious, complex, and withal not strikingly original. They pass for professor's music...' But it must also be said that the two were antipodal in almost all regards except their denigration of Nadia Boulanger.

Both men lived in Europe during the rise of Nazism. But while Sessions was alarmed by events in Germany, Thomson never mentions them, and in fact fled from Paris to Lisbon and New York only in July 1940, after the invasion of France. His friend Sherry Mangan had 'lectured [him] fruitlessly about the oppression of Jews, the scourge of fascism, the plight of the smaller countries Hitler was vanquishing... [but] he found Virgil shockingly detached'. Thomson's 'social attitudes' were 'essentially conservative', Tommasini says, and in the 1950s when Copland was being hounded because of his 'leftist' politics, his *Lincoln Portrait* banned by the Eisenhower inauguration committee, Thomson, almost alone among prominent spokespeople for the arts, did not speak up in his defence.

The book throws fresh light on Thomson's relations with Copland, partly by reprinting the beginning of Thomson's early (1932) *Modern Music* essay on this principal rival:

> Aaron Copland's music is American in rhythm, Jewish in melody, eclectic in all the rest. The subject matter is limited but deeply felt. Its emotional origin is seldom gay, rarely amorous, almost invariably religious. Occasionally excitation of a purely nervous and cerebral kind is the origin of a *scherzo* which led to, a jazz experiment. That has been his one wild oat. It was not a very fertile one.

Thomson was more harshly critical of Copland in their correspondence, as a letter on reading Copland's *What to Listen for in Music* shows:

> Your book... I... find... a bore. [It] contains a lot of stuff that I don't believe and that I am not at all convinced you believe... It... remains to be proved that analytic listening is possible even. God knows professional musicians find it difficult enough. I suspect that persons of weak auditive memory do just as well to let themselves follow the emotional line of a piece... which they certainly can't do very well while trying to analyze a piece tonally... I do not believe ... that the loose and varied sonata form practiced by the great Viennese has very much relationship to the modern French reconstructed form... You know privately that it is the most controversial matter in all music... I find it a little dull of you and a little unctuous to smooth all that over with what I consider falsehoods.

Copland's response begins with: 'Dear Virgil, It was lots of fun to get that long letter from you...'

In the fall of 1981, Composers' Showcase, a concert society formed by the Gershwin biographer Charles Schwartz, presented Stravinsky's *Histoire du soldat* in the Whitney Museum, with Thomson reading the part of the Devil, Sessions and Copland those of the Soldier and the Narrator. 'For this historic occasion', Tommasini notes, the two unreconciled eighty-five-year-olds 'behaved with civility'. Of course they would on stage, but as the conductor of the event, I can testify that the atmosphere during rehearsals was icy. On the first day, the soft-spoken Sessions and the deaf and stentorian Thomson shook hands and reminded each other of their last meeting, which turned out to have been embarrassingly long ago. Copland, on good terms with both, arrived a few moments late, but in time to help organise their positioning for a *Times* photograph. Copland, at eighty-one and struggling with the early stages of Alzheimer's, read his lines but spoke to his colleagues only to ask, 'Did I just say that?' Thomson stage-directed, revised the script (which needed it), and decreed that at the performance he should stand closest to the audience, Copland in the middle, Sessions somewhere in the remote interior.

Why, one wonders, did the trio consent to appear in an event marking the tenth anniversary of Stravinsky's death? Surely the answer is that Copland and Sessions wholeheartedly wished to pay homage. Both had known Stravinsky since the late 1920s, Copland in Paris, New York and Hollywood, Sessions in his late Princeton period and after that in New York where he visited the Russian composer at each opportunity and, incidentally, conversed with him in his native language. Thomson, who knew Stravinsky at least as well, but did not venerate him – he always referred to *Sacre* as 'that pretty little piece' – doubtless accepted the invitation for the very different reason that the occasion signified Thomson's recognition as one of America's most distinguished composers. Whereas the other two were inveterately established as such, most people must have thought of Thomson, especially in his years 'on the aisle', primarily as a critic. He knew, of course, that his writings would last, but the coveted accolade was that of composer.

Thomson and Copland could not have been more congenial to each other and to me when I became the third member of their Pulitzer Prize panel for the outstanding original composition of 1970. The deliberations, such as they were, took place in Thomson's digs at the Chelsea Hotel in March 1971, by which time the entries had been winnowed from perhaps 200 to about twenty-five. These were heard on tapes, or judged, chiefly, from qualities of craftsmanship in scores.

The final choice was widely reputed to depend less on merit than on personal predilections, which Copland's introductory declaration, 'I am a Del Tredici man', confirmed. But, unlike Thomson, who had done no homework, Copland had examined some of the manuscripts. Taking charge, Thomson proposed to exclude from consideration all graphic notation, verbal instructions for musical 'happenings', indeterminacy (the performer choosing which segments of a work he or she will play and in what order), and electronic pieces, which he called 'Engineering music: I've heard nothing of any interest in two decades of listening'. We concurred, but compromised in allowing a genre of interplay between electronic and live.

While admitting the absurdity of trying to compare a cantata and a skiffle trio for washboard, bassoon and guitar, we nevertheless proceeded to sample the tapes. Thomson napped through most of them but awakened periodically to endorse our opinions, exclaiming, after the first resoundingly negative ones, 'Another redskin bites the dust' and 'Got the varmint'. An anti-*Perspectives of New Music* bias became apparent when Copland proposed that two Milton Babbitt string quartets be interchanged in the middles of movements, presumably to prove that the pieces were indistinguishable. 'Virge', as Copland called him, thought this a jolly idea, but dozed off during the first experiment.

A mortified Copland, in the taxi uptown, promised a more professional session on the morrow. But it was much the same. Moreover, Thomson kept niggling me to review his newly published *American Music Since 1910* for *The New York Review of Books*. This was out of the question, largely because of his comments, some of them unintelligible, on many of the 106 composers whose biographies fill a large part of the volume: Irving Fine's music 'seems to remember without really resembling it the music of Henri Sauguet'; Foss's is 'more accomplished than convincing'; Dai-Key Lee's 'lacks charm and intellectual distinction [and] I frankly do not quite know how to place it'. (Then why was he one of the 106?) The longest biography, furthermore, is Thomson's own (eighty-six lines to nineteen for Gershwin), even though he has a whole chapter to himself, the only one with examples in music type. Worse still, the erratically chosen

106 include several non-Americans, as well as such oddities as the opera-composing bank president Avery Claplin, while omitting Scott Joplin, an immortal.

Tommasini clears up the hitherto confusing relationship between Thomson and John Cage. In a 1945 *Tribune* interview, Thomson had acclaimed the younger composer as the colossus of the age – 'genius as a musician... sophistication unmatched... original expression of the very highest poetic quality'. This was at the expense of Schoenberg, which infuriated Roger Sessions, yet Thomson's criticism of Schoenberg, so far as it goes, is irrefutable:

> The constricting element in atonal writing... is the necessity of taking care to avoid making classical harmony with a standardized palette of instrumental sounds and pitches that exists primarily for the purpose of producing such harmony... Cage has been free to develop the rhythmic element of composition which is the weakest element of the Schoenbergian style...

In 1949 Thomson decided that a biography of him was due, and he asked Cage to write it. The result was unsatisfactory. The author was unhappy with Thomson's editing of his prose, and Thomson objected to Cage's 'unfriendly' doctoring of musical analyses. The project came to nothing, but in 1955 Thomson approached Cage again, without revealing that he had already assigned the purely biographical part of the book to Kathleen Hoover, and that the musical part, in which Cage had no interest, had been relegated to him. When Cage delivered his 167-page typescript, in March 1956, Thomson pretended to be pleased with it, 'overall', but added that of course it 'would have to be completely changed'. Meanwhile, Hoover and Cage had met and discovered that they strongly disliked each other. Nevertheless, a book jointly under their names, *Virgil Thomson: His Life and Music*, was finally published (1959), not to wide acknowledgment or the approbation of its subject.

Thomson struck back years later in a *New York Review* essay,[3] ostensibly on four of Cage's books, including the one about himself written with Hoover. Much of this brilliant piece is devoted to Cage's mammoth collage of noises, *HPSCHD* (1967), from which Thomson concluded that

> The ultimate aim was to produce a homogenized chaos that would carry no program, no plot, no reminders of the history of beauty, and no personal statement... Cage wanted [to remove] all identifiable structure and rhetoric.

Cage was flitting from one inane extreme – the serialisation of every element (pitches, lengths, dynamics, timbres, modes of attack), which removed all freedom from composition – to another – its apparent opposite, aleatory, or indeterminacy, which would make music completely free, 'an achievement he was especially pleased with because it eliminated from any piece both the history of music and the personality of the composer'. Cage himself described his composing at this time as 'an activity characterized by process and essentially purposeless'.

Cage, Thomson notes,

> prizes innovation above all other qualities – a weighting of the values which gives to all his judgments an authoritarian, almost a commercial aspect, as of a one-way tunnel leading only to the gadget fair. [Composers generally] have considered the history of music as leading up to them, but Cage has no such view. He thinks of himself, on the contrary... as a prophet denouncing the whole of Renaissance and post-Renaissance Europe, with its incorrigible respect for beauty and distinction, and dissolving all that in an ocean of electronic availabilities.

Thomson then comes in for the kill:

---

3   *The New York Review of Books*, 23 April 1970, p. 9.

The truth is that Cage's mind is narrow. Were it broader his remarks might carry less weight. And his music might not exist at all. For with him the original gift, the musical ear, is not a remarkable one... A lack of urgency has been characteristic of Cage's music from the beginning... Whenever I have played his recorded works for students I have found that no matter what their length they exhaust themselves in about two minutes, say four at the most. By that time we have all got the sound of it... And there is no need for going on with it, since we know that it will not be going any deeper into an emotion already depicted as static. Nor will it be following nature's way by developing an organic structure. For if the mind that created it, though powerful and sometimes original, is nevertheless a narrow one, the music itself, for all its jollity, liveliness, and good humor, is emotionally shallow.

Like Thomson, Tommasini favours a vernacular vocabulary. The elderly Thomson's 'tummy' is enormous, while other things and people are 'wacky', 'hokey', 'fuss-budgety', 'snazzy', 'sassy', 'comfy'. But 'savvy' and 'sweeping', the redundant modifier for Thomson's innumerable 'generalizations', are overworked. The author of *The Sheltering Sky* is referred to at one place as 'Paul Bowels', and his estranged wife, Jane, is said to have died in Tangier, instead of the convent hospital in Málaga where she lived for years and near which, in the cemetery of San Miguel, she is buried. Some confusion exists between 1956 and 1957. In Venice, in the summer of 1957, Thomson's friend Roger Baker is said to have made an appointment with 'a handsome young painter' to see some (non-existent) 'Caravaggio murals' (not necessarily a slip for the Carpaccios in the Scuola di San Giorgio degli Schiavoni, since they are canvases), and in 'Venice that summer', the ballerina Tanaquil LeClercq was 'struck down by polio'. In fact this tragedy occurred the year before, in 1956. But no matter, the narrative is smooth and the book is indispensable to anyone concerned with American cultural history of the period.

Showing a new secretary around his apartment, Thomson, in his ninetieth year, instructed him: 'This is what you do if you show up and I'm dead. Don't call a doctor; it will be too late. Call the lawyer. He knows what to do. Then call the locksmith to come change the locks. Then call AP, UPI, and the *New York Times* – the culture desk, *not* the obit boys.' 'Do you want to be buried or cremated?' his friend Dick Flender had asked one day. 'Cremated,' Virgil said. 'Easier to ship.'

Thomson's own blurb for the dust-jacket of his 1966 memoirs is unstinting in its self-praise, but not misleading:

> Salty, witty, warm, and beautifully written... they tell of a Kansas City childhood, a Harvard education, a Missourian's adventures in Boston, New York, and Paris... Penetrating, powerful, and quirky, the book shows Virgil Thomson not only as an international gadfly stinging where he pleases but also as one who was certain to leave an indelible mark on the times that he so vividly recounts.

Chapter 13

On Music and Time

On 31 March 1948, I was in a Washington hotel suite with Igor Stravinsky (here to guest-conduct the National Symphony), his wife Vera, and W.H. Auden, who had come to deliver the completed libretto of *The Rake's Progress.* The 'Stravs', as Auden referred to them, had just arrived from the West Coast on a night train. Auden had come from the Cosmos Club rooms of Robert Lowell, the Consultant in Poetry at the Library of Congress. I had flown in early that morning from New York, at the composer's request, to establish a rehearsal schedule for a concert I was to share with him the following week in Town Hall, New York. He was gracious but crisp and impatient for quick, precise answers. Auden was edgy and dyspeptic, a consequence, I surmised, of having to explain his uncovenanted inclusion of Chester Kallman as his co-librettist. The prospect of hobnobbing with two of the century's great artists had frayed my nerves to the extent that I expected to collapse from metabolic depletion.

Auden opened the conversation with a pertinent reference to the historic debate of 'prima la parola/prima la musica'. But this conceit failed to engage Stravinsky, who responded with a non sequitur that has fascinated me ever since: 'Music is the best means we have of digesting time.' What did he mean by the alimentary image, and what did he mean by 'time'? Clearly not something to be passed through, what cosmologists now ridicule as the 'myth of passage' that transmutes the future to the past. More likely he was thinking of the creation of alternative time-worlds in musical forms, and therefore, in part, of the complex psychological relationships between musical time and real time. After all, the temporal dimensions of music are more interesting than the illusions of an empty infinity that lacks even an intrinsic metric. Another possibility could be simply that a musical thought for his new opera was already gestating. In fact, he had composed the Interlude to the Graveyard Scene in *The Rake's Progress* weeks before seeing even a synopsis of the libretto. He went on to say that a creative musician must possess natural gifts of measurement, and that the time-sense was the most acute and important of these. A year-and-a-half later I would hear the same from Arnold Schoenberg.

Unlike the other arts, music begins in time, moves in time, is realised in time, and ends in time, though of course its sound waves move through the air. Music also possesses perfect unity, and speaks an international language that everyone understands differently and no one can translate. True, the temporal exactitude of music is attainable only at the expense of an infinitesimal vagueness of pitch, since the frequency of a note, the oscillations that determine its pitch, interact with its duration. This suggests an analogy to Newton's discovery that a particle can have both a position and a momentum, and reminds us of his contributions to the physics of music, primarily his logarithmic calculations expressing the magnitude of musical intervals. Much more recently, of course, both Werner Heisenberg's Uncertainty Principle and Gödel's Incompleteness Theorem correct Newton on the subatomic level. In the words of the first, 'It is not possible to calculate with perfect accuracy both the position and momentum of a subatomic particle. Effectively, the more certainty with which its speed is measured, the less accuracy can be assigned to its position.'

Stravinsky's 'time-digesting' observation seemed to connect with Walter Pater's 'all art constantly aspires to the condition of music'.[1] Since Pater does not expatiate on the properties intended by his word

---

1   Cf. T.S. Eliot: 'We can never emulate music, because to arrive at the condition of music would be the annihilation of poetry.' *Poetry and Drama*, Harvard, 1951.

'condition', perhaps we may be justified in concluding that in music it is impossible to distinguish form and content. Pater's description of the emotional and intellectual experience of artists – 'To turn always with this hard, gemlike flame, to maintain this ecstasy...' – does not differentiate between composers and other artists, but it removes the confusion from Lessing's *Laokoön* that the poet is the interpreter of time, and that the painter, the sculptor and the architect are the interpreters of space. If Horace's 'painting is visible poetry' (*ut pictura poēsis*) seems merely to confound two media while illuminating neither, the calligraphy of some of the greatest Chinese poets does combine the two arts in one entity, hence the terms pictographic and calligrammatic.

Helen Vendler's *Coming of Age as a Poet* offers a good example of poetry aspiring to the condition of music. Her discussion of the 'reduplicative semiosis', in the eight short lines of the song of the mermaids concluding *The Love Song of J. Alfred Prufrock*, shows how alliteration, assonance and overlapping words effectuate music: sea, sea-ward, sea-girls, seaweed; sing, singing; *on* the waves, *of* the waves; white, white hair; blows, blown; back, black.

Of the many definitions of music, one we can all accept is found at the head of a sketch page of 'The Dance of the Earth' in *The Rite of Spring*: 'If there is rhythm, there is music.' Rhythm is the mode of the appearance of time in music, and musical *tempo* is rhythm's expressive mode. Without rhythm there would be no 'before', 'after' or 'evolution' in music. In his later years, Stravinsky revised this chronology of his own creative processes, claiming to be 'aware of intervallic combinations first', and finding that 'rhythms, which tended to come later, were subject to change, as intervallic ideas rarely are', though 'melodic' intervals imply a rhythmic relationship even if not notated.

But again, what did Stravinsky comprehend by 'digesting time'? Was he thinking along the lines of Levi-Strauss's[2] famous postulate that 'music obliterates time, transmuting the segment devoted to

---

2   Stravinsky had more than one discussion with him in New York during the early 1940s, and rated him as musically sophisticated.

listening to it into a synchronic totality, enclosed within itself. Because of the internal organisation of the musical work, the art of listening to it immobilises passing time'?

This would have attracted Stravinsky's mind more than such metaphysical musings as Auden's definition of music as 'A virtual image of our experience of living as temporal, without its double aspect of recurrence and becoming'. But Stravinsky agreed with the poet that time was linear, sequential, non-repeatable, and that 'the Crucifixion took place in historical time'. Auden regarded cyclical concepts of time as heretical, of course, but he conceded that the all-pervasiveness of linear time in the Western world today is largely the inheritance of Darwin and nineteenth-century evolutionary biology, and he mentioned that the concurrence of linear time (*chronos*) and cyclical time (*kairos*) in the *Epithalamion* – the time symbolisms and horological metaphors – should be ascribed to Spenser's conviction that mutability cannot endure forever, and must end with eternal perfection in which time itself shall cease.

More importantly, Stravinsky believed in Augustine's idea of a timeless God and an eternal present. 'Only the present really is,' Augustine wrote. Further, the composer believed that time was created when the world was created, which sounds like an adumbration of the Big Bang Theory. It follows that music can be created only in the present. In an interview in Belgrade in 1961 he declared: 'I can't stand modern music. Thus I don't compose it... I have already said so many times. There is no future. The past existed, but it has disappeared. The problem is what to do to make the present exist. This is what we labour for.'

In a 1963 film portrait of Stravinsky, on board the SS *Bremen*, the composer is seen affirmatively answering the question 'Was music present at the creation?' 'See for yourself,' he says, pointing to the booming bass drum in the ship's deck band. In his 'Creation' cantata, *The Flood*, God is always accompanied by a bass drum.

Augustine also believed that time exists as a concept because of change, hence time is dependent on change, though the question of the priority of one over the other seems to be unresolved. Kant transformed the problem by rethinking time as a 'form' in which the mind 'apprehends phenomena'. He did not mention that time presupposes change, but eventually concluded that time as a form of apprehending phenomena is independent of change, which led to the idea of 'subjective time'.

'Why was the world not created sooner?' Augustine asked, and answered himself with 'Because there was no sooner'. Bertrand Russell considered this 'a very admirable relativistic theory of time, a great advance on anything to be found on the subject in Greek philosophy', and 'a better and clearer statement than Kant's on the subjective theory of time'. Augustine's reasoning was that the present is a moment in time that can be measured only while the moment is passing, i.e., past and future can only be thought of as present. 'Past' is identified with memory, 'future' with expectation, but both are conceived during present moments. It follows that time is in the human mind, which expects, considers, and remembers, and that there can be no time without a created being; thus to speak of time before the Creation is meaningless. Augustine clarifies his position in Chapter XX of the *Confessions*: 'The present of things past is memory; the present of things present is sight; and the present of things future is expectation.' Not completely understanding this himself, he concluded his perturbations with a prayer for enlightenment: 'I confess to Thee, O Lord, that I am as yet ignorant of what time is.' Russell, of course, does not agree with Augustine's theory in that it makes time something mental, an aspect of our thoughts, but he affirms Augustine's anticipation of Descartes, Gassendi and Kant.

Stravinsky believed in memory as the primary creative source, a corollary from Augustine, whose work he read (the twentieth, twenty-eighth and thirtieth chapters of the *Confessions*) during his years at St Petersburg University and again decades later in California. In Paris, in the 1920s, he had been close to the Russian émigré philosophers Nicolai Berdyaev and Leo Shestov, and also came under the spell of Bergson and the idea of *Le Temps retrouvé*; but by this date Russell had demolished Bergson's theory of 'subjective' and 'intuitive' time with the simple elenchus: 'It confounds the memory of the past event with the past event itself, *the thought with that which is thought about.*'

Though William Blake was ahead of us – 'I see Past, Present and

Future, existing all at once / Before me' – now, in the twenty-first century, we have written off the distinction between the three as simply a matter of perception, or, as Einstein said, an 'illusion'. The B-theory of time, which defines the universe as a four-dimensional entity, rejects the argument of the 'presentists', namely that only the present moment is real. This is controverted in terms of transitory tense-properties.

All concepts of time are oppressive, compelling us to recognise the flux of perpetual perishing, hence the turning of the mind-set from time to space in the last few hundred years. In *The Concept of Dread*, Kierkegaard remarks that the 'spatialising of the moment brings the infinite succession to a standstill'. Gurnemanz in *Parsifal* sings that in the Temple of the Grail, 'Time becomes space': no wonder cyclical concepts developed, the parcelling into periodicities, the returns to identities, and to Vico's *Scienza Nuova*. But could human societies survive without structuring time? Life in the civilisations that developed astronomical – solar and lunar – systems is unbearable even to contemplate. What a relief to turn to the Greeks, who never tortured themselves with meditations on indefinite duration, and who, before Eratosthenes, in the third century, seem to have had little concern for chronology.

Chapter 14

George Balanchine

A Memoir

For a Balanchine Centenary Symposium[1]

My first Balanchine ballet was the audacious, body-suit-nude 'Bacchanale' in the Metropolitan Opera's *Tannhäuser*, at Christmas 1937. My first glimpses of Balanchine himself were in 1946, as a member of the Ballet Society, when I watched him rehearse Stravinsky's *Renard*. I first met him on 5 April 1948, at Stravinsky's apartment in the now demolished Ambassador Hotel, Fifty-Second Street and Park Avenue. The composer had arrived by night train from Washington only a few hours before. When I entered his hotel room he and Balanchine were vigorously discussing the forthcoming premiere of their new ballet, *Orpheus*. Balanchine was cordial to me but puzzled; Stravinsky always had a retinue of Nadia Boulanger students, but not in his hotel room. The choreographer was also very nervous and snorted like a cocaine addict.

One would have had to be Russian-speaking in order to understand the exchanges between the two men. They slipped into American only infrequently and very briefly, out of politeness to Balanchine's wife, Maria Tallchief, and myself. Not until the time of *Agon* (1954) would they become fully effective in their adopted tongue,

---

1   Presented at New York State Theater, 17 May 2004.

notwithstanding Stravinsky's heavily accented and maddeningly macaronic vocabulary, and Balanchine's anacolutha and tendency to omit verbs. By the time of *The Flood* (1962), they spoke fluent, resourceful, never quite correct English. But verbal language was not their principal means of communication: Stravinsky could articulate his musical ideas at the piano, Balanchine his choreographic ones through gesture and movement.

Balanchine had convinced Stravinsky to extend not only the *Orpheus pas de deux*, which even Diaghilev would hardly have dared to propose, but also to repeat the Prelude to *The Flood* near the end of the play, thereby changing its theology as well as its dramatic shape. How different was the relationship in 1937, when Stravinsky obliged Balanchine to change the décor in *Jeu de cartes* and amend bits of the choreography. People who knew both artists at that time – Lucia Davidova was one – affirm that the composer tended to treat his young collaborator imperiously, having only *Apollo* as proof of his genius. But I think that *Jeu de cartes*, with no *Adagio pas de deux*, and hence no love interest, did not inspire Balanchine.

Balustrade (1941) marks Stravinsky's new appreciation of the young 'ballet master', as Balanchine wished to be called even in his magisterial late years. Stravinsky rated the choreography of this ballet above that of all of Balanchine's other ballets up to *Movements*. In April and May of 1943, the two artists worked again in performances of *Apollo* revived by Lucia Chase's ballet company at the Metropolitan Opera. Their next collaboration was *Danses concertantes* (1944), under the auspices of Serge Denham's Ballet Russe de Monte Carlo. Balanchine had worked out the choreography in the summer of 1944 for a New York premiere on 10 September, and, according to Eugene Berman, the ballet's scenery and costume designer, revised it for a performance conducted by Stravinsky in Los Angeles in December.

———◆———

The change in the personal and professional relationship between the two colossi came in 1942 with the *Circus Polka*, for which Balanchine managed to wheedle a substantial commission for Stravinsky from the Ringling Brothers. At about the same time, Balanchine married

Vera Zorina, who, under his tutelage, became a fine dancing actress (Ariel in *The Tempest*) and film star (*I Married An Angel*; the *Goldwyn Follies*; *On Your Toes*). The scenario and dance numbers of the next ballet, *Orpheus*, were plotted in Stravinsky's Hollywood studio in June 1946, and it was there that Balanchine presented an original thirty-two-note melody to Stravinsky for his sixty-fourth birthday, together with a quatrain, or chastushka, of Russian lyrics in which each line begins with a letter of the name 'Igor'.

Stravinsky added three-part harmony to the thirty-two notes, thereby turning the piece into an acrostic for *a cappella* mixed chorus. Not anticipating a performance, he omitted rhythmic values and a tempo indication, but shaped the melody in an original way at the chorale-like cadences. On the centenary of Stravinsky's birth, 18 June 1982, Balanchine authorised a facsimile publication of the manuscript in *Dance Index*. The tiny piece exemplifies Stravinskian characteristics of voice-leading, contrary motion, octave doubling, preference – in tonic harmony – for the first inversion over the root position, and harmony that features major and minor seconds: twenty-six of the thirty-two chords include one or the other, ten of the twenty-six include two sets of them; and one includes three.

Balanchine's text could be translated as:

> This is the day of your angel and your birthday!
> Guests chatter and are joyful!
> We will get drunk on Grand Marnier!
> Don't forget to give me a glass!

The last line hints at Balanchine's social vulnerability.

Stravinsky's full realisation of Balanchine's musical gifts came in New York between rehearsals for *Orpheus*. On 20 April 1948, Stravinsky saw him conduct Tchaikovsky's string Serenade for a performance by Ballet Theater. In tempi, phrasing, flow and refinement, this was a lifetime experience, utterly unlike anything Stravinsky had ever witnessed. Balanchine could have become a great 'maestro', but fortunately was content to remain what he so perfectly was. It is still not generally known that in the early 1950s he occasionally conducted ballet orchestra rehearsals. With due respect to Leon Barzin, Robert Irving and Hugo Fiorato, the players told me they much preferred playing it under Balanchine.

In the period between *Orpheus* and *The Rake's Progress* (1951) we attended as many Balanchine ballet performances as possible and saw him with increasing frequency. Stravinsky played his new opera for him at the piano as he composed it and chose him to stage-direct the American premiere at the Metropolitan Opera in February 1953.

I next saw Balanchine in California in the summer of 1953, for the first time without Stravinsky. The New York City Ballet was in Los Angeles for a season in the Greek Theatre. Something called twelve-tone music was in the air at the time, and Mr B. was determined to choreograph an example of it by its creator. He telephoned Gertrud Schoenberg, the composer's widow, proposing to barbecue a dinner for her and her family to discuss the matter. When Balanchine was assured that Stravinsky would be in the hospital recovering from a prostatectomy on 29 July, he chose that date for the dinner. On the 25th, Mrs Schoenberg called and invited me, explaining that she knew nothing about ballet repertory and was apprehensive about receiving the celebrated choreographer. Would I help? Her daughter, Nuria, would bake a cake for me.

When I arrived at the Schoenberg home in Brentwood, Balanchine was presiding over the grill on the spacious side-lawn, the dinner already on the fire. He was embarrassed to be seen there by me. Not until we were seated at table was anything said about seeking permission to base a ballet on one of Schoenberg's twelve-tone pieces. Since Balanchine knew no music by Schoenberg after *Verklärte Nacht*, I suggested that the *Accompaniment to a Cinematographic Scene*, Op. 34, could be used for a ballet, partly because it is short, structurally simple (large arcs), drivingly rhythmic, and does not require a large orchestra. When Richard Hoffmann, Schoenberg's ex-assistant, questioned whether a ballet orchestra could manage such difficult music, an offended Balanchine replied that the New York City Ballet repertory was more difficult than the New York Philharmonic's, which was true. When Hoffmann insensitively countered with the non sequitur that 'Schoenberg's music is more difficult than Stravinsky's',

Balanchine began to bridle but said nothing. Soon after this he left with his wife Tanaquil LeClercq and her mother, but not until an agreement had been reached to produce Opus 34.

The following day, in the Stravinsky house – the composer was still in the hospital – I explained the pitch organisation of Opus 34 and its proportional scheme of tempi to Mr B., and we listened several times to a fuzzy tape of the piece by a German Rundfunk orchestra. He grasped the music's dramatic scheme immediately, but reasonably wondered why a twelve-tone composition began and ended in triadic harmony (E flat minor). We listened again the next day, and the next, and the happy outcome was the inception of his ballet *Opus 34*, first performed on 19 January 1954 by the New York City Ballet at the City Center of Music and Drama on West Fifty-Fifth Street. More exactly, the ballet was performed twice, both times with copious quotients of wrong notes, first to abstract choreography, second to a hospital scene inspired by *The Cabinet of Doctor Caligari.*

I was a catalyst for other Schoenberg-related Balanchine ballets, including his half of the Webern *Episodes*, and the Brahms Piano Quartet in G minor, in Schoenberg's 1937 orchestration, which Mr B. learned from my Chicago Symphony recording. Anna Kisselgoff describes the NYCB's current performance of the 'Gypsy' section of the last movement as 'sure-fire kitsch', which is true, and the reason the piece did not become, as Schoenberg had hoped, 'The Brahms Fifth'.

———

Agon, a turning point in ballet and music history, was commissioned in the summer of 1953. The collaboration was much closer than for *Orpheus*. Balanchine had now become the composer's co-creator, an equal partner from inception to execution. After working with Stravinsky at his home in Hollywood on 5, 6, 7, 9 and 17 June 1954, Balanchine told the *Los Angeles Times* that 'the building materials of *Agon* are twelve dancers and twelve tones. We constructed every possibility of dividing twelve,' meaning dance duos, trios, quartets, sextets. The next meetings took place two years later, in Venice, Stravinsky having committed himself to complete the *Canticum Sacrum* first.

Arlene Croce has referred to a chart that Stravinsky made during the 1954 conferences which listed the succession of dances with their titles. In fact, Balanchine dictated this to the composer, who drew stick-figures for the dancers in each piece – triangular tutus for females – then stapled and Scotch-taped his pages together lengthwise. The first *pas de quatre* was composed immediately after Balanchine's departure, starting with a fanfare notated in December 1953. The chart reveals that not all of the pieces had been decided in those first meetings, and that the 'Sarabande' and 'Gaillarde' were not entered until completed, months later.

Balanchine's seventy-fifth birthday present to Stravinsky was truly magnanimous: he wanted the composer to hear his new work ahead of its staged premiere, and consented to have it performed in a Los Angeles concert on the eve of the anniversary. From the first rehearsal, Balanchine perceived that the music had miraculously fused jazz idioms with seventeenth-century dance forms. He did not question, as I did, secretly, the recapitulation of the beginning at the end as facile, tacked-on, and hence abnegating.

———◆———

The Flood music was completed before Balanchine's reluctant agreement to choreograph the two dance movements – an incidental assignment, humiliating to him, but no matter, since the staging of the whole was ultimately his achievement. In fact, every aspect of the visual realisation originated with him, again in Stravinsky's pokey Hollywood studio on 14, 15, 16 and 27 March 1962. Ever since Tanaquil LeClercq, the fourth Mrs Balanchine, had been stricken with polio in October 1956, Balanchine had become devoutly religious. This accounts for the Orthodox Church framework of *The Flood*, the Iconostasis (altar screen), and the predominance of the Seraphim. When the New York City Ballet presented the American stage premiere during its Stravinsky Centenary celebration, in June 1982, Balanchine revived ideas he had proposed two decades earlier, including the one for the Garden of Eden. When illness prevented him from completing his work on the staging of this dance-play, John Taras completed it for him, a burdensome and thankless legacy. We owe the deepest gratitude to his memory.

Since my meetings with Balanchine in his post-Stravinsky years are too numerous to catalogue, I shall mention only a few of them. The first picture to come to mind is of him at the private Russian Orthodox memorial service for Stravinsky on the day of the composer's death. Balanchine was ashen, biting his lips. He kneeled for three or four minutes before the flower-mantled bier, then bowed to Mrs Stravinsky. Taking my hand, he quietly thanked me 'for all you did for him'. Wishing to avoid photographers, he did not attend the public funeral service in New York three days later. I saw him next on returning from the interment in Venice. This meeting took place in the garden gazebo of Lucia Davidova's Seventy-Seventh Street home.

Balanchine was eager to tell me of his project to present a week-long Stravinsky Festival the following year, starting on the composer's ninetieth birthday, and we spent hours discussing the orders of the programmes and of their ballets. He asked me to conduct the first and last evenings and some pieces in between. When we met again the next day I could not agree with some of his choices (the early Symphony in E flat, which is as full of hot air as a Montgolfier balloon), and still less with such omissions as *Renard*, *Les Noces* and *Petrushka*. I knew, of course, that the culminant judgement would be his, and that Stravinsky himself could not have prevailed on him to mount *Petrushka*, not for Mr B.'s avowed reason (his dislike of realistic Russian pictorialism), but because of personal issues. First, this ballet had created the legend of Nijinsky, whose saltatory Olympic style was remote from Balanchine's dedication to the art of classical choreography. The second obstacle was that at this time *Petrushka* was regarded as virtually the personal property of Leonid Massine, who, as a rival for the affections of Balanchine's former wife, Vera Zorina, was an unmentionable name. (I can say this because I was with her in a CBS recording studio on 14 January 1957, when Massine, appearing unexpectedly, so flustered her that she later confided the whole story to me.)

To return to the NYCB Stravinsky memorial week, I attended many of Mr B.'s piano, and all of his orchestra, rehearsals. He consulted me on questions of tempi and the minutiae of inflections within them. He was always fascinating to watch, and particularly so during orchestra rehearsals, telling the conductors, as well as the players individually, how to articulate, shape a phrase, adjust tone colours and intensities. One can only deplore that every moment of this was not filmed and recorded.

The programmes and sequences of ballets were constantly changing. At the dress rehearsal for the opening night, the order of the Symphony in Three Movements and the Violin Concerto was reversed, as should have happened from the beginning, chamber music faring better before than after a noisy symphony. I had suggested the violin soloist – Joseph Silverstein of the Boston Symphony – and we spent a morning with Balanchine 'fixing' the tempi. This, by the way, is the most difficult requirement for ballet conductors: the same speed must be maintained at every performance, which Stravinsky himself could not do. Mr B. shirked the onus of informing me, delegating Lincoln Kirstein instead, that the Symphony in Three, which I was to conduct, would follow the Concerto. I had understood from the beginning that Mr B. was intent on showing his Concerto choreography first, and was delighted with the decision.

One final incident in connection with that first Stravinsky Festival. The concluding work on the last night was not a ballet but a concert performance of the Symphony of Psalms, with the whole company seated on stage listening. I proposed to Mr B. that he invite Leonard Bernstein, that master of gala occasions, to conduct; but Balanchine pointed heavenwards and said: '*He* would want you to do it'.

I conducted during the Saratoga season that summer and naturally saw Mr B. many times. He failed to conceal his annoyance that his then guardian angel, Karin von Aroldingen, befriended me.

I saw Mr. B. in Moscow in 1962, when the Soviet government was trying to keep him and Stravinsky apart, and saw him in New York two weeks later, during a mid-tour break in which he discussed with the composer the ordeal of teaching *Agon* to a Soviet orchestra. In Hamburg in 1965, while I recorded Stravinsky's Variations, Mr B. worked with me, and more importantly, with Suzanne Farrell, who has charmingly described dancing the piece at a later date in the empty State Theatre for Mr B. and Stravinsky alone.

After Stravinsky's death, Mr B. consulted with me about his experimental cuts in the first part of *Apollo*. He flew to Los Angeles several times to be with Stravinsky during his later illnesses, and was ill himself when he began the centenary week, though he attended his, Vera Zorina's and my rehearsals of *Perséphone* and *The Flood.*

I heard the news of Balanchine's death in Venice, mercifully from a close friend, rather than from a newspaper. Having just returned from placing flowers on the twin Stravinsky graves in the cemetery island of San Michele, I recrossed the lagoon and placed a third bouquet next to theirs.

Chapter 15

Stravinsky, Auden and the *Rake*

A Memoir

Igor Stravinsky and W.H. Auden created the scenario of *The Rake's Progress* in the composer's Hollywood home between 11 and 18 November 1947. The subject was Stravinsky's choice, but the 'moral fable' concept and the three-act structure of the libretto in the draft completed together were Auden's work. Back in New York on 20 November Auden sent what he described as a 'bread-and-butter letter (how do you say that in Russian?)' to Mrs Stravinsky and a note in French to her husband explaining a necessary revision in the first scene: the hero's inheritance should result not from the death of his father, which would destroy the pastoral tone, but from that of an unknown uncle. Inspired by the story of the opera, but with no words to set, Stravinsky composed the Prelude to the Graveyard Scene in Act Three, completing it on 11 December.

I met Stravinsky for the first time in the same moment that Auden gave the completed libretto to him, in Washington, DC, on 31 March 1948. I kept a record of their changes in the *Rake* libretto that day: the line in the Cabaletta was amended to 'Or be forgotten'. A more important change was the addition of the pact between Shadow and Rakewell not found in the original. Auden titled this dialogue 'Orchestral Recitative' but Stravinsky wrote over it 'Recitative Secco'. Five weeks later, returning to Hollywood from New York, Stravinsky began work on the opera on 8 May, adding the title 'Festival of May', from the second line of the libretto, to his first sketches. When I visited him there at the end of July, he had completed the draft score through Shadow's line, 'You are a rich man' (scene 1), and in the quartet that follows was sketching Rakewell's part, underscoring it with a sprinkling of bass notes and an incipit of the string accompaniment. On my first day in Stravinsky's home, 31 July 1948, he played, sang and groaned the music for me, stripped to his sleeveless undershirt and the gold cross and talismanic religious medals that hung around his neck. The visceral intensity and concentration of his performance, reflecting the throes of creation, seemed too private to watch, and at first I wanted to escape the intimacy of the small, soundproofed room. His renditions of the soprano and tenor parts were, respectively, two and one octave lower than the written pitch, and in his struggles to find the orchestra's notes on the piano from his sketch-score, all sense of tempi and rhythm disappeared. He mispronounced every word ('Tom' came out as 'Tome') and since he had never overcome his born-to pronunciation of w's as guttural v's, or shed his thick Russian accent, the text was unrecognisable. At the end, bathed in perspiration, his face beamed with pleasure and pride.

I heard no more of the opera until February 1949, when he played the completed first act for Auden, Balanchine and me in a New York apartment. (The first scene was finished on 3 October 1948; the second was begun two days later; and the third is dated 16 January 1949.) By the time of my arrival at the Stravinsky house, 1 June 1949, he had written the *da capo* tenor aria at the beginning of Act Two. But he was puzzled about the next pieces to be composed, having reservations about Auden's *acte gratuit* explanation of Baba the Turk and Shadow's arguments for Rakewell to marry her, which he thought specious at best, infra dig at worst, and more likely to baffle than to convince an opera audience.

During the gestation of the last two acts, I enjoyed the privilege of being able to observe the external signs of Stravinsky's creative processes at close range, and in fact was directly involved in their first step. He would ask me to read aloud, over and over and at varying speeds, the lines of whichever aria, recitative or ensemble he was about to set to music. He would then memorise them, a line or a couplet at a time, and walk about the house repeating them, or while seated in his wife's car en route to a restaurant, movie, doctor's, dentist's or lawyer's appointment. The vocabulary was quite unfamiliar to him, but he soon learned it and began to use it in his own conversation, charging one of us with 'dilatoriness', or himself of having to 'impose' upon us, which sounded very odd from him. It can be said that his transformation from a primarily Russian- and French-speaking to an American-speaking artist took place in correspondence with the composition of the opera, and that after the *Rake* and until the end of his life, this voracious reader confined himself almost exclusively to books in English, with the exception of the *romans-policiers* of Georges Simenon.

In setting words, Stravinsky began by writing rhythms in musical notation above them, note-stems with beams indicating time values – crotchets (quarters), quavers (eighths), semiquavers (sixteenths), triplets and so forth. In the act of doing this, melodic, intervallic and harmonic ideas would occur to him, and be included in the same line or just above. In Shadow's 'giddy multitude' aria, for example, the pitches and harmony attached to the words 'ought of their duties' came to the composer's imagination during his preliminary sketch of rhythms, and remained unchanged in the final score. In the *Rake*, tonalities and harmonies were rarely revised from first notation to full score, whereas melodic lines, rhythms, note-values, metres and instrumentation were subject to alterations and last-minute refinements.

A fair number of 'X'-ings-out, followed by rewrites, are found in the sketches. If an ongoing melodic, harmonic or rhythmic development suggested itself after a draft had been completed, Stravinsky would add it in a blank space in his manuscript, squeezing it into a corner or cranny of even the most crowded page, circling it like a speech-balloon in a comic-strip, and drawing a line, sometimes long and winding but with arrows and road signs, to the place for insertion in the main sketch. Staves were drawn with his several different sizes of stylus (he did not use printed music paper) on large sheets of manila that he thumb-tacked or clipped to a corkboard on the music rack of his piano. The full orchestra score was written with a soft lead pencil on sensitised transparent music paper, sprayed to prevent smudging, and reproduced by the ammonia vapour Ozalid process. For this work he wrote at a slanted desk with the draft score on a stand just above, and would carefully plot the numbers of bars and score systems to fit each page. In passages of comparatively complex orchestration, he would scribble a trial bar or two in full score, in pencil, on loose sheets of yellow carbon typewriting paper. If his layout of a score page proved less than perfect, though this happened rarely, he would rewrite it in its entirety rather than erase. His well-known remark that music should be composed 'avec la gomme' is a criticism of the works of others, not of his own.

Composition was exclusively daytime work for Stravinsky in 1949–51. He began by playing the music he had written the day before. I often joined him in this, taking the treble parts, since he insisted on playing the bass himself. The task of orchestrating, not unduly onerous in his case, since he had already assigned most of the instruments and worked out the voice-leadings in the drafts, was reserved for the evenings. Quite regularly, at his request, I read to him during these soirées. From time to time he would interrupt me in order to concentrate on an intricacy of some kind, or to try out a chord on the piano, then say, 'And?' He was especially keen to hear Russian literature in English: Lermontov, Gogol, Shestov, Rozanov, Goncharov, whose *Oblomov* was one of his all-time favourites. But the first book that we finished was Frances Calderón de la Barca's classic, *Life in Mexico* (1843), in the Everyman edition. He remembered this at least as long as I did, which suggests that he had a compartmented mind, able to follow a narrative and mechanically copy and transpose a musical score at the same time.

Stravinsky entered indications for instrumentation in even the earliest sketches, and rarely revised them thereafter. Two instances of the latter come to mind, the initial draft of the reprise of the choral march in the Brothel scene specifies the second horn as the obbligato instrument. Not until writing the final draft did he recognise that the part would stand out more distinctly in the trumpet. Second, Shadow's entrances are associated with flourishes on the harpsichord. After the first of these, in response to Rakewell's 'I wish I had money', he pronounces the protagonist's name, whereupon a shorter flourish follows, played by cembalo in the original sketch and provided therewith keyboard fingerings. The final score transfers this to bassoon, partly because the wind-instrument 'echo' adds a parodistic element.

Stravinsky reshaped melodies as he worked. A small but stunning improvement in this sense is the rewriting, a third higher in the last version than in the first, of the last three notes for the line, 'the heart for love dare everything'. In its first form, too, the trumpet solo in the Prelude to Act Two, scene two, develops differently from the way we know it, and in the first sketch Baba the Turk's breakfast patter is purely rhythmic, acquiring a melody en route. In the early sketches the line is frequently interrupted by rests, until Stravinsky realised that breathlessness is the dramatic intent, which he then achieved by converting the quavers (eighth notes) followed by rests to semiquavers (sixteenth notes). I should also mention that this first Baba aria was composed after the second, the trumpet solo after the aria it introduces. Stravinsky did not always compose in the order of the libretto.

Yet what strikes us most about Stravinsky's composing procedures is not the discrepancies between first and final versions but the overwhelming degree of resemblance, despite the enormous growth of his powers as an opera composer from the early to the ultimate scenes. Consider only one aspect of this, the ever-greater naturalness of the word-setting. Thomas Campion's songs and those in Shakespeare's plays are words for music, words to be sung with or without an instrumental accompaniment. They do not express ideas and are as simple in thought as possible, unlike, for example, those lyrics of Donne's, which, if sung, would make their sense difficult to follow. The opening scene of the *Rake* follows the Shakespeare–Campion principle of simplicity and pure verbal music:

> *The woods are green, and bird and beast at play,*
> *For all things keep this festival of May.*

Collaborating with Henry Purcell on *King Arthur*, John Dryden complained of having to 'cramp' his verses. He accepted the constriction because 'operas are principally designed for the ear and the eye... My art ought to be subject to his,' to which Mozart added, a century later, 'Poetry absolutely has to be the obedient daughter of music'. At an opposite extreme, Pierre Corneille insisted that the true poet's inspiration 'is powerless when it depends for utterance on the capricious tunes of a musical dreamer; when it must take its laws from his strange whims... when rhymes must be adapted to every musical inflection'. Rhyming verse, we should bear in mind, is the norm in seventeenth-century French poetic drama, as blank verse is in English, Dryden himself being the qualified exception. The dialogue in his early rhyming-couplet plays is generally thought to be more 'natural' than the dialogue in his later blank-verse plays, of which *All for Love* is the most popular. In opera, Dryden advocated short, unrhymed lines for recitatives, longer lines for the 'songish parts'. Stravinsky, of the same mind, nevertheless sets the wordy narrative recitative about the forgotten uncle as an arioso.

By the time he began work on the opera, Stravinsky had steeped himself in Elizabethan music that offered precedents aplenty in the matter of accented weak syllables (Morley's 'and sweet wild ros*es*', Wilbye's 'with smiling glanc*es*'). Moreover, his preference for the French scansion of franglais words, as in the allocation of but one note to 'uncle' (*oncle*) – at the opposite extreme from Handel's German habit of pronouncing everything, even making a dissyllable of 'whole' – was an obstacle only when he first started to compose. But in Act Three, words and music fuse and complement each other. Accent and metre, syllable sound and vocal register, are in agreement. Here Stravinsky feels the right speeds and pitch range for polysyllables ('dilatoriness') and the orchestration that enhances verbal articulation, as in the accompaniment, *pizzicati* with crisp double-tongued trumpet notes, which make the consonants sparkle in the Bedlam chorus:

> *Banker, beggar, whore and wit,*
> *In a common darkness sit.*

The piping viola harmonics and high, rasping oboe in this same minuet, I should add, perfectly evoke the atmosphere of Bedlam.

To some extent the greater flow and continuity in the third

act than in the first two can be attributed to the reduction in the number of secco-recitatives, and to thematic and stylistic linkages from scene to scene, most obviously the varied forms of the Ballad-Tune (itself indebted to the Mozart A major Piano Sonata, K.331), and most profoundly the embellishments that stylise Rakewell's fear in the graveyard and, still more floridly, in the death scene ('A swan-like music'). Above all, Act Three has genuine musical and dramatic power, in the throbbing orchestral climax accompanying Shadow's 'I burn, I freeze', during his descent to Hell, and in the quiet, hollow unison, the only one in the opera, of the chorus's 'Madman, no one has been here'.

The First Performance

The premiere of the opera, in Venice on 11 September 1951, was an *ancien-régime* event befitting the period, subject and style of the opera. All pedestrian approaches to the Teatro La Fenice were cordoned off to segregate affluent ticket holders from members of the Fourth Estate who had come to gape at them. The super-rich arrived at the theatre's canal-side entrance in private gondolas and motoscaffi. The audience for this last great gala, as it seemed then and infinitely more so now, was 'Perfumed, well-dressed, And looking [its] best', as Shadow tells Rakewell he must be himself, as 'A bachelor of fashion'. The audience was in evening clothes, and the rustle of long silk dresses and the glitter of diamond necklaces and tiaras were sounds and sights that I have not heard and seen since.

The Fenice itself was pre-1789: red-plush loges with bouquets of white roses pinned to them, cherubs swinging from the Tiepolo-blue ceiling, and periwigged grooms in gold-embroidered livery holding candelabras at each entrance. Embedded like an oculus in the ceiling above the orchestra was a large round clock that had probably not kept time since the premiere of *Rigoletto* here 100 years earlier. How perfectly appropriate for Stravinsky's tonality-affirming, small-orchestra *bel canto* opera, alternating aria and harpsichord-recitative, as distinguished from the atonal, large symphonic, and quasi-spoken kind. At the same time, *The Rake's Progress* has proved as resilient to re-interpretation through period-changing and cultural transposition as any opera in the permanent repertory in which it seems to have won a place. Ingmar Bergman successfully made the opera nineteenth-century and Swedish, and Sarah Caldwell's 1968 updating, in which Shadow entered in a Rolls-Royce hearse, and Baba the Turk was a male transvestite who did a sit-in at Leonardo's *Last Supper*, was a 'smash hit'.

The Problems of the Drama

The hero's hypocrisy, fraudulence and dishonesty are exposed even before his first aria, when, after a brief encounter with his intended father-in-law, the latter exits and the former says of him, 'The old fool'. In the piece that follows, the hero sings: 'Why should I labour / For what in the end / She will give me for nothing if she be my friend?' Halfway through the opera, the Rake's betrothed comes to London to find him. They join in a love duet, musically one of the most moving pieces in the opera, but which he follows by revealing that he has betrayed her by marrying the freakish Baba the Turk, to whom he then brutally identifies his fiancée as 'only a milkmaid, pet, to whom I was in debt', thus making a mockery of the feelings he has just avowed. Fortunately the music stays with us and suggests that at some level the emotion is true, and the final scene of the opera confirms the love. But these earlier revelations of the hero as amoral, double-dealing and base perplex the audience and nearly destroy the opera.

Mother Goose's[1] London whorehouse, the setting of scene two, is the first step, *Le Plaisir* in Auden's scheme of Tom's progress. The words are Auden at his best, and they launch the *Rake* anew with some of the most felicitous verse in all opera. Having composed a fast-tempo chorus in which the whores and their clients sing of their wish to keep the aubade at bay, Stravinsky asked Auden for an additional stanza. In the one the poet provided – the *first* quatrain

---

1   'Goose' was Elizabethan slang for Southwark whore. Auden may have borrowed the term 'roaring boys', for the male clients in Mother Goose's establishment, from Thomas Dekker's play *The Roaring Girl* (1608).

below: Stravinsky had already set the one with the arresting last line
– staccato consonants and simple rhymes, abetted by syncopation in
the music, confer the utmost clarity on every syllable:

> *Soon dawn will glitter outside the shutter*
> *And small birds twitter; but what of that?*
> *So long as we're able and wine's on the table*
> *Who cares what the troubling day is at?*
> *While food has flavor and limbs are shapely*
> *And hearts beat bravely to fiddle or drum*
> *Our proper employment is reckless enjoyment*
> *For too soon the noiseless night will come.*

Half a minute further into the opera, Auden adroitly contrasts this
with a transfixing slow-tempo lyric, greatly enhanced in its musical
setting by the remoteness of the tonality:

> *Love, too frequently betrayed*
> *For some plausible desire*
> *Or the world's enchanted fire,*
> *Still thy traitor in his sleep*
> *Resumes the vow he did not keep,*
> *Weeping, weeping,*
> *He kneels before thy wounded shade.*

In the opening scene of Act Two, Rakewell, weary and alone in his
London house, sings of disenchantment with his life in the city,
ending his aria with the spoken line: 'I wish I were happy'. Shadow
enters initially in response, and unfurls a broadsheet likeness of Baba
the Turk, a bearded lady circus artiste, the librettists' substitution for,
and improvement on, Hogarth's merely rich Ugly Duchess. 'Do you
desire her?' he asks. 'Like the gout or the falling sickness.' 'Then marry
her,' Shadow says, going on to explain that happiness is obtainable
only through freedom from Passion and Reason, those 'twin tyrants
of appetite and conscience'. How happiness can result from being
shackled to an intolerable mate is not explained, but neither is the

insuperable problem of making dramatic sense out of this next step in Auden's scheme of Rakewell's progress, 'L'Acte gratuit'.

Inexplicably, Rakewell agrees to the 'joke', as Auden later referred to the episode, ignoring the pain that it will bring to his hero's forgotten fiancée. The audience does not believe Shadow's argument, of course, and cannot adjust to the jolt and the burlesque into which the opera then sinks, to rise again only in the final two scenes. To forestall criticism of this turn of events at the US premiere of the *Rake* (Metropolitan Opera, 14 February 1953), Auden (or Kallman, or both, or someone else) explained in a synopsis of the plot contributed to the programme book that 'since Tom is neither attracted to Baba nor obligated to her, he can therefore prove his freedom and obtain happiness by the completely unemotional and irrational act of marrying her'. But do irrational and emotionally indifferent acts hurtful to innocent others bring happiness to those who commit them? Addressing the same criticism again on a 1958 BBC Television broadcast of the last five scenes (i.e., after the marriage to Baba), Auden wrote a Prologue, to be spoken by Shadow, that further compounds the difficulty: 'Look on this portrait of strange womankind,' Shadow says here (in the opera he describes Baba as a 'Gorgon'), and

> *Marry her, Tom! Be happy and rejoice,*
> *Knowing you know no motive for your choice*
> ....
> *Perhaps you ask, dear viewers, how this man*
> *Could think of marriage and not think of Anne*
> *... but pride*
> *Soon won his guilty conscience to my side.*

The viewer does indeed ask why Tom does not think of Anne. But whereas vanity is a feature of Tom's personality at the start of the opera, it is not much in evidence by this time. In an afterthought, Auden diagnosed Rakewell as a 'manic-depressive', for whom (as with the rest of us) 'the anticipation of experience is always exciting and its realisation always disappointing'. The psychosis, he weakly pretended, 'allowed for musical contrasts of moods'.

Auden has written that 'the librettist supplies the words, the characters and the plot', and of these 'the words are the least important'. This is not true of *The Rake's Progress*. The plot is creaky, if not extravagantly so by operatic standards. 'Opera plots allow that sort of marvelous and surprising conduct which is rejected in other plays,' Dryden observed. Chester Kallman's notes for a 1964 record album recognised that the scene in which Tom dreams of a machine that will turn stones into bread and thus put an end to poverty is 'impossibly difficult to put across', not, presumably, because of the absurdity of the apparatus, but because credulity on such a scale is unimaginable, even in Tom Rakewell. Auden disagreed and defended the scene as showing Rakewell 'further removed from reality', forgetting that Rakewell becomes insane as a consequence of Shadow's curse, not gradually, as the result of events.

Kallman's hindsights further acknowledge that 'Anne is a soprano. Period.' Which is to say she is devoid of anything remotely like a psychological make-up. Auden's 1968 Salzburg lecture on opera concedes that Rakewell, far from being a Hogarthian toss-pot, is 'almost entirely passive', adding, however, that 'the more willful [an opera] character the better, the more passive the worse'. Still second-guessing, Auden went so far as to attribute Shadow's defeat by Rakewell in the card game to his 'over-confidence' – whereas the actual fault is his procrastination ('My own delay cost me my prey') – which is to imbue a supernatural being, who has the power to turn time backward, with a human weakness. Shadow, of course, is the opera's willful character.

This leaves Baba, who, in the previous scene, in befriending Anne and warning her to beware of Shadow, becomes the one endearing member of the ménage, a considerate person who does not linger over her wounds but determines to go back to the stage and bravely forward with her life.

———

Some of Auden's words inspired immortal music. Consider the perfect match of Anne's berceuse with flutes and the childlike simplicity and gentleness of

Lion, lamb and deer,
Untouched by greed or fear
About the woods are straying:
            And quietly now
The blossoming bough
Sway, sway, sway
Above the fair unclouded brow.

And consider the unification of the poetry and music in Bedlam, where mad Tom, thinking he is Adonis, embraces Anne, whom he imagines as Venus:

In a foolish dream, in a gloomy labyrinth
I hunted shadows, disdaining thy true love;
....
Rejoice, belovèd, in these fields of Elysium
Space cannot alter, nor time our love abate;
Here has no words for absence or estrangement
            now a notion of almost or too late.

Chapter 16

Stravinsky in Santa Fe

A Memoir

In midsummer 1950 Igor Stravinsky conducted two concerts, a week apart, in an Aspen circus tent. The first was the more memorable because of his attire: blue jeans, sandals, sleeveless and open-neck shirt with red bandanna. A spokesman explained that because the Stravinskys had driven from California in order to visit Yellowstone Park, he sent his concert clothes ahead by train, unaware of an impending railroad strike. The audience was amused by the predicament and even applauded him. On arrival in Aspen, the composer and his wife were greeted with Russian-style smooching and bear-hugging by their longtime friends, the duo-pianists Victor Babin and Vitya Vronsky, who were also performing there, and who invited them to their Santa Fe home during the intervening week. On the morning of 3 August we crossed the partly snow-blocked Independence Pass, reaching Taos in time to visit the pre-Conquistador Pueblo with its terraced, cube-shaped dwellings connected by ladders. The Indians, selling jewellery, pottery, serapes, woven Navajo rugs and rebozos, seemed curiously remote and incommunicative. D.H. Lawrence refers to them as 'a tribe of 600 Indians who have been there since the Flood'.

The Babins had told us that his young friends, Miranda Esperanza Masocco and Bob Davidson, would be joining us in Taos for dinner at the Sage Brush Inn. Miranda was an intimate of Frieda Lawrence, he said, and could introduce us to her, as well as to Mabel Dodge Luhan and the Hon. Dorothy Brett (still in thrall to Lawrence twenty years after his death), as well as, in Santa Fe, to Witter Bynner, the last of Lawrence's New Mexican friends.

The next morning we drove to Frieda's Kiowa Ranch, a few miles from Taos at the foot of the San Cristobal Mountains. She came to the door, a stoutish woman in a loose white frock, more *Hausfrau* than *Baronin*, blue-eyed, whitish-blond hair, welcoming us in a husky, penetrating voice. Her German-accented English resembled Stravinsky's in the v's for w's, but her *Gemütlichkeit* was too ebullient. (He used to say that he married Vera Sudeykina because of the softness of her voice.) While Frieda proudly exhibited framed samples of Lawrence's embroideries and crochet work – difficult to imagine him at such sedentary occupations – Capitano Angelino Ravagli entered the room. Everyone knew him as the real-life Lady Chatterley's lover, to which he had added a reputation here for canoodling with local girls. He was the first character *from* a novel I had ever met – and what a character, and what a novel, at least in the unexpurgated edition, which Lawrence referred to as 'full fine flower with pistil and stamens standing'.

As we left, Frieda urged us to see the small wooden chapel carpentered by Angelino on the crest of a nearby hill to enshrine Lawrence's ashes, brought from France in 1935. She laughingly described the New York Customs officials initially declining to admit the banned writer's immoral embers.

Though knowing of her continuing conflict with Frieda, we went on to visit Mabel. (Lawrence wrote, 'We are still friends of Mabel, but don't take this serpent to our bosom... another culture-bearer who hates the white world and loves the Indians out of hate.') We were kept waiting in the scorching sun while she finished dressing, and Miranda showed us in. Tony Luhan, Mabel's Indian husband, looked askance at us from the next room, but did not introduce himself. She was apologetic about her tardy appearance and remained gracious, no doubt assuming that these sophisticated Russians would know that John Reed (*Ten Days That Shook the World* and the only American buried in the Kremlin) had been her first lover. The painter Lady Brett was supposed to arrive, purposely late to show her superior social status, as Miranda later explained, but did not. We recalled that when she acquired a Chevrolet, in 1926, Lawrence warned: 'You'll run over Mexican babies, you'll go over the edge of the Hondo Canyon, and however will you hear when anything is tooting behind you?' The Stravs were ill at ease, however, and after a quick exchange between them in Russian, followed by an excuse in English, we rose to leave.

On the declivity to Santa Fe we were blinded at every turn by vistas of the azure Sangre de Cristo Mountains and the changing hues of the shimmering rutilant desert. In the car Miranda suggested that we drive beyond the city to the Santo Domingo Pueblo to catch the end of the Tewa Indian Corn Dance. We agreed, and soon discovered that this ritual might better be described as a binge. The ground outside the adobe church was strewn with inert, inebriated bodies, which we had to circumnavigate to catch a glimpse of the remaining corybantic celebrants. 'They are Catholics,' Lawrence wrote, but 'still keep to the old religion'.

Back in Santa Fe, the Stravinskys spent the night and the next three with the Babins, and I at Bishop's Lodge, a rustic inn in a piñon wood. Finding my way there became an adventure. In the moonless night I mistook an *arroyo seco* for a road, and drove along a *barranca* before realising that I was lost.

The next day Miranda took us to meet Witter Bynner, who presented a jade buckle to Stravinsky from a collection acquired in China while translating the T'ang poems of *The Jade Mountain* and writing a book on *Laotzu*. In September 1922, Mabel had met the Lawrences' train at Lamy and brought them here for their first night in Santa Fe. D.H.L. washed the dishes. Since his magnetism was the principal subject of our host's conversation, we were surprised a year later when his memoirs of Lawrence revealed so much spite toward him.

That evening Miranda told us that Bynner had been a surrogate father to her. She, her three older sisters and thirty-one-year-old mother had travelled from their birthplace in Venice to join their father in San Francisco. During the train-trip from New York her mother was stricken with an illness and died as they reached Albuquerque. None of the girls – of whom Aurora, the eldest, was only twelve – spoke any English, and in the grief, fear and confusion of the situation all of their documents were lost. Albuquerque did not have a convent and the orphaned children were taken to Santa Fe's Academy of San Loretto. When Aurora reached seventeen and married the Italian proprietor of 'The Thunderbird Shop', Miranda moved in with her and at a precocious but unknown age began to design turquoise jewellery. Bynner discovered her there and, intrigued by the child's intelligence and talents, virtually adopted her, educating her in both English and Spanish.

———•———

On the eve of our return to Aspen, the Stravinskys invited Miranda and Bob to visit them in their Hollywood home. They arrived sooner than expected, probably because Davidson, one of Bynner's poetry pupils, was intent on collecting money owed to him as a scriptwriter for Ralph Levy, a movie and television director best remembered for his numerous Jack Benny and Burns and Allen films. After several unanswered calls, Davidson went to Ralph's posh, momentarily empty Mulholland Drive home and, with my help, sank the patio furniture in the swimming pool.

As it happened, Miranda eventually married Ralph and resided in Hollywood one tier below the Stravinskys and one above Sunset Boulevard, a block east of the housing development on the newly terraced Doheny estate that Ralph jokingly referred to as 'the Jewish rice paddies'. In the 1960s Miranda frequently walked from her new address to the Stravinskys, sometimes bringing friends, among them Dorothy Parker and Roddy McDowell, who produced superb photo portraits of the composer. In 1969, after the Stravinskys sold their house and moved to New York, they entrusted Miranda to dispose of its furniture. The following summer she came to stay with them in Evian, and a year later, after the composer's death, spent weeks with his widow in Biarritz, helping to distract her.

———•———

It was from Miranda, in 1956, that we first heard of John Crosby and his dream of founding an open-air summer opera in Santa Fe. Because of the altitude, the remoteness, the sparse population and the quirky weather, it seemed an impracticable venture, but Crosby was determined. The idea of presenting Stravinsky's *Rake's Progress* near the beginning of the opening season (1957) was also Crosby's, who foresaw that the composer's presence – now a possibility through Miranda – would confer prestige on the new company and attract international publicity. Miranda flew to California to invite Stravinsky, but when he asked about the theatre and she had to admit that work on it had just begun, he dismissed the idea. Crosby persisted, nevertheless, and in a few months a see-through barn with a stage and lean-to roof was actually completed. By this time, the moment was propitious for the composer. He had finished *Agon* and on his seventy-fifth birthday heard it acclaimed in performance. The thought of a respite in Santa Fe, and the prospect of seeing his opera, appealed to him

The Stravinskys left Los Angeles on the 'Super Chief' on 7 July and were met at the Lamy station the next afternoon by Crosby, a welcoming committee, and myself. (I had come from the east the day before, after conducting three seventy-fifth anniversary concerts on Boston Common.) We learned that staging rehearsals for the opera had been underway for several weeks, and that the orchestral ones would begin on the morrow. Stravinsky was relieved to find that the *metteur-en-scène*, Bliss Hebert, had helped to stage Boston University's production of the opera for him in 1953, and that three principals of the cast had also sung it there with him. Only the weather was uncooperative. The dress rehearsal took place in a strong wind that caused an electrical failure. Crosby used to tell a story of trying to hold down one of the tarpaulins on the set and of suddenly realising that another hand helping him was Stravinsky's.

The premiere, slated for the eighteenth, had to be postponed because of thunderstorms, but this probably increased both the anticipation and the next night's 'standing, shouting ovation'. Two musicological footnotes should be recorded here. The composer was expecting to hear a harpsichord in the orchestra, but when the instrument had proved too soft in the open-air theatre, as well as prone to drift radically out of tune, a piano had been substituted. Stravinsky immediately began to rewrite the harpsichord part for piano and by curtain time had almost completed the transcription. Unfortunately he loaned his manuscript to the player, Vernon Hammond, who promised to return it but has not yet done so. (Since he was a Philadelphian, both as resident and in the Greek sense, it may still be recoverable.) The second item is that Stravinsky quashed an insect in a margin of his score, forgot to remove the corpse, and, discovering it years later, drew a tombstone around it with the legend, 'Santa Fe, July 1957'.

Meanwhile we had enjoyed an evening with Miranda and Paul Horgan, our first meeting with the Pulitzer-prizewinning author of *The Rio Grande.* On the 19th, Christopher Isherwood and Don Bachardy came from Malibu for the second and third performances. One of Isherwood's comments on the opera adds a fresh perspective:

> We saw *The Rake's Progress* twice... The opera grew on me. There is something heartlessly brisk in the music which suggests the eighteenth-century equivalent of *Bandwagon.* All aboard for London, sex, success. Oops – you fell off? Too bad! Goodbye – we won't be seeing you again...

Though I had spent many evenings with Miranda and Christopher at the Stravinsky home in Hollywood, I was amazed to discover only now that they had known each other at Bynner's long ago.

Shortly before we left Santa Fe, Crosby introduced Stravinsky to André Senutovitch, a wealthy part-time resident of Los Alamos who had sponsored the *Rake* and wished to commission another opera for the company. Stravinsky wrote to T.S. Eliot, proposing a collaboration – they had been discussing one in London – but his reply doubted that he had any talents for libretto-writing, while also making clear that he did not think Auden/Kallman possessed them in bountiful measure either. In any case, Senutovitch soon vanished into upper New Mexico's very thin air.

The First Twenty Years of the Santa Fe Opera, Eleanor Scott's generally reliable chronicle, relates that in 1958

> The Stravinskys attended a concert [the 'Eroica' Symphony,
> Stravinsky's *Danses concertantes* and Schoenberg's *Begleitmusik*]
> and spent part of the summer in Santa Fe, he composing and
> working with Craft on their book. Stravinsky was also seen
> prowling Woolworth's counters, and at noon, at his favorite table
> in La Fonda's outdoor patio beneath the cottonwood tree, a glass
> of Chivas Regal in his hand.

The composer has never been accused of abstemiousness, of course, and the locals knew of his habit of laying down a substratum of the favourite mead before degustation, but he was not *in* Santa Fe that summer. (I was, very briefly.) Still, the description would fit other years as well.

The phenomenal growth of the Santa Fe Opera dates from the conflagration that destroyed it in 1967 and the rapid reconstruction on a far grander scale. In this, Miranda was one of the chief fundraisers, though she would jokingly say, 'Well, I did the tin-cup thing', which was less important than bringing Stravinsky and Crosby together, thus giving the groundbreaking company – understaffed, only partly protected from the elements, and with a minimum of resources – an auspicious beginning.

Paul Horgan also deserves recognition for inducing Stravinsky to conduct an annual concert in Santa Fe's St Francis Cathedral. The first of these, on 12 July 1959, featured a performance of his *Threni*, a difficult work, painstakingly prepared by the Opera orchestra, chorus and soloists. I remember that a Star of David was placed in the keystone of the main arch to honour the Jewish community, which had helped to finance the building of the Cathedral in, remarkably, 1869.

We were in Santa Fe again in July 1960. This time Stravinsky conducted *Oedipus Rex* at the Opera, on a double-bill with *Gianni Schicchi*, the title role sung, if that is the word, by the actor José Ferrer. Stravinsky conducted the Symphony of Psalms in the Cathedral concert, which was preceded by Haydn's *Sinfonia concertante* and Mozart's 'Prague' Symphony conducted by me. We shared a table at La Fonda Hotel afterwards with Ferrer, his wife, Rosemary Clooney, and several members of the company. Ferrer made a speech that included a gentle dig about Stravinsky creating a futuristic opera and then having it translated into Medieval Latin.

In 1961, Vera Zorina came to Santa Fe at Stravinsky's invitation to perform the title part in his *Perséphone*. Brigitta, as everyone called her, was accompanied on stage by three lovely demoiselles from the Metropolitan Opera Ballet, Nancy King (Zeckendorff), Judith Chazin (Benahun), and Louella Sibley (Signora Cesare Siepi).

Crosby had been petitioning the US State Department to sponsor a tour of the Santa Fe Opera to West Berlin and Warsaw. This might be a possibility, he was told, only if Stravinsky conducted in both places. But the composer was not quite ready to cross the Iron Curtain. Thanks to behind-the-scenes manipulation by George Kennan, the American Ambassador to Yugoslavia, the venue was changed to Berlin and Belgrade. *Perséphone* and *Oedipus Rex* were performed on a double bill in both cities in September 1961. A review in the Berlin *Bildzeitung*, critical of Franglais pronunciations in *Perséphone*, provoked Stravinsky to a characteristically gallant response: 'Miss Zorina dances excellently in all languages.'

The performances were enthusiastically received, but our arrival in Belgrade was traumatic. A valise containing Stravinsky's manuscript sketches for his next opus, *The Flood*, had disappeared in Munich during the change of planes. Crosby managed to retrieve the precious cargo, but all we ever knew about the process was that Kennan and the US State Department were involved.

Stravinsky's press interviews in Belgrade's Hotel Metropol, switching from English to French to Russian, contain nuggets of his musical philosophy:

> They call me the Picasso of modern music. But though I appreciate deeply the genius of my dear friend Picasso, I can't stand modern music. Thus I don't compose it... I have already said so many times. There is no future. The past existed, but even it has disappeared. The problem is what to do to make the present exist. This is what we labour for.

> The audience prefers to recognise something rather than

to learn something. The audience is always lazy. It likes to recognise, but not to cognise.

[On *Perséphone*] Dance and Music have been bound together from the very beginning. The movement imitates the sound, and the sound becomes a more and more beautiful movement.

I like to travel. I have spent all of my life in travelling. Either me or my music. I like new environments, orchestras, landscapes, and new tones.

In 1962 a grateful Santa Fe commemorated Stravinsky's eightieth birthday. *The New York Herald Tribune* quoted him: 'Santa Fe is my family, and the celebration is like having my birthday at home.' As well as a festival of his music, lectures were delivered by Virgil Thomson, Milton Babbitt, Carlos Chávez, Thomas Messer and Roger Shattuck. Stravinsky directed his *Mavra* and *Renard* at the Opera and I his *Nightingale.* In the Cathedral concert on 19 August he conducted his 1952 Cantata, and I his arrangement of Bach's 'Vom Himmel hoch' Variations. On the 21st I also conducted two performances of *The Flood* in St Francis Auditorium. During that summer, in the sacristy of the Cathedral, Stravinsky began to compose *Abraham and Isaac.*

By this time I had become very good friends with two of the three ballerinas, and persuaded them to attend Milton Babbitt's lecture, promising that it would be brilliant, if a trifle abstruse. Understanding not a word, but sticking it out, they held me responsible for their intellectual ordeal, and came to my room afterwards to spill flour over my black-top table and inscribe it with their fingers: 'Professor Milton Babble'. I was forgiven later only by revealing the meaning of 'pulchritudinous' to them, the word having been used in a *Daily New Mexican* review describing their appearance in *Perséphone.*

In 1963 Stravinsky was in Santa Fe for the last time, ostensibly to hear the American premiere of Berg's *Lulu,* but actually to participate in a Cathedral concert, during which he was invested with the Papal Order of St Sylvester, a Knight Commander, with star ('*Inguarum*

Stravinsky Equitem Commendatorem Ordinus Sancti Sylvestri Papae').
As part of the ceremony, he conducted his Mass, which was preceded
by his favourite music, Monteverdi's Vespers. The accolade had been
bestowed on the composer by the recently deceased Pope John XXIII,
whom Stravinsky had known in 1956 as Patriarch of Venice. After
his elevation to the tiara, two years later, while the composer was
conducting in Rome, the Pontiff telephoned to him at the Hassler
Hotel, inviting him to the Vatican for a private conversation. When
Stravinsky said that he lacked the proper clothes, the Pope told him
to 'Come as you are'. 'I *are* in my pajamas,' he answered, and while
quickly dressing, gulped a large tumbler of Chivas Regal. During
their *tête-à-tête* the Pope confided that he was homesick for Venice,
that he did not care for some of his new obligations, and in truth
felt miserable in his exalted office. Worst of all, to whom could he
confess? To the composer, it seems. When the visit came to an end,
Papa Giovanni implored him to come again, and, 'Please, next time,
would you bring an autographed photo'.

2003

In July 2003, I was invited to attend a Festival in Santa Fe
commemorating the fortieth anniversary of this last Stravinsky
concert. On learning that the sponsor was 'The Desert Chorale', I
wondered what my role would be, besides that of a gerontological
observer at large. Then Craig Smith, the *Daily New Mexican* music
critic, called asking for comments on the Cantata and the Mass, the
featured pieces in the upcoming programme. He said that some Santa
Fe residents remembered the original occasion with emotion.

When Alva and I arrived in Albuquerque on the night of 5 August,
a loudspeaker summoned me to the information desk, where a spry,
attractive, white-haired lady said, 'I'm Nancee, don't you remember me?'
I did, but as a brunette. In 1968–9, when she was Mrs Ramiro Cortez,
wife of the composer, and also, for a time, Stravinsky's secretary.
During the ride, she filled in the agenda that would concern us, the
history of 'The Desert Chorale', the current social and operatic feuds,
and the recent biographies of people I had known well, too many of

whom had recently joined 'the gen'ral dance', to borrow a phrase from Stravinsky's Cantata. Vera Zorina had died recently, and John Crosby soon after, prematurely, during a bungled appendectomy. In spite of these painful losses, the first view of Santa Fe, glittering on the far side of the wide desert gulch, brought twinges of nostalgia.

Opening the curtains the next morning, I recalled D.H. Lawrence's description of the same experience after his first night in the city in September 1922: 'I saw the brilliant, proud morning shine high up over the deserts of Santa Fe... There was a magnificence in the high-up day, an eagle-like royalty... '

During a luncheon at La Fonda Hotel, Alva and I sat on a dais next to New Mexico's First Lady, Barbara Richardson, who introduced me. After this, members of the audience began to share their recollections of Stravinsky in the city. Seeing how these people had venerated him not only as a great composer but as a readily approachable human being was such a moving experience that I was scarcely able to control my own feelings. One of the speakers, Manuel Melendez, now Congressional Liaison to the Smithsonian Institute, had sung in the chorus under Stravinsky, and described it as one of the happiest, proudest, most meaningful experiences of his life. Don Manuel also warned us, however, that '*au fond*, Stravinsky was a tiger'.

We went next to Dorothy Massey's 'Collected Works Bookstore', where I became a commodity, merchandise of my concoction being on display. After an hour of talking with old friends from the Opera orchestra – one of them said that 'Stravinsky seemed grateful to us for playing his music, when it was we who were grateful to him to be able to play it' – we went to the dress rehearsal for the Cathedral concert, defying a notice at the entrance: 'Don't even think about opening this door.' The Chorale was of the highest quality, the tempi judiciously lively. The sky muttered minatorily throughout but cunningly waited until we were outside to spill its rain.

The surprise of the panel discussion that took place the next afternoon was the unannounced participation of my old friend Michael Tilson Thomas, music director of the San Francisco Symphony, who lives here in the summer. Sitting next to each other, much of our talk inevitably became semi-private conversation about past lives in

Los Angeles. Michael touched on topics to which only he was privy, observing that some of Stravinsky's later California compositions reflect the influence of music, old and new, that the composer had heard at West Hollywood's Monday Evening Concerts, citing *Agon* as an example. Michael spoke of the joy that he saw in Stravinsky's face during Schütz's Christmas Oratorio. His comments on Stravinsky the conductor were especially vigilant on the reflection of his physical gestures in the gestures of the music, but he also mentioned the habit of licking the left thumb before turning each page of the score, and the way he 'grabbed' chords from the orchestra and cued players with a simple nod. He also recalled Stravinsky conducting *Firebird* in a concert in Beverly Hills in 1967 and realising only after the first bar that the orchestra parts were for *Petrushka*. At this point a member of the audience sought to turn the subject to 'Stravinsky the man'. Here I deferred to Nancee, a former ballerina, asking her to act out her first meeting with the composer. She did, imitating his very slight, restrained introductory bow, and her own somersault solo-bow response.

The next afternoon Nancee drove us to visit Miranda, who had been prevented from attending the week's events because of a series of accidents. The road to her apartment led past the site of the Castillo Bridge, where, on 2 June 1945, Klaus Fuchs, the German-born Soviet spy, passed atomic bomb construction secrets to an agent for the Russian Vice Consul in New York, Anatoli Yakovlev. One night two weeks later, and 150 miles away in the Alamogordo Desert, 'the radiance of a thousand suns burst forth' (The *Bhagavad-Gita*).

Though decubital, bandaged, with two limbs in casts, her bed hemmed in by a wheelchair and crutches, Miranda was spunky, cheerful, anything but moribund. In fact, her spirits seemed to rise as she recounted each of the mishaps that had brought her to St Vincent's Hospital – 'St Victim's', as she called it. She told us that a fire had started in her living room (spontaneous combustion?), that she telephoned 'security', to no avail, then tried to extinguish the flame herself, moving furniture and books away, but fell in the process, breaking her left arm, four ribs, and the insteps of both feet. On regaining consciousness, she found herself surrounded by firemen and neighbours.

Our visit began with talk about the Santa Fe Opera. Her only experience of its stage was vicarious: her French poodle, Justin, had stolen the show in the Café Momus scene from an otherwise routine *La Bohème*. She then asked me if I would look around at her walls 'and tell me which Stravinsky drawings and photographs you would like to have when I croak'. I protested, of course, that the necrological order would be the other way around. I kissed her and she said, 'I am very happy this afternoon, thinking of that wonderful life with the Stravinskys'.

This led her to talk about the funeral of John Crosby. His brother had come from 'the East' with two relatives, and the ceremony took place in a hall with a closed casket placed on a table at the centre of a small stage. Since the deceased was a practicing Roman Catholic, Miranda had been expecting a religious service. She attributed the absence of even a secular observance to the embarrassment of his family over his notorious homosexuality. She was the only friend invited to the memorial, and, together with a representative from the Santa Fe Opera, the only other outsider. The family sat on the left side of the aisle; she and the man from the Opera sat on the right. After ten minutes of silence the mourners left the building and entered two limousines, the family in the first. They were driven to a glass chapel at the top of a hill in the Santa Fe cemetery. While inside, they heard volleys of rifle fire by members of the National Guard, an acknowledgment of John's Army service at the end of World War II. I asked if he is buried here, but she could not say and seemed to think that the casket was shipped East and interred in a family plot there.

She told this story with a bias: Crosby had done something for the musical world, but had not achieved recognition, let alone gratitude. Having been his confidante for fifty years, she was deeply grieved by his death and the injustices surrounding it.

Chapter 17

My Participation in Stravinsky's Late Music[1]

In 1998 Dr Felix Meyer, director of the Paul Sacher Foundation in Basel, asked me to take part in a symposium at the Morgan Library in New York on the extent of my involvement with the twelve major and fifteen or so minor pieces that Stravinsky composed between *The Rake's Progress*, 1951, and the end of his creative life, in 1968. I complied but soon realised that the request could never be fully satisfied. Certainly the exchanges of influence, above all in my function as sounding-board, are indistinguishable at this date. All that I can do now is to establish a few specific connections to specific works. I had lived too closely to Stravinsky for twenty-three years and, desirable as it might be to identify my meagre contributions, they are no longer distinguishable, especially in exchanges of influence and in my function as a sounding-board. We co-rehearsed and co-conducted concerts and recordings; listened to music together at home, at opera houses, theatres, concert halls; spent countless hours together in cars, steamships, trains and planes; and shared innumerable experiences of indescribable diversity. I read to him during evenings at home regularly throughout the years, and, of course, conversed with him daily in all of our activities. I enjoyed all of this immensely and

---

1   A lecture, revised and expanded from one read at the Morgan Library in New York in 1998, delivered at Harvard University Music Department in 2002.

regarded it as a great privilege. The hard part for me came in his later life when I was sometimes surrogated to fill his role as interviewee and to stand in for him in audiences at performances of his music, extremely awkward and embarrassing situations, needless to say. Worse still, when I began to share concerts with him and conduct their first halves, I was obliged to walk out on stage and be received by a dim flurry of applause, a buzz of inter-audience questioning, and once something like a groan. Sensitive to this, he offered to open our programmes by conducting a short piece, usually *Fireworks*, at the beginning.

The foregoing statements will fuel the negative criticism that has come to my ears through the decades from Stravinsky's family, friends, more-or-less secret enemies, and other observers, namely that I kept him too much to myself. I plead guilty, but I long ago destroyed the evidence that would have provided a brief for my defence: two very personal letters from the mid-1960s – Stravinsky could not talk face to face about intimate personal matters, but he could and did convey them, straight and pithily, in writing – both letters expressing fear that my confining life on Wetherly Drive had become wearying to me, that I might be thinking of leaving, and begging me to stay.

A major handicap in attempting to recall my connections with Stravinsky's music is that the originals – manuscripts, sketches, notebooks, pertinent correspondence – are in Basel, Winterthur, Geneva, the British Museum, the Bibliothèque Nationale, the Library of Congress, the Morgan Library, and dozens of university and music-school libraries in St Petersburg, Jerusalem, Rio de Janeiro, Stanford, Oberlin, Juilliard, Dumbarton Oaks, the Koussevitzky Foundation and many more. In addition, the contents of private collections are extensive and as yet unexplored.

Nevertheless, I began to consider Dr Meyer's request seriously after reading a comment by the composer Philip Glass in a turn-of-the-millennium *Time* article:

> In 1947 Stravinsky befriended Robert Craft, a 23-year-old conductor who was to become his chronicler, interpreter, and, oddly, his mentor in some ways. It was Craft who persuaded

> Stravinsky to take a more sympathetic view of Arnold
> Schoenberg's twelve-tone school, which led to Stravinsky's last
> great stylistic development.

'Oddly, his mentor in some ways.' Well, yes, but these ways must be spelled out in every individual case, which cannot be done in the confines of a single essay. Glass's statements indicated, however, that my role is still enigmatic, thus making it incumbent on me to shed as much light as I can on the scene of fifty to thirty years ago.

Let me begin with a few general remarks on the idea of an 'old-age style' in the visual arts, in music, and in Stravinsky's music in particular. Sir Kenneth Clark once suggested that the predominant qualities of Michelangelo's frescoes in the Pauline Chapel, one of the supreme achievements of an aged artist, are

> A sense of isolation; mistrust of reason and a belief in instinct;
> savage indignation (holy rage); pessimism; a retreat from
> realism. The artist of advanced age is also impatient with
> established techniques, and his work is imbued with a feeling
> of imminent departure, the 'I haven't got long to wait' sense of
> desperation that Van Gogh conveys in his furious battle with
> time, even though he was in his thirties.

Resignation, another quality of the old-age style, is exemplified in the Christ who sits motionless and with downcast eyes in Titian's late version of *The Crowning with Thorns.* Another example is the figure of Jerome in Titian's last *Pietà* (now accepted as a self-portrait). Clark nominates the Magdalene in the same picture, passionate and enraged, as the supreme example of an artist's *saeva indignatio.*

In music the characteristics of an old-age style are more diverse and more difficult to categorise. The composers, of course, are easily identified as Bach, Beethoven and Mozart, even though the last did not achieve longevity. Of the major composers who continued to create in their octogenarian years, Verdi, Schütz and Richard Strauss, the common link between *Falstaff,* the Christmas Oratorio and the Four Last Songs is simply that these works are their composers' culminating masterpieces, exhibiting greater stylistic purity than ever before in each case, and as much vigour, if not staying power. Yet several of the qualities named in connection with octogenarian sculptors and painters are pre-eminent in the music Stravinsky composed at the same age, though he may have been shorter of breath in his eighties than the others. Apart from *Agon*, which he wrote at seventy-five, all of Stravinsky's successive major works, but especially *Abraham and Isaac* and the *Requiem Canticles*, are steeped in the feeling of imminent departure. The first concludes with the most gentle portrait in all music of an old man on his retirement (Abraham's journey to Bathsheba). The dominant change of facture in the aged Stravinsky is the preponderance of contrapuntal devices: *Threni, Canticum Sacrum, A Sermon, a Narrative and a Prayer* and even *The Owl and the Pussy-Cat* depend on canonic form.

Surveying Stravinsky's septua- and octogenarian music as a whole, one is amazed by the composer's fecundity when in poor, at times precarious, health. Remarkable, too, is his variety of genres, both sacred and secular: a Requiem, a ballet (*Agon*), a dramatised biblical story conceived as a television play (*The Flood*), anniversary and memorial pieces, *a cappella* choruses, arrangements of works by older composers (Gesualdo, Bach, Sibelius, Hugo Wolf) as well as of music from his own younger years (Russian songs, female Russian choruses, the *Five Fingers*, the Concertino). Most astonishing of all is that the later works are all new-thought new music.

Finally, let me dispose of a question that many would probably wish to ask: Would Stravinsky have developed a serialism of any kind without my influence? The answer is that I am certain he would not have. This could be contested on grounds that he himself understood *The Rake's Progress* as an end, and that he had to find a new path. True, the discovery of Webern and Schoenberg had already begun in Germany, France and Italy by the time of my arrival in California in 1948, but virtually none of the late-period music of these two composers had been performed in California or even in New York. When I presented Schoenberg's Septet-Suite at Town Hall in 1950, my bass clarinetist, Eric Simon, told me he had played it in a concert in the 1937 Venice Biennale, and that Stravinsky, in the city to conduct his *Jeu de cartes*, attended one of the rehearsals and was fascinated by the instrumental virtuosity of the piece, but regarded the music itself as 'experimental'. When he heard it at the University of Southern California, in February 1952, conducted by me, he was overwhelmed by the power of the music's constructive logic, as well as by the demands of the instrumental writing. He attended more than twenty of my rehearsals of it for the USC concert, and as many afterwards in preparation for my 1953 recording.

One last introductory point is that Stravinsky's late music is difficult to perform, as well as to hear and absorb, much of it requiring singers with 'perfect pitch' and the keenest rhythmic sense, which explains why general audiences are still unfamiliar with it, and continue to stigmatise it as 'cerebral' and forbidding. For this we must blame a cultural ethos in which great art is purchased primarily for investment and the prestige of ownership – Veblen's *Theory of the Leisure Class* – a society that rates almost everything, be it art, politics, crime, or natural and national disasters, according to entertainment value. We must also blame a musical public with simple-minded ears, or, less aggressively, undeveloped listening habits.

My involvement with Stravinsky's 1952 Cantata began when he had already completed its first song, 'The Maidens Came'. He chose the texts himself from the Auden-Pearson anthology, *Poets of the English Language* (1950), which Auden had sent to him, without explaining that the poem had been edited by the Chaucer scholar E. Talbot Donaldson, who also supplied a second stanza. A line in the latter, 'Elizabeth, our quen princis, / Prepotent and eke victorius', tells us that this was part of the reason for Stravinsky's choice: he kept a portrait of Elizabeth on his studio wall and read everything he could find about her. The second stanza was obviously written after the defeat of the Armada (1588) and hence would be much later than the first stanza, the now widely accepted date for which is c. 1450.

My contribution to the song, which he wrote immediately after the Postlude in the *Rake*, was in persuading him to rescore it, adding a pair of oboes (oboe and English horn) to his original accompaniment of two flutes and cello. I supposed that he had been thinking of the two-flute lullaby in the Bedlam scene of his recently completed opera, and my arguments for the changes were that the middle sound space was too empty and that the sonority was both monotonous and tiring for the players. The thought that I could have ventured this criticism appals me, but Stravinsky said nothing, and the next time he showed the song to me, a week later, the score had already been rewritten for the expanded, five-instrument, ensemble.

Perceiving that the two stanzas of 'The Maidens Came' were different in style, Stravinsky saw that the appropriate setting for the second would be a declamatory dramatic recitative with instrumental, chordal punctuation. The meaning of the first stanza, 'The bailey beareth the bell away', the bridal song, has still not been fully explained.

At one point in the early spring of 1951 Stravinsky asked Aldous Huxley for help as to the meaning of the poem, and was told that 'the speaker is presumably a young bride awaiting her bridegroom, but the identity of the bailey and why he bears the bell away is not known. The poem is an excerpt from a much longer one, printed in full only in volume 107 of the *Archiv für neuere Sprachen und Literaturen*, in 1901, by the scholar Bernhard Fehr of Southgate-on-Sea.' Huxley's *Texts and Pretexts* comments: 'If we really knew what this fragment was about, we might come to like it less. Uncomprehended, it is lovely, and mysteriously haunts the imagination with its peculiar magic. Let us leave well alone and be thankful for it.'

Recent scholarship associates the verses with May Day festivities in and around Durham Castle, the 'glasse window' probably referring to the vitraille East Window of Durham Cathedral. A musical setting from the period reveals that the first line is really the title, and that the last line of the first stanza should be a repetition of the penultimate line. An earlier, ribald version of a fragment of the poem is found in John Taverner's XX Songes (1530). Here the refrain 'the baily beryth the bell away' has been interpreted as 'We maidens beareth the bell', i.e., we take the prize. The bell probably refers to the swelling of pregnancy. Since the idea of the crucifixion as Christ's 'dancing day' comes from the Gnostic Gospels, so too perhaps the bailey/bell has

Gnostic connotations.

Stravinsky began to compose Ricercar II, 'Tomorrow Shall Be My Dancing Day' (taken from *Sandy's Christmas Carols*, London, 1839), at the end of January 1952, after a six-month hiatus from composing, a period occupied by the premiere of *The Rake's Progress* in Venice, a European concert tour (Cologne, Baden-Baden, Munich, Geneva, Rome, Naples) and a month of *pourparlers* in New York concerning the production of the opera there. Webern's Orchestral Variations, heard in Baden-Baden in October 1951, conducted by the composer's friend Hans Rosbaud, made a profound impression on Stravinsky, but the Cantata employs neither 'serialism' nor 'atonality', and could have been written if these developments had not occurred.

The first notation for the Cantus Cancrizans of Ricercar II is dated 8 February 1952, and the movement was completed on 22 February. The duet 'Westron Wind', beginning with the rhythmic figure now appearing at the end, was composed before the Ricercar, in the week beginning 2 February, and was fully scored on 22 March. Work was interrupted by another European concert tour (Paris–Brussels, Holland) in late April–June, and the Lyke-Wake dirge was written in California in July. Stravinsky originally intended to compose a prelude, interludes and a postlude for instruments, but, impatient to begin work on the Septet, he opted for the repeated, less time-consuming, choruses.

Stravinsky had planned to complete the Cantata on his return from Europe, several months later, but by this time he had been musically transformed, stunned by the Webern he heard in the tape archives of the Süddeutscher Rundfunk in Baden-Baden. He had already chosen the subsequent texts. Back in California he decided to compose a chorus, as aforesaid, and place its four stanzas before and after the soloists' pieces. This was a grave miscalculation in that the poem makes little sense heard in four instalments, and the Phrygian mode becomes monotonous not only in its repetition but also because the mode is the same in the solo pieces. Moreover, the vocal pieces are all slow, except for the rapid final duet, whose tempo provides necessary relief, but whose text may not belong in a work that, after its first performance, Stravinsky would subtitle a 'sacred cantata'. The doubt here stems from Sir Thomas Browne's line about the 'conceptions' abetted by the 'subvantaneous' influence of the 'Westerne Winde'.

One of Stravinsky's most moving creations, the Cantata followed naturally from *The Rake's Progress*, and was in fact composed (the duet and the tenor Ricercar) with the voices of Jennie Tourel and Hugues Cuénod in mind, the Baba the Turk and the Sellem in the Venetian production of the opera. (Stravinsky may even have thought of the line, 'The Devil bade me make stones my bread', in Ricercar II, in some way correlated to the bread machine in the opera.)

Most of 'The Maidens Came' is accompanied by the woodwind quartet, without the cello, which is silent under the pairs of winds at the words 'how should I love?' (note the oboe high C), as it is again near the end of the prayer that concludes this lovely lyric. The tenor Ricercar, however, is the centerpiece and most innovative movement in the Cantata. The melodic line, containing only five different pitches, is exposed in a one-bar introduction in which the cello doubles the first flute melody, a sonority suggesting Renaissance instruments, while the second flute doubles it an octave lower. The tenor repeats the subject with changes in rhythm, then sings it in retrograde order (more rhythmic changes), inverted order, and retrograde inverted order, in which a sixth pitch emerges. In the nine canons that follow, the oboes and cello provide the counterpoint, as well as a drone accompaniment in the Cantus Cancrizans.

The three Cantus Cancrizans are in one tempo, the *ritornelli* and canons are in another. The music of the first two *ritornelli* is an abbreviated form of the *ritornelli* between the canons, which are the same throughout, as are the odd-numbered canons, 1, 3, 5, 7, 9. The even-numbered ones, in contrasting tonalities and, in canons 4 and 6, new rhythms, introduce dramatic musical images of the text. The beginnings of canons 6 and 8 return to the original tonality and melodic form of the Cantus Cancrizans. Canons 2 and 4 also derive from the Cantus Cancrizans. Canon 4, in a remote tonality, is marked *in motu contrario* – in the manuscript sketch Stravinsky drew isobar lines showing the relationships. The intervals are inverted (the third becoming a sixth, etc.), and jagged dotted rhythms and harsh dissonances are exploited programmatically. Canon 6 employs still wider leaps and more agitated figurations in the cello; it begins in C and ends in D sharp major. The most affecting harmonic moment in the piece occurs near the end of Canon 8 when the tonal centre rises from C to C sharp major at the words 'And rose again on the third day'

Ricercar II, with its four serial orders (original, retrograde, inverted and retrograde inverted – four forms of a succession of notes), is the most surprising innovation in Stravinsky's American-period music, a consequence of his study of the boustrophedonic idea in Schoenberg's Septet-Suite in January–February 1952 for a performance in the University of Southern California's Bovard Auditorium. But whereas Schoenberg's series comprehends the twelve pitches of the chromatic scale, without repeating any of them until all twelve have been sounded, the series in Stravinsky's Ricercar employs only six different pitches and immediately repeats them. I do not have to point out that the retrograde form was first introduced 650 years ago by Guillaume de Machaut – 'Ma fin est mon commencement et mon commencement est ma fin' – and that its most memorable appearance in the Classical-Romantic era is in Beethoven's 'Hammerklavier' Sonata.

Schoenberg did not integrate the full quadrilateral perspective until the mid-1920s, in one of the *a cappella* choruses of Opus 27. His 'atonal' revolution, pre-serial as well as serial, began in 1908 in *The Book of the Hanging Gardens*, in harmonic and melodic relationships beyond the conventionally recognised boundaries of the tonal system. In Stravinsky's Ricercar II, at the opposite extreme, tonal centres are emphasised and complete sections repeated. The fifth and ninth canons, for example, are identical with the first. Stravinsky's initial foray into serialism only reaffirms his tonal roots.

In retrospect, my incitation of Stravinsky to employ this four-form series in the second Ricercar is perhaps my single most important contribution to his later life as a composer. The decision to continue in this direction confronted him with a major crisis, and during a drive in the Mojave Desert, on 8 March 1952, he expressed a fear that he did not know how to compose without exploring the possibilities of a serial approach. Aware that he had not been composing at all recently, I suggested that he might orchestrate an earlier piece as a kind of warm-up exercise. I proposed the Concertino for string quartet, on the irrelevant grounds that he would be able to use twelve instruments, some from the Octet and some from the Mass, both pieces already programmed for a chamber-music concert in November. The Concertino had never reaped much success in its original form, partly because it was too thick in the low register (viola and cello), and offered little colour relief. I pointed out that a wind instrument ensemble could clarify the space between the Concertino's violin and cello obbligato parts, as well as set the two string instruments off in intimate contrasts. He said nothing, but achieved this new instrumental version of the six-minute opus almost overnight and emerged from his work on it refreshed and eager to complete the Cantata. In gratitude he gave to me as an Easter present the manuscript sketch page of 'Through the glass window shines the sun', inscribing it 'To Bob, whom I love'. It remains the most treasured of all my possessions.

My only connection with Stravinsky's next creation, the Septet, can be found on the verso of one of the sketch pages in the Sacher Stiftung, part of an illustration in my hand (in pencil, so that it could be erased) of how Schoenberg distributes the series of his Wind Quintet both harmonically and melodically, vertically and horizontally. I remember a twinge of disappointment with the Septet's first movement as being formulaic and retrogressively tonal, a return to pure neo-classicism. But the second and third movements were strikingly new. The second begins with a passacaglia theme – Stravinsky's series, like Schoenberg's, are thematic – which repeats the four orders of a series of sixteen notes, only eight of them different. The other eight notes are repeated, and the four remaining pitches are not sounded at all. In the last movement 'Gigue' the eight *different* notes from the second-movement theme become a fugue subject with two tonal centres: E at the beginning, the dominant of the key, and A at the end, the tonic. As a consequence of transpositions and cross-rhythms, the in-between music could be described as atonal, and it marks Stravinsky's most daring step in his new direction.

Apropos the 'Gigue', Erwin Stein, who was Stravinsky's editor at Boosey & Hawkes, pleaded with the composer to delete the marginal identifications of the 'rows' of the various instruments. I concurred with Stein and his argument that the rows were perfectly obvious and that to highlight them exposed Stravinsky to ridicule. Stein, I should have said earlier, had a considerable influence on Stravinsky, going back to *The Rake's Progress*, for which Stein prepared the piano score, but which Stravinsky changed dramatically in the proofs. We met Stein in Rome in April 1954, and he died soon after, to be succeeded by Leopold Spinner, a former Webern pupil. It seems ironic that the editing of Stravinsky's music from 1949 to 1968 should have been the work of, respectively, pupils of Schoenberg and Webern.

The next pieces, the Three Songs from William Shakespeare and *In memoriam Dylan Thomas*, do not pursue the explorations begun in the 'Gigue'. I thought the first song stiff and diagrammatic, and the third dangerously close to being 'cute'. But the rich texture and gently wavy counterpoint in the second song is one of Stravinsky's loveliest settings of any lyric. His first score of the third song inadvertently omitted two lines, but he quickly repaired the error by adding a repeat sign. He had also dropped a word from the first song that neither of us noticed until 16 November 1953. Part of my work for him was in vetting each page of manuscript as it came from his desk.

My input *vis-à-vis In memoriam Dylan Thomas* was more significant. In the first place, I was present during the Boston meeting of the poet and composer in which a collaboration was discussed. Second, a letter from me in Hollywood to Stravinsky in New York, now in the Sacher Stiftung, and underscored in red pencil by the composer, establishes that after Thomas's death I chose the text and asked Stravinsky to set it to music. Thirdly, he wrote the instrumental Prelude and Postlude for quartets of strings and trombones after hearing me conduct Heinrich Schütz's *Fili mi Absalom*. All that matters, of course, is that the lament for the young poet, using only five pitches in the confining space of a major third – nine pitches counting four more from the four orders of the series – is one of the most affecting pieces Stravinsky ever wrote.

My contribution to the *Canticum Sacrum*, Stravinsky's next opus and his first to include a full break with tonality, was simply in urging him to compose it. I was with him in Rome when a delegation from Venice approached him with the commission, but he had already conceived the idea of writing a Passion according to St Mark. W.H. Auden told him that Passion texts should be in the vernacular, that is to say, English, which would be an affront to the Venetian audience. With the *Canticum* Stravinsky completely immerses his feet in atonal waters, yet clings tenaciously to tonality for half of the opus. The introduction and first and last movements are purely tonal, and the twelve-tone tenor aria from the *Song of Solomon* is nearly so, in its repetitions of pitches before moving on, its melodic emphases on stepwise tonal intervals, its groupings of notes around tonal centres, and its ending in modal A minor.

'A' is also the first note of the twelve-tone series in the movement that follows, a series that has an obvious tonal aspect in its melodic ambitus and in the perfect fifth that demarcates its two hexachordal halves. The 'A' tonality predominates in the fourth movement as well, and its *a cappella* figure exploits the traditional entrance of the second voice at the fifth. Still another tonal aspect is that Stravinsky disregards Schoenberg's early 1920s practice banning octave doublings. Other novelties distinguish the *Canticum* as well, above all the instrumentation: organ, lower strings, brass – the traditional components of late Renaissance and Baroque Venetian orchestras.

On completing the *Canticum*, Stravinsky realised that it was too short to fulfill the requirements of the commission, and in order to lengthen the premiere programme by another dozen minutes, he orchestrated, and added a chorus to, Bach's 'Vom Himmel hoch' Variations, originally written in open score, or for organ. This was entirely my idea. On his return from Lisbon to Los Angeles in May 1954, I played the piece with him in the Philipp Spitta edition. Stravinsky began plotting his instrumentation immediately, even though the concert in Venice was more than two years in the future. He employed the instruments and chorus of the *Canticum*, but without the organ. No more need be said: the translation to the orchestra, the added canons, particularly in the fifth variation, are worthy of Bach. I conducted the unofficial premiere in Ojai, California, in May 1956, and Stravinsky conducted the announced premiere in San Marco, Venice, in September 1956. The arrangement, or recomposition, as Stravinsky called it, is dedicated to me.

My only tangible input in *Agon* stemmed from my performances of Schoenberg's Serenade: Stravinsky simply borrowed the mandolin that he had so much admired in that work. I was especially close to him during the composition of the latter part of the ballet, with its amalgamation of tonal and atonal serial elements,[2] when he was recuperating from the thrombosis that hospitalised him in Munich in October 1956, and I knew the music intimately by the time I conducted the Los Angeles premiere. Stravinsky's own recorded performance follows mine in tempo and in numerous details.

My involvement with *Threni* is limited to the choice of title, and of two instruments. When composing the Three Songs from William Shakespeare in 1953, Stravinsky had wanted to set the 'Threnos', the bird-elegy from 'The Phoenix and Turtle'. He abandoned the idea on discovering that the seven-syllable lines in trochaic meter, three in each of the five stanzas, would require exact duplication of the fixed strong–weak pattern in the music. But in 1957 he returned to Shakespeare's title, 'Threnos', and his English word, 'Threne', in the poem. *Threni* ('lamentations') is the Vulgate for the Greek *threnos* sung by the Muses at the burial of Achilles. As for the instruments, I was with Stravinsky when he heard Mr 'Shorty' Rogers play the flügelhorn in a Hollywood nightclub in February 1957; the instrument makes its appearance in the composer's sketchbook the next day. I also nudged him into incorporating the sarrusophone in his orchestra, an instrument he admired in Ravel's *L'Heure espagnole*, noting that its sonority would be more penetrating in the rhythmic recitations in the first *Elegia* than that of the contrabassoon he first had in mind. Trombones and harp play prominent roles, as could be anticipated in any Biblical opus by Stravinsky. But *Threni* is essentially a choral, not an instrumental, work. The upper strings do not play at all in more than half of it. One fine effect that should be mentioned is the doubling of the basso profundo's falsetto 'di-xi-sti'. Another is the solo string bass harmonic that leads to the four wonderfully hollow vocal chords of 'Ne timeas'.

---

2   This has been analysed by Pieter van den Toorn in his landmark study *The Music of Igor Stravinsky*, Yale University Press, 1983.

I rehearsed the orchestra, chorus and solo singers for *Threni* during two and a half weeks in Hamburg at the end of summer 1958, and Stravinsky followed my dress-rehearsal performance for the premiere in Venice. I rehearsed it with him before, indicating tempi and beating patterns, and conducted the dress rehearsal. But no matter, and no merit: the performance of the premiere, recorded live, is far from doing justice to the piece, and Stravinsky's studio recording in New York, a few months later, is much inferior to the performance in the Naxos recording.

Stravinsky's manuscript sketches show that he composed the five introductory bars on 29 August 1957, in Venice, the day after his arrival there by train from Paris. He worked on it for a month before embarking on one of his perennial concert tours, this one to Munich, Donaueschingen, Zurich, Paris, Rome. On his way home, he stayed for only a single day in New York, to attend a rehearsal for the premiere of Balanchine's *Agon*. Work on *Threni* was immediately resumed in Hollywood, and the score was completed on 21 March 1958.

Stravinsky accepted the commission to compose *Movements* for piano and orchestra partly for reasons I suggested to him, namely that he had composed enough (excruciatingly) difficult-to-sing choral music in the *Canticum* and in *Threni,* and written a sufficient number of complex canons for a lifetime; hence a purely instrumental piece, and one that could also serve for a ballet, would be in order. The *Movements* came as a major surprise, a 180-degree turn in the domain of rhythmic exploration as well as in serial technique. At the time of the premiere, January 1960, Stravinsky described the piece as 'anti-tonal', but the numerous octaves and fifths, and the many sustained pitches and pedal points, tend to contradict this. The twelve-note series, exposed in the piano part at the beginning, encompasses the intervals of a fourth and a fifth, both of which are highlighted in chord structures. Near the beginning, one pitch of the series is repeated after only three intervening notes, and 'free' notes, not part of the serial organisation, are interpolated soon after that. Liberties on behalf of tonality are also taken in the fourth movement, where at one place the serial order is switched to 7, 8, 9, 11, 10, in order to end with G, thus giving the implication of that tonality to this part of the piece. The ear takes precedence over the system.

My only involvement with the composition came when Stravinsky again realised, as in the case of the *Canticum Sacrum*, that it was too short. I suggested that he add the four brief, purely instrumental interludes. He intended them as introductions to the movements that follow, *attacca*, the tempo of the shorter pieces remaining unchanged in the longer one.

Further to comply with Dr Meyer's request, I should add that my involvement in Stravinsky's Gesualdo recompositions – the three 'completions' of sacred motets and the instrumentation of the *Monumentum pro Gesualdo di Venosa* (1960) – was substantial. The manuscript of the first of the motets, the seven-voice *Da pacem Domine*, shows that the transcription he worked from is in my hand, in pencil, which peeks out from beneath his calligraphic overtracing in black ink, a palimpsest. The same is true of the other two six-part *Cantiones Sacrae*.

My influence in the *Monumentum* could only be for Stravinsky himself to say. As a surprise gift, he placed a copy of his manuscript score on my plate at lunch one day, inscribed 'To Bob, who made me do it and I did it – with love I. Str. 1960'. Stravinsky chose the three madrigals himself, in each case because they inspired instrumental ideas, such as the four open horns in the first, the brass and double-reed combination for the Venetian-style *canzona* in the second, and the muted horns and *a l'antiqua ponticello* viola da gamba cellos in the third.

With the composer's guidance, I selected the texts of *A Sermon, a Narrative and a Prayer*. My notes accompanying the copy of the libretto in the Sacher Stiftung make clear that Stravinsky followed my suggestions 'to a T' concerning the overlapping of singing and speech and, in the first movement, the partitioning of the chorus, which Elliott Carter regards as 'one of the greatest inspirations in all of Stravinsky's choral writing'. A minor contribution of mine is in the 'aid' to the performance of different speeds of triplets in the *Prayer*. He had watched me teach orchestras to play three even notes in four-beat bars, by asking the performers to count twelve, the least common denominator, silently, playing or singing the second note of the triplet on '5' and the third on '9'. Webern's conducting score of Schoenberg's *Lichtspiel* music shows that he changed the notation of four crotchets (quarter notes) bracketed in the time of three near the end of the piece as four dotted eighth notes. Annibale Carracci's *Stoning of St Stephen* in the Louvre, and the *Lapidation de Saint-Etienne*, the ninth-century fresco in the crypt of Saint-Germain d'Auxerre, were visual inspirations for the *Narrative*.

In December 1961, on his return from Australia, Stravinsky was unhappily reminded that he had committed himself to compose a new piece for a concert in Mexico City three weeks later. I suggested that he orchestrate the eight short pieces, *Les Cinqs Doigts*, composed in 1921. The time was insufficient, he said, but nevertheless went to work recomposing the last of the set, Tango, for a wind ensemble. Since this is barely three minutes long, he arrived in the Mexican capital feeling guilty and expecting a scandal, if not the one experienced. Since the concert took place during the *Feliz Navidad* holidays, the subscription public and everyone else who could afford concert tickets was at Acapulco. The arrangement was played, nevertheless, even though we were bereft of an audience, except for the six or seven lonely souls who had wandered into the vastness of the Palacio de Bellas Artes. I conducted it. Back in Hollywood Stravinsky started to orchestrate other pieces of the opus he would call *Eight Instrumental Miniatures*. I performed the first four of them in a March Monday Evening Concert. After hearing them, Stravinsky added a small group of strings to the wind ensemble for the last four pieces, discarded the Latino version of the Tango, and conducted the suite complete on his eightieth birthday concert in Toronto, June 1962. I asked him to dedicate it to Lawrence Morton, since the Monday Evening Concerts had included so much of Stravinsky's own music, as well as his favourite works by other composers.

In the creation of *The Flood*, I was responsible for choosing the subject itself and the texts, from *Genesis* and the York and Chester

Cycles of fourteenth-century 'Mystery', or Guild, plays. Another important influence on the form and period of the work was Noah Greenberg, whose New York Pro Musica Antiqua had given staged presentations of the *Play of Daniel* and other medieval morality works that were paradigms for *The Flood*. Greenberg was introduced to us by Auden, whose album note for 'An Evening of Elizabethan Verse and Its Music' has become the superior essay in musicology on the subject. Noah Greenberg was an intimate member of Stravinsky's circle in New York and Los Angeles, where we attended his concerts, and where I visited him in hospital after one of the heart attacks that would kill him so prematurely.

I shall mention another, private influence on the choice of *The Flood*: my mother's given name, Arpha, was the name of one of Noah's daughters-in-law. As for my own participation, I wrote the line containing the words 'salt' and 'flood', which, as no one seems to have noticed, come from *Timon of Athens* in a similar conjunction.

The subject was close not only to Stravinsky's thinking at the time (1960), but also to his experience. He was interested in the archaeological work at Mount Ararat and happened to be reading a popular book about it, *L'Arche de Noë*, when Venice was almost drowned by one of the worst *aqua alta* inundations in its history. On 15 October 1960, the lobby of his hotel, the Bauer Grünwald, was flooded to the height of three feet, restricting him to his room and to a very limited selection of room-service food. Guests were few this late in the season, fortunately, but this must have been a harrowing experience for a claustrophobe who could not swim and was frightened in gondolas. The connection to the music is obvious. The movement called 'The Flood' conveys a sense of water steadily rising rather than of waves cresting and breaking, characteristic of musical representations of overflowing rivers and raging oceans. (I do not know whether or not Stravinsky was aware that in old age Richard Strauss had pondered the idea of composing a work on the subject of Noah in which the ark would be a haven-symbol for tonal composers in a stormy sea of atonality.)

Like *Agon*, *The Flood* is a synthesis of tonal and atonal, and as programme music it belongs to the genre of the 'Pastoral' Symphony, with which it shares imitations of warbling and chirping birds, thunder, and rain. My only musical input was the idea that the flood itself, the orchestral piece, should be retrograde in form, like the cinema music in *Lulu*.

Harmonically speaking, *The Flood*, with the *Requiem Canticles*, is the easiest to digest of Stravinsky's late pieces. 'God's' cadential chords, the sustained strings with the final 'curtain', the octave-unisons in 'The Building of the Ark' and the 'Covenant of the Rainbow' could have been written before Stravinsky developed his idiosyncratic brand of serialism. Much of the music, melodic or not, is unharmonised. Nearly half of the bars in 'The Building of the Ark' contain unharmonised notes, and a third of that half is *limited* to them. Two or three places in the movement contain some of Stravinsky's densest music, but the complexity is more rhythmic than harmonic. The Te Deum, near the beginning and at the end of the score, is largely restricted to a two note chant accompanied by a simple bassoon figure, and half of the thirty-five bars in 'The Catalog of the Animals', as well as more than that in 'The Comedy', Noah's abduction of his wife into the Ark, also consist of unharmonised lines.

The Flood's musical images include felicitous variations on conventions. Consider the Wagnerian-like characterisation of the serpent: two muted horns writhing in close harmony and moving in a stealthy, slithering rhythm; and the onomatopoeic carpentering in 'The Building of the Ark': different speeds and volumes of hammerings in percussion and trombones. So, too, in 'The Catalog of the Animals', the pauses between staccato bass-clarinet and short, biting trombone chords suggest, as the text tells us, the sudden stopping, and then running, of a squirrel.

I am responsible for the abbreviation of the text from Verdi's Requiem for the *Requiem Canticles*; the source was the contents page of the Eulenberg miniature score. At the time neither Stravinsky nor I was aware that the Vatican had recently censored the reference to the 'Cumean Sibyl'. For the second time Stravinsky traced over my pencil markings in ink, but, again, the pencil shows through. I also persuaded him, after the first rehearsal, to replace with muted horns the scarcely audible and nearly-always-out-of-tune harmonium of the original manuscript.

The melody of Sibelius's Canzonetta was the signature-tune of the Canadian Broadcasting Company Orchestra, played by strings during the fade-out of each radio concert. Stravinsky heard me conduct it at the conclusion of one of these in Toronto, and it stayed in his mind. Since the original, like *Valse Triste*, was composed in 1903 as incidental music to the *Kuolema*, Stravinsky could have heard it in his youth. When he was awarded the Wihuri–Sibelius prize in 1963, he rescored the piece for eight instruments, and gave his manuscript, in gratitude, to the Wihuri Foundation.

The stunningly new 'Fanfare for a New Theater', composed for the opening of the New York State Theater in Lincoln Center in 1964, began with a telephone call from George Balanchine enlisting my help in prevailing upon Stravinsky to write it; he was working on the Variations at the time and did not welcome an interruption, but accepted. The *a cappella* Russian Credo, rewritten in May 1964 at my instigation, imposes strict meters, and is a great improvement on the *faux-bourdon* of the 1932 original. The *a cappella* setting of Eliot's lines from 'Little Gidding' was, in truth, a gift to the poet, but the 1965 Introitus in his memory was Stravinsky's idea; I conducted the first performance and the recording session, which Columbia Records filmed, but a sound engineer mistakenly overdubbed a passage from *Oedipus Rex*, because it co-ordinated with my beat.

The orchestral encore-piece 'Canon' using the *Firebird* melody was a surprise. I conducted the premiere, in Toronto, but Stravinsky never heard the work. The 1966 *Owl and the Pussy-Cat*, for voice and piano (in which I played the piano in the first recording), was a personal work, composed for his wife. The only new music composed after it is the Two Etudes for a [piano] Sonata, which, though short, is a perfectly formed composition, and should be considered as part of the Stravinsky canon. The May 1968 orchestrations of the two songs from Hugo Wolf's *Spanisches Liederbuch* was my idea, but Stravinsky had chosen the Wolf pieces himself, in June 1967. I had no involvement in the two short memorial pieces, *Epitaphium* and the Double Canon *Raoul Dufy in memoriam*, composed in 1959. The former satisfied a request from Heinrich Strobel, music director of the Südwestfunk in Baden-Baden, which provided the orchestra for the Donaueschingen Festival of Contemporary Music. The patron of this annual event, Prince Max Egon von Fürstenberg, had known Stravinsky for only two years, but the composer and the Prince became friends, and the former was pleased to contribute a work in memory of the latter, in October 1959. Stravinsky also made the drawing of the Prince's *Grabmal* (tombstone) on the cover of the score. The proper title of the opus is *Epitaphium für das Grabmal des Prinzen Max Egon zu Fürstenberg*. As for the Dufy, Stravinsky never met the painter but admired his work. He composed the tiny memorial canon because he had been promised a picture by him, which turned out to be a throw-away ink drawing.

In conclusion, and to be rid of the tiresome refrain of 'my participation', let me quote Stravinsky himself on what is surely the most important part of our relationship. At a press conference in Tokyo in April 1959, he very kindly described me as 'a very good conductor of his works, the old ones, the new ones, and even those not yet written' (*Asaki Evening News*).

Chapter 18

An Interview for Radio Frankfurt[1]

You ask about my affiliation with Stravinsky, and whether our connection can be attributed to 'love at first sight'. It was for me, at any rate. One of his doctors, Max Reinkel of MIT, found affinities in our nervous systems and chemistries, and we shared a similar sense of humour, as well as equipollent provisions of sarcasm. Stravinsky was fast-moving, impatient, hyper-tense. So was I.

You ask whether I was Stravinsky's secretary. No. I helped him with his correspondence as early as March 1949, but his French- and English-speaking son-in-law, Andre Marion, who in the 1930s had been a purser for a French steamship company, was his full-time secretary during most of my first years in California. In the mid-1950s, he was employed by a travel agency in Beverly Hills, returning to the composer in his last years to manage his financial affairs. A man of superabundant energy, Stravinsky did most of his secretarial work himself. He actually enjoyed typing, especially on the Russian-language machine that Diaghilev gave to him in 1927. He also had a French typewriter with keys for the accents, and an American portable for travel. In late evenings, when both of us were working at the same time, he composing in his studio, I struggling with words in

---

1   An interview with Herr Backes in Mainz, Germany, recorded in Florida on 4 December 2000, and transmitted by National Public Radio, New York.

the adjoining library room, he would ask, retiring early and passing through my room, if I had anything he could type for me. In fact he typed all of our so-called 'conversations books', deleting what he did not like, and amplifying what he did.

Regarding your question about 'my contribution to Stravinsky's artistic horizon', I can claim to have introduced him to a large repertory of 'old' music, from Guillaume de Machaut and Josquin des Prez to Lassus and Schütz, to name only some of his favourite composers. I also acquainted him with the music of Schoenberg and Webern. After that he found his own way, discovering new directions in what he could do with hexachords and serial procedures, progressing slowly at first, by trying to tonalise atonal harmonies, then rapidly renovating and expanding his musical vocabulary. The *In memoriam Dylan Thomas* of 1954 exemplifies the emotion he was able to achieve with his new means, and the same can be said of *Abraham and Isaac* and the *Requiem Canticles*. I believe that these masterpieces will live as long as his early music. But, as you say, the larger public has not yet discovered them. I do not know much about the popularity, or otherwise, of his last-period music in Germany, but in the UK performances of *Movements*, *Abraham and Isaac* and the *Requiem Canticles* are becoming less rare, and in the US *Agon* has become the most popular of his ballets.

You ask about my programming policy as a conductor. The answer is that I have always tried to juxtapose works that reflect upon each other from different historical periods, as distinguished from programmes that depend primarily upon contrast and variety.

Your questions about the Prince of Venosa indicate that you have visited the village and castello at Gesualdo yourself, though you do not say whether before or after the restoration of the painting of the Prince of Venosa and his uncle, St Carlo Borromeo, now cleaned and placed in its proper position above the altar. The circumstances of my trip there with Stravinsky in 1956 were simply that we had eight hours in Naples during a stopover of our Patras-bound steamship, the SS *Vulcania*, and used the time to drive to Gesualdo with friends from Rome. Stravinsky and I visited the castle again in 1959, after a rehearsal for a concert in the Teatro San Carlo, Naples, this time with the photographer Robert Emmet Bright from Rome, engaged by Columbia Records.

When I came to California in 1948, Stravinsky, like most musicians at the time, was unaware of Gesualdo's music. The only book in English about him, by Philip Heseltine and Cecil Gray, both of whom are models for characters in D.H. Lawrence's *The Rainbow*, was long since out of print, and the music itself, except for one small German and two small Italian collections of only a few of the 150 extant madrigals, all three ineptly transcribed, had not yet been published in modern notation. Wrong notes are strewn throughout them, and some metres have been misconstrued. Incidentally, the Prince of Venosa's alliance with Philip II accounts for the copies, now in the Royal Library in Madrid, of madrigal score-books printed in Gesualdo's lifetime. Philip corresponded with Gesualdo in Venosa.

You ask whether the description in Aldous Huxley's *The Doors of Perception* of listening to music by Gesualdo under the influence of mescaline refers to my recording. The answer is 'yes'. The intonation, pronunciation and style of the performances leave nearly everything to be desired, though in my opinion the pure, 'white', ecclesiastical tone of present-day recordings is misapplied to the late-period madrigals. The treble parts of the music composed in Ferrara were sung by full, rich-voiced divas who probably exuded a vibrato that we would prefer to remove. I would like to live long enough to hear the lost book of six-voice madrigals, believing, as I do, that treasures of music and literature will some day be found in still-uncatalogued libraries and scuolas in Italy.

Turning to your remarks about W.H. Auden: he was easily the most fascinating figure in Stravinsky's American-period entourage. All that I can say about him now is that, mercifully, he did most of the talking. No one could keep up with him, let alone match his wit. In retrospect, I see that what I have written about him tends to focus more on his personal peculiarities than on his intellect, but he *was* eccentric, and in my view his biographers have been over-piously discreet on the subject. Why not admit that, in the early 1940s, while acting as administrator of his Brooklyn boarding house, he informed his fellow tenants that they restrict themselves in the bathroom to 'one square'?

Your question about Stravinsky's personality is too large for me. When composing he was like an exposed nerve. When he was thinking about composing he severed all connection with people around him and entered a private world, his face frowning if anyone talked to him. But his personality expressed itself in countless other ways as well, as in his fondness for fine apparel.

Yes – to answer your question – I rehearsed almost all of Stravinsky's performances for concerts and recordings, and from 1956 conducted the first halves of all but a few of his concerts. Passages from my rehearsal sessions were routinely incorporated in the master copies of the recordings, but I doubt they could be identified now.

Oddly, your question about Stravinsky and the USSR *after* his visit there in 1962 has never come up. He went there only reluctantly and tried to cancel. Once there, however, he was very active, very 'emotioned' – a favourite word of his – and protective, or defensive, of everything Russian. Alas, promptly on his return to Paris he reversed himself and said many disobliging things, particularly about the state of music in the USSR, all of which, of course, was reported in the French and then the Russian press. After that he never mentioned the Russian trip again. Nor did he ever comment on my diary of it, probably thinking it critical of him.

The answer to your question about Mrs Stravinsky in the Hollywood years is that if she had not been there, I could not have lived and worked with her husband. He was moody, critical of everything and everybody, a non-stop worrier, and an alarmist. She was steady, calm, forgiving, idealistic, a little spoiled and naïve, but with a great gift for 'smoothing over'. She and her husband conversed in Russian, and since her voice was very soft, an argument between them was an impossibility.

As for your question about Stravinsky's religion, I witnessed the fervour of it for the first time when accompanying him to his early morning birthday Confession, 18 June 1949. After fasting for twenty-four hours, he was in a fractious mood – certainly not in a solemn one – and did not speak to the two clerics who received him at the door and directed him to the centre of the room, where, to my amazement, he kowtowed (*proskynesis*) on the uncarpeted floor and remained in that position rigidly for twenty minutes. The Confession lasted about two hours and took place out of my sight in a side room. I have never forgotten that picture of Stravinsky, flat on the floor, and was shocked by it.

He stopped going to Hollywood's Russian churches about three years after my arrival; before my arrival came to be referred to as 'BC'. One reason could be that both places of worship were long drives from the Stravinsky home and the services themselves were lengthy. Another factor may have been that he did not like his confessors. His elder son and younger daughter having married Catholics and converted to the Roman Church, and after being given a Papal Knighthood himself, Stravinsky seemed to be moving in the same direction. But he remained Russian Orthodox. No, he did not receive extreme unction. Since his faculties were perfectly clear, Mrs Stravinsky thought that the rites – the rubbings of oils, and the pressing of the silver cross to the lips – would be a cruelty.

As for my own Stravinsky performances, I have recently re-recorded many of his works and intend to continue doing the same, trying to improve on my previous ones. To appraise Stravinsky as a conductor, I would have to say that he was not able to conduct his late music, though he could still give unsurpassed performances of his early ballets, imbued with a spirit that was uniquely his.

Your question about the wretched condition of Stravinsky's published music upsets me. In 1994, Dr Berke, the distinguished director of the publisher Bärenreiter, broached the idea of a *Gesamtausgabe*. I told him that was exactly what Stravinsky had most wanted. In Paris, in 1968, he had agreed to give the publication rights to all of his archives to Boosey & Hawkes in exchange for a commitment to issue a variorum edition of his music. Dr Berke was not seeking financial support – Paul Sacher had agreed to underwrite the undertaking – or compensation of any kind, simply wishing to do for Stravinsky what Schott has done for Schoenberg. In January 1995 Dr Berke came to London to discuss the project with Boosey & Hawkes, but returned to Germany empty-handed. I then wrote to Stravinsky's grandson, explaining the shameful condition of the music and begging him to enlist the agreement of the other family heirs to the publication of a critical, variorum edition, but he slammed the door on the project. I can only hope that the next generation will begin to appreciate the man to whom they owe their existences and their financial wellbeing. Some fraction of the three million dollars that the family heirs received from their suit against the Disney company for the use of *The Rite of Spring* in *Fantasia* (which did incalculable good for the recognition of the composer and the promotion of his music) would help toward the establishment of a corrected edition.

For only a single example of the disgraceful state of the printed music, the piano transcription of *Three Movements from Petrushka*, commissioned by Artur Rubinstein in 1921, lacks two bars in the fourth tableau. The error can be traced to Stravinsky's manuscript, in the Morgan Library in New York, an oversight on his part due to an interruption. But since the omission is obvious to anyone familiar with *Petrushka* as played by an orchestra, one wonders why in all these years it is still uncorrected in the printed score. A few years ago, in Milan, the *Three Movements* was a required work for the contestants in a piano competition. The judges included Maurizio Pollini, Bruno Canino, Charles Rosen and Elliott Carter. None of these acute, aurally well-endowed musicians noticed that the two bars, which complete a perfect sequence, were missing in every performance.

Chapter 19

A Note from Stravinsky on his Piano Concerto (1925)

The sketches for the Piano Concerto contain only a few dated entries: the music from [9] to [11], composed on 8 August 1923; the music from the beginning of the *Allegro* to [9], finished by 15 September; the section from a few bars before [39] to [40], completed on 5 October; the continuation to [45], on 8 October. The end of the movement is signed '1 December, Biarritz'. The second movement was completed (to [54]) on 16 December, the end of the second cadenza on 22 December, and the end of the movement on 24 December. The third movement is inscribed, in Russian, '13 April', and the full score '21 April'. The first performance, the composer as soloist and Koussevitzky conducting, took place on 22 May at the Paris Opéra. A public and a private performance of Stravinsky's reduction for two pianos were given, respectively, at a matinée in the Salle Gaveau on 15 May, and in the evening of the same day at the Princesse de Polignac's. Jean Wiéner played the second piano (the reduction of the orchestra). Stravinsky introduced each performance with a lecture that has not survived, though the following paragraph seems to have been part of it:

> The idea of the Piano Concerto was not spontaneous. This is to say that at the beginning of the composition I did not see that it would take the form of a concerto for piano and orchestra. Only gradually, while already composing, did I understand that

the musical material could be used to most advantage in the piano, whose neat, clear sonority and polyphonic resources suited the dryness and neatness which I was seeking in the structure of the music I had composed. I never said that my Concerto was written in the style of the seventeenth century. I did say, while composing it, that I encountered some of the same problems as the musicians of the seventeenth century, and also Bach. These problems are purely technical and refer to the form: how to build with the musical material that comes from my brain – themes, melodies, rhythms – everything that has a power in a spirit dedicated to musical creation. Beethoven had other problems, and you will readily see that those of my Concerto have nothing in common with his.

In June 1928, Stravinsky told a reporter for a Russian newspaper in Paris: 'Romantic music was a product of sentiment and imagination. My music is a product of motion and rhythm.'

The processional, ceremonial beginning of the Concerto, each of its thirty-two bars with an identical dotted rhythm, the most rigid rhythm Stravinsky ever wrote, has always and continues to puzzle audiences. The scoring, moreover, has been dismissed as 'muddy', and so it can seem when played too loudly and in a soggy, lugubrious tempo. But when the volumes are balanced, the dynamics properly contrasted, and the tempo lightened, the mood changes and the textures become transparent. In June 1929, in Berlin, Stravinsky, hearing Otto Klemperer rehearse these opening bars for a performance a day or so hence, shouted, 'No, no, it should sound like Savonarola',[1] by which, presumably, he meant austere.

Of the *Allegro* that follows, Stravinsky wrote that:

The short, crisp dance character of the Toccata, engendered by the percussion of the piano, led to the idea that a wind ensemble would suit the piano better than any other combination. In contrast to the percussiveness of the piano, the winds prolong

---

1   The sixteenth-century Dominican reformer who preached dark prophecies.

the piano's sounds as well as provide the human element of respiration. 28/XII/28

The sketches for the opus indicate that at first Stravinsky intended to restrict the winds to the reinforcement of motives and figures in the piano part, and gradually expanded their role. The almost exact repeat of the seventy-four-bar exposition endows the body of the movement with a formal firmness as well. In the concluding *Maestoso*, following the 'written-out', strictly measured, piano cadenza, the processional music of the introduction returns in the full orchestra.

The second movement is Stravinsky's last Russian song, as he called it in response to an unexpected questionnaire from his New York audience, for whom he had played the piece during his 1925 American tour. The New York agent for his pianola recordings wrote as follows to the composer's representative in Paris on 27 November 1928:

> We are extremely eager to have a commentary by Stravinsky on his Piano Concerto for a demonstration at an audiographic exhibition in January. It has been suggested that M. Dubois go to Stravinsky with a stenographer who could take his conversation by dictation. We could make the translation here and organize the annotations necessary to present this material in a film. As you know, the New York public's impression of Stravinsky is very special and not very favorable. We wish to change this by audiographic means and to make clear his principles as expressed by himself. To this end we have prepared a questionnaire. M. Stravinsky will be able to polish his answers before the document is placed in the Bibliothèque Audiographique.

Nineteen questions are introduced under the title *D'un Profane à New York à Stravinsky*:

> When you played your Piano Concerto in New York in February, 1925, we were stirred by the strength of the music but did not grasp its meaning. The critics failed us, moreover, saying that a

new beauty cannot exist if *they* have not perceived it. Thus we turn to the last source, the composer himself.

Stravinsky penciled a few marginal replies in French, adding a section-by-section analysis of the Concerto, then translated his texts into dictionary English. Here are a few extracts:

> *Prelude*, processional movement.
>
> *No. 35:* Leaving the theme No. 2, I build up a new period based on the rhythmical development following the same theme after its exposition.
>
> *No. 39:* Rhythmical piano-solo cadenza, in its first phase. In its second phase this determines the value of the metrical unit and allows me to place the processional music of the *Prelude* from the previous movement.
>
> *Second Movement:* I straight start with solemn and large song.
>
> *Third Movement:* I straight begin this *Allegro* by a theme which will be developed in fugato form.
>
> The 'large song' must be played softly in the wind instruments, and, to avoid a monotonous, dirge-like pulsation, played *con moto*.

The oboe solos that follow each of the piano cadenzas contain some of the most lyrical music of Stravinsky's early 1920s period. The last five notes in the piano right hand, ending the second movement, played much faster, become the opening theme of the third movement, a 1920s jazz piece, or parody of one.

Chapter 20

Petrushka: 1947 versus 1911

A comprehensive study of *Petrushka* did not become a possibility until 2006, when the autograph full score, the sketches, and an extensive draft for the first three tableaux were donated by Bruce Kovner to the Juilliard Library in New York. Whereas the original *Firebird* manuscript has been accessible to the public since 1920 (Geneva) and in facsimile for decades, and the principal *Rite of Spring* sketches since 1969, the *Petrushka* manuscripts have now come to light for the first time. The earliest sketches are stamp-dated 22 September 1910. The end of the second tableau is signed '11 February 1911, Clarens', and the third tableau '29 March 1911, Beaulieu'. The fourth is inscribed 'The end, Rome, 13/26 May 1911'.

Comparative studies between the first two ballets will no doubt begin to appear and their similarities, such as the marrying of the musical imagery and the action, as well as their differences discussed, namely the breakaway from the childlike *Firebird* fairytale into drama of great power in *Petrushka.*

Die-hard advocates of the original 1911 score of *Petrushka* over that of the 1947 revised version are still extant, partly because of a mystique about 'originals', but primarily because the earlier score is in the public domain and its performance requires no fees and yields no royalties. But the superiority of the later score is demonstrable, nor can it be claimed that the two texts manifest different aesthetics of different periods, since the 1947 revisions are technical, and only minutely substantive. The argument against the 1947 centres around the retrenchment in the size of the orchestra, the elimination of the fourth flute, oboe, clarinet, bassoon and trumpet, second harp, and second celesta *player* (*not* a second *instrument*). But in truth, the volumetric strength of the later score is generally greater.

Consider the twelve opening bars in both scores. In the 1911, a single flute plays the first melody, but in the 1947 this is doubled by the second flute on sustained notes, thereby adding rhythmic emphasis, articulation and accentuation. The accompaniment is the same in both versions, except that four horns and four clarinets oscillate in 1911, producing a less evenly sustained sound than at bar six in 1947, where the melody is given to the entire cello section; the difficult intonation in high register is more secure in 1911, but the result is a thinner more nasal tone. In sum, the 1947 accents and phrases the music, as the 1911 neglects to do. In bar eleven, 1947 transfers the original harp part to the piano, which increases both the volume and the clarity of line. The rhythm of the flute music accompanying this piano is less regular, an undeniable improvement, as is the change to marcato articulation.

The crucial difference between the versions in the make-up of the orchestra is not in the reduction by six instruments – strings, horns, lower brass, and most of the percussion are the same in both – but in the role of the piano. *Petrushka* was conceived as a concert piece for piano and orchestra, and the piano solo in the Second Tableau was the first music composed. But the piano is used sparingly in 1911 in the first part of the First Tableau, not at all in the Third, and in only a few *tutti* bars in the Fourth. In contrast, the piano remains integral to the sonority throughout the 1947 score. With xylophone and clarinet, piano is the main instrument in the chase music near the end of the Fourth Tableau, thereby emphasising the connection to the beginning of the Second Tableau. The piano, we must remember, represents Petrushka's soul, as the violin does the soul of the title character in *Histoire du soldat*.

The next major difference between the versions occurs at bar three of [3] in both scores. In 1911 the uppermost melodic line in the 7/8 and 5/8 metres is out-of-sync. In the 1947, having discovered that not all players can think in different metres from the orchestra as a whole, Stravinsky bracketed the notes as groups of 7s and 5s in, respectively, 3/4 and 2/4 bars. Moreover, the 1947 reinforces this line with the piano, which also adds a lower octave. In 1911, the harp plays glissandos throughout this entire episode, thereby muddying the texture and depriving the four distinct musical ideas of the clear relief with which the 1947 endows them.

A decided improvement occurs in the 1947 score at the beginning of the next episode ([13] in 1947, [7] in 1911). The 1911 metronome is forty-six for a dotted crotchet-tied-to-a-minim, combined in two unequal bars, 3/8 and 4/8. Not only is this tempo impossible to convey at the *beginning* of a passage, but the change bears the additional indication *stringendo*, meaning that the speed increases from the first beat. 1947, avoiding this unnecessary complexity, continues the steady pulsation from the preceding bars, and separates the two unequal ones. A further improvement occurs in this same place. Whereas each string section in 1911 repeats a single note of accompaniment for several bars, and confines the melody, at first, to barely audible bassoons, 1947 gives the melody to the violins in octaves and doubles it in the piano. 1947 also improves the articulation by shortening the tied-into note in the strings.

The next episode is introduced by an instrumentally heavy triplet figure in 1911, but by rapid arpeggios, snare drum, piano and cellos in 1947, a crisper, cleaner combination. In the organ-grinder's music, the 1947 implements three marked improvements: the melody is played by clarinets two octaves apart, a more effective spacing than in 1911; the figure of the two twittering flutes (one flute, one piccolo in 1911) is enhanced by a more interesting rhythm, adding distinctiveness, with a longer last note; and the in-any-case-unheard rhythmic groups of 7s and 5s in the string parts are rewritten as tremolos, which the listener does hear. But the faster metronome mark of 1911 for the organ-grinder seems preferable, and the *campanelli* for the music-box melody at [15] in 1911 may also be preferred to the celesta, except that the thick celesta accompaniment to the *campanelli* in 1911, with its trills, triplets and difficult-to-distinguish figuration, obscures the melody.

The music at [30] in 1911, [58] in 1947, is substantially the same, except that the 6/8 metre of the flute solo in the earlier score, with a fermata on every long note, does not tell the player precisely how to execute the rhythm. 1947 adds dynamic contrast and an accent on the penultimate note. Stravinsky wanted to control his cadenzas, it should be said, and he always conducted this one with a strict, steady beat.

The Charlatan's music is much the same in the two versions, except that 1947 eliminates the blurring harp scale and, with a harder-edged articulation, transfers the second bass note from cellos to harp. 1947 doubles the harp part with piano, and changes the harp glissando at the end to five measured and detached notes. In 1947, the trumpet parts at [62] are mistakenly assigned to instruments in C instead of to instruments in B flat – the error survives in the last printing of the score – but at this same place in 1911, these parts lack the important indication 'with mutes'.

The beginning of the 'Russian Dance' is brighter in 1947, thanks to the addition of trombones and non-arpeggiated harp chords at the ends of the first two phrases, as well as on a syncopated note. At [66] in 1947, the harp and piano parts of the original ([34]) are doubled by first violins playing *pizzicati à la* balalaika (strumming). The 1947 suddenly and effectively drops the volume of the full orchestra accompaniment to the oboe at [67]. At [76] in 1947 ([41] in 1911), the second violin part is transferred, with advantage, to the violas. What should most surprise 1911 loyalists are the *espressivo* markings in the *later* score and the absence, or misapplication, of them in the 1911; at seven bars before [43], the clarinet solo is marked *dolce espressivo* in 1947, and the second phrase, second beat, *piano subito*, this last versus the empty *crescendo* of 1911. The later score doubles the flute figure at [86] ([44]).

Stravinsky began the composition of *Petrushka* with the Second Tableau and followed it with the First, the Third and the Fourth. The function of the First Tableau as far as the entrance of the Charlatan, and of the Fourth Tableau as far as Petrushka's cry (muted trumpets in *crescendo* on one note), were to provide the 'real world' atmosphere of the carnival and the milling spectators. The drama in the inner world of the puppets is confined to the middle Tableaux and the final page of the Fourth Tableau.

The 1947 revisions in the Second Tableau are less significant than those in the First, Third and Fourth. Already in the first bar of this second scene, 1947 makes apparent that every note should be accented. In bar seven the single cymbal note with the piano is an improvement on 1911's two triangle notes and the jangle of cymbal and tambourine. 1947 reduces the accompaniment to trills and tremolos in all parts at [100] ([51]), eliminating the thick five-note figures in clarinets and bassoons and giving greater prominence to Petrushka's paroxysms in the brass. One of the oddest discrepancies between 1947 and 1911 is in the metronome markings at [152] ([102]) and [103] ([53]). The earlier score has, respectively, 54 and 168 for the quaver (eighth), the later score 80 for the quaver with no change for a considerable time. But in any case the 168 becomes humanly impossible in the piano part in bars five and six of [55]. The 1947 improvements at [108] are in the switch to trombones from horns, and in the piccolo and flute doubling violins and cellos on the second beat. The next bar has a different pitch in the trumpet parts on the penultimate note, which is not a copyist's error but a correction, and 1947 cancels the third appearance of the figure (cf., respectively, [109] and one before [57]). The clarinet cadenza at bar four of [58] is a rhythmically measured solo in 1947. In 1911 the five English horn notes at the end of this *ad libitum* bar lack the more precise *ritenuto* of 1947. A more important, indeed a major, difference is that in 1947 the second violins do not double the piano figure that follows (at [115]) on notes one, three and five, as the harp doubles them in 1911, but play these notes a half-step higher.

The Third Tableau in 1947 makes extensive use of the piano at the beginning as well as later, adding colour, giving edge to the chords, and, when doubling the lower strings, more definition. An incontestable improvement occurs at [128]-[129] in 1947 in the addition of timpani to clarify the triplet figure, and the switch from horns to bassoons in the echo effect that follows. The repetition of the figure, transferring the triplet from trombones to horns, provides a contrasting sonority to the trombones and trumpets at [130]

([67]). 1947 reinforces this brass music with the entire upper string orchestra. A few bars later, the sustaining of the chords at the ends of the trumpet figures by muted horns is an imaginative improvement. Surely, too, the combination of a horn with two bassoons three bars before [133], and thereafter, provides a clearer voicing of these triads than that of the three bassoons of 1911.

1947 adds dynamic nuances to the Ballerina's cornet solo, but the deletion of the word *grotesco* from the bassoon part in the original at the beginning of the Valse is a mistake, since present-day bassoonists contrive to make it sound 'beautiful'. In the bass counter-melody, later in the Valse, the off-beat quavers of the cellos sound fussy in 1911; the 1947 score wisely ablates them. At three bars before [151], the change from four notes-to-the-beat to six, in the trumpet and flute (an octave higher), indicates that Stravinsky had learned about triple-tonguing in the interim years. He had also perceived, at [151] ([76]), that a muted trombone is far more penetrating than the low register of the muted trumpet. 1947 improves the rhythmic spelling of the wind parts in the bar before [156] and thereafter, as well as the metrication from there to the end.

The most extensive 1947 revisions occur at the beginning of the Fourth Tableau. One factor in this is the strengthening of the string parts by reducing the *divisi*. But the first and most noticeable difference is that cellos play from the first bar, thereby providing solidity to the opening that 1911 lacks. Bar three, in 1911, has three solo violas playing a figure in contrary motion to three oboes, a messy, scarcely audible detail. But the whole first part of the Fourth Tableau sounds thick in 1911, as compared to 1947. At [166] ([87]), 1947 transfers the first group of 5s from French horn to English horn, a rhythmic support as well as a change of instrumental colour. A crucial reorchestration occurs at the curtain cue [167] ([88]). Whereas in 1911 the upper strings double the winds, a glutinous texture, in 1947 the fast notes are played by woodwinds alone, leaving the strings and piano to play the rhythmic–melodic figure, a separation that results in a better orchestral balance and that allows the music to breathe: the 1947 includes helpful two-bar phrase-markings.

One of the conductor Ernest Ansermet's objections to the

1947 score was that the accompaniment in the Wet-Nurses' Dance
had been changed from flowing phrases of legato clarinets and
bassoons to staccato trumpets. To him the new articulation seemed
inappropriate to the profession of the dancers at this point in the
ballet, but Stravinsky, an admirer of the female bosom, considered
this association absurd. (Stravinsky's elder son's memoirs describe
the composer personally sampling the fresh milk of a dozen or so
wet-nurses in a Lausanne clinic in 1914, before employing one of them
to service his newborn second daughter.) The only other significant
reorchestration in this dance occurs at [176] ([93]), where piccolo,
flutes and second violins double the melody of the first violins and
horns. At [196] ([102]), 1947 makes clear that the upward unison
string scales should be played glissando and not articulated.

1947 calls for a *ritardando* leading to the 'Dance of the Coachmen',
as 1911 does not. The 1947 accompaniment in this piece strengthens
the semiquaver figure with second and fourth horns. At [223] ([112]),
the responses of the three trombones are helpfully accented on the
first and last notes. At [228] ([114]), all of the upper strings and piano
play two semiquavers on the off-beats as against the lumpish quavers
of the original. At [234] the piano replaces the weaker celesta of the
original ([117]). In 1947 the configuration of the clarinet part in the
third bar is more interesting than in the original, and oboe and English
horn are added.

The bars from [239]–[240] in 1947 introduce an additional
punctuating chord, and improve this by adding harp and piano to the
winds. At [243] ([122]), 1947 deletes the scramble of semiquavers in
the lower strings and piano, and strengthens the melody. Students
of orchestration should study the distribution of *pizzicati* at [247]
in 1947 (bar four of [123]). Small rewritings are found in the music
of the Moor's pursuit of Petrushka, and three considerable revisions
in 1947 occur in the music that follows the puppet hero's death.
Contrabassoon is added to the accompaniment of the policeman, the
bass clarinet part is transferred to a third bassoon, and the 1911
score is not followed in doubling the three trumpets with strings; the
1947 withholds them for the 'sawdust' music. Finally, the music for
two trumpets at the end, scored for a trumpet in D and one in B flat

in the original, requires two trumpets in C in 1947, thereby improving
the balance and intonation.

Chapter 21

Movements, Abraham and Isaac

Stravinsky's... manner of construction [in *Movements*] remains as personal as the sound of his orchestra, and the result is a work which moves forward and is beautiful to listen to, which is brief yet highly concentrated, which at every part reveals a master who has both a precise and original ear and a fastidious mind to direct his ear. The wisdom of great age and experience speaks through this music, but there is no suggestion of relaxed mellowness; the music is taut and has something of the devotional intensity of *Threni*. (From a Cologne newspaper, 1960)

The late Zurich industrialist Karl Weber commissioned *Movements* for his wife, the late pianist Margrit Weber, in March 1958. The first movement was completed on 9 July, the second on 7 September 1958, the third on 14 February 1959, the fifth on 23 March, and the fourth on 30 July 1959. The four interludes were added between 31 July and 18 August 1959. The place-names 'Hollywood–Venezia–Hollywood' appear on the title page of the sketchbook, but ideas for the fourth movement and the interludes came to Stravinsky in Japan in April and May, from Noh, Kabuki and especially Gagaku music.

At the end of February 1959 Stravinsky sent the three completed movements to Frau Weber, who acknowledged them in a letter dated 4 March, but without commenting on the music. Thereupon Stravinsky wrote (23 March) asking her to tell him frankly whether the style and technique were alien to her, and, if so, offering to return the advance on the commission ($15,000). But the Webers kept to the agreement, and on 9 April Stravinsky wrote from Tokyo inviting them to come in late May to Copenhagen (where he was to receive the Sonning Prize and conduct a concert) to study the piece together. As it happened, the meeting in Denmark would be spent with Stravinsky correcting errors in the piano part discovered by Frau Weber herself. The solo part was not 'studied' with a view to performance until the week before the premiere in New York, when I coached Frau Weber in the beat patterns. While in the Danish capital Stravinsky also attended a lunch with Niels Bohr, met Isak Dinesen and received Pierre Boulez, who, following my advice, came from Paris to smooth the ruffled feelings that had resulted from the disastrous French premiere of *Threni* eight months earlier.

The interludes should be performed as introductions to the movements that follow them, as indicated by the continuation of the tempi of the shorter pieces in the longer ones and the absence of pauses between. The instrumentation of each of these four short bridges is markedly different and in contrast to the sonorities of the movements both before and after.

The movements are similarly distinguished by their instrumentation. Only the first and last employ the nearly full orchestra, respectively thirty-four and thirty-five of the thirty-seven instruments. The second is scored for a sextet of harp (vibraphone in the first sketch), trumpet and four solo strings, the third for a nonet of winds and harp, the fourth for flutes, clarinets, trombones and the lower strings. The piano and instruments alternate, as well as play together, at which times the instruments characteristically re-enforce pitches and rhythms in the piano part.

Movements is one of Stravinsky's least harmonically dense pieces. Chords of as few as three, four and five pitches are rare. Frequently they are formed by fanning out, or arpeggiation, note by note, then sustained. For much of the first movement the piano part employs a one-note-at-a-time style, alternating with passages of two- and three-part counterpoint in the winds and, later, violas and cellos. The single-note style returns at the beginning of the third movement, and in the last movement the piano part is largely, the orchestra part entirely, one-note-at-a-time. The piano and orchestra play together in only three places.

The first movement follows three principles of Classical form: the repeat of the exposition, with first and second endings; the contrasting slower-tempo, lyrical and legato beginning of the same-length second part; and the recapitulation toward the end of the movement, in celesta, harp and piano, of the rhythm of the string music near the beginning, with the return to the staccato style. The first movement is the only one with a metronomic change and tempo nuances (a ritard and four fermatas). The longest chord in the movement, the second of the three final fermatas, contains an octave (G), and octaves occur throughout the work, in one instance three times in the same bar (at the beginning of the fifth movement). Open fifths are also prominent, and the second interlude begins and ends with this interval.

Stravinsky enlarges his rhythmic vocabulary in a direction that he would explore further in *The Flood*, *Abraham and Isaac* and the Variations. Here groups of five and seven notes occur in the time of, respectively, two, three and four notes, and ten notes in the time of three. Generally the tactus, or 'felt' beat, obtains, but suspensions of it occur, most conspicuously and excitingly between bars 158 and 169. Changes of metre occur throughout the first movement, toward the ends of the second and third movements, and with almost every bar of the last two movements. Perhaps the most subtle rhythmic relationship in the piece is that of the first bar of the last interlude, a crotchet (quarter-note) triplet with a silent third component followed by a quaver (eighth-note) triplet with a silent first component. The crotchet triplet should be conducted as a 4/8 bar (cf. the beginning of *Surge aquilo* in the *Canticum Sacrum*), the quaver triplet as a 2/8 bar, since only in this way, i.e., against the beat, will the beat of the remainder of the interlude not be felt as a change of tempo. A new rhythmic, and stylistic, feature of *Movements* is in the exploitation of appoggiaturas, unprecedented since *Les Noces*. In the first and last movements they occur in almost every bar, chiefly, but not exclusively, in the piano part.

One of the most ingenious constructions comprises bars 82-3 in the third movement, an upward-directed oboe and clarinet figure of seven even notes in the time of two quavers answered by a downward-directed piano figure of seven even notes in the time of four quavers. The seven repeated G flats in the downward construction, followed by a long G flat in the next bar, momentarily establish the G flat tonality. So, too, a tonality is briefly accented at the climax of the piece, bar 183, through the iteration of the same chord seven times in rhythmic unison, a Stravinskyan pattern of an earlier period.

The many sustained pitches and 'pedal points', together with the numerous octaves and fifths, tend to undermine Stravinsky's claim at the time of the piece's first performance that the music is 'anti-tonal'. The twelve-note series itself, exposed at the beginning in the piano part, with a rest dividing the first six and last six pitches, contains the intervals of a fourth and a fifth, and both are evident in chord structures. Remarkable as well is Stravinsky's habit of piecing together small segments of the four serial forms (original, inverted, retrograde, retrograde-inverted) in a way that enables him to repeat the same pitches immediately, as in the F and E's in the flute near the beginning, or to repeat them with only three intervening notes, as in the case of the two C's in the same example. Furthermore, he introduces an interval that is not part of the serial organisation, the minor-third B flat to G, and in the fourth movement switches the serial order to 7, 8, 9, *11*, 10, in order to end the first half with G, thus endowing the whole movement with the implication of the G tonality.

Every movement makes use of 'pedal' notes: the C in the first ending of the first movement; the tremolo F in the harp part in the second movement; the clarinet tremolo and the repeated Gs in the harp in the last bars of the third. The four-note chords in high register harmonics in violas and cellos in the fourth, initially for nine bars, then for seven bars in different pitches, and again for nine more bars at the original pitches, form a classical symmetry. The fifth movement includes a sustained three-note cello chord under repeated minor seconds in the same pitches played by accelerating flutes. The effect here is of picking up speed for a plunge into the busiest (and best) music in the piece. Notated accelerations are found as well in a bar in the first movement in which the bassoon increases from three to four to five notes for the beat, the piano from two to four to seven, a reminder that Stravinsky had replaced 'subjective' ritards with exactly measured ones in his 1924 Sonata, which broadens the tempo at final cadences through notation.

The premiere of *Movements* took place in Town Hall, New York, on 10 January 1960. The European premiere took place in Cologne six months later.

Abraham and Isaac

Stravinsky had always been fascinated by the story of Abraham's non-sacrifice of his son, and when the commission came from the State of Israel to compose a work for the country's music festival celebrating his own eightieth birthday, he immediately chose the text of this narrative. As everyone knows, about 1800 BC God commanded Abraham, a rich nomad from Ur, in Mesopotamia, to move from the Euphrates valley to the land of the Canaanites between the Mediterranean and the River Jordan. There, as a reward for his obedience and belief in one God, the deity promised that he would have innumerable descendants, and to seal this covenant he and all the men of his tribe were to be circumcised. The difficulty in fulfilling this promise was that he was very old and his wife, Sarah, was a nonagenarian. She persuaded Abraham to father a child by her Egyptian maidservant Hagar, which he somehow managed to do, but after the birth of his son, Ishmael, Sarah miraculously conceived and gave birth to Isaac. At her bidding, Abraham sent Ishmael away to the wilderness of Beersheba, where God said that he would found a great nation in the deserts of Arabia.

God then set a final test of Abraham's faith, ordering him 'to offer your only child, Isaac, whom you love... as a burnt offering on a mountain I shall point out to you'. Abraham took Isaac and two servant boys to an outcrop of rock on Mount Moriah that God had designated. (The rock, sacred to three religions, Judaism, Christianity and Islam, is now covered by a golden dome.) When Abraham raised a knife to kill Isaac, God intervened and ordered him not to harm the boy, 'for now I know you fear God. You have not refused me your son, your only son, and because of this I will shower blessings on you, I will make your descendants as many as the stars of heaven and the grains of sand on the seashore...'

The story of Abraham's willingness to sacrifice Isaac is now generally regarded as a myth, but by Muslims and Orthodox Jews as literal truth; the Torah contains texts verifying it. Stravinsky, who believed in the jealous God and the Bible, composed his 'Sacred Ballad for Baritone and Chamber Orchestra' on verses 1–19 of Chapter XXII of the Book of *Genesis*, in which God summons Abraham to lead his son Isaac into the land of Moriah and sacrifice him. After the journey is enjoined, Abraham experiences a vision of the place of sacrifice from afar. When they arrive there, two servant boys, or sizars, gather firewood. In most artistic representations of the scene they do not witness the non-sacrifice. In Stravinsky's Ballad, Abraham is described binding Isaac and raising a knife over his body. After God recognises Abraham's intention of sacrificing his son, a ram is caught and slain instead, after which Abraham retires to Beersheba.

Stravinsky's friend Sir Isaiah Berlin prepared a Russian transliteration of the Hebrew text, and compiled a guide to Hebrew pronunciation and accentuation for him. Additional tutoring in pronunciation and word setting by the American composer Hugo Weisgall should also be acknowledged, since he was in Santa Fe when Stravinsky began the composition there in the summer of 1962. Stravinsky received Weisgall several times in his rooms in the La Fonda Hotel, and a chart of vowels and consonants and their equivalent pronunciations in English in his hand survives. Stravinsky entered both the Latin-letter transcription of the Hebrew text and the English translation in his manuscript, but the piece was composed to be sung in Hebrew only, the sounds of the words and the music, the appoggiaturas, quasi-trills, melismas and other stylistic embellishments being unsuited to any other language.

Completed in Hollywood on 3 March 1963, the score, dedicated 'To the People of Israel', is now in the Israel Museum, Jerusalem. Theodore Kollek, the then Mayor of Jerusalem, wrote to Stravinsky on 30 March 1965 recalling a dinner in Hollywood a few weeks before with the Stravinskys and 'our mutual friends Isaac Stern, Grisha [Gregor] Piatigorsky, and Bob Craft', asking him to give the manuscript to the Museum on grounds that, as compared to the Los Angeles County Museum, 'our setting is better, overlooking as we do the beautiful Byzantine Russian Orthodox Monastery and the eternal hills of the Land of Abraham and Isaac'. But Kollek had been given the wrong address and his letter was returned to him. He wrote again, on 16 May, but Stravinsky was on a concert tour and did not receive the letter until 15 July. He replied on the same day: 'The enclosed manuscript is my answer. I hope it will be not long before we meet again. All best, my dear friend.'

The full orchestra is never employed together, and purely instrumental music occurs only in the introduction and in the brief interludes that divide the narrative into six sections, each one further distinguished by a progressively slower tempo, as well as by different instrumental combinations. In order to give the words the highest possible relief, Stravinsky confined much of the accompaniment to a single line shared by instruments of different timbres. Thus the second part of the narrative, beginning with the words 'Avraham took two of his boys with him', heretofore scored for a single line of wind instruments, spreads to two parts. Here and elsewhere, God's words, related by His angel, are accompanied by strings only, at first by five tremolo chords in the upper register, a device that Stravinsky had associated with the voice of God in *The Flood*, his biblical opus of the previous year. The next section, a canon between the voice and a bassoon alternating with solo violin, is again restricted to a single instrumental line. The music associated with the departure of Abraham and Isaac from the two serving boys for the sacrifice is a flute cadenza punctuated by five string chords. The next, and longest, interlude represents the journey to the place for the infanticide; its even tread can be described as a march. It consists of a succession of chords of two-pitches in the bass register, with melodic fragments played by alto flute.

At the start of the next section, the point in the narrative where wood is collected for the fire, the vocal part is unaccompanied. It begins on C sharp, the referential pitch of the whole work. Octave-doubled in bassoon and bass clarinet and thrice repeated, this pitch becomes increasingly focal. The statement, 'God will provide the lamb', accompanied by trumpet and tuba, is introduced by the narrator briefly using *Sprechstimme* (partly sung, partly spoken). Father and son go together (two bassoons) to the place where God has bidden Abraham to build an altar. The next episode, the binding of Isaac to the pyre, and of Abraham brandishing his knife, begins with the English horn on C sharp and ends with the same note in the bassoon. The subsequent episode, the angel crying out of Heaven, is accompanied by flute and tuba, a combination that is an ingenious musical symbolism in itself. Harsh, *forte* chords in the full strings punctuate God's command, 'Do not lay thy hand upon the boy', as well as at the dramatic moment when God's angel says that 'Avraham has not withheld thy son, thy only one, from me'.

The programme music inspired by the capturing of the ram in a thicket evokes the friskiness of the animal by leaps and rapid notes in the bassoon, and by such irregular rhythms as twelve notes to be played in the time of five, eleven notes in the time of three, five notes in the time of three, and three notes in the time of five. The next episode, the naming of the place of Isaac's non-sacrifice as Mount Moriah (the hill in Jerusalem), is introduced by a slightly different form of the interlude before the ram-chasing. The music, a three-part canon for the narrator, the French horn and tuba, leads to the most passionate moment of the piece, a C sharp sustained in four octaves in the winds, followed by eight repeated C sharps in the vocal part with the words 'And they called the angel of the Lord to Avraham', accompanied by tuba and horn, first in alternation, then together. The rapidly repeated clarinet notes on one pitch here are Stravinsky's musical image for the multiplication of the seed of Abraham. The short chords, played by the wind instruments together, with the words 'Blessed is thy seed in all the nations of the earth', are a further instance of the composer's musical imagery. The ending, 'And dwelt Avraham in Beersheba', the most moving episode of the Ballad, is introduced and accompanied by three solo strings, replaced in the final phrase by two clarinets. The first and the last note of this final verse is C sharp.

The story of Abraham and Isaac has inspired great visual art (Ghiberti's and Brunelleschi's relief panels in twin frames, in the Bargello in Florence), great music (Stravinsky's) and great literature (Kierkegaard's *Either/Or*). Erich Auerbach's comparison in *Mimesis* of the story with Homer's account of the recognition of Odysseus by his nurse Erycleia should also be mentioned. Stravinsky was in his eighties when he composed this deeply felt, dramatically and musically original work. Its emotional power is conveyed at first hearing, but to understand and love its musical content requires repeated listening.

Chapter 22

The Rite of Spring Manuscript[1]

Some of the principal differences between the manuscript full score of *The Rite of Spring* and the revised versions in the current orchestral repertory are so substantial that portions of the original score would be scarcely recognisable to a twenty-first-century listener. Much of the music in its manuscript form would sound exasperatingly slow compared with the familiar 1967 edition, the metronome markings having been modified downward in rehearsals for the premiere, 29 May 1913. The work would also seem comparatively weak in volume to us at crucial places. This second differential pertains particularly to the 'Sacrificial Dance', which, in the original, drops at a pivotal point from a full orchestra *fortissimo* to a handful of instruments playing *pianissimo.* Additionally, the alternating modes of string articulation employed in the 'Sacrificial Dance', the rotation of *arco* and *pizzicato,* and the occasional use of *ponticello,* together with the continual shifting between *divisi* and *unisono,* exceeded the abilities of the 1913 players, hence the Dance, in its pre-World War I performances in Paris, London and Moscow, did not fulfill the composer's intentions. In all probability, therefore, the *Rite* has never been played as originally written. My own, June 2004, recording of the 'Sacrificial Dance', restores all of the original string articulations, but since the wind parts were not adjusted

---

1   The Elson Lecture delivered at Harvard University, 24 April 2003. Copyright Robert Craft, 2004.

accordingly, the differences are only sporadically perceptible until [186]. From there until the end, however, this (unreleased) recording offers a good transmission of the orchestral sound originally intended, one, I think, that should be generally adopted, since it reduces the volume to a dramatically effective hush that eerily intensifies the anticipation of the end. The studio recordings made by Stravinsky and Pierre Monteux in June 1929,[2] a sufficiently long interval for many of the *Rite*'s rhythmic innovations to have become familiar to the players – partly through other music by Stravinsky himself (*Les Noces*, the *Soldat*) – are in fact so shockingly poor that the listener can scarcely imagine the orchestral pandemonium of the 1913 premiere. Monteux's recording is superior to the composer's in many respects, as could be expected, since *le maître* is conducting his own orchestra and had had more rehearsal time; but his tempi are erratic, moping through the 'Sacrificial Dance' and the 'Evocation of the Ancestors', and racing helter-skelter in the 'Ritual of Abduction'. The tempi in the Stravinsky performance are generally too fast and they tend to accelerate – off the map in the case of 'Dance of the Earth'. His final dance is a struggle with the orchestra that turns into a donnybrook: virtually nothing is together. But the ensembles in both recordings are relentlessly ragged and balances are non-existent, recording technology not yet being in its infancy, but unborn. Thus the top line in the passage for six violas at [91] in the Stravinsky performance sounds close-up and the other five as if from a different room, whereas at [93] the off-beat cellos are loud, the on-beat violas inaudible. The bass-line is feeble in both performances, and the dynamics, high and low, are virtually the same. But the ragged performance of the comparatively simple rhythm of the chords in the first part of 'Dance of the Earth' is surprising, considering that most of the players had rehearsed and performed the work a number of times in the interim, the *Rite* having remained in the Ballets Russes repertory until 1929. Surprising also is that it was not neglected as a concert piece.

---

2   Stravinsky attacked Monteux bitterly in the race to make the first recording of the work, but the two friends were eventually reconciled, and on 19 March 1933 the composer conducted the piece with Monteux's Orchestre de Paris.

Since the Paul Sacher Stiftung in Basel has announced the forthcoming publication of a facsimile edition of the original manuscript score, the general public will be able to savour it as a calligraphic, as well as a musical, treasure, and to see that the layout of the score systems on the page is often more economical and better spaced than in printed editions. Stravinsky himself did not see much of his manuscript. Before the 1913 performances it was with a copyist in Leipzig, and after them, with engravers in the same city. The composer received the first proofs in Switzerland only a few days before the beginning of World War I, but the manuscript remained with the Russischer Musikverlag in German captivity until the composer managed to retrieve it in April 1915, hand-delivered to him in Switzerland by a German woman closely connected to his family.

After the War he returned it to the Leipzig engravers, vainly hoping to have printed scores and orchestra parts in time for Diaghilev's Paris revival of the ballet, 15 December 1920. But the original, error-strewn parts had to be used, and the composer's changes made during the rehearsals were so numerous that second proofs were required and publication delayed until June 1922. Post-World War I, the manuscript was in his possession only during proof-correcting in 1921-2, again in 1929, and during the first two weeks of February 1926, when he extensively revised the score for his own first performance of it, in Amsterdam on 28 February 1926. (From mid-month until this concert he was in Villefranche-sur-Mer, Toulon and Marseille, working with Cocteau on *Oedipus Rex*.) From March 1926 until October 1968 the manuscript was in the hands of his publishers, who returned it to him as an eightieth-birthday present.

An August 1922 letter from the Swiss conductor Ernest Ansermet, who was preparing an Errata, asks Stravinsky to restore the *pizzicati* in the *Sacrificial Dance*, on grounds that orchestral string-playing had improved since 1913, and that the varying articulation was a part of the original conception that should not be lost. He reminds the composer that the

> *pizzicati* were cancelled primarily because the strings already had quite enough to do with the music's rhythmic complexities.

> The crux of the matter is that the *pizzicato* strings are playing in *unison* and the *arco* strings *divisi*. But the doubling of the oboes by *pizzicati* produces a delectable dryness and rhythmic precision, while the bowed string notes are never short enough, and the sonority of the continual *arco* becomes thick and heavy.[3] The alternating *pizzicati* provide clarity and relief and they also go well with the muted horns.

Stravinsky replied in the margins of the letter and returned it to Ansermet: 'Since all orchestra players everywhere are *cons*, I must continue to suppress the *pizzicati* throughout the *Sacrificial Dance*. I ask you to note this in the Errata (the suppression of the *pizzicati*, of course, not the expression in red ink [*cons*]).' In 1924 Stravinsky relented in part, accepting Ansermet's proposal to the extent of writing in the margin on page 126: 'The *pizzicati* are to be played as originally printed in all of the string parts except basses, which continue to play *arco*.' In 1965, after attending several rehearsals for a performance in Vancouver, he cancelled the *pizzicati* again, and the last engraved score, 1967, does not include them.

The purpose of the June 2004 recording by the Philharmonia Orchestra was to restore the string (and other) articulations of the original manuscript to the 1967 score, and to correct the wind and percussion parts throughout in conformity with Stravinsky's final revisions, though only when they are obvious improvements over the original. The question of tempi was crucial, since some of those in the manuscript original were altered numerous times over the years. Whereas the metronome for the first dances in Part Two and the penultimate dance have become slower, some of the fast dances remain difficult to achieve.

On 5 March 1913, Monteux wrote to the composer requesting the score of Part One in order to study it before preliminary rehearsals in Paris later in the month. Stravinsky did not attend these, but Monteux

---

3   After hearing Ansermet conduct the piece in Berlin on 21 November 1922, Pierre Souvtchinsky wrote to the composer saying that the strings, and especially the violins from [196], were 'not rhythmic enough and they weaken the ending'.

sent a description of them, which arrived on 30 March. The next day the composer reorchestrated the music between figures [28] and [29], in which Monteux had found an imbalance during his tryouts. (The manuscript preserves only the first bar from the cancelled original version.) On 2 April, returning this manuscript, the conductor wrote that meanwhile he had 'received another score from your publisher in Berlin, but the last 20 bars are missing'. This score, a copy in Stravinsky's hand (now in the Bibliothèque Nationale, Paris) is not an exact duplicate of the first part of the manuscript, but, like it, is covered, for legibility, with large-sized metrical changes in blue and red pencil in Monteux's hand.

Since the Leipzig copyist, 'Th. O.', did not finish the 'Sacrificial Dance' until 1 May, the orchestra parts of those last twenty bars must have been extracted in great haste. Monteux would also have had little time to familiarise himself with the completed instrumentation. His correspondence indicates that he had first learned the music from a two-hand piano reduction.

Stravinsky arrived in Paris for rehearsals in the Théâtre des Champs-Elysées on 13 May. When not sitting with Debussy or Ravel during them – the two French composers were feuding at the time – he followed the score standing behind Monteux. The lore recounts a crisis in which the orchestra broke into laughter after playing an excruciatingly dissonant chord (the beat before [54]), whereupon Stravinsky angrily stopped the rehearsal, rushed to a piano, and analysed, from disintegration to recombination, the perfectly logical construction of the harmony. This edifying analysis was received with general applause. The harmonic vocabulary expands prodigiously with the chromatic beginning of Part Two. Of the fifty possible hexachords, the *Rite* employs thirty-five, as well as all of the thirty-eight possible pentachords.

Before and after the December 1920 revival – the performance on the 15th was conducted by Vladimir Golschmann, the others by Ansermet – Stravinsky vetted the proofs (now lost) for the first edition. But the major revisions that transformed the latter part of the score were not completed until February 1926, when he scored several entire pages in preparation for his own first performance (Amsterdam). These new manuscript pages were pasted over the corresponding published ones, and many smaller changes were inked in. This version was used for his first and second recordings, French Columbia, 7–10 May 1929 (five sessions with the Orchestre Straram),[4] and American Columbia, April 1940 (New York Philharmonic, 4 April, 2.30–6PM, after five rehearsals and one concert performance in Carnegie Hall). In 1930 Serge Koussevitzky's Russischer Musikverlag published a second edition of the 1922 score, restoring many but not all of the string articulations of the original manuscript. Stravinsky had corrected the first proofs of this score (in August 1929, in Talloires), and the second proofs (in October in Paris), but he never conducted from the edition, and used his 1926 part-manuscript score for his 1930s Paris performances and his 1940 New York recording. A further corrected edition appeared under the Boosey & Hawkes imprint in 1952, marked '1947 revision'. The composer continued to correct this in 1957 and 1965, and in 1967 a 're-engraved' edition appeared. Stravinsky's third studio recording, on 1 January 1960, in the ballroom of the Hotel St George, Brooklyn, attempts to incorporate the 1943 revision of the *Sacrificial Dance*, as does the pirated recording of a Swedish Radio Orchestra broadcast in 1961.

———◆———

Stravinsky was inspired by a vision of *The Rite of Spring* (*Holy Spring, Vesna Sviaschénnaiya*) while completing *The Firebird*. Soon after the *bouleversant* success of the earlier ballet, he wrote to Nicolas Roerich,[5] artist, archaeologist, ethnologist, whom he had

---

4   The famous film clip of Stravinsky recording an excerpt from *Firebird* was made at his performances of 8 and 10 May 1929 for Columbia Records, Paris.

5   'Who else could help me, who else knows the secret of our ancestors' close feeling for the earth?' Stravinsky wrote to the St Petersburg critic Nicolai Feodorovitch Findeyzen. Stravinsky's relations with Roerich seem to have been much closer than hitherto supposed, as the following excerpt from a letter indicates. It is dated 22 March 1939, and posted from Naggar, Kulu, Punjab, British India: 'The plane from Paris brought us the sad news of your tragic loss, your wife's death [on 2 March]. Please accept our deepest condolences. Despite the great distances that have kept us apart for so long, we often think of you and your whole family, thus this sad news is all the more sorrowful to us. Many friends from our generation have already died, and of late it seems that we have been receiving such sad bits of news more frequently. God keep you well in your service to your great talent. You are with us in our hearts.'

met through a nephew of Roerich who had been a fellow-pupil of Rimsky-Korsakov, sharing the vision and proposing collaboration in a 'choreodrama' on the subject. But during the late summer of 1910 the idea of *Petrushka* had seized Stravinsky's imagination, and in September when Diaghilev and Nijinsky visited him in Lausanne to discuss *Vesna Sviaschénnaiya*, they were astonished to hear sketches for the second tableau of a puppet drama. Fascinated by the *Petrushka* music and scenario, Nijinsky persuaded Diaghilev to postpone the *Rite*. Stravinsky explained the predicament to Roerich, but urged him to continue with the scenario of the *Rite*, and also to design its costumes and sets.

In Ustilug, Volhynia, in the summer of 1911, after the triumph of *Petrushka*, Stravinsky returned to the *Rite*, now subtitled 'Scenes of Pagan Russia'. Wanting him to see the Princess Tenisheva's collection of Russian ethnic art, Roerich asked the composer to meet with him at Talashkino, her country estate near Smolensk, to plan the structure of the ballet. Stravinsky's reply of 25 July reveals his first travel itinerary: 'Could some horses be sent to Smolensk to fetch me? Remember that my train arrives from Warsaw very early, I think at 5 o'clock in the morning.' On arriving at Brest-Litovsk, however, and learning that the next passenger train to Smolensk would depart only two days later, Stravinsky bribed the conductor of a freight train to let him ride in a cattle car:

> I was alone there with a bull! The animal was leashed by a single, not very reassuring rope, and as he glowered and slavered, I barricaded myself behind my one small suitcase. I must have looked an odd sight in Smolensk as I stepped from that *corrida,* carrying an expensive, or, at least, not tramp-like, bag, and brushing my clothes and hat, but I must also have looked relieved. The Princess Tenisheva put at my disposal a guesthouse attended by servants in white uniforms with red belts and black boots. I went to work with Roerich, and in a few days the plan of action and the titles of the dances were composed.

Surely this tauromachian encounter en route to the creation of a prehistoric ballet must have heightened the sense of realism in the composer's atavistic imagination.

———•———

The *Rite* was conceived as two equal and complementary parts, 'The Adoration of the Earth', which takes place in daytime, and 'The Sacrifice of the Chosen One', which takes place at night.[6] The orchestral Introduction to Part One represents the reawakening of Nature. The curtain rises at the end of it for the 'Augurs of Spring', in which an old woman soothsayer is accompanied by a group of virgins. 'The Ritual of Abduction' follows, then the 'Round-dances of Spring', the 'Ritual of the Two Rival Tribes', the 'Procession of the Sage', the 'Sage's Kiss of the Earth' and the 'Dance of the Earth'. As Stravinsky wrote to Findeyzen: 'I want the whole of my work to give the feeling of the closeness between the lives of man and the soil, and I sought to do this through a lapidary rhythm.'

An interview with Stravinsky by Ricciotto Canudo published in his Paris periodical *Montjoie!* on the day of the premiere[7] emphasises the religious character of the rituals, even referring to the Sage ('The Eldest and Wisest') as a 'Saint' and a 'Pontifex'. Stravinsky vehemently disavowed the article (an unfinished correction of which survives in his hand) but it sounds like him, above all his word for the kiss of the earth as a 'Benediction'. Stravinsky's title for the opus from its inception was *Vesna Sviaschénnaiya*, the 'sacred' or 'holy' spring. He was never happy with Léon Bakst's more memorable *Le Sacre du printemps.*

———•———

---

6   An undated letter from Roerich to Diaghilev, describing part of the scenario of the ballet, was sold at auction, Sotheby's, London, 21 May 2004. The probable date is February 1913, since Roerich refers to the completed Part One as he had seen it in a Nijinsky rehearsal, and since Nijinsky wrote to Stravinsky, 25 January 1913, saying he had choreographed Part One only.

7   The literature on the premiere is more copious than on that of any other single composition in music history. See T.C. Bullard's *The First Performance of I. Stravinsky's Sacre du printemps*, 3 volumes, University of Rochester, 1971.

In Part One, the original and the latest (1967) scores differ drastically in only a few places, in the accents and dynamics from [13], in the four bars before [59], and in the four before [72]. The original and revised versions of the last dances in Part Two are far more dissimilar in metre, instrumentation, dynamics, phrasing and accentuation. One of the important discrepancies is in the phrasing of the opening bassoon solo: the original clearly indicates a break after the second quaver (eighth) in bars two and eight; and in bar fourteen, just before the return of the bassoon, the English horn phrasing should duplicate the breaks in bars fifteen and sixteen. Also, the English horn part lacks the *accelerando* for the last four notes of bar two of [2]. On page three the manuscript lacks the *diminuendo* for the English horn, French horn and bassoon (bars four, six and seven). Further, at [10] the first two notes of the piccolo clarinet are slurred in all six statements but tongued in later scores, a major improvement. The latest revised printed score is in error in the fifth bar of [12]: the bassoon should continue to sustain the A flat on the first note, not move down to F. The manuscript makes this clear. Later in life Stravinsky would rewrite accidentals (flats, sharps, naturals) in parentheses for notes sustained over bar-lines; he had not yet begun this practice in 1913. In the manuscript, the tempo for the 'Augurs of Spring' – the original title was 'Fortunetelling' (*Gadonia*) – is 112 for the crotchet (quarter), as against a turgid 100[8] in some of the pirated scores.[9]

The manuscript from [18] to [22] is incomplete as compared to the four-hand score that Stravinsky marked for Nijinsky, indicating a pattern of jumps for the dancers, some of them anticipating the offbeat accents of the orchestra, some of them doubling the orchestra, and some in response to it. In effect, these choreographed accents are rhythm made visible. The manuscript at bar four of [19] lacks the *forte*, bar five lacks the *subito piano*, bar eight the *forte* on the second note, bar twenty the *piano* on the second note, and bar four of [20] the *forte* on the last note. At [21] the *subito piano* is missing on the

---

8   Monteux's 1929 recording begins this section too slowly but accelerates.

9   The *Rite* has never enjoyed copyright protection in the United States, which, like the USSR, did not sign the Berne Copyright Convention. The pirated edition of the miniature score published in 1933 by Kalmus was the most widely circulated until the 1960s.

second note. The 1967 score corrects these errors. In the original score, the bar before figure [22], the low F in the basses is sustained by a fermata and by the abbreviated word *ten.* (*tenuto*); the note is also doubled by a (penciled in) *secco* and a *Gr. C.* (*Gran Cassa*: bass drum) note marked '*sf*'. In the same place in the 1967 score, two tubas, an octave apart, and the bass drum play a sustained note. Two bars before [22], the G and C in the violas' quadrupal stop, deleted in 1913, were restored in 1967.

———•———

Leaving Ustilug for Clarens on 13 September 1911, Stravinsky wrote to Roerich:

> I have sketched the Introduction for *dudki* (reed pipes) and the 'Divination With Twigs'[10] in a state of passion and excitement. The music is coming out very fresh and new. The picture of the old woman in squirrel fur sticks in my mind. She is constantly before my eyes as I compose. I see her running in front of the group, stopping sometimes, and interrupting the rhythmic flow – I have also composed a smooth jointure of 'The Dance of the Maidens and the Divination With Twigs', with which I am very pleased.

Stravinsky followed, and improved upon, Monteux's advice at [28], cancelling four bars in 2/4 time and rescoring them in lighter and more transparent instrumentation on the next page. The principal difference between manuscript and final score in the eleven bars following is that the first note of the second beat of the second violins is B flat in the manuscript and C in the later scores, as well as in the sketches. The German script at the bottom right of this page identifies the score in the process of being printed as 'Igor Stravinsky's'.

In some of the published scores, bars two and three of [29] lack the manuscript's overarching phrase line above the trumpet parts,

---

10   Having no recollection of why this title was dropped from the score, Stravinsky wrote to Nijinsky, 'She enters at [15]'.

and the second beat of bar five in the trumpets is a quaver (eighth) instead of a crotchet (quarter) – a minor point but a correction not carried out in the latest score. At [30] the manuscript assigns the semiquaver (sixteenth-note) figure to '4 *sole viole*', and the *pizzicati* to the remainder of the viola section. At [31] in the original the second horn doubles the fourth horn in the four-note syncopated figures, whereas the 1967 score restricts the part to the fourth horn. The 1967 score corrects the manuscript in the bar before [33], which should duplicate the second bar before [33]. This correction is in the composer's hand in the present writer's score.

Some of the markings at [37] recreate the excitement of the rehearsals for the premiere, especially the cancellation of the too-fast metronome mark of 132 for the dotted crotchet,[11] and in the added piccolo trumpet. We know from Stravinsky's memoirs that this octave-doubling trumpet was suggested by Debussy, who had remarked that the strings overwhelmed the flute melody. At the same time, Stravinsky added the piccolo clarinet, hastily, and in pencil, but having already written *marcatissimo* over the passage, why did he write an accent for every note? In 1922 he added an oboe to the flutes. Musicians will wonder at what point he required the piccolo trumpet to double-tongue each note, though the idea obviously came from the flute and piccolo parts; and, conversely, when and why he removed the double-tonguing in the flutes in the revised editions. The manuscript shows that he neglected to complete the slur in the horn parts through the downbeat of [39]. The adjacent 4/8 and 5/8 bars at [39] are not combined into a 9/8, as they are in the 1967 score, and the tuba in the 4/8 bar is doubled in the manuscript by the third trombone. The barring here is enlightening for score readers, but the 9/8[ths]-in-three better accommodates the players.

The second half of bar one of [41] in the manuscript adds a tuba, with a rest on the second quaver, instead of a G, as the melody warrants. Stravinsky's response to Monteux's letter saying that this part did not come through in the two horns was to add the entire

---

11   The tempo in Monteux's 1929 recording is faster than this and the music becomes a blur of crossing lines and notes.

horn section and the tuba. He also retained the tuba for the last four notes, a revision in the manuscript not followed in the 1967 score! His '2 – 1 – 1 – 2' numbering above the strings changes the 4/8 bars into 2/4 bars, but leaves each 5/8 bar for a single awkward beat. Further examples follow in which 4/8ths and 5/8ths should be combined as 9/8ths played as three even beats.

The Russian word at [48] is *Khorovod* ('La ronde: round dance). The word *Andantino* and the slackening of the metronome from 108 to eighty-eight per crotchet are unexpected, but the tempo in Stravinsky's sketchbook is an incredible 144. The last note in the bass clarinet at [49] lacks the appoggiatura, perhaps intentionally.[12] In the manuscript the viola parts have been corrected in bar four of [50] and the horn parts in bars six and seven, in order to continue the octave-doubling of the flutes. The 1967 score confusingly drops the *f* from the direction at [53] in the manuscript, *Molto pesante ma non troppo f*, the intended meaning being 'not too *forte*', rather than 'not too *pesante*'.

Comparing the manuscript and the 1967 score at one bar before [54], we remark the absence of *ritardando* in the former. The tempo at [54], 160 for the crotchet, was reduced in the manuscript to 138 for the first performance. A similar reduction recurs at [56], from 108 for the crotchet to eighty-eight, and the *Andantino* is repeated. Stravinsky dates the bottom right corner of the page '30 January', which is Gregorian, as well as its Julian equivalent, '12 February 1912'.[13] At [57] the manuscript indicates still another reduction in tempo, from 168 for the crotchet to 146. The words *Allegro rigoroso* are in another hand than the *Molto Allegro*, which is unmistakably Stravinsky's. The editors of the 1965 score have neglected to erase the *con sord.* that Stravinsky deleted in his original score.

---

12   An editor of one of the later scores has mistakenly cancelled the appoggiatura in the piccolo clarinet instead of adding one to the bass clarinet.

13   In the twentieth century the Russian Orthodox, or Julian-style, calendar was thirteen days ahead of the Gregorian calendar, which was introduced in March 1582 by Pope Gregory XIII. The difference became fourteen days in the twenty-first century, and will become fifteen in the twenty-second, *ad infinitum*. The Julian calendar, devised in the same year by Joseph Scaliger, determines that the Julian period, 7980 years, began on 1 January, 4713 BC, the nearest year in which the solar, the lunar and the Roman cycles coincided.

The four bars before [59] are radically different in the manuscript and the 1967 scores, but the E in the bassoons, added in the 1926 score, is found in the earliest sketches. This E is missing in the Kalmus score, as are the G's in the timpani in the seventh and ninth bars of [58], and the *pesante* for the eighth bar. Stravinsky was always troubled by this passage, and his revisions of it do not solve all of the problems. The first of these is that the two sustained chords are too long. The fourth bar before [59] should be 2/2 not 3/2, and 2 bars before [59] should be 2/4 and not 3/2. Neither of these notes should have a *crescendo*, which sounds dull. Moreover, the exact repeat is uncharacteristic of the piece as a whole. One of Stravinsky's miniature scores marks each chord '*sfp*', which the present writer has chosen. The abolition of all tempo indications in the 1967 score is not convincing. In 1954, when Robert Rudolf was preparing his reduced orchestration of the *Rite*, which Stravinsky was powerless to prevent, the piece being in the public domain in the US, the composer nevertheless decided to improve these four questionable bars even for a pirated edition, partly by reducing the lengths of the notes in the horn and bassoons (!) triplet. We remark that in this 1954 rewrite the sustained chord is given to the bassoons and tuba, and that the harmony becomes an E flat triad, inverted position. Further, the dynamic of the sustained chord is *piano.* In the 1922 score the doubling of the seventh and eighth horn parts by the tuba is a considerable improvement.

The hurried writing of the two bars at [62], adding horn and trombone in pencil, suggests that this was done during a rehearsal. At [65] the first four horns are muted (as they are in the sketches), which must be mentioned for the reason that they are insufficiently *forte* even without mutes, to which Stravinsky changed the marking in 1920. The words of the hyphenated title 'moving-leading', which appears in Stravinsky's sketches above the music of what is now four bars before [62], were coined by him.

Critics have suggested that before Ravel's visit to Clarens in April 1913 to work with Stravinsky on orchestrating and editing Mussorgsky's *Khovanshchina*, the orchestral roster of the *Rite* did not include such percussion instruments as the *cymbales antiques*, earlier in Part One, and the *guïro,* or *rape-guero*[14] at [70], the great *tutti,* and at the end. The manuscript contradicts the contention. Stravinsky seems to have told Canudo that the deafening noise at the climax before the Sage's kiss was meant to convey the terror of the midday sun. At [71] the manuscript assigns the quavers (eighth-notes) to the solo *cello,* and the sketches add *pizzicati* violas on each quarter-beat, but Stravinsky transferred the part to a solo bass before the first performance, along with, in bar three of [71], the changes from minim (half-note) rest/fermata to crotchet (quarter-note) rest and dotted minim/fermata. The original tempo for these three bars, fifty-two for the crotchet, was reduced to forty-two before the first performance and retained thereafter. The Russian title proclaims the 'Procession of the Sage'. The 168-for-the-crotchet metronome in the manuscript for the 'Dance of the Earth' is a reduction from 184 in the sketches, but in 1913 the music was probably played slower than 168. The notes of the introductory bar of the bass drum *crescendo* at [72] (the 'stampede') are semiquavers in the sketches, but the manuscript changes them to triplets, a crucial improvement. Stravinsky preferred the part to be played on a drum with a single head, which produces a more hollow sound; he also preferred wooden to felt sticks.

The deleted handwriting in faint pencil between the two score-systems on page forty-two tells the copyist: 'Bis hier ist schon Abschrift / von hier Abschrift weiter'. ('The copy is complete until here / starting here the copy goes on.') 'Hier' refers to a thick demarcation sign four bars before [77]. The bold Latin-letter script in blue pencil above reads: 'Abschrift (Paris)' ('Copy (Paris)'). Bars six, eight and eleven of [75] in the cello part, each identified by an '**X**', are changed in the 1922 score to replicate bar four of [75]. From [75] to the end, the first note of each group of four semiquavers spells a whole-tone scale: C, D, E, F sharp, G sharp, A sharp. An important message to Nijinsky in the four-hand piano score annotated for him by Stravinsky says that the dance should emphasise the downbeat of each bar, *not* the orchestra chords. We note that the curtain cue was moved back to the bar before [78] for the premiere. The inscription under the last two bars says that

---

14   A large Cuban gourd, played with a scraper.

the full orchestral score was completed in Clarens on 16 February (Gregorian-style), 1912. Stravinsky informed Roerich that

> Part One will represent about three-fourths of the whole, and since the tempi are almost all madly fast, this has meant an immense amount of writing. But it seems to me that I have penetrated the secret of the rhythm of Spring and that musicians will feel it.

Exactly when Diaghilev realised that the *Rite* could not be finished and prepared for performance in 1912 and would have to be postponed until the spring of 1913 is not known, but it seems that he did not inform Stravinsky of the decision before 16 March, the date of the latter's letter to Roerich: 'I am awaiting Diaghilev and Nijinsky here [Clarens] on their way from Vienna after a triumphant tour.' At first the composer was rankled by the rescheduling, then relieved, recognising the impossibility of finishing the full score and preparing the orchestra parts in time for the 1912 season. He began the second tableau forthwith, however, and by mid-March had written most of the Introduction to Part Two. He then travelled with the Ballets Russes to hear and see his own ballets, as well as the premiere of Ravel's *Daphnis et Chloë* on 8 June, which had an effect on him, as the slow music near the beginning of Part Two of the *Rite* does not entirely succeed in disguising. On 29 May Stravinsky saw the ballet premiere of Debussy's *Faune*, with Nijinsky's scandalous masturbation scene that Rodin, at Diaghilev's instigation, publicly defended. On 31 May the magazine editor Louis Laloy invited Stravinsky to lunch with the Debussys at his home the following Sunday, 9 June 1912, the occasion of the famous four-hand play-through by the two composers of what had been composed of the *Rite*.

Stravinsky spent the first part of the summer at his home in Ustilug working on the remainder of the composition and the full score. He also completed the orchestra score of *Zvezdoliki* and wrote two of the *Three Japanese Lyrics*, music on the same high level as the *Rite*, though utterly different from it.

Part Two

Part Two, 'The Sacrifice', or as the composer called it, 'The Great Offering', begins after an Introduction to 'the secret night-games of the maidens on the sacred hill'. The music accompanying these mysterious rituals is quiet but foreboding. After two intimations of danger, effectuated first by sharp-edged muted horn chords, then by muted horns and trumpets, a wild dance erupts, followed by eleven savage drum beats and the 'Glorification of the Chosen One', leading without pause to the 'Evocation of the Ancestors', the 'Ritual Dance of the Ancestors' and the 'Sacrificial Dance'.

The *bouchés* marking for oboes in the manuscript is unique in Stravinsky's music, though he had used a muted oboe in *Zvezdoliki*. The string dynamic is missing at [80], but the *diminuendo* from there through the next bar indicates that it would be *mezzo-forte*. The mark at the top left of '44A', and in the centre of '44B', '44C' and '44D', refers to the renumbering of the pages added on 29 March 1913 to the Introduction to Part Two. Bars two and three of [81] are without slurs in the manuscript, but this is corrected in the published scores. In bar two of [82] the direction *sul ponticello sino al segno* is rubber-stamped, as are the indications for mutes and their removal in the strings, which means that they must have been added by an editor; Stravinsky's gadget-filled studio lacked these tools.

The *ripieni* violins in bar three of [83] are intended to play a B, parenthetically confirmed as B natural in the manuscript. Beneath bars two and three of [85], Stravinsky has autographed and dated the addenda 'Clarens 16–29, IV, 1913'. In bar seven of [86] the motive of the two muted trumpets has been inserted on a single small stave drawn by a tiny stylus between the horn and violin staves. The 1967 score should have specified 'straight mutes' – though no other kind existed in 1913 – and established the dynamic as *mezzo forte*.

At [89] the only difference between the manuscript and the 1967 score is the correction, probably during a rehearsal, of a parenthetical *poco* to the *più mosso*. The information that the curtain cue at the premiere was co-ordinated with the cello solo in bar four of [90] tells us that the orchestral Introduction to Part Two is the longest pre-curtain prelude Stravinsky ever wrote. At [91] and [93] the respective markings *très tranquille* and *Allegretto tranquille* are in Monteux's hand. The clarinet parts at [94] are marked *mf* in the manuscript, against *p* in 1967, and at [95] the oboe and bassoon lack the *piano* dynamic. The insertion of a fermata at the end of [103], in order to make a clean start for the 11/4 bar, is in Stravinsky's hand.

After noting the slip at [101] in the placement of the trumpets above the horns in the layout of the score, we remark that the first four pitches of the piccolo trumpet part at [103] correspond to the sketches, but have been incorrectly transposed (by Stravinsky) in the manuscript. The notes should sound D sharp, C sharp, C double sharp, D sharp (the trumpet in D sounds a whole tone higher than written). A letter from Vera Sudeykina to Stravinsky during his 1935 American tour says that she was playing his recording of the *Rite* one day when the volley of these mis-transposed trumpet notes caused their dog, Pilou, who had been wagging his tail, to flee to the bathroom and hide there until the end of the piece. The phrasing of the following bar's eleven beats into two groups of four and one group of three is Stravinsky's. The parenthetical 120-for-the-crotchet metronome seems to have been added to the manuscript during a rehearsal.

At [104], *Glorification of the Chosen One,* the metronome marking of ♩ = 144 implies that Stravinsky conceived the beating pattern as two plus three, though he conducted it, at least in his later years, as three plus two. This pattern holds throughout the dance in all 7/8 and 5/8 bars; the 9/8ths are of course always in three (three times 3/8).

In one of his copies of the 1922 miniature score Stravinsky deleted the first two notes of each of the five appoggiaturas in the flutes, which had formed a perfect octatonic progression. No doubt the 144 tempo seemed too fast to include all five before the second quaver, but later editions restore the deleted notes. In the same miniature score Stravinsky consolidates the bar at [106] with the bar before into a bar of 7/8. The curious Klee-like drawing above the last bar of this score outlines the composer's own callisthenic beating pattern. Bar three of [110] shows the beat, 3/8 followed by 2/4, as against the music; it should be 2/8 + 3/8 + 2/8; the same error occurs in bar three of [120].

At bar three of [116] the words *Molto Allargando* appear to have been a post-compositional directive. At [117], horn, trumpet and trombone parts are added by means of the composer's smallest stylus. The 1921 and later printed scores err in bar four of [117] in that the bass drum doubles the upper strings instead of the lower. (This obvious mistake was corrected in the 1967 score, but, astonishingly, the performance of the bar is wrong in all recordings made before that date,[15] as well as in many after it.) Stravinsky's sketches for this music repeatedly identify the maidens as 'Amazons', but whether he was thinking of Scythian females, or the ancestors of the more recently excavated ancient female warriors at Veronezh in southern Russia, is not known. In May 1963 Stravinsky saw the Budapest Opera's staging of the ballet in which the Chosen One emerged from a stone labyrinth encircled by six Amazons. He was very pleased and told the Intendant and the choreographer that the staging was correct for the first time in his experience.

According to the 'short score', 'Purification of the Sun' was the original title of the next dance. I do not know when this was changed to 'Evocation of the Ancestors', but the probable date is September 1912. The manuscript was sent section by section to the publisher in order to prepare the piano reduction eventually published in January 1913. Stravinsky's interview with Ricciotto Canudo tells us that the Chosen One must not 'touch' the sun, and that after her death the elders who lift her body towards the empyrean are also forbidden to 'touch' it.

As the manuscript reveals, the 'Evocation of the Ancestors' differs radically in rhythm and metre from the later published scores. Bar one at [121] is distinguished by a fermata, as are bars one and three of [122]. The metres in both scores differ as well. Before the entrance of the treble part in the wind instruments, the manuscript contains only seven crotchet beats, in a bar of three and a bar of four, as against twelve beats in the first published score. The treble melody is also differently accentuated in the manuscript, the penultimate note occurring on an upbeat, and the accent on the second beat of a 4/4 bar, as well as on the downbeat of the following three-beat bar.

---

15   A mistake I discovered when listening to a recording by Pierre Boulez.

The accents, doubled by string chords, recur in the same melodic-harmonic positions in both scores, but the metrication is different. Whereas the metres for the treble motive in the original are 4/4, 3/4, 4/4, 3/4, in the printed score they are 4/4 (2/2), 3/4, 2/4, 3/4. Anyone familiar with the music would feel that the manuscript version is against the grain.

In the 'Evocation', the sustained D sharp in the bass remains at triple *forte* in the manuscript, dropping to *pianissimo* only when accompanying the five bassoons at [125], which represent the five 'eldest and wisest'. Further, the manuscript requires two bass tubas, the printed score only one, doubled by the bass trombone. The manuscript metres at [123] are 4/4, 3/4, 5/4, 3/4, 4/4, 3/4 and 3/4, those of the 1967 score 2/4, 3/4, 2/2 (4/4), 3/4, 3/4, 2/2 (4/4), 3/4 and 3/4. The accents differ as well. The C major treble melody in the winds, echoed by the bassoons at the end and marked triple *piano*, is similar in both scores, but Stravinsky's revision of the first part of the dance is based on this bassoon version.

The 'Evocation' movement, the shortest in the *Rite*, was more problematic for the composer than any other except the final dance. The June 1922 miniature score, and the 1924 reprint – advertising the new score of the *Octuor* on the back cover – show him pursuing a different course than he would adopt in 1926, retaining the fermatas and consolidating the twos, threes and fours into larger units by lengthening the bars to 7/4, 8/4, 10/4 and 11/4. This can only be attributed to the complexities of the music for the players of 1913–14 and the 1920 revival. The 1926 revisions include an indication that the tempo of the quaver in the preceding dance is equal to the crotchet in the 'Evocation' (cf. the beginning of the first violin part at [121] in 1967).

Having mentioned the miniature scores, I should say that the one, now in Basel, signed on the cover 'Igor Stravinsky, Paris, Juin 1922', contains the composer's 'Invitation 2753 de la Théâtre des Champs-Elysées', for the 1913 premiere and, in blue crayon, the seat numbers 109 and 111. The composer's corrections are found on pp. 46–53, 55, 56, 58–61, 70, 71, 73, 75–7, 79, 80, 83, 85–91, 93, 95–102, 106–109, 111 and on every page of the 'Sacrificial Dance'.

At [129] in the manuscript ([128] in 1967), the 'Ritual Dance of the Ancestors', Stravinsky asks the bass drum to be played *Avec la baguette de bois – Touchez légèrement au bord, de façon à produire un si bémol environ*, an important directive missing in the 1967 score. Students of orchestration should be intrigued by the composer's decision to accompany the English horn and alto flute by horns and strings, rather than clarinets and strings. At [132] in the original score the trumpet phrases are slurred in bars one, two and five and tongued in bars three and four. At [134], on a very crowded page, the composer's tiny stylus enabled him to include the parts for the alto flute, three oboes, piccolo clarinet, trombone, and the third and fourth bassoons. The manuscript is dated '18 – 31 / X / 1912' beneath bar five of [141]. The violin and viola accents on the offbeats in bars four and five of [133] are not authentic Stravinsky.

———◆———

The 'Sacrificial Dance' began with an unpitched notation of the rhythm from bar two of [147] to bar two of [148]. The Russian script says 'this is the rhythm from which the "Sacrificial Dance" grew, written during a walk with Ravel in Monte Carlo in the spring of 1912'. The actual date was 15 April, the location was La Taverne Parisienne, Avenue de la Costa, and the paper was the back of a grey Russian telegram form. Ravel was in Monte Carlo for rehearsals of *Daphnis and Chloë*, scheduled for its Paris premiere in June. Monteux was also there, and also present on the 18th when Stravinsky played the not-yet-completed *Rite* for Diaghilev on the piano. The conductor wrote home that 'Before Stravinsky got very far I was convinced he was raving mad... The walls trembled as he pounded away, occasionally stamping his foot and jumping up and down.'

Remarkably, the manuscript at [142] lacks a tempo indication. This does not mean that the composer was uncertain of what it should be – 126 for the pulsation whether of the quaver or, later, in the 1943 revision of the dance, of the crotchet – but of the tempo at which the orchestra could play it. Another discovery here is that the fermata in bar one occurs on the first semiquaver rest instead of on the third, a mistake Stravinsky does not seem to have recognised until

1922. The manuscript evidence that Stravinsky wanted shorter notes, semiquavers for quavers, followed by semiquaver rests, is apparent throughout the dance: two bars before and two after [143]; one bar before [144] and three after; three and one bar before [146] and in the second bar of [146]; bar four of [169]; three and one bars before [170]; bar two of [171]; bar [172] and three bars before [173]. At [173] the bass trumpet and trombones should shorten their first note to a semiquaver and insert a semiquaver rest after it.

At one bar before [143] and two before [144] the trumpet chords on the downbeats, missing in the manuscript and added in 1926, provide the snarl in the downbeat. At [146] and [147] the absence in the manuscript of the minor-third ping-pong 'melody' in the timpani is surprising, but the timpani throughout that Dance are also not in accord with the final score in too many other places to mention. From bar four of [151] to [154], the first violins are muted, and the *senza sord.* at [154], missing in published scores, is another rubber-stamped directive. In the third bar of [152] the manuscript contains the marking *retouffé* (stop the reverberation) of the tam-tam, missing in the 1967 score, which adds *crescendi* to the sustained notes in the fifth and sixth horns in bar three of [157] and in bar two of [158]. The *accelerando* at [161], not in the manuscript, must have been added at a rehearsal. The first horn note in bar four of [166] should sound E flat on the second note; i.e., the first two horns play the same notes as at the end of the previous bar, a mistake in all scores. From [171] through [172] the bass drum doubles the timpani in the manuscript, but not in the 1967 score. At [173] in the revised score, the contrabassoon doubles the appoggiaturas in the bass part, as it fails to do in the original until [181]. At [174], bar three, the fourth horn plays the same-pitch rhythmic figure for three bars, but in 1967 is reinforced by horns two, four, six and eight. It should also be mentioned that when Stravinsky conducted the 1943 'Danse sacrale', in Stockholm in September 1961, he asked the cellos and basses to play the appoggiaturas *détaché* (not legato) for greater volume, an important revision.

The *pizzicati* resume at bar two of [180], but the most important difference with 1967 occurs at [186]. In February 1926, Stravinsky recomposed the passage, and some of the written pages, including this one, were re-engraved and rebound in his copy of the 1922 score. At [186] the manuscript exposes an abrupt drop in the dynamic level from the full orchestra at its loudest, to a small ensemble of *pianissimo* bassoons and horns, with the cellos playing a single *pizzicato* note softly. One deduces from this that the change must have coincided with a momentous event on stage, but neither the sketches, nor Stravinsky's performance instructions to Nijinsky in the four-hand piano reduction refers to whatever this might have been. In concert performances the sudden letdown in dynamics could only perplex the audience. In any case, the composer's idea was to begin a volumetric increase corresponding to the mounting rhythmic delirium and the registral, upper octave, expansions. The 1926 addition of bass trumpet, trombones, tubas at [186] follows the original thereafter, with sections of instruments entering individually in the order timpani, horns, trumpets, clarinets, bassoons, oboes. At [189] all of the strings play *pizzicati.* At the second bar of [184] they are *arco,* but two bars later return to *pizz.* From [190] to [192], the strings alternate *arco* and *pizz.* At [193] the basses alternate *arco* and *pizz.,* while the second violins and violas play *pizz.* With the re-entrance of the first violins at [195] the *arco–pizzicato* changes are too complex to be described here. From [189], the first violins and cellos are differently distributed in the manuscript and revised versions. The climax at [192] and [193] marks a return to *piano* in both the manuscript and 1967. Beginning at [192] the basses play the C's *pizzicato,* and the A's *arco.* Both notes are played *arco* in the third and fourth bars of [197] (not marked by Stravinsky). The C in the single bar of [198] is *pizzicato,* but the remainder of the bass part is *arco.* At [193], Stravinsky's revised version reverses Monteux's three-plus-two pattern for the 5/16 bars to two plus three. From [197] to [198] the piccolo appoggiaturas consist of five notes – B flat, C, D flat, E flat, E natural – as against three notes in the published versions.

The vaulting energy of the penmanship from [196] to the end (see Monteux's letter to the composer of 2 April 1913) reflects the force of Stravinsky's drive to complete the work. As aforesaid, these bars were received by the Leipzig copyist only in late April 1913. The note-stems, flags and beams in the string parts for the first nine of these bars are scarcely different, whereas those of the wind instruments steeply incline toward the right. From bar three of [198] the upper strings join in this onward surge. The bolder, larger notes were evidently written at high speed. Simply to see them is to be swept along with the feeling that a powerful creation is coming to its end. The stridulous *rape-guero* re-enters a fraction of a second before the last chord, which it plays with the orchestra, a fact that has escaped the editors of the 1967 score. To play this chord, the manuscript instructs the cellos to *descendez le 'la'* in order to sound the last G sharp, and the basses to lower the E string in order to produce the low D. To the right of the last bar, Stravinsky signed and dated the score '9–23 [*sic*], 4 April 1913'. His comment in the upper-right-hand corner of the final page translates from the Russian as follows:

> May whoever listens to this music never experience the insult to which it was subjected and of which I was the witness in the Théâtre des Champs-Elysées, Paris, Spring 1913. Igor Stravinsky. Zurich, 11 October, 1968.

Chapter 23

Monumental Musicology

The publication of Richard Taruskin's *Stravinsky and the Russian Traditions*,[1] twenty years in the researching and writing, is a landmark event in contemporary musicology. The book exposes the Russian roots of Stravinsky's musical language for the first time, and in so doing changes the way we think about the composer.

A promotional blurb anticipates 'heated debate', but without specifying the issues, presumably Taruskin's rectifications of the errors and, as he charges, 'mendacities', in Stravinsky's memories of his formative and early Diaghilev years. Certain to be challenged is the downsizing of the 'cosmopolitan' music of the composer's French and American periods. Here, Taruskin locks arms with Stalin's toady Tikhon Khrennikov, who had written, 'not inaccurately', Taruskin says, that 'Living... far from his homeland, [Stravinsky] became ever more remote from the national source that had so fruitfully nourished his creative imagination during the first half of his life'. So what should he have done with the second half: left Paris or Los Angeles for Russia and joined the Union of Soviet Composers? Controversy can also be expected over the coronation of Stravinsky rather than Schoenberg as the century's most representative composer, which Taruskin strangely justifies by purely extraneous criteria: 'most famous',

---

1   *Stravinsky and the Russian Traditions: A Biography of the Works through "Mavra"* by Richard Taruskin. 2 vols, Berkeley, 1996.

'most played', 'most recorded', 'most photographed', 'most talked about'. After all, an international elite of composers, performers, and music historians remains convinced that *Pierrot lunaire*, the Serenade, the Five Pieces for Orchestra and the Orchestral Variations manifest a musical imagination and finesse of facture on a level as high or higher than that of *The Rite of Spring*, and few would deny that Schoenberg's compositional technique comprises a larger and deeper spectrum than Stravinsky's, which is not to assert that one or the other is the greater composer.

Nearly 100 pages of background precede the entrance of Stravinsky himself. 'Igor' is Varangian in origin, from the Scandinavian Ingvar, Taruskin says, but the child was named for Saint Igor Olegovich, on whose commemoration day he was born. This obscure churchman was a Prince of Chernigov, the birthplace of the composer's father, Fyodor Ignatyevich Stravinsky, celebrated basso and member of the Russian gentry, who may also have made this choice because Fyodor's recital repertory included two arias from Borodin's *Prince Igor* (not Olegovich), one of which he had performed in Moscow only six days before his son's birth.

Thanks to the accessibility of new material from correspondence and the Russian press of Fyodor Ignatyevich's time, he emerges as a far more significant figure than the previous anglophone literature conveys. Unlike his successor and rival, Chaliapin, Fyodor made no recordings, but Taruskin cleverly attempts to compensate for this by deducing some of the singer's vocal endowments from the music he performed. Thus a song by Rimsky-Korsakov dedicated to him implies a strong middle register, excellent breath budgeting, and a pitch ambitus from E flat above the clef, both *forte* and *piano*, to the F sharp below. Fyodor was renowned as much for his histrionic as his musical talents, for which reason both Tchaikovsky and Rimsky chose him to create roles in their operas. He sang the part of Varlaam in the first *Boris Godunov*, and Mussorgsky was his sometime recital accompanist. On 5 April 1879, Fyodor shared the stage with Dostoyevsky, who read from *The Brothers Karamazov* to vociferous approval.

Of the father–son relationship, we learn that young Igor was a kind of mascot of the Mariyinsky Theatre, in which his father was a leading artist. Fyodor was additionally famous for designing his own costumes and drawing witty caricatures – graphic gifts inherited by his son, whose paintings at age eighteen, not mentioned in the book, are more accomplished than his musical endeavours of the same time. Taruskin censures the son for expressing enmities toward his father more than a half-century later, but without taking into account that the parent was tantrum-prone, severe and emotionally distant from the child, as he would be, in turn, with his own offspring. Stravinsky's 1904 song for basso, 'How the Mushrooms Mobilised for War', may have been written with his father (d. 1902) in mind, or so Taruskin believes on the fanciful grounds that the composer kept the work with him out of filial sentiment. The truth is that after its arrival in America, in 1949 crated with the bulk of the composer's manuscripts (not 'brought over by Soulima Stravinsky in June 1948',[2] as the book mistakenly informs us), he lacked the curiosity even to glance at it.

Though biography keeps breaking in, nothing is vouchsafed about the composer's mother, Anna Kyrillovna, an excellent pianist who failed to recognise her son's gifts[3] and so strongly discouraged his musical ambitions that on one occasion he sought refuge from her criticisms in the home of his older brother, Yuriy. Igor seems to have inherited his mother's resoluteness, but also her least sympathetic character traits: hubris, vindictiveness and a truculent tongue. Mrs Samuel Dushkin (d. 1996), who knew her in Paris in the late 1930s, pictured Stravinsky as constantly fearful lest she discover the secret of his bigamous life, as Stravinsky himself referred to it.[4] No wonder he became an intimate of the Rimsky-Korsakov household even before the period of his scheduled lessons with the master (Autumn 1905 to April 1908).

The next 300 or so pages cover the social and cultural Russian

---

2   When I met Soulima Stravinsky's Air France flight on its arrival in New York, he had no manuscripts with him. Nor were any sent from Paris until the spring of 1949.

3   In 1938 Samuel Dushkin, escorting her to a performance of *The Rite of Spring*, which she had never heard, jokingly said that he hoped she would not whistle, as the audience had done in 1913. She responded: 'No, because I don't know how to whistle.'

4   The memoir, *Au Cœur du Foyer* (Paris, 1998), by Stravinsky's daughter-in-law, the late Denise Stravinsky, reveals that the secret had been disclosed to the composer's mother by a family member.

scene from which Stravinsky sprang, but take the narrative only as far as the pre-*Firebird* music. Taruskin's one glaring oversight is that he fails to provide the political context, the effect on Stravinsky's early youth of the assassination of Tsar Alexander II in the year before the composer's birth, and of the unrest and revolutionary foment throughout the Russian Empire in 1905–07, the period of Stravinsky's first significant compositions and of his last years as a law student at the University of St Petersburg. Instead, Taruskin offers deft analyses and aptly chosen music examples illustrating 'the stylistic bedrock of Stravinsky's Russian manner', in particular, the way in which Rimsky-Korsakov's octatonic scale (alternating tone and semitone) borrowed from Liszt, who lifted it from Schubert, runs like a rudder through most of Stravinsky's creations, down to and including his last, *The Owl and the Pussy-Cat* (1966).

One of the more surprising of the book's revelations is the extent of young Igor's indebtedness to Glazunov, Stravinsky's lifelong *bête noire*. Indeed, the side-by-side music examples from Glazunov's Eighth Symphony and the one in E flat by the student Stravinsky might have brought accusations of plagiarism from the older composer.

The book opens with the history, aesthetics, stylistic features, harmonic and other practices of the two Russian traditions, the 'kuchkists' (the Mighty Five) and the Belyayevtsi (the circle around the music publisher, Mitrofan Belaieff). Both the folklorism of the former and the academicism of the latter were central to Stravinsky's art at the beginning, even though as a young man he 'knew little native folklore and may have wished to know even less'. Taruskin emphasises the young composer's docility in conforming to Rimsky's 'academic code', and the absence of any sign of rebelliousness throughout his apprenticeship. He won acceptance as Rimsky's private pupil with the Sonata in F sharp minor, in whose imitations of Rubinstein and Tchaikovsky Taruskin finds more merit than do the few pianists who have undertaken to learn the long, derivative exercise.

Stravinsky attended Rimsky's musical Wednesday evenings, at which both Classical and contemporary works were performed and discussed, and became a participant, playing, four-hands with Rimsky's wife, such varied fare as Schubert's symphony of the 'heavenly-lengths' (No. 9, the 'Great' C Major) and Glazunov's Fifth. On Christmas Day 1907, Stravinsky unveiled his Pastorale, a vocalise, accompanying his teacher's daughter, Nadyezhda, and charming the audience with the music; Taruskin correctly deduces that it would remain the only pre-*Firebird* opus that the composer cherished into old age. On the same evening, one of Stravinsky's songs to texts by the poet Gorodetsky was performed, despite Rimsky's known distaste for the writer's insidious 'modernism'. No doubt Stravinsky's mother, who was present, felt the same way. Rimsky's guests on his sixtieth birthday heard, and ridiculed, Debussy's *Estampes*, even though the host abominated the Frenchman's music as much as his most famous pupil loved it. The cantata that Stravinsky had composed for the occasion, however, earned the praise of his teacher, who confided it to his diary. After Rimsky's death, Taruskin remarks, Stravinsky's letters to the widow are a mixture of devotion and ambition to have his memorial piece for the master performed.

We are attracted to Rimsky-Korsakov by his personal generosity, perseverance as an autodidact, sympathetic discernment as a teacher, political and anti-clerical liberalism. The book's many music examples from his operas stimulate interest, but in contrast to the many discussions concerning their octatonic content, next to nothing is said about their dramatic viability. We learn that Rimsky did not consider Stravinsky's student symphony worthy of publication. Yet Taruskin defends its *Largo* movement as a more 'genuinely Tchaikovskian creation' than the 'chic pastiche', *Le Baiser de la fée*, a statement that exposes the book's Antaeian, everything-goes-back-to-Russia bias, and opens to question the objectivity of its musical judgements. This, in turn, raises the larger question of whether, by itself, a strictly analytical approach to music can ever explain its power. Most listeners – Taruskin rarely distinguishes the perspectives of the analyst and the listener – would argue that the beauties of the *Fée*, the ending above all, outweigh the banalities, as in the numbingly repeated first tune of the second tableau.

The chapters devoted to the first three ballets and *Les Noces* comprise the largest portion of the text. Their every aspect – mythological, anthropological, theatrical-historical, pictorial, musical, choreographic – is scrutinised and an ultimate-reference compendium amassed for each piece. Of what use this may be to concert audiences remains moot, for, in the view of many, no staging could ever complement the music, which, as Stravinsky and Balanchine concluded, stands best on its own, as music unencumbered by a programme. The essay on the *Rite*, nevertheless, like those on *Noces*, *Petrushka* and *Firebird*, is unputdownable, despite the bulkiness of the volume containing it. The one on *Noces* exemplifies a high order of critical acumen in its insistence on the 'balance between the artist's fancy and the ethnographer's conscience'.

Taruskin is at his most eloquent discussing the famous 'extra' bar of silence – the composer Andrew Imbrie's 'one measure of eternity' – in the coda of *Les Noces*. The bar does not appear in the first draft, which lacks three other bars of the ending, nor is it a part of the conclusion revised in the piano score. But Stravinsky consciously retained it in the full score,

> evidently regarding it as a legitimate accident. He took it as a gift... and made us the gift of it in turn. Pierre Boulez was completely wrong to assume that it was 'merely' a mistake... wrong to eliminate it from his recording of the work... and wrong especially to attempt to persuade Stravinsky (as he is shown doing [in a] documentary film) that it should be eliminated from the score for the sake of a consistency that is no less foolish for its being rational... the measure, whatever its origins, is now one of *Les Noces*'s glories, and Stravinsky's insertion of it, whether a considered invention or only a decision to keep a fluky acquisition, was an utterly characteristic stroke of his artistic genius.

The exordium to *Firebird*, showing how Stravinsky came to be 'chosen by fate as the protagonist of an extraordinary nexus', makes suspenseful reading. Among the principal intersecting trajectories are the redivivus of ballet, which Rimsky condemned as a degenerate art;[5]

---

5   'The language of dance and the whole vocabulary of movement are skimpy... there is no need for good music in ballet.'

the synthesis of the arts movement; Diaghilev's flight from stultifying Russian cultural politics and concomitant switch from opera to ballet following the sudden loss of Imperial patronage; and the unfavourable reception of the exciting music of the Ballets Russes presentations in Paris. As these developments converged on Stravinsky, 'History has shown us how ready he was'. The year before, in 1909, Diaghilev had entrusted him to orchestrate the first and last pieces, the Nijinsky solos, in *Chopiniana*, a measure of the impresario's confidence in the young composer before the *Firebird* commission. What no one foresaw was that this first Stravinsky masterpiece would establish the course for ballet as a medium of modernism.

Taruskin describes the musico-dramatic quiddity of *Petrushka* in fewer and better-chosen words than any other commentator known to this writer:

> Despite the musical infusion of natural artifacts in the form of folk and street music, the impression the ballet makes is anything but naturalistic. We never feel that we are observing an evocation of the real world... but a tug-of-war between inner and outer reality... Only the puppets have 'real' personalities and emotions. The people in *Petrushka* act and move mechanically, like toys. Only the puppets act spontaneously, impulsively, in a word, humanly.

Berating Stravinsky for his shift regarding Alexander Benois's role in creating the scenario, and the supposedly 'venal' motive behind the composer's failed 1929 lawsuit to block his collaborator's royalties from concert performances, Taruskin prosecutorially declares that Stravinsky's 'self-interested denials have enjoyed their undeserved authority long enough'. But since the original concept of the ballet, and the idea of the apparition of Petrushka's ghost at the end, which elevates it to the level of great theatre, were Stravinsky's inspirations, surely he deserves as much credit for the scenario as Benois. Further to disculpate the composer, one wonders what the libretto contributes to a concert performance of the *Danse russe*, or the *Three Movements from Petrushka* for piano solo, and why should the creator of the décors receive part of the royalties from the music?

The treatment of *Zvezdoliki* (1911–12), Stravinsky's choral setting of Konstantin Balmont's popular poem, is puzzling. Taruskin rightly contends that its 'surface features' owe something to Scriabin's *Poème de l'extase* and *Prometheus*, but the focus on his Seventh Sonata seems misdirected. Next to it, *Zvezdoliki*, with its 'elaborately symmetrical chromatic progressions... and their circulations through the octatonic collections' is put down as 'slapdash, unworthy of comparison with Scriabin's tightly if narrowly organized' opus. (Stravinsky's Verlaine song, 'La Lune blanche', is dismissed with the same word, despite a 'cerebrally conceived rotation *à la* Rimsky of ninth-chords around the pedal'.) But since *Zvezdoliki* was composed *before* Scriabin's Sonata, one wonders how the later work can have provided a 'stylistic paradigm' for the earlier, and how the 'organization' of a short, slow-tempo piece for huge orchestra and male chorus can be compared to that of a fast-tempo piano solo. Taruskin avers that the Sonata contains a 'marvelous' touch in the way that an 'unstable G-sharp' is made 'to replace the G-natural in the Coda', whereas Stravinsky's ending, with its 'apparent allusions to the opening of *La Mer*' – not apparent but pointedly, in *homage* – 'seems tacked on, quite out of joint with the rest of [a work that] comes off smacking a wee bit of charlatanry'. Nothing is said about the ingenious monotheistic symbolism of setting the text of the *Voice from Above* to vocal unisons, though to most audiences *Zvezdoliki* seems closer to Scriabin's theosophy than to his music. The stunningly new, never-repeated sonorities of the work, the amazing transparency of the wind chords at the centre, the high tenor timbres and choral humming, and the instrumental novelties (muted oboe) are not even mentioned.

But then, the only comments on the instrumentation of *The Firebird* are reserved for the *glissandos* of open string harmonics in the Introduction that Stravinsky borrowed from Rimsky by way of Ravel. These, in any case, as performing musicians know, are unplayable in the first violin part, and are always played an octave lower because of insufficient time to return the E string to pitch after the tuning down to D.

The book is more enlightening concerning the personal relationship between Stravinsky and Scriabin. The former's recollection of frequent encounters with the latter at Rimsky's is shrunk to only three, but Taruskin seems to be correct in attributing the younger composer's late-in-life objurgations against 'the only contemporary in whom he was interested' to Scriabin's failure to reciprocate. When the two men were together in Lausanne in October 1913, an abashed Stravinsky may even have hidden his *Zvezdoliki* score from Scriabin's eyes, Taruskin conjectures, though Stravinsky is hardly likely to have brought that score with him instead of the newer *Rite of Spring*, which had extinguished Scriabin's *flamme* in Paris only a few months before. Taruskin includes Stravinsky's account of this meeting in a letter to a friend in Russia but seems not to understand from it that Scriabin was plainly jealous of the excitement created by the *Rite* in Paris.

The chapter on the *Three Japanese Lyrics*, beginning with Stravinsky's meeting with Schoenberg in Berlin in December 1912, is disappointing. Taruskin acknowledges that Stravinsky could have retained only 'generalized gestural' impressions from a single hearing of *Pierrot lunaire*, as instanced in the rapid runs and arpeggiated figures in 'Mazatsumi', the second of the *Lyrics*. Music examples are juxtaposed, showing a six-note violin motive followed by a trill in the Stravinsky and a superficially similar configuration in 'Rote Messe' (*Pierrot*, No. 11) of great density and for several lines in rhythmic unison. But as we now know, 'Mazatsumi' was entirely composed in Russia six months before Stravinsky heard *Pierrot*. A letter to him from Nicolas Miaskovsky of 25 July 1913 (Old Style), expresses gratitude for 'sending the score of the "*Japanese*"', as Stravinsky referred to the opus, and Stravinsky would never have sent an incomplete score or sketch to this hyper-critical musician. In truth, the notion of a *Pierrot/Japanese* influence is *Boulez-blague*.[6] Only the last of the *Lyrics* postdated Stravinsky's experience of *Pierrot*, and this delicate piece, concluding in an F major triad, owes nothing at all

---

6   Taruskin quotes 'Pierre Boulez's typically bellicose characterization of the *Japanese Lyrics* as a "stupid misconstruction" of Schoenberg's innovations'.

to it. Taruskin should have mentioned that Stravinsky, completing the *Rite* two weeks before hearing *Pierrot*, was the only other composer – not Webern, not Berg – who could have, and to a considerable extent did, appreciate Schoenberg's achievement. Taruskin's account of the negative reaction to the *Japanese Lyrics* following a performance in Moscow only three weeks after the enthusiastic reception at the Paris premiere, explains the beginning of the cold war between Stravinsky and his compatriots.

The most eagerly awaited chapter in *Stravinsky and the Russian Traditions* examines Stravinsky's and Ravel's contributions to Diaghilev's production of Mussorgsky's *Khovanshchina*. Well aware that Rimskyites were incensed at the thought of Stravinsky replacing his teacher's version of the final chorus, Diaghilev slyly *retained* the Rimsky ending for the first Paris performance, with critics none the wiser, and postponed Stravinsky's until ten days later. Taruskin fairly describes Rimsky's ending as a 'banal Petrine meliorism with its gaudy orchestral apotheosis', and Stravinsky's as 'apt' in mood, though as a coda, a tail, it impudently wags the production to which it was appended. The unresolved ninth chord with which Stravinsky concludes the opera is an 'ineffably spacious, poignantly definite close *à la Zvezdolikiy*', which should have been said in the section dealing with the allegedly sub-Scriabin opus. Stravinsky's chorus was also neo-nationalist, hence 'implicitly anti-Western', and as such it opened a path to *Les Noces*. Taruskin mistakenly assumes that Stravinsky had once possessed the published vocal score of his *Khovanshchina* chorus, but his only copy, given to him in the late 1960s, was a photostat.

The chapter on *Histoire du soldat* sets out to debunk Stravinsky's claim that American jazz and jazz bands left their imprints on the rhythmic and instrumental aspects of the work. The true origin of the *Soldat* ensemble, the author proposes, is the shtetl band of the Ukrainian village (Ustilug) where Stravinsky spent his summers before 1914. This is contradicted by the composer's story, confirmed by Ansermet, of having started to compose for violin only and adding the other instruments one by one over many months. Taruskin also rejects Stravinsky's assertion that the *Soldat* marks a break with his

Russian traditions, though to most listeners the Argentine Tango, French Valse, American Ragtime, Swiss March and parody German chorales do not sound in the least Russian. In any case, the most delectable music in the *Soldat* is in the Pastorale, and its tiny reprise for clarinet and bassoon, rather than in the dances, the marches and the 'little concert'. No fragment of this duration for two instruments, one of them limited to only two different pitches, has ever conveyed as much atmosphere.

The chapter on the Symphonies of Wind Instruments draws parallels between its form and that of the Panikhida ritual (memorial service) of the Russian Orthodox Church, asking us to think of the piece as an 'instrumental evocation of liturgical chanting'. We learn that the three proportionally related tempi correspond to the litanies, the responses, and the acclamations of the liturgy, though whether Stravinsky was conscious of this, or aware in a deeper faculty, cannot be known. In conversation he referred to the two flute–clarinet duets as litanies one and two, and called them that in a programme note for his first performance of the revised version of the piece, New York, 11 April 1948. The musical examples show that the final chorale is based on a chant in the *Obikhod*, the Slavonic *Liber Usualis*, that he would have heard in his churchgoing childhood. With a memorial piece by Rimsky-Korsakov as precedent, Taruskin further speculates that Stravinsky may have borrowed a melody from the *Obikhod* in his lost *Chant funèbre.*

Taruskin attributes Stravinsky's adoption of his 'second style' to *Pulcinella* and to his work on reorchestrating the pieces for *The Sleeping Beauty*, with which 'Diaghilev succeeded in winning him to the cause of new classicism'. The present writer persists in dating Stravinsky's neoclassicism back to the puckish Valse for Erik Satie, composed in 1913, and followed through in the eight four-hand pieces (1914–17), the Etude for Pianola (1917) and the *Five Fingers*, all composed in the eight years before *Mavra* (1922). This last, the subject of one of the book's most illuminating explorations, is identified as the pivotal creation of the period. Taruskin astutely notes that the dramatic substance of this miniature comic opera is typical of a Chauves-Souris skit, and it is true that Stravinsky enjoyed the singing, dancing and satirical 'take-offs' presented by the Moscow theatre troupe relocated in Paris. His presumed presence at a Chauve-Souris evening on 19 February 1921 – after arriving in Paris from Rome the day before – together with Diaghilev, Boris Kochno and the latter's invited friends, Sergei and Vera Sudeykina, must be attributed, we are told, to the beguilements of Zhenya Nikitina, a Chauves-Souris dancer. But the author mistakenly has 'the Nikitina affair' beginning, not ending, on this occasion. The book's chronology for the progress of Stravinsky's lifelong infatuation with Mme Sudeykina wrongly dates it to the summer of 1921, and it confuses Zhenya Nikitina, *née* Landau, with Alice Nikitina of *Apollo* fame.

The Chauves-Souris influence on *Mavra* is evident in the flimsiness of the libretto concocted by Kochno and Stravinsky in lieu of a 'motivated music drama'. Whereas the absurdity of the libretto was undoubtedly the chief merit of the work in the eyes of its creators, as Taruskin correctly deduces, it was also partly responsible for the fiasco of the Palais Garnier premiere, the other part being that it was overwhelmed by *Petrushka* and *The Rite of Spring*, with which it shared a triple bill. Taruskin credits the libretto entirely to the teenage Kochno, apparently not having seen his *Mavra* notebooks describing meetings with Stravinsky, or Stravinsky's letters to him requesting changes: 'What you have sent me is not a duet (and what you brought me is not a quartet), it is a dialogue.' In the same letter, the composer announces one of the ways in which *Mavra* marks a musical watershed: 'I have managed to achieve a clarity and simplicity such as I have not been able to do before.' The music examples show how the new style looks back to Glinka and away from Rimsky, as indicated in the reduction to a single occurrence of a 'fully referential octatonic' construction.

Taruskin is a spunky, sometimes strident, critic, taking on the field and exultantly trumping even his closest colleagues. When he turns to the American years the tone occasionally slips into the combative, as when he says that Stravinsky may have written the 1965 orchestral *Canon* 'to impress his friends at Princeton' (then regarded as the Areopagus of musical sophistication); but why not simply say to 'amuse' these friends, since the composer neither wished nor needed to 'impress' anybody? Moreover, some judgements of the music of this period are superficial, such as the brush-off of the Septet, despite its 'octatonic leanings', as Derrick Puffett observes in the most brilliant analysis of any mid-to-late Stravinsky opus to date (*The Musical Times*, November 1995).

The author also asserts that at the time of Stravinsky's first book of 'Conversations' (1957), Pierre Souvtchinsky, a 'momentous intellectual influence' on him, 'was chiefly responsible for the brief close relationship (1956–1958)' between the composer and Boulez. In actuality, it was Boulez, visiting Stravinsky in Munich in November 1956, who smoothed the way, after an eighteen-year rift, to Souvtchinsky's reconciliation with his former friend Stravinsky. Souvtchinsky's motive 'in engineering the relationship', in Taruskin's breathtakingly patronising imputation, was that 'he wanted to see Stravinsky return to "usefulness"' – i.e., after wasting his time composing the two symphonies, the Mass, *The Rake's Progress*, etc. – 'and to creative activity worthy of his genius'.

No instance of Souvtchinsky's 'intellectual influence' is cited, and the expression itself begs questions. Stravinsky was an intuitive creative artist whose powers of mind were not invariably subject to logocentric rationality. ('In our discussions Stravinsky seemed completely free of the mind, and put the idea of art, and especially of music, so far above everything else that he amazed and moved me' – Valéry to Gide, 17 September 1939.) Outside the world of music, Stravinsky could be as readily persuaded by ideas as the next person, and was not susceptible to 'intellectual influence', as distinguished from the concrete kind effected through Nadia Boulanger, who introduced him to Machaut and the isorhythmic motet, Josquin and Lassus, Byrd and Monteverdi. More important errors are exposed in the further assertion that since Stravinsky's 'Conversations' began during Boulez's visit to California in March 1957, 'the voice that speaks to us [in them] was as much the creation of Pierre Souvtchinsky as the voice that had spoken in the *Poétique musicale*'. But the notion of Souvtchinsky speaking through Boulez, if that is meant, is preposterous, and if 'the voice that had spoken' in the *Poétique* was the anti-Thomist Souvtchinsky's, how can it also be the voice of his opposite, Jacques Maritain? 'The *Poétique* often lapses into virtual paraphrases of *Art et scholastique*,' Taruskin remarks earlier, unaware that Stravinsky had accepted Maritain's refutation of the dictum 'Music is powerless to express anything at all'. After praising the composer for his concept of 'the effacement of the individual by his achievements' (*askesis*), Maritain wisely maintained that 'There exists a creative emotion through which the artist unknowingly expresses himself in his works' (letter of 23 July 1934).

Souvtchinsky knew no English and was quite unacquainted with the contents of the 'Conversations', but he did send Vasiliy Yastrebtsev's diaries of the Rimsky-Korsakov years –Taruskin's primary source – to Stravinsky, thereby revising his perspectives, though not in time for him to revise his recollections.

Those who can afford Taruskin's two volumes should be advised that their biographical and historical parts, which comprise most of the text, are not only accessible to general readers but also lucidly and imaginatively written. Its analytical parts, meanwhile, are hobbled by such archaic locutions as 'occurses' and 'anent', and such up-to-date ones as 'anhemitonic tetrachord' and 'subtactile ictus'. For those who must await the paperback edition, one hopes that it contains a trailer correcting a profusion of small errors of fact and mistaken suppositions. The sketches for the unfinished Petrarch dialogue incorporated in *Perséphone* date from December 1932, not from the period immediately after the Symphony of Psalms. 'Apart from Monteux... and Koussevitzsky... no conductor had access to [the *Rite* score].' Ansermet certainly did when he assisted Stravinsky in correcting the first proofs, and Rhené-Baton when he conducted the ballet in London in July 1913. Nicolas Nabokov cannot be described as 'an old pal from the Diaghilev days' – the future *Partisan Review* days, rather; and Stravinsky, despite Taruskin's contrary claim, *did* conduct his *Scherzo fantastique* – in San Francisco in April 1958. Further, all references to the 'Sigmund Rothshild catalog' (1970) of Stravinsky's manuscripts, thrown together in three weeks for the purpose of establishing a low tax evaluation, should be changed to the 'Paul Sacher Stiftung, Basle'.

Stravinsky and the Russian Traditions is a lavishly produced book as well as an epochal, seminal, if now-and-then over-the-top one that testifies to a deep knowledge of Stravinsky's music. It is probably the most intelligent monograph of any composer since Wagner, though of course I have not read them all. I am grateful for multitudes of facts and insights learned from it.

Chapter 24

A Modest Confutation[1]

Walsh I

Stravinsky: A Creative Spring, by Stephen Walsh,[2] begins with a salvo aimed at me. To avoid possible backfire, he offers the placatory statement that without me, 'there probably would have been no *Agon*, no *Abraham and Isaac*, no *Requiem Canticles*'. Nothing is said about his backhanded compliment of cribbing more than 25,000 words from my writings on the same subject, so that, in effect, parts of his *Stravinsky* are glosses on mine.

Walsh's version of our acquaintance requires rectification. He did not spend 'several days' with me in London and Venice in 1995, as he writes, but, by BBC contract, a few hours during each of three days in each city. From this he claims to have acquired an understanding of 'the complex relationship' between Stravinsky and me, though his opening sentence referring to Stravinsky as my 'former employer' reveals that he understood it not at all. The relationship was symbiotic and filial, and in no way mercenary. I received no wages and was remunerated only for my work as Stravinsky's co-conductor, and then only toward the end of his life, his accountant having discovered

---

1 This (updated) review from *The Musical Quarterly* is reprinted here because it contains intimate aspects of Stravinsky biography that would not otherwise have come to light.
2 *Stravinsky: A Creative Spring, Russia and France, 1882-1934* by Stephen Walsh, New York, 1999.

a tax advantage to him in declaring payments to me as deductible expenses. A subsequent *Times Literary Supplement* review of my memoir, *An Improbable Life*,[3] by the composer-critic David Schiff, elevates me to a higher level of regard.

Having encouraged Walsh to undertake the biography and promising my co-operation, I corresponded with him both before and after 1995. When he asked to see the English translations that I had commissioned of the voluminous letters to Stravinsky from his first wife, I sent them – and still await their return. When he sought my assistance in obtaining oral histories, I imposed on Elliott Carter, Milton Babbitt, and others who had known Stravinsky and might be able to provide useful reminiscences, and to whom Walsh would not otherwise have had access. These favours were not acknowledged, and the interviewees reported to me that his sole interest seemed to be in gathering gossip possibly demeaning to me. Still, I continued to support his project.

When I finally met Walsh, he was ungracious at first, then rebarbative. My instinct was to withdraw, but for some reason I denied it and even recommended him as a symposiast in a Stravinsky festival I would conduct in Santa Barbara a few months later. There I introduced him to the composers David Raksin and William Kraft, friends of Stravinsky, and invited him to dine with us. Later, in London, after a talk that I gave at the Royal Philharmonic Society, he asked to borrow the forty or so letters to me from the late Isaiah Berlin that had been my subject. I not only obliged, but some time afterwards even sent a chapter of new material from forthcoming memoirs of my own. My suspicions were awakened only when letters began to come from him signed, oddly, I thought, 'love to you both', and asking to come to my Florida hideaway for more Stravinsky talk. The last of these arrived in July 1999, almost simultaneously with a review copy of his book.

Browsing through the introduction, I was disturbed to find that he was and had apparently long been my insidious enemy, and that to discredit me was virtually his *raison d'être*. What surprised me most

---

3   Nashville, Tennessee, 2002.

was that he would unmask his envies and ambitions so blatantly. Others noticed this as well, among them Andrew Clark, the music critic of *The Financial Times* (London), who telephoned to ask if I felt I had been 'stabbed in the back'.

Reading on, I found not only copious borrowings from, and evident paraphrasings of, my writings, but also ideas of mine presented as his. Some of the filchings were second-hand, of work taken from me by earlier writers that he attributes to them. I was and still am perplexed by the stratagems with which the predator obtained publishers' permissions to fleece from my work, while well aware that I, as the sole copyright owner, am alone entitled to grant them. My name does not appear in his Acknowledgements.

I responded to a critical notice of the book by John Warrack in the *Times Literary Supplement*, 30 June 2000, as follows:

Mr. Warrack's fair minded review article is in need of amplification. It is not Stravinsky who 'rewrote the facts over *The Rite of Spring*', but Mr. Walsh, whose book states that in Venice, August 1912, Stravinsky played *The Rite* for Diaghilev, who 'had by now heard some of the music at least three times and all of it at least once'.[4] 'All of it', as everyone knows, had not yet been composed. Walsh also challenges the accepted venue of this audition, the Grand Hotel on the Grand Canal, despite Stravinsky's photographs, dated by him at the time, of himself, Diaghilev, Nijinsky, and Misia Sert on the porch outside this hotel's music salon. Instead, Walsh supports Richard Buckle's whim that 'sets this play-through, perhaps rightly, in the Grand Hotel des Bains on the Lido'. No explanation is forthcoming for 'perhaps rightly'. Further, Walsh dismisses Stravinsky's 'I could play, but did not, at first, know how to write, the "Sacrificial Dance"', pretending that 'the sketches reveal little trace of this

---

4   Warrack does not quote the remainder of the sentence: '[Diaghilev] is supposed to have asked the composer, "Will it last a very long time this way?" to which Stravinsky is "supposed" to have replied, "Till the very end, my dear!"' But why 'supposed'? Stravinsky re-enacts the scene, saying exactly the same words, in a widely known CBS documentary film.

problem'. A closer perusal of them would have revealed the composer's initial uncertainty as to whether or not the first chord should fall on an upbeat, as it does in the first (1922) printed score. Nor did he know, in 1913, whether the three-beat bars should precede the two-beat, as in the 1943 revision. The earliest sketch, the notation of a rhythm without pitches, was not used at the beginning but 26 bars inland, and no one knows how many sketches had been discarded before the one incorporated in the sketchbook draft. On the question of Stravinsky's four-hand run-through with Debussy, Walsh fleers at the 'assumption of all authorities' that the 1913 date was a slip for 1912, and asserts that the event took place a few days before the premiere.[5]

Warrack writes that Stravinsky's pecuniary obsessions were 'at first understandable as an exile's insecurity'. On 3 September 1981, Tatiana Rimsky-Korsakov, the composer's granddaughter, spent an afternoon with me in her ancestral home testifying that this Stravinsky trait was already notorious in 1903–05. As a live-in witness to a long patch of Stravinsky history, I can confirm Warrack's judgment that Stravinsky could be vindictive and unkind to old friends, but he could also be generous to them. Certainly he was untruthful at times, as in Warrack's example, the use of Maeterlinck's *Les Abeilles* as a scenario for the ballet *Scherzo fantastique*. (Walsh might have noted that, in mysterious retribution, the composer's home in Nice, the Villa des Roses, has now been replaced by a compound called *Mélisandes*; Maeterlinck was his friendly neighbour there from 1924 to 1929.)

When Warrack refers to Stravinsky's 'violently distorted memories of his immediate family' (I can find no instance

---

5   Stravinsky attended the premiere of the ballet *L'Après-midi d'un faune* at the Théâtre du Châtelet, Paris, 29 May 1912. On 1 June, Louis Laloy, editor of *La Grande Revue*, invited him to lunch at his suburban home the following Sunday, saying that the Debussys would be there. On 25 June, Laloy published some remarks in *La Grande Revue* indicating that the play-through of *The Rite of Spring* had just taken place. Debussy recalled the occasion in a letter to Stravinsky postmarked 'Clarens, 8 November 1912'. The confirmed date of the four-hand play-through was 9 June 1912.

approaching violence), one should remember that Walsh's principal source is the 'Conversations' books, and that these were the recollections of a man of seventy-five to eighty-five. But Warrack has failed to recognise the *ignis fatuus* in Walsh's contention that the portrait of Stravinsky emerging from the 'Conversations' was the one he wanted. On the contrary, Stravinsky's goal in these books was to discuss the current musical scene. Mine was to persuade him to talk about his early years, his autobiography containing so little information about them. Without my urging he would not have discussed his Russian past at all. No documents were consulted, but the *sur-le-vif* immediacy and vividness of his memory seemed to me more valuable than the factual agenda that would inevitably be dug up. Walsh thinks that the composer sought, in that hoary expression, 'to reinvent his past'. What he sought, and did all his life, was to rejuvenate his art.

Warrack perceives that Walsh's discussion of Stravinsky's 'indebtedness' to Maritain is inflated. But the assertion that the composer's 'sudden assemblage of icons, votary candles and so forth [was no] more than a symptom of an exile's nostalgia' is nonsense. It is true that every morning, before composing, Stravinsky prayed before an icon that he had brought with him from Russia in 1910. Superstition was undoubtedly a large element in his religion, as in other people's, but the drawing of the Crucifixion attached to the flyleaf of the Symphony of Psalms sketchbook, the insertion of a copy of the Russian Orthodox Cross at the end of the Polymnia Variation in *Apollo*, and the Church calendar dates found in his other 1920s scores – 'I. Stravinsky, after Friday confession,[6] April 9, 1926' on the cover of the Serenade in A – are proofs of deeply felt obeisances. We know that he composed his uncommissioned

---

6   Walsh does not mention Stravinsky's confessor in Paris, Father Vassily, nor is anything said about Father Hieroskimonakh Gerasim, his spiritual advisor on Mount Athos, to whom the composer sent money and soul-baring letters (an especially fervent one on 12 July 1932). An icon of Father Gerasim stood on his night table, at home and on all of his travels, during at least the last thirty years of his life.

Mass for liturgical use, and that when it was performed by the Roger Wagner Chorus in a Los Angeles church for a Thursday noon 'Holy Day of Obligation' service in December 1949, Stravinsky knelt throughout.[7]

Finally, Warrack declares that, 'latterly, the position of Robert Craft in Stravinsky's life... has been a contentious one'. Not latterly, but from day one.

———•———

A Creative Spring ends in early autumn 1935. This corresponds to no climacteric in the composer's life, creative or personal, and severs too many lines of development too near their natural resolutions. The break should have been four years later, with the move to America, the changes of language and culture, and the second marriage. Moreover, readers not obsessed with the subject will find the book overly detailed with information about publishing agreements, rehearsal and concert schedules, wranglings over performance fees and royalties, unenlightening quotations from the press. Competent musicologists will object that it is also far from comprehensive, that it exchanges too many old errors for new ones, and is patently wrong in major questions of interpretation.

Another impediment is that most of the more interesting information is consigned to the 112 pages of fine-print footnotes at the back, belated discoveries, no doubt, that could not be worked into the main text without extensive rewriting. Some 950 of these notes refer to the peculations coyly described as the 'pragmatic use' made of my writings, but countless others are unacknowledged. For example, Stravinsky happened to be conducting in Rome during a

---

7   As an authority on Russian musical history, Warrack should have criticised Walsh's omission of any discussion of Stravinsky's *Sektantskaya* (1919), his first religious opus and the song on which he devoted the most labour. The composer was deeply interested in the Khlysty, the Russian heretical sect whose leader was Rasputin. Stravinsky suffered from the conflict between his Luciferian pride and his belief in, and strivings to attain, Christian humility. Rasputin preached that the spirit should abase itself before the flesh, the will before the impulsions of instinct, the intellect before the passions, and that to abandon oneself to sin is the truest humility. Stravinsky partly believed this inane doctrine when he began to break the seventh commandment after the resurgence of his wife's tuberculosis in 1914.

brief run, in the Teatro Odescalchi,[8] of *Histoire du soldat* in Luigi Pirandello's staging. Walsh's endnote reveals that the composer saw a performance of it on the same night as Benito Mussolini (28 April 1925), at which the two may have met, which would help account for the Duce's greeting to him in the Palazzo Venezia in May 1933: 'Maestro, je vous connais.'

Too many of the book's comments on Stravinsky's music suggest only the most superficial acquaintance with it. To begin with, its distinguishing emotions are never identified – the joy, the restrained pathos, the exaltation-in-belief in Symphony of Psalms; the feral ecstasy of the 'Élue' in *The Rite of Spring*; the tenderness in 'The Eternal Dwelling Place' from *The Fairy's Kiss*; the sense of time suspended in the coda of *Noces*, and of lustral purification in *Oedipus Rex* ('Lux facta est').

Walsh rates *Mavra* as Stravinsky's first significant work after moving to France from Switzerland in 1920. But discerning musicians have long since conferred this distinction on the Symphonies of Wind Instruments,[9] his actual first new composition in France, and an immeasurably greater creation than the operatic opusculum. In fact *Mavra*, a succession of parody arias, duets and a vocal quartet, is generally regarded as the least satisfactory of all Stravinsky's mature works, which does not stop Walsh from referring to the 'wizardry' in the music, understandably without offering a clue as to where it might be hiding.[10] This must be said if only because *Mavra*, 1921-2, marks the commencement of Stravinsky's fifty-year

---

8   Stravinsky had known Mme Odescalchi since 1917. He composed a melody for her in a copy of his *Easy Pieces*, and sent it to her through Alfredo Casella. She was a descendant of Prince Ladislao Odescalchi, the same who purchased *La Tentation de Saint-Antoine*, long misattributed to Pieter Brueghel the Younger, the picture that haunted Flaubert from 1845, when he first saw it in Genoa, until 1874, on the publication of his novel of the same title.

9   Walsh describes Stravinsky as 'messing about' with sketches of the Symphonies, but Stravinsky never 'messed about' with anything in his art.

10   Reviewing the premiere of *Mavra* (1922) at the Paris Opéra, Aldous Huxley described it as a *fiaschino* (*Westminster Gazette*): '*Mavra* is depressing in spite of its gaiety... depressing because, in its prodigious triviality, it simply isn't there, it doesn't exist. *Mavra* shows in a deplorable and unmistakable fashion [how] the influence of the young French musicians [Milhaud, Auric, Poulenc, *et al.*] has shamed the Russian out of his native seriousness and vigour... The man who wrote the *"Sacre"* now occupies himself with little musical jokes of no greater significance than *Ragtime* and *Mavra*... The result... [could] be the loss to Europe of one of its most interesting and original composers.'

love affair with Vera Sudeykina.[11] Of his other music of the time, the 1921 Fugato for two pianos, eventually the last variation in the Octet, is not mentioned, nor is the arrangement of *Three Movements from Petrushka* for piano solo.[12]

Walsh extends his *Mavra* gaffe by suggesting that *Pulcinella* might have been 'done, perhaps, with solo strings (as in *Mavra*)', forgetting that *Mavra* requires full cello and bass sections, and that the alternation of solo and ripieni strings is the basic conception of the *Pulcinella* orchestra. Walsh further misinforms the reader that the orchestra of *Nightingale* was 'slightly reduced for the ballet', when in actuality the woodwinds were cut by half, the strings correspondingly. He also maintains that the distinctively Spanish dance titled 'Madrid' (Four Studies for Orchestra) was really inspired by Naples, and that 'the character of *Apollo* was to some extent determined by outside money', without explaining how money, 'outside' or 'inside', can determine the *character* of a musical creation.

Even more awry regarding the most popular pieces, *The Firebird* and *The Rite of Spring*, Walsh criticises the former for its derivativeness: 'Today it is easier to hear *Firebird* as a hotchpotch of... folk-song setting *à la* Borodin, the "sparkling" academic ballet style of Glazunov, and a few exoticisms from Rimsky-Korsakov and Scriabin.' Surely no one else hears these things in it today. Now, as in 1910, the music is remarkable for the 'modernity' of its dissonances, syncopated rhythms and new sonorities (trombone trills, horn glissandos). One reads with amazement that the music is 'metrically rigid', which is certainly not the case at the end of Kastchei's Dance, or in the Finale, where threes and twos alternate within bars of seven-four. The principal rhythmic innovation in *Firebird* is not metrical, but the implementation of a proportional system that gives the same

---

11 In the early spring of 1921, when the title of the work was *The Little House in Kolomna* (Pushkin), Stravinsky gave the blue-cover sketchbook draft of the first scene to her.

12 The manuscript of this, in the Pierpont Morgan Library in New York, shows that the composer forgot to include a sequence in the Fourth Tableau. He has been faithfully followed in the mistaken cut by his publishers and by pianists ever since. The Babin and Vronsky four-hand arrangement of the piece restores the missing bars. I was present when they played it for Stravinsky in his Hollywood home and can testify that on this occasion he first discovered the mistake.

time-values to different note-values in different tempi, a guarantee against rigidity of metre and tempo. Walsh might have noted that the *Firebird* debut programme, 25 June 1910, included Grieg's *Kobold* in Stravinsky's instrumentation and danced by Nijinsky.[13]

The misinformation about *The Rite of Spring* is too copious for discussion here, but the notion that Stravinsky 'rescored' the 'Evocation of the Ancestors' in the first two months of 1926 must be corrected. What he did was to rebar the music and eliminate the fermatas from the bass part. The crucial reorchestration in *The Rite of Spring* does not occur here but in the 'Sacrificial Dance'.

Walsh's chapter on the 1925 American tour adds little and fails even to mention the Eighteenth Amendment, which would have constituted a hardship for Stravinsky in the US hinterland. Whereas wealthy New York hosts could provide excellent bootlegged Bordeaux, it was not available in restaurants, and otherwise only in speakeasies, the 'watering holes' of the time. Nothing is said about Joseph Steinway's dinner party for Stravinsky, with Sergei Rachmaninov, Josef Hoffmann, Fritz Kreisler, Leopold Auer, Alexander Siloti, Alexander Borovsky and other Russian musician friends with whom Stravinsky must at least have been pleased to be speaking the mother tongue. Think of all those Anglophone repasts and receptions, and the struggles with orchestras unable to follow his polyglot verbal instructions.

We are told that in Philadelphia, in 1925, Stravinsky and George Enescu met for the first time. Actually this had taken place in Paris in 1914, when Enescu played concertos by Bach and Mozart on the same programme with the first concert performance of the *Rite*. Walsh even presumes to denigrate Stravinsky as a conductor, naming five others who, in 1924, had 'a perfectly adequate grasp of his music and much better baton technique than he had or would ever acquire'. But how can Walsh know anything about the 'adequacy' of any performer's grasp of Stravinsky's music in 1924? (During the greater part of his conducting career Stravinsky did not use a baton.)

---

13 On 19 June 1910, Diaghilev, Karsavina and Nijinsky drove to Jacques-Emile Blanche's villa in Auteuil for a photography session by Eugène Druet. Blanche painted eight portraits of Nijinsky in his *Danse siamoise* costume based on these photos.

Wanting Stravinsky to have attended a performance of *Turandot* at La Scala in May 1926, where he was conducting in the same week as the premiere of Puccini's opera,[14] Walsh decides that he 'almost certainly' did. The shaky premises for the claim are that Stravinsky was 'fond of Italian opera', respected Puccini, and had 'an admiration for Verdi' – which at that time virtually precluded one for Puccini. In fact Stravinsky did not hear the opera, but on first hearing *Tosca* (Lyon, 5 February 1929), cared for it enough to attend a second performance in Lugano.

But the man, not the music, is Walsh's subject, and here the true lineaments of the composer's personality completely elude him. How could anyone pretend to understand anything about Stravinsky and still believe that '[w]hen the curtains at last closed down after the premiere of *The Rite*, the battle continued, amid competing applause and protests', in spite of which Stravinsky and Nijinsky 'took several calls'? This is simply not credible.[15] The explanation can only be that the reviewer (for *Comoedia*, 30 May 1913, the only source for the assertion in the vast press dossier) had already departed to meet a deadline. Stravinsky consistently testified that he went backstage as soon as the fracas began and did not return. To believe that he would have exposed himself to hecklers who had insulted his masterpiece is to comprehend nothing of his character.

Stravinsky's nimble wit and natural ludic sense elude the biographer *in toto*. Walsh suspects that the composer's 'gushingly expressed desire to play [Florent Schmitt's *Salomé*] "endlessly and madly from start to finish" does not ring entirely true'. Indeed, and as intended, it rings so false that the caution exposes the naïveté of the remark. Nor

---

14   '[Stravinsky] was in Milan for a week and a half in mid-May', Walsh assures us, but the actual duration was five days, during which the composer conducted two staged performances of *Petrushka*. Walsh has Toscanini 'already at work, preparing... *Turandot*' at the time of his 'March meeting' with Stravinsky. In fact, the two musicians did not meet in March: Stravinsky's train from Zagreb arrived in Milan on 24 March. He checked into the Hotel Cavour for the night and left for Nice the next morning.

15   In a re-enactment for a CBS documentary camera in the Théâtre des Champs-Elysées, 13 May 1965, Stravinsky identified the seventh row of the orchestra, second seat from the centre aisle, as the one he occupied at the beginning of the performance... He confirmed that soon after the beginning he departed through a door to the right, saying, though the music was so loud that no one could have heard him, 'Mesdames et Messieurs, vous êtes très gentils, merci, merci, good-bye, merde'. Mario Bois, *près de Strawinsky*, Paris, 1998, p. 157

can Walsh tell true from false in more important instances. He cites a passage from one of the 'Conversations' books about the composer's first wife, Catherine, who was his first cousin but is mentioned only once in his autobiography. She 'came into my life as a kind of long-wanted sister... We were from then until her death extremely close, and closer than lovers sometimes are, for mere lovers may be strangers though they love together all their lives'. Walsh's tone becomes perfervid: 'Nothing else in Stravinsky's memoirs rings so true.' The truth is that when the book first appeared, the composer's friends and family recognised that he would never have said this, and that the overcooking was mine. The claim 'until her death' is so false that anyone aware of the reality, through Catherine's begging letters to her spouse – on 26 November 1938, she expresses the desire to write to him daily about the health of their elder daughter (who died four days later), but 'I'm afraid you will scold me for wasting stamps' – cannot help but feel shocked by this misrepresentation of it. Every photo of Stravinsky in the family album memoir by Denise Stravinsky, the composer's elder son's wife, exposes a man who desperately wants to be elsewhere. His ill-concealed anger and boredom dominate not only all of the group portraits but also the solos. He never smiles and is usually looking away from the depressing scene surrounding him. A glimpse of him as he sees his son Theodore imitating his folded-arms pose catches the composer in mid-recoil. Folded arms can't embrace, of course, and not a single picture of him with his wife shows them even looking at each other, let alone holding hands. His are usually in his pockets.

The post-glasnost material in the book's account of the composer's Russian childhood and youth is meagre. In 1901 his parents, wishing to prepare him for a practical career, enrolled him in the Faculty of Law at the University of St Petersburg. (Tchaikovsky had been a student there.) He had not given proof of exceptional musical talent – compared to Prokofiev, ten years his junior but at that point far ahead of the greater composer. During the next five and a half years, he earned a half-course diploma, but of the fifteen branches of law available, we are not told those in which he was enrolled. Walsh speculates that Andrey Rimsky-Korsakov, elder son of the composer, 'was for a time perhaps even closer [to Igor] than [his brother] Volodya, a fellow law student'. But since *The Firebird* is dedicated to Andrey, this is a certainty, not a 'perhaps'.[16]

The one significant question concerning the St Petersburg years, the lost score of Stravinsky's memorial piece for Rimsky-Korsakov, is left dangling in a 'still-prevalent belief in Russia that the orchestra parts probably survive in the archives of the St Petersburg Philharmonie'. *Probably?* Then what inanition kept Walsh and his Russian confederates from undertaking a thorough search? And is it not possible that the score could still be with the Rimsky-Korsakov family? After all, the older composer's widow only reluctantly permitted Stravinsky to borrow the manuscript of his own Symphony in E flat. The book quotes reviews of the first and only performance of this lost musical epitaph (17 January 1909, conducted by Felix Blumenthal in the St Petersburg Conservatory); but to convey anything of value about a non-existent piece of music from a few contradictory reviews is impossible.[17]

In fact, the consequential Russian material in the biography comes from Stravinsky's 'Conversations' books. Walsh's Russian research reveals as much about Stravinsky's father as about young Igor, though most of this is inchoate. We learn that Fyodor Ignatievich's 20,000-volume library contained three Russian editions of *Das Kapital*, surprisingly not banned in czarist Russia, as well as a number of censored titles, including Alexander Herzen's complete works. (The biographer scoffs at the notion that the latter might have been read for content, as if anyone who had acquired Herzen's books and sampled a few paragraphs could fail to become engaged by his thought.) Some of Fyodor Ignatievich's traits of

---

16   This became apparent during the two occasions when Stravinsky and Volodya were together in Leningrad in October 1962.

17   Maximilian Steinberg, Rimsky-Korsakov's son-in-law, to whom, with his wife, the work is dedicated, remarks in a letter to Rimsky's widow after the performance: 'It is brilliantly scored but incredibly hard to play'. Richard Taruskin quotes the critic G.N. Timofeyev's description of the piece in a European newspaper: 'One seems to hear the sinister wail of a storm... and in the midst of it is heard... with gradually increasing volume, a beautiful theme, quite recognisably Russian in character. In the middle section there are melodic touches reminiscent of the portrayal of Caliban in Tchaikovsky's *Tempest*... It is orchestrated with great taste...'

personality, the parsimony and obsessively meticulous book-keeping, the fractiousness and intractable moods, the rampages and objurgations, were all supposedly replicated in Igor Fyodorovich. But the great shortcoming of the book is the failure to recognise that the unfavoured child, with his superstitions, hypochondria, anality, short-man's Napoleonic complex and near-megalomaniac ego, is a custom-made subject for a psychobiography, a genre Walsh disdains but occasionally slips into with references to 'Stravinsky's tendency to paranoia'. A psychoanalytically oriented writer would have studied the origins of the neuroses as far back as the nursery and emphasised the child Igor's fear of the father who 'at dinner never spoke to me'.

We read that Vera de Bosset, eventually the second Mrs Stravinsky, and her husband, Sergey Sudeykin, eloped from Moscow to St Petersburg in 1916. The actual time was the early spring of 1913, and the route Moscow to Paris, where Diaghilev had engaged Sudeykin as scene painter for *The Rite of Spring*.

The Walsh version of the first meeting between Igor and Vera, 21 February 1921, differs from the Stravinskys' in every particular. Stravinsky had returned to Paris from Rome on 18 February 1921, and the very next day, Walsh says, the composer, with Diaghilev, the Sudeykins, Boris Kochno and others, attended a performance at the Théâtre de la Chauve-Souris, where Stravinsky had fallen 'head over heels in love' with a 'voluptuous blonde' dancer, Zhenya Nikitina. 'It seems certain that there was an affair,' Walsh believes, but the correct name of the Chauve-Souris[18] dancer with whom Stravinsky actually did have a brief affair was Katinka. Afterward they all 'repaired to an Italian restaurant in Montmartre', where, Walsh imagines, the

---

18 In a 1922 *Westminster Gazette* article on the Chauve-Souris, Aldous Huxley describes it as 'an overrated institution... it has only done well what the Russian Ballet has done a good deal better. Take the décors. The Russian scenes designed by Sudeikin are charming and tasteful and amusing, but as works of art they cannot compare with the really grandiose creations of Goncharova and Larionov... the *Chauve-Souris* makes art out of art instead of out of life. It is sophisticated and literary to the last and most hopeless degree... The best things are undoubtedly the frankly comic items, [among them] Katinka dancing the polka... But "good" and "bad" are not the right terms in which to criticize the *Chauve-Souris*. At its best it is amusing, at its worst it is tiresome.' Katinka's 'Polka' was one of Stravinsky's four-hand piano pieces orchestrated by him for her and incorporating her Chauve-Souris theme-song in an added trombone part.

Sudeykins reminisced about their marriage in Yalta three years earlier. (Since they had been together every day since then, what would they have to reminisce about, especially in the presence of Stravinsky?) Walsh goes on to quote Artur Rubinstein's reliably unreliable memoirs about 'subsequent dinners at Fouquet's with the lovely Zhenya, the Sudeykins, and presumably Stravinsky'. *Presumably?*

Vera Sudeykina Stravinsky's account of these events is more believable. Having known Kochno (1903–1990) from the Crimea during the Revolution, she maintained that he came to her on the penultimate Sunday morning of February 1921, explaining that he had an appointment to meet Diaghilev later that day, and implored Sudeykin, whose catamite he would become,[19] to shave him, barber shops in Paris being closed on Sundays. In fact, it was Vera Sudeykina who had persuaded Diaghilev to meet the seventeen-year-old boy. Diaghilev telephoned the next day (21 February) inviting her, and not her husband, to dinner in the Montmartre restaurant and saying, 'Stravinsky will be there. He is moody today, so please be nice to him.' The meeting, which the Stravinskys celebrated annually, was a *coup de foudre* for the composer, whose behaviour she described as outrageously flirtatious. A day or two later, Stravinsky called for her at her apartment and sent a message upstairs: 'I am waiting for you in a car in the street below.' Walsh remarks that this note has 'not resurfaced', meaning that he has not seen it in the Paul Sacher Stiftung, Basel, catalogued on page 173 of the Vera Stravinsky correspondence.

Elsewhere Walsh says that 'however brutally candid [Stravinsky] could be with Katya about his affair [with Vera], his mother had to be kept in the dark', but Denise Stravinsky's *mémoires* now reveal that an unidentified family member had told the composer's mother about his *affaire.*

Walsh's chronicle of Stravinsky's romantic life is mistaken in other instances as well. 'According to Craft, there was a romance with Lydia Lopukhova,' Walsh writes, though he should have known the facts of

---

19   When Stravinsky and Kochno encountered each other in New York during the composer's 1937 American concert tour, Kochno told him that he was living there with Sudeykin.

this from other sources and from the published photographs of the pair together in Bordeaux on 8 September 1916, where Stravinsky had gone to embrace her on her return from New York. The composer himself always freely admitted to this 'affair'.[20] The autobiographical writings of Victoria Ocampo, who had been present at 'the *cataclysme apprivoisé*' (Cocteau) of the first *Rite of Spring* and who remained captivated by Stravinsky for the rest of her life, make clear that Walsh exaggerates the composer's romance with Coco Chanel. Ocampo, who knew the couturière over a long period, repeats a conversation in which Coco replies to her confession, 'I was once very jealous of you', with 'Who, Stravinsky?', whereupon Ocampo changed the subject but tells her readers that Chanel admitted to 'disliking sexual relations with any man more than two or three times'. Walsh further supposes that the consummations with Stravinsky (twice or thrice) would have taken place at Chanel's suite in the Ritz, unlikely as that seems, since it would have been tantamount to going public. Stravinsky's affair with Chanel began in 1919 and ended amicably when she moved on to the Grand Duke Dimitri in 1920. She continued to see Stravinsky and Vera throughout the 1920s and 1930s, helped the composer financially in hard times, and attended Diaghilev's funeral in Venice in August 1929, as Stravinsky did not. In New York, in February 1949, she dined with the Stravinskys at 'Maria's', on East Fifty-Second Street.

In contrast, nothing at all is said about Stravinsky's earlier connection with the beautiful Russian-speaking Brazilian soprano-cum-violinist (pupil of Enescu) Vera Janacopoulos, for whom he orchestrated two of his songs with piano. With the help of her uncle, the Brazilian minister of war, she had moved to Switzerland from her mother's home in Brussels at the outbreak of World War I, and met Stravinsky there shortly after he had composed *Pribaoutki* (1914). The resurgence of his wife's tuberculosis earlier in the same year initiated a succession of marital augmentations. He gave the original manuscript of the new piece to the young singer (who had learned

---

20   I witnessed the moving scene backstage in the Royal Festival Hall, London, in 1965, between a lachrymal Lopukhova (widow of John Maynard Keynes) and a perspiring but dry-eyed Stravinsky.

Russian from the poet Polonsky[21]) and Heitor Villa-Lobos copied it for her. She performed it in New York under Prokofiev[22] in 1919, then returned the manuscript to Stravinsky, who affectionately inscribed a printed score for her in Russian. In later years he gave the original manuscript scores to her of the 1924 orchestrations of his *Tilimbom* and *Pastorale* (a version with *flute,* oboe, clarinet and bassoon).[23]

The fling with Juana Gandarillas, the wife of the homosexual Tony, who served plovers' eggs at his dinner parties, must have taken place earlier than this, probably in Paris in 1919. Virginia Woolf describes her in May 1919 as 'very stupid, but so incredibly beautiful that one forgives it all'. Lytton Strachey gossiped that 'she had the finest underwear in Europe', and that Clive Bell had 'fallen madly in love with her'. Meeting Gandarillas at Harry's Bar in Venice in the 1950s and in the Grand Véfour in Paris in the 1960s, the present writer felt certain that this elegant gentleman was grateful to Stravinsky for cuckolding him.

Walsh wrongly places Stravinsky at a concert in the Salle Gaveau (it was the Salle des Agriculteurs) on 29 May 1923, and fails to remark that this was the tenth anniversary of the premiere of *The Rite of Spring.* Ostensibly Stravinsky had come to hear Janacopoulos sing pieces by Manuel de Falla, but in actuality he was there to see and hear her perform his own Japanese Lyrics, *Pribaoutki* and, for the first time, *Sektantskaya*, this last with flute obbligato, for which Stravinsky himself copied the part for Marcel Moyse. Though she later married Alexis Staal, a former official in the Kerensky government, Janacopoulos remained on close terms with Stravinsky, continuing to perform in concerts with him even during the early Vera Sudeykina years.[24] In 1951 W.H. Auden and Chester Kallman confided to the present writer that the director of La Scala had wanted Vera

---

21   One of Stravinsky's first cousins, Nicolai Yelachich, was married to Natalie Polonsky, the poet's daughter. Polonsky is best known today for his recognition of the genius of Isaac Babel.

22   Janacopoulos was the co-librettist of Prokofiev's opera *The Love of Three Oranges.* (Prokofiev was in his 'wild oats' period. He married in 1923.) Stravinsky responded tersely to Prokofiev's letter from New York about her: 'I know her very well.'

23   The manuscripts are in the Library of the University of Rio de Janeiro.

24   See her diary for 1927.

Janacopoulos to sing the lead in the premiere of *The Rake's Progress*, an idea the librettists managed to squelch in deference to Vera Stravinsky, having heard from Nicolas Nabokov of Janacopoulos's reputation as 'an ex-girlfriend of Stravinsky's'. (A self-proclaimed stickler for accuracy, Walsh misdates her birth by five years: she was twenty-seven in 1919.)

The biographer describes Igor and Vera as having 'drowned their scruples and travelled together from Paris [to Barcelona in 1924] in a wagon-lit', though by this time they had been living together for two years and had often journeyed together in wagon-lits. Same-sex sexuality offends the author's prudery still more, as when he refers to Anna Akhmatova as Olga Sudeykina's[25] 'flatmate (to put it no more strongly)', and wonders whether or not 'Stravinsky was aware of the true relationship of Gide and Marc [Allégret]', as if, alone in France, he might have been hoodwinked.

In 1922, when Vera left Sudeykin for Stravinsky, Diaghilev jokingly offered to 'compensate' the painter, a gesture Walsh describes as 'ghoulishly perverse'. More pertinently, the homosexuality of Stravinsky's younger brother, a matter of some significance in a biography, is referred to only by innuendo: 'Gury would never marry' and 'We still know curiously little about him.' What we do know, Stravinsky having talked openly about it, is airbrushed from the scene. Yet Igor grew up sharing a room with this favourite sibling and in June 1905 journeyed with him through the Gotha Canal and on to Oslo, where they happened to see Henrik Ibsen walking in the street. (Walsh incorrectly dates Stravinsky's first visit to the city in the 1930s.) Stravinsky's protectiveness toward his androgynous friends[26] – Cocteau, Eugene Berman, Poulenc, Henze, Boulez, Copland, Carlos Chávez, Charles-Albert Cingria,[27] Lord Berners, Auden, Isherwood, Spender, Edward James, Kopeyikin (Balanchine's pianist)

---

25 The painter's first wife.
26 Stravinsky's correspondence with the minor composer Maurice Delage is homosexual in tone, and Wilde's name comes up in it. In 1911 Stravinsky sent a frontal nude photograph of himself to Delage, and during a vacation in Delage's country hideaway, they were joined by Prince Argutinsky, a notorious homosexual.
27 Cingria was closer to Stravinsky than C.F. Ramuz. Cingria's close friendship with Amadeo Modigliani eventually led to his portrait painting of the composer.

e tutti quanti – surely reflects his relationship with his brother.

Walsh's hostility toward the composer leads him to such hyperbole as 'for once we can accept Stravinsky's own account as broadly accurate'. Only once? And why the tone: 'unless he was fibbing – in that fulsome way he was beginning to find socially convenient'? Stravinsky is chastised for the most trivial transgressions and defects of character, as if the object of a biography was to provide a compendium of its subject's delinquencies. If Walsh had known about Stravinsky's bivalvular obsession – that he had become addicted to *Marennes* in Brittany in 1910 and arranged to have iced packets of them sent regularly to his Swiss home – the indulgence would have been criminalised. When the composer was taken to a clinic in Neuilly two days after the premiere of the *Rite*, seriously ill with typhus from a bad oyster, Walsh's upper lip stiffens: 'an unpleasant illness, but only very briefly life-threatening'. In fact it is a grave malady that killed Stravinsky's younger brother.

'Strangely enough', in Brussels, in 1924, 'the composer continued to fret about money' (what is 'strange' about that?), and 'dispatched' Vera (as if she were a carrier pigeon) to Paris to borrow some. 'She was greeted on her return with champagne, as is the way with the superior poverty.' Surely such high-spirited people deserve better. Yet the gibes continue. 'After the First World War the composer began lying to journalists.' (A heinous thing to do, especially in that high-principled world.) 'On another occasion he prevaricated to a publisher' (truly unconscionable), and once even misstated his age, apropos the performance of an early Glazunov symphony.[28] '[Stravinsky] was eleven, not nine or ten as he had claimed,' when the symphony was played on 2 February 1894, Walsh announces. But to expect a man of seventy-five to set down a factually accurate record of a minor event from his early childhood exposes a lack of imagination. A high proportion of Walsh's boasted-about corrections of facts are on this level.

'The principal author of the view that [the composer Arthur] Lourié

---

28 Walsh's veneration for Glazunov provokes the nebulous remark that the young 'Igor played four-hands with his uncle – Beethoven, Wagner, and by implication... Glazunov'. But how can Glazunov be implied by the German giants?

exerted an overriding intellectual influence on Stravinsky is Robert Craft.' No. This view was Pierre Souvtchinsky's. I never met Lourié, knew neither his writings nor his music, and, for reasons not divulged to me, never heard his name mentioned in the Stravinsky household. Souvtchinsky stood firmly behind Lourié, but Walsh goes on with the crude remark that 'it was typical [of Stravinsky] to be more interested in the Jewish Lourié's practical value as an office boy...'

The chapter on Stravinsky's politics is seriously bungled in averring that he 'never performed in public under Fascist auspices'. The inconvenient truth is that he conducted in Franco's Spain, and in Italy in the 1920s, before it was considered reprehensible, and after that in Trieste, Venice, Florence, Turin, Milano, Rome and Naples. In this last he opened a concert in 1936 with the Fascist hymn *La Giovanezza*, promising the orchestra manager in writing that he would play it '*avec joie*'. Two and three years later he appeared at the Maggio Fiorentino (*Perséphone*, with Victoria Ocampo as *diseuse*), and in Milan and Rome.

Walsh's verbosity would tempt any competent editor to trim at least 50,000 words, many of them from an apparently inexhaustible fund of clichés and equivocations ('may have been', 'seems likely', 'perhaps', 'presumably', 'possibly'). German word order is not uncommon ('Here there met regularly a group of musicians') as well as atrocious imagery ('Nijinsky had to cut his teeth on Debussy's *L'Après-midi d'un faune*'). Of the numerous infelicitous expressions, the uncouth 'hard-nosed' is introduced on page one, and does not become more appealing after about forty reappearances. It is used throughout to characterise such different people as Diaghilev ('hard-nosed but soft-hearted'), Rimsky-Korsakov, and, of course, the 'usually hard-nosed' Stravinsky. Malapropisms are by no means rare: *viz*: an early critic 'gushed tautologically' that Stravinsky 'is a man of unmistakable talent', which is neither a 'tautology' nor long enough to be 'gushed'. Walsh prides himself on his 'retranslations' of letters, though most of these are not new renderings but paraphrasings of old ones and shufflings of word order. Some are out-and-out thefts from me, distorted to hide the fact, as when he claims to 'quote' Stravinsky criticising a performance of his Symphonies of Winds in

Brussels in 1924 as 'a bit flabby' (overweight, loose), but here he is caught red-handed, since the only source is Vera Stravinsky's diary, cited in a book of mine as 'not hard enough'. Walsh's version says exactly the opposite of what Stravinsky meant, namely a performance lacking in sinew, punch, attack.

Living longer in the United States than in any other country – 'Que devient-il ce cher Ygor Fedorovitch égaré dans cette Amérique puérile?' René Auberjonois wrote on 16 January 1942 – Stravinsky formed his own American idiom, of which his 'Conversations' preserve a few choice examples. When Walsh has him characterise Cosima Wagner, at the 1913 Monte Carlo *Parsifal*, as 'a right old piece of junk and a skinflint to boot', the Brit tone jars, as do the vulgarisms and scabrous language that Stravinsky did not know and would not have used if he did – 'buggered me up', for instance, and the Anglo-Saxon tetragrammaton that, like Henry James ('excrement, not to put it more shortly'), Stravinsky never used. His preferred locutions for the much-called-upon Russian word *govno* were *merde*, *ka-ka* and *Petrushka-ka*. Nor did he ever pronounce a translated version of the Russian *iebla* (fuck), and when John F. Kennedy employed it several times in male after-dinner talk during the White House reception for Stravinsky in January 1962, the composer was deeply shocked.

Postscript

Two years after the publication of the above review, Stephen Walsh resurfaced in a pamphlet, *The Stravinsky Project*, produced and distributed by the composer's music publishers, Boosey & Hawkes. His contribution, *Igor Stravinsky: A Timeline*, contains numerous errors of fact, and many more in choices of inclusion and exclusion: Walsh says that Stravinsky visited St Petersburg for the last time in 1912, but photographs show him there in the autumn of 1913. Walsh has Stravinsky conducting at the Edinburgh Festival in 1959. He *never* conducted there. The CBS Stravinsky documentary was directed by David Oppenheim, not Rolf Liebermann. Walsh writes that in 1920 Stravinsky 'moves from Switzerland, via Brittany, to Coco Chanel's villa in Garches'. In truth, Brittany was the composer's home from

July through November of that year. Picasso's portrait of him is signed 'Paris, 31 December 1920'. Stravinsky's family and his wife's in-laws, the four Beliankins, occupied Chanel's home in Garches for a few weeks in 1921, not 1920. Stravinsky himself was in central Paris throughout December 1920 preparing for the revival of *The Rite of Spring* on the 15th.

Walsh claims that Roland-Manuel spent 'months' with Stravinsky at Sancellemoz in 1939, preparing the composer's forthcoming Harvard lectures. Actually Roland-Manuel spent six days with him there, 7–13 May, and another six between the end of May and 7 June, the date of Stravinsky's mother's death in Paris.

Stravinsky and his second wife did not 'settle' in Beverly Hills in 1940 (or ever), as Walsh writes, but in a rented house in a ramshackle neighbourhood in Hollywood, and only for a few weeks. The important event of the summer of 1940 is that he travelled to Mexico in order to re-enter the US under the Mexican immigration quota, the Russian being closed. Returning to California, he immediately took out first papers for US citizenship.

In 1962 '*The Flood* goes out on T.V. with interruptions for shampoo ads,' Walsh reports. But can Stravinsky be held accountable for the commercialising of a film he never saw? His eightieth birthday was spent in Hamburg conducting the New York City Ballet in five successive performances of his *Apollo*.

Walsh II

Advance publicity for Stephen Walsh's *Stravinsky: The Second Exile (1934-1971)*[29] vaunts that 'at last the record has been set straight and countless errors have been corrected'. In reality, the record is more muddled than ever and far more mistakes have been added than corrected. I marked 400–500 of them on a quick read-through, but a limited space in a *New York Times* letter (28 May 2006) allowed me to cite only a few. Besides, correcting mistakes is not so much the issue. The whole book is wrong, an attempted exoneration of all the

---

29   *Stravinsky: The Second Exile, France and America, 1934-1971*, London, 2006

Stravinskys except Vera and even Igor.[30] The largest part of the text continues with the tatters of the ongoing campaign to discredit me, by the odd method of plagiarising, then distorting, my writings on the subject.

For example, Walsh says that 'Craft writes in *Cher Père* all the time as if he thinks that the fact of Marion's name on the Basle account made him the composer's heir. It is hard to believe that Craft really believes this, yet the alternative conclusion, that he is fabricating the whole assumption in order to represent Marion as a swindler is even more incredible.' (What really is hard to believe is how poorly this is written.) Marion's thefts from Stravinsky over a long period are documented in the New York City Surrogate Court.

Greg Sandow's *New York Times* review (21 April 2006) of *Stravinsky: The Second Exile* quotes Walsh to the effect that my work 'is riddled with bias, error, suppositions, and falsehood'. I maintain that these terms more aptly apply to his work. Sandow notes that 'Walsh is no longer courteous and when discussing Craft his tone shifts from sarcasm to outrage'. This hostility becomes evident in the caption to a photo taken in January 1947: 'Studying the score of *Perséphone* with James Fassett [the producer] and Robert Craft, who has sneaked into the photograph.' In reality, the undoctored original of this well-known picture shows several other people, now airbrushed out, standing between Stravinsky and me; in fact, I was at the end of a line-up, positioned there by the photographer herself.

I must acknowledge, however, that the book does pay me two or three unintended compliments. One of them says that during a long flight with his daughter and son-in-law (Marion), Stravinsky, 'without the company and stimulus of his alter ego,' was unable 'to organize his creative agenda in his own mind'. Another elevates me

---

30 No other enemy of Stravinsky would have thought of charging him with anything quite so gross as, in pasting the obits of friends in the sketchbook of *Requiem Canticles*, a 'self-conscious act, a gesture to the movie cameras of posterity. Waugh's death cannot possibly have affected him in any personal way,' Walsh righteously declares, knowing nothing of the composer's innermost feelings. The obits were intended as tributes, of course, not as famous people in a P.R. necrological album. 'Varèse, who [Stravinsky] saw from time to time in New York,' in Walsh's description, is also in the sketchbook. Stravinsky was deeply grieved by his death, as he was by that of Somerset Maugham, whom he did not know personally but admired in Christopher Isherwood's home films of him.

to a higher realm, quoting a letter from the composer's friend Pierre Souvtchinsky: 'among young musicians Boulez rates and fears only Craft and Stockhausen. He spits on the rest.'

Walsh relies heavily on oral tattle – with which the book is stuffed – but manages to avoid accurately informed people who knew Stravinsky well, such as Elliott Carter and Harold Shapero. A paragraph on Michael Tilson Thomas describing Stravinsky, taken from Dorothy Crawford's chronicle of the Los Angeles Monday Evening Concerts, should have suggested to the biographer that the conductor would qualify as a valuable source. While still a USC music student, Thomas was the keenest observer of everything about Stravinsky as conductor and composer, affectionately mimicking the older man's conducting gestures and his manner of speaking. Thomas attended not only Stravinsky programmes at the Monday Concerts, but most others when the master was in the audience. The younger man is able to point to passages from Schütz, Couperin, Tallis, and other Baroque and Renaissance composers in *Agon*. Thomas amusingly recalls Stravinsky's own California symphony concerts, including one in which he confused the program order and began beating the slow 12/8 of *Firebird* while the orchestra launched into the Fourth Tableau of *Petrushka*. Thomas brings Stravinsky to vivid life, as Walsh never does.

Other musicians who knew Stravinsky well and could have contributed new material include Gregg Smith, who prepared most of Stravinsky's choral music for his concerts and recordings in the United States, who worked closely with him on a translation of *Les Noces*, and who prepared the *Requiem Canticles* in Venice, performed at the composer's funeral. Another rich quarry would have been David Oppenheim, who played (clarinet) in some of Stravinsky's recordings, and who, in 1965, produced a documentary film in which he accompanied Stravinsky on a steamer from New York to Sweden, then shepherded him on a French-Swiss tour and two strenuous weeks in Warsaw. David was with Stravinsky in Rome, Venice, Chicago and Texas, and several times in both of his Hollywood homes.

Chortling triumphantly that Stravinsky's 1959-1960 concert series in New York left him 'out of pocket,' Walsh misses that important aspect of the composer's character: his financial foxiness. In actuality, Stravinsky realised a handsome profit from the series, by enlisting three different sponsors, unknown in that capacity to each other: the wealthy husband of his piano soloist in *Movements*; Goddard Lieberson, who was induced to increase Columbia Records' contribution; and the scrap metal tycoon Hans Popper, who had hosted the composer's 1959 Japanese tour (and was underwriting the Domaine Musicale in Paris). A further economy came from Aaron Copland, Roger Sessions, Lukas Foss and Samuel Barber, who waived their performance fees as pianists in *Les Noces*.

Having mentioned Sessions (another ignored intimate source, who occasionally visited Stravinsky in his last years for the pleasure of conversing with him in Russian), I am reminded of a splurge of errors in *The Second Exile* concerning Stravinsky's participation in a 1959 Princeton symposium. Walsh claims that the Stravinskys 'set off from Hollywood at the end of August and after a few days in Princeton... they flew on to London for discussions with Eliot'. In truth, the composer, coming by car from New York, spent a single day at the University, his purpose being to extricate me for an earlier departure to Britain. In order to release me from obligations in the symposium, Stravinsky talked to a class of students himself.

Walsh's inability to provide contexts and circumstances leads to innumerable misunderstandings, as in his account of a disruptive incident during the Stravinskys' 1959-1960 New Year's Eve party at the Gladstone Hotel (Walsh locates it at the Pierre Hotel, which did not enter the scene until a decade later). Uninvited, Lillian Libman, one of Stravinsky's concert agents, and her husband appeared at the door of the composer's tiny apartment to convey good wishes, but were not asked in, for the reason that an intimate party was in progress there for their friend Dr Max Edel and his new wife, who had flown in for the occasion from Los Angeles. What Walsh should have realised on his own was that Stravinsky scarcely knew Libman - and her husband not at all - having seen her only a few times since his return from Europe at the end of November and during preparations for the *Noces* concert.

In December 1966 the Stravinskys took a holiday for two weeks in Honolulu, a project planned by the composer's attorneys, William Montapert and his wife, who were in recluse there themselves at the time and had convinced the composer that it would be restful and healthy for him to join them. Another promoter of the project was a Russian-Swedish woman from San Francisco, Irena Arn, who had supplanted Libman after a scandalous mismanagement of the preceding summer. The principal attraction of the two Honolulu concerts that were part of the adventure was the appearance of the young Itzhak Perlman playing Stravinsky's Violin Concerto, with 'the dreadful local orchestra,' as Walsh insultingly refers to it. (It goes without saying that only a very competent orchestra could play this tricky piece.) The orchestra gave a lavish party for Stravinsky between the concerts on one of Oahu's west-coast beaches, at which the composer, to my eyes, seemed relaxed and happy, though he soon became restless again and eager to return to fulfil two concerts stateside. Walsh, who knows nothing whatever about the Honolulu sojourn, writes 'that Craft was the driving force behind this ever more alarming schedule could scarcely be doubted'. But Stravinsky in his eighties greatly enjoyed travelling and wanted more of it. Not being able to walk around the block, he could be transported to Johannesburg and New Zealand with little inconvenience.

Walsh lacks a talent for characterisation, describing Stravinsky's Dr Edel as 'a classic example of the old-fashioned cultivated physician with a personal touch and a beautiful bedside manner...' In fact, Edel, having lived in Communist Russia in the 1930s, had *no* bedside manner, but only a cocksure gift for inveigling attractive young women into the lap of this piece of furniture. One wonders why Walsh identifies Edel as 'the Viennese Jew' and why, eight years later, he blames Mrs Stravinsky for 'turning on' and dismissing the doctor for misdiagnosing her husband's thrombosis as gout, surely a perfectly justified response to this medical error.

The portrait of another close Stravinsky friend, Paul Horgan, is wholly misconceived. After Stravinsky's performance of *Threni* in

Santa Fe, Horgan, lauding the work to him, was met by the composer in a bantam mood grousing about the mistakes. This 'bitterness' is compared to 'a kind of post-coital emotional detumescence'. Poor Paul, a pious gentleman who had taken a vow of celibacy, and whose member may never have been tautened, even for manustupration, as Beckett put it, would have been horrified by the grotesque analogy.

The book's contribution to musical knowledge is both nil and baffling. What can be meant by the comment on a piece that 'Uncomplicated it may be, but transparent it remains'? And what is the point of saying that 'when Schoenberg had begun writing serial music in the early twenties, Webern had followed him – had even preceded him in some respects'? In which respects, please? The analogies become increasingly far-fetched, as when we are told that Stravinsky, fascinated by Krenek's 'manipulations' on a serial chart, added 'connecting lines and arrows on it... as if plotting cavalry movements at Austerlitz.' (Curiously, Krenek, a devout Roman Catholic of Czech origin, is also singled out as a 'Jew', as was Samuel Dushkin in Walsh I: 'Dushkin was Jewish in both appearance and in fact'.) I myself am pleased to learn, at the conclusion of an inventory of my shortcomings, that: 'Craft [is] edgy, complex, quick, almost Jewish'. (Quite so.)

A crucial shortcoming of the book is that Walsh's bias in favour of Stravinsky's family heirs against his widow deprives it of objectivity. In particular its vilifications of Vera Stravinsky, which contrast too radically with the views of all those who knew her as loving, warm, and generous to a fault. Here is Christopher Isherwood: 'Don and I agree that Vera Stravinsky is one of the most un-nastiest people we know. There seems absolutely nothing bad about her. She is sweet-tempered, funny, witty, kind, intelligent, and very industrious.' The bias is evident from the outset, since the book begins with a paean to the composer's sixty-year-old grandson, who has consistently blocked the publication of a variorum edition of his grandfather's works. It was Stravinsky's most fervent wish.

Chapter 25

'Après le Déluge, Moi'

Glimpses of Stravinsky in Paris, 1958–1968

My most surprising 2006 New Year's gift was a book, *près de Strawinsky*,[1] inscribed 'Un souvenir des jours heureux à Paris. Bien amicalement Mario.' In the thirty-eight years since I last saw him, Mario Bois became a television producer, Président du Conseil de la danse auprès de l'Unesco, and the author of a dozen books on ballet, music and *choses d'Espagne* – earlier in his career he had lived in Andalusia training to become a torero.

The handsomely produced and illustrated volume covers Stravinsky's sparsely documented 1960s sojourns in Paris. I read Bois' fragments of biography with pleasure, in spite of trepidations about references to myself, particularly in the chapter 'Véra, Pierre, Bob et les autres'. Pierre Souvtchinsky, a close Stravinsky intimate, happened to be with him when Bois first presented himself to the composer as the new French representative for his British music publisher, Boosey & Hawkes. Both men took to Bois, and Souvtchinsky became his mentor during most of Stravinsky's Parisian visits.

Bois begins by remarking on Vera Stravinsky's 'independent character', her *allures de grande dame* and her ability to pacify her husband during crises with a few calm exchanges in Russian. Bois

1   Mario Bois, *près de Strawinsky*, Paris, 1998

observes that she managed everything, baggage, air tickets, travellers' cheques, tips, telephones, taxis, passports, visas and money, whereas 'Bob ne s'occupait jamais de rien'. Bracing myself before reading on, I learned that I was 'thin, dry, with a sharp critical eye' and possessed both

> a quick spirit and unrivalled erudition. He is informed about everything, speaks perfect French, and is the epitome of the young American intellectual.[2] We were comfortable together and became good friends... Strawinsky thought very highly of him, and excused any lapse with a paternal sentiment. The composer often deferred to Bob – 'Bob said this... Bob thinks that...' – and repeatedly said 'Bob is my memory.' He placed total confidence in him and in truth Bob worked mightily for Strawinsky, travelling with him, sharing his concerts, rehearsing concerts and recordings for him, and writing articles and books with him.

'Souvtchinsky always defended Craft,' Bois explains:

> *Écoutez*, he can be insufferable, but he is very interesting. The Strawinskys are very fortunate to have him. He is a precious presence for them, young and intelligent, he distracts, informs, and stimulates them; without Bob they would have become *gâteux*. Can you imagine Igor cut off from the world, lost there in the backwoods of Hollywood?

And Bois concedes that 'After all, it must require a lot of patience to live with the Strawinskys every day.'

The book is primarily anecdotal and Bois gives examples of our quotidian repartee: 'One day, Souvtchinsky remarked that "Beethoven was very famous in his lifetime; his funeral cortege was followed by

---

2   The reader must bear with me for a few lines of this, since it ends with my ultimate humiliation in Bois' contention that 'the world accuses me of apostasy and of converting Strawinsky to serialism'.

twenty thousand people." Stravinsky responded: "Then Beethoven was almost as famous as Leonard Bernstein."' Another time:

> Bob came back from the kiosk with an armful of newspapers in several languages. 'The only major news in the world press today,' he announced, 'is that Dali has cut off his moustaches and sold them for two million dollars.' 'Bravo,' Strawinsky said, 'when one has moustaches like that, one would be a *con* not to sell them.'

près de Strawinsky brings a welcome freshness to the composer's biography. Though its author knew him only from meetings during his 1960s Paris stopovers, he gives a vibrant portrait of him and his ambience, bringing him to vivid life, painstakingly reproducing his conversational language, describing his body language, and even, now and then, penetrating to the depth of his character. The honesty of the narration, agreeably free of rhetoric, is immediately apparent. The book seems to me more amusing in French than it would be in English, and the direct, clear prose can be read by anyone with a year or two of school French. It is an affectionate antidote to much of the Stravinsky literature of recent years.

The material is sorted into thirty short chapters according to subject, and subsumed under an overall but not strict chronological order. The importance of the publication is that approximately half of the text is in Stravinsky's words, accurately quoted, as the present writer can testify, having been on the scene when a portion of them were uttered and recognising the fidelity to the thought and intention of the others. The author artfully describes Stravinsky's physical movements, evolving moods and repertory of facial expressions. For instance, he repeatedly mentions the composer's habit of cupping his hand behind his ear, and meticulously tabulating his alcoholic consumptions, not a swig going unnoticed.

Chapter 5, titled 'Strawhisky', begins with Bois arriving at the composer's hotel and being told by the concierge that 'Monsieur Strawinsky is downstairs in the bar'. When the author enters this favoured refuge, Stravinsky, 'in a ceremonious tone', directs the waiter to 'bring a double whisky for the young man' and another for himself. When the glasses are quickly emptied, Stravinsky complains that the next ones should be a little fuller: 'Je suis adulte.' (Stravinsky was in the habit of ordering his guests' drinks for them.) A year later, when a London physician banned whisky altogether, the composer, wilfully misunderstanding that alcohol in general was meant, switched to Dom Perignon, also two bottles at a time. Answering Bois' question about alcoholism among composers, Stravinsky awards top honours to Mussorgsky, but then stoops to a pun: 'The whisky I prefer is Whisky-Korsakov, but only up to *Sheherazade*.' Bois quotes him on the White House dinner celebrating his eightieth birthday. 'After it, President Kennedy asked me how I was, and I answered "Perfectly all right." He then said, "We are honoured to welcome here a man so famous." I added, "And so drunk."'

Bois might be the first to have observed that Stravinsky responded to toasts to his health – 'A votre santé, Maître!' – with 'A *ma* santé' (not 'à la vôtre'). This detail introduces a résumé of Stravinsky's health, from a severe attack of pleurisy at the age of thirteen, to a near-fatal nicotine intoxication in 1911, and a no less precarious bout of typhoid fever in 1913. The following year he contracted his wife's tuberculosis, which would later confine him to a sanatorium for six months, and remain dormant after that. His life was a constant succession of colds and influenza. In October 1956, while conducting a concert in Berlin, he suffered a major stroke. His doctors advised his wife that they did not think he would live more than a few months. He recovered, of course, while composing *Agon*, and went on to create a dozen other pieces of new-thought new music during the next fifteen years.

The chapter on Stravinsky and Money begins with a litany of complaints about 'le fisc'. He believed that the IRS was persecuting him for deducting his support of a granddaughter in a Swiss hospital, and exacting full restitution, in addition to a fine. His revenge was to deposit his European royalties in a numbered account in a Basel bank. He also began to seek out tax-free investments, one of them in an abandoned California goldmine, which he named 'Verigor' (for the *or*). 'Everyone knows that Strawinsky had the reputation of being miserly,' Bois asserts, recounting the origin of the composer's Italian cognomen, 'The Merchant of Venice', a result of publicity apropos his steep fees for works commissioned by La Serenissima. This amused the composer, who thereafter autographed restaurant bills and souvenir albums with a dollar sign for the 'S' in '$trawinsky'. 'At my age,' he said, 'one can compose only for God or for money.' Bois sympathises with the composer, arguing that he actually spent very little money on himself, lived in a one-bedroom bungalow, and, in contrast, when in Paris, regularly invited eight or ten people for lavish dinners. The author neglects to mention, but probably does not know, that Stravinsky supported more than a score of relatives for most of their lives, as well as Russian refugee friends in France and America. The conclusion of this chapter affords a glimpse into nuclear family financial relations. 'Late one afternoon I arrived at Strawinsky's hotel, but Souvtchinsky stopped me in the lobby. "Don't go upstairs; this is not the moment. Théodore [Stravinsky's elder son] is on his way down with a check for eight thousand dollars in his pocket, and Strawinsky is groaning."'

Bois appears to have been astonished by Stravinsky's belief, contra Goethe, that music 'touches the heart', and that the heart is the emotional centre of the human being. It is true that Stravinsky subscribed to the Greek idea that the liver was the centre of emotion. But then, Stravinsky sided with Dostoyevsky and D.H. Lawrence in thinking that 'the life implicit has "touch" and the life explicit has only ideas'. A composer, he believed, must 'touch the notes. A man who talks about music without being able to play an instrument is like a man who speaks about love without being able to make love.' This discussion follows another about the absurdity of such appellations as the 'Pathétique' Sonata, the 'Death and the Maiden' Quartet and the 'Trout' Quintet, which Stravinsky brings to an end by saying that he likes 'The Maiden and the Trout', adding that obviously the title of the '*Unfinished* Symphony' had to be by someone else. 'Incidentally, I love Schubert, the string music above all, the quintets and even the quartets, which are less well known but contain beautiful things. Of course the fifteen operas and the seven hundred lieder are too much, but within this prolixity we have great string music and great piano pieces.'

Some of the book's dialogues add to those of the Stravinsky of yore. Bois asks if he thinks composers are intelligent people. The answer is: 'To write an orchestral score one must have a certain sense of synthesis, of cerebral organisation.'

M.B.   And Prokofiev? Was he intelligent?

I.S.   A complete idiot. He was interested only in music. Serge, I said, one must be interested in other things. But he never was.

M.B.   And Georges Auric?

I.S.   Yes. He was the most intelligent of the French musicians. But he did not write any music.

M.B.   Was Mussorgsky's *Boris* orchestration 'thin' because he didn't know enough, or was this by design?

I. S.   Probably both. He was lazy, you know. And there was this (Strawinsky pointed to his bottle). But above all he wanted to give precedence to the voices, to the people. Boris is the second role, the chorus, the people, is the first.

M.B.   What music do you listen to?

I.S.   Bach, *le maître des maîtres.*

Bois then asks Stravinsky to help him choose music for his forthcoming wedding to the ballerina Claire Motte, but is sceptical when he suggests some organ pieces by Frescobaldi. Wouldn't that be too 'severe', the fiancé demurs, having something more 'decorative' in mind? Stravinsky snaps back with this: 'Méfiez-vous des musiques décoratives.'

Bois' account of the scandalous Salle Pleyel concert on 14 November 1958 is broadly correct but insufficient. The Orchestre Lamoureux and the chorus of the Jeunesses Musicales had not been adequately rehearsed. Stravinsky's *Threni*, which he conducted, was so alien to the standard fare of both organisations that, as Bois says, they could neither sing nor play it, but his word 'cool' for the audience reception is greatly understated. Actually, the music was loudly hissed and booed. Stravinsky sequestered himself in his dressing room, refused to return to the stage, and when Pierre Boulez implored him to do so, shouted at him, 'Go to Hell'. Stravinsky vowed never to appear in Paris again.

Perhaps the full story of this fiasco can now be told, Bois having begun the process. *En passant*, it exposes the rift between Stravinsky and Boulez. It was Boulez's organisation, the Domaine Musicale, that presented the concert, and he who had faithfully promised to rehearse and prepare the new work for the composer. After the full dress rehearsal, the only one conducted by Stravinsky, his friends unanimously urged him to cancel the concert, which would have been simple and because of his age excusable. But the ultimate cause of the personal problem was a maleficent arrangement to have a new book about Boulez containing his attack on Stravinsky (by A. Goléa, Stravinsky's nemesis among French reviewers), sold in the foyer of the Salle Pleyel on the night of the *Threni* premiere. Somehow a copy of this publication was placed on the piano in Stravinsky's green room before the concert. The composer did not see it, but Boulez did, and quickly snatched it out of sight. The beginning of the Goléa book tells the story of Boulez's role as instigator in an assault on Stravinsky in a festival of concerts devoted to him in Paris at the end of World War II.

On 11 June 1965, Stravinsky was taken to a crowded studio at Télévision Française for a screening of the *Sacre* conducted by Zubin Mehta. Seated in the front row, Stravinsky began to fidget during the Introduction, and when the lights went on at the end of Part One he stood up in a rage, reproaching the entrepreneurs responsible for exposing him to this 'complete misrepresentation of my work. The tempi are wrong and always unsteady.' He pointed to metronome marks in the score and sang the correct articulations: 'Il faut faire ta ta ta et non ti ti ti. Ça c'est sa musique. Ça n'est pas la mienne.' The startled audience, which had probably loved what it had heard, looked on silently and mystified as he stalked out of the hall - at the intermission, not at the end, as *près de Strawinsky* implies.

The book is not free of biographical errors of some significance. Visiting Venice after Stravinsky's death, Bois goes to the Hotel Danieli in search of elderly staff members who might have known him. The oldest concierge says that the composer was kind to the staff, and talked to them with genuine interest. The plaque on the George Sand room is mentioned, but Bois does not care to see it, saying that 'there should be one for Strawinsky'. Alas, Stravinsky never stayed at the Danieli, and only once dined there, as the guest of friends.

The statement that when Stravinsky died in New York on 6 April 1971 he had been living in the city for 'several weeks', and in a rented apartment, is not correct. Actually, the Stravinskys had moved to the city from California almost two years earlier, and in 1970 purchased the apartment in which he died the following year. (Bois' account of the Venetian funeral service mentions Nicolas Nabokov standing next to the widow, and wonders, 'Where is Souvtchinsky?' – a question that has troubled us all, since Stravinsky had been supporting him for the last three years.)

Another error is the statement about the composer having three sons (instead of two) and only one daughter, about whom the author says, 'No one speaks because *elle n'avait pas toute la tête*'. She nevertheless married, he goes on, and 'Strawinsky continued to contribute generously to her family needs.' But surely the composer's deceased granddaughter is meant, since his elder daughter died in 1938, and his younger daughter, still (in 2006) living in California, aged ninety-two, has always been normal. Further, the granddaughter did not marry until several years after Stravinsky's death.

Bois records that a journalist rang up one day and asked Mme Stravinsky the titles of her husband's latest works. '*The Flood*,' she said. But her husband corrected her: '*Le Déluge.*' She asked: '*Et après le Déluge?*' '*Après le Déluge, Moi.*'

Part Two: Literature
Mallarmé, Joyce, Eliot, Auden

Chapter 1

'Pardon's the Word to All'

Auden's Shakespeare Lectures

W.H. Auden did not write *W. H. Auden: Lectures on Shakespeare.*[1] Nor does this title, which could mean a book about the lectures, claim that he did. In the lectures, some of which I attended, he spoke impromptu from aide-mémoires no longer extant. The versions presented here are based largely on notes taken by Alan Ansen, the poet's intimate friend, later his secretary,[2] and the author of *The Table Talk of W.H. Auden,*[3] a collection of literary chit-chat from the same period as the lectures, 1946–7, and including some of the same observations on Shakespeare.

Arthur Kirsch's editing organises and amplifies Ansen's material, trying 'as much as possible to be faithful to Auden's voice in reconstructing' the texts. But to reconstruct what never existed is patently impossible, and understandably the voice rarely resembles the one in *Table Talk.* Each of the lectures, given to audiences of as many as 500 at New York's New School for Social Research, lasted an hour or more. Only a stenographer could have kept pace at this length, despite Auden's occasional stammerings and normally less-

---

1   *W.H. Auden: Lectures on Shakespeare*, edited by Arthur Kirsch, Princeton, 2000.
2   Ansen typed the first version of *The Rake's Progress* libretto.
3   Sea Cliff, New Jersey, 1989.

than-lightning delivery. (Why was a recording not made?)

This is not said to discourage readers but only to remind them that the language and style are not Auden's. Even so, Auden at second or third hand, edited, doctored, filled in, even misquoted, is preferable to no Auden at all. The wit, insights and intelligence survive. Professor Kirsch, to whom we are all indebted, has been charged with padding the book, but the primary culprit is the indefatigable anthologiser Auden himself. To support and extend many of his conclusions, Auden provides an abundance of poetry and prose from his personal pantheon. In the lecture on *Julius Caesar*, the excerpts from Epictetus and Kierkegaard (whose title *Fear and Trembling* comes from one of Falstaff's speeches), together with poems by Housman and Eliot, occupy almost as much space as Auden's text. All of this *littérature choisie* – Saints Paul and Augustine, Dante, Peele, Milton, Herrick, Blake, Baudelaire, Dostoyevsky, Whitman, Rimbaud, Hölderlin (*Sokrates und Alcibiades* in both German and English), Rilke's 'The Spirit Ariel', Lawrence, Yeats, Robert Graves – is delectable, though much of it seems irrelevant.

Auden without intermediary appears only in his underlinings and other markings in a copy of *The Complete Works of Shakespeare* edited by George Lyman Kittredge (1936), and in annotations, largely lexical/philological, for *Hamlet* and *The Tempest* found in an appendix. A single vintage Auden remark here contrasts strikingly with the prose of much of the main text: Following a stage direction, 'Enter Ophelia', Auden says that 'Nicolas Rowe [1709] put in *fantastically drest...*' but 'Mad people don't have special dresses to be mad in. You ought to have an originally good dress not put on properly. Obviously her slip is showing.'

Nuggets like this occur throughout the lectures, sometimes in preposterous statements: 'Why should so much poetry be written about sexual love and so little about eating, since it is just as pleasurable' – how was this determined? – 'and never lets you down'. (Was Auden never 'let down' by the texture and flavour of his lamb chops?) Elsewhere he announces that 'Sexual desire begins with the individual object but ends in bed where things are generalized'. This hardly squares with his assertion in the *Measure for Measure* lecture that 'Brothels depend on the desire for fornication', or with the one on Juliet's speech anticipating the consummation of her marriage, 'Oh, I have bought the mansion of a love, / But not possess'd it' that it is 'the speech of someone thinking of a particular person'. One doubts the irrefragability of many other sweeping statements: 'I don't believe people die until they've done their work'; 'People, as a rule, die when they wish to.'

Inevitably, the lectures are dated. Shakespeare criticism at the time (Dover Wilson, G. Wilson Knight, Granville Barker, Hotson) was chiefly concerned with analyses of character and plot structure, and with the perpetual search for historical connections. Auden follows the then accepted chronology of the plays and poems, which would change appreciably in the ensuing years, and has continued to change since then with, recently, a slightly later date for *Henry V.* But his evaluations and comments are for the most part original. He counters Eliot's exalted opinion of *Coriolanus* with the arguments that the play does not have a 'really sympathetic character' or even 'an exciting or interesting' one; the poetry is 'restrained'; and 'there is no music for private life'. But one suspects that Auden's anti-French bias – Belloc 'can hardly be unaware that the Crucifixion was actually performed by the Romans, or, to make it contemporary, by the French' – is the underlying reason for his dislike of this 'French' classical style play. The book will be treasured not for such wholesale judgements, but for its asides on language, as in the reference to the 'Latinized vocabulary in *Troilus and Cressida*, words such as vindicative, tortive, errant and prenominate'.

Auden would have been amazed to hear that Shakespeare scholarship in the twenty-first century has focused on the question of his connection to Roman Catholicism, though it has always been known that the poet's mother was an ardent Catholic, and his father an ambiguous one. Auden was less interested in the biography than in questions of obscurities of language and looseness of plot in the last plays, the subject of his final lectures. His explanations for the opacities in the collaborative plays and in *The Winter's Tale*, one of his favourites, differ substantially from those of present-day critics, who tend to think of them as deliberate and purposeful. We are also more concerned with dramatic and theatrical readings and interpretations today than a half-century ago, but here Auden was ahead of his time. Witness his sensitivity to the impact on Shakespeare's style of the move from the Globe to Blackfriars, from loud-voiced outdoor plays to quiet, indoor, candlelit ones, where whispering and softly spoken verse were intended to be heard and facial expressions seen. He was far ahead of his critic-contemporaries, too, in focusing on the supreme importance of music in the plays.

What dates Auden's lectures more than subsequent discoveries in Shakespeare studies is the pervasive influence of Freud, and, to a lesser but nevertheless conspicuous extent, Georg Groddeck. An aunt of Auden's, who 'detested pleasure', sprained her ankle just before she was 'to go on a holiday. Will is an element in such an accident,' he says. Othello is both a father-figure to Desdemona, and, as an outsider, 'paranoid'. Falstaff, a 'displaced person', wants to 'attach himself to Hal both as child and as mother'. Angelo in *Measure for Measure* 'demonstrates the difference between the superego and conscience', possessing the former but not the latter. Auden's discussion of the genesis of religious belief is borrowed from *Totem and Taboo*, as is the distinction between religious dogma, presupposition ('I believe in order that I may understand, *credo ut intelligam*') and myth ('a proposition about experience'). He tells us that 'by an aesthetic criterion' (not divulged), 'Freud's myth of the killing of the father is [a] better explanation of guilt' than St Paul's. Readers too young to recall, or know much about, the pre-eminence of Freudianism in America at the time of these lectures will be surprised to learn of the extent of Auden's immersion in it, despite the well-known couplet in his Freud memorial: 'to us he is no more a person / But a whole climate of opinion'.

The anti-feminism, or castration fear, in the lectures dates them as well. Auden cites Thurber's *New Yorker* cartoon, reprinted in *War Between Men and Women*, showing 'the headquarters of each with maps of the USA in the background. In the maps in the women's headquarters, the appendicular Florida has been cut off.' The misogyny becomes serious in the remark on *Twelfth Night* ('a horrid play') that society 'is beginning to smell gamey. The women are the only people left who have any will, which is a sign of decadence.' Add to this the claim that 'American culture puts a premium on youth in women, in its fashions and elsewhere,' while at the same time 'you have a culture with dominant homosexual traits'.

Auden kept a stable of hobbyhorse subjects that he groomed and trotted out in a diversity of contexts. 'Eros and Agape' was one, Marsilio Ficino's neo-Platonism, via Erwin Panofsky's *Studies in Iconology*, another, and twelfth-century courtly love, which 'gave new honesty to new feeling', still another. At the time of the lectures Auden could also be counted on to bring up a discussion of the three world-changing events of 1859, *The Origin of Species, Tristan und Isolde* and, though the date doesn't quite fit, *Alice in Wonderland.* He also gives considerable thought to the theme of what distinguishes major and minor artists. It is 'not necessarily the difference between better and worse,' he tells us. The minor artist 'never risks failure', but when he discovers his particular style and vision, 'his artistic history is over'. The major artist, in contrast, is 'engaged in perpetual endeavors. The moment [he] learns to do something, he stops and tries to do something else, something new, and not caring if it fails, like Shakespeare, or Wagner, or Picasso.' In fact, Wagner cared a lot, and unlike the others, each of his works belongs to a higher firmament than the one before.

In one of Auden's notes on *Hamlet*, he remarks that 'Last couplets are never important', and in the lecture on the sonnets he asks his audience to 'Notice how frequently the concluding couplets are poor... Shakespeare says what he wants to say and lets the sonnet end anyhow. But that is the fault of a major artist; a minor one always completes the work carefully.' This point is not without merit, when we think of the only sonnet that everyone knows 'by heart', number 129, or, in *Cymbeline*, of the embarrassing last line of 'Fear no more the heat o' the sun', but the reader should turn to Helen Vendler's *The Art of Shakespeare's Sonnets* for a study of the 'Couplet-Tie' relation, through repeated key words, to the dozen preceding lines.

The lecture on the Sonnets begins with the assumption that

> there must be a difference between Shakespeare's dramatic works and poems about experiences that were happening to him... How far is [a lyric verse] personal, how far is it dramatic?

> Most of these sonnets were addressed to a man... The Dark
> Lady was neither beautiful nor wise – she's therefore sexually
> attractive as an infernal genius. The young man is no nicer, but
> Shakespeare's thoughts about him are different.

Sonnet 76 has lately become tabloid news, with the discovery that clay-pipe fragments excavated from Shakespeare's Stratford-upon-Avon home contain cocaine, cannabis and myristic acid (a plant-derived hallucinogen). The Sonnet refers to a 'noted weed' and to 'compounds strange'. Vendler attributes no significance to the 'weed', but takes the word 'strange' to be 'an editorializing insertion by Shakespeare'.

Perhaps we know too much about Auden's ratings of the plays. His top ten were *The Tempest, The Winter's Tale, Love's Labour's Lost,* both Parts of *Henry IV, Much Ado About Nothing, Measure for Measure* ('the least unpleasant of the ripe plays'), *Hamlet, Lear, Antony and Cleopatra.* On reconsideration, Auden replaced *Hamlet* with *Othello,* and, of the rejects, explained that *Troilus* is unsatisfactory for the reason that 'In the great tragedies the knowledge of what they are doing is hidden from the heroes', whereas in *Troilus* 'the characters are and remain maniacs and are aware of it'. *The Taming of the Shrew* is 'a complete failure. The plot... belongs to farce, and Shakespeare is not a writer of farce.' As for *King John,* Auden does not mention that Faulconbridge's monologue contains Shakespeare's first conversational colloquies in verse. His only comment on the play is that he does 'not care for the first scene in Act IV' because 'little kids on stage are impossible. They should be drowned.' Coriolanus, with Macbeth as runner-up, is 'the most boring of Shakespeare's heroes... The best people in the comedies are Beatrice and Benedick. One feels absolutely confident of the success of their marriage... They have creative intelligence, good will, [no] sentimentality, and an ability to be open and direct with each other in a society in which such directness is uncommon.'

The main interest in the lectures is in observing Auden trying to think along with Shakespeare. Part of Auden's method of relating the plays to the present of 1947 is to typecast contemporaries from

Shakespearian models. Thus 'Cassius is a choleric man – a General Patton'; Patroclus is 'a 52nd Street queen', and his relationship to Achilles 'is reduced to sexual love'; 'Pistol is a nasty drunk – you can meet him at cocktail parties'; 'Hal is the type who becomes a college president, a government head, etc., and one hates their guts.' Equally trenchant is the characterising of Desdemona as 'a young schoolgirl, afraid of sex, but wanting above all to be a grown-up... a romantic girl out slumming'. Another Auden method is to become more personal himself. He makes frequent references to the New York scene, declaring that he 'can't dislike Tammany Hall. Under the circumstances of today, we must have a decently dishonest bureaucracy. If a policeman won't take a bribe, you're sunk.' Surprisingly, he readily refers to his religious convictions and practices, informing his New School audience that he will not be lecturing on Holy Saturday: 'When they told me Saturday wasn't a holiday, I told them it might not be for them, but it certainly was for me.'

Most of the lectures follow a schema that begins with a moral / social /philosophical digest of the play. Thus '*The Merchant of Venice* is about... a society that is related to and can't do without someone whom it can't accept', and *Measure for Measure* is concerned with 'the nature of justice, the nature of authority, and the nature of forgiveness'. These bleak précis are followed by résumés of the dramatic situations, and by analyses of the characters. The first lecture, on the *Henry VI* trilogy, begins with a commentary on the requirements of the chronicle play, chief among them 'an explanation of the causes and effects of events' rather than 'the mere depiction' of them. He reminds us in his last lecture that Shakespeare 'got his training in these plays', and he compares the speeches of Clifford and Jack Cade, who speak in the same way, with the differentiated speeches of Brutus and Antony. Contrary to current opinion *vis-à-vis* the Royal Shakespeare's recent revival of the trilogy in Stratford, Auden thinks Part Two the most satisfactory play dramatically, and he quotes from the rough, fleering language of the scenes of Cade's rebellion. Part Three contains Shakespeare's 'first great soliloquy' by his 'first big character', the not-yet-crowned Richard III, but is otherwise 'a little tedious'.

According to Auden/Ansen, the subject of *Richard III* is the distinguishing of the existential self from the essential self. Don Giovanni exemplifies the former in his indifference to the individuality of the females he seduces. The essential self, it follows, is represented by Tristan, who 'wishes suicidally… to eliminate the self and be absorbed into another'. What Richard III 'really wants is to be loved for himself alone… his essential self. Each person desires that. What people are in the habit of calling love is the reflection of their self-love, which is why we love or want to love people like us or like what we want to be.' (Debatable.)

Turning to the *Henry IV* plays, Auden does not comment on the alternation of prose in the scenes with commoners and of verse in the scenes centred on those of exalted rank. Instead, he detects 'a questionable religious atmosphere', especially in *Henry V*. 'Only scoundrels like Richard III and Henry V talk of religion,' he notes, adding that Henry's famous speech on sleep is 'terribly bad poetry'. Vintage Auden reappears in the remark that Henry 'doesn't know God in a personal way, but thinks he can manage Him'. But the assertion that Henry's 'cold and calculated wooing of Katherine is the most brutal scene in Shakespeare… and most shocking of all is Henry's certainty of success' can be contested by more terrible spectacles.

One of Auden's long-held convictions was that *Love's Labour's Lost* is the one Shakespeare play that could be made into an opera libretto, albeit with major surgery in adjusting it to operatic forms. Had he temporarily forgotten about Verdi's Shakespearian masterpieces, and even about his own favourite, Bellini's *I Capuleti e i Montecchi*? What will interest most readers in the lecture on 'L's L's L.' is the discovery that Auden was thinking of it operatically as early as October 1946, a quarter of a century before fashioning a libretto from it.

While not lacking in perspicacious observations, such as the distinction between 'being in love' – 'You find out who you are when you are in love' – and 'falling in love', the lecture on *Romeo and Juliet* is perverse. Auden had absolutely no understanding of young romantic love. 'The only explanation of the suicides is… a fear that the relationship cannot be sustained and that out of pride it should be stopped now, in death.' Further, 'If they become a married couple, there will be no more wonderful speeches – and a good thing, too. Then the real trials of life will begin...' Referring to his audience's incomprehension of the importance of the blood feud, he says 'We [Americans] do better imagining idealized fights, unless we're from Kentucky.' He pretends to think that 'Two families having a row over who borrowed the lawnmower would be interchangeable with the provincial feud in the town of Verona'.

The *Hamlet* lecture begins with a warning about 'a lot of grave defects'. These are ticked off with the doubt 'whether anyone has succeeded in playing Hamlet without appearing ridiculous'. Next, he complains that the subplot of Fortinbras is 'not properly incorporated into the play', and Hamlet himself is not 'well integrated, or adequately motivated'. His last speech 'has the same kind of vanity as a suicide note', and in the killing of Polonius, he 'shows a considerable lack of feeling'. His letter to Ophelia, moreover, is 'terribly conventional', but then, 'he is not really in love with her'. The Prince's age is 'a great mystery. If about thirty, as his conversation with the clown suggests, why is he still a university student, and how old, then, is Gertrude?' Auden's Hamlet would be 'short and tubby', but he does not say why, and seems to have forgotten that the 'too, too solid flesh' is Hamlet's, and that in the duelling scene Hamlet's mother refers to him as 'fat and scant of breath'. Furthermore, Ophelia's madness is not 'adequately motivated. She was not so wild about her meddling Papa, after all.' And 'Why wasn't she saved? The person who saw her drowning couldn't swim? A description [is] wanted.' Did the upper classes of the time lack natatorial skills?

The most valuable observations are literary: Hamlet 'speaks both verse and prose, verse to himself in his soliloquies, and in speeches of violent passion to others, as in the scene with his mother. Otherwise he speaks prose to other people.' The play shows a development in Shakespeare's use of the double adjective, which 'here combines the abstract and concrete'. But Auden's explanation that Shakespeare switched from writing comedy to writing tragedy because 'he was probably bored with the genre' is insufficient.

Othello wins Desdemona by 'tales of romantic adventures... She behaves as if she knows she is conferring a favor on him, because her color puts her in a favorable position.' Othello is 'a black outsider who wants to become a member of the community'. His suspicions are expressions of fear that people are ignoring him. 'Othello learns nothing – the big heroes in Shakespeare do not learn anything – and he cannot think why he did what he did, or realise what was wrong.' Cassio is a type of homosexual, 'the familiar type who gets on with women much better than with men'. He wants to be 'one of the boys', and 'Iago gets him to drink by playing on his wish to be just that. Bianca loves Cassio but he doesn't love her, and since she belongs to a lower class, he enjoys an unaccustomed feeling of power.' Iago is Shakespeare's 'portrait of the villain as an inverted saint, a saint manqué, the two representing similar psychologies'. Though Iago cannot 'explain his self to himself', he knows just how to treat Brabantio, repeatedly stressing the image of his beautiful, nobly born daughter in bed with a black man: 'Even now, now, very now, an old black ram / Is tupping your white ewe.' Iago is the incarnation of the *acte gratuit* as described by Augustine: 'I lusted to thieve, and did it, compelled by no hunger nor poverty... Nor cared I to enjoy what I stole, but joyed in the theft and sin itself.'

If compelled to choose, *Antony and Cleopatra* is the play Auden would save, chiefly because it contains 'more first-rate poetry than any other play in the canon; not a line of it is detachable from the context either of the scene in which it occurs or from the play as a whole'. He refutes the argument that, strictly speaking, the play is not a tragedy, since

> the title characters are passive: their flaw is general and common to all of us all the time: worldliness – the love of pleasure, success, art, ourselves, and conversely, the fear of boredom, failure, being ridiculous, being on the wrong side, dying. The physical attraction between them is real, but both are getting on, and their lust is less a physical need than a way of forgetting time and death. For that reason, they require the support of refinements and sophistication. But their relationship is therefore selfish and destructive and it doesn't work. *Antony and Cleopatra* presents a pleasure of experience. Shakespeare

needs this comprehensiveness to show the temptation of the world, the real world in all its kingdoms, all its glories. The one thing you will not find in *Antony and Cleopatra* is innocence.

The Tempest, the only great Shakespeare play with an original plot, is also the only one that observes Aristotle's unities of time, place, and action, 'which accounts for Prospero's long exposition of the plot at the beginning...' Auden emphasises Caliban's sensitivity to music, and the importance of music in the play: 'There is music to put people to sleep to and wake them, "solemn and strange" music at the banquet,' and as everyone knows, 'the isle is full of noises / Sounds and sweet airs, that give delight and hurt not...' The play is about forgiveness, Auden tells us, going on to say that 'Prospero tried to make Caliban a conscious person, and only made him worse'. But Ansen's off-the-cuff *ipsissima verba* conversations are more acute:

> Shakespeare really left it a mess – like all myths it has value independent of the way it is written about... No, I don't think 'Our revels now are ended' is such a purple patch or the one passage one would want to take as the high point of Shakespeare's art. It's all right, but *Antony and Cleopatra* is much better poetry... Prospero doesn't want to die rebelliously, but he'll be quite glad when he can go.

Many readers will find the lectures on the late plays, *Timon of Athens, Pericles, Cymbeline, The Winter's Tale*, the most enlightening. By this time Shakespeare's interests had shifted from character to relations: 'One can't talk about good and bad people, but only about good and bad relationships... The plays of the final period focus on feeling.' Common to all the late plays

> is the absence of any resemblance to the real world of time and place, the unimportance of physical appearance, the violence, the physical sufferings, the storms, the repeated shipwrecks – *Pericles* – the wish to shock, the indifference to audience appeal. In fact, the late plays appeal to lowbrows and very

sophisticated highbrows, but not to middlebrows, even to that aristocrat of middlebrows, Dr. Johnson.

Run-on lines are frequent in the late plays, and 'some of the best things occur not in climaxes, but in bridge passages, in little points'.

After nominating Act Three, scene three of *The Winter's Tale*, with its pastoral serenities, as 'the most beautiful in Shakespeare, not in words, but in its situation' – a Jamesian distinction – Auden concludes, gently:

> 'Pardon's the word to all' is the note of all the late plays, the note to which everything is made to lead up. The characters are not separate individuals in their own right, you are not fond of them as you are of Beatrice and Rosalind, and they are not terrifying as they are in the tragedies, where they are isolated in their own self-love. But like a fairy-tale story, this is the world as you want it to be, and nothing makes one more inclined to cry.

Chapter 2

'Because I'm Me'

Wystan Auden's *obiter dicta*, as transcribed by Alan Ansen,[1] are funny, brilliant, outrageous. Anyone who knew the poet – very slightly in my case compared to Ansen – must agree that the voice rings as true as the often preposterous pronouncements, whose authenticity is verified not only by the exclusion principle (no one else could have made them up) but also by the word-of-mouth survival of some of them in Auden lore.

Alan Ansen met WHA in 1946, while the poet was lecturing at New York's New School for Social Research, subsequently becoming his secretary. At age twenty-four Ansen seems to have had a prodigious knowledge of ancient and modern languages and literatures, as well as near-verbatim recall. Though about half of the entries are printed in dialogue form, the others as monologues, the young philologist is intrusive only on questions of scansion ('In "heavy like us" you could save the alliteration by syncopating the *ke* and positing the *k* as the fourth alliterating letter'). His own recondite contributions are accredited only through Auden's responses: 'Oh, did Hobbes do a translation of Thucydides?' 'You're right, Landor's epigrams do represent a further use of Greek models.'

The stream-of-consciousness sequence of subjects appears to have been preserved. But Auden's 'baltering torrent' (Joyce's 'irruent')

---

1   *The Table Talk of W.H. Auden* by Alan Ansen, edited by Nicolas Jenkins, New York, 1990.

better describes both the jumble of ideas later to be processed into essays and poems, and the reader's sense of a lonely man's exuberance in finding a receptive listener: Auden sounds high most of the time, hyperventilated by his own wit and intelligence. A typical entry (17 May 1947 – the other thirty are dated between November 1946 and April 1948) – jumps from Rimbaud to Churchill, from the rutting season of tomcats ('they have a rugged time of it trying to service so many ladies'), and a projected guide to England to the painter Paul Cadmus.[2] But the startling juxtapositions and droll non sequiturs help to establish the reader's sense of being in the poet's company. In addition to bits of background – occasion and location, the contents and conditions of Auden's apartment, the kinds and quantities of drinks consumed – Ansen provides a sprinkling of parenthetical stage directions ('smiling mysteriously', 'to the cat', 'to me', 'looking it up in the *OED* and finding he was right') and clues to enigmatic references: 'If you want special knowledge, there's just one place to get it from.' ('Presumably himself.')

The discussions alight most frequently on literary, sexual, political (antidisestablishmentarian) and religious matters ('I'm coming to doubt whether [Dante] really was a Christian'), leavened with gossip ('Did you see that Mary McCarthy has joined the anti-Homintern?'), snippets of autobiography ('My mother used to get ill every time I came home, which gives you some idea of the relation between us'), and observations on American and European differences of decorum ('For an Englishman coming over here to teach, the rudeness of the students is quite shocking'; 'Chester [Kallman] thinks that when I expect him to get a cab it's because I'm me, when it isn't at all. It's simply what an older person expects from a younger one'). A high proportion of Auden's conceits take the form of fiats and caveats beginning 'All', 'Everyone', 'No one', 'The only': 'The only way to spend New Year's Eve is either quietly with friends or in a brothel'; 'Americans ought to live in Europe.'

As expected, the Auden of 1947 was hardly a pioneering feminist; 'Women should be quiet. When people are talking, they ought to

---

2   Lincoln Kirstein's brother-in-law.

retire to the kitchen.' 'I am a convinced monarchist,' the newly sworn US citizen announces. 'Why doesn't the United States take over the monarchy and unite with England?... At least you could use it as a summer resort instead of Maine.' Contradictions of a sort arise when he disapproves of 'the American practice of allowing one partner of a homosexual act to remain passive – it's so undemocratic', and at the same time defends the supposedly 'European' view that 'the lower classes simply ought to go to bed when asked'.

The American presidents, Taft excepted because 'he was so fat', have not made a favourable impression. 'Jefferson, I think, must have been a great bore' and 'One wonders whether Roosevelt developed paralysis in order to become President... No one really good can get to occupy the position he did'. To be taken more seriously are the comments on American social distinctions: Americans who like Samuel Johnson tend to be 'nasty types of Anglophiles who think they have to be rude and are usually Republicans'; 'the important thing in America is not to have money but to have had it.'

Table Talk suggests that Auden's infamous Francophobia became more rabid with World War II: 'at the beginning of it the French lie down like a doormat, and afterward they're meanly vindictive... using German prisoners of war as slave labor'. Kallman, Italo- and Germanophile, operatically speaking, seems to have fuelled the prejudice. Even so, Auden's real trouble with the French is 'their terrible Cartesianism. To them, you agree or you don't agree. And that's perfectly logical. But it doesn't find any place for the irrational element which is always present.' Baudelaire 'was absolutely right when he talked about "*l'esprit de Voltaire*"'. (What Baudelaire actually said was '*Je m'ennuie en France, surtout parce que tout le monde ressemble à Voltaire*'.) But Auden's shocker on the subject, clearly intended as such, occurs in his introduction to the *Viking Portable Greek Reader*. 'The Crucifixion was actually performed by the Romans, or, to make it contemporary, by the French.' One pictures him trying this out on Kallman, for whose entertainment he probably concocted it.

Auden's remarks on French literature, Pascal's 'wonderfully malicious *Provincial Letters*' excepted, together with Balzac as 'a great writer on money', the 'extraordinarily clever' Cocteau, and the 'very intelligent' Valéry, also leave out rather a lot. 'I don't like Montaigne at all.' (Auden's *New Year Letter* dedication borrows an epigraph from him nevertheless.) La Rochefoucauld 'simply says what one has always known'. (Yes, but without him many of us would not have known that we knew.) Flaubert's pre-*Bouvard et Pécuchet* novels 'are so dull'. Verlaine 'wasn't so good'. Gide is 'really commonplace; imagine getting off with this Arab boy [and] stopping to say, "*Que le sable était beau*".' Even Racine 'isn't quite so fine as people say', while 'Mark Twain, bad as he was – I've read two books... and I don't want to read any more – [is] at least better than Corneille'.

Auden's best *bon mot* about music is apparently unintentional: the Kyrie in Bach's B minor Mass is 'marvelous for the first two [78 RPM] sides, and then you realize he's going on with the thing to the bitter end'. But then, Bach is a mere 'Alpha' composer, in comparison to 'the Alpha plus' Mozart. In any case, Auden's musical interests, as indicated here, are virtually confined to opera, even though 'the characters always manage to fall in love with unsuitable people'. *Tristan und Isolde* should be 'done' not by 'hetties' but by 'lizzies'. 'They eat each other up, try to replace the world. Isolde is the English mistress, Tristan the hockey mistress... Neither extreme, *Tristan* or *Don Giovanni*' – the Don being 'a certain type of male homosexual' – is 'compatible with heterosexual love'. Brahms is abused: 'Whenever I hear a peculiarly obnoxious combination of sounds, I spot it as Brahms and I'm right every time', but Liszt is accepted: 'The opening of *Totentanz* is so good. But why does MGM hire people to write music for them? Liszt has done it so well already.'

Auden's thoughts about Greek literature, expressed shortly before he began to compile his anthology, should be read more closely than anything else in the book, together with the passages on English prosody, too specialised for discussion here. The most remarkable feature of Greek civilisation is not, as we might have anticipated, the inquiring, sceptical intelligence and the unities of abstract and concrete thought and feeling, but 'the use of hypothesis in every subject'. What most puzzles is 'their failure to see the importance of freedom of choice', and their apparent indifference to the question of existence. What *did* the Greeks believe? 'I'm not talking about the

Roman period when it was generally held that the gods were allegorical personifications, but when people were serious about following the ritual. And yet they didn't seem to care whether their deities existed or not...' Auden's anthology essay bypasses the difficulty: 'The kind of god who is both self-sufficient and content to remain so could not interest us enough to raise the question of his existence.' Another crucial question remains unanswered: 'I don't see how Plato reconciled the Demiurge of the *Timaeus* with the vision of Er at the end of *The Republic* with its system of rewards and punishments. How far did he believe in either of them?'

Auden's Greek anthology lacks the variety and scope of the outline as exposed in *Table Talk*, which includes the thirteenth chapter of *Corinthians* and the *Romans*. Thucydides, not Aristotle, is Plato's 'real rival'. Auden seems to have downgraded Aristotle because 'I don't think [he] really liked poetry. I think he had a wife who liked to go to the theater and came home raving about the latest play.' Unlike Aristotle and Plato – 'a man of genius who's always wrong' – Thucydides 'did not deify the state but regarded it as a convenience'. Part of Auden's exalted opinion of the Atomists ('the people I really like') seems to derive from their influence on Thucydides.

Some of Auden's Petrine judgments on poetry are familiar: 'Blake's longer poems won't do'; Browning's lyrics are 'atrocious' ('I don't think Browning was very good in bed. His wife probably didn't care for him very much. He snored and had fantasies about twelve-year-old girls.'); Pope is 'the real test of liking English poetry... *The Rape of the Lock* is the most perfect poem in English... Some of his lines are wonderful – "Bare the mean Heart that lurks beneath a Star".' And *The Prelude* is 'a marvelous work... My landscapes aren't really the same as Wordsworth's. Mine... come from books first.'

Auden mentions Eliot more frequently than any other poet, primarily to distance himself. He achieves his goal by declaring his belief that 'poetry is predominantly frivolity. I do it because I like it. The only serious thing is to love God and' – he was a true Philadelphian – 'your neighbor'. Turning to specifics, he says that the chief difference between himself and Eliot is that, 'he thinks... society can be made into something good'. And,

> I don't know why Eliot is so unfair to Milton... I certainly disagree with Milton's beliefs as much as Eliot does, but that doesn't put me off his poetry... his unfavorable estimate prompted me to read Milton and find out how good he was. Eliot does know his meters quite thoroughly... You can't catch him out about the history of English prosody... Eliot wrote nothing but later poetry, after 'Gerontion' anyway.

Still,

> Eliot does realize his danger of falling into a Manichaean condemnation of the flesh per se. But our poetry is the product of our feelings. There's an awfully revealing anecdote about Eliot. A woman who was seated next to him at table said, 'Isn't the party wonderful?' He said, 'Yes, if you see the essential horror of it all.'

Auden's sex talk is largely directed toward Kallman, the absent philanderer: 'Sexual fidelity is more important in a homosexual relationship than in any other [where] there are a variety of ties. But here, fidelity is the only bond.' And with a papal gesture he divides the world into oral and anal. 'Americans are violently oral,' this practitioner of buccal coition says. 'Even the American passion for laxatives can be explained as an oral manifestation. They want to get rid of any unpleasantness taken in through the mouth... America is a very queer country... What the American male really wants is to be blown by a stranger while reading a newspaper...' Ultimately he decides that 'it's wrong to be queer', mainly because 'all homosexual acts are acts of envy'. Perhaps with this in mind he resolves to 'lead the life of a monk this summer, an absolute monk. Oh, one may drop in on a party for half an hour and eye it coldly with one's lorgnette.'

———◆———

Table Talk, an argosy of wit, has been ignored by the literary establishment, no doubt because of its improprieties. Lucy

McDiarmid[3] is among the few who have taken it seriously and intelligently. She notes that in *Table Talk*, Auden's remark that 'Shakespeare left *The Tempest* in a mess' means '*not* in a lustrum of love and forgiveness, but in disingenuousness and theatrical trumpery', adding that love in Auden's 'later poetics [is] a literary subject but never an emotion'. Further, she dares to expose the great man's vanity, quoting his homiletic on the nature of human egoism:

> Humility is easier for a poet or a novelist to acquire than for a critic, since the creative writer's subject is 'life in general', the critic's mere authors, human individuals. To say that 'life is more important than anything I can say about it' is easier than to say, 'Mr. A.'s work is more important than anything I can say about it.' But in an age of the usurpation of creation by criticism, is the critic's subject matter really limited to authors, and does the critic think of his or her work in relation to degrees of importance?

Auden's sin against humility, if that describes it, is elegantly absolved with the line from 'At the Grave of Henry James': 'Pray for me, and for all writers, / living or dead [...] because there is no end / To the vanity of our calling...'

---

3   *Auden's Apologies for Poetry*, Princeton, NJ, 1990.

Chapter 3

Sir Stephen by Himself

Stephen Spender's peregrinations as lecturer and symposiast in collegiate America, his quest for recognition, and his association with W.H. Auden are the principal subjects of his *Journals*.[1] Since the accounts of cultural conferences and romances on, or just off, campus are familiar in kind, the following remarks are mainly centered on his poet-colleague. But Spender's smaller, incidental subjects, his visits to the old and infirm, his encounters with artists and writers, are more attractive, and though he confesses to a 'lack of vitally experienced observation', his portraits of people confirm that he is a sensitive observer.

Both the reviews of the book and the letters protesting them have shown a remarkable absence of susceptibility to the rich appeal of the *Journals* as humour. Anyone who met Sir Stephen, and apparently anyone who was anybody did, will know that he himself is the favourite target of his highly developed gift for fun. Even to those unaware of the acuteness of this faculty in him, it must be evident that the witticisms at his own expense are conscious, the provoking of laughter intentional. Consider the following narrative in which he ridicules his desperate struggle to reach New York City in time for a dinner party the day after a lecture upstate:

---

1   *Journals 1939–1983* by Stephen Spender, New York, 1986.

I went to a place called Oneonta... I was met by a pleasant young man... Next morning, he called for me... took me... to the airport... We were told the plane could not take off unless there was visibility of at least a mile... In NY I had... to join... Jacqueline Onassis... at a restaurant... I simply had to get there. I enquired about taxis and found that Oneonta had just one... After an hour, an octogenarian taxi driver appeared... After a 100 miles or so... [he] made it clear that he did not want to drive me to NY... He said he would drive me to Albany... and there I could get an aeroplane... but there were no flights from Albany that would get me to NY in time... Finally I said the only thing was to find me another taxi... [When] I sat next to J.O.... [she] seemed to want to talk seriously... I asked Jacqueline what she considered her greatest achievement in life. 'Oh,' she said, 'I think it is that after going through a rather difficult time, I consider myself comparatively sane.'

Sir Stephen's failure to conceal his surprise at J.O.'s ability to rise above the level of unserious conversation is a minor lapse when measured against the proof, in revealing his maladroit question and her devastating reply, that he does not lack the courage of his candour.

In another droll story on himself, Sir Stephen dreams he is made pope:

I sat in a large room, waiting to deliver my first sermon before about a million people... Numerous flunkeys, autograph hunters... kept on interrupting me... My sermon was intended to bring the full weight of starvation, preparation for nuclear war, etc., into the consciousness of the people, so they would change the world... Everyone would be grateful if I spoke, say, for five or ten minutes... delivered some brief but tremendously moving exhortation.

So far from being confined to anecdotes, the Spender wit assumes a multitude of forms. One even suspects that some of the *Journals'* errors, factual and verbal, were intended simply for the fun of it. This is obviously the case with the footnote he attaches to a passage about the 'South Seas', with a reference to Tahiti and Gauguin, that relocates these waters in 'the Caribbean'. So, too, the misrendering of his line beginning 'Spender's simple spondees offer this...' as 'Spenders, simple Spenders, offer their...' has a special appeal, as does the anachronism in the entry of 4 September 1939, comparing King George VI's broadcast voice to an 'often interrupted tape machine', and the confusion elsewhere about other sounds: 'They played the Schubert Octet... oboes, flutes, clarinets always bring to mind...' But there are no oboes and flutes in the Octet.

On the verbal side, charmingly, disarmingly, the young Stephen, in one of his *Letters to Christopher*,[2] admits to 'not knowing one end of a sentence from the other', and vaticinates that 'If I go on writing badly enough, it will become one of my qualifications'. The *Journals* confirm the astuteness of the prediction. A tangle such as the following has a distinctiveness that could not survive a grammatically sorted-out version:

> I have the sense of an underlying depression like a large squid
> lying at the bottom of a tank, which if I don't act with resolution,
> will come up from the depths and embrace me in its tentacles.

W.H. Auden is referred to in the *Journals* more frequently and at greater length than anyone else including the author's wife and his American friend, B., about whom we are told only that he lives alone in a trailer. The reflections on Auden could be subsumed under the title that Spender expended on another book, *Love-Hate Relations*. 'Did I really like Wystan?' Spender asks himself, when someone puts this question to him. The complicated answer is unforthcoming. He

---

2   Santa Barbara, 1980. The *Letters* provide background for Spender's young friend Georg, not found in the *Journals* – he sat for 'an hour or so at my desk trying to copy my signature to see if he could forge a cheque successfully' – as well as editorial curiosities: Oliver Risdale Baldwin is identified as 'a biographer married to Victoria Sackville-West'. (Was Harold Nicolson aware of this?)

reflects on Auden's contempt when they were young. 'I imagine he laughed at me a lot behind my back.' (He certainly did when they were older.) And he reviews the less accommodating features of Auden's character: the dogmatism and arbitrariness, meaning the petrine approvals and disapprovals in accordance with one principle at the expense of all others; the hypocrisy of feigning indifference to his publicity; and the vanity ('They loved me', 'They were entranced'). Auden's blindness to painting is held against him, his vocation for religion dismissed as a subterfuge: 'The effect of cultivating a bad Christian conscience has been to free him of interest in social problems.' It now appears, as well, that there were two Audens, the mean and the absurd. A little of the former, surely, and lots of the latter, and in small doses the latter at least was entertaining. One may doubt, too, that Auden agonised from a bad conscience, or that he ever had any deeply felt, as distinguished from theoretical, interest in social questions.

The emergence of certain reservations concerning Auden's poetry is novel. In the early years it had an 'idiosyncratic sensibility', but lacked 'a center of his own personality'. Also unlike the later work, it was inimitable. Spender claims that a young poet able to match the technique of Auden's later periods could conceivably fill his carpet slippers in other ways as well, but the speculation is unarguable. Spender does not hide other feelings. 'Of our group – Auden, Day Lewis, MacNeice, myself – Auden has inspired teams of scholars and research workers.' In contrast, Sir Stephen has no confidence in even the one young man writing a book about him 'trying to support my reputation'.

Auden's homosexuality surfaces as camp, not as a factor of significance in Spender's life. Not long after Auden's death, Spender read an article about A.E. Housman's male Parisian prostitutes, and exclaimed: 'How I longed to tell Wystan'.

Some of the jokes are grammatically confusing: 'Wystan asked Bill to go to bed with him in the nicest way possible, so that it was easy to refuse.' So, too, a mock-serious discussion of Auden's aptitudes as husband and paterfamilias – unnamed friends had asserted that 'he was not gay' – is built toward a punch line that loses its quaintness without

Auden's high, cranky voice delivering it: 'What I hate is the fucking.'

Apart from Auden, the most abiding subject of the *Journals* is what Spender sees as the lack of a sufficient appreciation of his talents. Why does he feel 'such a resistance to writing poetry'? His answer could hardly be more frank: 'From the sense not so much of failure as of non-recognition.' When people ask 'if he is *the* Stephen Spender', he is ecstatic. 'The man at the desk asked whether I was related to the poet Stephen Spender. So I said "That's me." He looked pleased and said "Gee, a near celebrity."' That the matter is not a laughing one becomes apparent in a mirror scene headed 'Thoughts while shaving':

> A thing I am ashamed of is that I find suggested confirmation of my identity by reading my name in the newspapers. My heart really does do something journalistic – stops a beat, gives a jump – if my eye looks on the printed word 'Spender'.

The recommendation for a knighthood forces the question into the open: 'There comes a time when one craves for recognition – not to be always at the mercy of the spite, malice, contempt... of one's rivals.' But the slings and arrows, not all aimed by 'rivals', continued, and we only wonder how, after fifty years in the arena, Sir Stephen could have expected them to stop. Not his enemies – surely he has none – but his friends flinch with each of his cruel self-exposures: 'My life was in some ways ambiguous, like one of those photographs, which if you look at it from one direction has a different face from that which you see from another.' And, 'Being a minor poet is like being minor royalty.' Regardless of whether he can claim an assured place as one of the minors, Spender went on to say that one of the last of the majors wrote 'perhaps [his] greatest poem [*The Circus Animals Desertion*] when he was seventy-four. "I have four years then," I thought.'

For all of Spender's efforts to present himself as paranoid ('I imagine the young reading nothing of me but the bad notices other [*sic*] young critics write'), many of his self-criticisms, anticipating less-well-intentioned ones, are silver-lined. Sometimes the turnarounds and powerful upbeat endings occur in the same sentences:

Everything I had done – or nearly everything – seemed a failure, not that of a person who does not use his talents, but worse, does not use them enough even to discover how much talent he has. I also experience despair as the result of not having a disciplined mind [and of] feeling overwhelmed by the material and the uncontrollable rush of my own ideas.

Some of Spender's poems, memoirs, translations contributed to the formation of a period, which, to an extent, they now represent. Indeed, few lines express the feelings of the 1930s more memorably than

> *We who live under the shadow of war,*
> *What can we do that matters?*

Yet Stephen Spender himself stood taller than his work. The least insular writer of his generation and the most generous, he was a kinder man – *hypocrite lecteur!* – than most of us deserved.

Postscript

Dear Bob:

I have been sad my last few visits to N.Y. not to have seen you.[3] All my efforts at communication, through Barbara [Epstein] and others, have been in vain. It is therefore with great pleasure, and a sense of 'recognition' by you, that I read your review of my *Journals* in the *NYRB* – as though it were a letter written by you to me – which, I suppose, in a way, it was. I took all the points you made and I was touched by your last paragraph.

A *Journal*, of course, is not meant as criticism, it is a record of day to day reactions to people and events. Due to the limitations of the Journal form, I think you misunderstood

---

3   I was upset with him. Immediately after Stravinsky's death he wrote a beautiful poem on Stravinsky and I listening to Beethoven quartets together, dedicated it to me, and gave me the manuscript. I wrote and thanked him. But when the poem was published I was surprised to find that its dedicatee was Sacheverell Sitwell.

slightly my intentions in what I write about Wystan. When I wrote that his early poetry lacked 'a center of his own personality', I did not intend to express a newly discovered reservation I felt about this. I have always felt that his early poetry lacked an 'I' – and that its originality, its extraordinary bleakness and detachment lay in this – and in fact I've felt that immense as his achievement in his later work was to be, this strangeness, this feeling that the poetry someone emanated from the surrounding Nordic landscape, this 'clinical' objectivity was not developed in his later work – and that the failure to develop it was perhaps a loss.

I come back to the limitations of the Journal form. What I record mostly is things that strike me as extraordinary phenomena. It was extraordinary that Auden said to me after his visit to Milwaukee 'They loved me. They were entranced.' – but it struck me as being simply true. The idea that it exemplified his vanity did not occur to me until I read your review. When I wrote that 'the effect of cultivating a bad Christian conscience has been to free him of interest in social problems', I simply meant that this was the case. I did not at all mean to cast doubt on his Christian convictions, or suggest that they were held as a subterfuge.

I am not quite sure that I understand the sentence about the two Audens, 'the mean and the absurd'. I quote one example of his eccentric meanness (when he made me change a £1 note in order to buy a packet of cigarettes in Ischia), but I add in a footnote or a connecting passage that he gave me £50 to help buy Lizzie[4] a horse, that he left bottles of champagne in our home which we drank up. These outweigh two cigarettes, surely. I make this very clear. Perhaps you are using the word 'mean' in a sense more American than English. You may be referring to his remarks I quote made to Marianne Faithfull, but, again, I would not think of them as mean, though perhaps, in fact, they were rather.

---

4   His daughter.

My remark that Auden activated teams of scholars and research workers, whereas Day Lewis, MacNeice, and myself have not, is true, simply though carelessly expressed. I should have written 'Auden's work' and I should have added Isherwood to Day Lewis and MacNeice. I do not see that it reflects on Auden that works of exegesis and scholarship crystallized round it. I do think it sad that Isherwood should have had only one book about his work – by the plodding Bryan Finney – and Day Lewis by his boring son, and MacNeice by some other bore. I don't quite get the point of your 'unfortunately' – unless you think I am being jealous and spiteful here.

I am grateful to you for your remarks about my feelings of non-recognition, and still more for you own true and generous recognition of my work in your concluding paragraphs. Also for the trouble you have taken throughout in this review which I take as a sign of affection unfortunately not realized in recent years in our every meeting.

I am delighted to say that you misquote the two lines of poetry of mine:

We who live under the shadow of a war
What can I do that matters?

For if you had not done this where would I stand, with my many inaccuracies? Homer sometimes nods and Craft can sometimes be inaccurate!

My friend B. is an ornithologist and biologist, assistant to his professor at U.C.L.A., and one of the American team of scientists doing research into animal life in Antarctica, where he is at the present moment. He is intelligent, perceptive, imaginative, and affectionate, and is a person of great distinction. But of course I don't show this in my *Journals.*

Auden said that it is a sign that you regard someone as a friend if you find yourself smiling when you think of him. Remembering our visit to the [Kenneth] Clarks, to Stratford, and to David Jones, I always smile when I think of you, and

your miraculous friends – the wonderful Jamesian three of you
– I always feel pleased when you are praised, angry when you
are attacked – and I am sorry we do not meet more often.
Affectionately,
Stephen

Spender wrote to me on 4 May 1986 as follows:

Dear Bob: I stupidly misaddressed this letter to you. Also, Bob
Silvers, telephoning about your article, seemed concerned
whether I was distressed by your review of my *Journals*. So I
sent him a Xerox of my letter to you to show I have taken it
in good part. It will seem rude of me if you hear about Silvers
getting it before you have got it yourself. Best wishes, Stephen

Chapter 4

Aldous *Aun Aprendo*

A Memoir

The seventy-five *Westminster Gazette* articles on music in Aldous Huxley's *Complete Essays*,[1] not mentioned by his biographers and critics, reveal that music was no less essential to him than literature, philosophy, science and the visual arts. His fascination with its formal devices, and his innate susceptibility to its emotions, help to explain the loftiness of his adjudication that 'the *Grosse Fuge* is the most formidable piece of music that was ever written'. In 1930 he wrote to Paul Valéry: 'The Quartet in A minor and the Sonata Opus 111 are profound philosophical works, and Beethoven is the most complete of all philosophers, but music-philosophy is expressed only by music.'

Huxley's knowledge of the musical repertory was encyclopedic: Pérotin to Renaissance polyphony, Bach to Mozart, Schütz to Schoenberg, for Huxley did more than any other writer to enfranchise the truly new music of his own time. At the Salzburg Festival of 1922, he remarked on the 'wonderfully copious and varied musical invention' in Schoenberg's quartet with voice, and 'the long line of song, curiously curving through strange chromatics and modulations'. Webern, he added, 'might be quite good but his quartet was largely inaudible, being composed for the most part of infinitely pianissimo

---

1   Chicago (Ivan R. Dee), 2002.

pizzicati and the faintest catlike harmonics... His innovation tends towards soundlessness.'

As a small boy, Huxley was already aware

> of the enormous richness and complexity, the endless intellectual potentialities of music. After hearing Brahms's *Variations on a theme by Haydn* in a concert, I lived with these *Variations* for weeks at home poring over the printed music... I sat with the work for hours on end... trying to analyze and give a name to the logic which I could hear... but which I found it impossible to describe in words.

During my fourteen-year friendship with him (1949–63), his diet of Bach, Mozart and Beethoven expanded to the music of other cultures and as far back as Byzantine chant. In 1954 he came under the spell of the masses, motets and madrigals of the Italian and Flemish Renaissance court composers Dufay, Josquin, Ockeghem, Lassus, Marenzio, Monteverdi and Gesualdo,[2] this last becoming the subject of the most comprehensive of his writings on music, a survey of the madrigal in Ferrara at the close of the sixteenth century, before the Este city and lands were escheated to the Pope.

One of the *Gazette* articles deplores the absence in twentieth-century music of

> simple epical emotions, [the] unaffected and spontaneous grandeur, lucidity, and intellectual force, the simplicity and dignity, the spaciousness and serene greatness of Handel. What could give a nobler idea of the magnificence and grandeur of the human spirit than the great chorus 'For unto us a Child is born...'?

---

2   In September 1955 he wrote to Humphrey Osmond, who had introduced him to mescaline and administered his first dose of the drug: 'I have undertaken, rather rashly, to talk at one of the Monday Evening concerts on the [subject] of Gesualdo (the psychotic Prince of Venosa, who murdered his wife and could never go to the bathroom unless he had been previously flagellated) and on the Court of Ferrara, where he developed his utterly amazing musical style.'

He compares this example of Handel's 'objective' Christmas music with the meditative, introspective paschal music of Bach's *St Matthew Passion*:

> The religion [of Bach] seems to have been a very personal and inward religion, brooded over very tenderly, and at the same time with an extraordinary subtlety and refinement of emotion... which also characterize the form of [his] art, which was in the highest degree subjective and intellectual... [and] had very little epical faculty.

In 1957, after hearing some twenty-five Bach cantatas at the Monday Evening Concerts in Los Angeles, Huxley wrote of the composer as

> the only one who combined such miraculously enormous facility with consistently profound insight, copious production with unflagging originality of invention, prodigious learning with spontaneity and freshness.

Nothing is said of Bach's feral fecundity, the siring of more than twenty children (three of whom became major composers in a new and different style), which kept pace with his musical productivity. Early on, Huxley reached the conclusion that Russian music was shallow. Regular ballet-going had made *Sheherazade* 'intolerable' to him, and after a poor performance of Rimsky-Korsakov's *Capriccio* he resolved never to listen to it again. Scriabin's 'enormous pretentiousness' provoked Huxley to confess that he had 'grown heartily sick of Russian music', and though he conceded that Stravinsky could be listened to more than any of the others, he perceived that this composer's future development was in doubt. Also not a Wagnerian, Huxley reported that a *Parsifal* at Covent Garden,

> solemnly absurd as usual, was adequately sung but less well acted – granted that it is not possible to act in Wagner. [He] has no access to Beethoven's world of purity and subtlety, [being]

too much preoccupied with his eternal sex problems and his
visions of material splendour to be able to find the way into it.

Why did Huxley not pursue a music critic's career? One supposition
is his contempt for nearly all writing about music. He faults Dr
Burney for overrating C.P.E. Bach, and puts down the music entry
by Sir Donald Tovey in an *Encyclopaedia Britannica* supplement as
'non-committal and uninformative to a degree'. But the main reason
is surely the success of *Crome Yellow* (1921), his first novel, one of
whose laudatory reviewers was Marcel Proust: 'This grandson of
T.H. Huxley' occupies 'une place préponderante dans le monde de la
littérature anglaise' (*Sodome et Gomorrhe*).[3]

Aldous had been cruelly stricken three times in adolescence, first by
the premature death of his mother, Julia Arnold, Matthew Arnold's
niece; second by the suicide, *à la* Gérard de Nerval, of his next elder
brother, Trevenen, whose body was found, after eight days of search,
hanging from a tree with a note in his pocket from a young family
housemaid, who, instead of requiting his love, had 'given notice'; and
third by the *keratitis punctata* which, after three years of treatment,
left him totally blind in his right eye, and with only ten percent of
normal vision in the left, his 'half-blind eye', as he referred to it, a
stigma he would bear to the end of his life. He taught himself to read
musical notation as well as words in Braille.

As a child Aldous was taken to see Queen Victoria in her carriage
in Windsor Great Park, and, at age six, in the Natural History Museum,
to attend the unveiling by the Prince of Wales of a statue of Thomas
Henry Huxley, the boy's grandfather, 'Darwin's bulldog'. Feeling
queasy during the ceremony, young Aldous had to use his older
brother Julian's Eton hat as a receptacle.

The family tree, branching from Thomas Henry and flowering

---

3   Doubting that Proust had read the novel, though he could have and was always *au courant*
    concerning the English literary scene, Aldous was unable to explain the basis of the
    judgement.

through his son Leonard (an editor of Thackeray's *Cornhill* magazine), to the grandsons, Julian (the Darwinian biologist), Aldous, and their half-brother Andrew (Nobel Prizewinner in physiology), spreads to a twenty-first-century England in which numerous Huxley descendants excel in almost every field of human endeavour. But a Galton chart of the genetic history would be difficult to plot because of the quality of the collaterals, Matthew Arnold above all, but also the Huxleys-in-law, of whom Elspeth, wife of Gervas, may be the best known for her extensive writings on Africa.[4]

Aldous was a being apart in his physical dimensions as well, and he was convinced that his height had stunted his creativity: 'The brain is too far from the heart and the sexual center. Stravinsky, like Mozart, Schubert, Chopin, Wagner, is just right at five feet.' Virginia Woolf described him on their first meeting as 'infinitely long... [a] gigantic grasshopper... folded up in a chair'. A few years later, seeing him at a concert, she had the impression of 'a windmill and a scarecrow, more highbrow, purblind, and pallid and spavined than ever'. What surprises us is that none of Aldous's many medical and intellectual friends seems to have realised that, like Abraham Lincoln, he almost certainly suffered from Marfan's syndrome. The diagnosis applies to Huxley in several ways: the abnormal height, the long, thin fingers, the sunken sternum, the tisicky thinness, the fits of depression and the defective eyesight. Yet even in his last years, he stood as erect as a fugleman, never slumped or hunched.

Huxley biographers agree that their principal deterrents were the 1961 fire that destroyed his Hollywood home, library, diaries, correspondence and lifetime accumulation of personal papers; and the competition of Sybille Bedford's authorised biography, which draws on her 'thirty-year friendship with the Huxleys and has acquired the special authority and richness of a memoir'.[5] But in the 1990s, when the correspondence of the late Mary Hutchinson was made

---

4   See Ronald Clark's *The Huxleys*, London, 1968.
5   Bedford's 2005 memoirs, *Quicksand*, provide more about her early association with the Huxleys and an expanded and more open description of the Huxley ménage at Sanary, in Southern France. In this late book she describes Aldous's voice as 'silvery'. She died in 2006.

available, the picture of the life was radically altered. It revealed that from 1922 she was the lover of both Aldous and his wife Maria. The threesome occasionally shared a bed. A letter to Mary from Maria expresses 'a violent desire for [your] kisses', and reminds her of how Aldous 'can make your whole body quiver'. Maria's bisexuality has long been acknowledged, but not Mary's, a married woman as well as the mistress of Clive Bell.[6] Mary eventually confessed that

> Maria was the one I loved. Aldous was gentle, aloof, affectionate
> and even ardent sometimes, but it was Maria who attracted and
> charmed me... She always seemed to be sweetly scented, oiled
> and voluptuous.

Aldous was still corresponding with Mary in 1952, long after Maria had banished her as a nymphomaniac.

Aldous had met Maria Nys in 1917 at Garsington, that sanctuary for sexually wayward writers, including John Maynard Keynes, Lytton Strachey, E.M. Forster and Virginia Woolf. A war refugee from Belgium, Maria had been invited by the bisexual chatelaine herself, Lady Ottoline Morrell (Aldous: 'Lady Utterly Immoral'). Maria was not attracted to Aldous at that time, and when he asked her to marry him, fled to her parents in Florence, continuing to correspond with, but not seeing, him until two years later, when they were married at the Hôtel de Ville, Bellem, Belgium.

The paradox of the marriage is that despite its sexual openness it was nevertheless enduring, always tenderly affectionate, and, arguably, as firmly founded as a marriage can be. According to Bedford's biography, Maria usually arranged Aldous's extra-marital affairs for him, including the one with the Romanian Princess Henrietta Sava-Goiu,[7] who travelled in Burma with the Huxleys in 1925 and sailed with them from Hong Kong to San Francisco the following

---

6   A letter from D.H. Lawrence, Florence, 8 March 1927, to the Hon. Dorothy Brett, says that
     Mary Hutchinson was with the Huxleys on a recent visit. She 'seems nice and gentle, but
     very faded. Poor dear... Clive Bell and Co. must be very wearing.'
7   She was the model for T.S. Eliot's 'Princess Volupine'.

year. Maria wrote to Mary: 'I pointed out her attractions to him, and advised him to try his luck'.

———◆———

Near the beginning of the Stravinskys' early years in California, Aldous moved from Los Angeles to Llano del Rio in the Mojave Desert, where he lived an eremite's life and wrote the Hinayana Buddhist *Perennial Philosophy*. During excursions to Hollywood, the Huxleys visited the Stravinskys, and in 1942 both men were involved in Orson Welles's *Jane Eyre*, Aldous in writing a screenplay for it and Stravinsky in composing the score, though he soon withdrew. Often thereafter the two couples dined together at the Town and Country Market, and by 3 December 1946 Maria Huxley was writing to their son:

> Today we had a most delightful dinner with the Stravinskys. It was fascinating to listen to him. He pours out – what pours out is very intelligent and often very new – sometimes quite difficult to explain but always immensely worth listening to, and the French, not perfect, is intelligent and colorful... A vegetarian dinner for Aldous, just right, simple, good... Stravinsky is so extremely polite. The old school of politeness... I believe they have a real friendship for us. We like them very much...

From 1949, when Aldous and Maria moved back to Hollywood, they saw the Stravinskys two or three times a week, and became intimate friends. This has escaped the attention of biographers, who also seem not to know that in 1947 Huxley was responsible for Stravinsky's choice of W.H. Auden as librettist of *The Rake's Progress*.[8]

Stravinsky and Huxley regularly attended concerts and operas together.[9] Since the writer's library of recordings was much more extensive than the composer's, particularly in Baroque, Renaissance

---

8 Huxley could not have been very happy with the result. At any rate he said nothing about it, except to observe, apropos the line 'the marriageable girls... cover their charms a little or they will catch the rheum long before they learn of the green sickness', that if the ladies were really nubile, they would have known about the chloritic aspect.

9 The first of the latter was Britten's *Rape of Lucretia* in Los Angeles on 17 June 1947.

and Medieval music, they shared many evenings listening together in the Huxley home. Maria describes one of these sessions in another letter to her son, 13 May 1951:

> Vera Stravinsky rang up... they could not bear going to another cinema, could they visit us?... Stravinsky arrived in an enchanting costume, blue jeans and a blue jean zipper jacket open on a wine-red jersey, and silk scarf with pin... Always the same programme: Stravinsky, Aldous, and Bob Craft – almost an adopted son of theirs, 26, and very clever, knows everything, terribly nervous and not a pansy[10]– stay in the music room and Vera and I stay somewhere else. They play music and we chat. I am very fond of Stravinsky and I like her and we are very good friends. Bob too is very nice...

Both men favoured the old-music programmes of the Monday Evening Concerts (in a dreary West Hollywood school auditorium, with the American flag planted in a standard at the side of the stage), and favoured the rehearsals over the concerts, where public recognition was a nuisance. By this time the maunderings of the 'new music' provoked 'septic ennui' in Huxley, who nevertheless became a sponsor of these low-budget 'Monday' events. Dorothy Crawford's history of the concerts[11] notes that following a 1953 talk 'urging the audience to support ticket sales... only Aldous Huxley came forward'. In 1957, after hearing both sets of Thomas Tallis's *Lamentations of Jeremiah*, Aldous rated them as 'two of the noblest pieces of music ever written'. Eventually he lectured there, on a memorial programme for Dylan Thomas, and at a subsequent concert talked learnedly on the music of Carlo Gesualdo, Prince of Venosa, as well as on his uxoricidal and scatological proclivities.[12] Huxley had learned that the poet Milton

---

10 Mrs Huxley's report on my sexuality was from her much younger sister, Mme Rose d'Haulleville Wessberg.

11 *Evenings On and Off the Roof: Pioneering Concerts in Los Angeles, 1939–1971*, Berkeley, 1995.

12 Huxley gave his manuscript of this lecture to me; it is partly typed, partly in ink in his hand.

was interested in Gesualdo's music and had purchased several volumes of it in Italy, which he shipped to England from Venice. On another occasion, in Royce Hall, University of California, Los Angeles (UCLA), celebrating Stravinsky's seventy-fifth birthday, Huxley delivered a moving tribute to his friend.

———◆———

When the Huxleys dined at the Stravinskys' on 27 July 1949, I was impressed above all by his gangly movements and his altitude (six feet four inches: these measurements had been notched, as if for Procrustean readjustment, on the inside of a closet door in the den where I slept),[13] and by his dulcet voice, articulating the most beautiful English in sentences that flowed with perfect concinnity. Though he had been living in Southern California for more than a decade, his language had not been corrupted:

> Language is perpetually changing; the cultivated English I listened to as a child is not the same as cultivated young men and women speak today. But within the general flux there are islands of linguistic conservation; and when I listen to myself objectively, from the outside, I perceive that I am one of those islands. In the Oxford of Jowett and Lewis Carroll, the Oxford in which my mother was brought up, how did people speak the Queen's English? I can answer with a considerable degree of confidence that they spoke exactly as I do. [My] recordings of 1950 are at the same time documents from the seventies and eighties of the last century.

Malheureusement, the conversation that evening was entirely in French.

An expert hypnotist, Huxley cured Stravinsky's insomnia during a period (summer 1950) of 'composer's block' that also ulcerated

---

13 The measurements of the 'beat' poet Charles Olson, also incised there, exactly matched Huxley's; Olson was introduced to the Stravinskys by their mutual friend the Italian refugee painter Corrado Cagli; the Black Sun Press in Paris had published a volume of five poems by Olson and five pictures by Cagli.

him as he began to worry about finishing the opera before death could interrupt. I drove Aldous back and forth to these sessions and soon became a kind of mascot to him. Perhaps I should explain that from March 1952 I lived in a rented room in one of the poolside guesthouses of the Baroness Catherine d'Erlanger,[14] whom Huxley had known since 1918, and refers to as the 'culmination of English social success'. Palladio's Villa Malcontenta on the Brenta River near Venice was one of her residences, and another was a Palazzo on the Grand Canal, in which she gave opulent balls. (Cecil Beaton's Diary for August 1926 describes his unsuccessful connivings to procure an invitation to one of them.) Though remote from the Baroness's milieu, Aldous faithfully attended her Hollywood parties, to which I drove him and endured with him. From 1952 to 1957 I was the Baroness's reader and exegete, an activity that was then, at five dollars an hour, my sole source of income.

During the same period I was at the Huxley home almost daily, sometimes alone and always with the Stravinskys when they visited, occasionally reading to Aldous, proofreading for him, and walking with him in the wilds of the Hollywood hills north of Doheny Drive. He had forsaken his daily constitutional on the deserted sidewalks of residential Beverly Hills after the police detained him on suspicion of vagrancy. Because of his near-blindness, he sat in the front row at movies, concerts and lectures, and I with him. When we saw the 1953 British documentary of the Coronation together, he was scarcely able to remain in his seat as he railed against the continuing connection in Britain between church and state. (He later declined a knighthood from Elizabeth II.) Afterward, he said that he had been at school with the Archbishop of Canterbury, 'the most gormless creature' he had ever known.

I frequently drove Aldous to appointments, lectures, movies and concerts. He also liked to sneak off with me to the Beverly Hills 'Delhaven' for unhealthy banana splits, and, during the lonely period

---

14   She was the immensely wealthy descendant of a banking family that moved from Frankfurt in the early nineteenth century to Paris and London, where she became a Lady-in-Waiting to Queen Victoria. Shortly before the outbreak of World War II, feeling threatened by the Third Reich, she fled to Hollywood.

after Maria's death, would sit with me late at night at the 'Hamburger Hamlet' on Sunset Boulevard, consuming the illicit nominal item and enjoying his anonymity. When I first knew him, his social calendar was surprisingly full, and he apparently enjoyed dining at Mike Romanoff's, where he was treated like Russian royalty. I remember an evening there with Florence Heifetz, ex-wife of the great violinist and wife-to-be of the film mogul King Vidor. She annoyed Aldous by bringing up the old question of similarities between his *Point Counterpoint* and Gide's *Counterfeiters*, a forbidden subject. (There were other off-bounds areas concerning which I had not been forewarned, but which were commonsensical, such as my stupid question as to whether he had met Rudolf Carnap, the philosopher recently arrived at UCLA. This upset him, as I should have foreseen, his own metaphysics being so far removed from the logical positivists.)

The range of his talk, when I was alone with him in the car, was wider than when we were *en famille* with the Stravinskys, and often I had no inkling of what it was about. He would digress fascinatingly on the Latin poetry of Notker Balbulus, Charlemagne's friend and biographer, recite passages from *The Canterbury Tales* in what he said was the correct pronunciation, then perhaps shift to the moral perfectionist Gracián, or dip into scientific literature, Faraday (a hero), Ohm (the *Galvanic Current Investigated Mathematically*), Erasmus, Darwin, and then move on to eighteenth-century pornography (the *Amours du chevalier de Faublas*). Peacock, who had influenced him so deeply thirty years before, was mentioned repeatedly, and Aldous persuaded me to read *Headlong Hall*, *Crotchet Castle* and some others, though I was irritated by the frequent interspersions of Greek, and did not care for the limitation of substance to smart dinner-table conversation conducted by one-dimensional deipnosophists, each representing a single point of view.

Sex was a staple, and he returned again and again to the subject of stirpiculture, expounding on the Oneida experiment of teenage boys trained by post-menopausal women,[15] which was soon extirpated.

---

15 See *Desire and Duty at Oneida*, edited by R.S. Fogarty, Bloomington (Indiana University Press), 2000.

He did not believe in monogamy, and, a finer point, he claimed an ability to tell which of the nudes in Pascin's *Dessins Erotiques* had been drawn before, and which after, intercourse with the artist. In the company of daringly *décolleté* young women at the Stravinskys' parties, he would draw a special magnifying glass from an inner pocket and, unnoticeably, because of his height, leer appreciatively at their charms. Nuria Schoenberg was subjected to this scrutiny.

On one occasion the Stravinskys and I spent some days with the Huxleys in Escondido. Aldous had wanted to see a new avian specimen from Sumatra in the San Diego Zoo. He would stop briefly before each cage, moated pit, and glass tank to expatiate on the inhabitants' IQs and patterns of sexual behaviour, especially the love-life of crustaceans: 'crayfish copulate through their third pair of legs'. He believed, incidentally, that zoo inmates were better off than their kin in natural environments. During a crystalline night walk on the beach, he talked enlighteningly about the classes of celestial galaxies and identified as many stars in the constellations as were visible. His pseudonym, after all, was Autolycus.

I seem to be the only surviving friend who knows that when Huxley was preparing for trips to Brazil and Portugal in 1958, he learned the language in a few weeks and read the whole of Luis Vez de Camoens's *Os Lusiades.* (He had read Richard Burton's English translation in his youth, but he wanted to train his ear to the sound.) At that time he persuaded me to read two of Eça De Queroz's novels, *The Relic* and *The Sin of Father Amara*, in the only language in which I can read.

———◆———

In December 1951 a tumour was discovered in Maria Huxley's right breast, and on 12 January 1952 she underwent surgery. After the operation I drove Aldous from the hospital to the Stravinskys' for a meal. He told us that Maria had undergone a mastectomy. The next day we learned that the tumour was malignant, had already metastasised to the lymph nodes, and that the prognosis was poor. He dined with the Stravinskys almost daily during the next two weeks, but mentioned Maria's condition only to say that she was undergoing radiation treatment.

On 23 February 1952, Aldous asked me to witness his and Maria's last will and testament. Frail and pallid, she nevertheless looked on, and he thanked me with the gift of his copy of Apollinaire's salacious verses, *Le Jou Jou des desmoiselles*, inscribing it 'For Bob, to improve his knowledge of French,' telling me that it had been given to him for the same purpose in his adolescence. In 1917 he had written to his sister-in-law Juliette: 'I write in French only when I want to be *un peu scabreux*; it certainly is the best language for indecency ever created.'

I do not know when Maria became a spiritualist, but her visits to mediums became more frequent after the operation and for the first time she began to talk openly about them. She eventually persuaded Vera Stravinsky to join her in séances with these strange characters. Aldous was interested in the chicanery as well, and to some extent believed in it.

By September 1952 the cancer had spread to Maria's spine and she was again in the hospital. Aldous pretended that it was only 'a particularly painful lumbago', but soon thereafter her forearm had bloated to double its normal size and she was wearing specially made sleeves and cuffs. In 1952, as well, the wholly unselfish Stravinskys relinquished their Escoffier chef, Marie Le Put, to the Huxleys. She became very close to Maria, and would care for Aldous long after her death. Marie Le Put was the widow of the chef of Le Deauville, the best of the Baroness's three Hollywood restaurants.

During this period the Huxleys made secret trips to Mexico, where Maria received injections of cells extracted from unborn calf foetuses, a fashionable Hollywood treatment at the time, outlawed in the United States. Huxley's doctor, Sigfrid Knauer, who made the arrangements and accompanied his patients, was a Baltic Russian married to a Russian Hindu who had taken the name Indra Devi. He acupunctured the Stravinskys, the Huxleys, and, from August 1959, myself. Indra instructed Stravinsky in yoga.

On 4 May 1953, Aldous swallowed a half-gram of mescaline, dissolved in a glass of water. The results were very different from what he had anticipated, not having considered that he was a poor visualiser. What he saw was anagogy, 'the miracle of existence', the 'Isness', or *Istigkeit* of Meister Eckhart, the haecceties and quiddities.

His mind was 'perceiving the world in terms of other than spatial categories... with being and meaning'. Nicholas Murray wrote, perceptively:[16]

> All this was happening because the massively functioning Huxley brain was being outwitted and bypassed. The cerebral reducing valve (mescaline diminishes the supply of blood sugar to the brain) was preventing access to 'Mind at large'.

The reader wonders whether this drug-taking, which continued to the end of his life, might be thought of simply as escapism from the realisation of Maria's illness, or as merely another step in the adventure of *Aun aprendo* ('I am still learning').[17] Clearly she was not much in his thoughts during the hallucinogenic episodes. In describing his first experience of *Les Paradis artificiels* to the Stravinskys and me, Aldous talked exclusively about the heightened intensities of colours, and what sounded like mirages and emanations. Soon after, he asked Stravinsky to take the drug, wanting the reactions of a mind and temperament so different from his own, but the composer declined, saying he did not wish to disturb his senses.

The next month Maria was strong enough to drive her husband to National Parks, starting at Yellowstone and the Tetons, then to the Pacific Northwest. We received postcards from them, one of which, surely intended as a joke but disturbingly irrational, proposed that we open a restaurant together. On returning to Hollywood, Aldous wrote *The Doors of Perception*, which would mark the beginning of the steep decline in a reputation that had been foundering since the publication of *Ape and Essence*, and would reach its nadir in his last novel, *Island*, the intended Utopian counterpart to *Brave New World*.

---

16   *Aldous Huxley: An English Intellectual*, Boston (Little Brown /Time Warner Books), 2002.
17   In the first paragraph of his book, Murray says that this Huxley motto was the 'legend hung around the neck of a ragged scarecrow of a man in a painting of Goya'. In actuality the 'painting' is the well-known black chalk drawing, thought to be a self-portrait of the artist, numbered 54 by him in his first Bordeaux album, and probably executed in 1826. The title, in Goya's hand, is '*Aun aprendo*', and the 'legend' is not 'hung around' any neck. Moreover, the aged Goya in the portrait may be hoary but in no way resembles a 'ragged scarecrow'.

In April 1954, Aldous and Maria went to St Paul de Vence, ostensibly to recuperate, though a short drive to Palm Springs would have been incomparably less strenuous. They were soon en route again, this time to Ismailia, where Aldous could study the methods of a Dr Roger Godel[18] in, of all inanities, 'teasing psychosomatic symptoms from his patients'. After a week or so in Egypt, the Huxleys proceeded to Beirut; the real purpose of this exhausting trip was for a 'medical' appointment with a certain Tahra Bey, a fakir whom they had known in Bandol in 1930, when D.H. Lawrence was dying there.[19] In Aldous's résumé, Bey was

> a Lebanese M.D. who learned all the tricks of the dervishes and has made a living all these years by giving demonstrations of being buried alive, running skewers through his flesh, stopping and starting bleeding... doing telepathy, etc.

A year before, Tahra Bey had inveigled the Huxleys into promoting two public demonstration appearances for him in Los Angeles. He also convinced Aldous that Maria could be healed by his methods. After three evenings with Tahra Bey in the Huxley home, 22 and 24 July and 6 August 1953, the Stravinskys and I concluded that this confidence trickster and stunt artist was also a scrounger. We nevertheless attended the first of his performances in the staid Wilshire Ebell Theater, which was filled with Huxley camp-followers, and which turned out to be lewd exhibitionism. Bey failed to turn up in Lebanon, and was totally unknown to the sources he had provided. Only then did Aldous realise that he had been duped by a self-proclaimed miracle worker. Gullibility was Huxley's abiding weakness.

The Huxleys journeyed on to Jerusalem, Cyprus and Rome, where

---

18 Director of a hospital for the Suez Canal Company.
19 The Huxleys, who were with Lawrence during the last two weeks of his life, believed in a supernal relationship between the writer and birds and animals. Both Maria and Aldous testified that the farm animals were strangely subdued. Dogs, horses and cows stood outside the window of his room in silence and would not eat.

they met with Aldous's sister-in-law, Juliette, who questioned him about Maria's health:

> 'Well, she has little nodules coming out.'
> 'That's frightening.'
> 'No, no. It's quite all right. It's normal.'
> 'How serious is it?'
> 'Oh, no. It's not serious at all.'

Realising that someone of Aldous's medical sophistication could not be unaware of Maria's actual condition, Juliette testified that 'Of course he knew. But he pushed it away... He was protecting himself from a truth that was unbearable.' Six years later Aldous would deal with his own cancer in the same way, discussing it with his surgeon but with no one else.

In Rome, Maria met Laura Archera, Aldous's future wife, supposedly for the first time. Sybille Bedford, also present, wrote that 'Maria took Laura to one side and spoke to her out of earshot', [deducing that] 'Laura was being told that Maria is dying'. But a confidence of this nature implies that Maria had known Laura for some time, probably since 1948, during Laura's and Aldous's first meeting. Bedford affirmed that his marriage to Laura was 'engineered by Maria'. All three women, Maria, Bedford and Laura, were lesbians.

Maria died on 12 February 1955. Aldous privately performed his 'rites of passage' for her (a description of them – from the great Bardo Thodol, the Mahayana office for the dying – is given in *Island*), but he also followed her wish for a Catholic funeral service. Gerald Heard's wise and humane *The Poignant Prophet* says that Huxley managed to hold back his tears through the whole ordeal, but this is not literally true. His eyes were red and tearful. He leaned for support on the arm of Maria's dry-eyed mother, who led the recessional with him.

The New York postmark on a communication from Aldous addressed to me shows that by late June of that year his spirits had revived:

Dear Bob,

Thank you for your letter and the good news about the whole family. I expect to return to L.A. in September but shall (I hope) have to come back here in November for rehearsals (if there is a production in December or Jan., which I hope, but don't yet know).

I could take a modest part in your programme some time in October – say the second half. There will be time to discuss details in September.

There is a wonderful loan exhibition at the Museum of Modern Art – pictures in private collections from Cézanne to Picasso. Such marvels! And on the floor above is a show called 'The New Decade' – five or six acres of non-representational ennui, produced since the end of the War. How very cruel to juxtapose the two shows! And why on earth should these last years have been so fearfully barren? Unanswerable question.

My love to you all,

Yours, Aldous

The Stravinskys and I were not privy to Aldous's life with Laura, and were as surprised and jolted as everyone else by the news of their marriage, in March 1956, at a drive-in wedding chapel in Yuma, Arizona. The Stravinskys, whatever they felt, invited the newlyweds to a dinner with Maria's loyalist friends Gerald Heard and Christopher Isherwood, who remained stiff, remote and barely polite.

In 1961 a hillside fire destroyed the Huxley house and most of its contents. Aldous did not seem badly shaken, and his wit was not shaken at all: his first words to us after the conflagration were, 'Well, it *is* rather inconvenient'. He wrote to his old friend Robert Hutchins, president of the University of Chicago: 'It is odd to be starting from scratch at my age – with literally nothing in the way of possessions… I am evidently intended to learn, a little in advance of the final denudation, that you can't take it with you.'

In 1962 Aldous was found to be afflicted with a carcinoma of the tongue. The Stravinskys and I did not know this, although we saw him several times in the spring of 1963. Then on the day before our departure for Rome in November, Gerald told us that Aldous would not be alive when we returned. We heard the news of his death, competing with reports of President Kennedy's assassination on the same day, in Naples, during a stop of our Messina to Rome train. Stravinsky, composing his orchestra Variations at the time, dedicated the piece to the memory of his friend.

Back in Los Angeles, Gerald told us that on his last visit to the Huxleys, to give his own new book to Aldous, he quoted one of George III's sons' remarks to Gibbon on receiving the last volume of *The Decline and Fall*: 'What! Another big, fat book!' Aldous, barely able to whisper, corrected the quotation: 'Another *damned* thick *square* book.'

———◆———

Of Huxley's posterity, *Brave New World* (1932) was the first choice in a 2000 poll of literary people for the most important book of its century. (It was quickly replaced by *Ulysses*.) Though radically out-of-date, this portrait of a dystopia has nevertheless held up longer than any of his other novels, probably because so many of its predictions – soma, alpha-beta types, test-tube babies – have come to pass. But Aldous never thought of himself as a novelist. He protested a blurb for a proposed dustcover of one of them with: 'I am [not] a "great novelist" – I am a sort of an essayist sufficiently ingenious to get away with writing a very limited kind of fiction'.

As claimed, *Texts and Pretexts*, published immediately after *Brave New World*, is 'one of the most delightful anthologies of verse ever compiled', and one of the broadest in scope, including poems in nine languages. It is also an avowal of the author's profound belief in poetry: 'Literary language is richer, more expressive, and ultimately more penetrating than the algorithmic codes of science.' He perceives that 'nature' is supernatural, that epistemologies are 'language-dependent', and that 'all of our experiences have a kind of linguistic tinge to them', the view ultimately adopted by Wittgenstein. Huxley's prose commentaries are always worthy of his choices of poetry, *viz.* his gloss on Donne's 'Whoever loves, if he do not propose / the right true end of love':

All of Shakespeare's heroes and heroines propose the right

> true end... Reading through the plays, I realized to my dismay
> that platonic love is not a subject with which Shakespeare ever
> deals. Spenser is our only considerable Platonist. The other
> poets of importance agree at bottom with John Donne.

He concludes with 'One admits the wisdom of Dante, who platonically loved a memory while living with a perfectly solid and actual wife', and he rated him 'second only to Milton in unpleasantness'. At the end of the anthology Huxley proposes an extraordinary answer to the religious question: 'If we must play the theological game, let us not forget that it is a game. Religion, it seems to me, can survive only as a consciously accepted system of make-believe.'

This reminds us of Docetism, the heresy according to which the Lord was born, lived and died only symbolically, so that his coming and going should edify men's souls.

It seems incredible that a decade after *Brave New World* the author had become a Mahayana Buddhist leading a cenobitic life in a California desert, and exchanging his precise, lucid language for the involuted vocabulary of mysticism: *viz.* (from the Sanskrit) 'What is the That to which the Thou can discover itself to be akin?', which is by way of instructing the reader how 'intuitive knowledge of Thusness may be achieved'. Yet even after penetrating 'the mists of science and mysticism', Aldous continued to believe that 'life is an unfathomable mystery'. He seems not to have commented on his grandfather's coinage of the word 'agnostic', which comes from the Greek original of St Paul's 'To the unknown God', or on the lines his grandfather's widow inscribed on Thomas Henry's tombstone:

> Be not afraid, ye waiting hearts that weep,
> For still he giveth his beloved sleep.
> And if an endless sleep He wills, so be it.

What had happened to Aldous in the years between his native scepticism and his conversion to Buddhism? His late 1920s essay on Pascal shows that the transition had begun earlier than is generally assumed. But did it have anything to do with the 'inexplicable exaltation' of Hitler that he had denounced in 1932? Aldous's alliance in the early 1930s with England's growing Pacifist movement is often held against him, though when war became inevitable, he was among the first to warn that 'mass persecution' would follow. His essay *One and Many* – mono- and polytheism – was denounced by monotheists for its endorsement of Renan's 'new religion of Life', which 'will have many Gods' since 'life is diverse'. Huxley's 1926 book on India was attacked for its 'colonialism', since he saw

> no good in Indian independence; the people, though victims of oppression, are incapable of self-government: There are certain things about which it is not possible, it is not right, to take the reasonable, the utilitarian view.

Nor was his reputation enhanced by his proselytising for the sociology of Vilfredo Pareto, the Italian philosopher being generally regarded as a precursor of fascism. But with the opening of the Mondadori archives in 2002, the report of a publisher's reader revealed that Huxley's *Ends and Means* (1937) had been rejected for Italian translation 'primarily because of its... political and moral criticism of today's world conducted from the perspective of democratic principles and the humanitarian ideologies that make up most of the English mentality'.

Though not generally regarded as a political activist, Huxley supported progressive causes throughout his years in America, marching on a picket line in a film studio labour dispute, joining lobbies for human rights and ecological causes, and taking time to testify before the State Legislature in Sacramento. On 23 May 1951, the House Committee on Un-American Activities was told that Huxley was 'one of a number of writers involved in an organization called "Friends of Intellectual Freedom"', whose purpose was 'to help former Communist writers to rehabilitate themselves'. Two years later the FBI revealed that he had been monitored until found to be 'far removed from any Communist Party sympathies'. He never became a US citizen, refusing to take the oath to bear arms. The near-blind seer was then in his late fifties.

Perhaps the early social satire novels and, of the later ones, *Time Must Have a Stop* and *After Many a Summer Dies the Swan*, will continue to be read. But the essays, elegant and erudite, will be relished longer than any of the fiction. *Vulgarity in Literature* is the finest of these pieces, I think, and the early ones on Chaucer and on the limpid Latin of Magister Gratias's *Epistolae obscurorum virorum* are not far behind. After teaching Latin for eight years, Huxley believed that

> The only point of learning the language is to gain an intelligent understanding of the vocabulary of our own and other languages today. The Latin vocabulary is still alive; Latin syntax is as dead as Tully. Yet children are made to waste their energies in learning the rules of this devilish syntax, when they might with comparative ease and pleasure learn all the Latin they need to know – which is simply the vocabulary – in the Obscure Men of the Middle Ages. It was the Humanists [who] bequeathed to us the intolerable superstition of 'pure Latinity'.[20]

Huxley used to do an amusing send-up of Baudelaire's Latin translations, calling the poet the 'last and most eloquent of the Fathers of the Church', who 'made the Medieval masters sound like Racine'.

The French histories, *Grey Eminence*, *The Devils of Loudun* and the long essay on Maine de Biran have become primary sourcebooks on their subjects. Yet *Letters of Aldous Huxley* is his greatest book, for the wisdom and humanist spirit on every page, and for the nonpareil writing.

Isaiah Berlin was with the Huxleys in India in 1961, and wrote to us from there. He should have the last word:

> He was a humanist in the most literal and honorable sense...
> he was interested in, and cared about, human beings as objects

---

20   Compare T.S. Eliot: 'When I was a schoolboy, it was my lot to be introduced to the *Iliad* and the *Aeneid* in the same year. I had, up to that point, found the Greek language a much more exciting study than Latin. I still think it a much greater language: a language which has never been surpassed as a vehicle for the fullest range and the finest shades of thought and feeling.'

in nature in the sense in which the *philosophes...* had done. His hopes for men rested on the advance of self-knowledge... He bore the frequent accusations of betraying his original rationalism in favor of a confused mysticism, of a sad collapse into irrationalism as a means of escape from his own private miseries... He inspired in one a lasting affection and a degree of respect bordering on veneration... the recollection that will remain in my mind for the rest of my life is that of a wholly civilized, good and scrupulous man, and one of the greatest imaginable distinction.

1879. Pauline Schoenberg with her children, Arnold and his sister Ottilie.

1883. Schoenberg, aged nine, showing a remarkable maturity.

Top: c. 1900. 'Visit Portrait' of Schoenberg.
Bottom: 1908. Portrait of Schoenberg in his Mödling apartment, by Richard Gerstl.

Top: 1911. Schoenberg in his studio with his paintings on the wall. The picture is inscribed: 'Dear Mr. Kandinsky, I am discharging in musical tones an obligation I have long wished to fulfil. 12 December 1911.' It includes the first seven notes from the vocal part of the last movement of the Quartet, Op. 10.

Bottom: 1911. Portrait of Schoenberg, looking directly into the camera, with the caption 'after an amateur *aufnahme*'.

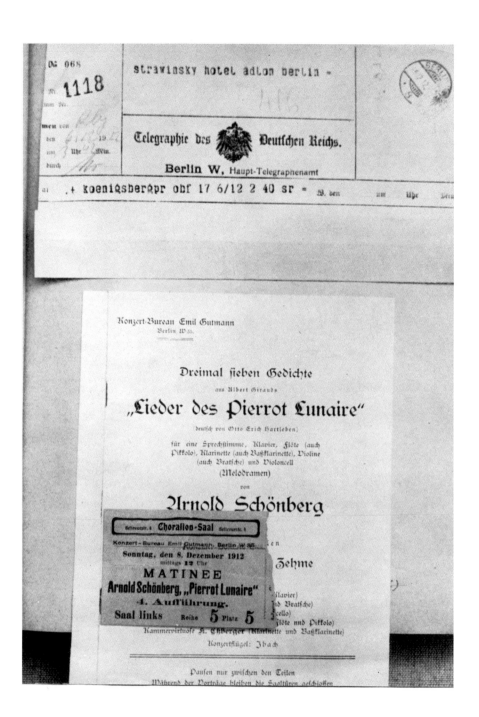

November 1912. A telegram from Diaghilev to Stravinsky in the Adlon Hotel in Berlin apropos a forthcoming performance of Schoenberg's *Pierrot lunaire*, together with Stravinsky's ticket stubs and programme for the concert, 8 December 1912.

1917. Portrait of Schoenberg by Egon Schiele. Black crayon and tempera on paper. The whereabouts of this drawing, a sketch for the portrait, in oils, is unknown. Unlike the painting, it includes the left arm and torso and is titled 'Arnold Schönberg' by the artist.

Top left: 1921. Schoenberg in Prague.
Top right: December 1927. Paris. Schoenberg by Man Ray.
Bottom: Summer 1927. Kandinsky and Schoenberg with their wives, Nina (left) and Gertrud (right), at Pörtschach on the Wörthersee.

October 1933. Schoenberg, his wife, and their dog Witz arriving in New York from France.

April 1, 1934. Schoenberg and Albert Einstein at Carnegie Hall after a concert, at which Schoenberg conducted his *Verklärte Nacht* and Einstein spoke, to raise money for Jewish refugees.

Top: 1935. Brentwood, California. Portrait of Schoenberg by Edward Weston.
Bottom: 1936. Brentwood, California. George Gershwin painting a portrait of Schoenberg.

DIE GLÜCKLICHE HAND

DRAMA MIT MUSIK

VON

ARNOLD SCHÖNBERG

OP. 18.

UNIVERSAL-EDITION A.G.
WIEN   LEIPZIG.

COPYRIGHT 1916 BY UNIVERSAL-EDITION

U. E. Nr 5670.

Before its performance in Town Hall on Oct. 21, Erika von Wagner rehearses the Sprechstimme of Arnold Schönberg's Pierrot Lunaire with Robert Craft conducting members of the Chamber Art Society. Drawing by B. F. Dolbin

Top left: 1939. Schoenberg on the lawn of his home in Brentwood Park, with his dog Roddie.
Top right: Schoenberg's inscription on the author's copy of *Die glückliche Hand*. The date, 6 July 1951, is one week before the composer's death.
Bottom: 21 October 1950. Cartoon by F. Dolbin (a pupil of Schoenberg in 1908–09) of the author conducting *Pierrot lunaire* in Town Hall, New York. Eduard Steuermann is the pianist, Isadore Cohen the violinist, Seymour Barab the cellist, and Erika Wagner-Stiedry the *Sprechstimme*.

Top: 1912. Vienna. Anton Webern.
Bottom: Spring 1910. St Petersburg, the 'English Club'. Vaslav Nijinsky is seated to the left of the samovar; Igor Stravinsky, centre rear, stands to the right of it.

April 1917, Rome. Drawing of Stravinsky by Picasso.

Spring 1912, Monte Carlo. Sketches of the unpitched rhythm for Stravinsky's 'Sacrificial Dance' (*The Rite of Spring*).

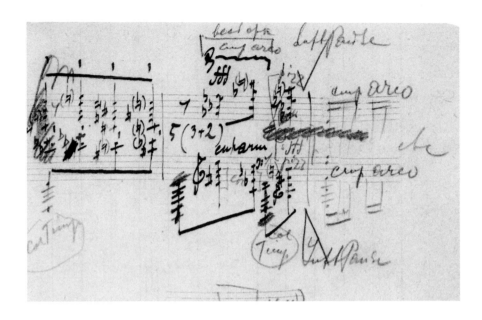

Top: 1912. Ink sketch of the same music as on opposite page, near the beginning of the 'Sacrificial Dance', with harmony and indications for instrumentalists and articulation. The pencil sketches are for later episodes in the piece.
Bottom left: May 1913. Paris. Portrait of Stravinsky by Saul Bransberg.
Bottom right: May 1913. Paris. Portrait of Stravinsky by Gerschel.

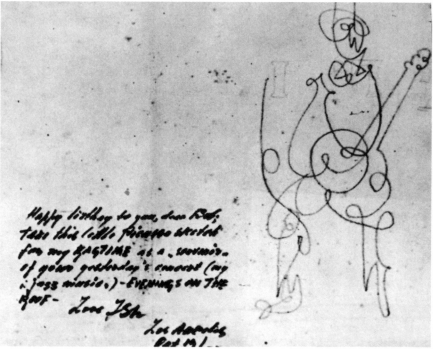

Top: 1920. Stravinsky by Picasso, *'Paris, 31 Décembre 1920'*.
Bottom: Picasso's single-line priapic drawing of a man, intended for the original cover of *Ragtime*, was rejected by the publisher. Stravinsky inscribed it to the author on his thirtieth birthday.

IGOR and VERA
STRAVINSKY

1923. Igor Stravinsky and Vera Sudeykina seated on a park bench in Fontainebleau.

Top: September 1925. Stravinsky on a train from Nice to Venice, where he would play his Piano Sonata. Note the glove on his left hand to protect an abscessed finger. Photo by Vera Sudeykina.
Bottom: 22 January 1930. With Otto Klemperer, who conducted two concerts in Berlin featuring Stravinsky as piano soloist in his Capriccio (22 and 30 January). The first programme included Mozart's G minor Symphony and the second Brahms's First Symphony and the Chaconne from Gluck's *Orpheus*.

9 December 1931. Stravinsky in Frankfurt.

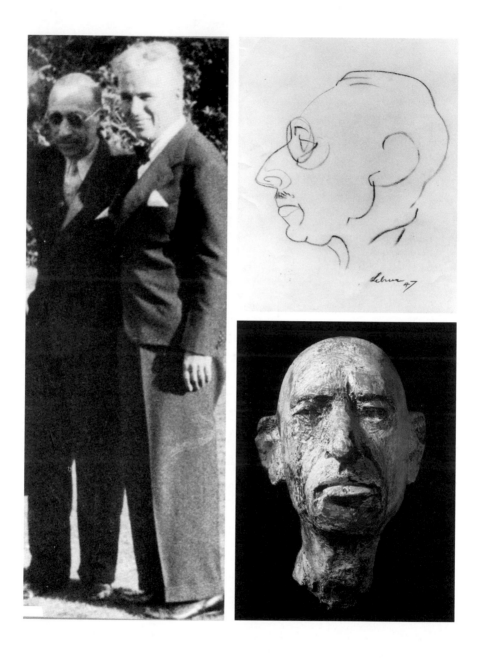

Left: March 1937. Hollywood. Stravinsky and Charlie Chaplin. Photo by King Vidor.
Top right: 1947. Hollywood. Charcoal drawing by the painter Rico Lebrun (1900–1964).
Bottom right: 1950. Head in bronze by Marino Marini, New York, May 1950. Now in the State Gallery, Munich.

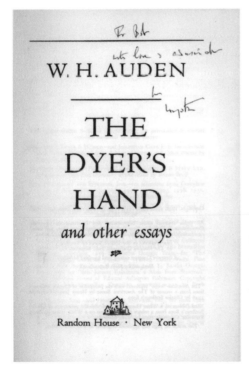

Top left: September 1951. Stravinsky with W.H. Auden at La Scala, Milan, during a rehearsal of *The Rake's Progress.*
Top right: March 1952. North Wetherly Drive, Hollywood. Photo by Sanford Roth.
Bottom left: 1958. Title page of *The Dyer's Hand*, inscribed by W.H. Auden to the author: 'For Bob with love and admiration from Wystan'.
Bottom right: March 1953. New York. Listening to playbacks during a recording session of *The Rake's Progress.* Photo by Don Hunstein.

Top: October 1959. Naples. Hans Werner Henze greeting Stravinsky on his arrival at a party in the German composer's apartment.
Bottom: September 1961. Backstage at the Stockholm Royal Opera during the interval in *The Rake's Progress*.

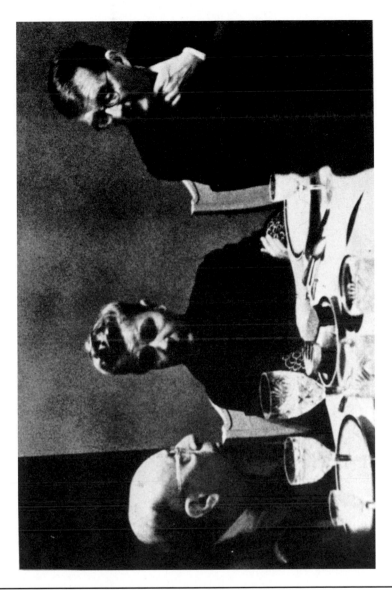

1 October 1962. Moscow, the Metropole. Encounter with Dmitri Shostakovich at a dinner hosted by Madame Furtseva, the Minister of Culture, seated between the composers. Shostakovich 'is thinner, taller, younger, more boyish-looking than expected. He is also the shyest, most nervous human being I have ever met, chain-smoking, chewing not merely his nails but also his fingers, twitching his pouty mouth and chin, wiggling his nose in the constant adjustment of his spectacles, looking querulous one moment and ready to cry the next. He stutters, too, and his hands tremble – when he shakes hands, his whole frame wobbles, which reminds me of Auden. When he stands to express his welcome to Stravinsky, his knees knock audibly and his colleagues, Khachaturian and Khrennikov, regard him with trepidation. He has a habit of staring, and of rapidly and guiltily turning away when caught. All evening long he peeks illicitly at I.S. around Madame Furtseva's nicely rounded corners. But the thoughts behind those frightened, intelligent eyes are never betrayed – or at least I cannot read them.' (From the author's *Stravinsky: Chronicle of a Friendship*)

Stravinsky with Virgil Thomson at an eightieth birthday party for I.S., New York, June 1962.

1954, Hollywood. Aldous Huxley.

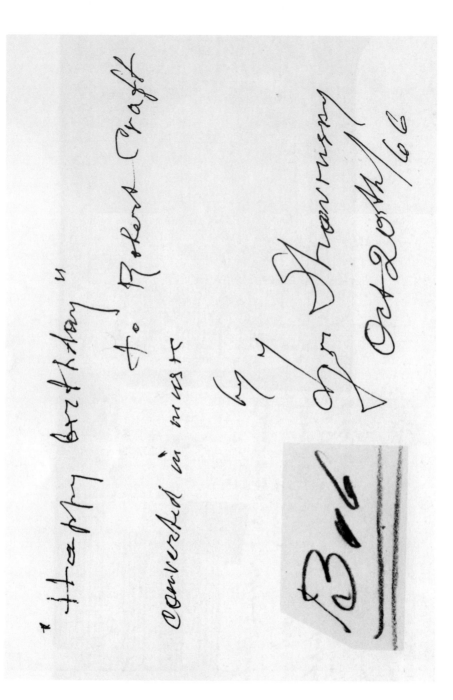

Above and right: October 1966. Hollywood. Stravinsky's birthday greetings to the author set to the principal melody of the Introduction to *The Rite of Spring*.

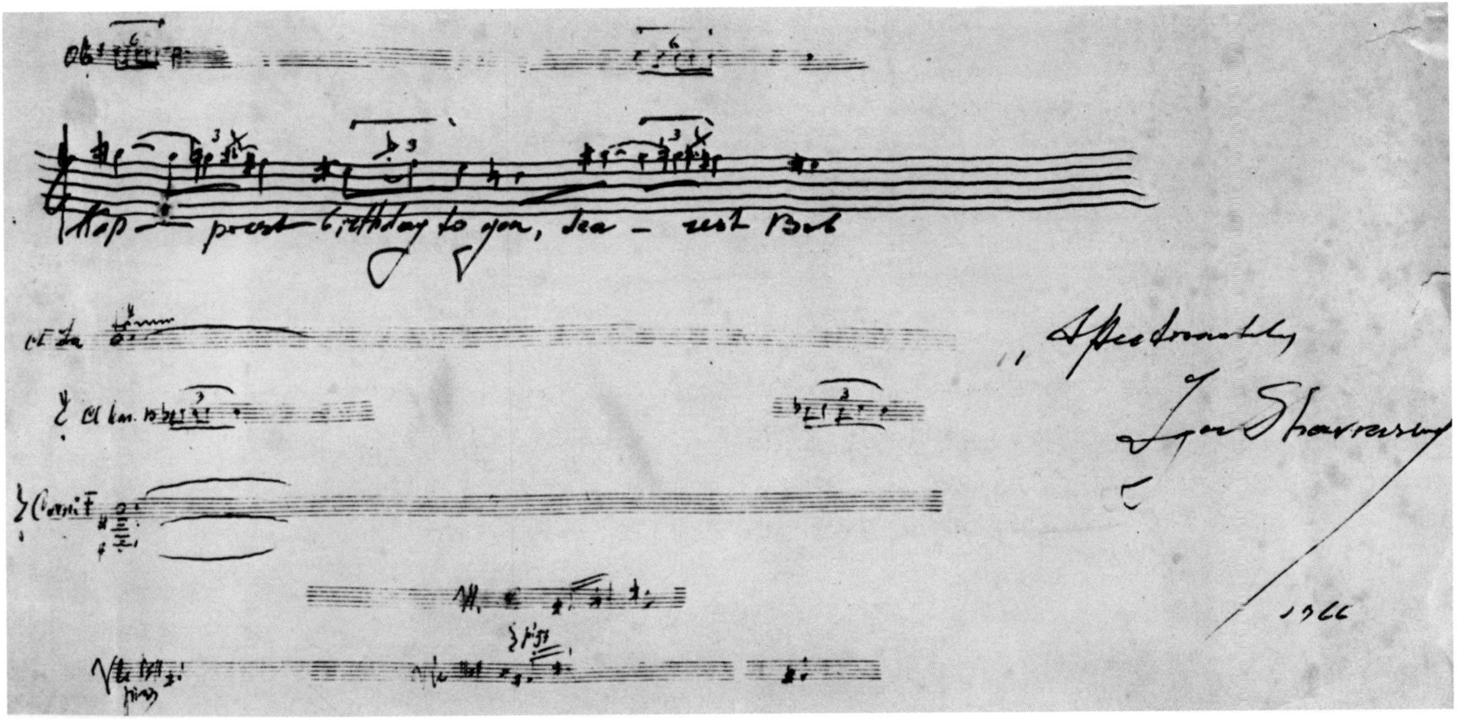
Hap – piest birthday to you, dea – rest Bob
Affectionately
Igor Stravinsky
1966

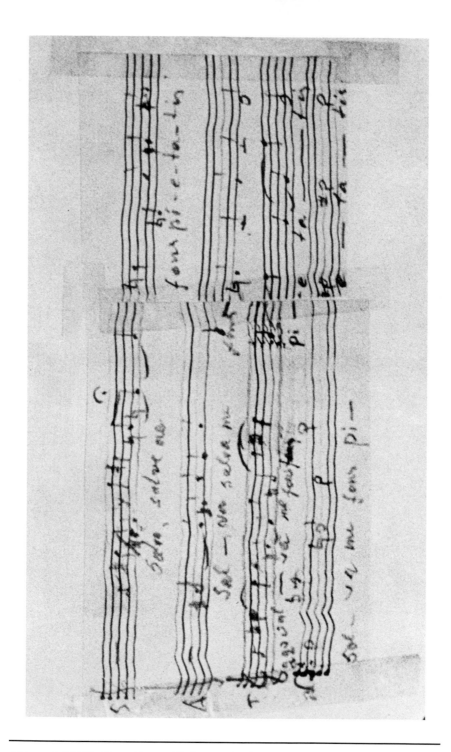

Above and right: The *Times* obituary of Evelyn Waugh published a photo of him that Stravinsky placed in his sketchbook for the *Requiem Canticles*.

Obituary

MR. EVELYN WAUGH

ARTIST IN SATIRIC PROSE

Mr. Evelyn Waugh, the novelist, died at his home at Combe Florey yesterday. He was 62.

Waugh was essentially an artist in prose. In an age where care for the exact word, for the form of a sentence and for good grammar are all too rare, Waugh set himself from the first a high standard of writing. Whether he was engaged on his earlier works of unreal and high spirited satire, on one of his more serious books of later life, of a defence of religion or even some casual *piece d'occasion* of a sharp letter to the press one could always be certain that his conscience would require him to find for it the exact phrase. Though not himself a deep classical scholar he had a great reverence for the disciplinary virtues of the Latin language—of that which " had fought and conquered the centuries "—and felt that those who had " little Latin and less Greek " were likely to fail in piety towards the English language. He thought such disrespect for language almost the supreme sign of a failing culture. It was this disrespect which he found in the younger writers and which was the main cause of his distaste for them. He did not conceal his dislike of the movement within the Catholic Church for the substi-

tution of a vernacular for the Latin liturgy, thinking that with the loss of Latin the Mass would be robbed of much of the sense of awe which it had held throughout the ages.

He himself professed to find this carefulness for the exact phrase, more clearly than in any other modern writer, in Monsignor Knox, whose biography he wrote and for whom his admiration was high, but Monsignor Knox expressed himself most naturally in parody or in translation. Waugh expressed himself most naturally in satire. He imposed upon himself a most strict economy of language. None of his books are long. He believed in saying what he had to say and then closing down. The same is true of his sentences. No long speeches are put into the mouths of his characters. They say what they have to say in a sentence or two. He had no ear for music and he imposed on himself the same discipline which he imposed on his characters in his own descriptive passages. He had no belief in irrelevant padding to create an atmosphere. He never told the reader anything that was not strictly necessary for the understanding of his story. There were no literary allusions or cultural references. His own opinions were only discoverable through his mockery of the follies of his characters.

IN HIS BLOOD

The second son of Arthur Waugh, sometime chairman of the publishing firm of Chapman and Hall, and younger brother of Alec Waugh, the novelist, Evelyn Arthur St. John Waugh was born on October 28, 1903, and educated at Lancing and Hertford College, Oxford. Literature was in his blood and from the time of his coming down from Oxford he gave himself to writing. His first book, a study of Rossetti, appeared in 1928, and this was followed shortly after in the same year by his first novel, *Decline and Fall*. It is as a novelist that he is mainly remembered.

In his earliest books—*Decline and Fall* and *Vile Bodies*—he appeared before the public as the chronicler and satirist of the Bright Young People of society's life, holding up to scorn with exquisite wit the futility of their lives. His second period—the period of *Black Mischief*, *A Handful of Dust* and *Scoop*—was a period of transition. Of the characters in those books some were what might be called two-dimensional characters, figures of farce, too unreal

Top: Christopher Isherwood.
Bottom: 3 December 1958. Stravinsky with the T.S. Eliots in London.

Top: March 2001. The author in Banteay Shrei, Cambodia.
Bottom: The Stravinskys' graves, San Michele Cemetery, Venice.

Top: Archidiskodon, L'Aquila.
Bottom: Columbus monument, Seville Cathedral.

Chapter 5

Evelyn Waugh

A Memoir

At the beginning of September 2004, a category-five hurricane was approaching the east coast of Florida. After days of rampageous seas, gusting winds and obnubilating skies, police came to our door with a mandatory evacuation order. They said the tempest had changed course, heading directly for our Gulf Stream shore. Landfall was expected in two hours, by which time the drawbridges connecting our key to the mainland would be raised. The threat of electrical outages required the immediate closing of storm shutters, and since towering ocean surges and flooding were anticipated, the police advised us to take our movable valuables upstairs. In our case this meant armfuls of books, but in my haste, the first load toppled midway up, spilling some papers and a packet of letters from a small volume. Retrieving these and tucking them into an overnight bag, we set out for Sarasota, where Alva had managed to reserve a hotel room. Since most of the Everglade vegetation is higher than its traversing Tamiami Trail, the only vistas are from the Miccosukee Indian villages. Vultures and hawks hovered overhead, and warnings of panther crossings appeared intermittently on the roadside, though they only emerged at night. At the west-coast highway intersection dense refugee traffic brought us to a near standstill and we reached the bearded-oak boulevard to our hotel only in late evening.

Delving into my bag that night, I discovered that the book bulging with papers was a copy of Evelyn Waugh's 1926 *P.R.B.: Essay on the Pre-Raphaelite Brotherhood 1847-1854*, inscribed to me in the author's gracefully drawn letters, and dated by him 'April 1949'. The brown-paper packet, postmarked 'Stinchcombe, Gloucestershire', is also addressed to me in his hand: 'Robert Craft, Esq., 41 Johnston Avenue, Kingston, New York, U.S.A.' The other communications are an enveloped letter on notepaper of 'The Plaza, Fifth Avenue at 59th Street', postmarked 'New York, Jan. 28, 1949'. The text, in Waugh's hand, says: 'Mr. and Mrs. Evelyn Waugh have great pleasure in accepting Mr. and Mrs. Stravinsky's kind invitation to dinner at the Ambassador Hotel on Friday, February 4'. The other communications are on postcards with the printed heading: 'From Mr. Evelyn Waugh, Piers Court, Nr. Dursley, Glos. Dursley 215'. The first of these says:

> Very many thanks for your letter of Nov. 12, just received. I was in the U.S.A. when it was written and it lay here awaiting my return. I should have been most prone to meet Mr. Stravinsky. I shall be back in New York (Plaza Hotel) for a week from January 28. But, alas, I shall not be there on February 25. I must confess that all music is positively painful to me. But please let us meet and let me not miss the great honour of meeting Mr. Stravinsky.
> E. W.

When I first met the Stravinskys, in Washington, DC, in March 1948, their travel reading was Charles Morgan's *The Fountain* and Simenon. On parting, three days later, I urged them to try *Brideshead Revisited* and presented them with a copy. Not only did they become admirers of Waugh's mellifluous prose, but it changed their lives. After eight years in America, English began to supplant French.

On a visit to Stravinsky's Hollywood home a few months later, I found him fascinated with *The Loved One* to the extent that he asked me to take him to see Forest Lawn and the Pet Cemetery. I disliked the book myself, and feared that its stale vernacularisms - ain't, heck, gotta, kinda, screwy - might corrupt his increasing knowledge of English. Curious to meet the author, he asked me to send an invitation to him for the New York concert premiere of his Mass. The composer did not know that Waugh hated music, and may have been misled by a description in the book of Forest Lawn obsequies accompanied by 'strains of Handel'. The writer was frequently in the USA at the time, lecturing, meeting movie moguls and Catholic dignitaries, including, the spokesman, paradoxically speaking, for the Trappist monks of Gethsemani, Kentucky, Father Thomas Merton, author of *The Seven Storey Mountain*, which Waugh was editing (mostly deleting) when we met him.

On the basis of an evening or two with Waugh in Hollywood, Aldous Huxley had warned us that Mr W. could be 'prickly, pompous, and downright unpleasant', and indeed the collaboration with Merton soon ended acrimoniously. But the composer, who could hold his own in any company, remained undaunted and persisted with the invitation. Since the mention of 'Feb. 25' in his reply refers to the date of the Mass performance, his word 'alas' at being unable to attend was not truthful. In any case, the dinner took place, and I tried to describe it in my diary:

> **February 4, 1949.** New York. The Waughs arrive at the Stravinsky suite in the Ambassador Hotel[1] in full evening apparel, 'for a late party at the Astors,' they say, apologetically. The elegance of her gown and the crispness of his tuxedo accentuate our awareness of the crumples in our own everyday togs, which bothers me but not the Stravs. Mrs. W. is fair and lovely, Mr. W. ruddy, pudgy, smooth-skinned, and surprisingly short, barely an inch taller than I.S. He enters the room commenting favorably on its temperature, and complaining that he leaves his windows at the Plaza wide open in order not to suffocate, a statement that may help to account for both his icy exterior and his inner, intellectual heat. I.S. responds in French, attempting to excuse the change in language with a compliment on the French dialogue in Mr. W.'s *Scott-King's Modern Europe.* At this point he interrupts, disclaiming conversational command of the tongue,

1   Park Avenue at Fiftieth Street, long since demolished.

whereupon Mrs. W. contradicts him: 'That's silly, darling, your French is very good.' This provokes so harsh a reprimand from her spouse that it shocks and embarrasses us.[2]

We had been expecting to ask Mr. W. about the credentials of H.H. Prince Vsevolode, a pretender to the Russian throne and the dedicatee of Waugh's *Wine in War and Peace.* The soi-disant Prince had negotiated an agreement whereby the vintners, Saccone and Speed, would reimburse the writer with 12 bottles of champagne for each 1000 words in the book, a tax-dodge for Waugh. But we never come near the subject, and as conversation flags, I switch to Mr. W.'s lecture in Town Hall last week on Graham Greene's *The Heart of the Matter,* the coolest performance of the sort I have ever witnessed. He spoke without notes, in incisive, impeccable prose, and glared challengingly at the audience throughout, with such detachment that he was able to convey several ruthlessly observed details in his descriptions of three people who walked out.

Mr. W. prefers to converse about U.S. burial customs and the mortician business, which had recently imposed a ban on burying him should he, as the industry must fervently hope, expire on American soil, an eventuality he had already obviated by arranging to be buried at sea. Keenly interested in my own (non-existent) interment plans, he asks whether my *beaux restes* are destined for a family vault. While explaining that my origins are too humble for that, I become aware that this down-to-earth talk has made I.S. uneasy, and change the subject.

A new crisis emerges when Waugh refuses the S.s' vodka and caviar, not because of his rudeness – 'I never drink spirits before wine' – but because the S.s exchange two *sotto voce* observations in Russian, a pardonable recourse for them in many instances, but not now, since Mrs. S.'s pretense of discussing the cigarettes she makes a show of rummaging for in her handbag does not delude Waugh, who understands that the subject is himself.

---

2   When introduced to Paul Claudel, Waugh famously feigned total ignorance of French and demanded an interpreter.

Still another obstacle arises when our distinguished guest asks I.S. about his American citizenship, adding that he deplores everything American, beginning with the Revolution. Here I.S., taking the offensive, praises the Constitution, which he had learned by heart before taking the oath to become an American citizen. He then proposes that we go to dinner, thus bringing the abstemious and uncomfortable half-hour to a close, except that he switches the venue, from the posh Ambassador restaurant implied in our invitation, to 'Maria's', a small, crammed, artists' café, good enough for Chanel when we dined here with her, but wholly wrong for the Waugh swankiness.

Mr. W.'s mood takes an upward turn during the freezing and, in his case, coatless, block-and-a-half walk from the hotel, and the sight of the Funeral Home at the corner of Lexington and Fifty-Second restores his *joie de vivre* to the extent that he actually takes leave of us, gallivanting to the back of the building to explore the service entrance. The starchiness and sparring that the S.s think of as the normal British method of making acquaintance vanishes with the first bottle of Valpolicella, which the temperature-sensitive Mr. W. mulls. It seems to me, too, that, like everyone who meets Mrs. S., the novelist is succumbing to her charm. In fact he becomes positively courtly, and even the suspicion in the glowering glances he directs to I.S. diminishes. (Heretofore, or so I imagine, he has regarded I.S. as one of Maritain's converts from Judaism.) But a new gaffe occurs over the menu when I.S. recommends the prosciutto and Vera S. the Italian-style chicken. 'It's Friday,' the offended Mr. W. exclaims.

With the fettucine the conversation turns – no apparent connection – to the Church. Here I.S. shines, showing himself to be as ultramontanist as Mr. W., or at least as well read in Chesterton and Péguy, and as ready to believe in the miraculous emulsification of St. Januarius' blood. But another crisis occurs with a reference to the origins of tonight's encounter, the invitation to attend the premiere of the Mass. I.S. says: 'One composes music for a march to help men keep step. It is the same with my Credo: I hope that the music will help men to concentrate on the prayer. The Credo is long – there is a great deal to believe – which is the reason it is also fast.' I feel very proud of him.

Mrs. Waugh handles this politely, sincerely regretting that they have already 'booked passage home.' Lest the conversation continue in this dangerous direction, her husband adds, with a bluntness that seems to show that he has been inwardly lacerating all evening from the thought of I.S.'s cacophonous art: 'Music is painful to me.' The declaration can only be ignored, as V. does, graciously, with a compliment to Mr. Waugh on *his* art, and a comparison between his *Decline and Fall* and Sade's *Justine*. At this, Mr. W. realizes that his hosts have read everything he has published, and a new character surfaces in him, as magnanimous and amusing as the old one was supercilious and priggishly precise.

If the novelist does not brook the literary talk of literary types, he seems to enjoy it from outsiders like (though no one is 'like') the I.S.s, and even from semi-insiders like (there are many 'like') me, for I consider *Handful of Dust* an excellent novel and no longer object that chance and arbitrariness play too large a part in Waugh's fictions. We seek to draw him out on other writers but are rewarded with only one acidulated reference to his lecture-touring compatriot, Osbert Sitwell, and the commendation of Christopher Isherwood as 'a good young American novelist,' with the last two adjectives wickedly emphasized.

The meal concluded, Mr. W. asks permission to smoke a cigar. Choosing one from a case in his breast pocket, he holds it under his nose, where it looks like a grenadier's mustache, circumcises the sucking end with a small blade, passes a match under the other end as if he were candling a pony of precious cognac, avidly stokes and consumes it. Holy Smoke!

The next morning a lavish bouquet of white flowers arrives from the Plaza.

—◆—

I wrote to Waugh again after that to thank him for the Pre-Raphaelite book and received another card from Dursley, dated 25 January 1950, dealing with some questions of mine regarding his early writings:

> 'Antony who sought things that were lost' appeared in an undergraduate magazine, but has not been reprinted and will not be in my lifetime. It is jolly decent of you to be eager to disinter my early work, but my instinct is to suppress or destroy more and more juvenilia. *Work Suspended* has too few stories I wish to put out. Best wishes from Evelyn Waugh.

He also sent an inscribed copy, this time adding my middle initial, of the deluxe edition of *The Loved One*. I failed to appreciate the illustrations, particularly the drawing of a cadaver in a full dress that included a monocle.

Stravinsky did not encounter Waugh again, but on his premature death in 1964 the composer pasted the (London) *Times* obit in the loose-leaf sketchbook for *Requiem Canticles*.

Chapter 6

Christopher Isherwood

A Memoir

Between August 1949 and September 1969, when the Stravinskys moved from California to New York, I saw Christopher Isherwood regularly, had an affectionate *en famille* relationship with him, and even dedicated a book to him. Only now, with his second posthumous memoir, *The Lost Years*,[1] have I realised that I knew him only as a writer and was quite unaware of his private life. Not that his sexuality, publicly acknowledged in the 1977 autobiography, *Christopher and His Kind*, was ever covert. His friends and readers always understood that it was central to his work. During the early years of our friendship I rarely heard him allude to the sexual experiences that are the principal subject of the new book.

I turned first in *The Lost Years* to 1951, expecting to find an account of the 28 November Broadway premiere of *I Am a Camera*, the bonanza that led to the long-running, much-revived, and cinematised *Cabaret*. I had described the evening in my diary and waited fifty years to read his version. On Thanksgiving Day, he and W.H. Auden, with whom he was staying in New York, drove to Idlewild, the pre-JFK airport, to welcome the Stravinskys on their return from Rome, the

---

1   *The Lost Years: A Memoir 1945-1951* by Christopher Isherwood. Edited and introduced by Katherine Bucknell, London, 2000.

first reunion between the librettist and composer since the Venetian opening of *The Rake's Progress* two and a half months earlier. During dinner afterwards at the Lombardy Hotel (mutton chops, no turkey), Isherwood expressed reservations about the stage adaptation of his *Berlin Stories*, adding that he intended to boycott the gala opening a few days hence. *The Lost Years* implies that his real objection to the script was simply that he had already entrusted the work to his friend, Speed Lamkin, when the play's producers prevailed on the professional John van Druten to undertake the dramatisation.

Far from avoiding the event, Christopher was at the door greeting the glitterati, one of whom was the elfin wunderkind Truman Capote, and, in the foyer during intermissions, revelling in the success. Since *The Lost Years* does not mention the occasion, may I say that for some of the audience the most theatrical moment of the evening was the entrance of Stravinsky, escorted by Christopher down the centre aisle, when the composer's friend from Berlin in the 1920s, Marlene Dietrich, leapt from her seat and flung her arms around him, without noticing poor starstruck Christopher.

But *The Lost Years* ends in June 1951, and the text is chiefly concerned with the breaking-up of Isherwood's four-year affair with Bill Caskey, and with numerous sexual comings and goings: Andrew, Barry, Bill, Brad, Cliff, Denny, Frank, Jack, Jim, Keith, Mike, Mitchell, Peter, Rod, Russ, Speed, Steve, Tito, Tony, Vernon, 'a boy', Tom, Dick and Harry.

The prepublication flyer warns that the material is 'raw' and has 'an unpolished directness', which is a well-polished understatement. Katherine Bucknell's introduction includes a helpful character analysis of the often cantankerous Caskey. We learn from it that Natasha Moffat, finding herself seated next to him at a Charlie Chaplin dinner party, made an innocuous but resonant reference to 'pansies'. Caskey retorted: 'Your slang is out of date, Natasha, we don't say "pansy" nowadays.[2] We say "cocksucker".' Whereas her word had silenced the guests, noisy cover-up conversation rapidly followed Caskey's. In my

---

2   'The words "fairy" and "pansy" were considered to be in bad taste. It was fashionable to say that a person was "gay".' Gore Vidal, *The City and the Pillar*, New York, 1948.

limited experience of Hollywood dinners, I remember language of this sort exchanged by the likes of Bette Davis and Groucho Marx, and can testify that the after-dinner talk in the JFK White House (18 January 1962), after the retirement of the ladies, was no less exotic. Still, one wonders why a verbal artist as sensitive as Christopher Isherwood chose to repeat *ad nauseam* such vulgarisms as 'fucker', 'fuckee', 'screwing', 'rimming'.

Isherwood's descriptions of his promiscuous encounters are equally monotonous. The scenario is always the same: the pick-up, the flirtation, dinner, bed. Sometimes the partners are the wrong size, or otherwise incompatible. Parts of the book might have come from a manual on homosexual intercourse. Having been gratifyingly 'massaged' and 'milked' by a Yin partner, he describes his attempts to imitate the technique by flexing and unflexing his own sphincter. Christopher also tells us of his discovery that onanistic orgasm can be enhanced by pressing the thumb against a nerve at the root of the penis. But enough. The consequences of his promiscuity included haemorrhoids, two cases of clap, two of gonorrhea, and a penile constriction requiring surgery that resulted in impuissance.

In view of his crowded sexual agenda, Christopher's literary productivity is astonishing, He writes film scenarios and scripts, articles and essays (some of them collected under the unpromising title *Exhumations*), contributes dutifully to Vedanta Society tracts, works on his unreadable life of Ramakrishna, as well as on his often brilliant elucidations of Swami Prabhavananda's translation of Patanjali's yoga aphorisms. The publication of his translation of Baudelaire's *Intimate Journals* is not mentioned, presumably because it had been trashed by academic critics. Furthermore, the schedule of his social life with actors, directors, film writers, and his escorting of such visiting literary luminaries as Tennessee Williams and Norman Mailer around the Hollywood studios, must have been strenuous.

The book is a trove of diverting tittle-tattle of the 'with whom' variety, particularly in Ms Bucknell's glossaries. Though strewn with catastrophes, these little tales are perhaps the best starting point for queasy readers, but it should be noted that the Balanchine ballet is *Four Temperaments*, not *Four Temptations*, and that the bar in which

Tony Bower picked up the young man who later murdered him in his Park Avenue apartment could not have been 'on Fifth Avenue in the West Forties'.[3] Some of the glossaries provide thumbnail histories of hitherto unknown sexual attachments between prominent people. I, for one, dined with Alexis Saint-Léger (St.-John Perse) and Mina Curtiss without the slightest suspicion that they were 'long-time lovers'. I was also surprised to read that Sam Langford, the companion of Brian Howard, himself the original of Evelyn Waugh's Ambrose Silk, 'died in his bath when he was gassed by a faulty water heater' and that 'Howard killed himself a few days later'. Nor did I know that Erika Mann 'asked Isherwood to marry her and provide her with a British passport', and that 'he felt he could not, but contacted Auden', who accepted. We are told that the ex-movie actress Thelma Todd owned an establishment on the Pacific Coast Highway that incorporated 'a restaurant, a gambling casino, and a whorehouse, in which she was murdered'. After escaping from Germany, Hellmut Roder and his friend, Fritz Mosel, 'designed jewelry, especially for opera costumes, and dealt in metal and feathers [until] Mosel committed suicide, after which Roder apparently did the same'. Ms Bucknell reveals that William Randolph Hearst, partying on his yacht *Oneida*, shot the film director Thomas Ince, 'mistaking him for Charlie Chaplin, who was having an affair with Hearst's mistress, Marion Davies'; that Jack Hewit, 'the English dancer and spy', was the lover of Guy Burgess and, in succession, Anthony Blunt and Isherwood; that the film star Ramon Navarro was the lover of Richard Halliburton, until the latter was 'lost at sea in the Pacific'; that Norman Fowler was 'the boyfriend of Peter Watson and heir to most of Watson's estate…' When Watson drowned in his bath in 1956, Fowler was in the flat, but was not considered a suspect. Fowler then 'bought a hotel in the Virgin Islands, called it the Bath Hotel… and lived there until he himself drowned in his bath in 1971' – which sounds like one of Evelyn Waugh's 'sad stories'.

This litany also informs us that Evelyn Hooker, an intimate friend of

---

3   Fifth Avenue, a north-south thoroughfare, is not *in* the West Forties. It borders ten West Forties blocks but the building numbers on the West Forties streets begin west of, not on, Fifth Avenue.

Isherwood's, was one of the first psychologists and psychotherapists to view homosexuality as a normal psychological condition. After working with and studying homosexuals in Los Angeles for several years, she presented the results of her research at a conference in Chicago in 1956, the first to claim that the percentage of psychologically well-adjusted homosexuals was as high as that of heterosexuals.

Isherwood's duplicity and bigotry – 'Christopher's anti-Semitic feelings', which he admits to, and the present book amply confirms them – are no less disturbing than they were in the first volume of his diaries. He gives a party for Benjamin Britten and Peter Pears, who were in Los Angeles on a concert tour. Strictly faithful to each other, they pay no attention to the 'boys' Christopher has invited for the musicians' vicarious pleasure – as the last Austrian Archduke offered his male diners a post-prandial harem – but the diary describes these illustrious guests as 'just a pair of slightly faded limey queers'. Christopher accepts Victoria Ocampo's hospitality in Argentina, writes respectfully about her in one of his best books, *The Condor and the Cows*, but insults her in *The Lost Years* as 'a bullying old cunt'. Returning from his second visit to his mother after World War II, he vents his disgust with her for remarking that 'I want grandchildren': 'At seventy-eight, with one foot in the tomb, she could say this – without the slightest consideration for the wishes of her two sons she professed to love! But, of course, this wasn't Kathleen speaking, it was the matriarch cunt, death to all decency, demanding that its gross fleshly will be done.'

A blurb describes the book as 'Isherwood's own account, reconstructed in 1971–1977 from datebooks, letters, and memory, nearly thirty years later, of his experience during those missing years'. But the meaning of 'reconstruction' is not always apparent. The 1946 chapter begins with the statement: 'Since there isn't any day-to-day diary... I shall have to describe the happenings of that year much more vaguely and impressionistically.' Here one wonders if 'I' is always Isherwood, and never a stand-in. Clearly the writer of the 1949 diary is in some places a friend of Isherwood's who has heard him reminisce but taken it down carelessly. Vera Stravinsky, we read, 'found time to paint pictures and to help run a boutique'.

But Isherwood knew very well that she did not begin to paint until a later date and that her art gallery, La Boutique, had ceased to exist years before she knew him. The writer goes on to say '... Igor was well known [for] his avariciousness. Auden, who had had business dealings with him when writing *The Rake's Progress,* complained of it often. Christopher was never exposed to it.' Stravinsky never had 'business dealings' with Auden, who said just once, in a letter to me, that he and Chester Kallman thought they were entitled to a share in the lump sum the pococurantist Italian cultural bureaucrats had agreed to pay to Stravinsky (but never did in full) for his travel and hotel expenses and for conducting the opera. The libretto was commissioned and paid for by Stravinsky's publishers. The music was not commissioned.

Isherwood uses the third person adroitly in other books, but why, having eschewed the device in previously published diaries, does he employ it in an admittedly 'reconstructed' one? Whatever the answer, the switching from 'Christopher' to 'I' is distracting: 'Christopher felt and I still feel...'; 'Since Christopher now had less than three weeks... I agree that...'; 'Christopher bought three numbers of the magazine *Camera Work*, which Stieglitz had published in the early 1900s... As I remember, Georgia [O'Keeffe] charged him quite a lot for them.' Why not 'charged me'? At least once the author himself seems to have been confused: 'John was watching Garbo, and wondering what she was thinking and what *he* was thinking about her.' Surely John must have had an inkling as to what *he* was thinking?

After long stretches in which Christopher's life seems to be dominated by sex to the exclusion of all else, it is a relief to come upon his footnoted comments on his reading: Conrad's *Nostromo* is 'noble and masterly but unmemorable'. In another 'unmemorable' work by this 'beloved writer', *The Shadow Line*, 'Conrad combines startlingly realistic moments of physical experience... with the artificiality of a cultured foreigner talking English at a literary tea'. Ford Madox Ford's *Parade's End* provokes the observation that the author's 'disingenuousness is part of his charm'. *The Bostonians* is Christopher's 'favorite long novel by James – indeed the only one I really like'. His reviews of contemporaries are more prickly: 'I find

Venus Observed – and the few other Christopher Fry plays I've read –
piss-elegant posing.' '*Homage to Catalonia* is certainly a noble book; I
honor grim old Orwell far more than I enjoy him...' '*Miss Lonelyhearts*
– that's a different matter; I neither honor nor enjoy Nathaniel West.'
Thornton Wilder's *Ides of March* is put down as the work of 'a scholarly
closet queen'. Camus's *The Stranger* is 'as phoney as *No Exit*. It is a
French novel and nothing but a French novel; one of the classic bogus
masterpieces of this century.' I can vouch that this does not square
with Isherwood's outspoken admiration for *The Plague* and most of
Camus's later work. Cyril Connolly's *The Unquiet Grave* is

> his most maddening and snobbish book and, for that very
> reason, his most fascinating and self-revealing. It contains a
> passage which I keep quoting to myself: 'the true function of
> a writer is to produce a masterpiece... no other task is of any
> consequence'. Obvious though this should be, how few writers
> will admit it [and] lay aside the piece of iridescent mediocrity
> on which they have embarked.

Chapter 7

An E.M. Forster Garland

This belated volume of E.M. Forster's critical writings and opinions[1] is more amusing than its predecessors, *Aspects of the Novel* (1927), *Abinger Harvest* (1936) and *Two Cheers for Democracy* (1951), and at least their equal in critical acumen. The quality of the writing – compact, graceful, unobtrusively witty – is consistently of the highest. How regrettable that such *bijoux* can have remained scattered and unknown for so long.

The 'tale' of the title is that of Prince Giuseppe Tomasi di Lampedusa (1896-1953), whose novel, *The Leopard*, is the only piece in the collection with which readers are likely to be familiar, since it was published as the preface to a modern edition of the book. A single comment of Forster's on the English translation of the book is so sensitively observed that one regrets he does not discuss it at greater length. Describing an intimate scene in which the peasant-girl mistress of the author's *de facto* great-grandfather addresses her lover as 'Principone', Forster observes that the word 'combines the feudal with the erotic' in a way that 'My Prince' does not.

An essay on Virginia Woolf's earliest novels and stories confirms Forster's largely negative view of this literary rival. She 'cannot create character or, for that matter, tell a story or weave a plot,' he says,

---

[1] *The Prince's Tale and Other Uncollected Writings* by E.M. Forster. Edited by P.N. Furbank, London, 1998.

adding that her 'chief characters are not vivid… when she ceases to touch them they cease, they do not stroll out of their sentences, and even develop a tendency to merge…' *Orlando* is 'a fancy on too large a scale', and 'after the transformation of sex things do not go so well'. *Kew Gardens* has 'no moral, no philosophy, nor has it what is usually understood by Form. It aims deliberately at aimlessness, at long loose sentences, that sway and meander…' Later, in his memorial lecture on the writer (published in *Two Cheers*), Forster dismissed the 'Invalid Lady' myth and emphasised the toughness: 'She was always civilized and sane on the subject of madness.' Declaring his preference for her biographies, of *Roger Fry* and Elizabeth Barrett Browning's dog *Flush*, he concludes that she will be judged by her novels alone, while allowing for the possibility that a new generation might discard them altogether as 'tiresome'. But her chatty literary essays and gossipy letters have weathered the turn of the century better than those very dull biographies.

So it is surprising to find in *Two Cheers* that Forster nominates Woolf, together with Lytton Strachey, T.E. Lawrence, D.H. Lawrence and Joyce, as 'the leading writers of our age', by which Forster means 1918–39. He ventures only the word 'curious' on *Ulysses*, but quotes 500 purplish ones on the death of Victoria from Strachey's novelised biography of the Queen. Forster was apparently not considering continentals (Kafka, Musil, Broch) for his passé pantheon, and he seems to have been deaf to new voices, Evelyn Waugh's, for instance, as well as to Americans, apart from Sinclair Lewis, who, to Forster's delight, 'mistrusts the Y.M.C.A.', and is 'against heartiness', although, like other 'quick, spontaneous writers', Lewis is 'apt, when the spontaneity goes, to have nothing left'. Lewis, nevertheless, 'lodged a piece of a continent in our imagination', but the tiny article in which this statement occurs, 'Sinclair Lewis Interprets America', is not included in *The Prince's Tale*, no doubt because someone observed to Forster that his opening statement, 'I have never been to Gopher Prarie [*sic*], Nautilus, Zenith, or any of their big brothers and sisters,' misspells the essential word.

As might be expected, Forster is more enlightening on an English bestseller, Jan Struthers' *Mrs. Miniver*, than on any of Lewis's books.

He notes that 'the little lady' of the title lacks 'some grace or grandeur, some fierce eccentricity'. Her class 'strangled the aristocracy in the nineteenth century'. But now that 'the castles are gone' and 'we have to live in semidetached villas... let us at all events retain a Tradesman's Entrance'. This seems inconsistent from a writer who snipes at Woolf's snobberies.

'Forster believed that "good writing can only be learnt from good writing",' P.N. Furbank's elegant introduction notes, yet the subjects of this collection are by no means confined to this ideal. Forster castigates Clayton Hamilton, the author of a book called *Materials and Methods of Fiction*, for having read with too wide a catholicity, and, since he has 'neither emotion nor taste, [he] cannot provoke those qualities in others'. Quoting a paragraph from a biography by Sidney Lee that is hopelessly entangled in misrelated pronouns, Forster warns the reader, before trying to push ahead, to assign 'the 'his-es' to their proper owners'. In contrast he praises a passage from one of Ouida's letters for having 'no hesitation, not a word out of place, the rhetoric rising naturally out of the emotion'. Even Proust, to whom Forster credits the 'epic' of the early twentieth century, comparable to Dante's of the early fourteenth, does not escape grammatical and stylistic ridicule. A sentence 'undulates and expands, parentheses intervene like quick-set hedges, flowers of comparison bloom', and 'three fields off crouches the principal verb... making one wonder... what is its relation to the main subject... half a page back, and proving finally to have been in the accusative case'.

Furbank alerts us to Forster's skill in taking his metaphors to what seems the furthest possible limit. A book of insipid verse by Ella Wheeler Wilcox stimulates this aspect of his talent; viz.: 'The quiet stream of her life joins the impetuous torrent of his at last, and they flow on together in one mighty river of broadening emotion towards the sea, whence... they will one day re-emerge in the form of dew...' An anthology called *The Elizabethan Home* prompts him to ask: 'Do you wish you had lived in the days of Queen Elizabeth?' and to answer: 'I am thankful to have escaped them'. He avers that the two attractions of the age are 'lyric beauty and quaintness', and that the latter 'disappears entirely when we form part of it'. The Queen, 'a portentous figure shaped like a dinner-bell', closed every vista. 'The hard reverberations of this creature filled the air... she made... rude metallic jokes... she was a public virgin.' Spenser, Sidney and Raleigh 'accepted the dinner-bell as a solid woman; they did not venture to think. There was very little thought in those spacious times...'

The Elizabethans 'were at once too violent and too hazy to contribute much towards the development of the human mind'. What they were responsible for was the discovery of continents, the exercise of 'vigour and swagger', and the emergence of an England that began 'to splash and send ripples all over the world'. No more is said about the farthingale, but the lack of thought is neatly attributed to the choice of the other option. The Elizabethans 'plumped for the native hue of resolution'.

Forster's essays on Mrs Gaskell and Ford Madox Ford should be read as supplements to *Aspects of the Novel*, which does not mention them. The former is acclaimed here as 'a great Victorian novelist'. Her unfinished masterpiece, *Wives and Daughters*, 'believes in the goodness of human nature', and Forster prefers the company of its heroine 'to that of any fictional maiden of her century', partly because 'she learns from experience quicker than any Jane Austen heroine'. As a sampling of the book's prickly dialogues, Forster quotes the following exchange between an earl and a countess, not mentioned hitherto:

> 'Preston's a clever, sharp fellow.'
>
> 'I don't like him,' said my lady.
>
> 'He takes looking after but he's a sharp fellow. He is such a good-looking man, too, I wonder you don't like him.'
>
> 'I never think whether a land agent is handsome or not. They do not belong to the class of people whose appearance I notice.'
>
> 'To be sure not. But he is a handsome fellow: and what should make you like him is the interest he takes in Clare and her prospects.'
>
> 'How old is he?' said Lady Cumnor with a faint suspicion of motives in her mind.

As for Ford, his hit-and-run *The English Novel* is condemned as capricious, impertinent, cavalier in its treatment of facts, and irritating in its assumption of 'the air of the repository of artistic traditions', by which Forster can only mean the high court of opinion in all matters pertaining to the Flaubertian as well as the English novel. These defects are not offset by the book's meritorious 'swiftness' and its power to 'aerate' our minds, or by a publisher's blurb intended to forestall these objections by pretending that the author is not so much writing criticism as 'thinking aloud'. But when Ford's survey of the English novel is compared to an academic one, priggishly subtitled *Intellectual Realism, from Richardson to Sterne*, which, Forster grants, 'delivers the goods', he finds the academic work 'dull, badly written, and conventional in its judgements'. It inclines us 'neither to hear about Sterne nor to read *Tristram Shandy*,' Forster says, as he returns 'with renewed appreciation to Mr. Ford'.

Like many other critics, Forster is at his best when reviewing the second- or third-rate. He dissects a literary corpse by Georges Clemenceau, the same who 'urged millions to die' for France, writing that

> the Tiger in 1898 was off his feed, so he turned out a novel... Pinch the book where you will, and it does not move. Not only are the characters 'dead'... being mere bundles of qualities, but the scenery, the social face of Paris, is also defunct... He, to whom all sections of society must have been open, reads as if he had never been anywhere or seen anything... Hum of life, vividness of details – he transmits neither.

The review of C.M. Doughty's long narrative poem *Mansoul* would have to be quoted in full to convey the full flavour of its fun. Forster reminds us that Doughty's *Arabia Deserta* was 'highly but mysteriously spoken of by a small circle'[2] and 'sometimes praised but

---

2   A 1925 letter from D.H. Lawrence to a friend that had come into the possession of Forster says that 'I don't do much: but slowly wade my way through the sandy wastes of Doughty's *Arabia Deserta*. I read it on and on and on without quite knowing why.'

seldom opened'. His prose is 'gnarled, [but] what will be the fate of his verse?' he wonders, exhibiting an incomprehensible specimen:

> Wherefore be those too much to blame, that pinch;
> Of malice, rankling in ungenerous breast;
> (Which might themselves a cattle-crib uneath
> Devise:) at master-ártificers work;
> And with the venom of crude lips, deface;
> Who moved of hearts devotion, vows to Heavens
> High service a CATHEDRAL.

'What does "uneath" mean?' Forster asks, and 'why in the last line but one is there no apostrophe for the possessive in "hearts" and "Heavens"?' One would renew the attempt to read the poem if,

> beneath the tiresomeness, there was a beautiful or intellectual general purpose. But no beauty or intelligence can be discerned in the general purpose of *Mansoul.* It is the old hackneyed business of a visit to the under-world – so tiring, such a getting downstairs, so dark, magic mirror, etc. First of all we meet the Kaiser, 'a loathly leprosy blots his werewolf's face', then others of the dead. The conversation is such as is usual on infernal occasions. The shades ask the poet, with whom are associated two things called Mansoul and Minimus, how he came to be here while still alive, and he replies to them at length. Then they give their opinion on man's destiny. Zoroaster, Confucius, Buddha, Socrates, and the other heavies each utter appropriate redes. To hear them, we have to burrow backwards and forwards under the earth, sometimes tunnelling the Mediterranean.

The three 1920 pieces on H.G. Wells's *The Outline of History* are no less shrewdly observed for being long out of date. The book's failure lies in its being 'a history of movements, not of man'. Like most scientists, Wells 'confuses information with wisdom'. But, 'Who is to educate our scientists?' That is, who will teach them not to work for politicians and invent yet more terrible instruments of war? Further, Wells's intelligence, which was always 'both subtle and strong... cannot quite supply his lack of imagination'. Wells's principal complaint against the past is that it was so ill-informed:

> He notes the uneducated tendencies of the reptiles, who might have averted extinction had they taken appropriate steps... The Chinese invented printing, but made no use of it owing to some mental blur. The Alexandrians had a library, but their books were shaped like pianola rolls, and consequently awkward to consult.

In all of Wells's 700 pages, Dante is mentioned only once, and then in an irrelevant connection, hence Wells's 'ideas of what is supreme in human achievement can never coincide with ours'. But neither can Forster's, when he names Shakespeare and Voltaire as the two people he would choose 'to speak for Europe at the Last Judgement'. Voltaire rather than Beethoven?

In *Aspects of the Novel*, Forster was rightly critical of D.H. Lawrence's preaching and nagging, 'so that in the end you cannot remember whether you ought or ought not to have a body, and are only sure that you are futile'. But Lawrence's bullying – 'I think you *did* make a nearly deadly mistake glorifying those *business* people in *Howard's End*' – occupies for Forster only the foreground of Lawrence's 'blend of vision and vituperation', while 'his greatness lies far, far back... with a power of re-creation and evocation we shall never possess...'[3]

Not surprisingly, the piece in this collection about the debate, via pamphlets, between Lawrence and the Home Secretary, who had kept *Lady Chatterley* and its author's paintings at bay, has lost all pertinence. But Forster fixes a common ground between them in their inability to define pornography. The Home Secretary 'considers everything related to sex evil with one exception: marriage'. To turn from him to the writer of genius is 'to turn from darkness into

---

3   After Forster's three-day visit to the Lawrences in their Sussex cottage in February 1915, D.H.L. wrote to Bertrand Russell: 'There is more in him than ever comes out... We were on the edge of a fierce quarrel all the time... he seized a candle and went to bed, neither would he say good night.'

light', Forster says. Lawrence 'has dealt a blow at reformers who are obsessed by purity and cannot see that their obsession is impure'. To make his point, Lawrence had quoted two poems, both obscene, with 'devastating effect', 'My Love is like a red, red rose', and 'Du bist wie eine Blume'. Whereas 'Burns sends his emotions outwards to mingle with human beings and become passions, Heine shuts his up in a circle of self-enclosure, where they fester'. Heine, not Burns, Forster argues, 'is the modern man. He is a typical product of repression...' The Home Secretary 'wants to suppress everything except marriage, and Mr. Lawrence to suppress nothing except suppression...'

The book reviews are more diverting than the sections labeled 'Diversions', the 'Political Thirties', 'Memoirs' and 'The Arts in General'. Forster had an ear for music, but on the evidence, no eye for painting. The best of the other pieces are on India, a subject on which 'it is impossible to be too intricate'. All nine articles on its intricacies are still worth the time of anyone planning to visit the country. Even the earliest of them, on train travel in 1913, is still apropos; the iron horses do occasionally leave and arrive on time. The 'trial of unpunctuality' occurs when 'passengers forget to get in or those who are in forget to get out, and the train stops again while they alight screaming; or it stops for social reasons, so that the guard may chat with his friends...'

In declaring his Hindu bias, Forster sounds like a disciple of Christopher Isherwood: 'Hinduism, unlike Christianity and Buddhism and Islam, does not invite [a man] to meet his god congregationally; and this commends it to me':

> There often exists inside [the Indian temple's complexity] a tiny cavity, a central cell, where the individual may be alone with his god... The exterior of each temple represents the world-mountain, the Himalayas. Its top-most summit, the Everest of later days, is crowned by the sun, and round its flanks run all the complexity of life – people dying, dancing, fighting, loving – and creatures who are not human at all, or even earthly. That is the exterior. The interior is small, simple. It is only a cell where the worshipper can for a moment face what he believes.

He worships at the heart of the world-mountain, inside the
exterior complexity. And he is alone.

The uncharacteristic fervour reminds us that Forster believed that
the Maharaja of Dewas, whose secretary he had been, and one of the
loves of his life, was a saint.

Forster emphasises the impossibility of drawing a definite line
between Buddhism and Hinduism. The main issue between the
religions, he says, is the social one of the caste system. By condemning
caste, Buddhism became a 'missionary religion', in China, Ceylon,
Siam, Cambodia, Java, Japan, whereas Hinduism, 'rooted in caste,
stayed home'. Hinduism 'modified Buddhism and complicated it,
then exported it'. He highlights the two religions' similarities in a
1953 article extolling the Gupta period in architecture – a 'classic'
in the sense of the word describing a degree of perfection never
established before or since – and observing that Hindu and Muslim
art occasionally blend together, as in a Muslim tomb near Golconda
and the mosques of Ahmedabad.

In contrast, another essay explains, irenics in any form between
Islamism and Christianity are unimaginable because of the 'permanent
stumbling block' of the Trinity; the Mohammedan cannot logically
'exchange his one God for a God who is both one and three'. Moreover,
the central mystery of Christianity – 'For God so loved the world that
he gave his only begotten Son' – is actively repulsive. The Islamist is
shocked by the idea that 'God should love a world, that he should be
a Father, and that he should allow his Son to die'.

Forster's account of how he lost his Church of England faith, though
he seems never to have been overburdened by it, is gentle and low-key.
When he was a boy, the Reverend Hutchinson told him and his widowed
mother that 'in the very next road there lived a man who did not believe
in God called Mr. Huxley', whereupon the young Forster 'wondered
whether the house of anyone so inconceivable would have a special
shape'. Later he lost his Christian faith partly because of 'the general
spirit of questioning' associated with G.E. Moore's *Principia Ethica*.
He also became aware of his lack of sympathy towards the character
of Christ, having no 'desire to meet [Him] personally', and finding

that his 'preaching and threats and absence of humour' contrasted unfavourably with 'Krishna, that vulgar blue-faced boy', who admits 'pleasure and fun and jokes and their connection with love'.

Christ, furthermore, 'is nearly always in pain... the sufferings, we are told, are undergone for our sake, [but I hope that] none of this has been undertaken for my sake'. Christendom turned to the Virgin Mary in the Middle Ages because she gave birth to the child, 'saw him grow up and saw him killed', which is 'immediately comprehensible' and 'to which we can accord heartfelt pity'. If there is such a thing as Salvation, it has now (1959) 'disappeared from my thoughts, like other absolutes'.

Forster's review of Tolstoy's pamphlet on poverty, and on property as the root of all evil, contends that evil lies in possessions, for the simple reason that 'they clog the life of the individual'. Furniture and ornaments, he says, are 'wearisome forms of wealth far more tiring than balances at the bank'. The present writer recalls an afternoon spent with Forster in 1961 in his book-cluttered rooms at Cambridge, as the elderly ascetic indulged, between awkward pauses and hiatuses, in moral self-reproach while deciding which objects – the shabby William Morris armchairs, ancestral portraits, crocheted shawls, solitaire board – he could most readily do without.

But why did Mr Furbank omit Forster's delightfully downplaying Introduction to the *Aeneid* in the Temple Classics Series (1916)? It observes that Virgil himself was 'greatly dissatisfied with the poem' and that in the last six books the hero is 'if possible, duller than ever'. Forster even questions Virgil's dedication to Augustus, since there was 'little in the emperor that should attract an elevated mind'.

Chapter 8
Lytton's Letters[1]

It struck me that letters are the only really
satisfactory form of literature.
L.S., 1916

Strachey's outgoing mail, oppugnant, contumelious, scabrous, blasphemous, is far more entertaining than his novelised biographies. Moreover, his lexicographical virtuosity roves with greater freedom and license away from the high formal style and the eye of the censor, which obliged the great historian to substitute asterisks or other stepping-stones in place of sexual descriptions and *gros mots*. On the other hand, his contempt for Christianity is vented with superior sophistication in the true storybooks, as when he tells us that Philip II, when called to his maker, was met not by God but by the Trinity.

Most of the first part of this selection of Strachey's correspondence is addressed to Leonard Woolf, his closest heterosexual friend at Cambridge, then serving as colonial administrator in Ceylon. Lytton kept him apprised of events back home, above all of local gossip about copulations, especially his own. Few details about existence on the island can be gleaned from Lytton's responses, and next to nothing about the man whose

---

1   *The Letters of Lytton Strachey*, ed. Paul Levy, assisted by Penelope Marcus, London, 2005.

future wife would establish his family name in the pantheon of twentieth-century literature. Nothing of Leonard's personality surfaces in the letters, and the same is true of Lytton's other closest correspondent, Dora Carrington, the Bloomsbury painter, his worshipful disciple, love of his life, and principal participant in the latter part of it. She inspired his most poignant letters, disclosing the pejorationist's surprising gentleness. In fact, Virginia Woolf had described him as 'The most interesting and sympathetic friend to talk to... curiously sweet-tempered, considerate; and if one adds his peculiar flavour of mind, his wit and infinite intelligence – not brain but intelligence – he is a figure not to be replaced by any other combination.'

Though the quality of Lytton's wit remains at peak level throughout, the most droll, i.e., malicious, examples are found in his early, impecunious years, long before his renown as a biographer. After witnessing a Greek play at Cambridge, he writes that 'The chorus was composed of the twelve ugliest undergraduates dressed in mauve gauze, looking like a melancholy band of harlots who had grown too old for work'. Apropos the marriage of Clive Bell to Vanessa Stephen, Virginia Woolf's sister, he remarks that 'She's very intelligent: how long will it be before she sees that he isn't?' A part ingratiating, part vituperative letter to Virginia, referring to her presumed nemesis, Katherine Mansfield, one of the few females to whom Lytton himself was sexually attracted, depicts her as

> decidedly an interesting creature... very amusing and sufficiently mysterious. She spoke with great enthusiasm about *The Voyage Out*, and said she wanted to make your acquaintance. She has an ugly impassive mask of a face... cut in wood, with brown hair and brown eyes very far apart; and a sharp and slightly vulgarly-fanciful intellect sitting behind it.

Lytton is scathing about nearly everyone except the great thinkers whose company he solicited, Maynard Keynes, G.E. Moore, Bertrand

Russell[2] and Wittgenstein. Other people are 'boring, tedious, tasteless, hideous, brainless, cretinous, ugly, oafish, stupid, and incapable of two seconds of consecutive thought'. One of his Cambridge lovers, Henry Lamb, is both 'stupid and slimy'. Another has become 'pale and inanimate, hardly more than an incompletely galvanized dead body'. Occasionally Strachey's sense of fun at his own expense breaks through: 'Went to dinner with the Freshfields on Friday and was (to their minds) properly brilliant.' At times he laughs at his own sexuality, conjecturing whether he will be counted among the male or the female invitées at an upcoming party. The *Letters* reveal that he also had a certain bisexual inclination, however limited. Carrington finally managed to seduce him, and years before that he was erotically attracted to Maria Nys, the future wife of Aldous Huxley[3] ('how I might have put my hand on her bare neck, even up her legs, with considerable enjoyment'), and he confessed to being 'a good deal taken' with Princess Marie-Louise, that 'utterly crazed scullery maid'.

It seems to have been Lytton himself who invented the expression 'Cambridge: The Higher Mathematics and the Lower Sodomy', and his *Letters* are a major contribution to the sociology of buggery as well as an index of some of its most illustrious practitioners. He was the lover of innumerable men, and as he grew older suffered increasingly from the rejections of younger ones. His few *real* love letters are shamelessly sentimental and much less absorbing that his countless callous reports of 'copulations'. Moreover, the turnover is far more rapid.

Lytton's longest-lasting and deepest affair was with Keynes, and when the great man abandoned him, the budding writer's vindictiveness and vitriol emerge in parlous force. He portrays the

---

2 Though Lytton admired him unreservedly, a letter of his to Virginia Woolf about the philosopher concludes that 'I can only suppose that he dislikes me - pourquoi?' The Huxleys blamed Ottoline Morrell's break with him on his notorious halitosis, though of course the real reason was simply that he had taken a new lover. Lytton did not support Russell in the debate over admitting Wittgenstein to the 'Cambridge Apostles', and endorsed the latter's demolition of Russell's Platonist view that logic was the study of independently existing entities and realities, persuading him that it was the study of the consequences of linguistic connections.

3 Strachey found the young Huxley 'incredibly cultured', but they never became close. Still, one is convinced that both Huxley and Eliot owed their discovery of Thomas Lovell Beddoes - 'I've huddled her into the wormy earth' and 'A wedding-robe and a winding sheet / A bridal bed and a bier' - to Strachey's essay on him. Lytton had discovered *Death's Jest Book* and Beddoes' mastery of dramatic blank verse as early as 1905.

century's leading economist working in his garden 'wearing a scarlet knitted wool cap looking like an effete Pasha':

> Poor old Keynes is absolutely sunk... and by God I think he deserves his fate. Looking back I see him hideous and meaningless... a malignant goblin gibbering over destinies not his own. He imagines that he's reached the apex of human happiness – Cambridge, statistics, triumphant love, and inexhaustible copulations.

Lytton tattles to Vanessa on his replacement, Duncan Grant: 'I copulated with him this afternoon and at the present moment he is in Cambridge copulating with Keynes.' A groovy university, indeed.

Strachey's art criticism seems of little value apart from its brilliant language, and is far inferior to his literary criticism. As a reviewer for *The Spectator*, he claims to have 'shrieked' at every page in a book on Shakespeare, except that the editor 'won't allow anything but a very veiled frenzy'. He dreams of writing a new dunciad.

After dining with Picasso and Derain in 1919, Lytton demeans the occasion, arranged by Diaghilev, as 'not so enjoyable'. During a tour of 'hydrotrophic' Holland, he visits the Hague Museum but hones in on only one picture, a pseudo-Rubens 'with swans interlacing rather improperly in the background'. After viewing a London exhibition of Rodin, during which he managed to glimpse the sculptor's 'red-grey beard', Lytton remarks that the large-scale plaster model of *The Thinker* 'thundered above the ladies and gentlemen in evening dress... Very violent':

> My theory is that the French imagination is nearly always *material*. Rodin is *grossly* so. Imagine, if Shelley had been a sculptor, how he would have done *Le Baiser* – a winged Eros just touching the earth; Rodin has a thick man cuddling a thick woman. *Le Penseur* is rigid banks and heaps of muscle. The imagination of Michael Angelo was 'spiritual' in some way that Rodin's isn't.

Platitudes and clichés provoke a low-keyed sarcasm that sustains the reader through less glittering patches, as, for instance, in Lytton's account of a lecture by the painter Sir William Rothenstein, from whom 'you may be glad to learn that in his opinion "the artist interprets life"'. On a new French magazine he reports that the prose is 'inconceivably vile... formless, clumsy, and intolerably dull. There was an article on Rome by Maeterlinck who said that Rome was a very beautiful place and full of objects of interest, also an article on Napoleon by Jean Moréas, whom I can only imagine is an imbecile...'

The book sags during the years of the Great War, particularly in the discussions of anti-conscriptionism and Suffragism. Lytton does not attend meetings of the latter, of course, but strolling by Trafalgar Square one evening, he notices an 'appallingly large' congregation presided over by 'two hags'.

In 1911 Lytton writes from Devon to his friend, the philosopher G.E. Moore: 'Have you read Whitehead on mathematics? I enjoyed it very much, though my brain reeled.' Since it is unlikely that this little 'Home University Library' book (1911), a model of lucidity and still accessible to today's general readers, could have strained the Strachey cerebellum, the reader would like to know the actual capacities of his mathematical mind. A letter from Lytton to Moore, September 1912, severely criticises the latter's *Ethica*, and in some detail. Another letter, dated November 1912, interests us for its intimate description of Russell's squabble to keep Wittgenstein to himself, as his pupil, and of Keynes's triumph in recognising Wittgenstein's 'genius', thereby obliging Russell to admit him into their 'Apostolic' circle.

The glimpses of some of the greats of the time are among the book's main attractions. Lytton's portraits are deft, compact, and percipient. He wrote to his brother in 1909:

> I've seen Henry James twice. Both times exceedingly remarkable... He came in here [Mermaid Inn, Rye] to show an antique fireplace to a young French poet... the poor man absolutely [gasping] and all the golfers and bishops sitting

around quite stolidly munching buttered buns. He has a colossal physiognomy, and it's impossible to believe that such an appearance could have written *The Sacred Fount.* I long to know him. He seemed infinitely conscientious and immensely serious, and this was especially so the second time I saw him – at a window in his house; he had just come there to look more closely at a manuscript – and then the polite worry of it all! I think he must be quite extraordinarily slow.

Twenty years later Lytton informed E.M. Forster:

> I've just reread *The Awkward Age.* It is all very strange. His cleverness is positively diabolical, and the artistry, and so on. What's so odd is the vulgarity of mind in combination with this. He's most distressing about sex and money... It seemed dreadfully boring, too – one had to force oneself to go on, which can hardly be right... One does somehow feel, in spite of everything, that there was something distinguished about him – something big; but one doesn't quite see what.

Early in their relationship, Lytton was not an admirer of Forster himself:

> His new novel [*The Longest Journey*, 1907] has come out. I think it's a good deal worse than the last, and it certainly contains things infinitely more foul. The morals, the sentimentality, and the melodrama are incredible, but there are even further depths of fatuity and filth...

These execrations ceased a decade later when the writers were Lady Ottoline Morrell's fellow guests at Garsington. Forster is then referred to as 'delightful, more feyish than ever, having had a complete success with a member of the lower classes, aged 24'. Later still, in

1927, daring at last to be candid about Virginia Woolf,[4] Lytton writes to Forster:

> I enjoyed *Lighthouse* more than *Dalloway*. But it is a most extraordinary form of literature. It is the lack of copulation – either actual or implied – that worries me... there is some symbolism about the *Lighthouse*, etc., but I can't guess what it is.

———◆———

Like many others, Strachey was overshadowed by the young T.S. Eliot, though he first referred to him (December 1917) as a 'spouting poetaster', and was annoyed by Lady Sands's opinion that *The Hippopotamus* was the height of brilliance and wit'. Writing to Carrington from Garsington on 14 May 1919, Lytton tells her of 'A long and interesting conversation with Eliot... He's greatly improved – far more self-assured, decidedly intelligent, and, so far as I could see, nice. I hope to see much of him, but the circumstances are difficult.' Vivienne was 'not at all bad' but had a 'painfully vulgar voice'. A propos the same Garsington weekend, Lytton wrote to another friend, Mary Hutchinson: 'Poet Eliot is altogether not gay enough for my taste. But by no means to be sniffed at.'

Lytton's first letter to Eliot of February 1920 lauds his essay on Blake, and concludes by sending 'my love', which must have annoyed him. A second letter, containing reflections on *Prufrock*, provoked a 'grim' reply (Strachey's word), a tutorial on letter writing that nearly ended the new friendship:

> ... the good sentence, the good word, is only the final stage in the process. One can groan enough over the choice of a word, but there is something much more important to groan over first. It seems to me the same in poetry – the words

---

4   The recently discovered (2004) letters of Virginia Woolf to Lady Aberconway mention an 'unintelligible' new book ('Anna Livia Plurabelle'), the meaning of which might 'swim to the surface with the help of morphine'.

come easily enough, in comparison to the core of it – the tone – and nobody can help in the least with that... You are very ingenious if you can conceive of me conversing with rural deans in the cathedral close. I do not go to cathedral towns but to centres of industry...[5] [I] regard London with disdain and divide mankind into supermen, termites, and wireworms. I am sojourning among the termites...

On 13 July 1920 Strachey invited Eliot to spend the next weekend with him at his Tidmarsh 'Mill House'. The letter provides train timetables and other renseignements about the journey. Strachey mentions that his sister and husband will be there, and regrets 'not having seen you for so long, Yours ever, Lytton Stratchey' [sic]. But Eliot did not come, and seems not to have done so after being invited again the next week. In 1921 the poet asked Strachey to contribute to *The Criterion*. His refusal, containing the enigmatic remark, 'If only my make-up were of a different sort', must have enraged Eliot.

Then comes the great surprise, Eliot's encomium in the *TLS* for *Elizabeth and Essex: A Tragic History*. Here are only two excerpts:

One of Mr. Strachey's peculiar gifts, besides that of lucidity, is his cunning ability to accelerate or reduce the speed of his narrative. It is difficult to see how, with such slight means, this is done; but it is part of his dramatic gift to be able to give us the feeling, and the impatience of intolerable delays and shifts and changes, and the rush of sudden events as well. For this reason we want to read the book at a sitting; we could no more insert a bookmark until tomorrow than we could see a play by going to a different act each night...

Once we have allowed Mr. Strachey his dramatic license for intensification and isolation, we must admit that his characters seem to us otherwise true to history. His character of Elizabeth is particularly just. He takes a middle path between those who

---

5   Eliot was employed at Lloyds Bank in London at this time.

represent her as merely a puppet moved by the scheming Whig nobility created by her father... and those who picture Elizabeth's ministers as merely intelligent servants. The power of these intelligent servants Mr. Strachey does not diminish; and indeed one of his most powerful figures is that of Robert Cecil – always kept behind the arras, and always precarious, always maintained by indefatigable attention and consummate diplomacy. And had the character of Elizabeth not been a strong one, and had it been different from what it was, her ministers could not have played the *role* they did play. Mr. Strachey's presentation of his chief figures is as near to the right historical judgment as posterity can ever achieve.

———•———

Strachey seems to have read as much French as English literature, though he maintained that he never conversed in French. (The lunch with Picasso and Derain could only have been in that language.) He claimed that Saint-Simon, Voltaire and Proust provided his support system, yet he says nothing substantial about them, and why is his English translation of *Le Bateau ivre* unobtainable? He had borrowed an edition of *Les Liaisons dangereuses* with marginalia in the hand of Baudelaire ('In reality wickedness has won. Satan has become innocent. Evil knowing itself so is less ghastly and nearer being cured than unconscious evil. George Sand is inferior to Sade'). More editorial information would be useful here. The letters abound in commonplace French expressions, but also in a plethora of irritating English ones: 'By the bye', 'Oh! Oh!', and 'God Almighty', this last being an unbefitting term for a militant atheist.

The night before Dora Carrington married the third member of their triumvirate household, Ralph Partridge, Lytton wrote to her:

You realize that I have varying moods, but my fundamental feelings you perhaps don't realize so well. Probably it is my fault. It is perhaps much easier to show one's peevishness than one's affection and admiration... You know very well that I love you as something more than a friend, you angelic creature, whose goodness to me has made me happy for years... my love for you, even though it is not what you desire, may make our relationship a blessing to you – as it has been to me.

A decade later, on 21 January 1932, when Strachey died from an undiagnosed tumour that had perforated the colon, he confessed that he had 'always wanted to marry Carrington', who at that very moment was failing in an attempted suicide. She would succeed a few weeks later on realising that she could not live without him.

———◆———

Music, meaning Bach, the operas of Mozart (particularly *Seraglio*, *Figaro*, *Così fan tutte*, over and over), and the Master of Bonn, was Lytton's passion. After listening to a recording of Mozart's G minor Symphony, he told Roger Senhouse, his publisher, 'I've always thought that music was the salvation of life'. Modern music is not mentioned, except for a piece by Ravel from 1921 that seems to have meant nothing to him. Returning from a concert, Strachey wrote:

> Yesterday afternoon the [Beethoven] C Minor was being performed; I couldn't resist it and went... The Symphony wrecked me, just as usual, and in the same place, the sudden plunge into infinite glory at the beginning of the fourth moment.

Chapter 9

Lady Keynes in Bloomsbury

Lydia Lopukova (1892-1981) was 'not really a great ballerina, nor was she among the most technically expert,' Sir Frederick Ashton confides in this volume of tributes to the Diaghilev dancer.[1] But dancing is not the subject of the book. What Milo Keynes offers is the story of her unlikely but nevertheless successful marriage to his uncle, John Maynard Keynes. The Lady Keynes side of the book much outweighs the Lydia Lopukova side.

In the one entirely candid contribution, Quentin Bell reveals that until shortly before the marriage, Keynes's constant companion was a certain Professor Sprott, 'a very elegant and seductive youth' sometimes referred to as 'Maynard's wife'. Sprott's union with Maynard 'never caused the slightest difficulty with Maynard's other friends,' Bell tells us, unnecessarily, since this is Bloomsbury. But Lopukova's arrival did create a fuss. Describing her as a 'half-witted canary' and remarking that having children would be '*too* improbable', Lytton Strachey, an earlier lover of Maynard, reported that 'he actually seemed to be in love with her, and she with him'.

One wonders less about the bisexual Keynes's conjugal life with Loppy, as he called her,[2] than about how this gamine of unexceptional

---

1   *Lydia Lopukova.* Edited and with an introduction by Milo Keynes, New York, 1984. The review appeared in *The New York Times*, 29 April 1984.
2   Stravinsky called her 'Lopushka'. See his correspondence with her in the autumn of 1928, when she was seeking his help in obtaining rights to produce *Histoire du soldat* in London.

intellect, limited education and incompatible social background provided companionship for one of the most brilliant men of his time. Even while assuming that he could not have considered the consequences of marriage, his friends plotted to avoid the 'catastrophe', as Virginia Woolf foresaw it, adding that 'I should rather like her for a mistress myself', a wish that, in a 1923 photograph of the two women together, might have been on the way to fulfilment. The wedding, on 25 August 1925, was followed by a honeymoon in the USSR. The reader is not told what became of Professor Sprott.[3]

Milo Keynes refers to the twenty-five-year marriage as a 'happy association', and his book convinces us of the truth of the claim. Loppy diverted and charmed her husband. She also nursed him, both before and after the heart attack that left him a semi-invalid during the last nine years of his life. His niece, Polly Hill, says that even after his marriage, he would 'call for his mother when ill'. Hill quotes a friend: 'He enjoyed a nursery atmosphere,' and added that he never outgrew 'his own precocity'.

The nineteen contributors to the book may not have been maliciously intentioned *vis-à-vis* Lady Keynes, but the kindness of their courtesies toward her are less memorable than the barbs in their anecdotes about her. Isaiah Berlin, avowing that Keynes was 'certainly the cleverest man I have ever met', describes a scene in the British Embassy in Washington on the night of Roosevelt's election to a fourth term. As a group listened to radio reports of the election returns, Loppy was bored and restless:

> Do you like the President? Roosevelt? Rosie? Do you like Rosie?
> I like Rosie. Everybody here likes Rosie. Do you like Rosie, too?
> Shoosh, Lydia, not now, said Keynes... She turned to me again,
> Do you like Lord Halifax? The Ambassador was sitting about
> a yard from me at the time... Keynes did not shoosh her this
> time, but stared straight in front of him with a faint smile on
> his lips... Lord Halifax looked faintly, very faintly, embarrassed,

---

3   He became one of Lytton Strachey's lovers and travelled with him to Venice and in the Netherlands.

rose from his place, patted his little dachshund... and... strode from the room.

Quentin Bell tells a similar story of amazement that Keynes 'made not the slightest attempt to stop Lydia from making a fool of herself, [when with] some very slight exercise of that incredibly brilliant mind of his, he could have set everything straight'. Clive Bell, Quentin's father, provides a clue: 'Keynes's hubris was as dominating as his brain.'

In such situations, Lady Keynes seems to have been less to blame than her husband, being not so much tactless as without any notion of the meaning of the term. Her insensitivity, vanity, exhibitionism, and, as Frederick Ashton says, 'fiendish rudeness', are more difficult to excuse. Many of the contributors describe her as 'witty', but their illustrations of this are generally confined to some unamusing malapropisms. David Garnett gushes about her 'enchanting use' of English, but a reader undeterred by her non sequiturs and digressions can judge this for him- or herself in the reprinted radio scripts and newspaper articles and in the excerpts from her letters to her husband.

John Gielgud remembered that Lopukova had a strong accent, but does not identify it as Russian. What kind was it? We learn that she had studied English in, of all places, 'the Catskills', but precisely where and how she came to be there are not divulged. None of this would matter except that she pursued a career as an actress and appeared on stage in English-language plays, including some of Shakespeare's. She received favourable reviews in the publications that Keynes owned, the other kind elsewhere. But why did he encourage her?

As an audience member talking loudly and embarrassingly, Loppy seems to have caused aggravations on the opposite side of the footlights as well. Ashton recalls an occasion when the curtain went up and all was quiet until Lydia's voice rang out: 'Oh, Maynard, look at her mouth. It is indecent. It looks as though it belongs somewhere else.' Yet E.M. Forster, a 'favourite friend', sitting directly behind Lydia during a performance of a stage-adaptation of *A Room With a View*, is said to have been amused by her comments 'made in a fairly loud voice'.

The book subtracts from ballet history in, for example, its

mistaken or misleading versions of such well-documented areas as the conception of *Petrushka*. Balletomanes will notice a prodigious number of errors, and the editor has failed to see that the reproduction of Picasso's portrait of Lopukova on the dust jacket, signed by him 'Londres 1919', is dated on the infold 'Rome in 1917', which is correct. The level of much of the writing is exemplified in a remark about 'the first public performance in English of Stravinsky's *The Soldier's Tale*, called at that time *The Tale of the Soldier*'.

Chapter 10

On Mallarmé

I was trying to like Mallarmé again the other day, but couldn't, because it's Jesuitical poetry, even the Swan *and* Hérodiade. *I'm... in mourning for the integrity of a pendu and emission of semen, what I find in Homer and Dante and Racine and sometimes in Rimbaud.*

Samuel Beckett, 1932

Mallarmé and Whistler

Stéphane Mallarmé, with Henri de Régnier, was in Prince's Hall, London, on 20 February 1885 for James McNeill Whistler's 'Ten O'Clock' lecture, but painter and poet did not meet until three years later, in Paris, introduced by Claude Monet. By that time, Mallarmé, tastemaker of the continent, was translating, and hence bestowing literary permanence on, *Le Ten O'Clock.* Whistler made a lithograph of him, engulfed in tobacco smoke, as in Edouard Manet's 1876 portrait. Whistler and Mallarmé became close friends.

The origins of the Whistler–Ruskin scandal of 1877 are well known. Ruskin's *Fors Clavigera*, which had so powerfully influenced the social, political and moral philosophies of Tolstoy, Gandhi and G.B. Shaw, trashes Whistler's *Nocturne in Black and Gold: The Falling Rocket* (Detroit Institute of Arts): 'I have seen much of Cockney impudence before now but never expected to hear a coxcomb ask 200 guineas for flinging a pot of paint in the public's face.' (Ruskin had evidently not stopped to consider that paint in 'a pot' could only be monochrome.) The writer had already ridiculed the same painting in *Val d'Arno* (1874), but this time Whistler sued. Asked in the course of the trial to justify the 200-guinea price tag 'for two days' work', he famously answered: 'I ask it for the knowledge of a lifetime,' and was loudly applauded. Though Whistler won the case, and the trial publicised his vision of a new kind of painting, thus enabling him to publish a book, *Whistler v. Ruskin: Art and Art Critics*, the court costs bankrupted him. Critics, meanwhile, had exposed the inconsistency between Ruskin's championing of Turner's 'misty' pictures, such as *Abingdon Morning*, and his denigration of Whistler's smudgy, blurring Nocturnes. After the trial, Ruskin resigned his Slade Professorship at Oxford.

Oscar Wilde was also present on that February night in 1885. Though nominally a friend of Whistler's, he subscribed to Ruskin's aesthetic of truth to nature as the artist's duty. Wilde's review of the proceedings appeared in the next day's *Pall Mall Gazette* under the title *Rengaines* ('Same old story'):

> Mr. Whistler... spoke for more than an hour with really marvellous eloquence on the absolute uselessness of all lectures of the kind. The scene was in every way delightful; he stood there, a miniature Mephistopheles mocking the majority! He was like a brilliant surgeon lecturing to a class composed of subjects destined ultimately for dissection, and solemnly assured them how valuable to science their maladies were, and how absolutely uninteresting the slightest symptoms of health on their part would be. Nothing could have exceeded [the audience's] enthusiasm when they were told by Mr. Whistler that no matter how vulgar their dresses were, or how hideous their surroundings at home, still it was possible that a great painter, if there was such a thing, could, by contemplating them in the twilight and half closing his eyes, see them under really picturesque conditions, and produce a picture which they were not to attempt to understand, much less dare to enjoy... Then there were some arrows, barbed and brilliant, shot off... at the

art critics who always treat a picture as if it were a novel, and
try to find out the plot...

Having thus made a holocaust of humanity, Mr. Whistler
turned to Nature, and... spoke of the artistic value of dim dawns
and dusks, when the mean facts of life are lost in evanescent
and exquisite effects...

What Whistler actually said was:

> Nature contains the elements, in colour and form, of all
> pictures... But the artist was born to pick and choose, and group
> with science these elements, that the result may be beautiful...
> That Nature is always right is an assertion, artistically, as
> untrue, as it is one whose truth is universally taken for granted.
> [Mallarmé: '"La nature a toujours raison" est une assertion
> artistiquement controuvée, que la verité en est universellement
> prise pour l'argent comptant.'] Nature is very rarely right, to
> such an extent even, that it might almost be said that Nature
> is usually wrong: that is to say, the condition of things that
> shall bring about the perfection of harmony worthy a picture is
> rare... seldom does Nature succeed in producing a picture.

One supposes that this homily, widely understood as perverse,
irritated Wilde as much as it delighted Mallarmé. Wilde's review does
not attempt to counter it but shifts to a secondary theme, 'the dictum
that only a painter is a judge of painting'. The asperity is open and
personal: 'I say that only an artist is a judge of art; there is a wide
difference. As long as a painter is a painter merely, he should not
be allowed to talk of anything but medium and megilp...' Wilde's
conclusion begins with a hollow conciliation, an over-preparation for
an embarrassingly inferior Parthian ending.

> Not merely for its clever satire and amusing jests will [the
> lecture] be remembered, but for the pure and perfect beauty of
> many of its passages – passages delivered with an earnestness
> which seemed to amaze those who had looked on Mr. Whistler

> as a master of persiflage merely, and had not known him, as we
> do, as a master of painting also. For that he is indeed one of the
> very greatest masters of painting is my opinion. Mr. Whistler
> himself entirely concurs.

Whistler responded civilly (23 February), but his rage is ill-concealed, while Wilde's acknowledgement (the same day) is insufferably patronising. Yet the two men remained on first-name terms, Oscar and James ('Jimmy' in pre-feud correspondence from America). The next letters are venomous on both sides, and Whistler talks not to Wilde but about him. Surprisingly, these are dated nine months after the first exchange, while the successive round of still more poisonous missives follows a three-year silence, leaving the reader to wonder about the causes of the sudden flare-ups. In the final round Whistler accuses Wilde of plagiarism, and warns him that in America he would be 'criminally prosecuted, incarcerated, and made to pick oakum', which sounds like a premonition of *Reading Gaol.*

In 1906, after the deaths of both men, a private press in London published 400 copies in quarto and 100 in octavo of the *Pall Mall Gazette* pieced together with the aftermath literature under the title 'Wilde v. Whistler, Being the Acrimonious Correspondence in Art Between Oscar Wilde and James A. McNeill Whistler'.

Henri de Régnier tells us that Mallarmé had instantly succumbed to Whistler's magic on that 20th of February, 1885,

> touched, as though by a conjurer's wand, by the ebony cane
> which this great dandy of painting wielded so elegantly.
> Everything in Whistler justified the curiosity and affection
> which Mallarmé felt for him: his mysterious and pondered
> art, full of subtle practices and complicated formulae, the
> singularity of his person, the intelligent tension of his face,
> the lock of white hair amid the black, the diabolical monocle
> restraining his frowning brows, his prompt wit in the face of
> the scathing retorts and cruel ripostes, that ready and incisive
> wit which was his weapon of defense and attack.

Mallarmé's *Le Ten O'Clock de M. Whistler*, published in 1888, played an important part in posterity's endorsement of the American painter's esthetic philosophy over Ruskin's. The poet inscribed a copy of it to his critic friend: '*A Félicien Champsauer, Ses amis Whistler et Stéphane Mallarmé*'. In 1891, when Mallarmé wrote to the Belgian publisher Deman concerning a collected *Poésies*, he stipulated a frontispiece by Whistler.

Mallarmé and Manet

Mallarmé's 'The Impressionists and Edouard Manet' is the least known of the poet's prose writings. After failing to obtain the admission of his friend Edouard Manet to the *Salon*, the poet expanded his arguments in this causerie, the most lucent analysis of the Impressionist movement at the time (1874). The manuscript was lost and the essay was first published in English in *The Art Monthly Review*, London, September 1876, after Mallarmé corrected and approved the translation. Retranslation into non-Mallarmé French, ludicrous as this seems, nevertheless took place, and though incomplete, the French version was not withdrawn until 1968. The English original was reprinted in 1986 in a book on Mallarmé, Manet and Redon, now difficult to find.

The essay begins by extolling Baudelaire, who 'loved all arts and lived for only one of them'. [Manet's] 'strange pictures at once won his sympathy. An instinctive and poetic foresight made him love them; and this before their prompt succession and the sufficient exposition of the principles they inculcated had revealed their meaning to the thoughtful few of the public many.'

The next admirer of Manet was 'the then coming novelist Emile Zola. With that insight into the future which distinguishes his own works, he recognised the light that had arisen, albeit that he was much too young to define that which today we call Naturalism.' Thereupon Mallarmé dispenses with the Naturalists and addresses himself to 'that absolute and important sentiment which Nature herself impresses on those who have voluntarily abandoned conventionalism'.

Mallarmé's discourse concludes with a description of Manet

during a personal chat with him in his studio. The painter's language was 'brilliant', he wrote, but 'the meaning of it is in the Painting':

> Each work should be a new creation of the mind. The hand, it is true, will conserve some of its acquired secrets of manipulation, but the eye should forget all else it has seen, and learn anew from the lesson before it. It should abstract itself from memory, seeing only that which it looks upon, and that as if for the first time; and the hand should become an impersonal abstraction guided only by the will, oblivious of all previous cunning.

Further,

> when Manet recognized the inanity of all he was taught, he determined not to paint at all or to paint entirely from without himself. Yet, in his self-taught insolation, the masters of the past appeared to him, and befriended him in his revolt. Velasquez and the Flemish School particularly impressed themselves upon him and the wonderful atmosphere which enshrouds the compositions of the grand old Spaniard, and the brilliant tones which glow from the canvases of his northern compeers, won the student's admiration, thus presenting to him the two art aspects which so reveal the Masters and give painting based on them living reality instead of rendering them the baseless fabric of abstracted and obscure dreams.

Mallarmé describes Manet's *Olympia* as a 'modern work' and 'the first non-traditional, unconventional nude'. The picture's surroundings and accessories are 'truthful but not immoral – in the ordinary and foolish sense of the word – but they were undoubtedly intellectually perverse in their tendency'.

Surprisingly, the great poet turns to Degas, Manet's nearly exact contemporary, for a contrasting example:

> M. Degas can be as delighted with the charms of three little washerwomen, fresh and fair, though poverty-stricken, and clad

only in camisole and petticoat, bend their slender bodies at the hour of work. No voluptuousness there, no sentimentality, the wise and intuitive artist does not care to explore the trite and hackneyed view of his subject.

Much of the essay takes the form of an inner dialogue. 'Why is it meaningful to represent the open air of gardens, shore, or street,' Mallarmé asks, 'when it must be admitted that the chief part of existence is passed within doors?' One of his answers is that 'In the open air alone can the flesh tints of the model keep their true qualities, being nearly equally lighted on all sides... No artist has on his palette a transparent and neutral colour answering to open air...'

> There is no painter of consequence who during the last few years has not adopted or pondered over some of the theories advanced by the Impressionists, and notably that of the open air, which influences all modern artistic thought. The pointillists – Monet, Sisley, Pizzarro [sic], Césane [sic], all look alike because they endeavour to suppress individuality for the benefit of nature. Claude Monet loves water, and it is his especial gift to portray its mobility and transparency... I have never seen a boat poised more lightly on the water than in his pictures. The work of a genius abjures singularity.
>
> If we turn to natural perspective, not that utterly and artificially classic science which makes our eyes the dupes of a civilized education, but rather that artistic perspective which we learn from the extreme East – Japan, for example – and look at the sea pieces of Manet, where the water at the horizon rises to the height of the frame, which alone interrupts it, we feel a new delight at the recovery of a long-obliterated truth. This is the picture and the function of the frame is to isolate it.

English Pre Raphaelitism, if I do not mistake, returned to the primitive simplicity of the medieval ages. The scope and aim of Manet and his followers is that painting should be steeped again in its cause, and its relation to nature.

Mallarmé on Fashion

Improbable as it may seem, in 1874 Mallarmé became the author, editor and designer of a women's fashion magazine, *La Dernière Mode*. The text of this fortnightly review, which published eight issues, was almost entirely written by Mallarmé under the pseudonyms of Marguerite de Ponty (fashion), Miss Satin, (representing the great fashion houses of Paris), and Ix, a male reviewer for books and the theatre. Each issue also included sample menus by Mallarmé under the name 'Le Chef de bouche chez Brébant', and black and white engravings of *à-la-mode* costumes designed by Mme de Ponty. Under this *nom-de-plume* Mallarmé also provided dress patterns and a correspondence column, which he filled with letters purportedly coming from figures in high society. The magazine had an attractively designed cover, displaying vignettes of women at the Opéra, and was handsomely printed. It was a successful commercial enterprise with de facto subscribers, and the poet himself personally collected subscriptions and even invested some of his own money in the venture.

Why is this publication of one of the greatest writers of the Modernist era, produced at the height of his powers – *L'Après-midi d'un faune* followed – all but unknown? And why was Mallarmé 'obsessed' (his word) by the art of fashion? In fact, he had studied it at a *lycée* in Paris in 1871, and had reinstated French representation at the International Exhibition in London later that year and the next. His theory was: the only style that had existed since the eighteenth century was the Empire, which was depressing. Innovation had been lacking, and the future would have to engender new forms.

Some renowned French literary figures had also written about fashion, Théophile Gautier, for one (*De la mode*, 1858), and most famously Baudelaire (*Sur Modernité* in *Le Peintre de la vie moderne*). The latter contended that the primary aim of his essay was to extract the mysterious beauty of the modern, of the fugitive, the contingent and the transitory. The language of fashion of any epoch, he maintained, is a matter, not merely of dress design but of gesture and facial expression and manners: 'It is futile to laugh at past fashions; the transition from one fashion to another follows a clear logic, like that governing the changing shapes of animals.'

Mallarmé's philosophy of fashion is in direct opposition to Baudelaire's, although Manet was the central figure for both. 'Evil is natural,' Baudelaire wrote. 'Virtue, by exact contrast, is always artificial, and it is possible to consider custom and fashion as one of the signs of spirituality and of longing for the ideal.' For Mallarmé, there is no difference between nature and art. 'Nature is a false concept. Nature and the man-made are not to be distinguished. Women, in particular, have a duty to use all arts to elevate themselves above Nature, and, among them, "make-up"... But they should employ it for the right motive, which is to imitate the beauty of Nature... Make-up needs to be frankly what it is, a challenge and rebuke to Nature.'

One of the favourite tropes of both Mme Ponty and Ix is that the high-life *monde* is perfectly synonymous with the everyday *monde.* What continues to amaze us is that Mallarmé made himself a fashion designer and a parody of a 'fashion journalist'. The first issue of *Mode* contains some of his richest prose, and jewellery is his subject. 'Plain gold earrings' are recommended for a walking dress, and a necklace 'in extremely pale coral'. Everyone should wear a good-luck bracelet on their arm, he writes, one made of

> simple gold or with pearls and turquoise; on their finger a ring, just one, always simple, without brilliants or emeralds. For a *corbeille de mariage*, one would begin by including a pair of ear-drops all in gold, long ones... a second *parure* in lapis-lazuli (a stone much in favour these days), and a third and more elaborate one... of garnet in the shape of pears or apples with diamond-studded stems.

'What can a fashion journalist talk about when fashion itself is in suspense?' Mme Ponty interposes. The disappearance of the bustle is a major subject. The French have two separate words for this garment (not to mention the risqué soubriquet, *le cul de Paris*). The bustle did in fact disappear in 1875.

Each issue of *La Dernière Mode* contains a black and white drawing of two fashionable ladies with exquisitely designed *toilettes*; an editorial on Fashion by Mme de Ponty; a Chronicle by Ix; some pages about interior decorating; a poem and a short story; a Gazette of forthcoming events for the fortnight (books, theatres, travel); correspondence with subscribers. Some of the poems and stories are written by Catulle Mendès, Alphonse Daudet and Théodore de Banville. Fortunately the editors and translators, P.N. Furbank and B.M. Cain, have added comments of such elegance and perception that to all but a very few the book would be unreadable without them. In a discussion of what Mme de Ponty calls 'an absolute revolution in the bustle', for instance, they quote a vivid passage from Proust, apropos Odette and Swann, that reveals a close temperamental affinity with *La Dernière Mode*:

> In spite of her being one of the best-dressed women in Paris, so much did the corsage, jutting out as though over an imaginary stomach and ending in a sharp point, beneath which bulged out the balloon of her double skirts, give a woman the appearance of being composed of different sections badly fitted together, to such an extent did the frills, the flounces, the inner bodice follow quite independently, according to the whim of their designer or the consistency of their material, the line which led them to the bows, the festoons of lace, the fringes of dazzling jet beads, or carried along the busk, but nowhere attached themselves to the living creature, who, according as the architecture of these fripperies drew them towards or away from her own, found herself either strait-laced to suffocation or else completely buried.

Ix opens his first causerie under the heading 'Paris Chronicle', but questions the title: 'A chronicle requires a past, but we arrive on the scene unknown, with only a future.' Why, he asks, are seaside holidays as much a feature in the social calendar as château entertainments and the pleasures of the hunting-field and river? Do not say that those who go on them are seeking 'escape' (for they cannot escape from themselves); do not say they are in quest of 'Nature', for they hurtle through Nature blindly on express trains. What impels them to spend long hours on the beach... is fashion... The principle of fashion is instant and universal change.

Ix, or rather the 'Le Chef de bouche chez Brébant', suggests a menu for a seaside luncheon, beginning with oysters, shellfish *en buisson*, Fillet of sole *à la* Saint-Malo, Lobster suprême; or perhaps turkeys, terns, Mutton cutlets Maintenon, or Chicken *à la* Duroc. The wine list includes Haut-Brion and Léoville. As is well known, Mallarmé himself was both gourmet and gourmand, and huge meals were habitually served in his household.

Another entry, attributed to 'Parc Monceau', advises gardeners in surmounting the constrictions of August: 'The sun, which caused the garden to flourish, has failed it.' A few touches of red are recommended (Pelargonium Diogène).

The first issue concludes with a detailed list of *costumes* for 'formal visiting' in the summer (1874), 'for the races', 'for walking', for the 'country', for a 'promenade concert', for 'visiting', and for 'a grand ceremonial occasion'.

In the sixth issue Mallarmé wears his own clothes and speaks in his own voice as a critic of music:

Scarcely a century old, music today reigns over every Soul. A religious cult for some of you, who are completely under its sway, and for others simply a pleasure, it has its catechumens and its dilettantes. Its prodigious advantage is to stir, by artifices reputedly denied to words, the subtlest or the most sublime reveries; and furthermore to entitle the listener to fix her gaze for minutes at a time, smiling in silence, on a blank spot in the ceiling, bare even of painting. The whole life of 'Society' is summed up there: the care it takes to hide the finer emotions, for which the imagination was created, or even (sometimes) to pretend to have them.

Who would dare to complain that music, that incorporeal Muse, made up of sounds and sensations, that goddess – no, that nimbus, that adorable scourge – should invade the town's theatres one after another.

A Death in the Family

Has too much importance been given to the tomb-in-words that Mallarmé dreamed of erecting for his son, Anatole, dead at age seven, in 1879, too little to the poetry in which the father actually did immortalise his child? Paul Auster tells us that the 202 fragments, republished with his translations,[1] are not poems but 'notes for a possible work, a long poem'. Two of them are titled 'Notes', while others are accompanied by reminders such as 'idea there', 'general effect', and 'etc.', as well as blank spaces for words in blocked-out lines. Yet by any criteria, some of these fragments are poetry.

The evidence that Mallarmé projected an epic work is more effectively supported in the fragments themselves than in any testimony about it, least of all the memoir by his daughter published in 1926, from which Auster quotes two sentences: 'In 1879, we had the immense sorrow of losing my little brother... I was quite young then, but the deep and silent pain I felt in my father made an unforgettable impression on me: "[Victor] Hugo," he said, "was happy to have been able to speak [about the death of his daughter]; for me, it's impossible."' Fragment 129 reveals something of Mallarmé's conception:

non mort – tu ne le	no death – you will not
tromperas pas –	deceive him –
je profite de	I take advantage of the fact
ce que tu le trompes	that you deceive him

---

1   The fragments were first published in Paris in 1961 under the title *Pour un tombeau d'Anatole*, Jean-Pierre Richard, editor. *A Tomb for Anatole* by Stéphane Mallarmé, translated with an introduction by Paul Auster, was published in San Francisco.

- pour son heureuse	- for his happy
ignorance à lui	ignorance
- mais d'autre part	- but on the other hand

and

malade à la-	sickness one
quelle on se	clings
rattache, désir-	to, want-
ant qu'elle	ing it
dure, pour l'avoir	to last, to have
lui plus longtemps	him longer

and

moment où il faut	moment when we must
rompre avec le	break with the
souvenir vivant	living memory,
pour l'ensevelir	to bring it
- le mettre en bière	- put it in the coffin,
le cacher - avec	hide it - with
les <u>brutalités</u> de	the <u>brutalities</u> of
la mise en bière	putting it in the coffin

Auster's introduction translates the passages from Mallarmé's and his wife's letters referring to Anatole and his illness (childhood rheumatic fever complicated by an enlarged heart), the false convalescence, and the fainting fits that began shortly before the death (presaging the poet's own death, following an attack of suffocation). Writing to a friend who had sent a parrot to Anatole, the poet complains of being unable 'to do anything literary', yet he bedizens his description of the bird, Sémiramas, whose 'auroral belly seems to catch fire with a whole orient of spices'.

The Introduction might have said something about the characteristic forms of the fragments, their short - never more than six-syllable - lines, the frequency of sequential pairs as well as the occurrence of the larger sets (3, 4 and 5), and the use of some of the same indicia as in the manuscripts for the so-called *Livre de Mallarmé*, the hoax of the unfinished masterpiece ('Il n' y a pas là d'héritage littéraire'). A satisfactory translation of Mallarmé is scarcely conceivable, and this attempt injects the wrong tone (cf. 'clearly/dearly'):

... 1)	... 1)
vous qui verrez	you who will see
bien, ô ma – bien	clearly, O my – dearly
2)	2)
aimé...	beloved...
je te le reprends	I take it back from you
pour le tombeau idéal	for the ideal tomb

That the dead, including Anatole, do not know they are dead ('– pour son heureuse / ignorance à lui') is one of the fragments' recurrent themes. Another is the merging of identities, of the son continuing to live in the father. Reading these fragments, one thinks of Stephen Daedalus on Shakespeare playing the ghost in *Hamlet*: 'To a son he speaks, the son of his soul, the prince, young Hamlet and to the son of his body, Hamnet Shakespeare, who had died in Stratford that his namesake may live for ever.'

Another of Mallarmé's themes is that of his guilt for failing to endow his son with a stronger body, of wanting to form him to continue his own task ('the man you would have been'), of wanting too much from him ('hésitant de cette merveilleuse intelligence filiale', which reminds us of Rodin's comment after Stéphane Mallarmé's funeral: 'Combien de temps faudra-t-il à la nature pour refaire un cerveau pareil?'). Still another theme is that of the boy's clothes:

trouver <u>absence</u>	to find <u>only</u>
<u>*seule*</u>–	<u>absence</u>
– en présence	– in presence
de petits vêtements	of little clothes

and

petit marin-	little sailor-
costume marin	sailor suit
quoi!	what!
- pour grande	- for enormous
traversée	crossing
un vague t'emportera	a wave will carry you

The explanation for the interest in the Anatole fragments can only be that despite much that is 'obscure', 'elliptical' and 'unintelligible', some lines are more direct and immediate than any to be found in Mallarmé's certified poetry, where, of course, he would never have published such raw, wrenching expressions of emotion as:

je le veux lui - et	I want him - and
- non moi	- not myself
genoux, enfant	knees, child
genoux - besoin	knees - need
d'y avoir l'enfant	to have the child here

The fragments expose the poet's imagination in the act of engendering possibilities of making Anatole's death survive in art, Mallarmé having lost his faith ('nous ne sommes que de vaines formes de la matière'):

- je ne veux pas	- I do not want
fermer les yeux -	to close his eyes -
- qui me regar-	- that will look
deront toujours	at me always

of creating his survival through poetry, the reality in the image. The critic Leo Bersani suggested that Mallarmé could not write the poem because 'of a reluctance to reduce life to the trivialising nobility of a redemption through art'. But the word 'reluctance' in this indictment of the aesthetic of art elevated to religion implies a voluntary decision. Mallarmé, as these *cris du cœur* show, was stricken beyond the power of his art to help him:

tu peux, avec tes	you can, with your
petites mains, m'entraîner	little hands, drag me
dans ta tombe – tu	into your grave – you
en le droit –	have the right –
– moi-même	– I
qui te suis moi, je	who follow you, I
me laisse aller –	let myself go –

Chapter 11

A Note on Sylvia Beach

I

The publication of some 200 pieces of correspondence by James Joyce was a major literary event,[1] but the editors' claim that 'these letters give witness to the unguarded moments' is true of only a few of them. The large majority attest to Joyce's punctiliousness in even the briefest statement; to his powerful prescience of the electronic age; to the exquisiteness of his vocabulary.

This said, it must be allowed that Joyce's importuning pervades the book, and that Sylvia Beach, for all her adulation and dedication, must have dreaded the sight of his handwriting in her mail. Not many of the letters are without requests for money. In addition to her duties as Joyce's banker, Beach became his telephone exchange and answering service, his social and business secretary, public relations director, delivery and errand girl, and post office. Many of his letters contain lists of changes to be inserted in his proofs, one of them with no fewer than sixty. Moreover, Joyce's requests are to be attended to 'the sooner the better'. Even the message of thanks on the publication of *Ulysses*, the day of Joyce's laureation, concludes with a nuisance assignment for her.

---

1   *James Joyce's Letters to Sylvia Beach*, 1921-1940. Edited by Melissa Banta and Oscar A. Silverman. Foreword by A. Walton Litz, Bloomington and Indianapolis, 1987.

A choice of letters from Beach's side would have provided helpful perspectives. Ms Banta explains that the Joyce family withheld access to some of these, but she does not quote from a 'revealing' unsent letter, dated April 1927, now in Buffalo and apparently available. Nor does Richard Ellmann's biography quote from the 'angry letter' that Beach sent Joyce in the spring of 1923, a period represented by a gap on Joyce's side. The most evident source of friction in the letters printed here is in Joyce's occasionally over-zealous promotion of *Ulysses*.

Joyce's relentless work of correcting the French and German translations of his books is a principal subject of the letters. A related one is his failing eyesight. He described this to T.S. Eliot who answered: 'I shall mention you in my prayers, if you do not consider that an impertinence'. Nevertheless, the quantity of his reading remained prodigious, and the subscriptions to magazines and books that Joyce ordered from Beach's Shakespeare and Company would make a bewildering library: all eight volumes of *The Complete Peerage*, Bury's *The Life of St. Patrick*, a monograph on César Franck, Joseph Clouston's *The Lunatic at Large*, and much more.

In Ostend, in 1926, Joyce was pleased to be able to talk to a small girl in Flemish. He was equally fluent in Dutch, and in the Hague a few years later, was amused on Bloomsday (16 June) when a waiter told him that a certain wine was called 'Een bloem'. Joyce would have been ecstatic if he could have known that this collection of his letters would be published in Bloomington, Indiana.

Eliot wrote an obituary for Sylvia Beach in the [London] *Times*, 13 October 1962, saying, in part:

> ... I do not know how Joyce could have survived or how his works could have got published [without her]. In the early thirties Joyce discovered that for reasons connected with the legality of his testamentary disposition he needed to spend a period of two or three consecutive months in England. Being the man he was, he rented, for this brief sojourn, an unfurnished flat: a dreary little flat, for which he then proceeded to buy some still drearier necessary pieces of furniture. (How he eventually disposed of

flat and furniture I do not remember.) It then transpired that he had no bank account; it was Sylvia who acted as his banker. When he needed money he wrote to Sylvia, who promptly sent a banker's draft, which he would then give to me to cash for him at my bank. What the financial arrangement may have been between those two, or what accounts were kept, I never knew.

II

The *James Joyce-Paul Léon Papers* catalogued in the National Library of Ireland and published in 1992 include disappointingly few letters actually by Joyce, as distinguished from paraphrases and précis of his words. The book is useful to Joyce biography as an agenda of people who corresponded with him through Paul Léon, but of Joyce's prose only a few phrases are worth noting. One of them occurs in a letter about George Moore's funeral.

III

1988

To The Editors of *The New York Review of Books:*

May I add a note to John Kidd's 'The Scandal of *Ulysses*' on the related ruckus over corruptions in the Gilbert and Ellmann editions of Joyce's letters? The publishing histories of the novel and the letters are not parallel, the corruptions not similar in kind: in the novel the disappearance of an aposiopesis and a dieresis - dittography replacing what was mistaken as haplography - and, in the letters, misreadings of words. But the errors are sufficiently numerous and bizarre to mandate rescension of the entire Joyce correspondence.

Gilbert and Ellmann include only 13 of the 211 known communications from Joyce to Sylvia Beach. On this meagre sampling, Gilbert, though less circumspect than Ellmann, does not stray as far from the plausible.

So much for the two authorities on *Ulysses* most familiar with Joyce's handwriting. But Melissa Banta, editor, with

Oscar Silverman, of *James Joyce's Letters to Sylvia Beach*, who exposes their several errors, does not inspire confidence. Ms Banta refers to Joyce's 'financial strai*gh*ts', and passes over his – though surely *not* his – 'rue G*uy*-Lussac'.

Mr. Kidd should know that the title of Sweelinck's variation cycle is '*Mein junges Leben hat ein End*', not '*eine Ende*'. A few lines above that, he writes 'neither... are mentioned, and, some paragraphs further above, 'The "Eumaeus" episode is cliché, euphemism, redundancy, and mashed metaphor ambered in a gooey sentimentality.' Whether or not the last two words are redundant, 'ambered' is a non-existent verbal form of the noun. Further, the hard substance cannot be preserved in the soft. To amber in goo?

Chapter 12

Amorous in Amherst

Austin and Mabel, Emily and Susan

The more than 250 of the thousand or so extant love letters between Emily Dickinson's brother and Mrs David Todd quoted in Polly Longsworth's *Austin and Mabel*[1] may well be the most explosive correspondence ever published concerning social and sexual mores in nineteenth-century America. Although protective Emily-ites have ignored its revelations, one of the poet's biographers, Richard B. Sewall, confirmed the book's importance because the events 'happened so close to Emily Dickinson'.

Though *Austin and Mabel* was published two years before the centenary of the poet's death (1886), the relationship between the pair was virtually ignored during the anniversary. Without naming Mrs Longsworth's book, Cynthia Griffin Wolff[2] issued the verdict that 'this all-too-well documented love affair' is 'entirely irrelevant save for one fact: Mabel Loomis Todd played a crucial role in getting Emily Dickinson's poems into print'. *The* role, surely, since Mabel not only transcribed most of the 800 poems from the undated, untitled and unsigned manuscripts found by Emily's sister Lavinia after the poet's

---

1   *Austin and Mabel. The Amherst Affair & Love Letters of Austin Dickinson and Mabel Loomis Todd*, New York, 1984.
2   *Emily Dickinson* by Cynthia Griffin Wolff, New York, 1986.

death, but even changed words 'to make them smoother'. Added to the feat of Mabel's transcriptions is her achievement in convincing her co-editor, T.W. Higginson, of their worth. But precisely because Dickinson's biography offers so little 'in the way of striking occurrence', as Wolff put it, her brother's liaison had to have been a momentous happening in her life, not a casual one to be so easily dismissed.

Sewall went on to claim that the diary of Millicent Todd Bingham, Mabel's daughter, takes us further: 'The effect on Emily? She was glad that Austin had found some comfort after his all but ruined life. In my mother's words, "Emily always respected real emotion." 'Some comfort' means four years of illicit, three-to-four-times-a-week coition. Yet Bingham herself was responsible for the long suppression of the Austin–Mabel correspondence, her disclosure taking place sixty-five years after Emily's death. To understand the circumstances of the affair it is essential to know that Austin's marriage to Susan Huntington in 1856 had been very unhappy. Nevertheless, they did produce three children, and his adulteries with Mabel began only in 1882, when he was twice her age. The Dickinson that Susan loved, however, was Emily.

Sewall assures us of the solid basis for Longsworth's comment that 'The Dickinson sisters were not only aware of their brother's intimacy with Mabel, they were accessory to it'. But he offers no supporting evidence, either here or in connection with his assertion that 'Emily, fully aware of what was occurring in her house, rejoiced in Austin's renewed happiness', and that 'dozens of notes exchanged attest to Emily and Mabel's mutual affection'. Surely a selection of these notes could have been transcribed, especially since, in the only one that is, Emily greets Mabel as 'Brother's and Sister's Friend', i.e., not as her own. Of the fewer than a dozen published communications from Emily to Mabel, only two can fairly be called letters; five consist of only one sentence, others are incomplete sentences.

Mabel was determined to meet Emily, but never did. After playing the piano and singing in the Dickinson 'Homestead', 10 September 1882, Mabel wrote: 'Miss Emily in her weird white dress was outside in the shadow hearing every word… I know I shall see her'. She did not see her until four years later, when Emily was in her weird white casket. It can be safely inferred that Mabel asked Austin to arrange a meeting, both because this would have been characteristic of Mabel, and because of a remark in her journal: 'No one has seen her in all these years except her own family.' Since Emily did receive those whom she wished to receive, this untruthful explanation probably came from Austin. After 13 December 1883, a face-to-face encounter would have been unthinkable, but the reasons for Emily's refusal before that date can only be conjectured. Was she intimidated by the worldly, gregarious, self-assured and literary-dabbling Mabel, her exact opposite?

On that 13 December, Austin Dickinson, fifty-four, married for twenty-six years and the father of three, became the lover of Mabel Loomis Todd, thirty years younger, married for four years, and the mother of Millicent. The consummation took place in the Dickinson sisters' dining room, where Emily sometimes did her writing. The diaries of Austin and Mabel reveal that their extra-marital rites were repeated thereafter about twelve times a month, then somewhat less frequently until Austin's death in 1895. In Lavinia's 1896 lawsuit against the Todds, the testimony of Maggie Maher, the sisters' housekeeper, places a higher estimate on the number of rendezvous, adding that they took place 'sometimes in the afternoon and sometimes in the fore-noon... sometimes for three or four hours, just as their consciences allowed them'. (Who said anything about consciences?)

On two occasions, Maggie apparently stumbled on the pair *in flagrante delicto.* Why Austin's wife never did the same can only be attributed to fear of her husband, and to a wife's powerlessness at the time. Susan rarely crossed the yard from her home, the 'Evergreens', to the Dickinson 'Homestead', only a few hundred feet away, but to enter and leave the latter unobserved from the window of the former would have been even more difficult a century and a half ago than it is in the overgrowth of today. Guarded by Emily and Lavinia, the 'Homestead' dining room was to remain the scene of the assignations, except for Austin's carriage during a fair-weather turn in the great outdoors, and in each others' houses when the spouses were away – as well as when hers was not. Even before the consummation, Emily wrote, surely not without irony: 'My brother is with us so often each Day, one almost forgets he passed to a wedded Home'. Yet when Emily was grieving over the death of her friend Judge Otis Lord, Mabel, but not Austin, seems to have had compunctions about using the dining room.

The correspondence supports the true-love view of the affair, as well as its passionate intensity – what Yeats said the worst of us are full of. But Mabel's diary – which also records her continuing, some eight-times-a-month, sexual relations with her husband David – blights any aura of romance, at least for non-Mormon readers. Since she usually confined her sexual activity to the 'safe' last ten days of her menstrual cycle, Mabel was perforce entertaining both men on several of the same days. Longsworth straight-facedly calls attention to Mabel's 'energetic physical commitment', but does not elaborate on her remark that Mabel's diary – surely destined one day to appear with a lurid cover as a bestseller paperback – is less specific about lovemaking with Austin than with David. Nor are particulars given of arrangements in the 'Homestead' dining room. Was the table used, or would this have inhibited the saying of grace at mealtimes, the pious adulterers reciting a prayer in unison?[3]

'Home is a Holy Thing,' Emily once wrote to Austin, and 'nothing of doubt or distrust can enter its sacred portals'. Apparently we must believe in Lares, Penates and the tutelary spirits. Love, moreover, must be 'consecrated', and laws obeyed. 'We die,' said the Deathless of Thermopylae, 'in obedience to the Law.' So Emily wrote to Mabel, after brother and brother's friend had broken the Seventh Commandment, upheld by law, society, religion and private moral codes.

Mabel had discovered at a precocious age that she 'was born with a certain lack of something in my moral nature'. She was quick to recognise, as well, that her 'strength & attractive power & magnetism' were 'enough to fascinate a room full of people'. In addition to being a talented painter, actress in amateur theatricals, musician – she had been enrolled at the New England Conservatory – Mabel was endowed with a sense of literary discernment, presumably cultivated by her

---

3   After 1875, 'meals were eaten in the kitchen, or at a little table set up in the hallway,' Mrs Longsworth wrote to the present writer, 12 May 1987. The same letter reveals that 'in winter, when the parlours were closed off, the dining room, with its couch, fireplace and desk, became a sort of winter parlour handy to the kitchen'.

father, who had known Thoreau and Whitman. She read and she wrote, publishing short stories and accounts of her travels; she was the first woman to climb Mt Fujiyama. Whereas Emily, in Washington, DC, with her Congressman father, avoided every social function, Mabel, thirty years later, was the hostess for Chester A. Arthur at a White House reception.

Unlike Mabel, Austin had no inkling of his sister's genius. Said to be Emily's 'closest confidant' – 'Tho *all others* do, yet *I* will not forsake thee,' she wrote to him. But what did she foresee as provocations from the others? When Mabel was about to leave for Boston in connection with the publication of Emily's poems, Austin asked vexatiously what she meant by 'the poems', and dismissed them as of 'no consequence'. Yet when he expressed reservations about the publication of Emily's letters, saying that she 'posed' in some of them, he could be believed.

Barton Levi St Armand's chapter[4] on Austin as an art collector reveals that his father, Edward Dickinson, while executor of his brother-in-law's estate, 'loaned' himself more than enough from the trust to pay for expensive renovations to his own house and to construct a new one for his son. As St Armand says, Dickinson *père* played 'fast and loose' with his sister's money. Or call it extortion. Longsworth's statement that Edward Dickinson 'had the most irreproachable [*sic*] record in the region' merely indicates what the region did not know. Austin bequeathed half of his estate to Mabel, not as part of his will, but by instruction to Lavinia to carry out his wishes. Though describing her to Mabel as 'utterly slippery and treacherous', he failed to realise that his death would unleash his wife's vindictiveness towards his mistress, and that families in such situations traditionally close ranks against the outsider. As might have been expected, Lavinia went back on her word, as well as on her promise to burn Mabel's letters to him, relenting only to the extent of giving Mabel and David a plot of Dickinson land. At this point Susan convinced Lavinia to sue the Todds on grounds that they had obtained her signature on the deed by misrepresentation and fraud. The Todds lost the case in

---

4   *Emily Dickinson and Her Culture: The Soul's Society*, Cambridge, 1986.

court when Mabel unaccountably failed to produce Austin's note to her confirming his intentions. But since Lavinia repeatedly perjured herself, the Dickinsons also lost the moral battle.

Dickinson biographers agree that Susan became 'spiteful' with age, but do not suggest that Austin might in any way have contributed to this unhappy development. Before the inaugural date of the affair, Mabel said that 'Susan stimulates me intellectually more than any woman I ever knew', but, when she did not acquiesce as David had done, was soon praying for her rival's demise. More importantly, Emily also had a high opinion of Susan's intellect, over the years sending her nearly 300 poems. Longsworth classifies these communications as 'love letters' that 'do not far exceed' the nineteenth-century tolerance for 'intimacy between unmarried females'. The subject was examined more closely by seventy-five scholars at a conference of the Emily Dickinson International Society at Mount Holyoke College, apropos the publication of the poems and letters exchanged between the sisters-in-law.[5] The conclusion was that an erotic attraction, as well as a literary collaboration, existed between the two women. It is difficult to form a clear impression of Susan, partly because of the warning in Emily's unflattering verse about her:

> To pity those that know her not
> Is helped by the regret
> That those who know her, know her less
> The nearer her they get.

David Todd, the oddest character of the other triangle, a direct descendant of Jonathan Edwards and of the New England of scarlet letters, was perversely, kinkily, submissive. Here the reader should take into account a history of mental illness in David's mother's family, for which, like her, he was eventually institutionalised. During the last three days of the countdown to 13 December, he and Mabel decided together that she would become Austin's mistress. David may

---

5   See *"Open Me Carefully": Emily Dickinson's Intimate Letters to Susan Huntington Dickinson,* edited by Louise Hart and Nell Smith, Ashfield, Massachusetts, 1998.

have been concerned about his tenure as professor of astronomy at Amherst College, where Austin was all-powerful, but as a philanderer himself, during as well as before his marriage, he was not in a position to insist on his spouse's fidelity. In a journal of 1890, Mabel noted that her husband was capable of 'falling immensely in love' and of 'having a piquant time of it'. Three years earlier he had begun to receive other women in the Todd home, and he once used 'lustful language' in a letter to one of them that he purposely failed to seal so that Mabel could read it, which somewhat redeemingly implies that he might have been jealous.

When the Todds moved into a new house in the autumn of 1885, Mabel and Austin made love there on ten or more Sundays in the presence of, as Austin recorded, 'a witness', who could only have been David. A few months earlier, while Mabel was in Europe and the two grass-widowers were constantly together, Austin wrote to her, sending his letters to her through David to thwart post-office gossip. One of them said: 'I think we three would have no trouble in a house together in living as you and I should wish'. David did not object to Mabel wearing Austin's wedding ring on her right hand. Like his wife and her lover, he kept a diary, in his case a record of his masturbations.

———◆———

The 'Homestead' today is 'one of the country's landmarks', Wolff's book begins – though today it has been surpassed by the 'Evergreens' as a period relic and tourist attraction (T-shirts, etc.). But Emily Dickinson's bedroom

> is unrefurbished with the lingering personality of its former occupant. It is something of a puzzle… that so many readers regard this House almost as a holy place, making the trek to western Massachusetts as if to a saint's shrine… What they ask about is seldom the work. They want to know about the *woman*.

Is this strange? Mabel's first words about Emily in 1881 established a legend:

> A lady whom people call the Myth. She has not been outside of
> her own house in thirty-five years. She dresses wholly in white,
> and her mind is said to be perfectly wonderful. She writes finely
> but no one ever sees her.

Mabel forgot to add that the poet disdained publication, which she described to Thomas Henry Higginson as 'the auction of the mind'. He responded by visiting her and reported that she spoke in a 'soft, frightened, breathless, childlike voice'.

Is the literary persona not related to the woman who created it, despite artists stepping aside and paring fingernails and poetry as an escape from personality, and despite the gap between human frailty and the strength of art, mortality and immortality?

And what is so puzzling about the pilgrimage? The poet's ever-ascending reputation has already reached an altitude near the level of Whitman's or even Eliot's. The Dickinson story, as Wolff herself says, 'seems to have become central to American life'. Wolff's book, showing that the poems lend themselves to depths, and occasionally to mere tangles of interpretation, indicates that appreciation is still far from complete.[6] Feminist critics are clearly not finished with a poet who, conquering the barrier against women – and over Hawthorne in 1855: 'America is now wholly given over to a damned mob of scribbling women' – is a legitimate feminist cause.[7] More will be said, too, by historians of modernism, for as Oscar Williams and other modern poetry anthologists understood as long ago as the 1940s, Dickinson should be considered the first of the breed.

If Emily's 'personality' does not haunt her bedroom, the visitor can still divine her physical presence. The white dress displayed in a glass case, now as much a part of American lore as the white whale, is even smaller than expected from her own and other people's descriptions. 'I have a little shape'; 'I am... small, like the Wren'; 'A

---

6   Thomas H. Johnson's chronological order into which the forty fascicles of the poems were sewn has been disputed since 1955, when his first edition of them was published, but in the variorum edition by Ralph W. Franklin that superseded it (Harvard University Press, 1999), the author argues that the fascicles are random compilations, and he accordingly revises many dates and factual details.
7   See *Emily Dickinson* by Helen McNeil, London, 1986.

little plain woman... in a clean white piqué'; 'A tiny figure in white'.
Whether she began to wear white after her father's death, or because
of a religious association – the multitude in white 'who stood before
the throne in Revelation' (Wolff); white was the dress 'of her inner
"Calvary" drama of renunciation' (Northrop Frye). She considered it
the proper attire for Death:

> This sufferer polite –
> Dressed to meet you
> See – in white.

A sense of Dickinson's solitary existence can be experienced in her
bedroom, in the west window view toward the 'Evergreens' and, on
the south side, Main Street, where a circus once passed the house: 'I
[still] feel the red in my mind.' The poignancy of her life as a recluse
is most intensely felt at the sight in one of the windowsills of a small
basket with a string for lowering her gingerbread and cookies to
her niece and other children. By 1876, Emily 'looked ill... white and
mothlike' from 'living away from the sunlight,' Helen Hunt Jackson
told her during a visit.

Wolff regards Dickinson's reclusiveness as unexceptional and of
little significance. There were precedents, she says, and in support
quotes George Whicher's *This Was a Poet*: '[Reclusiveness] has always
been a possible way of life for New England spinsters', as well as for
J.D. Salinger, Thomas Pynchon and others far from there. Moreover,
Emily and Lavinia could afford, monetarily, not to marry, and hence
'would not have to confront the rigors of childbearing', as if remaining
single were strictly a matter of choice.

Susan's obituary for Emily in the *Springfield Republican* makes
clear that their Amherst contemporaries did not see the self-
sequestration as ordinary; otherwise, her 'seclusion', Susan's word,
would not have had to be mentioned and excused. By attributing it
to 'the rare mesh of her soul', and to 'the realization that the sacred
quiet of her own home proved the fit atmosphere for her... work',
Susan may have been trying to bury speculation both about Emily's
nervous or mental illnesses ('the mad woman in the attic'), and about

Austin's adulteries. Amherst residents who had glimpsed the ghostly woman in white apparently writing by candlelight next to her window[8] must have wondered about the nature of the work. If tongues wagged that 'the intimacy existing between [Austin] and Mrs. Todd is as great as ever', they must also have talked about Emily's eccentricities. After all, almost no one knew that she was a poet.

By 1867–8, Emily was no longer 'a regular churchgoer', Wolff tells us, though she had stopped going to church at a significantly earlier date. Her absence from her father's funeral disturbed her niece: 'And where was Aunt Emily? Why did she not sit in the library with the family...?' That Emily also did not appear at her mother's funeral can be established from her invitation to Mabel to attend.

Emily seems to have been withdrawing from society ('Society for me is my misery') as early as July 1853: 'I sat in Professor Tyler's woods and saw the train off and then ran home again for fear someone would see me.' This suggests a physical stigma, blemish or disfigurement, as does her habit of talking to guests from behind a partly closed door or from the top of the stairs. Psychological roots and causes are more apparent in later years, in, for example, her wish to have the letters she sent addressed in someone else's handwriting. Whatever it was, including a possible experience beyond the known facts, *something* had happened to this twenty-two-year-old girl who had been socially active only shortly before – 'Amherst is alive with fun this winter,' she wrote in 1850 – participating in church gatherings and cooking contests, attending lectures and concerts. Yet before the end of the decade, she writes that 'someone rang the bell and I ran, as is my custom'. A prison, she said, 'gets to be a friend'. How was she traumatised? Could she have been sexually abused?

Analysis of the daguerreotype portrait of the teenage Emily indicates that she suffered from divergent strabismus (right exotropia), a congenital condition of the eye more prevalent in women than in men. Her mother and sister were also afflicted, though less

---

8   See 'Eyes Be Blind, Heart Be Still', by Sewall and Dr Martin Wand in *The New England Quarterly*, Fall 1979: 'Dickinson frequently wrote by candlelight; sometimes a line would go off the page, as if she were writing in the dark.'

severely than Emily, who is thought to have had a fifteen-degree deviation. Wolff mentions the diagnosis, but not that the Boston ophthalmologist Henry W. Williams, Emily's doctor in 1864 and 1865, had written papers on the subject, not about the reclusiveness but solely in relation to the 'eye contact deprivation', which, Wolff theorises, may explain the far-from-perfect relationship between the infant Emily and her mother.

That Emily stayed seven months with her cousins in a Cambridge boarding house is astonishing in the light of her intense homesickness nine years earlier during the few weeks with her father and sister in Washington.[9] Quite apart from what happened in Boston – Williams asked her not to write (the entire period is represented by only ten letters) and even not to walk alone – the extended time there must have been very difficult for her.[10]

No biographer, not even St Armand in his comprehensive treatment of the sun and sunset poems, seems to have attached any significance to the lines

> Before I got my eye put out –
> With just my soul –
> Upon the window pane –
> Where other Creatures put their eyes –
> Incautious – of the sun –

---

9   *Emily Dickinson: Letter to the World*, published by the Folger Shakespeare Library, establishes the dates of Dickinson's arrival in Washington and visit to the National Gallery. The booklet also includes a fascinating account of railroad travel from New York to Washington in 1855, and a fine poem by Richard Wilbur.

10 After the second visit she wrote to a friend: 'a woe, the only one that ever made me tremble... was the shutting out of all the dearest ones of time, the strongest friends of the soul – BOOKS'. Surely one of them contained Emily Brontë's poem about death:

Oh for a time when I shall sleep
Without identity
...
Three gods within this little frame
Are warring night and day;
Heaven could not hold them all, and yet
They are all held in me,
And must be mine till I forget
My present entity!

But if Emily was walleyed, or had some other eye impairment, why did Austin not mention this to Mabel, and the poet herself to T.W. Higginson in that first letter, as well known now as any of her poems, in which she reveals the colour of her eyes? Clara Green, who saw her in 1877, wrote that 'We were chiefly aware of a pair of great dark eyes set in a small, pale, delicately chiselled face and a little body'. Whatever the other factors behind Emily's withdrawal from society, the decisive one is that her genius required it.

Was Dickinson a 'Puritan to the last', as Northrop Frye believed? Wolff's well-documented argument is that by 1850 the Puritan tradition had been supplanted by Unitarianism, Revivalism and the Trinitarian belief in 'natural theology' that dominated the academic milieu to which the young Emily belonged. Whatever the truth of this, Wolff obliges the reader to accept her conclusion that Dickinson sought 'a true covenant of faith... not in... Christianity, but in... the passion between a man and a woman'. Dickinson herself says so:

> The Sweetest Heresy received
> That Man and Woman know
> Each other's Covenant
> Though the Faith accommodate but Two –

Furthermore, no other explanation can account for the secrets of the dining room in the Tanglewood tale of Mabel and Austin.

'The Bible was the text Emily most consistently sought to undermine,' Wolff goes on. Not 'the Bible', one thinks, but its unreliable Christ

> I say to you, said Jesus – That there by standing here –
> A Sort, that shall not taste of Death –
> If Jesus was sincere –

and its vindictive, arbitrary, cowardly God, who, after wrestling with Jacob at Peniel, 'retreated from us forever rather than risk combat again'. The upside of this is that 'Dickinson was deeply moved by the

fact that God, in apparent humility, had elected to become one of us':
'When Christ was divine, he was uncontented till he had been human.'
By the mid-1860s or early 1870s a 'poetry of faith had emerged'.
Looking back, 'the poetry described a long pilgrimage to faith'.

Dickinson's preoccupation with death has been put down as a 'natural
complement of an intense love of life'. Much more than that, it is an
obsession not found to the same extent in other intensely life-loving
poets. Death, the deep Stranger, is her abiding theme, the predominant
one in both frequency of references and in the inspiration of her
greatest poetry. Her vocation for dying began at an early age:

> I noticed people disappearing
> When but a little child –

She wrote conventional verse about it, even nodding toward
Cymbeline:

> This quiet Dust was Gentlemen and Ladies
> And Lads and Girls –
> Was laughter and ability and Sighing
> And Frocks and Curls

observed details of burial ceremonies

> And even when with Cords
> 'Twas lowered like a Weight –

and wondered

> Do people moulder equally,
> They bury, in the Grave?

She knew the pain of loss:

Father does not live with us now – he lives in a new house. Though it was built in an hour it is better than this. He hasn't any garden because he moved after gardens were made, so we take him the best flowers, and if we only knew he knew, perhaps we could stop crying.

She rehearsed her own dying

> To die – takes but a little while –
> They say it doesn't hurt –
> It's only fainter – by degrees –
> And then – it's out of sight –

and recognised the sensation of it

> A Wounded Deer – leaps highest –
> I've heard the Hunter tell –
> 'Tis but the Ecstasy of <u>death</u> –
> You'll find it – when you try to die –
> The easier to let go –
> She knew that death and love go together: '*is*
> there more? More than Love and Death? Then
> tell me its name.'

> If just as soon as Breath's out
> It shall belong to me
> Think of it Lover! I and thee
> Permitted – face to face to be –

But the greatest of her poems of death are those from the other side,[11] from within the upholstered coffin with the 'rafter of satin – and roof of stone', in the quiet of the tomb:

---

11 See St Armand, *op. cit.*, on Harriet Prescott Spofford's 'I Must Have Died at Ten Minutes Past One'.

> Let no Sunrise' yellow noise
> Interrupt this Ground –

Here is absolute genius of the word:

> I died for Beauty – but was scarce
> Adjusted in the Tomb
> When One who died for Truth was lain
> In an adjoining Room
> And we talked between the Rooms
> Until the Moss had reached our Lips

The personas of the poem and the poet unite, the mortal Emily Dickinson in her white dress and white casket – Higginson said that the fifty-five-year-old looked no more than thirty, her face without a wrinkle, head without a grey hair – carried 'through the grass field to the family plot' by the six Irish retainers who had worked at the Homestead:

> 'Twas just this time last year, I died
> I know I heard the Corn,
> When I was carried by the Farms.

Chapter 13

Remembering Helen Jones Carter

On 15 September 2003 I read the following memorial tribute for my dear friend Helen Carter at the Century Club, New York.

For Helen Jones Carter
July 4, 1907 – May 17, 2003

As we all know, Elliott dedicated his 'Boston Concerto' to Helen, choosing the perfect epigraph for it from William Carlos Williams:

As the rain falls, so does your love
Bathe every open object of the world.

The ovation that greeted Elliott and his new Concerto at the Proms in August 2003 acclaimed him, in Andrew Porter's words in the *Times Literary Supplement*, 'the world's greatest living composer'. This has been recognised by the musical elite since the death of the preceding titleholder in April 1971, who had himself been among the first to perceive the stature of his successor.

On 15 July 1966, the Lincoln Center Stravinsky Festival presented a staged performance of *Histoire du Soldat*, with Elliott as the Soldier, Aaron Copland as the Narrator, and – typecasting a bit – John Cage as the Devil. Three days later, Helen and Elliott dined with the Stravinskys at La Côte Basque. As always with this combination, the two composers talked about music, and so intently that neither of them noticed the famous face, better known as 'the voice', approaching their table. Helen, the first to identify the intruder, nudged Elliott, but Stravinsky saw only that a piece of paper and a pen, with which to inscribe his name on it, had been placed next to him on the table – by no means the first time this had happened to him. When he endorsed the paper without bothering to look up, Helen and Elliott were shocked. Frankie, unaccustomed to this newfound anonymity, retreated to his secluded table and rejoined Mia Farrow, who would fly with him the next day to Honolulu and become Mrs Sinatra. Situations of this kind were not new to Helen and Elliott, who had witnessed many curious incidents in their adventures with the Stravinskys.

But then, Helen and Elliott were the closest longtime friends of the Stravinskys in the American musical world, especially during the last years of the older composer's life, after his move from California to New York. Vera Stravinsky's diaries are the source of an extensive but far from complete agenda of visits, dinners, concerts, ballets, *vernissages*, experienced together with Helen and Elliott in Rome, Berlin and Dartington. I should add that George Balanchine and Nicolas and Dominique Nabokov were also frequent companions during Stravinsky's last years. Helen and Elliott, along with Balanchine, were among the very few who attended the private evening funeral service for Stravinsky on the day of his death.

'Call Helen' was Elliott's response when a difficulty of any kind arose, and call Helen we did. When Alva and I were negotiating to purchase an apartment in Venice, Helen returned us to reality with an inimitable remark: 'Just try to have a light bulb changed!'

When the tenor selected for our performance and recording of *The Rake's Progress* in New York proved incapable of learning some of the rhythmically intricate passages, and clearly had to be replaced (two days before the dress rehearsal) we turned to Helen in despair. 'Get John Garrison,' she said, knowing that he was familiar with the role. We explained to her that Garrison was vexed with us since we had chosen him for the Shepherd's part in *Oedipus Rex* instead of the title role. Helen volunteered to arrange the matter herself, and within a half hour we had an excellent as well as bonhomous 'Tom Rakewell, Esquire' for the part.

The very next day our Anne Trulove developed laryngitis, or said she did. Again, we called Helen. She proposed Lucy Shelton, but unfortunately Lucy had a previous engagement. A substitute was found, and though she was no Lucy, achieved a creditable performance.

Needless to say, Helen and Elliott were there encouraging us throughout the opera. Later, Elliott wrote praising our recording of it, and adding with his habitual perception:

> *The Rake* is wonderful. It avoids the dragging gait of the Stravinsky recording, which hurts the Third Act especially... I had forgotten that pervasive melancholy that surrounds the whole in some strange way, but adds a beauty... Perhaps Bedlam is the true artist's place in capitalist society.

———◆———

One day Alva was lamenting her inability to lure me out of the house for some exercise. She called Helen for advice, and was told: 'That's simple. Just open the door and *push* him out. I do that every day with Elliott.'

Helen's spunkiness was one of her most endearing qualities. One evening at a Fifty-Eighth Street bistro, Elliott must have sensed that Helen was on the verge of mentioning someone whose name he apparently thought impolitic to pronounce in the present company. Then suddenly Helen said to her beloved husband *sotto voce*, but distinctly: 'Don't you *dare* kick me under the table again'.

I think of Helen and Elliott as the French poet, Charles Maray, in the 1970s, thought of the Stravinskys:

> *Un Couple de Légende*
>
> *Depuis dix-neuf soixante-onze, dès que les premiers jours du printemps arrive à Venise, on voit débarquer une grande dame distingueé, qui aussitôt descendue sur les quais, se dirige vers San Michel.*

Madame Véra Stravinsky vient régulièrement se recueillir sur la
tombe de son mari...
Dans les allées, sous les cypres, se perpétue une belle légende
d'un couple hors de destin:
d'un couple qui a trouve son oasis, sa paix sous le ciel de
Vénise,
d'un couple de créateurs, lui, musicien, et elle peintre,
dont toutes les œuvres sont inspirées
d'un air étrange, féerique, d'une Venise d'un autre monde.

In 1922, shortly after his arrival in Taos, D.H. Lawrence wrote to the widower of a recently deceased friend:

> I knew Sallie was turning away to go. And what can one do. Only it hurts, the inevitable hurt... And if Sallie had to go to sleep, being really tired, having gone a long way... well, the rest of the journey she goes with us, but as a passenger now, instead of a traveller. Nevertheless, one uses words to cover up a crying inside one.

A few weeks later the same writer, on hearing the news of Katherine Mansfield's death, wrote to her husband:

> I had sent a new book I wanted Katherine to read. She'll know, though. The dead don't die. They look on and help.

Chapter 14

Evenings with T.S. Eliot

8 December 1956. After an afternoon at Hampton Court, where the hedges, fountains, fir trees and stone animals are draped in fog, we return to the Savoy for tea with T.S. Eliot. This rencontre has been organised by Stephen Spender, who fetches the poet and on arrival chases upstairs to escort the Stravinskys from their suite, leaving me feeling awkward in the lobby alone with the potentate of poetry, to whom I have not yet been introduced. When Spender returns with the Stravinskys, we proceed to the center of the virtually deserted Grill Room and sit around a circular table, the Stravinskys facing Eliot, Spender to his right, next to Vera, and I, at greater propinquity, to his left, next to I.S. After an inhibited, tentative, soft-spoken beginning, during which Eliot's right-hand fingers tap a paradiddle on an adjoining table, I.S. orders Scotch and Eliot sherry. Eliot tells I.S. that having seen him on stages and concert podiums, he had expected a much taller man. This being a sensitive subject, I.S. does not respond, but he is obviously pleased when Eliot says that he was greatly impressed by a staged performance of Stravinsky's *Oedipus Rex* at the Hamburg Opera. Attempting to forge a connection to Eliot's work, I.S. says that he was introduced to it in the early 1920s by Jacques Rivière, Maritain, Paul Valéry and St-John Perse.

What threatens to be a deadening pause follows, until Vera breaks the formality: 'Mr. Eliot, my husband's *Canticum Sacrum* owes something to you.' When she adds, 'Murder in the Cathedral', Eliot bolts upright and looks alarmed, until she explains that 'Your play was *Time* magazine's heading for a review of the premiere of the work in the Basilica of St Mark's', whereupon he thrusts his head back and laughs, a slow 'ha, ha, ha'. She goes on to say that Cardinal Roncalli, later Pope John XXIII, made the concert available to everyone by arranging for its broadcast in the Piazza San Marco, where, even after midnight, a throng had gathered waiting for Stravinsky to emerge. He was deeply moved by the warm applause that greeted him.

Hunched, head bent forward and down from a lifetime of reading and writing, Eliot stiffly twists his neck along with his head when turning in Spender's direction and in mine. His slowly measured speech is livelier in French, in which, two or three times, I.S. seeks refuge. The voice is weary, mournful, and as bleak as the December afternoon – when he speaks at all, that is, for most of the talk issues from I.S., and Spender alone initiates subjects and adds chips of kindling under expiring ones. Of these, the *Rake* generates a few sparks, giving I.S. an opportunity to describe Auden working, how the librettist would start out each morning noting down the composer's ideas, trying to imagine a scene and construct a plot. He went about this, I.S. says, 'as anyone else would go about drafting a business letter'.

Suddenly Spender proposes a subject for a play, based on one by Euripides, outlining it to Eliot in a few sentences. 'But you must write it yourself, Stephen,' he says, in a tone that seems to convey the meaning 'your sort of thing but not mine', yet it is evident that Eliot is fond of him personally. Not afraid of big topics, Stephen broaches the question of Wagner's influence, apart from *Tristan* in *The Waste Land*, and Eliot admits that Wagner once had a powerful effect on him. We wait with baited breath for more, but the subject dies with the statement, having been made in a way that seems to forbid extenuation.

Wagner leads to Germany and an opportunity for I.S. to describe his recent experiences in a Munich hospital. He does this partly to account for his considerable intake of liquids, the whiskey having been followed by a second and a third and by beer and tea. Unlike Eliot, I.S. gestures as he talks, and he employs his hands to illustrate the sludgy texture of his blood. 'The doctors say that my blood is so thick it could turn into crystals, like rubies, unless I drink a great deal', and he moulds the air so that we imagine jewels forming. Eliot's eyes indicate that he was struck by the image, but he responds morosely with 'A doctor in Munich once told me I had the thinnest blood he had ever tested', which brings a half-suppressed smile to Spender's face.

Both Eliot and I.S. complain about autograph seekers and requests for photographs. I.S. says that he ignores such letters unless the photo, envelope, and stamps are enclosed, 'because they cost money', a remark confirming his notorious lack of magnanimity that embarrasses V. He goes on about publicity as a major nuisance in his life and says that this very morning he was awakened by a call from the BBC requesting a comment on a broadcast performance of one of his pieces. 'I told them that we never listen to the radio,' V. says, which earns a chuckle from Eliot, who is beginning to thaw and become almost convivial. Alas, just then I.S. excuses himself saying he has an appointment with his doctor for a venesection. When we stand, I notice that he is at least two feet shorter than Spender and a foot-and-a-half shorter than the stooped Eliot.

3 December 1958. London. We are taken by limousine to a reception for Eliot and I.S. at the Faber offices. Many photos are taken of the two men and their wives. After the party the Eliots escort us to their favorite restaurant, L'Ecu de France.

8 December 1958. Dinner with the Eliots in their Kensington Court Gardens ground floor flat. The name does not appear on the tenants' roster, but they are holding hands in the open door when we arrive. The walls are bare, except for Wyndham Lewis's portrait of the poet, and numerous bookshelves, some of them in the dining room, 'which is where arguments come up,' Eliot says, 'and the reason that dictionaries and reference books should be kept there'. As if to illustrate the claim, and in response to some speculations by I.S. concerning the word 'paraclete', T.S.E. fetches a well-worn Liddell and Scott from behind his own chair, but before opening it offers a synonym ('the comforter'). He helps again when I.S. is unable to recall the name of the monastic order on San Lazzaro degli Armeni in Venice. 'The Mechitarist Fathers,' Eliot says, adding a curious tale about their history. He provides lapidary translations for his wife of the foreign expressions that occur regularly in I.S.'s talk but denies ever having been a linguist: 'I only pretended to be one in order to get a job in a bank.' A quiet man, he deliberates his every word, and his sentences trail off in *diminuendo*. But the life in him is not in his voice but in his clear, gray, piercingly intelligent eyes. He breathes heavily and harrumphs a great deal, 'Hm, hmm, hmmm', each 'm' deepening the significance, it seems. His high-pitched laugh is too slow, and we cannot protract our own merriment long enough to cover it. Eliot's fingers are constantly folding and unfolding, or touching tip to tip, which makes me aware that I.S.'s hands, otherwise remarkable for the large spread between the knuckles, are the steadiest, least tremulous, I have ever seen.

Eliot carves and serves the meat, and, to refill our glasses, walks around the table like a sommelier. His manner is always formal, reserved, parsonical, his every comment carefully cogitated, and he tends to restrict himself to implications. In comparison, I.S. seems to think with the tip of his tongue. Asked about public readings, Eliot says, 'I cannot recite my poetry from memory because it was rewritten so many times that I forget which version was final'. Most of his stories are self-deprecating:

> One day in a New York taxi with Djuna Barnes, I noticed that the driver had become engrossed in our conversation. After she left, he asked me whether "that woman was a writer". On one occasion, during a grounding at Gander, I became aware of a young, academic-type female watching me and hovering ever closer. I invited her for tea and accompanied her to a counter, fearing the worst – what had I *really* meant by such and such a line. Then it came. She was preparing a thesis on Virginia Woolf, and, since I had known her, what did I think of her novels?

When the talk turns to mutual French friends, Eliot is interested above all in I.S.'s recollections of Jacques Rivière and brother-in-law, Alain-Fournier. 'Cocteau was very brilliant when I saw him last,' Eliot says, 'but I had the impression he was rehearsing for a more important occasion.' During a tense interval I mention Hugh Kenner's *The Invisible Poet.* T.S.E. has not read the book and fidgets nervously until I say that it is insightful on the plays. I.S., in a similar situation, is always fortified with killing comebacks.

Table talk, otherwise, is about taxes – much mortifying V. when her spouse expresses guilt on learning that tonight's dinner is not deductible – and on Valerie Eliot's friend, Dylan Thomas. T.S.E. says that 'He had the richest gift of humor of any contemporary poet,' and 'two or three of his war poems remain unsurpassed. He might have written a good comedy, though whether he could have concocted a libretto I am unable to say.' The only other poetry mentioned is the incidental verse in Scott's *The Heart of Midlothian,* which Eliot deems the best that the novelist ever wrote.

We drink sherry before, claret during, whiskey after dinner, at which time Eliot brings a scrapbook bulging with photographs and clippings and asks I.S. to compose something for it, saying that he writes in it himself every night.

> *A time for the evening under lamplight*
> *(The evening with the photograph album)*

During the return to Claridge's, I.S. says: 'If not the most exuberant man I have ever known, he may be the purest'.

6 September 1959. London. The Eliots for dinner at Claridge's. T.S.E. looks younger and *is* livelier than last year, though he seems to think of himself as a hoary ancient with little time left. Social obligations are the bane of his existence, he says. 'I cannot accept lectures because the people who pay for them expect me to attend cocktail parties at which I am caught between someone wanting to know what I think of Existentialism and someone asking what I meant by this or that poem.' When Mrs Eliot asks if we have read 'Edmund Wilson's attack on my husband' T.S.E. describes Wilson as a brainpicker. I know, because he once tried to get me drunk and pick mine. He is insanely jealous of all original writers, and his only good line must have come from personal experience or been told to him by someone else. In one of his stories, a man stroking a woman's back remarks on how soft it is. She says: 'What did you expect, scales?'

'There are more Chinese characters than ever in Pound's new *Cantos*,' Eliot observes. 'Ezra is becoming the best Chinese poet in English.' After I.S. gives some of his impressions of Japanese theater, Eliot says he once watched a Noh dancer in Yeats's *The Hawk's Well* and was persuaded by the performance: 'One really could believe that the dancer had become a bird.' He asks I.S. about Japanese tastes in Western theatre: 'Ionesco, I suppose, and Tennessee Williams?' When Büchner is mentioned, Eliot astutely remarks that '*Wozzeck* is too simple for a play, just simple enough for an opera.'

He gazes at each of us in rotation, and slows down to beam affection toward his wife each time around. He drinks a gin and tonic before, claret during, and whiskey after his dinner (partridge), for while it is evident that he enjoys sniffing the cheese platter, after some hesitation and a final moment of indecision, he does not actually choose one. When Aldous's name is mentioned, Eliot says, unkindly and unnecessarily, 'I don't read him, of course; I am much too fond of him for that. He was pessimistic when we saw him last. Too many people in the world and more all the time. So there are, indeed, indeed.' One looks for a hidden twist in the echoed word.

Telling us about plans to visit his Missouri birthplace, he says that the house doesn't exist any more. 'A plaque would surely go to one of the neighbours.'

16 October 1961. Zurich to London. Coincidentally on the same plane with Otto Klemperer and his daughter, Lotte, we arrive just in time for dinner with the Eliots at the Savoy. More stooped than when we last saw him, the poet leans forward when he stands, as if from a yoke, with legs apart, like a skier ready to start down a slope. His colouring has changed, too: the lips and large ears are damson, the lines of his face leaner and sharper, reminding me of one of those ceramic birds we have just seen in the exhibition of Hittite art in Zurich.

He complains of the nuisance of having to refuse invitations to the Tagore centenary.

> I took a volume from the library the other day to be certain that I had not made a mistake, but I could make nothing of it. Difficult to tell that to the Indians, though, or to admit that one does not put their man with Dante or Shakespeare. Bill Yeats claimed to admire Tagore, but he was making a case for 'the East' at the time. I receive regular shipments of the works of new Indian poets, together with letters inviting my comments. Once I replied, ripping the thing apart, only to find my by-no-means-complimentary letter appearing as a preface to the published poems.

(This is not an unheard-of response, Gauguin having printed a critical letter from Strindberg in an exhibition catalogue.) 'In payment I received a Kashmir shawl, which I returned. Soon after, another and much better shawl came with a note that the first one had not been worthy of me.'

Tonight's dinner has been arranged to discuss a proposal that I.S. set 'two lyrical stanzas', as Eliot identifies them, from 'Little Gidding', though he expresses doubt 'that they can be set'. But nothing of this is mentioned, and instead the poet and the musician talk about favorite *romans policiers* and about Voltaire's tragedies which they have not read. 'I knocked down a complete Voltaire at auction when I first came to England, but never went to pick it up. That has been on my conscience ever since.'

Both artists are Simenon addicts. I.S. estimates that he must have read at least sixty of the novels, and Eliot confesses that 'I can read about Maigret when I can read nothing else'. Another mutually admired sleuth is Perry Mason, partly because 'the author knows California law, but Chandler was a better writer' – this from Eliot. Concerning the debate in a recent *TLS* on mistranslations in the *New English Bible*, Eliot admits to 'enjoying this sort of thing, when I know, as I do now, that I have the right end of the stick'. When Pound's name comes up, Eliot confides that

> Ezra was always a poor judge of people, and indeed of most things except poetry. He really did believe that his monetary ideas would change the world. And weren't we all tarred by that brush? But he had great gifts, and I owe more to him than to anyone else. Which reminds me that I owe him a letter; hm, hm, difficult to know what to say.

A noncommittal 'Yes?' escapes Eliot's lips during each pause in the conversation, until V. recounts some of our Yugoslavian adventures, and at the same time voices some criticisms of Switzerland, including Rilke's 'It is a waiting room on the walls of which Swiss views have been hung up'. At this Eliot interposes a whole sentence: 'I see what you mean, but I like it because more than any other country it resembles what it used to be.'

28 May 1963. London. The Eliots come for a dinner at the Savoy. Apropos my Russian diary in *Encounter* – knowing that he has read it nearly ruins my evening – he says that the British Arts Council asked him to receive Yevtushenko, but that the meeting was not a success: 'I am unable to speak through a translator I do not know. Incidentally, Igor, one of your Russian "r"s reminds me of the variety of "r" sounds in Sanskrit that Indians do not recognise as differentiations but nevertheless pronounce.'

29 May 1963. From a fiftieth-anniversary performance of *Sacre* conducted by Pierre Monteux at Albert Hall, we go to the Eliots' for late-night cheese, apples and single malt-Scotch, this in preference to a party given in I.S's honour by Ian Fleming. The Eliots had heard the concert 'on the wireless' and enthusiastically applaud the composer as he enters. T.S.E. compares tonight's ovation with the reception of the ballet in London in 1921 and adds, 'In general, the English think it is polite to laugh when confronted by something serious they do not understand'. The conversation turns to this afternoon's Derby: 'I used to wager in the Calcutta Sweepstakes,' Eliot says, 'but I never drew a horse. During a visit to Stockholm in 1948 I put some money on a long shot called Queen Mary – out of loyalty, of course, not because of a hunch – but we came in last.' Before we depart he inscribes my copy of his new essay on George Herbert, remarking that 'Herbert is one of the very few poets whom I can still read again and again. Mallarmé is another, and, hm, so is Edward Lear...'

11 December 1963. New York. We fetch the Eliots at the River Club on East Fifty-Second Street in a roomy limousine. He has become frail, and, with his wife Valerie, I help him descend the winding staircase from his suite to the lobby and down the front steps to the car. Entering it, he declares that 'This is New York's most convenient street, because it is a dead end.' On the way to the 'Pavillon' a glimpse of the United Nations building provokes a denunciation from the poet as 'the centre of an anti-European conspiracy'. At table he eats almost no food and drinks nothing, but from time to time sits upright and focuses those unforgettable eyes on each of us in turn, calling me 'Robert' for the first time. 'I am rereading *Nostromo*,' he says, adding that 'After first reading Conrad it was a terrible shock to hear him talk. He had a very guttural accent.' 'Like mine?' I.S. asks, but Eliot evades this with: 'Yours, Igor, is easier to understand.' At one point, complaining of the overheated room, Eliot removes his jacket and the blue sweater underneath, exposing bright red suspenders. The room briefly becomes silent, but his wife quickly helps him back into his jacket. To distract the attention of other diners, I interject the unneeded information that Conrad's and I.S.'s fathers were born a few versts apart, in Chernigov, Eastern Poland, and that both the novelist and the composer came to English via French, as their third culture, that both were patricians who hated the regimes from which they had exiled themselves, and that both remained aloof from Western politics. *Under Western Eyes* is a disappointing book, Eliot adds.

On the subject of languages, Eliot says: 'My Italian was quite fluent when I was at Lloyds, but Dante's Italian is not the most suitable instrument for modern business phraseology. I had a smattering of Rumanian, too, and of demotic Greek, for which reason the manager of the bank insisted that I must also know Polish, indeed, not to know it was illogical.'

When we leave, full of presentiments that this may be our last meeting, Stravinsky and Eliot walk arm in arm to the *vestiare*, where the maître d'hôtel remarks very audibly to the attendant: 'There you see together the greatest living poet and the greatest living musician.' Since the statement has been overheard, V. shields the two men from embarrassment by saying in exactly the right tone: 'Well, they do their best.'

Chapter 15

'An Excellent Pass of Pate'

Eliot's 1926 Clark Lectures at Cambridge and the abbreviation of them as the Turnbull Lectures, read by him at Johns Hopkins University in May 1933, shed a glimmer of light on his feelings towards his first wife, Vivienne.[1]

F. Scott Fitzgerald was Eliot's fellow houseguest at the Turnbull estate in Towson, Maryland, while the poet delivered the Turnbull Lectures. Fitzgerald wrote to Edmund Wilson that he liked Eliot 'fine', that he had read, presumably on Eliot's request, some of Eliot's poetry for an evening gathering, but that Eliot himself seemed 'very broken and sad and shrunk inside'. Ronald Schuchard reveals that on 14 March Eliot wrote to Ottoline Morrell, informing her that he had asked for a Deed of Separation from Vivienne: 'For my part, I should prefer never to see her again; for hers I do not believe that it can be good for any woman to live with a man to whom she is morally, in the larger sense, unpleasant, as well as physically indifferent'. The syntax seems to make the last phrase say the opposite of what he so obviously means: that *he* finds *her* physically repugnant.

Eliot's lectures are less concentrated than his essays, and most critics rate the two series of talks, dating from the same tour that brought him to Harvard (*The Use of Poetry and The Use of Criticism*),

---

1   *T.S. Eliot: The Varieties of Metaphysical Poetry.* Edited and introduced by Ronald Schuchard, London, 1993.

the University of Virginia (*After Strange Gods*), and Johns Hopkins (the Turnbull Lectures), as his weakest books. When Ezra Pound wrote in the *New English Weekly*, June 1934, that the Harvard lectures should not have been published, Eliot responded in the same periodical, 'wholeheartedly' agreeing with him – 'an unsatisfactory attempt to say something worth saying' – but tore into the manner of his criticism, ending with a parody of Pound's backwoods prose. When the Virginia Lectures appeared in the same year as *The Use of Poetry and The Use of Criticism*, the reaction to Eliot's extreme rightist views and blatant anti-Semitism was so negative that they were never reprinted.

In contrast, the Clark Lectures are perhaps too concentrated, in spite of their wide range of allusions to, for a sampling, the music dramas and influence of Wagner, the Spanish mystics as psychologists, the German mystics as heretics (the school of Eckhart), the French poets, Baudelaire, Laforgue, Corbière, Verlaine, Mallarmé, Rimbaud – without whom Eliot doubts whether 'I should have been able to write poetry at all' – and even, 'in their peculiar mode of escape from life', the surrealists. What the reader doubts is that even the most sophisticated audience, and Eliot's included A.E. Housman, Sir G.F. (*The Golden Bough*) Frazer, G.E. Moore, A.N. Whitehead and I.A. Richards, would grasp many of the references in Eliot's arguments. Indeed, without Schuchard's guidance some passages are scarcely coherent. He identifies and corrects quotations; provides translations for most of those in Latin, Italian and French; footnotes references to Eliot's other writings relating to the same subjects; and cross-references the British and Baltimore texts. Schuchard's clarifications of meanings, his account of the background, the origins, the composition and reception of the lectures, and his history of the manuscript, are indispensable to the reader's comprehension of them. Heretofore the Clark Lectures have been available to only a few scholars, none of whom conveyed any idea of the richness of the contents and the new areas of Eliot's 'cranial lodgings' that they open up.

As in all of Eliot's criticism, the theoretical parts are less engaging than the close-up analyses of individual poets, in this case Crashaw, Cowley and Donne. 'Lectures on Donne', Eliot's title for his 1931 essay 'Donne in Our Time', extend and amplify his caustic earlier

(1921) remarks on 'The Metaphysical Poets' ('Keats and Shelley died, and Tennyson and Browning ruminated'); the appellation is Johnson's, who vividly described this species of poetry as one in which 'heterogeneous ideas are yoked by violence together'. The 'force of this impeachment', Eliot observes, 'lies in the failure of the conjunction, the fact that often the ideas are yoked but not united'.

Eliot turns to Johnson again in the lectures for help in structuring the meaning of 'metaphysical'. He elaborates on his own that 'the tincture of human emotions by philosophy... is essential to metaphysical poetry' and that metaphysical poetry is not likely to issue from the 'political cosmologies of the immediate future' or 'from a philosophy which lays under cultivation only the more social emotions and virtues'. The metaphysical poet must be subjective, he goes on, reminding us that 'it is not for nothing that the *Divine Comedy* is related in the first person'. His distinction between this metaphysical subjectivism and Milton's 'self-dramatizing' kind is that 'Milton... expresses his feelings towards the world through a dramatic figure', whereas 'the metaphysical poet deals with his feelings directly... One is the attitude of the theater, the other that of the confessional'.

The largely negative 1931 essay, 'Donne in Our Time', should be read as a corrective to the lectures and a gauge of the change in Eliot after his reception into the Church of England (June 1927). He now decides that 'Donne's poetry is a concern of the present and recent past rather than of the future'. Furthermore, Donne is 'not even an absolutely first-rate devotional poet', and his sermons, less original than his satires, 'will disappear as suddenly as they have appeared'. Donne's '"scoffing at the fickleness of women... comes to me with none of the terrible sincerity of Swift's vituperation of the human race'. (In the lectures, Swift is 'the colossal'.) Donne had a legal, rather than a theological or philosophical, mind, and might today 'have been a very great company lawyer'.

The lectures devote less space to Crashaw, and still less to Cowley, whom Eliot characterises as a 'pathetic little celibate epicurean, paraphrasing Horace on the virtues of a country life', and providing 'an analogy to Saint-Evremond and the French freethinkers'. Only a few months after writing this, Eliot took a vow of celibacy himself, an ostentatious action, one would think, for an inaction that might well have remained private.

Eliot soon withdrew his Crashaw essay, regrettably, if only for the loss of his observation on the poem 'The Tear' of the Blessed Virgin:

> Faire Drop, why quak'st thou so?
> 'Cause thou streight must lay thy Head
> In the Dust? O no;
> The Dust shall never bee thy Bed
> A pillow for thee will I bring
> Stuft with Downe of Angels wing.

Eliot wryly notes that 'There is no warrant for bringing a pillow (and what a pillow!) for the *head* of a *tear*'.

One of the lectures examines some lines from the same poem,

> What bright soft thing is this?
> A moist spark it is,
> A watry Diamond,

and concludes that '"soft thing" is good, for a tear, "moist spark" is still better, and "the water of a diamond" is an excellent pass of pate', this last phrase describing Trinculo's display of wit in *The Tempest*. One of Eliot's own excellent passes of pate occurs near the beginning of the third Clark lecture: 'The human mind, when it comes to a terminus, hastens to look up the next train for almost anywhere.'

Chapter 16

Vivienne

I

Eliot inscribed a copy of his *Poems, 1909-1925*: 'For my dearest Vivienne, this book, which no one else will quite understand.' One of his biographers asserts that

> without knowledge of Eliot's first, tragic marriage, a complete appreciation of his poems is impossible. No matter what Flaubert, Valéry, and Eliot may have said about the objective impersonality of art, the full heartrending meaning of *The Waste Land* and *Ash Wednesday* depends on it.[1]

Carole Seymour-Jones's biography of Eliot's first wife[2] adds further notes toward the definition of her mysterious spouse, and explores a fresh cache of bisexual Bloomsbury gossip that significantly amplifies the portrait of him. 'Viv' predeceased 'Tom' by eighteen years, a creatively fallow period also covered by the book. *Painted Shadow* has been denigrated as part of a 'campaign against Eliot', but the campaign it exposes is the one to ignore his first wife, presented

---

1   *T.S. Eliot, An Imperfect Life*, by Lyndall Gordon, London, 1998.
2   *Painted Shadow: A Life of Vivienne Eliot, First Wife of T. S. Eliot, and the Long-Suppressed Truth About Her Influence on His Genius*, New York, 2001.

here as his troublesome sometime muse. On several points the new book controverts Lyndall Gordon's semi-authorised biographical studies, in which Vivienne receives only half the index space given to Emily Hale, Eliot's Bostonian friend whose personal connection with him was immeasurably less close than that of the tenacious English woman with whom he somehow managed to live most of the time between their wedding in 1915 and separation in 1933. Vivienne, of course, does not really have a biography apart from Eliot. What the book offers instead is a surprisingly unexplored intimate perspective based in large part on Vivienne's correspondence, her contributions to *The Criterion*, her writings still in manuscript and unpublished diaries, of which only 1919 is complete.

—•—

Vivienne Haigh-Wood was born in 1888, four months before Eliot, in the Lancashire cotton-mill town of Bury, to which her parents had journeyed from London for a one-man exhibition of her father's paintings. He had studied at the Royal Academy School in London, become an Academician himself, and, born into a prosperous family, was not dependent on his art for his livelihood. His Anglo-Irish wife also had financial expectations, which must be said because Vivienne's material position was superior to Tom's, a calculated factor perhaps in their impulsive and clandestine marriage, which Eliot's family had opposed, as they did his choice of a possible career as a writer in England over that of a philosophy professor in America, for which he had been educated at Harvard. The nascent poet was obliged to accept support at one period from, among others and most generously, his Harvard mentor Bertrand Russell, whom he had re-encountered on a street in Oxford in October 1914.

The sexual and temperamental incompatibility of Vivienne and Tom is an overworked subject, but the book contains new material on this as well as on her background and childhood. As a young girl, Vivienne was subject to a variety of disorders, including tuberculosis of the bone, for which, more than once, she underwent surgery. A more disruptive affliction was that of her too frequent, unpredictable, and painfully protracted menstrual periods, accompanied by abdominal cramps and severe mood swings. It is now thought that she suffered from a hormonal imbalance, curable today by the contraceptive pill, but whatever the cause, menstruation, the subject itself taboo at the time, was a torment for her, bringing on crying fits and disabling attacks of nerves. The drugs prescribed seemed to exacerbate her maladies, which in later years included colitis – 'Tom,' Virginia Woolf thought, 'was inclined to particularise the state of Vivienne's bowels too closely' – neuralgia, migraines and hallucinations of demons who emitted 'groans, shrieks, and imprecations'. (Vivienne's best writing is in her descriptions of illness.) A victim of insomnia as well, she was dosed with bromides, chloral and other addictive remedies.

That Vivienne was also intelligent and physically attractive is established by her close relationship with Bertrand Russell. Though not educated to the highest levels, she had attended exclusive schools, was taken by her parents to France and Switzerland, and learned to speak fluent French. She met Eliot at an Oxford social function through a mutual American school friend and her current suitor, Scofield Thayer (whose 'wife had a baby daughter by the poet e.e. cummings, whom she later married'.) Vivienne soon fell in love with the complex, shy, silent Eliot, and he, however ambiguously, with her. As all the world knows, the marriage, perhaps unconsummated,[3] was a disaster.

One of Seymour-Jones's theses is that sexual and marital dysfunctions notwithstanding, Vivienne became both the source and the subject of some of Eliot's poetry, stimulating, if not directly inspiring, his creativity. As late as 1936, three years after the Eliots had separated, Virginia Woolf, the first to perceive that part of *The Waste Land* is the autobiography of the marriage, admitted to Clive Bell that Vivienne was 'the true inspiration of Tom'. But Virginia could also write cruelly about her: 'Was there ever such torture since life began! – to bear her on one's shoulders, biting, wriggling, raving, scratching... This bag of ferrets is what Tom wears around his neck.'

---

3   Logan Pearsall Smith maintained that 'Eliot had compromised Miss Haigh-Wood and then felt obliged as an American gentleman, the New England mode being stricter than ours, to propose to her'.

Bertrand Russell realised this as well, observing that the couple was perfectly matched. As a prime source of succor to the Eliots through a long patch of their troubles, he came to the conclusion that 'their troubles were what they most enjoyed'.

The account of Vivienne's collaborative assistance to Eliot in *The Waste Land* and her contributions, under aliases, to *The Criterion* holds some surprises. Eliot's remark to his friend Sydney Schiff, on finishing a draft of 'The Fire Sermon' (*The Waste Land*) in November 1921, acknowledges the first part of this: 'I do not know if it will do, and I must wait for Vivienne's opinion.' This letter, sent from a clinic in Lausanne, also attests that Dr Vittoz, the psychiatrist and guru noted for his talent in achieving 'transference' between therapist and patient, was succeeding in Eliot's case.[4] Vivienne, meanwhile, lived with the Pounds in Paris, where Ezra took her three times to visit Joyce, who was 'wearing a long coat and tennis shoes', and whom she described as 'cantankerous'.

Vivienne either wrote the following lines in *The Waste Land* or is being quoted verbatim:

> My nerves are bad tonight. Yes, bad. Stay with me.
> Speak to me. Why do you never speak. Speak.

In view of them, her demand that Eliot delete the line, 'The ivory men made company between us', as too revealing of their lack of communication, seems inconsistent.[5] Though Pound cut most of Vivienne's contributions to the poem, he retained her improvements to the Cockneyisms in the Lil/Albert scene, as well as the line, in her hand in the manuscript, 'What you get married for if you don't want children?' Vivienne is as central to *The Waste Land* as is the illusory Jean Verdenal (*Phlébas le Phénicien*), Eliot's lost same-sex love.

Vivienne's writings in *The Criterion* of 1924–5 are a focal subject of the book. She chose the arrogant title of the publication, helped

---

4   Julian Huxley, a patient of Vittoz's the year before, confirmed Eliot's favourable opinion of him.
5   Eliot restored it from memory in 1960.

to edit its contents, and to prepare each issue with her husband in their own home. On 24 February 1924 Eliot wrote to Schiff: 'We have both been working at top pitch for the last five weeks to get out the *Criterion*'. She reviewed books, and published her poems, stories, and diaries, always under an alias, of which her favourite was 'Fanny Marlow', the surname being that of the residence Russell had put at the Eliots' disposal, the first name that of the most enticing to the great logician of her anatomical features. To judge from the quotations in *Painted Shadow*, her best writing did not appear in *The Criterion*, but in the unpublished 'Diary of the Rive Gauche', an original and perceptive piece about an American in Paris. Eliot's own observations on Americans abroad – almost always 'very immature' – are supercilious, as in a remark on seeing his old friend Conrad Aiken in London: 'stupider than I remember him; in fact, stupid.' Perhaps Eliot had heard that Aiken referred to him as 'the Tsetse fly'.

Vivienne's verse, though not wholly without merit, is affected and too imitative of her husband's: 'One's soul stirs stiffly out of the dead embers of winter – but toward what spring?' Eliot felt compelled to defend her work to *The Criterion*'s assistant editor, Richard Aldington:[6] 'She is very diffident and very aware that her mind is untrained but she has an original mind. In my opinion a great deal of what she writes is quite good enough for *The Criterion*.' Eliot also trusted her literary judgement concerning his poetry. He wrote to his brother Henry in December 1922: 'I consider my Sweeney poems as serious as anything I have written... I do not know anyone who agrees with me... except Vivienne and William Butler Yeats, who have both said much the same thing about them.' At this date (1924) she was an asset to him, not only by filling up columns of short reviews, but also, in Seymour-Jones's words, by 'sparkling at literary gatherings, where her spontaneity provided a refreshing contrast to the thrusts and parries of the literary-minded guests'. What disturbs us are her confession in a 1924 letter to Pound that she had written 'nearly the whole of the last *Criterion*', and the revelations that she ghost-

---

6   Aldington, almost alone, recognised Eliot's *The Sacred Wood* (1920) as 'the most original contribution to our critical literature during the last decade'.

wrote 'On the Eve', published in the January 1925 *Criterion* under her husband's name.[7]

Vivienne's symptoms of growing mental instability began to increase at the beginning of the 1930s, together with a penchant for humiliating Eliot in public. W.H. Auden used to tell a story of arriving at the Eliots for dinner (in 1932), of being received by Vivienne, of saying 'We are very pleased to be here, Mrs Eliot', and of her response: 'Tom's not pleased'. At one dinner party, according to Seymour-Jones, 'both Eliots directed streams of hatred at each other throughout the meal,' until embarrassed guests began to depart. '"There is no such thing as pure intellect," Eliot declared. Vivienne interrupted angrily: "What do you mean? You know perfectly well that every night you tell me that there is such a thing: and what's more that you have it, and that nobody else has it."' Eliot scratched back with 'You don't know what you're saying'. But Conrad Aiken later reported that 'Vivienne did not appear mad to me'.

The final chapter of Vivienne's life is both the climax of the book and a complete blank: her nine-year incarceration in an asylum for the insane. In July 1938, the police found her wandering in a London street at five in the morning and in a state of mental confusion, saying that she was hiding from mysterious people and had heard that 'Tom had been beheaded'. Her brother, Maurice Haigh-Wood, came to fetch her and to obtain a magistrate's warrant for her commitment to Northumberland House, a home for the mentally ill. Maurice informed Eliot, who, not so coincidentally, perhaps, was vacationing with Emily Hale in Gloucestershire, but he refused either to come to London or to share the responsibilities. On several occasions in 1980, Maurice recounted the full proceedings to Michael Hastings, author of the play *Tom and Viv.* The following excerpt calls Eliot's involvement into question:

---

7   Vivienne's papers were deposited at the Bodleian Library in 1947 by her brother, but the black notebook containing the drafts of her stories, with editing in T.S. Eliot's hand, has been missing since 1990.

> It was only when I saw Vivie in the asylum for the last time I
> realized I had done something very wrong. She was as sane as I
> was. I did what I hadn't done in years. I sat in front of Vivie and
> actually burst into tears... What Tom and I did was wrong... I
> did everything Tom told me to.

One would like to think that the poet had Vivienne in mind years later when he wrote: '... the shame / Of motives late revealed and the awareness / Of things ill done and done to other's harm...' but this seems improbable in view of the mindset he had maintained for a decade. Obviously he hated her, and on hearing the news of her death seems not to have allowed any remorse to spoil his sense of relief.

In the presence of two doctors who apparently did not know Vivienne, Maurice signed the certification papers. But Maurice insisted that the confinement was instigated by Eliot, who clearly wished to eradicate Vivienne from his life.[8] In 1932, when Eliot was invited to give the Norton Lectures at Harvard, Vivienne accompanied him to Southampton. Months later he wrote to his London solicitor asking him to obtain a legal separation from her on grounds that she had become a nuisance and embarrassment to him. On his return to England in the summer of 1933, when by prearrangement he and Vivienne met for the last time in the solicitor's office to sign papers, she held his hand but he would not look at her. Henceforth he went into hiding, constantly changing addresses to avoid her, and refusing to receive her at his Faber office.

In fact Vivienne did encounter Eliot a second time. On 18 November 1935, at the *Sunday Times* Book Fair in Lower Regent Street, she accosted him as he was walking to the platform to give a lecture. 'Tom,' she said, whereupon he seized her hand and said, 'How do you *do*,' loudly, so that anyone overhearing would suppose this to be a first meeting. She stood next to him throughout his talk, wearing her Fascist black Macintosh and black beret, then handed three of

---

8   In 1944 Eliot told Mary Trevelyan (see below) that Vivienne had been made a Ward of Chancery at his instigation, and that because of the 'V2 bombs' he had tried to have her moved to an institution farther from London, but Maurice, whose permission was necessary, was with the British Army at an unknown location in Italy.

his recent books to him to sign, and asked him to come with her. He could hardly refuse the signatures in front of a queue of autograph seekers but said, 'I cannot talk to you now', and as soon as possible departed with an unidentified young man.

The biographer believes that Vivienne's condition did not justify permanent confinement, virtually severed from all contact with the outside world. On two occasions, she had been a patient in an establishment for nervous disorders in Malmaison, France, one of them jointly with Eliot, and been discharged as stabilised both times. She seems to have been treated well there and was much liked, and the same was true of the Eliots' stay together in June 1927 (not mentioned in *Painted Shadow*) in a sanitarium for mental disorders at Divonne-les-Bains, near Geneva. One alternative was that Vivienne's family inheritance, administered by Maurice and Eliot, was substantial enough to have made home-care an option. Eliot's widow, Valerie, has testified that 'restraints were sometimes necessary', which she can have known only from him, and once Vivienne had attempted to escape.

Eliot seems to have made no inquiry regarding the conditions of Vivienne's care and well-being.[9] He did not contact her – her letters to him at Faber were returned unopened – yet must have heard something about her from Enid Faber, the publisher's wife, who visited her faithfully throughout the war. But no word of these meetings has ever appeared in print. Seymour-Jones suggests that Vivienne may have attempted suicide with hoarded pills, difficult as that would have been under close surveillance. This thought makes the reader wonder about the withdrawals from the drug dependencies and the ether,[10] which, for years before her incarceration, had been supplied daily by her family physician. The biography does not mention medications, or indeed anything else about the life of the inmate.

---

9   On hearing the news of Vivienne's death, in January 1947, Eliot told Mary Trevelyan that it was 'unexpected. She was supposed to be in quite good physical health.'

10 Maurice denied that she ever took ether, but Virginia Woolf detected it, and Aldous Huxley testified that at times the Eliot house 'smelled like a hospital'. Cyril Connolly (*Sunday Times*, 7 November 1971) said that Leonard Woolf had told him Vivienne was addicted to ether.

II

Seymour-Jones assembles a parallel portrait of Eliot during the Vivienne years and beyond. One of her first glimpses is via Lady Ottoline Morrell, the wife of Philip Morrell, a wealthy member of parliament (who fathered a son on his secretary, and another on his wife's parlourmaid). Ottoline, who was introduced to the young poet by her lover, Bertrand Russell, nicknamed Eliot 'the Undertaker', and said he was 'dull, dull, dull':

> He never moves his lips but speaks in an even and monotonous voice, and I felt him monstrous without and within. Where does his queer neurasthenic poetry come from, I wonder... I think he has lost all spontaneity and can only break through his lock up by stimulants or violent emotions... He was better in French than in English. He speaks French very perfectly, slowly and correctly.

In another letter she remarks that his 'carefully enunciated English sounded false', but as Dame Helen Gardner observed, 'he lost his American accent without ever developing English speed and English slurring and English speech rhythms'. Osbert Sitwell was 'struck by the contrast between his diction, the slow, careful, attractive voice, which always held in it, deep and subjugated, an American lilt and an American sound of r's'. Russell thought that Eliot's 'slowness is a sort of nervous affliction. It is annoying – it used to drive his wife almost to physical violence – but one gets used to it.'

On first meeting Eliot, on 15 November 1918, Virginia Woolf recalled a patrician, even a 'polished, cultivated, elaborate young American'. Before long she discovered that he was also 'sinister, insidious, eel-like'. By August 1922 she perceived him as 'sardonic, guarded, precise, and slightly malevolent...' and confessed to 'growing boredom with his troubles and his tedious and longwinded American way... I could wish that poor dear Tom had more spunk in him, less need to let drop by drop of his agonized perplexities fall ever so finely through pure cambric.' When ruffled, 'he behaves like an old maid who has been kissed by the butler'. Mrs Woolf's dislike grew with her awareness of his hypocrisy. She had seen a performance of *King Lear* with him, at which they both 'jeered', but which, in the next *Criterion*, he praised as 'flawless'. A crisis occurred when he took *The Waste Land* and other poems away from the Woolfs' Hogarth Press and furtively placed them with his new company, Faber. She thought that he had treated her and her husband 'scurvily... Leonard thinks the queer, shifty creature will slip away now.' Eliot's conversion horrified her – 'most shameful and distressing... Tom Eliot may be called dead to us from this day forward. He has become an Anglo-Catholic, believes in God and immortality, goes to church...[11] There is something obscene about a living person sitting by the fireside and believing in God.' She would have applauded Harold Bloom's observation that 'To have been born in 1888 and to have died in 1965 is to have flourished in the age of Freud, hardly a time when Anglo-Catholic theology, social thought and morality were central to the main movement of mind'.

In March 1929, at age forty, Eliot took the Church's 'vow of chastity',[12] which seems like making a virtue of necessity, and an admission that he was impuissant. Why was it necessary to proclaim this private matter in a public document, unless he was attempting to nullify his marriage? (The vow would have constituted a diriment impediment.) The 'King Bolo' verses, published (incomplete) in the volume edited by Christopher Ricks, *Inventions of the March Hare: Poems 1909–1917*, bring Eliot's sexuality to the surface, though the poor quality of some of the verse disturbs us more than the adolescent ribaldry. Why, one wonders, was Eliot so eager to preserve them, since they reveal so much of what he most wanted to hide?

Seymour-Jones's depiction of Eliot as having homosexual

---

11   In a Christmas letter to Harriet Shaw Weaver, Joyce took a more amused view of the conversion: 'Eliot is dusting pews in an Anglo-Catholic church round your corner. Ask him to have an A.-C. mass said for the three Joyses.'

12   A line in the poem *Marina*, written in this period, echoes the interdiction: 'Those who suffer the ecstasy of the animals, meaning / Death.' Harold Nicolson, in *Journey to Java*, drolly recounts his sudden recollection of the successive line in the same poem: 'As I sit there, on the deck of the *William Ruys*, basking in the sun, a line of T. S. Eliot's swoops down like a black crow upon me: "Those who sit in the sty of contentment [meaning / Death]". I rise quickly and walk back along the promenade deck... flagellating myself in self-contempt. Epicure, I mutter, *de grega porcus.*'

tendencies is convincing, but she omits the most important evidence for it, the verse that Ezra Pound, who probably knew more about Eliot's sex life and inclinations than anyone else, sent to him after reading *The Waste Land*:

> *These are the poems of Eliot*
> *By the Uranian muse begot;*

(The word may have been better known then, owing to contemporary circulation of Wilde's line, 'To have altered my life would have been to have admitted that Uranian love is ignoble'.) But was Eliot a practising homosexual? The book's chronicle of his activities in this regard from the mid-1930s is scarcely believable, but fails to present any evidence beyond the comings and goings in his apartment of younger men, and his six-year shared residence with the 'not altogether masculine' vicar Eric Cheetham at Emperor's Gate in South Kensington (from 1937). Eliot had certainly fallen in love with Jean Verdenal in Paris in 1910–11,[13] but even the author thinks that, given the poet's inhibitions, 'the relationship... was unlikely to have been a physical one, notwithstanding the constant homosexual theme of the [Bolo] verses'. The prayer concluding *Ash Wednesday* ('Spirit of the river, spirit of the sea...') invokes Verdenal, not Vivienne, the original dedicatee,[14] as, of course, do the three mentions of Phlébas, all of them mistaken in that Verdenal's war record makes clear he did not drown while standing in waist-high water on a landing beach in the Dardanelles helping to evacuate soldiers, but died later, on 2 May 1915, while attending a wounded man on a battlefield. Yet how do we explain Eliot's tantrum in 1952, forcing the publisher of an essay that speculates on the nature of the Verdenal friendship to withdraw it? Eliot's furibund response seems out of proportion to an untruth.

His ability to terminate relationships with the people closest to him is a more enigmatic aspect of his character. Seymour-Jones notes that he 'abandoned' John Hayward, his muscular-dystrophic housemate

---

13   None of Eliot's letters survives. Verdenal's are in Harvard's Houghton Library.
14   Eliot removed her name from the second edition.

of eleven years, 'with the same abruptness and moral cowardice with which he left Vivienne'. In Hayward's version, Eliot entered his room early on 9 January 1957, asked him to read a letter that he handed to him announcing his immediate departure and imminent elopement with his young secretary. Hayward read it and said that he was not angry, whereupon Eliot leaned forward, put his arm around him, and kissed him. (Hayward later recorded that 'since I am the most un-homosexual man in London, I found this a most offensive gesture'.) But why, after the marriage, did Eliot sever relations with this trusted friend and respected literary scholar who had helped him with critical advice in the composition of 'Little Gidding'?[15] Not long before, Eliot had chosen him as his literary executor, instructing him that 'I do not want any biography written or any intimate letters published... Your job would be to discourage any attempts to make books of me or about me, and to suppress everything suppressible.'

Emily Hale, Eliot's friend from his Harvard years, had thought of herself, not without some justification – since he seems to have given her reason to believe he would marry her if Vivienne were to die – as his 'fiancée presumptive'. When the poet's brother wrote to ask if there was any basis to this, the reply was affirmative. Emily had accompanied Eliot on his visit to Burnt Norton in 1935, but neither of them attached any significance to this. Back in Boston, after Vivienne's death, Eliot informed Emily that he could not marry her, hence her shock at the news of his nuptials in 1957 to his secretary Valerie Fletcher. Emily reacted by depositing at Princeton the thousand or so letters he had written to her over a period of fifty years, and wrote to him offering to 'excise' any intimacies in them. His response was to ignore her letter and impose an interdiction against accessibility until 2020. When she wrote again to say that Princeton wanted to reduce the time of the ban, he did not answer but instead burned her letters to him, which seems like an unnecessarily harsh punishment. Like

---

15 This should be qualified: Eliot invited Hayward and Rosamond Lehmann to a lunch for Robert Frost, which is curious in itself, Frost having publicly disputed a statement in one of Eliot's 1930s Harvard lectures. Hayward did not hide his irritation with Eliot during the repast but returned the invitation, which Eliot honoured. In the 1963 reprint of *Four Quartets*, Eliot removed a note of acknowledgement to Hayward that appears in the original.

Vivienne, Emily died in a mental institution.

Eliot's treatment of Mary Trevelyan, his London companion since the late 1930s, was shockingly factious. Mary and Tom saw each other for dinner or drives in the country regularly for twenty years. She was a confidante of John Hayward's as well, and tried, with him, to protect the poet from the impression of arrogance and omnipotence that he had begun to make. In 1955 she wrote to Hayward concerning the deification: 'I have noticed of late his immense indignation with anyone who disagrees with him.' In 1958 – after the marriage to Valerie – Mary wrote angrily that 'Tom is a great "runner-away". He is extremely deceitful when it suits him and he would willingly sacrifice anybody and anything to get himself out of something which he doesn't want to face up to.' Nonetheless, Mary sent two letters conveying every good wish to him in his new life, only to receive an outraged reply accusing her of 'gross impertinence'.

Painted Shadow tells us that 'the intimate letters between Pound and Eliot' of the early 1930s reveal a 'shared anti-Semitism', which may explain why successive volumes of Eliot's letters have not followed the one that appeared on his centenary, September 1988. Seymour-Jones does not dwell on the issue; fails to mention John Maynard Keynes's April 1934 letter to Eliot expressing approval of the infamous *After Strange Gods*; and says less about Eliot's Jewish friends, the sculptor Sir Jacob Epstein,[16] Leonard Woolf, Sydney and Violet Schiff,[17] and Margaret (Margot) Cohn, owner of the House of Books on Madison Avenue, than the reader would like to know. The Eliots stayed with Mrs Cohn in her Manhattan apartment during five of their New York sojourns.[18]

Writing before the discovery of the correspondence (1927–60) between Eliot and Horace M. Kallen, the Jewish social philosopher and Zionist at the New School for Social Research in New York, Seymour-Jones quotes part of Isaiah Berlin's 1951 letter to Eliot showing the

---

16   In 1935 Eliot wrote that 'the work of Mr Epstein is now so familiar to the common man that he no longer stops to ask what it is all about'. Epstein sculpted the largest penis in modern art; it now adorns the home of Lord Harewood, Queen Elizabeth II's first cousin.

17   She was the sister of Ada Leverson, the novelist.

18   The present writer knew Mrs Cohn and acquired most of his Eliot library from her.

writer hurt and indignant at the asperity of the poet's anti-Semitism as revealed in *After Strange Gods.* Berlin quotes Eliot's words back at him: 'Reasons of race and religion' make 'a large number of free-thinking Jews undesirable', and protested that

> You thought it a pity that large groups of 'free-thinking Jews' should complicate the lives of otherwise fairly homogeneous Anglo-Saxon Christian communities? And that it were better otherwise? And it would be better for such communities if their Jewish neighbours... were put beyond the bounds of the city.

Eliot responded that 'The sentence of which you complain would of course never have appeared at all... if I had been aware of what was going to happen, indeed had already begun in Germany'. But surely by 1933–4, when the book was written and published, Eliot, as an editor in central London, had to have seen what was happening. His post-War letter to Kallen, dated 2 April 1955, is more specific:

> You speak of 'Jewish Education': do you suggest that there should be separate schools and colleges? I should not disapprove of religious foundations, but any segregation on the basis of race seems to me undesirable. I am interested in the conservation of Jewish culture not as representing a race so much as representing a religion.

Late in life Eliot discontinued publication of *After Strange Gods*, but refused to delete the ugly references to Jews in reprints of his collected poems, or the poems themselves, and, in the case of *Gerontion*, to change the spelling of the word from lower to upper case.[19] No critic seems to have noticed the anti-Semitic slight in Eliot's *Arnold and Pater* essay: 'Arnold Hellenizes and Hebraicizes in turns; it is something to Pater's credit to have Hellenized purely.'

---

19 Eliot may have decided to use the lower case after reading *Ulysses*, where Haines says in the first scene: 'I don't want to see my country fall into the hands of German jews'; and, a little later: 'England is in the hands of the jews. In all the highest places: her finance, her press... as we are standing here the jew merchants are already at their work of destruction.'

Some errors, obscurities, and the omission of significant aspects of Eliot history should not be overlooked. Thus Seymour-Jones introduces a 'Princesse di [*sic*] Bassiano', apparently unaware that the publisher of *Botteghe Oscure*, and the wife of Don Roffredo Caetani, Prince of Bassiano, was the St Louis-born Marguerite Chapin, a cousin of Eliot's on his mother's side. The author also fails to identify the model for Eliot's 'Princess Volupine', the Romanian aristocrat Henrietta Seva-Goiu, described by Aldous Huxley, after a fling with her in Burma and on a trans-Pacific cruise in the mid-1920s, as 'bitchy' and a 'philosophizing cock-teaser'. Seymour-Jones's account of Eliot's stay with Frank Morley, his co-director at Faber, after returning from America in the summer of 1935, does not include their ten-day tour in Wales, which inspired the lovely poem *Usk*. And the biography is confusing and uninformed about the connection with the Culpin family. After the untimely death of his Oxford companion, Karl Culpin, early in the 1914 war (on the German side), Eliot transferred his friendship to Karl's brother Jack, who, after the war, married a German woman called Rexi, who, in 1932, submitted a novella, *The Dead Image*, to Eliot at Faber. He declined to publish it on grounds that it was too short for a novel and too long for a periodical. Writing to her from America, he asked her to visit Vivienne from time to time. In 1959 she again submitted the novella, this time in her own English – the 1932 version was a translation from the German – but he again refused it.

The book says nothing about Eliot's longest verse opus, his translation of St-John Perse's *Anabase*, and Perse himself, a close friend, is not mentioned. Robert Sencourt, who is, does not receive adequate space given the importance of his role in Eliot's life as a co-patient in Vittoz's Swiss clinic in 1921 and as the only friend to have been a houseguest of the Eliots at Clarence Gate Gardens near the end of their marriage. Sencourt foresaw this development and wondered how the two could have stayed together at all. He describes Vivienne as 'wayward, unpredictable, finding fault in everything, subtly thwarting Eliot at every turn'.

Djuna Barnes merits more attention than the three brief references to her suggest, and the biographer misses an opportunity to use Eliot's friendship with this patroness saint of lesbianism to support the idea that his attraction to masculine women was another component of his sexuality. Barnes became a cherished friend of the poet, whose letters address her as 'Darling' and 'Dearest'. When she told him that she had 'wasted her life', he answered gently that she 'may have wasted some of it, but should look very carefully at what [she] had done when [she] was not wasting it', meaning her novel *Nightwood*, which he published and made famous in a preface to the American edition. (Another publisher had rejected it because of the 'welter of homosexuality'.) One supposes that her conversation amused him, *viz.* 'Everyone hates old ladies because they aren't good for anything. They aren't pretty and they can't screw.' Eliot published her play, *Antiphon*, in spite of not liking it, no doubt for the reason that, as Seymour-Jones recognises, it is 'the revenge drama Djuna Barnes wrote after seeing Eliot's *Family Reunion*'.

Seymour-Jones does not mention Mary Butts, another bisexual female writer, said by Eliot scholars to have had 'intense and intimate encounters with Eliot'. When she died, in March 1927, he wrote to her executor: 'I felt if she had lived she might have made some remarkable contribution to literature.' Perhaps she did in her posthumous – 1929 – *Armed with Madness*.

Eliot biographers seem to have little to say about Prince D.P. Svyatopolk-Mirsky, the intellectually distinguished White Russian who was a frequent Eliot visitor in the 1920s and early 1930s.[20] In 1924 the Woolfs published the *Autobiography of the Archpriest Avvakum*, with Mirsky's introduction claiming this seventeenth-century life as the most significant work in Russian literature between the twelfth-century *Lay of Igor* and the late eighteenth-century odes of Lomonosov. Eliot would have read it for the additional reason that one of its translators from the Russian was a long-time friend, Hope Mirrlees, in whose family home at Shamley Green, Surrey, he resided for part of each week during most of World War II.

---

20 Prince Mirsky, who wrote his monumental *History of Russian Literature* in English, was the editor of *Versti*, the Russian periodical launched in Paris in May 1927. His collaborators there included Pierre Souvtchinsky, Alexei Remizov, Marina Tsvetayeva, Leon Shestov and Arthur Lourié, all of whom were close to Stravinsky, who, incidentally, was a friend of the Diaghilev dancer Serafina Astafieva, the model for Eliot's 'Grishkin'.

One useful book by Eliot remains unpublished, a sampling of his work as a Faber editor, including his 'blurbs', one of which was for *The Tropic of Cancer*, another for Durrell's *Black Book*, and his letters rejecting manuscripts for publication. To judge by the wise and witty fragments that have appeared in the catalogue of the Humanities Research Center at the University of Texas, Austin, these may be his most interesting letters. A propos some poems by Keith Douglas, Eliot queries the phrases 'interesting waves', asking 'why?'; 'dim water', wondering 'whether the water was dimmer than most sea-water'; and next to the words 'bright Pacific', writes 'No force in this adjective'.

We are indebted to Margot Cohn for the following excerpt from one to Allen Tate on 19 August 1943, on the reasons for rejecting some poems by the young Robert Lowell, over which Eliot claims to have 'brooded' for four months:

> ... I don't feel that his religious convictions have yet sunk down through the surface to that unconscious level of experience which I think such convictions have to reach to rise again as material for poetry. Something similar seems to be lacking still in his verse as poetry. I don't think he has altogether assimilated his models, and his words in general seem a little self-conscious, but I would like to hear more of him from time to time as he is obviously something out of the ordinary.

Another wished-for publication would be a miscellany to include words whose prominence in Eliot's poetry – 'velleities', for example – have made their use by other writers unwise. This collection should also contain his contributions to the Revised Psalter of the *Book of Common Prayer*. In the Twenty-Third Psalm, Eliot insisted on retaining the phrase: 'Though I walk through the valley of the shadow of death, I will fear no evil,' despite the Hebrew original's limitation to 'the valley of deep darkness', together with an account of his help in preserving the Coverdale text, and in lambasting the concurrent publication of *The New English Bible*. In this last he objected most sharply to the updating of 'bear the burden of the heat of the day' to 'sweated the whole day long in the blazing sun', to the mistranslation of St Luke's Greek word for 'virgin' as 'girl', and to 'neither cast ye your pearls before swine' to 'do not feed your pearls to pigs' – 'swine' still being in common usage as an insult – the point not being the animal's nutrition but its inability to appreciate beauty. Lastly, a delightful booklet could be made of Eliot anecdotes: Robert Giroux: 'Aren't most editors failed writers, Mr. Eliot?' 'Yes, and so are most writers'; and apropos Shakespeare: 'Scholars and critics must be ready to change their way of being wrong.'

> Not far into the future, one hopes, when the Eliot biography is completed, and placed on a hard-to-reach shelf, the poet Eliot will prevail, 'the greatest poet', as Auden wrote on December 8, 1941, 'that his country has the honor to have produced... whose professional example [is] to every other and lesser writer at once an inspiration and a reproach.'

Chapter 17

Eliot on Prose Fiction

Late in life, T.S. Eliot reaffirmed 'the general aversion to prose fiction which I share with Paul Valéry', claiming that

> with the exception of one article and two prefaces, and a very few pieces of literary journalism which remain uncollected, I have never attempted criticism of prose fiction; it follows that I have no special competence to criticize criticism of prose fiction.[1]

In truth, Eliot's writings in the category are substantial. His range, ancient to modern, is prodigious: Apuleius (in the translation by Aldington,[2] 'an imperfect Latinist but a master of Tudor prose'), in whose 'ecstatic debauch of words, the late Latin and the Tudor mind meet'; Sir Philip Sidney, who 'wrote one of the dullest novels in the language',[3] though not in prose; Thomas Nashe, 'a very great writer indeed [whose] *Unfortunate Traveller* is the first really interesting English novel';[4] and the peerless fictions of Swift: *The Voyage to the Country of the Houyhnhnms* 'seems to me one of the greatest triumphs that the human soul has ever achieved'. Nor is French fiction neglected, since Eliot goes back to Marivaux, whose *Marianne* and *Le*

---

1   Foreword to *Katherine Mansfield and Other Literary Studies*, by J. Middleton Murry (1959).
2   Hands's *Sources for T.S. Eliot's Poetry* gives Walter Pater's translation as the one Eliot used.
3   *Athenaeum*, 4 April 1919.
4   *The Listener*, 19 July 1929.

Paysan parvenu 'deserve more attention [than his plays]', [5] and still further back to Rabelais, if only to remember that 'there is an *esprit gaulois,* an element of richness... which may qualify our judgment of the wholeness of Racine or Molière...' The most regretted unwritten Eliot essay is one on Proust, particularly since Eliot's exalted opinion of him is well known: '*Ulysses* still seems the most considerable work of imagination in English, in our time, comparable in importance to the works of Marcel Proust.'[6]

Some of Eliot's verdicts surprise us with their seeming remoteness from his interests: 'Hans Christian Andersen [is a] frightening writer, not suitable for children';[7] O. Henry is 'still unappreciated and unknown [in England]';[8] for Flannery O'Connor, 'My nerves are just not strong enough.'[9] But his evaluations, powers of distinction, and focus on the quiddities are beyond compare:

> ... the less 'realistic' literature is, the more visual it must be. In reading *Pride and Prejudice* or *The Wings of the Dove* we hardly need to visualize at all; in reading Dante we need to visualize all the time.[10]
>
> ... since Defoe the secularization of the novel has been continuous... In the first phase, the novel took the Faith for granted, and omitted it from its picture of life. Fielding, Dickens and Thackeray belong to this phase. In the second, it doubted, worried about, or contested the Faith. To this phase belong George Eliot, George Meredith and Thomas Hardy.[11]

---

5   *Arts and Letters,* Spring 1919. Elsewhere Eliot remarks that 'Marivaux's world is a very stripped world; there is no moral earnestness, and no sentimentality. It does not deny emotions; it analyses them.'
6   *Horizon,* March 1941.
7   *Yorkshire Post,* 29 August 1961.
8   *New Statesman,* 29 July 1916.
9   Letter to Russell Kirk, 20 February 1957. One supposes that Eliot's friend, the editor Robert Giroux, introduced him to O'Connor's work - *The Wise Blood,* and the stories in *A Good Man Is Hard to Find* - but the poet may have been shaken by O'Connor's blasphemous rejection of the Eucharist Symbol, 'If it's a symbol, to hell with it,' and her comments on Simone Weil, whose life 'is the most comical life I have ever read about'.
10 *The Egoist,* 1917.
11 'Religion and Literature' (in *Faith That Illuminates*), 1933.

Eliot's critical genius *vis-à-vis* contemporary fiction first appears in his early recognition of the stature of *Ulysses*. Only two months after its publication (February 1922), he wrote in *La Nouvelle Revue Française*[12] that it is 'A book of such significance in the history of the English language that it must take its place as an integral part in the tradition of the language. A book of this caliber revivifies at the same time the totality of its forebears... I hold this book to be the most important expression which the present age has found.'[13]

> Mr. Joyce's parallel use of the *Odyssey* has great importance... No one else has built a novel upon such a foundation before: it has never before been necessary. I am not begging the question in calling *Ulysses* a 'novel' and if you call it an epic it will not matter. If it is not a novel, that is simply because the novel is a form which will no longer serve... The novel ended with Flaubert and with James... Mr. Joyce has written one novel – *The Portrait of the Artist as a Young Man*,

though 'it appears to me that *A Portrait* is the work of a disciple of Walter Pater, as well as of Cardinal Newman.'

Elsewhere Eliot explains that 'The essential of tradition is... in getting as much as possible of the whole weight of the history of the language behind [the] word... Joyce has not only the tradition but [also] the awareness of it';[14] and, Joyce 'did not compose a novel through direct interest in, and sympathy with, other human beings, but by enlarging his own consciousness so as to include them'.[15] Further, '*Ulysses* bears the unique literary distinction... of having no style at all [in the sense that] it has none of the marks by which "style" may be distinguished.'[16] 'It is not... periods and traditions but individual men who write great prose.'[17] In 1923 Eliot propounded

---

12   1 May 1922.
13   *The Listener*, 14 October 1943.
14   *The Three Provincialities* (1928).
15   *The Listener*, 14 October 1943.
16   *Dial*, July 1923.
17   *Athenaeum*, 2 May 1919.

the opinion that '*Ulysses* is as distinct a precursor of a new epoch as it is a gigantic culmination of an old.'

Eliot did not endow *Finnegans Wake* with a comparable testimonial, though he describes the final passage, when 'the dreamer of the book approaches waking consciousness', as 'tragic eloquence', a paean compromised to an extent by his acclamation of St-John Perse's *Anabasis* as 'a piece of writing of the same importance as the later work of Mr. James Joyce, as valuable as *Anna Livia Plurabelle*'. The crucial aspect of Eliot's Joyce criticism, nevertheless, is in his comparison of *Finnegans Wake* and *Paradise Lost*:

> Joyce's imagination is not naturally of so purely auditory a type as Milton's. In his early work, and at least in part of *Ulysses*, there is visual and other imagination of the highest level; and I may be mistaken in thinking that the latter part of *Ulysses* shows a turning from the visible world to draw rather on the resources of phantasmagoria. In any case, one may suppose that the replenishment of visual imagery during later years has been insufficient; so that what I find in [*Finnegans Wake*] is an auditory imagination, abnormally sharpened at the expense of the visual.

Even in the *Wake*, 'Joyce maintains some contact with the conversational tone,' Eliot goes on: 'But it may prove to be a blind alley for the future development of the language.'[18]

'After *Ulysses*,' Eliot maintained elsewhere, 'we feel abandoned by our writers... despite our admiration for James and Conrad,[19] they are not close to us... a gulf of taste separates us from Wells, Bennett, Chesterton, and Shaw.... Kipling has become the complete English

---

18 Oxford University Press, 1936.
19 Eliot never brings the reader close to Conrad, and fails to identify any of his merits, while censoring minor faults: 'Conrad did not master all the refinements of the language', as in 'his clumsiness in the frequent use of *could* or *would* instead of might'. One evening in New York with Eliot in November 1963, the present writer heard Stravinsky – whose father, like Conrad's, was born in Chernigov – ask if *his* accent was more difficult to understand than Conrad's. The reply was 'No, no, Igor, Conrad was far more difficult to understand'. This seems to be Eliot's only mention of having known Conrad, though the poet's correspondence for the years 1922–5 has not yet been published.

equivalent of the *pompier*. The same *NRF* essay comes down harshly on The new Americans', who are only 'symptomatically interesting. Their novelty and ingenuity of form give expression to thought that is ordinary and conventional in spirit... they cannot overcome such forces as the vices and stupidity of their country. Other novelists' characters, compared with James's, seem to be only accidentally in the same book.' For Eliot at this time the consequential Americans were Poe, Whitman and Hawthorne. Revisiting St Louis in 1953, he changed this to Poe, Whitman and Mark Twain.

Eliot's first published criticism of any prose fiction was a review of a book on Hardy's Wessex novels.[20] The young reviewer remarked that the slaughter of Sue Bridehead's children in *Jude the Obscure* is 'horror nearer to Cyril Tourneur than to Sophocles', a statement that suggests *Sweeney* ('Agamemnon's cry'), as well as the epigraph from Conrad in the first draft of *The Waste Land* ('The horror! The horror!'), and the phrase 'handful of dust' from Conrad's *Return*.[21] Eliot later wrote:

> In a world without meaning there can still be horror, but not tragedy, [for tragedy] belongs to a world in which right and wrong, and the soul and its destiny, are still the most important things.[22]

After Hardy's death Eliot grandly remarked that 'If any man was ever worthy to be buried in the Abbey on grounds of literary greatness alone, it is the author of *The Dynasts*, *The Mayor of Casterbridge*, and *A Group of Noble Dames*.'[23] *The Mayor of Casterbridge* 'always seemed to me his finest novel as a whole – he comes the nearest to producing an air of inevitability, and of making the crises seem

---

20 *Manchester Guardian*, 23 June 1916.
21 The expression also occurs twice in Conrad's *Youth*, in the fourth of the Meditations in Donne's *Devotions Upon Emergent Occasions*, and in the fifth section of Tennyson's *Maud*.
22 *The Listener*, 18 September 1941.
23 *After Strange Gods* praises Hardy's short stories as 'masterly', asserting that one of them, *Barbara of the House of Grebe*, introduces us 'into a world of pure Evil', as distinguished from 'a world of Good and Evil' in works by Sophocles, Conrad and James.

the consequences of the character... '[24] Yet Eliot's criticism became increasingly stringent: 'What again and again introduces a note of falsity into Hardy's novels is that he will leave nothing to nature but will always be giving one last turn of the screw himself.' Hardy's philosophy, as expressed in his blank-verse poems, struck him as 'uncongenial',[25] whereas

> The philosophy of the novels seems to be based on the mechanism of science. I think it is a very bad philosophy indeed, and I think that Hardy's work would be better for a better philosophy, or none at all... Has he not exploited determinism to extract his aesthetic values from the contemplation of a world in which values do not count?[26]

'The scene in *Far from the Madding Crowd*[27] in which Bathsheba unscrews Fanny Robin's coffin... seems to me deliberately faked,' Eliot wrote in 1957,[28] yet the following year he suspected that the 'liquid siftings' in 'Sweeney Among the Nightingales' was 'suggested by the rain dripping' on the same coffin.

Few English novels are 'really well-written', Eliot thought,[29] rating the best of them well below those of Stendhal. He accepts as axiomatic that poets wrote the best prose, the poet having 'a power over the word' that the prose writer lacks.[30] His discussions of English prose styles virtually ignore novelists. Thackeray is a qualified exception, but unhappily the man who could 'write such good prose as the

---

24 *After Strange Gods.*
25 In the *Granite Review* (Summer 1962), Eliot said he was eighteen or nineteen when he read Hardy's novels, 'but I did not know of him as a poet until years later'.
26 *Bookman*, February 1930.
27 *Sunday Times*, 16 April 1958.
28 *Saltire Review*, Summer 1957.
29 *Egoist*, April 1918.
30 *Spectator*, 23 February 1934. Here Eliot breaks ranks with Valéry, who maintained that the purpose of prose 'is to convey a meaning, to impart information, to convince of a truth, to direct action... So with walking or running: our purpose is to get to a destination... But the purpose of the dance is the dance itself.' Eliot proposed a brilliant exception: 'The purpose of a war dance, I believe, is to arouse the dormant pugnacity of the dancers.'

Steyne episode' [*Vanity Fair*] hadn't brains enough to find out what he could do well, which was high society sordidness, and do it'.[31] The finest prose 'of the nineteenth century' is Cardinal Newman's, says the pope of Russell Square, whereas Pater, the peer of the stylists, 'is restricted by a limited emotional range'. And though Samuel Butler 'is not even an artist', Eliot asked his mother to read *The Way of All Flesh* 'for the character of Christina, one of the finest pieces of dissection of mental dishonesty that I know anywhere'.

The author of *Amos Barton* 'is a more serious writer than Dickens',[32] Eliot wrote, admitting that Rosamond Vincy in *Middlemarch* frightened him more than Goneril and Regan. In a 1918 letter to his mother, Eliot found *Jane Eyre* and *Wuthering Heights* 'amazingly good stuff, but I cannot endure George Eliot'. A month later, preparing a lecture, he wrote home again: 'I have been cramming George Eliot... I was surprised to enjoy her much... I think my memory is based chiefly on one story – *Amos Barton* – which struck me as far and away ahead of the rest. I read *The Mill on the Floss*, *Scenes of Clerical Life*, *Adam Bede* and *Romola*' – but not *Daniel Deronda*? Later still he wrote to a friend: 'George Eliot had a great talent, and wrote one great story, *Amos Barton*, and went steadily downhill afterwards.' This high claim for *Amos Barton,* her Opus One, written even before she had adopted the George Eliot nom-de-plume, is difficult to explain. Eliot may have been impressed by the pure realism and even by the masculine voice of the writer, her talents as ventriloquist not yet having developed the androgynous tone. Or did the poet admire *Amos Barton* so much because of the

---

31   The young Joyce concludes his centenary essay on Dickens with 'Is not Thackeray at his finest greater than Dickens?'

32   *Dial*, December 1920. Eliot overuses the word 'serious', not, of course, in the unforgettable remark, 'If I had thought that death was final, it would seem to be a far less serious matter than it does' (*Time and Tide*, 12 January 1935), but in comparing degrees of the saturnine disposition in literature, viz., 'Molière in some lights is more serious than Racine'; 'Wycherley is as serious as Marlowe'. Eliot's Introduction to Valéry's *The Art of Poetry* (1958) asserts that Valéry is not concerned with relating a poem to the rest of life 'in such a way that the reader will undergo not merely an experience, but a serious experience'; Valéry's seriousness resides not simply 'in the value of the materials out of which the poem is made', and 'no agreement shall ever be reached about the extent to which the seriousness is in the subject', although 'the seriousness of Valéry's finest poems is self-evident' and some of them are 'very serious poems indeed'.

skilful rendering of the character's mediocrity and self-satisfaction?

In the introduction to his mother's play, *Savonarola* (1926), Eliot says that unless *Romola* 'gave a faithful presentation of Romola's time to George Eliot's contemporaries, it would have little to say to us about George Eliot's time'. By comparing the period described in *Romola*, as we know that period, with George Eliot's interpretation of it, 'we cannot write a purely literary criticism of George Eliot... unless it is admittedly a very imperfect criticism, for as the interests of the author are wide, so must be those of the critic'.[33] Eliot pictures his namesake 'walking in the garden and denying God as she affirmed the Moral Law with fuliginous solemnity'.[34] In the same year he announced that 'George Eliot est un romancier philosophique, Dostoyevsky un romancier psychologique, Henry James un romancier métaphysique',[35] but did not elaborate on the distinctions.

Eliot's strongest affinities are with Dickens, a 'visual writer'[36] primarily, who 'knew best what America looked like'. This puzzling assertion is contradicted by the young Joyce's centenary essay on 'the great Cockney', which argues that whenever he went 'far afield from London to America (*American Notes*) or to Italy (*Pictures from Italy*), his powers of observation failed him utterly'. Eliot concurs in declaring that 'Anything drearier... than the American chapter of *Martin Chuzzlewit* would be hard to imagine'. But his primary attraction to Dickens was in his language, as was revealed in the discovery that the cancelled subtitle of *The Waste Land* was 'He do the Police in different voices' (*Our Mutual Friend*); and in the cat, in *Cats*, who 'will do / As he do do', an 'echo' of the 'solid and eternal Podsnap';[37] and the temporary borrowing from *Pickwick* of an epigraph for *Burnt Norton*.[38] Eliot's successful instantiations of lines and phrases from the whole of Western literature is one of the poet's most remarkable achievements. He asserts that 'Dickens's figures belong to poetry,

---

33 *Tradition and Experiment*, Oxford University Press, 1929.
34 *Nation*, 23 March 1918.
35 *Nouvelle Revue Française*, March 1926.
36 *Vanity Fair*, July 1923. Three years later, Eliot remarked that 'the majority of readers of novels have their taste impaired by an indulgence in visual detail' (*TLS*, 29 August 1926).
37 *Dial*, April 1921.
38 Helen Gardner, *The Composition of "Four Quartets"*, London, 1978.

like figures of Dante or Shakespeare, in that a single phrase, either by or about them, may be enough to set them wholly before us.'[39] Eliot's early criticism contains many references to Dickens: *viz.* the practice of doubling parts in sixteenth-century plays 'affected the plots of the Nicholas Nicklebys of the time';[40] 'Little Em'ly is not nearly so moving to me as the chancery prisoner in *Pickwick*';[41] Henry James's Mr Striker (*Roderick Hudson*) is 'too suggestive of Martin Chuzzlewit';[42] and Henry Adams 'remains little Paul Dombey asking questions'.[43]

The poet's taste for detective fiction partly accounts for the comprehensive essay on Wilkie Collins and Dickens. In fact, Eliot continued to review detective fiction – twenty-six books in the first half of 1927 alone – during a period when he devoted only one essay to a major novelist, D.H. Lawrence, and that less as literary than as religious and philosophical criticism.[44] Less attracted to mystery stories *per se* than to the detectives in them, and to the pitting of wits against those of an Arsène Lupin,[45] on whom the poet once promised to devote a full study, Eliot's precepts for writers of detective fiction are worth recalling:

> The sleuth must not be so highly intelligent that we are unable to keep pace with his inferences; love interest holds up a story; the characters need not be fully drawn, the most satisfactory kind being just real enough to make the story work. Also to be avoided are elaborate stage properties; involved mechanical business; the prestidigitatorial, the occult (including ghosts); scientific

---

39   *TLS*, 4 August 1927.
40   *TLS*, 8 December 1927.
41   Preface to Charles Louis Philippe's *Bubu of Montparnasse* (1932).
42   *Little Review*, August 1918.
43   *Athenaeum*, 23 May 1919. Nevertheless, the line in Eliot's *Gerontion*, 'In depraved May, dogwood and chestnut, flowering judas', is indebted to the beginning of chapter 18 of *The Education of Henry Adams*.
44   Eliot's views on Lawrence as novelist, on his 'romans splendides et extrêmement mal écrits', are found in the *Nouvelle Revue Française*, 1 May 1927.
45   'I like detective stories, but especially the adventures of Arsène Lupin,' Eliot wrote in the *Harvard College Class of 1910, Seventh Report*, June 1935. A 1960s *Report* says that he has come to prefer Inspector Maigret, a change of taste that had occurred at least a decade earlier: 'I never read contemporary fiction – with one exception: the works of Simenon concerned with Inspector Maigret, of which I may mention the most recent, *L'Amie de Madame Maigret*.' (*Sunday Times*, 24 December 1950)

discoveries; dependence on disguises; and bizarre characters and motives - *Dr. Jekyll and Mr. Hyde*, in which the literary craftsman is too obviously the manipulator of the scene.[46]

Turning to Sherlock Holmes,[47] to expose some of his inconsistencies and illogicalities, Eliot describes him as a mere 'formula and not even a very good detective'. He has no 'rich humanity', moreover, no 'knowledge of the human heart', and none of 'the reality in any great character in Dickens or Thackeray or George Eliot...' Yes, but surely the reality of Holmes is created by the vividness of such other characters as Mrs Hudson and Dr Watson, and of the London of gaslights, hansom cabs, and fore and aft caps. Even so, 'every critic of the novel who has a theory about the reality of characters... would do well to consider why Holmes... is just as real to us as Falstaff or the Wellers'.[48] Exasperatingly, Eliot reveals neither his own theory about this, nor, in another article,[49] the nature of his doubts about *The Turn of the Screw*, though he refers to 'that transfinite world with which Henry James was in such close intercourse'.[50]

In 1928, Eliot thought that H.G. Wells 'has positive self-contained gifts for one or two types of imaginative fiction which are peculiarly his own. His imagination depends upon facts. When he uses the facts for imaginative purposes he is superb, when he uses his imagination to expound facts, he is deplorable.'[51] Wells's 'triumphs' in science fiction are attributed partly to his scrupulous observances of the limits of the genre.[52] A dozen years later, Eliot stigmatised Wells as

---

46 Eliot complimented Chesterton on his observation that 'though this story is nominally set in London, it is really taking place in Edinburgh!' (*Nation and Athenaeum*, 31 December 1927).

47 'At the mention of the name, [Eliot] lit up like a torch: "I flatter myself that I know the names of... even the smallest characters" (Lawrence Durrell, *Atlantic Monthly*, May 1948). Curiously, Eliot never acknowledged borrowing the word 'grimpen' in *East Coker* from *The Hound of the Baskervilles*, as well as the following lines from *The Musgrave Ritual*: 'Whose was it?'- 'His who is gone.' - 'Who shall have it?' - 'He who will come.' - 'What was the month?' for *Murder in the Cathedral*: 'Whose was it?' - 'His who is gone.' - 'Who shall have it?' - 'He who will come.' - 'What shall be the month?'

48 *Criterion*, June 1927.

49 *Little Review*, August 1918.

50 *Dial*, August 1922.

51 *Cambridge Review*, 6 June 1928.

52 *Criterion*, June 1927.

one of 'the loudspeaker voices of our time', though 'some of his short stories, such as "The Country of the Blind", and certain scenes from his romances, such as the description of survival on the moon in *The First Men in the Moon*, are quite unforgettable'.[53] Two decades later Eliot told an interviewer that:

> Wells had marvelous imagination... The *Time Machine* is a fearful, though a wonderfully imaginative piece. It is a great story... There is much that I respect about Wells. He seems to me a tragic figure... Shaw seems complacent. I don't think Wells was, in his later years... Wells, I think, had more imagination, and I think that 'The Country of the Blind' is one of the greatest short stories ever written.[54]

———◆———

Eliot failed to reveal his debt in *The Waste Land* for several lines from D.H. Lawrence, and his borrowing in 'Burnt Norton' from Lawrence's preface to *New Poems* (1930) for such motives and images as 'Now, now, the bird is on the wing...', 'of before and after', 'the quick', and 'beginning and end'. Eliot trashes J. Middleton Murry's thesis in *Son of Woman* that Lawrence cannot be judged as a pure artist because he did not think of himself as one, and because 'he had an axe to grind':

> to be a pure artist is by no means incompatible with having 'an axe to grind'. Virgil and Dante had plenty of axes on the grindstone; Dickens and George Eliot are often at their best when they are grinding axes... Unless there was grinding of axes, there would be very little to write about... [55]

Further, if Lawrence was not trying to make works of art, he should have been:

53   *New English Weekly*, 8 February 1940.
54   *Yorkshire Post*, 29 August 1961. Eliot appropriated a line in *Ash Wednesday* (1930) from Wells's *The Sleeper Awakes*.
55   *Criterion*, July 1931.

The less the artist, the less the prophet; Isaiah succeeded in
being both... The false prophet kills the true artist... Only the
greatest, the Hebrew Prophets, seem to be utterly caught and
preserved by God, as mouthpieces; in ordinary human poets the
human personal loss, the private grievance and bitterness and
loneliness must be present. We envisage... a Villon... holding
nothing back in a passionate cry to God – and there is, in the
end, no one else to cry to.[56]

A sampling of other Eliot comments on Lawrence expose a divided
mind:

D.H. Lawrence, who discovered [James Fenimore] Cooper late
in life [actually he was thirty-one] [wrote] probably the most
brilliant of critical essays on him.[57]

The most objectionable feature of *Lady Chatterley's Lover* is
surely the view of the male as merely an instrument for the
purposes of the female.[58]

He still theorizes... when he should merely see. But there is
one scene in *Aaron's Rod*... in which one feels that the whole is
governed by a creator who is purely creator, with the terrifying
disinterestedness of the true creator.[59] In *Aaron's Rod* is found
the profoundest research into human nature... by any writer of
our generation.[60]

Not only are there magnificent descriptions... but there
are marvelous passages... of dialogue and narrative in which
Lawrence really gets out of himself and inside other people...
In one story, 'Two Bluebirds',[61] he states a situation which no

---

56 *Literature and the Modern World*, November 1935.
57 *To Criticize the Critic* (1965).
58 *Revelation*, 1937. In fact Lawrence says nothing about the feelings and sensations of
    Mellors.
59 *Dial*, August 1922. 'What gives Machiavelli's book its terrifying greatness is the fact that he
    does not seem to care.' *Twentieth Century Verse*, November/December 1937.
60 *Vanity Fair*, July 1923.
61 For the connection between Lawrence's story 'The Shadow in the Rose Garden', analysed in
    After Strange Gods, and *Burnt Norton*, see Gardner, *op. cit.*

one else has ever put... He is a great tragic figure, a waste of
great powers of understanding and tenderness.[62]

Lawrence's 'egotism, spiritual pride, and heresy' repelled Eliot, but
also compelled him to mention his own Unitarian background,
perhaps to avoid an imputation of bigotry. Furthermore, Lawrence
was 'ignorant', which Eliot later changed to 'uneducated', in an essay
elaborating on the novelist's search for 'a religion of power and magic,
of control rather than propitiation... Being educated means

> having such an apprehension of the contours of the map of
> what has been written in the past as to see instinctively where
> everything belongs, and approximately where everything new
> is likely to belong; it means, furthermore, being able to allow
> for the books one has not read and the things one does not
> understand.[63]

'On the subject of education,' Eliot wrote, two weeks after Lawrence's
death, 'there are some helpful remarks in Lawrence's *Future of the
Unconscious*.'

Religious questions do not enter into Eliot's earlier criticism of
fiction, but his expatriate prejudices anticipate them. His special
vantage provides the main interest in his remarks on American
writers and is surely responsible for the unusual perspectives in his
comparisons of French, Russian and English novelists. In his view, the
uniquely American qualities result from the environment:

> The granite soil which produced the essential flavor of
> Hawthorne is just as inevitably the environment which stunted
> him... Hawthorne, Poe, and Whitman are all pathetic creatures

---

62 *Criterion*, July 1931.
63 *Revelation*. cf. Paul Elmer More's belief in an 'imagination in its power of grasping, in a
    single, firm vision, the long course of human history, and of distinguishing what is essential
    therein from what is ephemeral'. Eliot singled out this statement in his review of More's
    Aristocracy and Justice (*New Statesman*, 24 June 1916). Also compare Eliot's remark, 'By
    education, I do not mean erudition but a kind of mental and moral discipline' (*Nation and
    Athenaeum*, 17 September 1927).

not because of the lack of intelligent literary society, this being much more certainly responsible for some of their merits. The originality of these men... was forced out by the starved environment.[64]

The handicap of Americans is that 'their world was thin, and, worst of all... secondhand...a shadow'. Yet comparing 'Ulalume'[65] with 'The Witch of Atlas', Poe's poem is 'more creative' than Shelley's, just as *Leaves of Grass* is 'more creative and original, at least in single lines', than Browning's 'Dramatic Monologues' [*sic*]. A similar judgement favours *The Scarlet Letter* over *Adam Bede*. As for Henry James, he 'is understood by very few Americans and very few Englishmen.[66] To understand James we should know America at least as well as he knew it, and the England that he knew (and the rest of England) perhaps better than he knew it.'

If Americans were offended by these haughty homilies and their accompanying jibes at Boston ('the Puritan traditions of Beacon Hill' and the 'views of the Irish-American bishopric'), many a former fellow countryman must have been indignant on being told that 'the essays of Emerson are already an encumbrance', and that Hawthorne 'gets New England, as James gets a larger part of America, [but] none of their respective contemporaries get [*sic*] anything above a village or two, or a jungle'. The reader is left wondering what can have been intended by the claim that 'Hawthorne grasped character through the relation

---

64 *Little Review*, August 1918.
65 In *La Nouvelle Revue Française*, March 1926, Eliot compares 'Ulalume' to '*Un coup de dés*', in that both poems 'replace philosophy with incantation'. The young Eliot tended to disparage Mallarmé, stunningly characterising his poetry as 'mossified'. On 29 May 1963, in his Kensington apartment, Eliot told the present writer that Mallarmé, George Herbert and Edward Lear were the only poets he could still read.
66 And some of him, surely, is understood by no one, as in the ambiguous passage that Eliot quotes from *The Ivory Tower*: 'However, he didn't mind thinking that if Cissy should prove all that was likely enough their having a subject in common couldn't but practically conduce; though the moral of it all amounted rather to a portent, the one that Houghty, by the same token, had done least to reassure him against, of the extent to which the native jungle harboured the female specimen and to which its ostensible cover, the vast level of mixed growths stirred wavingly in whatever breeze was apt to be identifiable but as an agitation of the latest redundant thing in ladies' hats.' Eliot's comment on this is that 'a torturous style, when its peculiarity is aimed at precision (as with Henry James), is not necessarily a dead one...'

of two or more persons to each other, [as] no one else except James has done.' Apart from dialogue and pure narrative, what other means are there? Hawthorne, of course, is a part of the American psyche.

On Poe's most famous poem, Eliot amusingly notes of the 'stately Raven of the saintly days of yore', that

> Since there is nothing particularly saintly about the raven, if indeed the ominous bird is not wholly the reverse, there can be no point in referring his origin to a period of saintliness... We have just heard the raven described as *stately*; but we are told presently that he is *ungainly*, an attribute hardly to be reconciled with *stateliness*. The bird is addressed as 'no craven' quite needlessly except for the pressing need of a rhyme...[67]

After lauding Poe as 'a critic of the first rank... an heroically courageous critic... who wrote some masterly criticism',[68] Eliot offers an appraisal of his stature:

> Poe makes the world different from what it would be if we had never read him. There are a dozen poems and more than a dozen stories, which... we never forget... It will seem puzzling that, with such a narrow range of emotion, such a lack of ordinary human passion and sympathy, the author of so few poems should be more than a minor poet. But, in the first place, his poetry is original. That is to say, his vision of life, though limited, was peculiar and coherent and his idiom unmistakable. He takes you into a world different from that of any other poet. And he has the integrity not to attempt to write about anything outside of his own world, or to do anything that any other poet has already done.[69]

Peculiarly American, in Hawthorne and James, is a concern for what the latter called 'the deeper psychology':

---

67   *The Nation and Athenaeum*, 21 May 1927.
68   *Ibid.*
69   *The Listener*, 25 February 1943.

> Neither Dickens nor Thackeray, certainly, had the smallest
> notion of this; George Eliot had a kind of heavy intellect for
> it... but all her genuine feeling went into the visual realism of
> *Amos Barton.*[70]

To improve on Eliot's metaphor for Jamesian criticism would be difficult: his 'technique has received the kind of praise usually accorded to some useless, ugly and ingenious piece of carving which has taken a long time'.[71] The same essay claims that James was not concerned with the portrayal of character in the usual sense, and that critics have failed to understand that 'character is only one of the ways in which it is possible to grasp reality'. Ultimately James is 'more pertinent for the present age than Dostoyevsky', and 'no less profound', though his 'criticism of books and ideas is feeble'.[72] The 'profundity of Meredith', for comparison, is 'profound platitude'. By the 1930s, James's reputation had declined to the extent that, in a draft for *The Family Reunion,* one of the two characters says 'the jolly corner', then apologises for having alluded to 'an author whom you have never heard of'.

Among Eliot's elders, the fictionalists for whom he had the highest regard were Kipling,[73] Conrad and, as aforesaid, Hardy. Eliot's writings on the first extend from 1919 to 1959, and the titles of two of his poems are indebted to Kipling (*The Love Song of J. Alfred Prufrock* to *The Love Song of Har Dyal*[74] and *The Hollow Men* to *The Broken Men*[75]). In a 1909 college essay, 'Defects of Kipling', Eliot rated *Without Benefit of Clergy* 'perhaps the best thing which Kipling has done'. Ten years later, he described *Plain Tales from the Hills* as 'the

---

70 *Little Review,* August 1918.
71 *Vanity Fair,* February 1924.
72 *Egoist,* January 1918. In the same issue, Eliot derides Meredith's ideas as 'a facile substitute for observation and inference', and argues that style is more truly an acquirement than an endowment'. Nowhere does Eliot admit that the last line of his poem 'Cousin Nancy'- 'the army of unalterable law' - is a magpie borrowing from Meredith's sonnet 'Lucifer in Starlight'.
73 Lord Birkenhead's biography of Kipling (1978) revealed that Eliot had advised Mrs Bembridge, Kipling's daughter, against publishing the book.
74 *Kipling Journal,* March 1959.
75 In a letter to the *TLS,* 10 January 1935, Eliot said that *The Hollow Men* combines Kipling's title with that of William Morris's *The Hollow Land.*

one perfect picture of a society of English, narrow, snobbish, spiteful, ignorant, vulgar, set down absurdly in a continent of which they are unconscious',[76] an opinion not contradicted in the introduction to his World War II selection of Kipling's verse. Kipling was 'the greatest master of the short story in English',[77] whose 'genius... lay in his powers of observation, description and intuition. That he was an intuitive[78] and not an intellectual may account for his being underrated by intellectuals who are not intuitive.'[79]

Eliot rarely mentions historical novels, but his comments on one of them demand quotation: Ford Madox Ford's 'admirable, unappreciated novel *Ladies Whose Bright Eyes* teaches us to see the Middle Ages as we see our own time, just as Scott taught his age to see the Middle Ages as it saw or wished to see itself. An historical work not only tells us more – or what is more authentic – about the age in which it is written than about the past...'

In 1922 Eliot encountered the disturbing new genre of the psychoanalytic novel through May Sinclair, who had extolled Eliot's poetry from the time of *Prufrock*. Five years earlier he had published an anonymous short review of her philosophical book, *Defence of Idealism*,[80] and he had mentioned his friendship with this older woman to his mother. The first issue of *The Criterion* publishes her short story, 'The Victim', next to *The Waste Land*, and in 1922 she was one of three organisers of a fund-raising project to help support Eliot and rescue him from his time-and-energy-consuming job at Lloyd's Bank. In the same year, discussing her book, *Life and Death of Harriet Frean*, in the *Dial*, he refers to psychoanalysis as a 'dubious science', adding that the 'soul of man under psychoanalysis' is an 'evasion of the problem of evil'. But the review is more interesting for an incidental comment on Oscar Wilde, who 'through

---

76 *Athenaeum*, 2 May 1919.
77 *Criterion*, October 1926. On the connection between Kipling's story 'They' and *Burnt Norton*, see Gardner, *op. cit.*
78 According to Chambers, and most grammarians, the word is not a noun.
79 *Kipling Journal*, March 1959.
80 *New Statesman*, 22 September 1917. A letter from Rebecca West, 3 November 1962, to Sinclair's biographer describes her as 'a delightful human being' but doubts a love affair between her and Richard Aldington.

the whole experience of his life remained a little Eyas, a child actor'.

Eliot's criticism of his older French contemporaries deplores that 'There never was a time, I believe, when those who read at all, read so many more books by living authors than books by dead authors; there never was a time so completely parochial, so shut off from the past.'[81] He observes that Gide's writings 'belong to a class of literature... in which the author is moved partly by the desire to justify himself. The greatest authors have never written for this reason...'[82] If Eliot's characterisation of the novels of Léon Blois as 'violent and rhapsodical'[83] is apt, not many will share his opinion of Bernanos's *Sous le Soleil de Satan* as 'a novel of great interest'. Eliot was more involved with Paul Bourget, in whose *Lazarine* and *Essais de psychologie contemporaine* he finds a subconscious fascination with a plot in which the hero, in fortuitous and undiscoverable circumstances, shoots his estranged wife – the uxoricide theme that reappeared in *The Family Reunion*.[84] Otherwise, *Lazarine* is dull, Bourget having failed to make us understand 'particular feelings at particular moments'. His novels derive from the 'talent of analysis in company with the talent of curiosity', but in *Lazarine*, the sense of curiosity has evaporated, and only analysis remains.[85] In 1926 Eliot had written that 'Passionate curiosity in individual man... together with a complete detachment from all theory, all faith, all moral judgment, go to make the peculiar talent of Sainte-Beuve'. Three years later he wrote that 'What is permanent and good in Romanticism is a curiosity – a curiosity which recognises that any life, if accurately and profoundly penetrated, is interesting and always strange'.[86] Earlier, Eliot had remarked that 'With such anatomists as Racine and

---

81 'Religion and Literature', 1933.
82 *Revelation.*
83 *TLS,* 8 November 1923.
84 Eliot's fascination with murder warrants analysis beyond literary criticism. 'A man murders his mistress,' he wrote. 'The important part is that for the man the act is eternal, and for the brief space he has to live, he is already dead... He has crossed the frontier. Something is done which cannot be undone... a possibility which none of us realize [sic] until we face it ourselves... The medieval world, insisting on the eternity of punishment, expressed something near the truth' (*Little Review,* May 1917).
85 *New Statesman,* 24 June 1916.
86 *Athenaeum,* 2 May 1919.

Stendhal, life has an interest to which analysis is never adequate; there is always something unexplained'.[87]

It seems that Eliot's Rhadamanthine powers of judgement desert him only in grading the fictions of personal friends such as Djuna Barnes, Charles Williams and Wyndham Lewis – 'the most fascinating personality of our time'; the characters of his *Tarr* are 'immortal for literature'.[88] His encomiums for the genius of Djuna Barnes, whose *Nightwood* he claims to have read 'a good many times', are no less wildly inflated: it is 'so good a novel that only sensibilities trained on poetry can wholly appreciate it... a great achievement of style, beauty of phrasing'.[89] His introduction to *All Hallows' Eve*, after having 'read all of Charles Williams's novels as they were published', amounts to an empty puff: Williams 'is a mystic of Love' who understands 'the depths and intricacies of human nature', who shares affinities with Sheridan Le Fanu and with the Chesterton of *Man Who Was Thursday*, which, incidentally, 'we can enjoy... simply because of the swiftly moving plot'.

Eliot's recognition of David Jones's *In Parenthesis* as 'a work of genius' goes some way in balancing the Lewis hyperbole, but the kudos for Virginia Woolf in the *Nouvelle Revue Française* (1937) contrasts oddly with the embarrassing avoidance of any judgement

---

87 *New Statesman*, 27 August 1917.
88 *Egoist*, September 1918. The same is true of Eliot's pronouncements upon the poetry of his friends, as when he asserts that 'There are poems by Mr. Herbert Read and Mr. Aldington which endure' (*Dial*, March 1921). (One wonders which ones.) Eliot's 1955 *Hudson Review* essay on Lewis's *Monstre Gai* declares a preference for it to the 'less mature' *Tarr*, but continues to praise the author-painter, comparing him favourably to Picasso in the latter profession: 'Mr. Lewis, unlike Picasso, Dior or other fashionable designers, has never been concerned with finding a new style for next spring'; and even to 'Leonardo, that formidable and unpleasant personality (the simpering madonnas and epicene saints of his famous canvases are obviously phantoms of the same brain that conceived the flying machine, the submarine, and other subversive [*sic*] contraptions)'. In another essay of the same period, Eliot says that 'perhaps we need not too much regret that Raphael did not [further] multiply his Madonnas'. Eliot was obviously forgetting Fenollosa and Pound and their comparison of the 'quiet mysterious smile of a Japanese Buddha to the smile of the *Mona Lisa*'. Obviously the great poet had no 'eye' for the visual arts; indeed, he was actually unaware that frescoes are not painted on canvas. One wonders how the ex-editor of *The Criterion* could conclude that 'Mr. Lewis is the greatest prose master of style of my generation.' To this writer, the prose of *Monstre Gai* is awkward and inept: *viz*. the description of a character who emerges from a WC with a 'deliberate bashfulness', words that do not go together, while another, 'opinionated as a rhinoceros', offers to 'give you the low-down'. 'Thanks awfully,' another 'gushes', though two words cannot be gushed.
89 *Criterion*, April 1937.

on her work in Eliot's *Horizon* obituary for her, which begins with the odd disclaimer, 'I have never been able to interest myself in criticizing contemporary writers', and ends by saying no more of her novels than that 'the future will arrive at a permanent estimate of their place'.[90] As for Gertrude Stein, to whom Eliot had written in 1925, 'I am immensely interested in everything you write,' he was soon predicting that *The Making of Americans* will 'remain unread... Miss Stein's... work is not improving, it is not amusing, it is not interesting, it is not good for one's mind...'[91] He was scathing about her 'school', averring that 'a society which has [patronised] such novelists as Mr. Thornton Wilder [and] Mr. Hemingway... is decidedly decadent'. 'Mr. Frost's... verse is uninteresting, and what is uninteresting is unreadable, and what is unreadable is not read' (*Dial*, May 1922). In contrast, *The Great Gatsby* seemed to be 'the first step that American fiction has taken since Henry James'.[92]

Eliot's kinship among the Russians was with Turgenev, partly as the exemplar of the writer living abroad:

> Turgenev's grasp of the uniformity of human nature [and his] interest in its variations made him cosmopolitan and made him a critic. He did not acquire those two qualities in Paris, he brought them with him.[93]

Eliot is 'not sure that the material of Turgenev – this perfect proportion, this vigilant but never theoretical intelligence, this austere art of omission – is not that which in the end may prove most satisfying to the civilized mind'. Turgenev 'used Russian material naturally, with the simplicity of genius turning to what its feelings know best'. But his form par excellence is the *conte*, not the novel. He

could not get lost in a character,[94] could not become possessed

---

90 May 1941.
91 *Nation and Athenaeum*, 29 January 1927.
92 Letter to F. Scott Fitzgerald, published in *The Crack-Up* (1945).
93 'Dostoyevsky is none the less universal for having stopped in Russia' (*American Literature and the American Language*, 1953).
94 This could be contested in the case of *A House of Gentlefolk*.

by the illusion that any particular creation was, for the time being, the center of the universe. His detail, therefore, is not that of the exaggeration of the trivial in an abnormally stimulated consciousness, but really a way of setting the balance right. Hence the importance of the frequent interruptions of external nature, and the interruptions always come to correct the seriousness of life with the seriousness of art.[95]

'A curious trick of the Russian novel [is] of fastening upon accidental properties of a critical situation, and letting them in turn fasten upon the attention to such an extent as to replace the emotion which gave them their importance.' With Dostoyevsky, too, and in contrast to Balzac, the

most successful, most imaginative flights are projections, continuations of the actual, the observed... [Dostoyevsky's] point of departure... is a human brain in a human environment.[96] [Yet] so much of Dostoyevsky's effect is due to apparent pure receptivity, lack of conscious selection, to the irrelevancies which merely happen and contribute imperceptibly to a total impression.[97]

Moreover, Dostoyevsky had

the gift, a sign of genius in itself, for utilizing his weakness; so that epilepsy and hysteria cease to be the defects of an individual and become the entrance to a genuine and personal universe. I do not suppose that Dostoyevsky's struggles were fundamentally alien to Flaubert's.[98]

At the same time, Dostoyevsky is a dangerous model, since the 'method is only permissible if you see things the way that Dostoyevsky

---

95   *Egoist*, December 1917.
96   *Athenaeum*, 30 May 1919.
97   *Egoist*, September 1918.
98   *Egoist*, December 1917. Both men were epileptics.

saw them'.[99] Eliot had first read *Crime and Punishment*, *The Idiot* and *The Brothers Karamazov* in French translation in 1911, under the influence of Alain-Fournier.

The essay 'Beyle and Balzac',[100] the centrepiece of Eliot's art-of-fiction criticism, challenges Victor Hugo's[101] formula of the 'union of imagination with observation'. 'The greatest artists do not bring these two together,' he says, and in Balzac the combination produced little more than an 'aura':

> Balzac, relying upon atmosphere, is capable of evading an issue. The greatest novelists dispense with atmosphere. Beyle and Flaubert strip the world[102] and they were men of far more common intensity of feeling, of passion. It is this intensity... and consequent discontent with the inevitable inadequacy of actual living to the passionate capacity which drove them to art... The exposure, the dissociation of human feeling, is a great part of the superiority of Beyle and Flaubert to Balzac.[103]

This is the familiar 'impersonality' creed of the most personal and autobiographical of poets. The reader is hardly surprised to be told that Stendhal's mind was 'an instrument continually tempering and purifying emotion'.[104]

Despite his professed 'aversion to prose fiction' and disavowal of any 'special competence to criticize it', Eliot's Introduction to *The Adventures of Huckleberry Finn* is criticism of a high order:

> Other authors had achieved natural speech in relation to particular characters – Scott with characters talking Lowland

99 *Dial*, August 1922.
100 *Athenaeum*, 30 May 1919.
101 Hugo 'had no gift whatever for thinking' (*Cambridge Review*, 6 June 1928).
102 In *Time and Tide*, 19 January 1935. Eliot cites Rémy de Gourmont's 'La Vie est un dépouillement' (Le Problème du style), adding that 'To be free we must be stripped, like the sea-god Glaucus...'
103 In a review of Charles Whibley's *Literary Studies*, Eliot states that in addition to the standard tools of the critic, comparison and analysis, the artist must have 'the dissociative faculty' (*Athenaeum*, 12 December 1919).
104 *Athenaeum*, 4 July 1929.

Scots, Dickens with cockneys - but no one else had kept it up through the whole of a book. Thackeray's Yellowplush, impressive as he is, is an obvious artifice in comparison. In *Huckleberry Finn* there is no exaggeration of grammar or spelling or speech, there is no sentence or phrase to destroy the illusion that these are Huck's own words...

Turning to the river that 'gives the book its form'–Twain's river is 'the universal river of human life, more universal [*sic*] than the Congo of Joseph Conrad' – Eliot does not conceal his emotions, and even alludes to his own poetry:

The river with its strong, swift current... is a treacherous and capricious dictator. At one season... it runs with a speed such that no man or beast can survive it. At such times, it carries down human bodies, cattle, and houses... In my own childhood, it was not unusual for the spring freshet to interrupt railway travel... The river is never wholly chartable... the Boy is also the spirit of the River.

Huck

would be incomplete without Jim, who is almost as notable a creation as Huck himself. Huck is the passive observer of men and events, Jim the submissive sufferer from them; and they are equal in dignity... the River makes the book a great book. As with Conrad, we are continually reminded of the power and terror of Nature, and the isolation and feebleness of Man... But Mark Twain is a native, and the River God is his God. It is as a native that he accepts the River God, and it is the subjection of Man that gives to Man his dignity. For without some kind of God, Man is not even very interesting.

Chapter 18

On Eliot's Philosophy at Harvard and After

Apart from his 1916 doctoral dissertation, *Meinong's Gegendstandstheorie Considered in Relation to Bradley's Theory of Knowledge*, widely reviewed but little read at the time of its belated publication,[1] Eliot's writings on philosophy have not been collected and are little known. This dereliction is the more remarkable for the reason that he taught philosophy at Harvard for three years, and his principal comments on the subject, contemporary with his first mature poems, reveal more autobiographical glimpses than his literary essays. One of these is found in an article on Gordon Craig written a half century later. In 1955 Eliot recalled that he first read Craig 'while I was an undergraduate at Harvard - probably in 1907 or 1908. Other discoveries of the same period were Manet and Monet, Japanese prints, the plays of Maeterlinck, the music of Debussy, and above all the combination of Maeterlinck and Debussy in *Pelléas et Mélisande*.' This establishes the year as 1908, the date of the opera's debut in New York, the only place in which Eliot could have heard it, since his first visit to Paris was in 1910, but the recollection helps to flesh out a portrait of him as a student.

Of Eliot's Harvard teachers, William James, George Santayana, Josiah Royce, Bertrand Russell, the last had, if not the greatest intellectual influence on him, the largest role in his personal life. But

---

1   1964, under the title *Knowledge and Experience in the Philosophy of F.H. Bradley.*

Eliot admired qualities in the others, more as men, perhaps, than as philosophers: William James   .

> had great curiosity, and a curiously charming willingness to believe anything that seemed preposterous to the ordinary scientific mind. He hated oppression in any form; the oppression of dogmatic theology was remote from him, who lived in the atmosphere of Unitarian Harvard; but the oppression of idealistic philosophy and the oppression of scientific materialism were very real to him. Many of James's ideas may be due rather to this antipathy to other people's narrow convictions than to convictions of his own... [The] footnotes... show that James was already struggling toward the philosophy barely outlined at his death, the 'Radical Empiricism' which he considered more important than his Pragmatism...

> The two points made and elaborated in the body of the James [Ingersoll Lecture of 1898] are the 'transmission' theory of psycho-physics and the futility of the objection to immortality as an appalling and tiresome multiplication of souls. On the latter point, he is characteristically democratic, genially drawing a picture of a future life which includes animals and savages and our primitive ancestors. The former point, the theory that the function of the brain is not to generate consciousness but to 'limit' it, has since been made familiar by Bergson's *Matter and Memory*... There are difficulties in the theory which James does not face: the greatest of these perhaps is that we do not clearly conceive what it is, according to the theory, that is transmitted; what 'consciousness' is, apart from its actualisation through the brain into thoughts and words and acts... he says that after death the 'sphere of being' which *supplied* the consciousness would remain intact. Personal immortality always tends to evaporate in this way... But James has an exceptional quality

of always leaving his reader with the feeling that the world is full of possibilities...[2]

In 1908 Eliot attended Santayana's course in the 'History of Modern Philosophy', and in the next year the more advanced one, 'Ideals of Society, Religion, Art and Science in Their Historical Developments', which kindled the nascent poet's lifelong fascination with Dante. In 1926 Eliot's lectures on *The Varieties of Metaphysical Poetry* at Cambridge University refer to Santayana's *Three Philosophical Poets* (Lucretius, Dante, Goethe) as his 'most brilliant' work, but conclude that Santayana is 'more interested in poetical philosophy than in philosophical poetry'. Still, 'Mr. Santayana and myself... have both, I imagine, a prejudice in favor of the clear and distinct; we mean a philosophy which is expressed, not one which is inexpressible... Further, I should agree with Mr. Santayana that Shakespeare is not a philosophical poet.' Eliot returned to his Santayana theme in 1933, in the Johns Hopkins Turnbull Lectures, which to an extent are a recension of the Harvard Norton Lectures delivered in the previous months: 'It is clear that for Mr. Santayana a philosophical poet is one with a scheme of the universe... Dante and Lucretius expounded explicit philosophies, as Shakespeare did not.'

The phrase 'ends not with a bang' (the 'Hollow Men') comes from Santayana's Dante essay (in *Three Philosophical Poets*), and in the preface to his own essay on Dante, Eliot acknowledged a debt to Santayana's study of Goethe for the apt classification 'a philosophical poet' – although regretting 'Goethe's philosophy [as] that which the nineteenth century took up with... Love, Nature, God, Man, Science, Progress'.[3] Santayana also seems to have coined the term 'objective correlative', which became an Eliot nametag.

Eliot's references to Royce – 'my old master, now mostly forgotten, but a great philosopher in his day' – are similarly respectful and, on occasion, even affectionate. Eliot's introduction to his mother's Dramatic Poem, *Savonarola*, recalls that his unpublished 1913 paper

2   'William James on Immortality', *New Statesman*, 1 September 1917.
3   *New English Weekly*, 6 June 1935.

on *The Interpretation of Primitive Ritual* was intended 'for the eye of that extraordinary philosopher, Josiah Royce'. Eliot had participated in Royce's seminar on comparative methodology, and Royce graded Eliot's thesis on Bradley 'the work of an expert'. In 1955 a fellow seminarian, H.T. Costello, of Trinity College, Hartford, published a recollection of Eliot saying that he wanted to know the meaning of 'interpretation' as opposed to 'description', and that his year's work, 1913–14, 'circled around this question of the truth of interpretations'. Following Bradley, Eliot had maintained that no simple statement was absolutely true, thereby provoking a fellow student to inquire if Eliot thought *his* statement could apply to itself. An altercation threatened when Eliot replied that 'You can't understand me. To understand my point of view you have to believe it first.' At this, Royce, as referee, rung down the curtain with 'We can never make a simple statement'.[4]

It was in this period that Eliot read Hegel, whose phenomenology Royce had ridiculed as a *Bildungsroman.* The more tolerant Santayana, with 'his imperial and slightly amused gaze', had shown a 'tender reverence and admirable restraint' toward Hegel, whose Idealist philosophy Eliot condemned as a 'colossal and grotesque achievement'[5] that 'constituted the orthodox doctrine of American universities, [where] it had begun to turn manifestly mouldy'.[6] Hegel, Eliot goes on, was 'the most prodigious exponent of emotional systematization, dealing with his emotions as if they were definite objects which had aroused those emotions', but he blames the Hegelians, not Hegel, for believing 'that words have definite meanings, overlooking the tendency of words to become indefinite emotions':[7]

Compare a seventeenth-century preacher with any 'liberal' sermon since Schleiermacher, and you will observe that words have changed their meanings. What they have lost is definite, and what they have gained is indefinite… when everyone knows a little about a great many things, it becomes increasingly

4   *The Journal of Philosophy*, 1956.
5   *The Listener*, 23 March 1932.
6   Introduction to *Leisure: The Basis of Culture*, by Josef Pieper (1952).
7   *The Sacred Wood.*

difficult for anyone to know whether he knows what he is talking about or not. And when we do not know, or when we do not know enough, we tend always to substitute emotions for thoughts.[8]

At this point, two other philosophy teachers from Eliot's early Harvard years, Irving Babbitt and Paul Elmer More, must be mentioned, since at that time they seemed to him 'the two wisest men that I have known', though neither warrants discussion here, since Eliot's essay on Babbitt is still in print[9] and More was never formally Eliot's teacher. A fellow St Louisan, he 'had known my family, and if he had remained there a few years longer, he would have taught me Greek as he had taught my brother'.[10] Eliot met More at the Harvard home of Babbitt, but recalled that it was not until the publication of the later volumes of More's *The Greek Tradition* that 'I came to find an auxiliary to my own progress of thought, which no English theologian at the time could have given me...'[11]

One of Eliot's most precise statements about a philosophical position of his own occurs in his first article on More:

> The fundamental beliefs of an intellectual conservatism, that man requires an askesis, a *formula* to be imposed upon him from above: that society must develop out of itself a class of leaders who shall discipline it; distrust of the premises of the future, and conviction that the future... must be built upon the wisdom of the past - that is what we find in all of Mr. More's writings.[12]

More developed in a direction that Eliot found 'painful', a position

---

8   *Ibid.*

9   'The Humanism of Irving Babbitt', *Selected Essays*, 1932.

10   Although Eliot described his Greek as 'inadequate to the appreciation of Pindar's Odes', E.R. Dodds (*The Greeks and the Irrational*) attested that the young poet's command of the language as revealed in a seminar on Plotinus' *Enneads*, was equal to that of the best scholars. Eliot deprecated his own knowledge of languages - 'I began with a public school knowledge of Latin, a traveler's smattering of Italian' (Preface to *Dante*, 1929), but admitted to enjoying Lallans, even though 'I read [it] with difficulty'. (Letter to Hugh MacDiarmid)

11   *Princeton Alumni Weekly*, February 1937.

12   *New Statesman*, 24 June 1916.

which, ironically, he disclosed in part to Babbitt on their last meeting in London, before Babbitt's death in Boston in 1933.

Before turning to the 'emancipated Puritan', as Eliot famously characterised Russell, we should look to Henri Bergson, Eliot's deepest pre-Russell philosophical involvement having been with him and his lectures at the Sorbonne in 1910–11. On Eliot's graduation from Harvard in the former year – not Phi Beta Kappa – he fled to France. Surely William James had influenced Eliot in this, the pragmatist and the French mystic having corresponded as early as 1902, and James having hosted Bergson in intellectual society in New York and Boston. Both men were fascinated by the origins of religious experience and by new studies in psychology, as was the young Eliot. *Prufrock*, his masterpiece about indecision, borrows two lines from Bergson's *An Introduction to Metaphysics.* Later, in the 1920s, Bergson defined the fundamental difference between his philosophy and James's, but meanwhile Eliot had perceived that Bergson's 'creative world-will' did not 'provide an answer to the question of whether reality might be found in the object or in the consciousness';[13] that Bergson's use of science sometimes concealed 'the incoherence of a multiplicity of points of view'; and that his exciting promise of immortality was 'a sometimes meretricious captivation'.[14] But while Eliot rejected Bergson's time doctrine for inherent '*fatalism* which is wholly destructive',[15] Bergson, in the following passage, says much the same thing as the first part of *Burnt Norton*:

> Time, as we ordinarily envisage it, is a division of reality into existent and non-existent parts. From the reality which now is, the reality which will be is excluded. Duration knows no such distinction. The past exists in the present which contains the future. The concrete and ever-present instance of duration is life, for each of us living individuals in his own time.

13   Unpublished paper on Bergson, Houghton Library, Harvard.
14   *Criterion*, October 1927.
15   *Vanity Fair*, February 1924.

Looking back, an almost wistful Eliot wrote that

> to have truly understood the Bergsonian fervor, one must have
> gone, regularly, every week to the Collège de France, and the
> full hall where he gave his courses. (It was necessary to arrive
> an hour and a quarter ahead of time...)[16]

At a still greater distance, Eliot continued to express a 'longing for the
appearance of a philosopher whose writings, lectures, and personality
will arouse the imagination as Bergson aroused it forty years ago'.[17]
Eliot retrospectively perceived that 'the reason for my dissatisfaction
with philosophy as a profession I now believe to lie in the divorce
of philosophy from theology',[18] but this could have been portended
from his earliest philosophical reviews, which are preoccupied with
theology. His precocious attraction to Leibniz is also attributable to
the great monadist's 'strong devotion to theology'. Leibniz 'had the
mind of a doctor of the church,' Eliot wrote, and a power of intellect
in which he is 'the equal of Aristotle or Plato, though for all the
curious fables of *Timaeus* or the *Physics* [Plato and the Stagirite] were
more secure, better balanced, and less superstitious'.[19] Nevertheless,
Leibniz's theory of mind and matter, body and soul, 'is in some ways
the subtlest that has ever been devised. Matter [for him] is an arrested
moment of mind, "mind without memory"',[20] or what Bergson called
'mind running down'.[21]

In the autumn of 1911 Eliot was back at Harvard as a candidate for
a doctorate in philosophy, but the philosophy he began to study was
Indian, as taught by Professor J.H. Woods. Following his conviction
that the great works of literature and philosophy must be read
in the language of the original, Eliot learned enough Sanskrit to

16 *What France Means to You* (1944).
17 Introduction to Pieper, *op. cit.*
18 *Ibid.*
19 *Monist*, January 1916.
20 *Ibid.*
21 Unpublished paper on Bergson, *op. cit.*

make his way through at least some of the ninth-century *Sankara*.

Not until 1914, with Russell, did Eliot begin to form his belief that although

> no philosopher can be judged entirely on his prose, a good deal of light can be thrown on a philosopher by holding his work up to the standards of literature. For literary standards help us to perceive just those moments when a writer is scrupulously and sincerely attending to his vision... The point is, where is Mr. Russell's insight, his peculiar vision, to be found; is it equally present everywhere? For where that is, there will the style be; and where the style does not convince, the vision will be lacking... His style... neither increases nor dissimulates the difficulty of the subject. The liberation of English philosophy from German influence[22] will have been the work, not of Mill (who is an amateur), but of Mr. Russell; he is a philosopher who has invented a new point of view; and a new point of view is style.[23]

Apart from syntax, Eliot thought that good prose required precision, ordonnance and adequation, though he never used the last term (I think), so dear to Coleridge and so perfectly defined by Eliot's own iconic master of prose, Lancelot Andrewes: 'There are the words uttered as true, when there is a just adequation between them and the mind.'

In Russell, Aristotle, Plato, Spinoza and fragments from only two or three others, the philosophy can be called a work of art: 'Mr. Russell's essay on "Denoting"' is 'clear and beautifully formed thought.' But Eliot proceeds to criticise Russell's prose at its second best by reminding him that the possibilities of lyricism for his purposes are

---

22 'Russell and Bradley, between them, have nearly laid metaphysics in the grave.' (*New Statesman*, 29 December 1917).

23 *Nation*, 23 March 1918. In this article, Eliot refers to the *Principia mathematica* without mentioning Whitehead. In a later essay (*Bookman*, February 1930), Whitehead is acknowledged as 'one of the greatest... exponents of formal logic', but the compliment is a prelude to an attack on Whitehead's 'summoning of Shelley and Wordsworth to prove something in connection with a philosophy of nature... [While] poetry provides intellectual sanction for feeling, and aesthetic sanction for thought... [it] cannot prove that anything is true.' In a later paper Eliot denounces 'Whitehead's God' as a 'sentimental monstrosity'.

limited. Quoting a weak passage, Eliot remarks that elsewhere, 'Mr. Russell has made us *feel* "the passionate splendor" of Time and Fate and Death; here he has merely told us about it.' Moreover, 'there is certainly something a little disconcerting at times about Mr. Russell's exposition. It is so convincingly the subject explaining itself, rather than a writer explaining the subject.' Eliot offers three quotations from *Mysticism and Logic* as examples of Russell's ability to be 'paradoxical without meretriciousness, or which have the impact of paradox without its cheapness'. Here is the shortest: 'Not only is it doubtful whether Euclid's axioms are true, which is a comparatively trivial matter, but it is certain that his propositions do not follow from the axioms which he enunciates.'

Russell himself identified Eliot as the author of this unsigned article, as, incidentally, he recognised himself as the satyr in Eliot's poem 'Mr. Apollinax':

> *I heard the beat of centaur's hoofs over the hard turf*
> *As his dry and passionate talk devoured the afternoon.*

The continuation of the story is well known, and sometimes falls into tabloid quality. In 1924 Eliot attacked an inane pronouncement by Russell that 'Science is the only claim to distinction'[24] of the nineteenth century (not Beethoven?), but Eliot weakens his rebuttal by failing to name other claims and by limiting his ammunition to writers and painters). We now see this exchange as the opening skirmish in the war of 'the two cultures'. Later that year Eliot concluded that Russell had

> never been really convinced that philosophy was possible at all
> – the mathematician in him [being] impatient of the philosopher.
> Hence his history presents the curious spectacle of a very powerful
> mind... at war with itself... destroying not so much other men's
> systems (though Russell laid flat a good many) as his own.[25]

---

24   *Vanity Fair*, February 1924.
25   *Criterion*, April 1924.

Eliot nevertheless continued to revere Russell's intellect, which 'would have reached the first rank even in the thirteenth century'.[26]

The ten reviews of philosophical publications in the *Monist* in 1917 and 1918, first identified as Eliot's in 1977,[27] reveal a hitherto unknown link with Russell. On his recommendation, Philip Jourdain,[28] his pupil and the English editor of *Monist* (Chicago), invited Eliot to review 'all books on philosophy and science [not of] a formal character'. The exhumed writings date from Eliot's 'Russell period', which began in 1915 at Merton College, where the poet spent most of his time on the *Principia mathematica* ('It gave me a sense of pleasure and power, manipulating those curious little figures'), and moved on to a 'Dear Bertie', 'Dear Tom' stage, during which Eliot adopted the view that 'the truths of mathematics are not true absolutely, but are true and proper for the human mind'. In 1920, asked whether his essay 'The Perfect Critic' was philosophy or criticism, Eliot leaned on Russell's argument in the *Principia* (Chapter 2, on 'The Theory of Types and the Cretan Liar') that 'the statement of Epimenides does not fall within its own scope, therefore no contradiction emerges'.

The best of the recovered *Monist* pieces relate closely to Eliot's developing beliefs as known from other writings. Thus his presentation of Sorel on violence, read in T.E. Hulme's translation, is similar to views propounded in *For Lancelot Andrewes*:

> The reaction against romanticism which is one of the most interesting phenomena of our time... [the hatred] of middle-class democracy... the skepticism... which has developed the craving for belief... Sorel longs for a narrow, intolerant, creative society with sharp divisions. He longs for the pessimistic, classical view... It is not surprising that Sorel has become a Royalist...

---

26 'The Renaissance Platonists [were] inferior to the scholastics of the thirteenth century, scientific thinking having displaced philosophic thinking' (*Times Literary Supplement*, 6 December 1926). He should have mentioned Fibonacci, who is still an influence on composers.

27 By Alan Cohn and Elizabeth Eames. See *The Papers of the Bibliographical Society of America* 70, no. 3 (1977), 420-24.

28 See their correspondence, *Dear Russell, Dear Jourdain*, London, 1977.

Nor, reading this, is it at all surprising that Eliot would become one, too. Another of the *Monist* reviews, of Harris's *The Ascent of Olympus*, a history of the thunder-god from phytomorph (the oak tree is the kind most often struck by lightning) to anthropomorph (Dionysus and Apollo), points to *The Waste Land*. But Eliot was already familiar with the thunder fable (Datta, Dayadhvam, Damyata), in Sanskrit (the Brihadaranyaka Upanishad), or in German (Deussen's *Sechzig Upanishads des Vedas*), but also possibly in the English *Hindu Law and Custom as to Gifts* by C.R. Lanman, one of Eliot's Sanskrit professors.

Yet another *Monist* review, of a book of Jainist texts, questions the differences between the precepts of *ahimsa* (non-violence to all living beings) in Jainism, and, in Buddhism, between the dualism of the former and that of early Sankhya. But the most aggressive of the ten articles is aimed at Durkheim, whose 'group-consciousness' Eliot did not believe to be 'capable of articulate expression', and whose theory of the genesis of knowledge 'has doubtful philosophical implications... Durkheim leaves epistemology... precisely where it was before'. Jourdain's requirement that Eliot sign his pieces with his cognominal initial in Greek (*eta*) undoubtedly helped to hide them all these years, which is a shocking comment on the decline of cultural standards.

———◆———

Eliot's notes on his reading in the Harvard years show that his other main interests were mysticism and the psychology of religious experience. After his conversion to Anglo-Catholicism (1928), he excluded mysticism as a nostrum for the present: 'Mysticism nowadays' is simply a 'warm fog',[29] he writes of Baron Von Hügel's letters, after admitting that he has not read, partly because the style is so difficult, *The Mystical Element in Religion, as Studied in St. Catherine of Genoa and Her Friends*. '[Hügel's] feelings were exact [but] his ideas were often vague' – partly because he was

---

29   *The Listener*, 2 April 1930.

> neither a great philosopher, nor a theologian... Mysticism is
> not the issue of our time. We demand of religion some kind
> of intellectual satisfaction... True mysticism is so rare and
> unessential and false mysticism is so common and dangerous
> that one cannot oppose it too firmly.[30]

Eliot nevertheless commends Hügel for having decided on his own that 'the thirteenth century was a grander epoch than the sixteenth century'. Dante and Giotto vs. Montaigne and Michelangelo?

Nevertheless, the doctrine of John of the Cross ('perhaps the greatest psychologist of all European mystics'[31]), the denial of self in the love of God, was to be the foundation of Eliot's faith in the years immediately before World War II, a period during which he also accepted the *Dhammapada*, recognising that the belief in karma and reincarnation 'was so deep in the mentality [of Buddha's followers] as to be a category of their thought... His teaching assumes its truth.'[32] In 1917 Eliot had written: 'It seems to me that Buddhism is as truly a religion from the beginning as is Christianity.'[33]

Though Eliot discusses his espousal of 'classicism in literature' in several texts, he wrote very little about his 'royalism in politics'. His remarks on the legal issues of the abdication of Edward VIII (in the *New English Weekly*, 27 February 1937) may have some connection to his friendship with Ernest Simpson, Wallis's divorced husband. Here Eliot challenged the roles both of the press ('seldom edifying... whether righteous and sanctimonious or demagogic') and of public opinion ('When we cannot trust our own feelings, which might vary several times a day, why should we put faith in the collective feeling?'). He concludes with the warning: 'Those who saw in Edward a more democratic conception of the monarchy are enjoying the vision of an idealised past and preparing the way for a certainly not democratic

---

30   *Dial*, February 1928. The last sentence in this quotation is an observation by Bossuet that Irving Babbitt repeated to Eliot. Two years later Eliot explained that 'true mysticism is a gift of grace', the false kind produces 'pathological ecstatics'. *The Listener*, 12 March 1930.
31   *The Listener*, 2 April 1930.
32   *Revelation* (1937).
33   *The Humanism of Irving Babbitt*.

future... "When that the poor have cried, Caesar hath wept."[34]

On 8 October 1923, Eliot wrote to Richard Aldington, then his assistant editor at *The Criterion*: 'If I can write English prose... it is due to two causes: an intensive study of two years of the prose of Bradley, and an inherited disposition to rhetoric [which] gives my prose, I am aware, a rather rheumatic pomposity...' (In another aside[35] Eliot noted that 'A spirit such as mine is too inclined to measure everything according to the rules of a dogmatic conception and tends to become more and more rigid and formal.') But where Bradley was concerned Eliot had a blind spot, and the passage from *The Principles of Logic* that Eliot praises[36] contains at least one embarrassing locution: 'an unearthly ballet of bloodless categories'.

In his review of *The Oldest Biography of Spinoza*,[37] written by a French refugee in Holland who knew the philosopher there as a 'man of great reticence', a man 'of intensively private life', Eliot writes:

> The figure of Spinoza has been almost more important in the last hundred years than the philosophy of Spinoza. Few have mastered the *Ethics*, but everyone knows that Spinoza polished lenses; few people have read the *Tractatus Politicus*, but the whole world has been impressed by his excommunication from the Jewish Church. He has been almost a Saint of Deists: and even for those to whom he is hardly a 'Saint' he is unquestionably a hero, a symbolic hero of modern Europe. So that the celebration of the 250th anniversary has a different meaning from the anniversary of an Aristotle, an Aquinas, or a

---

34 On being awarded the Order of Merit, Eliot read *The Waste Land* in Buckingham Palace to assembled royals, who were apparently surprised that a poet did not have a uniform. A journalist published a description of the occasion attributed to the Queen: 'We had this rather lugubrious man in a suit and he read a poem. I think it was called "The Desert". At first the girls got the giggles, then I did, then even the King.'
35 *Nouvelle Revue Française*, 1 April 1925.
36 *For Lancelot Andrewes*, 1928.
37 *TLS*, 21 April 1927.

>Kant; it is the recognition not so much of a philosophy as of a
>personality in which certain human ideals seem to be realized.

Eliot tells us that as a young man he had considered the beginning
of the Third Book of Spinoza's *Ethics* 'especially brilliant',[38] but he
supported Leibniz's refutation of Spinoza's theory of the relation of
mind and body: 'With Spinoza the reason does not possess ideas,
it is an idea.' The switch of focus from Spinoza's philosophy to his
personality provokes the remark, 'A study of Spinoza worship from
Goethe, Renan, and Arnold on one side, and Rousseau on another would
show a considerable influence affecting liberal theology'.[39] Yet Eliot
himself had romanticised Spinoza, as in the following daydream about
Shakespeare: 'In the middle of a rowdy seventeenth-century playhouse
pit, the thought of Shakespeare, the feeling and the shuddering personal
experience of Shakespeare, moved solitary and unspoiled; solitary and
free as the thought of Spinoza in his study...'[40]

In his continual ratings of philosophers, Eliot tells us almost
as an aside that Descartes 'is inferior to Leibniz and Spinoza', but,
redeemingly, shows 'traces of later scholasticism, of Occam and the
nominalists'. Descartes remains 'the great typical figure of modern
heresy'.[41]

As he had done in the 1917 Russell article, Eliot continued to
evaluate philosophers by the quality of their writing. He cites Dewey's
'ungrammatical' thinking[42] as symbolic of the 'dark labyrinths of the
American philosophical mind', and condemns Péguy because

>his style... is not a style to think in; it is too emphatic, too
>insistent. His sentences, a dozen pages long, convey an emotion,
>but thought is submerged. It is a style with a refrain which
>compels one to lock step...[43]

---

38 *Athenaeum*, 4 April 1919.
39 *TLS*, 21 April 1927.
40 *Athenaeum*, 14 May 1920.
41 *Ibid*, 8 November 1928.
42 *TLS*, 2 September 1926.
43 *New Statesman*, 7 October 1916.

Péguy has a 'sensibility for the emotional value of words, completely unrestrained by either logic or common sense'.[44] He was handicapped in coming from a Paris 'surfeited with criticism [and with] radical and reactionary movements which were largely movements for the sake of moving'.

So far from being the exception to the rule of clear writing, Nietzsche's

> philosophy evaporates when detached from its literary qualities... Such scholars always have a peculiar influence over the large semi-philosophical public, who are spared the austere effort of criticism required either by metaphysics or literature.[45] Confusion of thought, emotion, and vision is what we find in *Also sprach Zarathustra*.[46]

Since Wagner's on-and-off disciple did not have a theory of knowledge, let alone a 'consistent moral policy', Eliot seems to have been drawn to Nietzsche primarily because of his 'pessimism with respect to the future of art evinced in *Human, All Too Human*'. Nietzsche's

> world-will is creative, like Bergson's, but, more sincerely than Bergson's... Sometimes the world appears malleable in the hands of humanity. Sometimes the world is conceived as something quite unconscious, and consciousness as epiphenomenal.

Even so, *The Birth of Tragedy* is quoted in *The Waste Land*.

Apart from the thesis on Bradley, Eliot's own style in his philosophical writings is admirably lucid and grammatically smoother than in some of his other prose. To an extent this may be the result of the tutoring (1916) of Harold Joachim, to whom Eliot acknowledged a 'debt for instruction in the writing of English... He taught me to avoid

---

44 *Cambridge Review*, 12 December 1928.
45 *International Journal of Ethics*, April 1916.
46 *The Sacred Wood* (1920).

metaphor and taught me the importance of punctuation'.[47]

Eliot's philosophical reviews are enlivened by skewering remarks: a certain Professor Parker 'has come by philosophy to conclusions which most thinking people have absorbed from the atmosphere';[48] by epigrams: 'Every significant philosopher is a man who has had one insight, or two or three, which no one before him had had; one new insight which excuses a hundred new errors';[49] and by a vividness that makes even the 'bald millionaire, *maestro di color che sanno*', seem to be our contemporary:

> In reading Aristotle... we are in touch with a mind that has regarded the world quite freshly and independently; when we read him carefully, we discover the world again with him, and find him, halting, stumbling, too intent upon the truth, at any moment, to be always consistent: sometimes at a dead stop in the face of insuperable difficulties.[50]

> One must be firmly distrustful of accepting [Aristotle] in a canonical spirit; this is to lose the whole living force of him. He was primarily a man of not only remarkable but universal intelligence; and universal intelligence means that he could apply his intelligence to anything... Aristotle had [no] impure desires to satisfy; in whatever sphere of interest, he looked solely and steadfastly at the object; in his short and broken treatise he provides an eternal example - not of laws, or even of method, for there is no method except to be very intelligent...[51]

---

47 *Times* (London), 6 August 1938. Eliot never completely mastered punctuation, and though he claims that 'correct language is civilisation' (*Listener*, 9 April 1930), his own language is (infrequently) careless: 'The modern world suffers from two great disasters,' he wrote, 'the decay of the study of Latin and Greek and the dissolution of the monasteries. These defects can be supplied' ('The Modern Dilemma', published in *Christian Register*, Boston, 19 October 1933). *Supplied?* Surely *remedied* is meant. See Robert Graves's and Alan Hodge's dissection, in *The Reader over Your Shoulder*, of the first three paragraphs of Eliot's essay on Massinger, and G.H. Vallins' analysis of a paragraph in Eliot's *The Use of Poetry and the Use of Criticism*, which exposes a misrelated participial phrase (a 'floater'), the misuse of an accusative and an infinitive, and the misrepresentation of 'many people' and 'they' by the first person possessive plural 'our'.
48 *New Statesman*, 13 July 1918.
49 *Ibid.*
50 *New Statesman*, 29 December 1917.
51 'The Perfect Critic', p. 9.

Eliot's own critical genius is in differentiating:

> For the Greek, the human was typically human, individual differences were not of scientific interest; for the modern philosopher, individual differences were of absorbing importance.[52]

Eliot is unduly harsh on Hobbes,

> one of those extraordinary little upstarts whom the chaotic notions of the Renaissance turned into an encumbrance which they hardly deserved and never lost. Hobbes was undoubtedly an atheist and could hardly have been unconscious of the fact; but he was no Spinoza and would hardly have been willing to sacrifice his worldly prospects for the sake of establishing consistency in his arguments.[53]

Hobbes is guilty of cynicism in this haughty homily, and of relying on an out-of-date anthropology, but this is broadly true of others, all of them much lesser writers than Hobbes. Eliot's review of Wundt's *Elements of Folk Psychology* condemns its animistic totemism, the 'diremption of primitive soul ideas into the corporeal soul and the breath- and shadow-soul'. The soul is regarded as 'a bird, a snake, or a lizard'.[54] Some of Eliot's own anthropological speculations warrant reprinting:

> It is possible to assert that primitive man acted in a certain way and then found a reason for it. An unoccupied person finding a drum may be seized with a desire to beat it; but

---

52 *Monist*, October 1916.
53 See the essay on John Bramhall in *For Lancelot Andrewes*, where Eliot berates Hobbes for 'confusing the spheres of psychology and ethics', and for rejecting the 'noble faith' of 'the divine right of kings', in favour of the divine right of power, however come by. Eliot unintentionally, I think, compliments Hobbes for at least two characteristics: He wishes to preserve 'the activity of human legislation in his deterministic universe'; and his philosophy is an 'adumbration of the universe of material atoms regulated by laws of motion, which formed the scientific view of the world from Newton to Einstein'.
54 *Monist*, January 1918.

> unless he is an imbecile he will be unable to continue beating
> it... without finding a reason for doing so. The reason may be
> the long continued drought. The next generation or the next
> civilization will find a more plausible reason for beating a
> drum. Shakespeare and Racine – or rather the developments
> which led up to them – each found his own reason. The reasons
> may be divided into tragedy and comedy. We still have similar
> reasons, but we have lost the drum.[55]

Distortions naturally occur in gamuts that extend from Maimonides to G.E. Moore, Heraclitus to Husserl (from whom Eliot's 'Triumphal March' borrows the line 'The natural wakeful life of our Ego is a perceiving'), Pantanjali to Frobenius ('The *Schicksalskunde* is an example of modern mind in its most unpleasant form'[56]). But within the bounds of general reading, the great poet scores a high proportion of 'right judgments', remote though many of them are from those prevailing at the time when he published.

Apart from *Le Neveu de Rameau*, Diderot, for one, was a mere 'echo of a name' when Eliot wrote:

> The Diderot problem is that he did not write a masterpiece. The
> *Letter on the Blind* and the *Letter on the Deaf and Dumb* are... as
> an exposition of sensationalism, inferior to Condillac's systematic
> treatise.[57] [Yet] wherever the intellect of the century stirred,
> Diderot dropped a grain into the ferment; he provided leading
> ideas which force the scientist to look in certain directions,
> which force the artist to develop certain forms... Whosoever
> wishes to understand how the nineteenth century sprang from
> the eighteenth must read Diderot as well as Rousseau.[58]

Eliot distinguishes the century of Newton, which could 'achieve a synthesis', from that of Giordano Bruno, which could not, in the 'mind

---

55 *Nation and Athenaeum*, 6 October 1926.
56 *New English Weekly*, 14 June 1934.
57 Ninety years later, we prize Diderot more for his equally unsystematic art criticism.
58 *New Statesman*, 17 March 1917.

of Montaigne, [who] is so much himself [but] also representative of some permanent attitude of the human spirit'.[59] Montaigne 'is a very highly civilized man, indeed', Eliot continues,

> but I must confess that he is rather too civilized for me and that I prefer cruder forms of literature... I hope that some of you[60] have at least looked at Florio's translation of Montaigne's *Essays*: you may even have read the *Apologie de Raimond Sébond* and then re-read *Hamlet*... Montaigne, in his essays, is a personality: one feels that he is quite willing to give himself away, to admit his defects and peculiarities with a humorous detachment, and an entire absence of self-consciousness, vanity or pose, which is the mark of a highly civilized person.

On entering the Anglo-Catholic church, Eliot readjusted his perspectives and his criteria of Montaigne. Supremacy must now be given to Pascal, but the language of the reversal is weak and evasive:

> Montaigne is a fog, a gas, a fluid, insidious element. He does not reason, he insinuates, charms and influences... Pascal studied him with the intention of demolishing him. Yet, in the *Pensées*, at the very end of his life, we find passage after passage... almost 'lifted' out of Montaigne, down to a figure of speech or a word... Had Montaigne been an ordinary, life-sized sceptic, this 'influence' would be to the discredit of Pascal; but if Montaigne had been no more than Voltaire,[61] the greatest sceptic of all, he could not have affected Pascal at all.[62]

Aesthetics was the one branch of philosophy that Eliot deliberately avoided,[63] for the reason that

---

59 *Athenaeum*, 10 October 1919.
60 Readers of *The Listener*, 26 June 1929.
61 Eliot was fond of quoting Baudelaire on the author of *Candide*: 'Je m'ennuie en France, où tout le monde ressemble à Voltaire.'
62 Introduction to *The Pensées of Pascal*, 1932.
63 *Nation and Athenaeum*, 12 January 1929.

abstract studies which turn upon the practice of one's art are dangerous. Aesthetics may make us conscious of what operates better unconsciously... The great characters of drama and prose fiction may themselves provide material for study to psychologists, but out of the psychologists' abstractions no character can be put together. The dramatist must study, not psychology, but human beings...[64]

As to Aristotle's aesthetics, Eliot wrote that the great philosopher 'did not have to like so many things as we have to like merely because he did not know so many things. And the less you know and like, the easier to frame aesthetic laws.'[65]

After his Anglo-Catholic conversion, Eliot repudiated all 'one-man philosophies', even that of the *Summa*:[66]

The whole truth of Christianity [does not] depend upon the validity of the philosophy of St. Thomas Aquinas – [an] impression which, I suspect, some of his main apologists have sometimes given.[67]

For Eliot, Maritain, the 'lyricist of Thomism', was not 'an original thinker... [but] a propagator [who] stimulates the intellect without always satisfying it [and who] persuades us before we have reasoned'.[68] Neither Eliot nor Maritain seems to have been prepared to admit that late in life Aquinas had a mystical experience, an 'infused contemplation', after which he renounced his former

---

64 *New English Weekly*, 14 June 1934. Earlier, in the *Athenaeum*, 6 August 1920, Eliot wisecracks that 'Hegel's *Philosophy of Art* adds very little to our enjoyment or understanding of art, though it fills a gap in Hegel's philosophy.'

65 *The Sacred Wood, op. cit.*

66 Eliot read the *Summa*, or at least the first 'Tome' of it, *Dieu*, in French, in the A.D. Sertillanges translation (Paris, 1925). He wrote 'T.S. Eliot' on the flyleaf in 1925, but 'R.S. Gordon George' inscribed his initials and pseudonym beneath Eliot's signature. On '27.iv.58', Eliot wrote in the centre of this page: 'P.S. I don't know how this book came to have Gordon George's (i.e., Robert Sencourt['s]) signature but it now belongs to my friend William Turner Levy.'

67 *The Listener*, 6 April 1932.

68 *TLS*, 8 March 1928.

intellectualising.[69] In the twenty-first century Aquinas is generally presented as more philosopher (empiricist) than theologian, and many endorse his view that the intellect has no immediate understanding of its own nature. But how is the contemporary mind to accept arguments of this sort together with, for example, Aquinas' chapter on the role of angels in the management of the world?

Eliot reserved his eloquence for opposing all 'world view projections of the personalities of their authors':

> Was [Blake] a great philosopher? No, he did not know enough. He made a universe; and very few people can do that. But the fact that the gift is rare does not make it necessarily valuable. It is not any one man's business to make a universe; and what any one man can make in this way is not, in the end, so good or so useful as the ordinary Universe which we all make together.[70]

---

69 Eliot's Clark Lectures contain the following curious statement: 'I should by no means say that Aquinas accounts for everything in the thirteenth century. But it is surely one of the differences between the new world and the old; and in its various mutations it either accounts for or is related to the causes which account for a great many of the phenomena even of our own time. The work of Marcel Proust, for instance, could hardly have appeared without it.'

70 *Nation and Athenaeum*, 7 September 1927.

Chapter 19

Isaiah Berlin's Philosophical Bestiary

Like *The Hedgehog and the Fox*, the essay that established his American reputation more than fifty years ago, Isaiah Berlin's *Conversations*[1] reveals his continuing preoccupation with categorical opposites. In this 'memoir in the form of a dialogue', with Iranian philosopher Ramin Jahanbegloo, the zoomorphic metaphor – hedgehogs (Marx, Dostoyevsky), who know one big thing, and foxes (Goethe, Herzen), who know many small things – becomes ichthyomorphic, on the incompatibility of absolute liberty and absolute equality: the rich and powerful are pikes, the poor and meek are cyprinid carp. A spin-off of this method of measurement is introduced, dividing nineteenth-century philosophers according to their probable sympathies during World War II: 'Tocqueville might not have collaborated,' Berlin says, 'but I don't think he would have joined the underground.' The main sorting-out is of monists, who explain all phenomena by one unifying principle, or as a manipulation of a single substance, and pluralists, who explain all phenomena in terms of many principles or embodiments of various substances. Sir Isaiah maintains that 'Every classification throws light on something'.

The making of distinctions is the task of all philosophy, of course, but few do it with the perspicuity and finesse of Isaiah Berlin. Comparing ideas of liberty, he reminds us that in Socrates' Athens anyone could

---

1   *Conversations With Isaiah Berlin*, by Isaiah Berlin and Ramin Jahanbegloo, New York, 1992.

bring charges against anyone else, and that the modern concept of liberty conferring a certain measure of privacy is rarely encountered in ancient thought. Comparing individual philosophers, he contrasts Spinoza, 'a rigid determinist' with 'no sense of change and evolution', and 'no sense of history', with Leibniz, an anti-determinist with 'a sense of the continuity of history and of the uniqueness of each moment'.

Machiavelli is a seminal figure for Berlin in that he recognised the possibility of two opposed value systems, two kinds of social morality, the antique Roman, which he clearly preferred (*virtù*, stoicism, self-assertion), and the Christian (humility, freedom from worldly ambition). As a dualist, in this sense, Machiavelli was the first to 'break the monist tradition', and 'once you have two equally valid possibilities you might have more'. Machiavelli perceived that a powerful and efficient state cannot be built on the morality of the Gospels, and this undermining of the idea of a Christian state is at least as important historically as his advocacy of bad means to successful ends.

The *Conversations* includes some discussion of philosophers about whom Berlin has written little – Thomas Hobbes, who was 'more monist than anyone', and Benjamin Constant, 'A thinker whom I greatly admire... a genuine liberal'. But the ideas that receive his closest scrutiny are the familiar ones of Giovanni Battista Vico, 'the first man who understood (and told us) what human culture is', and who 'taught us to understand alien cultures', and of Johann Gottfried von Herder, who goes beyond Vico in the pursuit of cultural empathy. Hegel, the target of Berlin's *Historical Inevitability*, is refuted yet again:

> Once people say: We should do this or that because history demands it [and] anything which gets in the way must be swept aside... you tend to trample on human rights and values... I do not believe in historical determinism... history as an autobahn from which deviations cannot occur.

In the Hegelian system, 'all footsteps point one way'. But when Berlin boasts that 'everything I have written has usually been attacked from both sides, from the Right and from the Left, with equal vehemence', one's impression persists that the more vociferous opponents were fellow-travelling Hegelian-Marxist Leftists.

Like Vico, and Edmund Burke, Berlin does not believe in a universal human nature, but he does believe in 'universal human values' that 'a great many human beings in the vast majority of places and situations at almost all times do in fact hold in common'. The apparent inconsistency may be attributable to his phobia against analogies between the life of a society and that of a biological organism, which have 'led to irrational and brutal forms of nationalism and intolerance'. All the same, Irenaus Eibl-Eibesfeldt's *The Biology of Human Behavior* is said, by E.H. Gombrich, among others, to demonstrate convincingly that certain human reactions are undeniably universal.

For many readers the most absorbing parts of the book will be the passages on Zionism, the 'very civilized' origins of which, in the ideas of the nineteenth-century German socialist Moses Hess, have lately been derouted in 'a nationalistic phase'. Hess understood Herder's principle that 'people can only create if they are independent and they can only be independent if they have a land of their own... a homeland'. Berlin became a Zionist as a schoolboy in Petrograd, having realised quite early in life that 'Jews were a minority everywhere... that there was no Jew in the world who was not, in some degree, socially uneasy', even if 'genuinely integrated' – which is an impossibility, as the 'deep assimilation' of the German Jews demonstrated.

Berlin feels 'free' in Israel, he says, and 'I don't particularly feel like a Jew'; but 'in England I do'. One can only suppose that this saddening remark is related to his fear that 'today's young... seek absolutes', which 'sooner or later... ends in blood'. He draws our attention to the failure of Saint-Simon, Marx and Lenin to predict the rise of nationalism over the entire globe during the twentieth century, and to foresee that nationalism and religious fanaticism would become the most powerful forces of our time. And he warns that at the end of 'one of the worst centuries of human history... there is a world shift to the Right. I wish it were not so. I am a liberal.'

Among twentieth-century philosophers, Sir Isaiah admires G.E Moore, 'an acute and totally honest thinker [who] converted Bertrand Russell to the belief that what we see and hear and touch and smell and taste, must, in the end, be the basis of all we know of the external world'. He finds Heidegger 'unreadable', and 'cannot understand a word of the philosophical writings of... Adorno [and] Derrida'. The anfractuous prose introduced by 'German and French philosophers' after the Second World War was evidently not 'intended to be generally understood'. He remains personally sympathetic to Leo Strauss, while rejecting his beliefs, but zaps Hannah Arendt as an 'egregious' lady who produces

> no arguments, no evidence of serious philosophical or historical thought... [and who] moves from one sentence to another without logical connection... *The Human Condition* [seems to be] based on two ideas, both historically false... I am not ready to swallow her idea about the banality of evil. It is false. The Nazis were not banal. Eichmann deeply believed in what he did; it was, he admitted, at the center of his being.

Asked about the usefulness of philosophy, Sir Isaiah says that it can 'teach us to see through political rhetoric, bad arguments... every kind of chicanery and disguise'. Philosophers 'clarify ideas; they analyze the words and concepts and ordinary terms in which you and I think'. One of the aims of philosophy is 'to understand the relationships of men, things, words to each other', and the aim of political theory should be to concern itself with the real 'goals of human existence'. In a book that tells us more about himself than ever before, Berlin avows that 'Anglo-American philosophy and Kant formed me', and admits to being 'hopelessly secular'. The values of the Enlightenment, 'what people like Voltaire, Helvétius, Holbach, Condorcet preached are deeply sympathetic to me. Maybe they were too narrow, and often wrong about the facts of human experience, but... they liberated people from horrors, obscurantism, fanaticism... [T]hey were against cruelty, they were against oppression... '

The five conversations are presented as if they followed in chronological order, but the text does not always bear this out. Thus Herder's *Einfühlung* appears twice in the first conversation (differently spelled), but is not translated (as 'empathy') until the last. Vissarion

Belinsky is identified only at the fifth reference to him; and when Berlin says to his interviewer, 'I don't know if you have seen my lecture on the Agnelli prize', can he have forgotten their supposedly earlier discussion of it? In the interests of greater cohesiveness and avoidance of repetition, passages on the individual philosophers might have been collated and grouped together, rather than spread throughout the book. Occasionally, too, a statement might have been clarified by a minor edit: 'The neglect of the ambiguity of the word "in" when we speak of an image *in* the mirror, can lead to philosophical confusions.'

The *Conversations* are free of jargon ('as' instead of 'qua'), and of what laymen think of as typical philosophical subject matter ('Why does the universe exist?'). The scope is broad, if not compendious, and while we are not surprised at the absence of the monist Kierkegaard, the pragmatist C.S. Peirce, the Marxist Antonio Gramsci, and the sociologists Emile Durkheim and Max Weber, we would have welcomed some comment on Ortega's concept of dehumanisation – and more on the structure, the volutions, of Berlin's own metaphor of history moving in 'spirals'. Also for our enlightenment, Jahanbegloo might have posed a question about Vico's autobiography and the exemplification of the philosophical method in the life; and a question about ancient prototypes of historical inevitability, such as the notion, in the later writings of Polybius, of Tyche (Fortune) sending all of the world's affairs in one direction.

What one most regrets is that Berlin's humour does not come through as frequently as it does in his unrecorded torrential talk. One example of it – the twinkle is in the qualifying clause – can be heard in his response to a question as to why Alexander Herzen turned his back on the Slavophils and towards the West. 'In Russia people were at the whim of landowners or officials, beaten violently or sent to Siberia. In the West, by and large, they were not.'

We can say of Isaiah Berlin, as he says here of the late Andrei Sakharov: 'Herzen's great liberal voice is heard again'. But the tribute he deserves was published long ago by a writer whose name will make it permanent. In 1955 T.S. Eliot declined to lecture on 'The Relation of Political Philosophy to the Practice of Philosophy' because 'it was alarmingly precise. It is a subject to demand all the learning, profundity, and eloquence of such a philosopher as Mr. Isaiah Berlin.'

Isaiah Berlin in His Letters

Postscript from the *Times Literary Supplement*, 3 December 2004
Isaiah Berlin's Letters 1928–1946 will be relished by anyone interested in mid-twentieth-century history from the perspective of a highly placed insider of unusual intelligence. Berlin's correspondence with his parents should be read both for evidence of the dominating symbiotic relationship with his mother, and for glimpses into the growing Zionist movement in World War II America. Those primarily interested in the foundation of Oxford logical positivism will find the new material disappointingly meagre, but it explains Berlin's decision not to pursue philosophy as a career, a consequence, it seems, of an entire semester in unresolved debate with J.L. Austin on a point of logic, and on having to respond to such of his questions as 'Do illocutionary forces exist?'

'Berlin didn't really write all that brilliantly,' Clive James recently remarked, and the letters, never as good as the best essays (*J.S. Mill, Montesquieu*), reveal Berlin struggling to polish his style. 'I can't, do what I will, make my words less like sticks and convey something'; 'God knows why I go on maundering this way.' The style, of course, is determined by the subject matter, *viz.* Berlin's exhilarating account of his visits to Moscow and Leningrad in November 1945, and by the addressee, as seen in the adroit application to Lord Halifax for a wartime position requiring Russian expertise.

Mr James also made the unverifiable assumption that Berlin, though flirtatious, was 'sexually inoperative'. The letters contain admiring references to young men: the 'very good-looking' Stephen Spender, the 'extremely handsome' Adam von Trott zu Solz, and a most attractive 'old friend', Guy Burgess. But how, in July 1940, could Berlin have travelled clandestinely from Liverpool to Quebec, en route to Moscow, with the notoriously dissipated, promiscuous and politically suspect Burgess?

Part Three:
Travel Diaries 2001–2004
Cambodia, Italian Vignettes, Seville

'… about must, and about must go…'

Donne (*Satyre 3*)

Chapter 1

Cambodia

'Khmer studies are going through a period of great intellectual excitement,' Michael Coe declares, in *Angkor and the Khmer Civilization*,[1] his contribution to the ferment and the most comprehensive general book on the subject to date. It covers the geology, natural history, pre-history – the petroglyphs of Homo sapiens, odd-looking, triangular-headed chaps – as well as the chronicle of the peoples, their languages and religions, the beginnings of rice cultivation, the development of commerce in the Mekong Delta, the early kingdoms, and the high empire. The survey includes remote areas like the Cardamones and the Elephant Mountains in the southwest, and remote people like the Montagnards.[2] The discussion of the period extending from the Portuguese discovery of the Angkor ruins in 1580 through the period of French colonial rule in the second half of the nineteenth century, gives full recognition to the achievements of French scholars, above all Etienne Aymonier, who transcribed, translated and catalogued the Sanskrit and Khmer inscriptions in all of the Angkor buildings, a mind-boggling task completed in 1901.[3]

Coe draws comparisons between the Mayan stepped-temple pyramid

---

1   London and New York, 2003.
2   See *Un Barbare en Asie* by Henri Michaux, Paris, 1933.
3   An English translation of this monumental work appeared in Bangkok in 1999.

(200 BC), from his previous archaeo- and anthropological research in Meso-America, and the similar structure, built more than a millennium later, at Angkor, as well as between rituals of human sacrifice in both cultures, the carditic evisceration in the Aztec, and the crushing of the victim between huge granite slabs in the Khmer. Furthermore, Coe's contexts include parallels with European civilisation, reminding the reader that the Khmer and Carolingian cultures were contemporary. One of the book's illustrations is a synthetic radar image from the space-shuttle Endeavor, in which the Angkor temples and their outstretching galleries look like orange flames in a forest fire. Angkor and the Great Wall of China are the only man-made structures on the planet Earth visible from outer space.

As I write, the *condition humaine* in Cambodia is desperate, despite such glimmers of hope as the American telemedicine project, begun in September 2003, and enabling Cambodian hospitals to send photographs of cardiograms, X-rays and ultrasound images for diagnostic help to M.I.T. and Harvard Medical School. The worst of the situation is that the impoverished people, living under the shadow of famine, poorly educated if at all, are in the throes of a rapidly growing AIDS epidemic, concerning which *Médecins sans Frontières* says that 'patients sell their farm animals and even their land to pay for ineffective herbal potions, or for Western treatments they cannot afford to continue'.

In the tradition of the Hindu epics, the abuse of the female continues. Teenage girls become prostitute slaves as an alternative to working eleven-hour days in textile factories for a few dollars a month. A number of incidents have been reported of the disfiguring of attractive young concubines kept by powerful married men, whose betrayed wives have flung acid in their rivals' faces, an action not regarded as criminal by courts that also absolve the husbands of culpability.

The government, nominally a parliamentary monarchy, is actually controlled by a Prime Minister, Hun Sen, a former Khmer Rouge leader who defected to the Vietnamese enemy, helped them defeat the Khmer Rouge, and tolerated their occupation of the country for a decade. Hun Sen has successfully blocked UN investigations of Khmer Rouge war criminals and is again forestalling a trial demanded by the 55,000 refugees from Pol Pot's 'agrarian utopia' living in Long Beach, California, who want the skeletons of Khmer Rouge victims, now stored in a charnel house in Phnom Penh, to receive Buddhist burial rites that would 'release their souls'. The prosecution opposes this on grounds that the ossuary is its main evidentiary source for the crimes. But what justice or retribution could be expected from the trial of six or seven septuagenarian ex-Khmer Rouge fanatics for crimes committed nearly forty years ago? Cambodia has not had an elected government since 27 July 2003, apart from one session of the National Assembly that convened for fifteen minutes, failed to reach a quorum vote, and dissolved itself.

Subsequent political crises overtook the country. On 22 January 2004, Chea Vichea, the leader of the principal workers' union, was assassinated in mid-day on a street in Phnom Penh. Hun Sen charged the murder to the head of his opposition party, Sam Rainsy, who responded by accusing Sen of intending to eliminate three other members as well. Ostensibly for medical reasons, Norodom Sihanouk, the king, fled to Beijing, then in October 2004 returned to Phnom Penh and abdicated in favour of his son Norodom Sihamoni. Meanwhile, another son, Prince Ravariddh, seems to have made a secret deal with Hun Sen. In November 2004, the Cambodian government announced that a tribunal would be formed for the trial of two of the most heinous Khmer Rouge criminals now in custody, Ta Mok and Kaing Guck Eay, the latter world-renowned under the name of 'Douch' in François Bizot's bestseller *The Gate.* Comrade Duch (actually pronounced Doik), commandant of the infamous Khmer Rouge prison Tuol Sleng (no survivors), is the subject of a new (2005) book *The Lost Executioner,* by Nic Dunlop, who after a long search found Duch working as the district chief of education in a remote western Cambodian village. He had become a baptised Christian and was helping refugee groups with his knowledge of English.

To backtrack slightly, it should be noted that during a quiet interlude in the political anarchy, in December 2002, the manager of Siem Reap's Grande Hotel d'Angkor, keenly aware that the Angkor tourist industry had risen to over a million visitors a year, organised a *son et lumière* extravaganza at the entrance to Angkor Wat. One thousand people, at $1500 a seat, were invited to a spectacle advertised as the 'José Carreras Charity Concert'. Except for the 900-year-old temple and a troupe of bayaderes, who might have stepped out of the stonework relief sculpture apsarases, everything, including champagne (in this 100-degree heat), food, electrical wiring, coloured laser lights, the Singapore Symphony, the tenor and CNN, had to be imported.

———◆———

En route from Paris, Alva and I were deposited at the wrong De Gaulle terminal for Bangkok, and since porters are non-existent, or *en grève*, we had to propel our over-stacked, minds-of-their-own metal carts more than a kilometre, lift their contents on, and soon off, a bus, then inch them forward in long queues for check-ins, Immigration and Security friskings. Perhaps this exhausting exercise helped us to sleep more soundly. We awoke during the descent over snaky rivers and mangrove-swamp shores.

The new Bangkok terminal connects to an elevated expressway that blocks the views of the klongs and their teeming boat markets, heretofore second only to harlotry as Thailand's main attraction. (On my first visit to the city the shed that served as a terminal was roped-off until Jimmy, Rosalind and Amy Carter were air-lifted to a border camp of refugees from the Khmer Rouge.) Since the exchange rate favours the dollar, the Oriental Hotel proves to be not only the most luxurious inn on our itinerary but also the most affordable. Guests are greeted by teenage hostesses with the *žwai* gesture of obeisance (hands, palms together, raised to bowed foreheads), then lassoed with fragrant leis. Our rooms, which overlook the Chao Phraya and its barges, sampans, and newly motorised ferries, are literally breathtaking with flower bouquets. When baskets of tropical fruit arrive, and an ice bucket with champagne, we feel that only a 'Just Married' sign is wanting.

From a picture-book history of the hotel we learn that until quite recently tiffin, not lunch, was served at noon, and that until the 1950s, with the installation of electric ceiling fans, Punkah wallahs were imported from India to wave palm fronds. Joseph Conrad assumed his first command of a ship here in 1888, but being beardless he is unrecognisable in a photo of that date. The greatest surprise is a 1916 family portrait of Nijinsky, his wife and elder daughter, here on a cruise. Hotel records and a souvenir programme show that he danced in its theatre, but the Nijinsky literature, including the catalogue of the recent Musée d'Orsay exhibition, makes no mention of a cruise, which could have taken place secretly in May/June 1916, or later that summer, when the Nijinskys were supposed to have been at Bar Harbor, Maine.

The history of Siam ranges from its luxuriating plant life (35,000 species of both epiphytic and terrestrial orchids) to its sexual mores. The oldest European report about the country, by Tomas Pires, a clerk in the Portuguese trading post in Malacca in the late 1400s, notes that the king has 'upwards of five hundred wives'. The Reverend Samuel Purchase's *Pilgrimage* (London, 1617) tells us that 'adulterie is common' in the Siamese state of Pattani, the reason being 'the women's unbridled lust'. More remarkable is a letter from Siam nineteen years later by one Thomas Herbert:

> The Siamese have been wicked Sodomites, and to deter them a Queen commanded that all male children should have a tiny bell of gold put through the prepuce, which in small time will become a musical ornament. When they have a mind to marry, he has his choice of what maid he likes, but beds her not till the Midwife presents a sleepie ophiated potion, during which the bell is loosed from the flesh and fastened to the foreskin, which hinders not but titillates. In green years they give the too forward maids a virulent drink; whose virtue (vyce rather) is by a strange efficacy to distend their mullebria so capaciously that the bells ring too easily; and, which is worse... the women here are not ashamed to go naked to the middle (the better to allure men from Sodomitry).

———◆———

The flight to Siem Reap is held up in Bangkok by a kerfuffle over visas, during which we read that radiocarbon datings testify to human habitation in the Angkor area in 6000 BC, and that in the Oc Eo area, the ancient trading centre in the Mekong Delta, a gold medallion portrait of Antoninus Pius has been unearthed, as well as one on a silver coin of Marcus Aurelius – which will not surprise readers of the British Library's *Silk Road*, which tells us that Roman gladiators are depicted in tapestries excavated near Khotan in the Taklamakan desert. It seems that a maritime silk-road existed between Persia, India, China and the Mediterranean. Oc Eo was Chinese in the first and second centuries AD, and the territory was known as Funan. It was also Buddhist, and remained so until the fifth century, when a Hindu ruled, though both Indian religions coexisted, with Sanskrit becoming the court language, Khmer the language of the people. This helps to account for the high percentage of simple two-syllable words in Khmer, though in the written language no breaks occur between words, and the left-to-right writing is alarmingly sesquipedalian in appearance. Khmer is a non-gender language with a subject–verb–object word order and modifiers following.

Sanskrit, with its abstract vocabulary, is the culture's legal and literary language. At Angkor stone inscriptions in Sanskrit date from the beginning of the ninth century, incised on door jambs and freestanding stelae. The texts are chronicles, inventories and censuses.

We step from the rickety airplane into what feels like a blast furnace, and walk from tarmac to tiny terminal to enter the Kingdom of Cambodia swooning in the quivering heat. The Immigration officials, military uniforms with holstered revolvers, are unwelcoming, deliberately slow in stamping passports and in comparing photos to the realities. In the absence of a carrousel and porters, young girls schlep our bags to the suffocatingly under-air-conditioned jeep of Mr Lol, our Abercrombie and Kent guide. Cambodia is a left-side-drive country, but this makes little difference on the narrow, cratered road, where bicycles are the only other traffic. Both sides are flanked most of the way by in-construction hotels.

The Royal Angkor is not yet fully functioning, but the lobby is cool and the music of the roneat, played with soft mallets by a boy in white clothes, turban and red sash, is soothing. Ten Iron Age prototypes of this marimba-like bamboo instrument have been excavated. At Reception, we sip chilled tangerine juice and listen to an explanation that all transactions are in US dollars. Cambodian currency can be exchanged, but the riel is an unmanageable 4,000 to the dollar. Mr Lol, coppery-skinned, about thirty-five, tells us that because of the intense midday heat, we must visit the ruins in early morning and late afternoon.

We climb back into his jeep to look for a pharmacy in 'downtown' Siem Reap, but find that nothing of the sort exists. The village is simply a marketplace of open food stalls, thatched-roof huts, dusty, unpaved streets, and barefoot, ragged, prematurely aged people; it does not 'bustle'. Though comparatively fluent in French, Mr Lol will not resort to it because he was 'hired to speak English', in which, haltingly, syllable by syllable, he begins each utterance with 'I mean' and substitutes the word 'right' for punctuation. Everything we are to see next is 'much more better' than what we just saw. He needlessly warns us not to venture into Siem Reap after dark because holdups are common and the thieves murderous. The hotel receptionist had already explained that they should not be resisted, since foreigners' pocketbooks are usually returned with the documents in order and only the cash missing, most of the robbers being off-duty Immigration Police in civvies. He had added that the ongoing hazard of landmines is a 'Thai invention intended to frighten off tourists'. But we pass two clinics where children are trained to use artificial limbs, and are told that about seventy-five people a month are still killed by Khmer Rouge mines. Coe's book identifies roads known to be still mined.

The Royal Angkor's restaurants are presided over by 'the renowned chef Supachai Verapuchong'. Nusara Thaitawat's *The Cuisine of Cambodia*[4] mentions such culinary favourites as 'sliced pork fat', the large mygale spider, a prized delicacy, and 'stir-fried insects' (cicadas and tarantulas). According to Mr Lol, the scene in *Indiana Jones* of people spoon-feeding on the brains of still-living, strapped-down monkeys is an actuality hereabouts. We share the dining room with a party of frequent-flyer Americans counting their points. A half-hour after indicating our choices on a disconsolatingly limited bilingual menu, the maître d'hôtel explains that the 'salmon cooked

---

4   *Nusara and Friends*, Bangkok, 2000.

to perfection' is not available today, and the only option is a less-than-scrumptious-sounding prawn and pineapple soup. Ultimately our meal consists of bread, ice cream, and slugs of a twelve-year-old malt, followed by an eighteen-year-old one, an incremental improvement commensurate with the rise in price.

An open-air performance of an episode from the *Ramayana* takes place afterwards on a wooden platform in the gardens, dance-mimed by young male transvestites with undulating bodies, tapering, carefully choreographed fingertips, and blank, mask-like faces. They are colourfully costumed, but the hieratic-ritual aspect is excruciatingly slow-moving, and anyway we are soon fleeing indoors from the torpid night air and a cloud of Kamikaze mosquitoes.

The remainder of the evening is spent boning up on Khmer cosmology. The time-cycles are virtually the same as those devised in Mesopotamia many millennia earlier. In Brahmanical numerology the universe is divided into four successive Kalpas, or yugas, which are repeated over and over. We live in the fourth and worst kali, the human lifespan being the shortest, famines and wars the most frequent, morality the lowest, degeneration general. Luckily it lasts only 432,000 years, and since it began on Friday 13 February, 3102 BC, has a mere 426,941 years to go.

———•——

The hammering of about twenty construction workers on the roof of a new wing of the hotel begins at dawn, long before the arrival of our jeep. The traffic of bicycles on the Angkor road, some with pigs in pokes attached to the handlebars, competes with motorbikes hired by young people who sit on the pillions behind the drivers. The main obstructions are ox carts lumbering back from the Siem Reap market and rickety tourist buses shuttling to and from the ruins. The dust is choking, and the noise drowns out Mr Lol's memories of his life as a small child during the Khmer Rouge reign of terror, 1975-9. It seems that he was hidden in a foxhole dug for him by his mother, and during this period of privation never ate cooked food. Even a wisp of smoke would have brought Khmer Rouge guerrillas.

The road borders the Siem Reap River, a murky creek, the only aquifer for a vast system of canals, irrigation ditches, reservoirs and the moat on which, according to Bernard Groslier, the 'hydraulic city' of Angkor depended. The Khmer had devised a means of water retention for the summer monsoons, which in the dry season could be spread across the land through a multitude of ditches.

On a patch of road under construction, young women swing pickaxes and push wheelbarrows of heavy stones. Why, in this matrilineal culture, are females the only hard-labourers? The social system developed in the seventh century mandates inheritance through the king's sister's son. Since the kings were polygamous, primogeniture could not exist, and the descent through the female line became the rule. But Royal Khmer genealogy is an intricate subject.

Nearing Angkor we stop at a tollbooth on a patch of blistering pavement to fill out forms, pose for ID photos, and pay $80 admission fees. The road beyond is bordered by a forest of tall and slender Borasso palms, the national tree; dipterocarps, from whose smooth trunks resin is extracted; and gum trees, which should be avoided, since the hills of termites surrounding their boles are said to be likely places to encounter cobras.

Angkor Wat, the temple city, and its stagnant moat, come into view next, but we continue beyond to Angkor Thom, 'the great city' – the population in AD 1200 is calculated to have been at least a million people – to visit the Buddhist temple of Bayon, the centre of a three-mile walled complex. This was erected by the emperor Jayavarman VII (1181–1219); 'Jaya', the honorific suffix, means victory, 'varman' protector. More impressive than the Bayon itself is its southern entrance, the Gate of the Dead. We pass through it on a two-lane road under a beautifully corbelled arch (each higher stone projecting over the one below until the sides meet at the top); Buddhists believe that 'voussoir vaults never rest, only corbelled vaults can sleep'. Immediately above the arch is a huge (seven by ten feet) sculpted face, flat-nosed, slumberous-eyed, square-jawed, thick-lipped, and enigmatically smiling. It represents the Bodhisattva Lokeshvara, 'Lord of the World', and is traditionally thought to be a portrait of Jayavarman VII's father. But the monks regard it as an icon of the Buddha and believe in a karmic alliance through it with the god, feeling something of his presence at no matter how great a remove. Paul Mus's *Iconography of an Aniconic Art*[5] reminds us that no model for the Buddha ever existed: 'India in the pre-Angkor period did not make use of images, but was represented by such nonfigurative symbols as the stupa and the wheel.' This 'Buddha' face, and three replicas at the same level respectively looking in the other cardinal directions, are crowned by a Shiva tower.

Within the Bayon complex the same large countenance smiles in the same directions from fifty-eight structures, wherewith one feels constantly watched. At one vantage twelve of these are visible at the same time. The face is also found at the Banteay Kdei temple-monastery, which, until recently, was inhabited by a herd of wild deer, as well as at the shrines of Ta Som (*Ta* means 'grandfather' or 'ancestor'), where it is entwined in the roots of the sacred pipal tree. Not uncommonly it is hidden in the midst of densely carved façades and at elevated, difficult-to-discern levels.

The Cambodian source-culture is accepted as having been the Gupta state of north-central India, which had returned to the Vedic (Hindu) tradition and revived the Sanskrit language. Of the Hindu divinities Shiva, Brahma and Vishnu, Shiva was the most powerful, yet images of him are outnumbered by those of Krishna, Buddha's eighth avatar, perhaps because of his superhuman strength. A *contrapposto* from Phnom Da shows Krishna nonchalantly lifting Mount Govardhana with his left arm to protect shepherds from rains. The mythology, god cults, cremation burial, architectural traditions (brick and stone), rectilinear town planning, and water systems – canals, irrigation ditches, reservoirs – are all Hindu transpositions to Southeast Asia. But the Khmer never adopted the Hindu caste system, maintaining, until the arrival of the French in the mid-nineteenth century, a classless bartering economy.

---

5   A chapter from his unfinished *Les Masques d'Angkor* was published in *Res*, Autumn 1987, the Peabody Museum of Archaeology and Ethnology, Harvard University. The twenty-three Buddhist caves, called Pandu Lona, near the Hindu holy city of Nasik (100 miles south of Bombay on the banks of the sacred Godavari river), are famous for their symbolisations of the Buddha's presence by empty thrones with footstools or steps, as well as by stupas that are reliquary mounds, and *chakras* (prayer-wheels). The art, dating from the first century AD, is in the Hinayana style, which prohibits statues of the Buddha.

The road beyond the Gate of the Dead crosses a dry moat on a causeway with railings that incorporate fifty-four sculptures, *devas* (gods) on the west and, opposite them, *asuras* (antigods), whose bulging round eyes are a demon feature, as are their thick eyebrows and fangs. Each side pulls the body of Vasuki, the snake deity, in a contrary direction, north (the *devas*) and south (the *asuras*), in accordance with the solstices in Brahmanical astronomy. The axis of the causeway is said to run in the direction of Mount Meru, the home of the gods and the Hindu centre of the universe, represented here by the central tower at Angkor Wat. The legs of the figures on the *asuras* side of this cosmic tug-of-war are bent at the knee, all exactly the same, like the chorus line at Radio City.

Beyond the bridge is a taxi-rank of elephants for those who elect to circumambulate the Thom compound from the outside, but after watching the howdahs pitch and toss like small boats on rough seas, we decide to walk.

Angkor Thom was the guest home from August 1296 to July 1297 of Zhou Daguan, a member of Genghis Khan's commercial mission to the country. Zhou described life in Angkor at both high and low social strata in a vivid, sometimes salacious memoir:

> Many Chinese sailors had settled in Bayon because the floating rice was cheap. It grew four inches a day and yielded three to four crops a year. Another incentive was that the always topless women were 'easily persuaded'. Thousands of women bathe naked in the Siem Reap River and show themselves from head to foot to any bystanders who may appear. The Chinese often treat themselves to the spectacle and many of them enter the water to take advantage of whatever opportunity offers.

No guidebook warns that ambulation inside the Bayon requires caution. One of the most popular complexes in the seventy square miles of the Angkor kingdom, doorways and walls seem to threaten imminent collapse. In 1947 the ceiling of a gallery at Angkor Wat actually did cave in, fortunately at night and without inflicting any injury. Pavement stones vary greatly in size, are awkwardly tilted, and dangerously declivitous. Since the full restoration of the Bayon said to be underway seems a hopeless goal, such temporary safety measures as the installation of a plank board over an abyss might have been undertaken. As is, the visitor must hop like a mountain goat from one sizzling rock to another.

The present Bayon, a three-tiered temple-mountain, was built in the late twelfth century by Jayavarman VII, the pre-eminent figure of Khmer civilisation. A text incised on one of the steles reveals that his legitimacy was properly established on the distaff side, and that his deeds include the expulsion of the Champa (Vietnamese) from Cambodia, after they had invaded and plundered Angkor. At one time this devout Buddhist ruled the entire region between India and China. Two statues of him in the National Museum at Phnom Penh portray, respectively, a heavily built young man, with coarse features and hair pulled into a chignon (not to be confused with the cranial protuberance of the Buddha), and an older, more slender contemplative figure.

The Jayavarman dynasty began in the seventh century and continued, with interregnums, for seven more. Jayavarman I proclaimed his divinity in 664, and thereafter kings assumed the style of gods. All that is known for certain about the reigns of Jayavarman VII's successors, Indravarman II and Jayavarman VIII (1243–95), is that a Shivaite iconoclasm took place. Zhou Daguan's testimony contradicts this, maintaining that at the time of his arrival (August 1296) saffron-robed monks were everywhere, and the population was largely Buddhist. Indravarman III abdicated in 1308 and was followed by two minor monarchs, during whose reigns Sanskrit inscriptions were no longer continued. The decline of Khmer culture is commonly attributed to annexation by the Siamese Empire, but this does not mean that Angkor was abandoned, a common assumption. Some of the buildings were inhabited until the eighteenth century.

In three registers of bas-reliefs on the south side of Bayon, a marching army is depicted against a forest background. The foot soldiers carry javelins and round shields, their generals, mounted on elephants, hold bows and arrows. Musicians, including one who pounds an enormous drum with two sticks, accompany the procession.

Civilians and families follow with supply wagons very like the yoked ox-carts on the Siem Reap road this morning, and with the same lateral brakes. Three princesses with richly ornamented tiaras are portrayed riding in palanquins, and the carvers have included a Chinese junk and a group of Chinese traders in animated discussion.

Among the most interesting reliefs, some 11,000 figures in all, are the scenes from daily life: a circus with jugglers, acrobats, tightrope walkers; a game of checkers; gamblers tensely watching cockfights, a low-caste amusement; a woman giving birth, another combing her hair before a mirror, and another delousing her beau. Criminals and dacoits with cropped ears and amputated toes are represented, as are people being chased up trees to escape tigers, a man bellowing a fire, and flunkeys with fly whisks, which the Buddhists employed to 'warn away' (not to harm) the pest.

We exit through the east gate to the Elephant Terrace, a wall of carved reliefs 300 yards long depicting gladiators, wrestlers, jugglers, polo players and elephants pinning down a tiger. Royal regalia – standards, pennants, parasols (status symbols) – is the paramount subject here. Next to this gallery is the Terrace of the Leper King, where royal cremations are believed to have taken place, and where thousands of people came to watch the great royal processions. Zhou describes one of these:

> headed by the soldiery, the flags, the banners, the musicians. Girls of the palace, 500 of them, with flowers in their hair and tapers in their hands, are massed together in a separate column. Other girls carry gold and silver vessels from the palace, and still more girls, the bodyguard of the palace, holding shields and lances. Following them came chariots drawn by goats and horses, and ministers and princes, protected by scarlet parasols, mounted on elephants, and accompanied by royal wives and concubines. Finally the sovereign appeared standing upright on an elephant whose tusks are sheathed in gold... The music came from drums, copper cymbals, and various other percussion instruments, long trumpets, horns, conches, and flutes with a delicious sound.

Angkor Wat was built of sandstone blocks hewn in the Kulen Hills, loaded by elephants on barges, and floated to Angkor via Tonlé Sap, the Great Lake. The Angkor Wat temples were built by the Hindu Suryavarman II (1113–50), who intended them as his mausoleum. The causeway spanning the moat from the mainland to this artificial island is an improvement on the pathways of the Bayon, but the risk of stumbling on the irregular projections of stones and in the gaps for missing ones is still high. A wide-brimmed straw hat with blue-ribbon chinstrap, purchased from a roadside vendor, shields my head from the scorching sun, but adds to the heat. We would like to look ahead toward the quincunx of towers symbolising the levels of Mount Meru, but must keep our eyes to the ground and step squarely on each disjointedly spaced rock. The end of the walk is marked by the famed sculptures of the multiple-headed serpents whose uncoiled bodies form the bridge's balustrades. The Khmer measured the crossing as 432,000 cubits, the number of years of the rule of the antediluvian kings of Babylon, according to cuneiform records – a cosmological coincidence?

Sanskrit treatises on religious structures associate Vishnu with the setting sun, which accounts for the westward orientation of the architecture, and for the co-ordination of every sculpted stone with the sun and moon in time cycles along west–east and north–south axes. The central tower is perfectly aligned with the position of the sun on the day of the spring equinox.

The temple adjoining the front entrance shelters a large Vishnu statue in his aspect as Suryavarman II, except that it has acquired a Buddha head. The room is also inhabited by a colony of bats, despite official claims that this and all other buildings have been cleared of them, and that their excreta has been cleansed from walls and floors. The scraping and rustling of their wings is louder an hour and a half later when we return from the buildings of the interior, but by then we can hurry through, most tourists having departed. In 1901 Pierre (*Ramuntcho*) Loti described these mammals as 'velvet pouches which hang suspended from stone ceilings by their claws, and want but the slightest noise to unfold and become a whirlwind of wings'.

A still longer causeway leads from the Vishnu shrine to a second terrace of galleries in the interior, and from there to a third, which ascends to the central tower. Angkor is as widespread as Bayon is tight and constricting. On both sides of this elevated stone bridge scrawny white bovines (zebus) graze in what are assumed to have been bathing pools for royal elephants. The windows in the libraries at the end of the covered corridors are shuttered with carved rounded balusters placed close together to suffuse the sunlight. One of the chief occupations of the Wat (monastery) was the copying of sacred texts. The galleries here are embellished with bas-reliefs illustrating episodes from Indian mythology, 2,000 feet of them with an estimated 18,500 carved figures of men and animals, including several hundred elephants. From cursory examination, none of these is as fine as the relief-sculpture in Buddhist Bayon, and the replication seems increasingly mechanical and monotonous. The Khmer scholar Claude Jacques writes that 'the notion of the perpetual repetition of an image takes us to the very essence of Khmer art'.[6]

Most of the Bayon and Angkor Wat reliefs have been filmed in a concerted effort to interpret them iconographically. Students from the *Fachhochschule* in Cologne laid elevated rails on which to run a Seitz rotating camera through the galleries photographing the carvings. This had to be done when all natural light was eliminated, between 2.30AM and daybreak, but a greater impediment was the variable two- to three-centimetre depth of the reliefs, and the necessity, which required a laser, of establishing the perfect alignment of the rails, since the slightest irregularity would produce vibrations. The photos are clear but in need of separating out and of greater magnification of details.

Some of the remoter galleries are occupied by Buddhist monks who sit in lotus positions on mats before their fire grates, meditating, praying, and burning joss sticks for pilgrims they have successfully importuned. Loti aptly characterised these monks as 'a diminutive humanity, at once infantile and old'. Older bonzes would of course not be capable of crossing the causeways carrying their cooking pots, hammocks, and mosquito nets, and then recrossing at daybreak, however creepy to us

6   *Angkor*, Paris, 1990.

the thought of spending a night here among Chiroptera, centipedes, and orthopterous insects (the *blatta orientalis*).

We do not attempt to climb the final, 196-foot flight of the staircases – on the outside, as in Mayan temples – partly because the tiny room at the top is vacant except for the spirit of Vishnu, but mainly because the steps are narrow, steep, irregularly spaced, and still in blazing sunlight. It seems that only kings and the highest priests were permitted to make the ascent.

We concur with Claude Jacques that the superior Khmer art is sixth- and seventh-century pre-Angkor. A Buddha statue in the Phnom Penh Museum strongly supports this conclusion. The earlobes are extra-long, the eyes lowered, the curls flat on the cranium, the *ushnisha* head lump, perfectly placed, the *uttarasanga* (mantle) draped over the left shoulder, the right hand in the *vitarka*-Mudra ('teaching' position). This majestic figure represents the Bipanhara-Buddha, the historical Gautama approaching enlightenment.

In later Angkor-period sculpture, legs are straight, stiff, heavy, the feet turned sideways, as if to avoid the third dimension. In fact, as Louis Finot explains in *Ruins of Angkor: Cambodia in 1909*,[7] the Cambodian sculptors were unaware of the art of foreshortening. (A facsimile edition of this photograph album was published in Hanoi that year, when the Thais ceded suzerainty of Siem Reap province to the French Protectorate.) By the ninth century, legs are rigid and figures have lost their suppleness. By the twelfth, Khmer Buddhas are over-decorated, their diadems over-ornate.[8] Not many Khmer bronzes are found in museums, surprisingly, because their creators possessed wax techniques lost to Europe at the time.[9]

Most fourteenth-century Khmer treen art has also fallen victim to insects and time, though a horde of poplar toothpicks survives from the sixth century. One exquisite wood statue of a kneeling

---

7   Chicago, 2000. The book's architectural terminology is oddly nineteenth-century classical (edicules, peristyles, plinths, pilasters).

8   Paul Mus writes that 'The art of the Buddha is the exact opposite of what, in our own art, is decorative'. *Res*, pp. 1–27, 14, Autumn 1987, *op. cit.*

9   The technique of smelting copper and tin ores came to China from the Near East. The Bronze Age is roughly dated from 500 BC, with the discovery that the process requires a much lower temperature than the smelting of iron ore.

woman with polychromatic traces, hands joined in prayer, can still be seen in the Phnom Penh Museum. Vittorio Roveda says that the decorative elements in the Banteay Srei palace 'give some idea of the masterly workmanship of Khmer woodcarvers',[10] and Jan Myrdal's *Angkor: An Essay on Art and Imperialism* persuasively argues that the forms of Angkor's buildings point back to the secular pre-Angkor timber architecture, now mouldered away. Only temples were made of stone.

During siesta we read the anthropologist Geoffrey Gorer, whose hypothesis that the ancient Khmer were 'opium-soaked' seems credible, since the drug must have been at least as popular of yore as now, when most of the young bonzes we see smoke what smell like 'joints'. But he is quite wrong about the celestial dancing maidens, or apsarases, whom he describes as 'extremely voluptuous, curved and adorned with an obvious appreciation of human beauty, but with no desire'. In truth, their bared, cantaloupe-sized bosoms are factory-identical, and they do not tilt in correspondence with their less-than-upright dance positions. Unlike Gorer, the only statuary that affects my id is the three-dimensional figure of Shiva's consort in the Phnom Penh Museum. Leaning on her right leg, she exposes appealingly wide hips, a narrow waist and opulent curves. Nudes are rare in Khmer art, but I respond to the one in the Musée Guimet (Paris) in the same way as Bernard Groslier: 'We can still feel the hand that shaped it, caressing it lovingly, coming back again and again to the full curves, the silky incline of the hips, flesh vibrating, sensual and proud, as one would wish embraces to be.'[11]

In 1923 the twenty-two-year-old writer-adventurer André Malraux appropriated six cornerstone apsarases from one of the shrines at Banteay Srei, transported them in ox-carts to Siem Reap, and accompanied them from there by boat to Phnom Penh, where he was arrested for his desecrations and attempted thefts. In the absence of a jail, he was free to live in the city until his trial, scheduled for July 1924, but long before this date, his wife, together with André

---

10 *Khmer Mythology: Secrets of Angkor.*
11 *The Arts and Civilization of Angkor* (1957).

Breton and other influential friends in Paris, obtained his release by publicising the corruption in the *École Française d'Extrême Orient* and its complicity with French colonial administrators intent on keeping the lucrative art traffic for themselves.

The plundering continues. In 1964, a hoard of 300 bronzes, discovered in a burial chamber under a Buddhist temple in the Prahan Chai precinct, was smuggled out of the country overnight by agents of the flourishing antiquities market. In 1993, five heads were broken off from the Angkor Thom causeway and sold to Western dealers. A recent review of the depredations estimates that about forty percent of the finest Khmer sculpture is now in private, mainly American and Japanese, collections. Meanwhile, Malraux's apsarases have been returned to Banteay Srei, where tourists take turns photographing each other next to them, and Malraux himself has been exonerated by the recent archaeological discovery that the thesis of his *A Royal Way* is accurate. 500 miles of conjoined major traffic arteries have been found exactly where his 1930 book predicted.

Banteay Srei, dedicated to Shiva and known as the Citadel of the Women, is now the most popular of the temples, partly because of the roseate glow of the sandstone and the quality and profusion of the carvings, many of them purely ornamental: vines, swags, fritillaries, foliage scrolls, and mythological animals. A jolting half-hour ride from Siem Reap on a rutted, gullied road and through a thick heat haze, the temple complex, a square surrounded by a moat, is smaller than most Khmer temples, and correspondingly claustrophobic. The entranceways to the miniature structures are only four to five feet tall, but the low positioning of the relief sculptures brings them closer to the eye. The feature of the place is that so many of the carvings are three-dimensional. Forty years ago, Sacheverell Sitwell, in *The Red Chapels of Banteai Sri*, wrote that 'Visitors were few, wild elephant herds, now extinct, lived in the surrounding forests, and countless small gray monkeys scampered on the ground'. Today all pathways are overpopulated, and at entrances and exits swarms of barefoot children plead for alms.

Inscriptions found at the site date the construction of Banteay Srei from AD 967, but the refinement of the carving and the lavish decoration suggest the thirteenth or fourteenth centuries. The most striking relief sequences depict scenes from the Ramayana, and the most impressive of these for us is one of Krishna about to kill his brutal uncle Kama by splitting him in two. All but one scene in this dramatic seven-part frieze portray the perturbation that the impending execution provokes in Krishna's palace, the human figures anxiously clinging to one another, the chariot horses chafing at the bit, forelegs prancing high.

The scholar Bernard Groslier believes that Banteay Srei court life had a gay nucleus: 'Jayavarman V, who built this temple, with all its lacy pink sandstone, preferred young male guardians to all those celestial apsarases.' The reference is to the high-relief sculptures of *dvarapala* (guardians), gently smiling, young, smooth-skinned ephebes who stand at the four corners of the great linga shrine, each holding a lance and a lotus bud. It has now been established that the Khmer accommodated same-sex sexuality, and that homosexual men openly solicited in the marketplace. The famous River of a Thousand Lingas is not far from Banteay.

———◆———

Visiting Ta Prohm, half ingested by its surrounding jungle, is a surreal experience as well as a potentially dangerous one. A sign warns visitors to 'Beware of the small but deadly light-green Haluman snake, which emerges after rainstorms'. The French surveyors of a century ago wisely decided against any attempt to restore Ta Prohm. The aerial roots of huge *tetrameles* and banyans have erupted the buildings' massive stones and smashed their walls, at once strangling and holding them together in an arboreal death grip. These dendritic tentacles, some smooth, some arthritically gnarled, look like streams of lava petrified in mid-flow. They clutch the masonry with giant skeletal fingers, entwine the sculptures, and insinuate themselves in the fissures between the layers of stone. Inside the compound, smaller trees and plants sprout from crevices, from ruptures in the pavements, and from ledges and roofs. The temples are eerily empty and in crepuscular shadow, the doorways and windows black and lugubrious. Visitors are advised to equip themselves with compasses as well as flashlights. Mr Lol's lantern enables us to see the least expected of Angkor's surprises, a relief sculpture of the supposedly extinct stegosaurus, a species lacking the serrated dorsal ridge. Nearby, attached to the limb of a tree, are two human skulls painted a luminescent white, as if for a Halloween party, but here a macabre sight, or hallucination, that hastens our departure from the premises, picking our way over seemingly slithering serpentine forms, and praying that they are roots only.

In Jayavarman VII's time, more than a hundred hospitals, spread throughout his kingdom, were administered from here, by a staff of 1,640 men and women. The extensive pharmacopoeia, which included 930 boxes of haemorrhoid salves, is inventoried on pediments and stelae, along with a census revealing that during the early-thirteenth century, Ta Prohm was the home of 12,640 monks, and that 79,365 retainers lived in the city outside. The royal family possessed five tons of gold tableware, 512 silk beds, 523 parasols, and uncounted numbers of mosquito nets.

On the path outside the exit, young boys dangle frogs from cords, hoping to sell them for suppers, while women nearby hull rice. Farther along a man plays a silk-string *klimae* (violin). The sound is sweet but barely audible against the sussurations of the darkening jungle.

Back in the hotel, we finish Loti's melodramatic and mendacious *Pilgrimage to Angkor*. Later, in 1912, he published a *Journal intime* that retrospectively lengthens what was in fact a mere two-day visit to the ruins (28–30 November 1901), and makes clear that he was never alone, as the 1901 book pretends, the King having provided him with an elephant and military bodyguard. Still, his romanticised memoirs, together with Paul Claudel's negative ones, are the only accounts that convey a sense of what Angkor feels like. Predictably, Claudel, who saw it from an airplane, hated it, comparing the lotus towers of the temple architecture to 'pineapples', and vilifying the place as 'one of the most evil that I know... Was this perhaps the Devil's own temple before me, and had the earth refused to support it?'[12]

---

12 The Claudel quotation is from Jean Lacouture's text in Marc Riboud's photograph album, *Angkor: The Serenity of Buddhism.*

Chapter 2

Italian Vignettes

Island Cemetery

As our flight approaches Venice, the clouds break at the point where the Brenta disembogues into the lagoon. Since our last visit, the runways at Marco Polo have been lengthened to accommodate bigger airbuses dumping ever larger hordes on the sinking Serenissima. Mercifully, the unwelcoming buildings of the new terminal, La Porta di Gehry, are still far from complete. After the scuffle to evacuate our plane, we are obliged to wait in a queue for a van to transfer us to the motoscaffo docks.

The pigeons perch on channel pilings like sentries, pointing to the graffiti on the walls of the Fondamenta: 'We hate Americans. We love Iraquis.' The high watermarks from the last *diluvio* stain the lower floors of buildings, and restorations are everywhere underway. Half of the Grand Canal side of the Palazzo Ducale, next to the Ponte Sospiri and the oubliettes, is still draped by a *trompe l'oeil* scrim, as it was a year ago.

The only familiar face at the Gritti Hotel is that of a kindly porter who after thirty years still greets me as 'maestro'. What worries us about our quarters is that the bathroom, at an elevation higher than the floor, poses a risk of falling during the night, should we forget which hotel we are in. The Adam and Eve in the painting above the bedstead have already 'fallen', to judge by the exaggerated concealment of pudenda with the weeds of postlapsarian Eden, but whether this is to be construed as warning or enticement we cannot tell.

Dinner with our Venetian friends, Francesco and Chiara Carraro, is less than festive because we become engaged in a discussion with Biennale acquaintances of theirs concerning the merits of La Porta di Gehry. The local Arts magazine *Leo* explains that the roof will consist of 'wavy, crumpled, metallic undulations', and that the architect's intentions are 'to bring the air terminal directly in touch with the lagoon' (it already was) so that it will 'interact in the Venetian setting with the historic waterways by using them as an essential part of the architectural space. Though the new entrance starts on the mainland, it never ends, and the whole world has always aspired to pass through a gateway on the water to the geographical and historic infinite.' Who writes this twaddle?

Auden was mistaken: the 'Island Cemetery' need not 'stay the size it has always been'. Indeed, landfill has already extended the Lido side by a third. The interior has been radically reapportioned as well and its denizens are being redistributed. The entrance has been diverted from the moorings by the church to the gravel walk near the florist's, where, in the withering heat, only artificial flowers are for sale. A bronze nameplate, 'Igor Stravinsky', framed by a bouquet of real purple hyacinths, marks the shaded gate to the Reparto Greco. The walls bordering the paths leading to it are stacked with ossuarial filing cabinets: A line from Beddoes comes to mind: 'After all, being dead's not so bad after one gets into the knack of it.' Alva says she wants a berth next to mine, but my mind is changing and I might prefer to go out in a puff of smoke.

A floral altar has been erected against the wall behind Stravinsky's horizontal tombstone, itself strewn with flowers, votive candles in red glass cups, and epistles from venerators in divers languages, held down by pebbles. A newly planted juniper tree (an angel touched Joshua as he slept under a juniper tree) separates the grave from the land beyond and its rapidly filling sarcophagi and mausolea. The new tenants' names here are neither Greek nor Slavic and their dates are twentieth-century. The plot next to Vera Stravinsky's is no longer occupied by Aspasia, Queen of the Hellenes, whose regally ornamented headstone now lies against the corner wall in a pile of putrescent refuse, but by some male bones with an ordinary Italian name and no credentials. This baleful exhuming and reburying, from wherever, suggests a macabre game of subterranean musical chairs. Overgrown shrubbery and cypress trees obscure the Diaghilev monument, where ballerinas' waterlogged slippers litter the open space beneath the marble baldachin, but whereas his gold nameplate still glitters, the gilt on the Stravinskys' crosses needs replating. In the neighbouring Protestant/Jewish wing, the headstone for Joseph Brodsky looks toward the ivy-covered grave of Ezra Pound and Olga Rudge. A transparent plastic envelope containing a copy of Pound's poem, 'for her and her violin', has been newly attached to the marker.

An insomniac night, which starts with a further discussion between Alva and me on the merits of cremation and final combustion. The San Michele visit has upset me – all those letters seeking communication, and in so many languages: one is signed 'Prazike Jaro', another 'Patricia Rossignol'. No less distressing is the memory of that day in the bright sun and cold wind, 15 April 1971, when I vowed to return every spring. Recently, in New York, the British conductor Christopher Lyndon-Gee told me that the news of Stravinsky's death reached him in Rome, that he took the next train to Venice for the funeral, and after it stood on the Ponte Fondamenta Nuova when the hearse gondola glided beneath.

I still feel impulses of wanting to convey personal news to the Stravinskys, and wanting to hear their voices, her lilt, his basso profundo: 'I aask vaht you are doing?' Some memories, especially when listening to 'The Eternal Dwelling Place' in *Le Baiser de la fée*, continue to move me, to sentimentalise me. In June 1971 I secured a plot for myself in the Reparto Greco because Stravinsky used to say 'We are a trio con brio'. Am I beginning to accept Auden's predestination theory of my life with them, by which he must have meant that our destinies lie in the strengths of our desires? Passing the Hotel Bauer on the return to the city, I envision the living Stravinskys, not as revenants or wraiths, waving to me from the porch of their corner room above the mob seated at the canal-side terrace tables. What patricians they were, which I say only because the populace now seems so *moche*, a much used word of theirs.

The Aquila Archidiskodon

Since the completion of the Gran Sasso Tunnel, the drive from Venice to Rome via the Adriatic coast is faster and more spectacular than the one through Bologna and Florence to the Via Flaminia. The traffic is lighter, moreover, except at Rimini during sunbathing season, when the beaches are covered with nearly, and sometimes entirely, nude, if not sylph-like – too many carbohydrates – young women. The Abruzzi, still capped with ice from the last age of glaciation, are even higher than the Italian Alps. This way, too, one can stop at the Sabine city of Ascoli Piceno, and the caves inhabited from the Upper Palaeolithic to the Bronze Age, and stop again at Téramo, with its recently excavated amphitheatre and seventh-century-BC pit tombs discovered in 1967.

L'Aquila, the capital of Abruzzo province, is west of the highest slopes of the Gran Sasso, midway across the peninsula; the actual watershed between the Adriatic and Tyrrhenian seas is north of Aquila. The city is somewhat eerily secluded in the mountains, in a region that resembles no other in Italy. Like Téramo, it was ruled by the Aragonese Kingdom of Naples (Alfonso I), which increases the curious feeling of remoteness from Rome, only two hours away. This isolation is also the reason that on 12 September 1943, a German paratrooper unit was able to fly to the plateau of Campo Imperatore, above and east of the city, to pick up Mussolini, then held captive here, and fly him to Salio on Lake Garda, where Hitler awaited him.[1] The tableland, inhabited today by herds of wild horses, is still accessible by an aerial ropeway, used by skiers in winter and in summer by tourists who wish to visit the scene of the Duce's *deus ex machina*, a perfectly timed and daringly carried out feat filmed by the Germans and now occasionally shown on the History Channel.

---

1   King Victor Emmanuel III had arrested Mussolini on 25 July and confined him to a prison near L'Aquila. On 26 July General Badoglio formed a new government and on the 28th disbanded the Fascist Party. He flew to Lisbon on 2 August and negotiated an armistice with the Allies, which was signed in Sicily on 3 September by the Allied Command and the Italian government. Badoglio fled to Brindisi with the Royal family, but by this time the Germans had occupied all of the strategic positions in northern and central Italy, including Rome.

L'Aquila was founded by Etruscans, then annexed by Rome. Sallust, who was born at nearby Amiternum and who accompanied Julius Caesar during the Jugurthine wars (Flaubert's *Salammbô*), came here to die, after the loss of his famous gardens (*horti*), of which the Pincio formed a part. The city had been refounded in the thirteenth century by Federico Secondo, the *stupor mundi*. Two centuries later it was governed by the condottiere Braccio Fortebraccio for the Aragonese. L'Aquila remained Spanish territory under the Habsburgs, and the Spanish Castle/Fortress (1530) still dominates the city. It shelters the Museo Nazionale, which includes a sixteenth-century auditorium, whose perfect acoustics can be savoured during performances by the Società Aquilana dei Concerti. The immense building is entered by a drawbridge spanning a wide and deep fosse, recalling that of the Spanish palace at Venosa, and leading to a monumental gate surmounted by the escutcheon of Charles V, whose illegitimate daughter, Margaret of Austria, governed the Abruzzi in the mid-sixteenth century.

Though renowned for its Romanesque churches, fountains and library – printed books appeared here from 1482 – L'Aquila's main attraction is the skeleton of the Plio-Pleistocene proboscidean displayed in one of the three huge bastions on the castle's main floor. This *Archidiskodon meridionalis vestinus mammuthus* fossil was uncovered by Professor A.M. Maccagno in 1954 in the nearby Saniarelli quarry, Madonna della Strada, near Scoppito. The mammal's cranium and ribcage were found almost intact, and the supplementation by plaster casts is minimal. The first efforts to reconstruct the skeleton took place at the site of the discovery, after which it was taken to the laboratory of the Museum of Geology and Paleontology at the University of Florence. Continuing there until 1987, the reconstruction was completed in June 1992 on the site of its present domicile in the Castello.

The progenitor of the proboscidean species, the Archidiskodon became extinct at the end of the Villafranchian (Plio-Pleistocene) era. It is the only fully reconstructed specimen exhibited anywhere; one tusk was still in place in the skeleton when it was unearthed. Fragments of a *meridionalis vestinus* and an *Elephas antiquus* have been found at Pietrafeltra, Umbria, and in twenty-five more *loci* between the L'Aquila basin and the eastern foot of the Gran Sasso and Adriatic coastline – which, in the Cenozoic era, must have undergone an unimaginable act of diastrophism. In recent history, the seventh-century-AD mosaics at Ravenna depict the now inland city as a port. Other incomplete specimens in the Natural History Museum in Florence are known as, respectively, 'Pietro', discovered during the planting of a vineyard near the Borro al Guercio Creek in Tuscany, and 'Linda', discovered in 1973 in a sandpit near Arezzo. Pietro's weight is estimated to have been about sixteen tons, and his most remarkable features are a large narial opening in the anterior of the skull and the advanced development of the dentition. All of the fossils in the Gran Sasso area were found in lacustrine sediments, and all date from the Early Pleistocene (two to three million years ago). An International Congress at Rome in 2001, *La Terra degli Elefanti*, published a map of proboscidean-bearing sites from Téramo to L'Aquila, and Pescara to Chieti. Of recent finds, the most important is a mid-Pleistocene elephant skull from Pratola Peligna in the Sulmona basin.

Disappointingly, implements fashioned by prehistoric Homo sapiens have not been found in Italy in conjunction with elephant fossils, which must be said because of the discovery in Kent in June 2004, during the construction of the Channel Tunnel Rail Link, of a 400,000-year-old giant elephant skeleton surrounded by tools – stones with sharpened edges – used by *Homo heidelbergensis* to carve it up for food. Since fire was first introduced 125,000 years later, the elephant meat had to have been eaten *à la carpaccio*. This revelation should help to upgrade the growing respect for Neanderthal man since the discovery that these human ancestors (350,000 years ago) possessed hearing abilities comparable to ours, and the discovery, in an Israeli cave, of a hyoid bone (500,000 years old) nearly identical to ours and essential to the mechanics of the vocal system. The Neanderthal throat could shriek, express joy, fear, pain, and even speak. Moreover, new techniques of measuring carbon dioxide levels in the Neanderthal period of 150,000 years ago indicate the temperature of the air and the correlation of the earth's atmosphere to its carbon dioxide content.[2]

The L'Aquila Museo provides no information about its prize exhibit, no brochure, even no postcard, which is surprising in that human habitation in Abruzzo has been established as Lower Paleolithic, and that Neolithic remains have been found throughout the region, particularly in the caves of the Fucino basin. Photos of the various stages of restoration fill only a small part of the wall space and are accompanied by skimpy, Italian-only captions. One of the photos shows six men struggling, with the aid of pulleys, to lift the edentated second tusk of the Archidiskodon, found on the ground nearby; the tusk now lies on the platform beneath its in-place partner. The shape, size and weight of the tusk indicate whether the animal dug for food in roots, or munched on tree branches, as African forest elephants still do. Artists' depictions are exhibited of what they imagine the animal's habitat to have been, moving from forest to savannas to alluvial environs. Teeth from other fauna found at Scoppito, including those of bears, hippopotami and rhinoceroses, are displayed in vitrines, together with beautiful fossil imprints of plant tendrils.

The migratory path of the Elephas is predicated to have been north from East Africa through Arabia to Europe and Asia, the largest number migrating south to an Italy very differently configured than at present, Lombardy being a narrow isthmus – diastrophism again. Projections of the evolutionary stages of the Archidiskodon's cranium are also displayed, but one wonders about the creature's huge claws, since present-day elephants have comparatively dainty toes. It seems unlikely that the animal could have become romantically involved with dinosaurs at any stage in their evolutions.

Although most elephant fossils have been found at high topographies, the animal also flourished at lower ones. Several *Elephas Paleologica antiquus* (as well as rhinoceros and hippopotamus fossils) were discovered in the red clays of Capri during the reconstruction and enlargement of the Quisisana Hotel, which means that in the Late Middle Pleistocene, Capri was not an island but part of the Sorrento

---

2   See Stephen H. Schneider's *Global Warming*, Cambridge (Lutterworth Press), 1990

peninsula, a determination supported as well by the discovery of Achulean artifacts in the uppermost level of the clays, similar to those found at Torre in Pietra, Rome. Inventories of the Quisisana fauna have been published, but the hotel has successfully resisted every attempt to begin excavation.

Field and laboratory research, *vis-à-vis* the many fossil remains of endemic dwarf elephants found in Quaternary deposits in Sicily, show that smaller elephants are older than larger ones, and that the dwarf of the species may have been an ancestor of our Archidiskodon. A much smaller proboscidean – the size of a small Hindu Ganesh – the *Phosphatherium escailliei*, discovered in Morocco in 1996, was also eons older, having lived 59 million years ago.

In his introduction to Claudine Cohen's *Fate of the Mammoth*, the late Stephen Jay Gould nominated paleontology as 'the most fascinating subject in the universe', and so it will seem to readers of Ms Cohen's lucid and comprehensive history. What one additionally learns from her book is that a paleontologist must also be a geologist – plenty of scope here, since the earth is 4.5 billion years old – a zoologist, seismologist, an expert in glacial and periglacial landforms; and in stratigraphical and tephrachronological correlation, glaciers being measured in stadials and dated from tephra deposits in seismic faults, as well as, since 1950, by radiocarbon, and by stratigraphical correlation with climatic curves. Oceanic isotopes have established that the large animal fauna of Central Italy maintained a cold-temperate character during the last glaciation (Late Pleistocene), and that analysis of fauna fossils indicates a milder climate on the Tyrrhenian side of the peninsula than on the Adriatic. Seismogenic faults run the entire length of Italy, and surface faulting in the Apennines is not uncommon, though the last instance of a high-magnitude eruption was the 1915 Fucino (Avezzano) earthquake that killed 33,000 people. A recent study of the paleoseismicity of the Ovindoli-Pezza fault shows that a powerful, previously unrecorded earthquake occurred between AD 800 and 1300.

Chapter 3

Seville

Cristóbal Colón and El Cancionera de la Colombina

Our mid-winter flight through the livid, contused sky of Gatwick to cerulean Seville is shorter than the drive from London to the airport, with its ticketing, baggage check-in and Security 'pat-downs'. Aloft, we read in George Borrow's 1830s *The Bible in Spain* that

> The higher class of Andalusians are probably the most vain and foolish of human beings, with a taste for nothing but sensual amusements, foppery in dress, and ribald discourse. Their insolence is only equalled by their meanness, and their prodigality by their avarice... Such are the sleek, highly-perfumed personages who walk in languishing attitudes about the streets of Seville.

A travelling salesman for the English Bible Society in a country that considered the possession of the book a capital offense – the Council of Toulouse (1229) had forbidden laymen to read the Scriptures – Borrow, some of whose nights in Spain were spent in jail for peddling the sacred Testaments, never loses his bonhomie. Moving from village to village, hovel to hovel, he is routinely arrested, but quickly reprieved because of Lord Palmerston's signature in the miscreant's passport.

During his mouchings in Gascony and Provence, Borrow learned to distinguish *langue d'Oc* dialects, and in Spain he noticed similarities between Basque and Sanskrit, as well as the elimination of initial consonants from the Sanskrit words the Basques were appropriating. On reaching Madrid, he translated the Gospel of St Luke into Basque. In Seville, his multilingual talents further distinguished him. Meeting a stranger and surmising from his mustache, clothing and accent that he must be a Hellene, Borrow, with only a smattering of demotic Greek, nevertheless managed to converse with him. (Untranslated words in Classical Greek occur throughout his writings, irritatingly.) In Seville he attended services in the Cathedral, not so much to hear the sermons as to detect their mistranslations of Biblical quotations.

The route of our taxi from the airport to the Alfonso XIII Hotel is deliberately roundabout, diverting from a boulevard bordered by flowering jacarandas and orange trees bursting with fruit to the riverside Paseo Cristóbal Colón at the Torre del Oro. The centre of the city is exotic and electrically bright. The professional women at street corners are not slatternly but well dressed – neither over- nor under- – and they do not pace up and down as they do in New York and London. In contrast to our driver, no one on the hotel staff – porters, concierge, receptionist – speaks any English, which was the case when I first stayed here with the Stravinskys forty-nine years ago. I still recognise the palatial gate from that visit, and the neo-Mudéjar architecture, the lobby, and even the rooms. In fact, nothing seems different, and the art-nouveau bathroom walls, inlaid with strips of blue, white and copper-coloured *azulejos*, the cane-seat chairs, the heavy mahogany table with cabriolet legs, look less démodé than when I first saw them.

Restaurants, cafés and even some tapas bars in Seville do not open before ten o'clock. Descending at that hour to the hotel's Fernando Dining Room, we fail to attract the interest of the major-domo, his waiters and bus boys. Richard Ford, Borrow's friend and sponsor, rightly remarked that 'imperturbable incuriousness' is a Spanish national characteristic. A quarter of an hour elapses before the maître d'hôtel and the waiters approach us to take our order. The head honcho speaks no English and no French, Italian or German

– is the hotel for natives only? – and his underlings are no help. Failing to dredge up the Spanish words to order the food we want, we eventually receive a pasta procured by histrionic means. Returning to our rooms, we find a bottle of excellent Manzanilla, courtesy of the hotel manager, Señor Hector S. The television activates directly on scenes of robotic pornography.

———◆———

Hominids inhabited Andalusia a million years ago, and Homo sapiens for the last 25,000, as cave art verifies. The great sculptured head of the Lady of Elche, now in Madrid, confirms that a high Iberian civilisation flourished during the Iron Age. Tartessius was the Greek name for Seville, which marks the point where the Guadalquiver ceases to be navigable. The Phoenicians ruled it until ousted by Scipio Africanus' Romans, who, after their victory over Carthage in 206 BC, founded the nearby town of Italica, the birthplace of both Trajan and Hadrian. A century and a half later, Julius Caesar gave Seville the name Hispolis and the status of a colony that during the Augustan Pax Romana became one of the most important cities in the Empire. The Visigoths arrived early in the fifth century, and in 589 were converted to Christianity by the beatified brothers Leandro and Isidoro, whereupon Seville became a political and religious centre. The Moorish conquest began in the eighth century and lasted until the thirteenth, when Ferdinand III re-established Christian rule. The surrender of Boabdil, the last Moorish king in Spain, was negotiated in a Granada mosque.

The Inquisition that began in Seville as early as the fourteenth century (1391) seems to have been as brutal as anything that took place in Europe in the twentieth century, and in proportion to the populations of the periods was no less horrible. Tomas de Torquemada officially instituted it on 29 October 1484, after a Papal Bull of 1478 decreed that unbaptised Jews were compelled to wear distinctive clothing, confine themselves to certain professions, and live in separate dwellings, where they remained under curfew from sunset to dawn. Converted Jews, Maranos, convicted of secretly following Kosher laws (washing the blood from their viands), or of keeping the feast of Esther, as their forefathers had done since Ahasueras, were burned alive. To save themselves the Jews proposed to donate 30,000 ducats to help Ferdinand and Isabella evict the Islamites from Grenada. When Torquemada learned that the sovereigns were ready to accept the bargain, he appeared before them with a crucifix in his hand and said: 'Judas first sold his Master for 30 pieces; your Highnesses think of selling Him again for 30,000'. Supported by a large armed force, Torquemada intimidated the monarchs and soon became Grand Inquisitor of both Castile and Aragon. He appointed the Archbishop of Seville as Judge of a permanent Inquisitorial tribunal, or so we learn from George Eliot's notes for *Daniel Deronda.* The first *auto-da-fé* began in 1481, and by the end of that year the bishopric of Cadiz had murdered 2,000 people by incineration. Thereafter, more than a million Jews converted to Christianity. Owing to the great numbers sentenced to death by burning in Seville, the prefect designated a field outside the city called Tablada, and had a scaffold of stone constructed there, called Quemadero, on which statues of four Old Testament prophets were placed. This still exists, but taxi and tour-guide drivers are unwilling to take visitors there, pretending not to know how to find the site.

Our day begins with an excursion through and beyond the city, an exasperating experience in that the driver's only language is German. The cramped streets and alleys, the wedged-together shops and cafés, the whitewashed rococo houses with wrought-iron grilles and balconies, the refreshing fountains in courtyards and plazas, and the flowers everywhere, contrast with the wide boulevards and forested parks, above all the Maria Luisa with its sanctuary of white doves, and equestrians preparing for a gymkhana. The sense of homogeneity, architecturally and in other ways, results from the successful blend of new and old. Medieval walls with parapets and crenellations intersect modern business and commercial districts quite naturally. We go first to the Washington Irving house. As the first official US representative to the country, he is still revered here, and his biography of Columbus is still read. He describes Andalusian summer nights as 'ethereal', but says little about molten post-meridian heat.

During the Mérimée/Bizet period, the eighteenth-century tobacco factory, a massive edifice with a Churrigueresque façade, employed

3,000 female workers, testifying to the pervasive dependence on the weed. Richard Ford tells us that 'tobacchose epicures' smoked two dozen cigars a day, holding them between lettuce leaves to heighten the narcotic effect. Of the many Iglesias in the Macarena district, we visit only San Gil, a repository of the flamboyantly dressed and bedizened Madonna dolls borne through the streets on white-flower floats in the Semana Santa procession, accompanied by boys wearing Ku Klux Klan hoods and robes.

From the front terrace of our hotel rooms, the Cathedral's full length is in view: pagoda-like pinnacles on the roof, graceful flying buttresses, and the Giralda tower, whose lower two-thirds are a minaret. The upper third is a Renaissance belfry topped by a weathervane and a bronze female figure named Faith, somewhat resembling the Statue of Liberty. Most of the buildings surrounding the Cathedral have weathervanes, as well as television antennae.

We approach the Cathedral via the Royal Alcázar, walking around a hack-stand line-up of tourist curricles with black wheels and yellow spokes. Memories of arriving here with the Stravinskys in 1955 – directly from Badajoz, a long, lonely drive – come crowding back. A priest was enthusiastically awaiting him, having heard on a broadcast from Lisbon that the composer had been awarded the Sibelius Prize and was in transit to Seville on his way to conduct concerts in Madrid. Introducing himself in French as the Cathedral's organist, the musical padre guided the weary composer through the vast, dark church for more than an hour, intermittently lighting a few feeble lamps, and taking us to the organ loft to play the antiquated creaky instrument; the reverberation time was a full five seconds.

Today we enter through the back door, the Puerta del Perdón, the only one open because of restorations underway in the others. A ticket counter request to show proof that I am at least sixty-five years old gives me an unexpected lift. A claustrophobic Romanesque tunnel leads to the immense, majestic interior, with its sixty fluted and massive columns, 186 feet tall and twenty feet in circumference. These support the ceiling from the five naves, and the Gothic vaults are the building's other most awesome feature. The many side chapels, particularly the Capilla Real, with its representation of the last Arab king surrendering at the foot of Fernando III, are no less impressive. In contrast to 1955, my present complaint is that the restorers' floodlights are sometimes blinding, though thanks to them we can see the stained-glass German Renaissance windows, and the carvings of Calvaries and reredoses in cedar, laburnum and almond woods in the chapels and choir, the gold and silver pyxes, monstrances, and tabernacles, and the Arabic-style modillions. The replica of a stuffed crocodile suspended from an entrada ceiling, the gift of the Sultan of Egypt in 1260 to the daughter of Alfonso the Learned, would be more appropriate to an old curiosity shop than to a great house of worship.

The Columbus monument of 1902, in the south transept inside the Princes' doorway, is a realistic waxworks-style funeral cortège. Larger-than-life polychrome effigies of four crowned figures shoulder a silver coffin on a plinth above the presumed site of the explorer's grave at a six-foot elevation on a layer of black marble atop an alabaster pedestal. The four pallbearers represent the royal macebearers of Aragon, Castile, León and Navarro. The forward pair bear the head of the casket on their shoulders, while holding lances perpendicularly, each with blade at the base and cross at the top. They gaze heavenwards, whereas the faces of the rear figures are fixed on the ground. These last two wear chain mail beneath tunics woven with designs of fleur-de-lys, flying bats and clumps of chains, the last an allusion to Columbus's return in shackles from his third expedition to the New World. The rubbing fingers of a century of pilgrims on the toe of a shoe of one of the front figures have polished the bronze into shining gold.

The monument haunts us, partly because the realism of the tanned, flesh-coloured faces of the four men are so out of place among the white marble figures reposing on the lids of the medieval sepulchres positioned throughout this indoor cemetery. Curiously, the artist's name, Arturo Mélida, incised in his own handwriting at the base of his creation, is not identified in the guidebooks.

In George Eliot's epic poem, *The Spanish Gypsy*, Columbus says, 'I ask but for a million maravedis: Give me three caravels to find a world'. On 3 August 1492, he and his three crews, thirty-two in all, including the Hebrew linguistic scholar, Luis de Torres, attended a Mass in a small church on a bank of the Rio Tinto before boarding their tiny vessels and sailing from the Gulf of Cadiz to the Canaries, the westernmost landmass of the known world. But one wonders how much Columbus knew of geography beyond Greek, Roman and medieval maps, and whether or not he saw the Portolan Chart, Juan de las Cosa's parchment map, since it was only hypothetically dated 1492. Even more pertinent, was he aware of Ptolemy's mathematics in calculating planetary positions using a single epicycle for each one? At this time it was not known that Ptolemy's spherical globe miscalculates the Earth's circumference a full quadrant too small. The Arab astrolabe, invented in the eighth century in North Africa but not known to European celestial navigation until five centuries later, provided a measurement of latitude. Columbus had an astrolabe as well as an altitude dial, which was used to tell time by calculating the height of the sun above the horizon. But the unanswered question remains: if Ptolemy had not positioned the Canaries seven degrees in error, Columbus' probable reason for supposing that India was closer to him on the Western than the Eastern route, would he have undertaken the voyage to cross what, after all, was called the *mare tenebrarum*? Did he suspect that the earth was oblate, rather than a flattened prolate sphere?

On 6 September the three small ships continued westward from Las Palmas into the unknown. About twenty-five days later birds and vegetation were sighted, but on 11 October a mutiny broke out and had to be quelled. The next day, land was in view, a small island at the twenty-fourth parallel in the Southern Bahamas, now called Guanahai[1] (San Salvador) or Watling Island, and anchors were lowered. The Spaniards soon sailed on to Santo Domingo (Hispaniola), where they

---

1   In 2005, Aruba, an island close to the one of Columbus's landing, attained international fame for the murder of a young American woman, but the 'media' coverage failed to mention that these waters were the site of the discovery of the New World.

remained for two and a half months. From there Columbus returned to Europe in glory, and, in twenty-first-century style, published his diaries (Basel, 1493) under the title *Regarding the Newfound Islands*. In October of that year he was back in Hispaniola with seventeen ships and 1,200 men – including mapmakers (Juan de la Cosa was with him on the second, not the first, crossing),[2] missionary priests, and a few of the women Shakespeare referred to as 'ease-flesh'. Columbus was back in Spain in 1496, but two years later, during his third visitation, was brought back in irons and in disgrace, as a result of his recommendation that the island populations of the lands he had discovered could be enslaved. Quickly pardoned by Queen Isabella, he eventually succeeded in organising a fourth voyage, after which he retired to Spain, where he died in Valladolid in 1506.

The vicissitudes of Columbus's mortal remains suggest parallels to those of his life. They were taken from Valladolid to Seville, and hence, thirty years later, to Santo Domingo, in accordance with his supposed wish to be buried 'in the Americas' – though how he could have known the name, which first appeared in print a year after his death, remains a mystery. In 1795, Santo Domingo was ceded to the French, and the coffin was exhumed and shipped to Havana, where it remained until 1899, when the newly independent Cuba sent it to Seville, where he had spent most of his life in Spain, including his years of study at the Franciscan monastery La Rabidá. The *beaux restes* were interred in the Seville Cathedral in 1902.

Or were they? In 1877, excavators in Santo Domingo Cathedral unearthed a lead casket inscribed 'The bones of the illustrious and distinguished Don Cristóbal Colón'. These bones showed signs of the rheumatoid arthritis from which Columbus is known to have suffered, whereas those in Seville betrayed no trace of the affliction. On Columbus Day 2004, the Dominican Government rejected an appeal by scientists for DNA testing, as did the Spanish authorities for the bones in Seville. In response to this, scientists at the laboratory

---

2   The mid-sixteenth-century world map by Ortelius, now in Seville, actually does bear a degree of verisimilitude to the northern hemisphere. By this time Panfilo de Narvarez (1478–1529), the Vallisoletano, had explored much of Florida.

of Rome in Tor Vergata began taking genetic (DNA) samples from the remains of the explorer's second son, Fernando, also buried in Seville Cathedral, and other possible descendants and concluded that the bones of Cristóbal Colón in Seville were the real ones.

The tomb of Fernando Colón (1488-1539), distinguishes a small chapel next to the Puerta del Perdón. He had bequeathed the several thousand volumes of his Biblioteca Colombina to the Cathedral, which officially acquired them in 1552. The collection includes Columbus's annotated copy of the *Tractatus de Imagine Mundi*. The library in the nearby Lonja includes 36,000 files of documents concerning the discovery of America and the administration of Spain's New World territories. (More information could still be found here about Alfonso de Molina, the prodigy taken to Mexico in 1523 to learn Nahuatl, the Aztec language. Molina published a Spanish–Nahuatlan dictionary and a translation in the latter language of Thomas à Kempis.) The musically educated Fernando collected ninety-five music manuscripts, from which he assembled a book of sacred and secular pieces composed during the lifetime of his father (1451–1506), and which he dedicated to his memory as *El Cancionera de la Colombina*. Richard Ford remarks that 'If he had not been his father's son, he would be one of the greatest names in Spanish history'.

Just beyond the Puerto del Cristóbal exit from the Cathedral, in a bookshop bordering the 'orange grove', we are ensorcelled by the sound of early Renaissance music, a recording, it turns out, of pieces from the *Cancionera*. We purchase the CD and spend the evening listening to the *villancicos* of Juan del Encina; the Ockeghem–Cornago 'Qué's mi vida preguntáys'; the polyphonic music of Johannes Urreda, court composer to Ferdinand V, whom he accompanied to Seville in 1487; and a lament for the iniquitous Duke of Alba, who executed ten times more people in three years than the Inquisition during the whole of Philip II's reign. The disc jacket reproduces a painting of a crescent-shaped lateen-rigged caravel much resembling the morion helmet of the conquistadors. A dozen or so men are huddled on deck as the ship approaches a rocky fantasyland coast, with a barren beach foreground, and a Spanish hill town in an unperspectivised distance. Two men on horses have come to the water's edge as if to investigate a rumour. Conceivably the picture could be a portrait of the *Santa Maria* and of what might have been described to the anonymous artist as the world's first transatlantic encounter.

Fifty-three of the compositions in *El Cancionera* are anonymous, but major polyphonic composers are included, among them Johannes Ockeghem, Louis XI's choirmaster during his visit to Spain in 1469-70. Some of the contents are duplicated in two other collections of the time, the *Canciones Musical del Palacio* and the *Montecassino Song Book*, the latter certifying to a connection with Aragonese Naples (Alfonso I). In fact, Juan de Triana, the most abundantly represented composer in the *Colombina*, collaborated with another of the collection's best-known composers, Juan Cornago, the two musicians evidently having become acquainted in the Parthenopean court. On his return to Seville, Juan de Triana was rewarded with a prebendary for his long service on the staff of Pope Sixtus IV in the 1470s and 1480s.

The passionate and learned music lover Charles V, greatest of the Habsburgs, married Isabel of Portugal in Seville in March 1526. Much less renowned for his musicality than for his association with the Plateresque style, and renowned, above all, as the subject of some of Titian's greatest portraits, Charles nevertheless relinquished the throne and spent his last years in a monastery, in order to hear the motets and Masses of the great Flemish masters sung by a chorus he helped to coach. (Delacroix's subtly imagined portrait of him there can still be seen in the artist's studio in the Place Furstemburg.) But Seville, musically speaking, is famous above all for Domenico Scarlatti's years here as court composer and clavicembalo teacher to the Princess of Asturias.

The ideology of the *Colombina* songs is that of courtly love, and the verses are in the tradition of the twelfth-century Provençal and Occitan troubadours. Here is one of the most beautiful texts, not entirely ruined by the penultimate line:

> Tell us, mother of the Squire,
> What did Gabriel tell you?
> Tell us, maid, you who gave birth,
> How did you conceive the son of God?

... When I believed the divine message
Of the angel who visited me
Then the son of the ternary God
Took form within me.

Sebastian, our driver for an excursion to Italica, is outgoing, cheerful, knowledgeable. His English is not seriously fractured, but he unctuously rounds out the vowel in the word 'right', which he employs as punctuation.

Publius Cornelius Scipio founded Italica, about five miles from Seville, as a retirement complex for veterans of his Punic Wars. Cicero describes his later years here as devoted to study and learning. The only surviving relic of the civilisation is the huge, elliptical – as chariot racetracks must be – amphitheatre. It is said to have seated an audience of 25,000, which hardly seems feasible judging from its present condition, but Sebastian explains that the upper three tiers and much else were removed to build Islamic Seville. The coliseum echoes with the horrors it has heard. The Romans stocked the rectangular pool at the centre of the arena with crocodiles, piranhas, sharks and other man-eating fish. Fallen gladiators and laquearians were thrown to them. The drainage system is still intact, but the only other artifact of the ancient world is a still-legible bronze accounting plate just outside the arena, a tabulation of monies paid to the victors.

George Borrow reached the ruins by crossing the Guadalquiver to Triana on a pontoon bridge, the 'permanent' one having been destroyed by an inundation, and walking to the city, the birthplace of Silius Italicus. The amphitheatre, he wrote, lies in a lee between two declivities, and has

two gateways fronting the east and west. On all sides are to be seen the timeworn broken granite benches, from whence myriads of human beings once gazed down on the area below, where the gladiators shouted, and the lion roared. All around, beneath these flights of benches, are vaulted excavations from

> whence the combatants, part human, part bestial, darted forth
> by their several doors. I spent many hours in this singular
> place, forcing my way through the wild fennel and brushwood
> into the caverns, now the haunts of adders and other reptiles,
> whose hissings I heard.

The hills above the amphitheatre, the patrician neighbourhood of the city, are noted for the floor mosaics in the excavated homes, but this underfoot art has never been, and is still not today, protected from the elements, and in consequence is almost totally faded. Zodiacs, birds and fish are depicted – mullets, crustaceans, wasse, dolphins – along with crocodiles. The views from this height of the meandering Guadalquiver and its fertile shores are worth the exertion of climbing the hills.

On the return to Seville, where kayaks dart down the river rehearsing for a race, we negotiate with Sebastian to drive us to Cadiz on the morrow. He is not enthusiastic about the proposal, but when he calls late in the evening to say that he had forgotten about a previous commitment, we are disappointed and annoyed. The excuse is false. Hourly basis driver-guides prefer to wait outside museums rather than expend gasoline and energies by going farther afield. All the same, my interest in Cadiz is special. The sack of the city in 1596 by the Earl of Essex's flotilla, with John Donne and Raleigh among his 'gentlemen voluntaries', was immortalised in Shakespeare's reference to Essex's full square beard, which became popular in London as the 'Cadz-beard' (*Henry V*, III, vi, 80: 'a beard of the general's cut'). But Cadiz is most important to me in that Joseph Haydn's 1786 meditation *The Seven Last Words* was commissioned by the canons of the Cathedral, and first performed there. Haydn complained that 'the task of writing seven *adagios,* each to last about ten minutes... was none of the lightest', and Cosima Wagner tells us that the piece deeply attracted her spouse. Did it influence the pace of *Parsifal*?

Our last stop is at the Plaza de Toros de La Maestranza, and at this point I turn to *Gatherings from Spain* (1846) by that good writer Richard Ford. After expounding on the selection of bulls for the arena, he offers a history of the ritual:

In vain did St. Isidoro write a chapter against the amphitheatre...
in vain did Alfonso the Wise forbid attendance. The sacrifice of
the bull has always been mixed up with the religion of old Rome
and old and modern Spain, where [ticket sales] are classed
among acts of charity, since they support the sick; therefore all
the countrymen of Loyola hold to the Jesuitical doctrine that
the end justifies the means.

This last proverb is followed by what mistakenly seems an even more
anachronistic usage, a reference to the 'lower orders' as 'the great
unwashed'. Then Ford begins with a description of the accoutrements
of the dramatis personae, the picadors, the *chulos*, 'arrayed like Figaro
at the opera', the matadors, who are university-trained hidalgos, and
'the caparisoned team of mules, which is destined to drag the dead
bulls from the abattoir'. The drama begins with the appearance of
the bull:

> Let loose from his dark cell, he seems amazed at the novelty of
> his position; torn from his pastures, imprisoned and exposed,
> stunned by the noise, he gazes around at the crowd, the glare,
> and waving handkerchiefs, ignorant of the fate which inevitably
> awaits him... It is in truth a piteous sight to see the poor
> mangled horses treading out their entrails... The miserable
> horse, when dead, is dragged out, leaving a bloody furrow on
> the sand... A universal sympathy is shown for the horsemen in
> these awful moments; the men rise, the women scream, but all
> this soon subsides. The picador, if wounded, is carried out and
> forgotten... If the flank of the horse is only partially ruptured,
> the protruding bowels are pushed back – no operation in hernia
> is half so well performed by Spanish surgeons – and the rest is
> sewn up with a needle and pack-thread. But neither death nor
> lacerations excite the least pity [and] the bloodier and more
> fatal the spectacle, the more brilliant it is pronounced. Foreign
> tisickyness is considered objectionable by the Spaniards, who
> resent the interruption of their favorite sport.
>   The matador, from being alone, concentrates in himself all the

interest as regards the human species... He advances to the bull, in order to entice him... and stands confronted with his foe, in the presence of inexorable witnesses, who would rather see the bull kill him twice over than that he should kill the bull. But he presents a fine picture of fixed purpose and concentration of moral energy. Seneca said truly that the world had seen as many examples of courage in gladiators as in the Catos and Scipios.

The matador endeavours rapidly to discern the character of the animal. Nor has he many moments to lose; a mistake is fatal, as one must die, and both may. Often even the brute bull seems to feel that the last moment has come, and pauses when face to face in the deadly duel with his single opponent. The slayer is arrayed in a ball costume, with no buckler other than skill, and as if it were a pastime: he is all coolness, the beast all rage. Could the beast reason, the man would have small chance. Meanwhile, the spectators are wound up to a greater pitch of madness than the poor bull, who has undergone a long torture. The matador must be quick and decided. He must not let the bull run at the [red] flag above two or three times; the moral tension of the multitudes is too strained to endure a longer suspense. There are many ways of killing the bull, the principal one is when the matador receives him on his sword when charging; then the weapon, which is held still and never thrust forward, enters just between the left shoulder and the blade-bone. A firm hand, eye and nerve are essential... The bull-fight terminates when the day dies like a dolphin and the curtain of heaven hung over the bloody show, is incarnadined and crimsoned. This glorious finish is seen in full perfection at Seville, where the plaza is open toward the Cathedral, which furnishes a Moorish distance to the picturesque foreground... the congregation depart... All hasten to sacrifice the rest of the night to Bacchus and Venus.

An estimated 17,000 bullfights take place in Spain yearly, with box-office receipts exceeding a billion dollars.

Index

A

B